Eleven Plays

An Introduction to Drama

Eleven Plays
An Introduction to Drama

Edited by

Gerald Weales

UNIVERSITY OF PENNSYLVANIA

W · W · NORTON & COMPANY · INC · New York

FOR

Bill and Helen

Contents

Contents

A Chronological List of the Plays

Preface

The two most common approaches to the drama anthology for beginning students are the historical and the generic. The first presents a chronological selection of plays chosen to represent the liveliest periods in the history of theater; the second, avoiding chronology, uses exemplary plays to fit carefully defined categories. Both are legitimate ways of talking about drama, but neither is particularly congenial to me. Although I have taught from both kinds of text, I have never used the books as they were organized. For me, the most important thing about a play—especially when it is being offered to a student who is just beginning to study drama—is the way it works; although historical and generic considerations must sometimes be introduced to clarify that working, it is the play's individuality that I prefer to stress. The plays that follow were chosen primarily because they are good plays, eminently teachable, each of which demands consideration in its own terms. Still, at least as I read them, the plays have two things in common: (1) they do not fit comfortably into any of the definitional molds; (2) they are all modern in tone. The first of these is a way of emphasizing that every play is its own man. The second provides the student with a useful ideational handle, a way of taking hold of a work which is unfamiliar in form.

Any number of plays might embody the generalizations of the paragraph above. In making my choices, however, I tried to consider a wide possibility of approaches to the material. First of all, these are plays that I admire for some reason and that I like teaching; they are arranged in the order that I would probably use in the classroom, one based primarily on the increasing difficulties among them. For those who prefer the chronological approach, there are plays which, for all their modernity, can be seen as products of their own time—*Troilus and Cressida, The Country Wife, Camille and Perdican*. The modern plays are spread from the 1880's (*The Wild Duck*) to the 1950's (*The Lark, The Matchmaker*), and there is a second table of contents to make the chronology of the collection immediately clear. Since plays that fit no mold are plays that touch many, those who want to teach genre, using conventional terminology or the definitions from the introduction, can find the examples they want. For farce, there are *Rococo* and *The Matchmaker*, although the latter can join *Arms and the Man* and *The Country Wife* in exemplifying very different kinds of comedy. Although there are no pure examples of melodrama, both *Arms and the Man* and *Tonight We Improvise* make use of melodramatic

xi

conventions and certain devices of melodrama are used seriously in *All My Sons*. The death of Joe Keller in that play makes it possible to consider it in relation to tragedy as the deaths of Hedvig and Hector allow for the same exercise with *The Wild Duck* and *Troilus and Cressida*. Those who prefer to talk about theater in terms of technique or who like to dwell on the split between the realistic and the nonrealistic can find plays here to illustrate their points. *The Lark* and *Tonight We Improvise*, for example, offer two very different ways of approaching nonrealistic staging. For those who like to stress thematic comparison, there are considerations of war and heroism (*Arms and the Man*, *Troilus and Cressida*, *The Lark*), truth and illusion (*The Wild Duck*, *Tonight We Improvise*, *The Country Wife*), the idealist in a corrupt world (*The Lark*, *Camille and Perdican*, *All My Sons*), the masks of love (at least half the plays).

Having too often had to break my way out of a tight editorial frame or skirt excessive pedagogical apparatus, I decided that my job as editor was simply to gather the plays and then get out of the way and let the instructor do with them what he wants. He would do that anyway, but now he does not need to do it over my dead body.

GERALD WEALES

Eleven Plays

An Introduction to Drama

What Is a Play?

Dramatic Instinct

"The theatrical game is inherent in the existence of any living being."
—JEAN-LOUIS BARRAULT

Once I stood on a street corner in downtown Atlanta and watched a group of high school boys attempt to terrorize passing women. There were four or five of the would-be tormentors, huddled under the marquee of a department store. When a likely woman approached, one of the boys—always the same one—moved quickly out of the group to get close to the victim. As she went by, he brought his foot down heavily on the sidewalk just behind her, his crepe sole giving off a resounding *splat*. "Got it," he shouted, a look of triumphant horror on his face. Behind him, the other boys tried to register terror. Ideally, the woman screamed.

This was a play of sorts.

Once I sat on a hillside in Stratford, Ontario, and watched a group of boys, say ten to twelve years old, playing baseball. I did not know one team from another nor which one was ahead. I was less interested in the fact that they were playing baseball than that they were playing at playing baseball. Both pitchers used the same gestures—the contemplative twist of the ball in the glove, the shoulders hunched in preparation, the suspicious half-turn to watch the runner on first, the sudden spin and sharp throw to the baseman. Both catchers bounced springily, thigh to calf, pounding their mitts and repeating a tribal invocation about "the old apple" and "the old plate." Every runner used the same teasing half-step to take his lead off base.

This was a play of sorts.

Psychologists these days talk a lot about role-playing, which is their way of saying that most of us spend a great deal of time acting and being acted upon. The ordinary business of life is a progression from one scene to another in which the leading character (yourself, of course) pretends to be whatever the situation demands—a son, a student, a lover. The motivations that go into any performance, as the psychological technicians will tell you, are many and complex. To an ordinary, uncomplicated mind, however, the everyday actor seems to be doing one of two things: he is trying either to fool someone else or to fool himself. That crepe-soled killer of mythical monster insects belongs in the first category; I am less sure about the Canadian ball players.

There are any number of reasons why we want to fool other people. Those boys in Atlanta were obviously doing it for the fun of it, the artist's pleasure of having a performance recognized and applauded (the screams were applause). So a child may pretend to be blind or a cripple and accept the applause of a sad reprimand; a woman shopping may pretend to be a potential customer and accept the applause of a special display of merchandise; two grown men, made childish by a spring day or a stiff drink, may suddenly begin to talk a made-up foreign language with only an occasional lifted eyebrow to pass for the clapping of hands.

Often, however, when a man performs—while making application for a job, or trying to get a day off from work—he is intent on getting something much more specific. Consider this line: "My wife doesn't understand me." Or this one: "Of course, I'd respect you."

As these two lines suggest, much of day-to-day acting involves the repetition of and the reaction to standard phrases. The occasion, more often than not, is much less insistent than the ones suggested at the end of the last paragraph. In the simplest kind of social situation, a conventional line demands a conventional response:

"How are you?"

"Fine. And you?"

You can probably hear that exchange even in a ward for terminal cases. The question and answer are a kind of play, a small and not very interesting drama in which each speaker assumes a role and recites a line that has been given to him by social convention, acting as playwright.

Under more complicated conditions, the same kind of performing takes place. An instructor in college who says to a class, "Now, tell me frankly what you think of this course," is providing an occasion for a variety of poses, from the sycophantic to the abusive, in which the poser chooses his role according to his interpretation of the part the instructor thinks he is playing. As the complications increase, the line between acting to fool the other man and acting to fool oneself gets a little hazy. A student assuming that "frankly" is the key word in the instructor's invitation might put on a man-to-man guise, a role that in its turn could elicit an attempt at camaraderie, at being just one of the boys, from the instructor. Neither of the pretenders may be trying to fool the other. Both of them may be tired of the conventional roles that the pattern of student-teacher relations makes them play, and on the assumption that a change of role is a step closer to communication, they go into their acts, for themselves more than for each other, and find themselves still masked, facing new masks. Even so, the role that each takes is built of familiar mannerisms—physical, verbal, psychological—and there is comfort for the player in his part. This I think accounts for the behavior of those baseball players in Stratford. Take the pitchers, for instance—either one of them, since they were both carbon copies. All the players on the opposite team must have known every gesture the pitcher made; they were all out of the folklore stockroom of American athletics—so no one was taken in. Except perhaps the pitcher himself. He knew how pitchers were supposed to act, and he acted that way; surely that made him a pitcher. Surely that is the way a man knows he is a doctor, a lawyer, a merchant, a chief.

If you are reading these pages, chances are you are a student beginning the study of drama (or playing that role), and you should be allowed one querulous question: What has all this to do with an anthology of plays? A person who is not a regular theater-goer or reader of plays sometimes approaches a play, in performance or on paper, tentatively—as though it were a strange beast that only the initiate can ride. This is plainly not true. A play is simply an organized extension of the kind of pretending that all of us do daily; it is a collection of fragmentary sketches, like those we take part in, given artistic form by a playwright who wants his finished play to tell a story, make a point, embody an idea more neatly, more completely than life ever can. To enjoy a play (which means to understand it and respond to it as deeply as possible), the man in the audience (in the theater or holding the book) has only to recognize and react to those clues that the playwright gives him or that the characters (with the playwright's help) give him. One should be able to step as naturally into Joe Keller's backyard (in *All My Sons*) as into a neighbor's backyard. When we step into the neighbor's backyard, we carry with us a fund of prior knowledge and a habit of observation which allows us to absorb the existing variation on a familiar situation. What this introduction will do from here on is to discuss the way plays are written in the hope that such a discussion will help you accumulate a fund of knowledge, acquire a habit of observation, make you operate easily in Joe Keller's backyard (or Raina's bedchamber in *Arms and the Man* or Ekdal's studio in *The Wild Duck*). If you know that the meaning of a line like "I don't care if I never see her again," whether you say it or have it said about you or simply overhear it, changes meaning according to speaker, object, surroundings, and tone of voice, you are already half way there.

The Performer's Tools

Language is the most important tool for the dramatist, as it is for the novelist and the poet, but the playwright has other tools at hand, those that have to do with the play in the theater rather than on paper. Before we get to a discussion of the way language is used on stage, it would be valuable to discuss the performer's tools and the playwright's use of them. They may include anything that contributes to the production of a play, from the theater building to the smallest gesture of an actor's hand. They belong properly to the director and the actor, to the designer and the sound engineer, men and women who are committed, ideally, to using their talents and their imagination to give flesh to the play-wright's work. Knowing the performer's tools, however, the playwright is able to anticipate. He can write into his play effects that will be made by means other than words. In actual production, of course, the director or the designer may decide that he can get the desired effect by an action or a device other than the one the playwright has suggested.[1] This fact of the practical theater is not our concern here. In reading a play, it is more important to recognize the playwright's own use of the performer's tools and to understand how that use has affected the shape and the substance of the play.

The Theater. Let us begin with the theater itself. Its size and location and the kind of stage it provides are necessarily limits within which the playwright must work. Unless he is a closet dramatist, a man who writes without ever expecting to see his work performed, the playwright does not operate as the ideal artist, giving his work the perfect shape the material demands. Instead, he manipulates his material to fit the kind of theater in which it is likely to be performed. It may later be adapted, by the play-wright or by someone else, for use in another kind of theater, but the marks of its first home are evident.

Take Paul Green's *The Lost Colony* as an example. Anyone reading it might say—and with some justice—that it is simply a bad play. Green's account of the disappearance of Virginia Dare and the Roanoke Island settlers is almost as obvious as the patriotic one-acters that junior high schools do on George Washington's birthday. The characters are one-dimensional, the comedy is broad, the plot scenes are confrontations so simple that they can be conveyed by stock gestures; the play seems to exist primarily as an excuse for the spectacular scenes—the battles and the dances. Yet

1. Sometimes the actor or the director falsifies the playwright's intention through misinterpretation or self-aggrandizement, but that is inevitable in an art that must depend on the cooperation of many people. That's the chance you take in show business.

The Lost Colony has been drawing audiences to Manteo, North Carolina, for more than twenty-five years. It might thus be worth the trouble to consider the very special kind of theater for which it was conceived. It was the first of the outdoor dramas now so popular with summer vacationers, and it was written to be performed in a large amphitheater, seating 1,500 people, with the sky for a roof and real landscape for a backdrop. Under such circumstances subtlety never had a chance.[2] By contrast, consider William Butler Yeats's *At the Hawk's Well*. This is a dance drama designed to be performed in a room where there is no stage, only an improvised playing area, and before a small audience, presumably a sympathetic one which does not need to be won over by the play. The poetry, without being formidable, is difficult enough to demand that every line be heard and absorbed; although the characters, since they come from myth, are recognizable extensions of everyone in the audience, conventional identification and sympathy are discarded both through the action, which is symbolic, and through the stylized depiction of the characters—the use of masks, formal movement, other dehumanizing devices. Although the play should have an emotional effect on the audience, particularly at its climactic moment, when a solo dance takes over from speech, the resulting experience is primarily intellectual. The play's effectiveness depends on keeping it small. The nuance, the suggestion that gives it its quality is lost when the play is moved into a large theater, when a stage comes between the play and the audience. *The Lost Colony* and *At the Hawk's Well* are plays in which subtlety or lack of it is a direct reflection of the size of the theater and the kind of audience for which the play was intended. Both, however, are special cases, plays by men who, unhappy with the theater of their time, branched off from the stream of Western theatrical history and attempted a new kind of theater, based in part on borrowing from other traditions (Green from the Greeks, Yeats from the Japanese).

The Stage. There are obvious differences among playwrights who stayed within that stream, differences that mirror the changes that the stage has undergone in the history of theater. Compare, for instance, two plays from this anthology: *Troilus and Cressida* and *The Wild Duck*. Shakespeare, writing for the open Elizabethan stage where there was no place for an elaborate set, could write

2. It might be argued that the Greek plays which were also performed in large outdoor amphitheaters achieved a high degree of psychological subtlety. This is true, of course, but the Greek theater that we know comes from the page, and we tend to read, say, *Oedipus Rex* with the kind of precise examination of each line that should be rightly used in reading *The Wild Duck*. I cannot help suspecting that a slave or two, up near the back of the amphitheater, missed some of the subtleties. They could follow the plot certainly— it was usually bloody and besides it was already familiar—and they could enjoy the song-and-dance (the Chorus speeches) even if they did not always pay attention to what was being said.

in short scenes where place and time altered with the entrance and exit of characters. Movement and speed are essential to his play because the stage not only allowed the actor to move easily but demanded that he do so. There is no barrier of any kind between the audience and the play; although the characters are involved with one another, they are aware that they are being watched, and they feel no embarrassment in addressing a line or a long speech to the audience. Ibsen, on the other hand, is boxed in by his stage where permanent sets are built to show us that each act is in a particular place; the blocks of action may not be much longer than those in Shakespeare's play, but when they follow one another, within a single act, they must be presumed to follow immediately in time. Ibsen, then, must find a reason for bringing in each of his characters; the audience will want to know why they are in that place at that time and why they choose to exit when they do. They cannot tell us, of course, because the audience does not exist so far as the characters are concerned. They go about their business, and we watch them through an imaginary fourth wall that stands between us and the action. The proscenium arch, the frame that divides the stage from the auditorium, is a kind of picture frame that emphasizes the separation between the actors and the audience.

There is not room in a short introduction for a history of the changes in theaters and in staging. Let me reduce the process to the kind of short, succinct statement that looks impressive on examinations: The development of the theater from Shakespeare to Ibsen was a business of boxing in the play and forcing the audience to look in from outside. A variety of forces shaped that development—one probably was that the audience just wanted to come in out of the rain and sit down—but the most important certainly was a growing desire, on the part of the writers and the actors, to make what went on on stage as real as possible, to make the illusion complete by pretending that there was no illusion. It was not an immediate change, of course. The Country Wife, for instance, is played against sets that depict (or suggest) real rooms, but the play opens with an aside of Horner's and ends with a summarizing verse from him, both of which are directed at an audience which may not be as close to the play as Shakespeare's was, but is certainly not ignored.

The realistic stage triumphed in the nineteenth century, but no sooner was its victory won than playwrights became restless and began to try to kick their way out of the box they had built. As Eugene O'Neill expressed it: "We are ashamed of having peeked through so many keyholes." Mrs. Levi, in The Matchmaker, does not step forward and make her "Money! Money!" speech directly to the audience simply because the play is based on an old-fashioned farce; she does so because Thornton Wilder, like O'Neill, is one of the playwrights who does not ask the audience to look through a keyhole. In *The Skin of Our Teeth*, he kidded the whole idea of an enclosing set by having the room put together by one of the character's pulling on a rope. In our time, one of the results of the desire to get away from the kind of theater for which Ibsen wrote has been the development of theater-in-the-round, in which the actors are completely surrounded by the audience.

There is a tendency among playwrights and directors to commit themselves to one form of staging or another. A reading of the plays in this volume will explode the myth that there is just one correct form. In approaching any play it is a good idea to try to understand what kind of theater the playwright was writing for; that recognition will explain many of the things the playwright does, things which might seem odd if you began with the assumption that all plays were designed for the high-school auditorium in which you first performed.

The Director and the Actor. This section of the introduction opened with the suggestion that we consider the ways the playwright uses the performer's tools. The one I chose to begin with, the theater, uses the playwright as much as he uses it. The most obvious of the performer's tools, the actor's presence—his body and his voice—may be said to use the playwright, too, but the playwright can at least indicate the way in which he would like the actor to heighten the meaning of his words. Within a few minutes of the curtain's opening on *Arms and the Man*, Raina speaks her lines *dreamily, ecstatically, remorsefully,* and *with dignity*; Catherine speaks *indignantly* and *authoritatively,* Louka *secretly* and *carelessly.* Or so they should if they follow Shaw's stage directions. The directions he has given to Catherine may be a little misleading, since she is only playing at being the careful mother in the opening scene, but with Raina and Louka he is already on the way to the characterization of them that the play as a whole calls for. His lines alone do that, but he obviously felt the job could be done more efficiently if he could command the way those lines should be read; after all, Shaw liked to direct his own plays. Similarly, in the last act of *The Wild Duck*, Ibsen (who was also a director) does not indicate that Hialmar "wanders about restlessly" because he wants a little stage action, but because the character's wandering comes at a moment of indecision. Sometimes when I read a play, the stage directions seem to get in the way of the production I am putting on in my head. You will probably find the same thing true as you read through the plays in this volume (except for *Troilus and Cressida* and *The Country Wife*[3]), but

3. The playwright did not begin to provide extensive stage directions until the middle of the nineteenth century. The main reason for this change—

it is at least worth remembering that the playwright does not direct the actress to droop her head, the actor to walk slowly, both of them to speak softly unless the droop, the slow step, the soft words seem to the author to be necessary to that moment, that situation.

The effectiveness of an actor on stage depends not only on the way he uses his body and his voice, but on the way he disposes them in relation to the other actors. I once saw a good offstage example of clever staging at a three-day seminar I attended outside of Paris. The participants were students from universities all over France, and between formal sessions they tended to huddle together in animated conversation. One striking looking girl with long, straight blonde hair and an unmistakable look of existential despair on her face was always outside the group. She managed to place herself within a few feet of a chattering cluster of students so that her silence and her singleness caught and held the eye of anyone coming into the room. She contrived to be the center of attention without ever being at the center of anything. You might say that she was the director of a play which only she and one or two interested observers knew was going on. For it is the director's work, in the theater, to dispose the bodies so that their spatial relations imply something about their relations within the play. Usually the playwright does very little about arranging the characters on stage, other than to tell the reader when one character moves to another to deliver a particular line or to make a gesture; once in a while, an author does draw a complete picture. At the end of *Riders to the Sea*, for instance, when the body of the drowned boy is brought in, John Millington Synge explains the order in which the characters enter and arranges the spots on which they are to kneel, so that the mother is separated from her two daughters and the three of them from the townspeople whose involvement in the death is real but peripheral. In Act II, Scene 3, of *Troilus and Cressida* it is up to us to do our own arranging if we want to establish a gulf between Achilles' tent and the group of Greek leaders who come to persuade him.

The Set. The set is not simply a convenient enclosure for the actors to walk around in; it, too, is one of the performer's tools that can help the playwright create his effects. When the curtain

which is partly a printing convention —is that the director arrived on the theatrical scene at that time. There had always been someone whose job it was to put the play on, but until the nineteenth century it was the author or an actor who took care of the staging. With the appearance of the professional director, a figure whose control of theatrical production has increased with the years, the author was forced to release his creation to another man for staging. In apparent response, he began to add detailed directions which indicated the way in which he thought the play should be performed. Those playwrights who have also been directors—Ibsen, Shaw, Barker—are particularly meticulous in their suggestions.

In the case of *The Alcestis*, as with any Greek play you read in English, the stage directions are all written by the translator.

goes up on a play, the set strikes the audience before a line is spoken. If the set designer has done his job properly, has converted to wood, cloth, and paint the playwright's idea of where his characters live, the spectators are in the play before it actually begins. A play in print can only offer a descriptive substitute for the visual first impression that one gets in the theater. Sometimes—particularly in the acting edition of a play—a dramatist will limit himself to practical matters, pointing out where the exits belong and what furniture is necessary to the action of the play. More often, however, the playwright turns himself into a miniature novelist, trying to make the set he describes a setting in more than a physical sense. Shaw's description of Raina's bedroom, Ibsen's of Werle's study, Miller's of the Keller back yard, Wilder's of Horace Vandergelder's living room—each of these tells us something about the economic standard, the tastes, the pretensions of the characters to whom the room belongs.

The sets mentioned in the paragraph above are all realistic, at least as they are described, but there is a wide range of possibilities in the theater—from the complete absence of set to one that is meticulously exact in its realistic detail. In Shakespeare's theater, as the Chorus in *Henry V* says, " 'tis your thoughts that now must deck our kings." Settings were created out of the characters' words. "Alack, alack," moans Friar Laurence in *Romeo and Juliet*, "what blood is this which stains/The stony entrance of this sepulchre?" He not only conjures up an imaginary tomb, but he lets the audience know, as Romeo has earlier ("Thou detestable maw, thou womb of death"), how they should react to it. At the opposite extreme, one finds *The Governor's Lady*, a play by Alice Bradley, which would long ago have been forgotten if its producers had not been so intent on realistic staging; in the Broadway production of 1912, a complete Child's Restaurant, accurate to the smallest detail, was constructed on stage as setting for the play's very brief Epilogue.

Between these two poles, great variety in sets is possible. There is, for instance, the conventional set, suitable to any number of plays. An historical example is the street with the house fronts behind it on which Italian Renaissance comedies were usually played. The bachelor's apartment and the suburban living room of Broadway comedies today are so standardized that they too are a convention, an easy indication to the audience of the kind of play to be prepared for. Such convention is, of course, basically unrealistic, even if the set pretends to be an actual room. A more vital reaction against realistic sets, however, is the current tendency, particularly in the production of serious plays, to use suggestion, to allow the designer's imagination to reach out toward that of the spectator. An abstract tree becomes a forest; a few exposed uprights and a little color become a room. The mechanical devices of the modern theater—the revolving stage, the moving belt—can shift sets and, ideally, can combine the fluidity of the Elizabethan stage with the solidity of the picture-frame stage.

Lights. The lighting, like the sets, has a variety of uses. It can control the flow of action and focus the spectator's attention. A lowering of the lights, for instance, can indicate a passage of time. A spotlight, placed on a particular performer, makes him for the moment the center of attention; usually, the character in the spot does the talking, but sometimes it is his silence that needs emphasizing—as at the end of *The Glass Menagerie*, where Tennessee Williams indicates that he wants Laura lighted throughout Tom's last speech, for it is, after all, more a play about her withdrawal from life than his escape into it. The blackout, the sudden extinguishing of all stage lights, can indicate that an action has come to an abrupt end, but it can also suggest that an action too brutal for exposure (a rape, a murder) is continuing in the darkness.

One of the most obvious uses of lighting, of course, is to tell us what time of day it is in the play we are watching. The lights become a mechanical shorthand for the work the playwright once had to do with words. Let's go back to that graveyard in Verona where Friar Laurence's speech built a sepulchre. The scene opens as Paris and his page walk on stage, and Paris' first words tell the audience that it is night: "Give me thy torch, boy." As soon as artificial lighting became efficient enough, such lines could be dispensed with. Of course, the dispensation did away with the need for the kind of ingenuity that let the playwright convert a practical necessity into a poetic statement. No longer did the lover need to say

> The moon shines bright. In such a night as this,
> When the sweet wind did gently kiss the trees
> And they did make no noise—in such a night
> Troilus methinks mounted the Troyan walls
> And sighed his soul toward the Grecian tents,
> Where Cressid lay that night.

as Lorenzo does to Jessica in *The Merchant of Venice*, for the electrician could turn on a bright moon, masked a little by a romantic filter. "The moon shines bright," the words that open the scene, say that it is night as surely as does Paris' need for a torch, but it is clear from the quotation as a whole that Shakespeare wants to set up an atmosphere which becomes part of the love scene.

Lighting can be used to prepare such a mood, and later playwrights, aware of the technical facilities at their disposal, wrote their plays with the potentialities of lighting in mind. Once it became possible to bathe the stage with artificial eeriness, no sensible playwright would send a character on stage to say, "Boy, it's creepy around here," unless he wanted a laugh. Mood lighting is just a step away from symbolic lighting, the kind in which the light itself represents something specific (Tinker Bell in *Peter Pan*) or something abstract (the "flickers of a white radiance" that lighting makes of the distant mountains at the opening of Tennessee Williams' *Camino Real* presumably suggest the possibility of escape to the audience before the play explains the nature of the trap).

Props. Properties (as they are correctly but almost never called) are tools like sets and lights which are capable of doing both practical and suggestive jobs. Since any object on stage, from an armchair to a cigarette lighter, is a prop, it is clear that a prop's first business is to cater to the actor's need, to give him a place to sit or something to light a cigarette with. Although the playwright frequently selects the furnishings for his imaginary room, he does so, as I indicated in the discussion of sets, to suggest what his characters are like. For the most part the director and designer have no hesitation about making substitutes for the author's choices. In a few cases—the bureau drawer where the confession letter is hidden, the sofa cushion with the stolen money in it, the glass containing the knockout drops—a prop becomes part of the action, has a function so important that it cannot be removed or changed. When Death comes to get Eurydice in Jean Cocteau's *Orphée*, she leaves her gloves behind—"well in evidence on the left-hand table"; the audience should know, before the explanations are made, that Orphée will use the gloves to win his wife away from Death.

Used best, this kind of prop not only fulfills a mechanical necessity in the plot, but foreshadows events for the audience, occasionally even builds suspense. The important thing, in providing such a device, is that the audience's attention is drawn to the prop and that, whatever else goes on on stage, that awareness never disappears. Sometimes a playwright's invention seems better than it really is. At the end of Sidney Kingsley's *Detective Story*, Charley, the burglar, snatches an exposed gun from Detective Callahan's back pocket and, in an attempt to get away, kills the play's leading character. When one reads the play, it is possible to see how carefully Kingsley prepares for that final scene. As soon as Charley comes into the precinct station, the detectives, who know that he is faced with a life sentence, hide their exposed pistols in desk drawers or safe side pockets; all, that is, but Callahan. To build suspense, Kingsley directs that Charley should keep his eyes on Callahan's pistol whenever the two are in the room together. Unfortunately in the theater—at least from the balcony from which I saw the play—none of this was clear; Charley's last big leap was a surprise. By contrast, in the movie version of the play, the point was made neatly by having the camera occasionally glance at the pistol in closeup. In examining the props in any play (or the sets, or the lights, or anything else for that matter), it is well not only to understand what the playwright wants to do, but to consider what his chances of success are.

Sometimes what he wants to achieve with a prop is something more than a practical contribution to the movement of the plot. The way a prop is used on stage can make a statement about one of the characters. The example I am going to offer here is a director's idea, but it will illustrate the kind of thing that can be done. The title character of Bernard Shaw's *The Simpleton of the Unexpected Isles* is a complacent and self-indulgent young clergyman who becomes so impressed with himself as the play progresses that he takes to lecturing his elders and betters. There is a scene in Act II in which Iddy joins the rest of the characters at tea and proceeds to try out a sermon on them. In directing the play, I discovered that I could let the actor begin to speak as soon as he stepped on stage; by the time he reached the tea table, accepted his cup, and started to sugar it, he was well into his first long speech. It was a simple matter to time the movement so that he put five or six spoonfuls of sugar in his cup while he spoke the line, "The notion is that you can't have too much of a good thing; but you can." The props, and the use of them, became not only a joke, but a kind of character definition. A look at the opening of Act II of *Arms and the Man* will show how Shaw suggests getting just such an effect. Here he uses the breakfast table props to underline one difference between Petkoff and Sergius.

A prop, then, can have a meaning for the audience which it does not have for the character. It can, however, have an emotional meaning within the play, can become a dramatic symbol which is clear to audience and characters alike. Shakespeare makes such symbolic use of a prop in *Richard II* when Richard, in the scene in which he is deposed, calls for a looking glass and uses it as a device both to proclaim his unhappiness and to suggest the past falseness of those around him; after Richard smashes the glass, solid Bolingbroke, for once as witty as his cousin, extends the idea of the mirror to accuse him of pretense: "The shadow of your sorrow hath destroyed/The shadow of your face." The piece of china that Lady Fidget brings in after having been closeted with Horner in *The Country Wife* is the same kind of prop; at least, she and Horner and the audience know what she is talking about when she says, "for we women of quality never think we have china enough." Costume   There are other performer's tools that work in much the same way as those I have described. Costume, for instance. A playwright can tell us much about a character simply by describing the clothes he wears when he first walks on stage. If he is a soldier, a policeman, a member of the Salvation Army—anything that requires a uniform—we can learn his vocation at a glance. There are other, less obvious uniforms that the stage makes use of; a street walker, for instance, can usually be recognized by what Eugene O'Neill, describing Margie and Pearl in *The Iceman Cometh*, calls "the usual tawdry get-up." It is sometimes possible, if the play and its author are not too sophisticated, to tell the good guys from the bad guys by the clothes they wear; for years, the hero of Western movies wore a white hat and was clean-shaven, while the villain wore a black hat and had a neatly trimmed moustache. Even a sophisticated playwright, one who wants to show, as Shaw and Ibsen usually do, that skimmed milk masquerades as cream, can use costume to suggest that a character is a dandy, a slob, a pedant whether he stays that for the whole play or not.

Sound. Sound can contribute to the meaning of a play or the development of its plot as the other performer's tools do. It can be the muffled shot in the other room at the end of Anton Chekhov's *The Sea Gull* that tells us that Trepleff has shot himself again; it can be the ominous knock on the door in Ibsen's *The Master Builder*, which indicates not only that Hilde Wangel has arrived at Solness' house, but that youth has come to overthrow an earlier generation. The sound can be on stage, of course, like the steady plod of the silent Alison's iron in John Osborne's *Look Back in Anger*, a noise that helps goad Jimmy to heights of nastiness. Once in a while a play is designed so that a continuing use of sound is an intricate part of what is happening; in Eugene O'Neill's *The Emperor Jones*, for instance, the beat of the drums, increasing in speed and in loudness becomes not only a reason for but an indication of Jones's disintegration.

The Writer's Tools

Language. For all the incidental richness that the writer can achieve by borrowing the performer's tools, a play stands or falls finally on his use of his own tools—words and those elements (characterization and plot) that grow out of the proper marshaling of words. It is probably best to begin a discussion of the playwright's words by considering the kind of language—more properly, the many kinds of language—suitable to the stage. The plays in this volume display a wide range of language—from Arthur Miller's attempt to reproduce colloquial speech in *All My Sons* to Shakespeare's use of blank verse in *Troilus and Cressida*. Somewhere in between lies Bernard Shaw's use of prose. Although any playwright must consider how his lines are going to sound when they are spoken on stage, Shaw is the English prose dramatist most conscious of movement within a speech and balance between speeches.

Claire Bloom, who once tried to play Shaw's Cleopatra on television, told an interviewer (New York *Times*, March 4, 1956): "Shaw has such rhythm. It's not verse; it's prose, but when something is missing, the rhythm is off and you know it's missing." Although we have no examples in this volume,[4] stage speech can go a step farther into artificiality and need the accompaniment of real music—as in opera or musical comedy.

The kind of language used may depend on any number of things —on the total effect the playwright wants his play to make, for instance, or on his own limitations as a writer. In most cases, however, the choice of language is a conventional one. Shaw once said that if he had lived in the seventeenth century, he would have taken to blank verse and given Shakespeare a run for his money. Whatever Shaw's claim may say about himself or about Shakespeare, it reminds us that blank verse was the conventional theater language of the Elizabethan period. Shakespeare may have written it better than his fellow playwrights because he was Shakespeare, but he wrote it because he belonged to his own time. Actually, there is almost as much prose as verse in *Troilus and Cressida*. Although we usually think of the Elizabethan plays as verse plays, many of the speeches, usually those of comic characters, are written in prose; the verse belongs to the serious or the romantic characters. Prose and poetry, like the funny and the serious, were usually mixed within a play in the Elizabethan period. The plays of the late seventeenth century, after the Restoration, reflected the same division between prose and poetry, but by this time the mixture no longer appeared in a single play. *The Country Wife*, for instance, is in prose, except for a song or two and the rhymed lines that signal the end of an act; the serious plays of the period, which seem less serious today than the comedies, were usually written in rhymed couplets, a device borrowed from the French theater of Corneille and Racine. Verse remained the language of the serious play well into the nineteenth century; even Ibsen used it in his early plays. It was Ibsen, however, who helped prove the suitability of prose for serious drama and, within our century, prose has become the conventional stage language for any kind of play. In most cases, when verse is used today, it is because the author (T. S. Eliot, for instance) was a poet before he was a playwright or because an author who is not a poet (Arthur Miller in the early version of *A View from the Bridge*) wants to make a conscious identity with a "great" theatrical period (in *View* with Greek tragedy) and thinks that the verse, being outside contemporary convention, will heighten the analogy with the earlier time.

There are still critics, poets, theater-goers who believe that we

---

4. Tyrone Guthrie once directed a production of *Troilus and Cressida* in which Pandarus' last speech was sung to a jazz-blues background.

can never have a great theater without verse, but the quarrel between prose and poetry need not detain us here. There are dangers in any kind of language in the theater. Prose can become so colloquial, in the playwright's attempt to make the characters sound like ordinary people, that it lapses into inarticulateness, flatness, and dullness. Verse can become so entranced with its own pretty face that it becomes simply decoration, poetry for its own sake not for the play's. For our purposes, it is more important to consider what language does on stage, how it works within a particular play.

Ordinary speech, on stage or off, shares with the most literary of languages those devices, such as metaphor and simile, which are sometimes called poetic. Hesitation in the face of metaphor in poems, or in stage poetry, is largely the result of putting a technical name on a device that is commonplace. When the mother says, "Now don't be a pig," the child knows what she means as simply as he knows years later what his fraternity brother means when he says, "Don't take her out; she's a pig." This kind of metaphor is at home in the first drama we know, the movies and television. "You got me, you rat," mutters Edward G. Robinson, and a generation of small boys stumble across backyards imitating his death. Paddy Chayefsky can turn such simple metaphor into pathos, as in *Marty*, where the hero assures the girl: "So you see, dogs like us, we ain't such dogs as we think we are." It should be a simple matter to move from the conventional metaphor of one's own slang to metaphor made for an occasion. When Troilus says, "Fools on both sides, Helen must needs be fair/When with your blood you daily paint her thus!" he is, in fact, comparing Helen, beautiful by reputation, unfavorably to Cressida, beautiful in fact, in a scene in which he refuses to go on fighting Troy's war when Cressida is going to be turned over to the Greeks. But the metaphor does more than that. It contains an implicit comment on the foolishness of the war by reducing the blood of the dying Trojans to the rouge that flatters Helen's face. It also suggests, although Troilus is not aware of it, that blood can paint a woman in more ways than one, that his blood (his desire) has given Cressida her beauty. A metaphor then may be a casual thing, as it is in ordinary speech, or a language device that allows a line to say more than one thing at a time. It can be chosen, too, to contribute to the feel of a play as a whole. The play that Robinson Jeffers made out of Euripides' *Medea* is stuffed with animal metaphors to emphasize the wildness of his heroine.[5] At best, a metaphor on stage is not simply a language device; it is related to a symbol that has been established within the play. Toward the end of Enid Bagnold's *The Chalk*

5. According to Caroline F. E. Spurgeon, in her *Shakespeare's Imagery* (Macmillan, 1935), the dominant images in *Troilus and Cressida* are about disease or food.

Garden, Miss Madrigal says to Mrs. St. Maugham, "When will you learn you live on chalk?" They are supposedly talking about the soil in the garden, but they are talking, too, about the sterile life the old woman has lived. The wild duck is that kind of metaphor; so, too, is the chocolate soldier, although it is not as central to *Arms and the Man* as the duck is to Ibsen's play or the chalk garden to Miss Bagnold's.

Lines in the theater—metaphorical or not—take on special meaning according to whom they are spoken. Some speeches are obviously meant for the audience. In the W. H. Auden-Christopher Isherwood play, *The Dog Beneath the Skin,* characters introduce themselves the way characters often did in the medieval plays: "Here come I, the Vicar good/Of Pressan Ambo, it's understood." In each act of *The Matchmaker,* the action is interrupted to allow one of the characters—Vandergelder, Cornelius, Malachi, Mrs. Levi—to step to the footlights and confide in the audience. In the last few years, it has become quite usual for the playwright to introduce into his play a character who speaks only to the audience, one who has no connection with the action or the other characters beyond commenting on them for the audience's benefit. Jean Anouilh is apparently so fond of that kind of character that he not only used him in *Antigone,* but introduced him into a translation he made of *Twelfth Night.* I do not mean to suggest that direct address to the audience is limited to medieval and modern plays; it flourished in the years between—for instance, the Chorus speech that opens *Henry V.* In those years, however, two popular speech devices developed which allowed the characters to speak to the audience indirectly. One of these is the soliloquy, the long speech in which a character apparently talks to himself, and the other is the aside, a short remark spoken to no one in particular but aimed at the ears of the audience. Neither of these is much used any longer because playwrights today tend either to take the audience into their confidence completely or to pretend that it does not exist.

Most of the lines in any play are spoken by one character to another. Still, if we in the audience are to know who the characters are and what they are up to, a great deal of information has to be provided. The playwright must do the providing, and if he is writing in the realistic tradition in which the audience is presumably not there, his job is that much more difficult. The trick of exposition is to write lines that might really be exchanged between characters but to fill them with information that the audience needs more than the characters do. Sometimes the playwright solves this problem by bringing on stage a stranger who needs to be told everything, or by sending a character off on a vacation, as Chekhov did Dr. Dorn in *The Sea Gull,* so that he has to be filled in on events when he returns. One of the old devices, so standard that it has become a joke, is to begin the play with two servants in conversation; Ibsen uses this in *The Wild Duck* as he does in many other plays. Since all exposition is contrivance, the best a playwright can hope to do is to make the artificial seem natural. He fails when the audience recognizes the unlikelihood of a line. To take a clumsy example, Arnaud d'Usseau and James Gow, the authors of *Deep Are the Roots*, have one character say to another, "You're also a novelist, aren't you?" only to reduce the line to silliness by having him admit in his next line that he has read the man's most recent novel. By contrast, Philip Madras' "Is my mother still staying here?", spoken to his uncle's maid at the beginning of Granville Barker's *The Madras House*, only appears to be inept exposition; by the time we have met Mrs. Madras and learned something of her complicated relations with her husband and her son, it becomes clear that the introductory line was already hinting a great deal about Philip's attitude toward his mother.

The kind of subtlety implied in the Barker line above brings us to the problem of language as it is handled by the best playwrights. Language on stage, like language off stage, is as often a failure at communication as it is a means to it. There are playwrights, of course, who want the audience to take their characters' speeches at face value, but the plays in this volume are not all that simple. In many speeches, the character does mean what he says, and the hearer understands and accepts the words as they are spoken. More often, however, the speech is shaped by either the speaker's or the hearer's conscious desires. Ulysses' famous speech in Act III, Scene 3, of *Troilus and Cressida*, the one beginning, "Time hath, my lord, a wallet at his back," is a good example. On the surface it seems to be a typical bit of Nestor-like moralizing, a sermon on the shortness of fame, used, in this instance, to comfort Achilles for having been snubbed by the other Greek warriors; we know that Ulysses arranged the snub, as he stage-manages almost everything in the Greek camp, and the speech—whether its moral message is true or false—becomes simply a rhetorical device to persuade Achilles onto the battlefield. A much funnier example of Ulysses' manipulation of language comes in Act II, Scene 3, in which he plays on Ajax' self-importance, hoping finally to use him as a lever to pry Achilles out of his tent. Ajax, of course, is a perfect example of the way a hearer's own desires affect his hearing; he is so convinced that he deserves the praise he receives that he is never aware that Ulysses is both making fun and making use of him.

A still more complicated kind of speech is one in which the speaker himself is not aware, or is only half aware, of what he is really saying. Take Joe Keller's apologia in *All My Sons*, the speech beginning "You're a boy, what could I do! I'm in business, a man is in business . . ." On one level, he is saying that he was not at fault for shipping out cracked cylinder heads, that some abstraction—the business world, the system—made him do it. His shift from the personal *I* to the impersonal *a man* and his use of the unspecific *you* in much of the rest of the speech are unconscious emphasizing of what the words actually say. I'm Joe Keller, a nice guy, a family man, he is saying, and I could not have killed all those pilots; it was a *they* or an *it* or a *you* that did it. But he is also saying, to save his own life, *I did not kill Larry, I did not kill my son*, and since this is a *mea culpa* as well as an apologia, *forgive me, Chris*. Chris, who can hear only with Chris's ears, understands no more than that his father is guilty and answers as accuser, not as son. In listening to any speech on stage, then, it is necessary that we consider who is speaking and who is listening and what each of them thinks he wants and what the playwright wants us to suspect they really want.

Characterization. The *who* brings us to the characters and to another of the writer's tools, characterization, which is so closely allied to language that it is difficult to separate the two. Characters, like speeches, range from the obvious to the subtle, from the conventional to the complex. In the old Morality plays the characters were simply abstractions, personified qualities such as Ignorance or Wisdom. Such abstractions still occasionally turn up in plays, more often than not in contemporary religious drama, but for the most part, even when the abstract label is used, the character becomes more than the name he bears. In *Grab and Grace*, a Christmas play by Charles Williams, Grace is a mischievous boy; the abstraction has become a stereotype. *Stereotype* is a kind of dirty word these days, a bad name which implies lack of imagination or invention. Such usage, however, assumes that the creator of the supposed stereotype is attempting to produce something else, a character or a situation which at least has the look of reality. This assumption, and the criticism based on it, are valid only when an author is working in the realistic tradition. As often as not, a playwright will use stereotyped characters quite consciously. In Charles Williams' case, the playwright is interested in his slapstick allegory in which Faith, through Grace, saves Man from Pride and Hell. His turning Pride into a *femme fatale* and Grace into a cheeky little boy simply feeds the fun of the play; Man alone has a certain psychological complexity, a characterization which enriches the play in more ways than one.

The stereotype, then, is an honorable dramatic convention. Certain stock characters—the braggart soldier, the irascible father, the cunning servant—began in Greek comedy and have turned up regularly—in the Roman theater, on the Elizabethan stage, on Broadway today—changed a little by time and place, but easily identifiable. Our own list of familiar types, those who people today's plays, films, and television is a long one: the dumb blonde, the spinster aunt, the boy on his first date, the private eye, the possessive mother. A stereotype, of course, is really a person seen from one angle only, so that one prepossession, one characteristic, even one tic is continually reiterated. The use of such a character is a kind of theatrical shorthand which avoids complication where it is not needed; the audience, after a first glimpse, knows what the character is and what to expect of him. This kind of characterization is frequently used in plays in which the working out of the action, whether comic or dramatic, is more important to the playwright than his characters. It is useful, too, to men with a message or with a verbal gift for wit or poetry who believe that what they have to say or the way they say it is likely to interest an audience more than the vehicles through which they say it. The ability to recognize a stage stereotype is useful to the man who reads or sees plays, but it is not enough to stop at recognition. It is necessary to go on and see whether or not the playwright is consciously using stereotype and, if he is, to understand why he is. In choosing to do over a nineteenth-century farce in *The Matchmaker*, Thornton Wilder obviously believed that stereotypes could be used—as they have always been used—to tell some of the truth about all of us. He knew, I assume, that all the great figures of myth are (or become) stereotypes.

One of the problems about stereotype is that it is difficult for a character to remain one. As soon as a playwright begins to work his variation on a type, individuality sets in, and there is the beginning of a character. The converse is true, of course. No character, however complex, can quite escape being a stereotype. In the early scenes of their respective plays, both Troilus and Romeo are stereotypes of young men in love, but Shakespeare lets the pressure of events turn them into characters (Romeo more obviously than Troilus). Whether a character remains simply one-dimensional (which is what a stereotype does) or takes on complexity, the playwright uses the same means to display him to the audience. The character exists by virtue of what he does, what he says, and what is said about him. Unless the play is simple-minded, by accident or by the playwright's choice, it is necessary not only to register the three methods of characterization, but to measure them against one another.

Action might seem to be a simple way of pegging a character, but the problem of motivation muddies the simplicity. A kiss looks much the same whether the man involved is a lover or a seducer; a shooting looks the same whether the man with the gun is a psychopathic killer or a patriot. Any act has to be seen alongside other acts and in conjunction with words spoken during or about it. This is especially true of the large dramatic moments in any play. The small things, the gestures, the apparently unconscious movements can be more revealing. In Act V of *The Wild Duck*, for instance, when Hialmar lets breakfast sidetrack his determination to leave Gina he proves, as Robert Martin Adams once said, that "He is one of nature's *noshers*, not her noblemen." A character's speeches, as the earlier paragraphs on language indicate, may be lies to another character, as with Ulysses, or to himself, as with Joe Keller; lying can reveal character as well as truth-telling, but the observer, to read the character right, has to know whether or not to believe the lines. Of course, to know whether or not to believe the lines, he has to know something about the character. This is not an insoluble paradox: it is simply a warning not to take any character at face value until a series of scenes has suggested the ways in which he may be deceptive or self-deluding. In *Arms and the Man*, Shaw provides that a scene between Sergius and Louka follow immediately and put into perspective the one in which Sergius and Raina exchange romantic commonplaces. If it is not an easy matter to judge a character by his own acts and words, it is not a certain help to listen to what the other characters say about him. With such testimony, there is the same problem of interpretation. It would make a difference whether a compliment was spoken by Iago or Othello. The more complex a character becomes, the more subtle the playwright must be in his use of language and his devising of action. If you watch what is done by, said by, and spoken of a character and come up with an adequate one-sentence description, you will probably have captured a stereotype; if he slips through your fingers, he may be a real character, which means an approximation of that elusive thing, the human being.

Kinds of Dramatic Action

Plot might be called a third writer's tool. If I were Aristotle, I would give it first billing, call it "the First Principle, and as it were the very Soul of Tragedy." And comedy, too, I suppose. It is not necessary, however, to classify the elements of drama according to importance. It is enough to know that plot, character, and language work together in all plays, harmoniously in the best of them, one often dominant over the other two in less successful plays.

Whether it gets top billing or not, *plot* needs to be defined. It is, simply, what happens in a play. Often, of course, a number of things happen, but unless the play is badly put together, the variety contributes to a unity. The small incidents feed the main event.

A subplot, whether it be extensive or not, can, by comparison or by contrast, heighten the effect of the main plot. *King Lear* provides probably the most famous example. Gloucester's story, his rejection of his good son and betrayal by his bad one, cuts in and out of Lear's story, his rejection of his good daughter and betrayal by his bad ones, in a way that comments on and makes much stronger Lear's foolishness and his pain. The best description I know of the way a subplot works comes in Jean Giraudoux's *Electra*. In the midst of the disaster that Electra is about to force on Argos, the President of the Council decides that his wife is unfaithful to him. "This little scandal within a great one can't displease you!" he says, and the Beggar answers, "No. It's like the squirrel in a big wheel. It gives the right rhythm." One of the pleasures of reading or seeing a play is to decide, to take a particular instance, how Ermengarde's elopement is related to the adventures of Barnaby and Cornelius and how they contribute to the "right rhythm" of *The Matchmaker*.

Although I preceded my definition of plot above with the adverb "simply," what happens in a play is not quite that easy. There are two kinds of dramatic action[6]—external and internal, the events and what they do to the characters. To illustrate them, let me invent a situation: An eight-year-old boy comes home from school one evening, winded, in tears, dirty, the leg of his pants torn. His mother wants to know what happened, so he tells her:

> When I left school, I went down Barker Street, to walk Mary Jane home. We'd only gone a block or two when this gang of guys—older guys, you know, twelve and like that—came up, and they began to say things. I got mad. I told them. But they just laughed at me. They knocked me down—that's when I tore my pants. Then they told me to go on home, and they threw rocks at me until I ran out of sight. Mary Jane just stood there and watched.

The external action is clear enough. The internal action—the embarrassment at being belittled in front of the girl, the frustration at not being able to fight back, the guard, the shame perhaps, that makes him keep his story on the level of events—is implicit.

Any situation, any event, then, may be considered in terms either of external or of internal action. The internal can be expressed only through the external, for even words that pass from one man to another are external action. For this reason, any play can be reduced to the externalities that it contains. *Hamlet* is a play about a man who gets killed in the successful attempt to kill the man who murdered his father. If *Hamlet*, for all the external action it contains, fails to reduce comfortably to a sequence of

6. I prefer the word *action* to the word *plot* for what goes on in a play, but the words are used interchangeably in this introduction.

events, there are plays enough which never want to go deeper than externalities.

The recognition of the two kinds of dramatic action can be of value in solving one of the most confused problems that faces any discussion about the theater: that is, the definition of theatrical genres. The problem was already out of hand by the beginning of the seventeenth century when Shakespeare let Polonius praise the players for their ability with "tragedy, comedy, history, pastoral, pastoral-comical, historical-pastoral, tragical-historical, tragical-comical-historical-pastoral . . ." Shakespeare knew that no play fits comfortably under a single label, unless, like *Oedipus Rex* wearing Aristotle's tragic label, the play sits as model for the definition; that no genre can really keep from lapping over into a neighbor's yard. Since that is the case, a bare minimum of hair-splitting should suffice for this volume. We will pretend that there are only four major dramatic genres—farce, melodrama, comedy, and tragedy— and that no play fits comfortably in any of them.

The division among the four is obvious enough. Farce and melodrama are mainly concerned with external events; comedy and tragedy with internal. The other separation, the one between farce and melodrama or between comedy and tragedy, is harder to make. Both farce and melodrama are constructed of a sequence of interlocking events in which there is always the possibility of disaster, either physical or social, although the disaster is ordinarily avoided. The chief impact of either genre is at the level of events (will he be found out?), but the audience's reaction in farce is to laugh, in melodrama to gasp. The most popular examples of melodrama at the moment are the mystery story and the spy thriller; fifty years ago, melodrama, as farce still is today, was likely to be built around a sexual infidelity, real or imagined. The strongest evidence of the fineness of the line between farce and melodrama lies in those aging melodramas about the unfaithful wife; today, most of them could only be played as farce. The characters in both farce and melodrama are ordinarily stereotypes, for as soon as characters begin to develop complications, our attention is drawn away from the events to their impact on the characters; when this happens, farce moves toward comedy, melodrama toward tragedy. At best, a certain sentimentality is allowable, but it asks the audience to shed a tear not over a person, but over a type—a good girl wronged, the boy who loses his innocence, the desolate old mother. Farces, like melodramas, ordinarily end with a comfortable suggestion of normality—insurance for the audience. They have, however, a tendency to edge toward violence, and in a few cases— Granville Barker's *Rococo*, for instance—the violence is strong enough to suggest that the playwright knows that the man in the audience, for all his conscious passion for order, has a longing for chaos too. The words *farce* and *melodrama* are sometimes used to condemn a work, to suggest that it lacks seriousness. In a way, it does, of course, but since these genres so obviously touch people where they live, on the edge of the subconscious, they deserve the respect of anyone who plays at being a student of the theater. They certainly have the respect, not always acknowledged, of playwrights. No dramatist in this collection fails to use some of the techniques of farce and melodrama, some of their artificial manipulation of events (that letter in *All My Sons*), and at least one playwright, Wilder with *The Matchmaker*, has adapted farce for his own purposes.

The separation between comedy and tragedy, which has a bad habit of disappearing, is similar to that between farce and melodrama. A paraphrase of one of the sentences in the paragraph above should get us started. Both comedy and tragedy are constructed of a sequence of events in which there is always the possibility of disaster, either physical or social; in comedy the disaster is usually avoided, in tragedy it is not. The important difference is in the nature of the events. In farce and melodrama the events tend to be outside the characters, a chain that may move logically from link to link, but which almost certainly begins in gratuitous accident. In comedy and tragedy, although accident is sometimes the trigger, the events appear to be the necessary result of the confrontations of particular characters. In farce and melodrama things happen to characters; in comedy and tragedy, characters produce events and are changed or destroyed by them.

Any generic definition is simply a tool to approach a work of art. To call a play a tragedy or a comedy is a way of beginning to talk about it. *Alcestis*, since it is by Euripides, is traditionally one of the Greek tragedies, but it has been interpreted as a satirical play. So, too, has *Troilus and Cressida*, although in the quarto edition (1609) it was called a "historie," and in the folio (1623) it was called a "tragedie." Ibsen called *The Wild Duck* simply a "play in five acts" when he published it, but he once told an interviewer, "It is to be tragi-comedy, or else Hedvig's death is incomprehensible." I am not suggesting that generic terms have no meaning, but that plays are elusive things that escape their labels. Since Aristotle defined tragedy more than two thousand years ago, the genres have been defined and refined, the definitions changing color with the centuries, the shift in theatrical conventions, the philosophic orientation of the aestheticians. I find it useful to consider plays in terms of the two kinds of action I suggested above; for me, *drama of internal action* (which would include both comedy and tragedy) and *drama of external action* (which would include both farce and melodrama) are convenient generic ways of taking hold of a play. The important thing is that each play be looked at first as an individual; its family connections can be considered after that.

Ways of Seeing

There are other labels that have to do with the theater which are sometimes as misleading as the generic terms discussed above. Some of them—the word *realistic*, for instance—have already turned up in this introduction because it is almost impossible to talk about plays and the staging of them without some recourse to these words. Although terms such as *naturalism* and *expressionism* grow out of a particular historical context and have—or at least once had—a specific meaning, for our purposes precise definition is not necessary. Realism, for instance, is the attempt to put an actual representation of life on stage, while naturalism is a kind of realism which has its philosophical base in a belief in determinism, economic or psychological usually. In practice, the fine line disappears and the word *naturalistic*, describing a set, say, means the same thing as *realistic* does.

Most of the words of this kind have to do with a way of seeing, a way of expressing what passes for truth with the playwright. Although there are a vast number of labels floating around, most of them can be comfortably lodged under one of two main divisions: realistic or nonrealistic. Since theater is by nature a form of pretense, since every play is an artificiality (in the sense that its order is imposed by an artist), a fairer division might be that between the *unreal real* and the *real unreal*. Eugene O'Neill used the first term in a letter to Joseph Wood Krutch, commenting on the kind of play-writing he wanted to escape from, "What I mean is freedom from all modern formulas that restrict the scope of the theater to the unreal real . . ." O'Neill's pejorative use of the phrase implies the kind of play in which the dramatist has taken great care to have his characters speak and dress as they should and walk through rooms that they might frequent, but has manipulated them so that what they do is designed for a shocking or tearful curtain and not out of any attempt at psychological validity. Since we are not burdened with O'Neill's need to attack one kind of theater in defense of another, we can borrow his phrase and give it a more general application. However accurate the playwright (and his set and costume designers) in his attempt to put a believable environment on stage, he is still dealing in make-believe. However carefully he organizes his play so that nothing appears incongruous or unacceptable, he is still using a neat form that would be impossible in reality; even the "slice of life" plays that were once so popular had an end and a beginning, which incidents in life, so far as we know, do not have. The unreal real, then, is the way of seeing that demands that the surface of a play have the look of actuality about it.

The real unreal is the opposite way of seeing. There is a wider range of possibilities within this category, but all of them can be seen as attempts to state some kind of truth about life (the real) by means of a surface presentation that has little or no desire to recreate the actual (the unreal). A fairy story on stage (Strindberg's *Swanwhite*) is such a play; so is the romantic costume comedy (Edmond Rostand's *Cyrano de Bergerac*). Plays in which characters speak in verse or in song (all opera, all musical comedy) belong in this category; so, too, do plays in which the characters can talk directly to the audience (*Tonight We Improvise* is an extreme example). Expressionism and all its offshoots (dadaism, surrealism, the theater of the absurd) belong here because any kind of subjective presentation of the objective world, dream or fantasy or just kidding around with stage tricks, produces an unreal surface whatever psychological or mythical reality it expresses. If Saint Joan is most herself in her moment of triumph, then Anouilh in *The Lark* has to destroy conventional form to give her the coronation.

The realistic theater (the unreal real) is usually assumed to be the dominant form of Western theater, at least since the middle of the nineteenth century; actually the nonrealistic (the real unreal) is just as persistent, and at the moment it seems very definitely to be on top. In this volume, for instance, only *All My Sons*, *The Wild Duck*, and *Arms and the Man* belong to the unreal real tradition; with a little effort, using as tools the symbolism of the *Duck* and the suggestion of parody in *Arms*, we might be able to move the last two into the other camp. My metaphor is a little unfortunate. Two ways of seeing there may be, and in the history of the theater they may sometimes have seemed like armed camps, but both kinds of play-writing attempt to say something true and significant about man. One group (the unreal real) believes that the minute details of life are an entry way into truth; the other (the real unreal) that truth can only be reached by an imaginative penetration which ignores, sometime defies our surface existence.

The Spire of Meaning

To be able to identify a genre, to be able to tell a realistic comedy from a romantic tragedy, a verse melodrama from a prose farce, is a virtue when one begins to talk about a play, but precision in the pasting of labels is no easy matter. It is a perfectly respectable aesthetic game, to be avoided only when the label hunt distracts you from what is happening in the play and what that happening adds up to. It should be possible, for instance, to get an argument going over whether *The Matchmaker* is a farce, which is what

Wilder calls it, or a comedy. Such a dispute, however, is about as unnecessary as the one at the beginning of Eugène Ionesco's *Rhinoceros* in which the townspeople argue over whether the rhino is bicorned or unicorned when they should be wondering how it got on their village street and what it means. To appreciate *The Matchmaker*, then, it is less important to decide whether or not Wilder was right in calling his play a farce than it is to consider how accurate he is when he says, "My play is about the aspirations of the young (and not only of the young) for a fuller, freer participation in life."

This introduction has dealt, for the most part, with how the playwright does his work. Before I call a halt and let you get on to reading plays, a more useful activity than reading introductions, I want to speak a word about the play as an artistic whole. A discussion that emphasizes the elements that go into a play, as this one has had to do, is in danger of suggesting that a play is simply a collection of fragments—a verbal effect here, a plot device there, a lighting effect in the upstage right corner. This is a false impression. In so far as a play is a successful work of art, it embodies an idea. "A drama must be shaped so as to have a spire of meaning," John Galsworthy once wrote. "Every grouping of life and character has its inherent moral; and the business of the dramatist is so to pose the group as to bring that moral poignantly to the light of day."

We may suspect the word "poignantly," knowing that there are more ways than one to expose a moral to the light of day. We may even suspect the word "moral," for it suggests that the play's function is to teach a lesson. Many plays do; many playwrights use the theater as a platform for the dispensing of political, social, or religious propaganda. A play may be a call to action, as many plays were in the thirties. A play may be a conversion device, as it is in the hands of a few of the contemporary religious playwrights. It may be the presentation of an argument proving or trying to prove that society should adopt a particular attitude toward poverty, alcoholism, homosexuality, mental health, or, *pace* Mr. Miller, one's responsibility to all one's sons. Thesis drama, the name given to the kind of play that takes a narrowly argumentative position, is drama at its least interesting because, for the sake of argument, it often ignores the richness, the complications that are inherent in the juxtaposition of ideas and human beings.

No play—not even the most trivial manipulation of stereotype characters—can escape containing an idea. No playwright, however careful he is to people his play with characters who reflect a variety of attitudes, can escape making a statement of some kind by the way he maneuvers those characters. Nor does the playwright want to escape. What he might like, though, is to have the reader, the man in the audience avoid reducing the play to its theme (theme is a common synonym for idea in a literary work). Irwin Edman used to tell a story about a composer who, having just finished playing a piano concerto, answered the question, "What does it mean?" by sitting down and playing it through again. Keep that composer in mind as you approach the plays in this volume. I assume that you will become quickly aware that *Arms and the Man* and *Troilus and Cressida* have a theme or two in common, share some ideas about the nature of war and its relation to love, real and romantic. Once you have climbed that spire of meaning, however, do not imagine that you can plant a flag on top claiming the play for one idea or another. A play has meaning, but it is more than its meaning.

All My Sons

ARTHUR MILLER

All My Sons, which was two years in the writing, opened in New York on January 29, 1947. It was Arthur Miller's first successful play. Its popularity is obvious from the length of its run—328 performances (42 weeks); its critical reception is evident in the fact that it received the Drama Critics' Circle award. In considering the play's success, it is worth remembering that it was produced soon after the end of World War II when the returning veterans still hoped that they had come home to a better world— even those less idealistic than Chris Keller, those who would find in his speech about the kid with dry socks the kind of sentimental nonsense that had filled wartime movies. Not that the play should be pinned forever to its historical moment. In the introduction to his *Collected Plays* (New York: Viking, 1957), Miller writes:

> That the deed of Joe Keller at issue in *All My Sons* is his having been the cause of the death of pilots in war obscures the other kind of morality in which the play is primarily interested. Morality is probably a faulty word to use in the connection, but what I was after was the wonder in the fact that consequences of actions are as real as the actions themselves, yet we rarely take them into consideration as we perform actions, and we cannot hope to do so fully when we must always act with only partial knowledge of consequences. Joe Keller's trouble, in a word, is not that he cannot tell right from wrong but that his cast of mind cannot admit that he, personally, has any viable connection with his world, his universe, or his society. He is not a partner in society, but an incorporated member, so to speak, and you cannot sue personally the officers of a corporation. I hasten to make clear here that I am not merely speaking of a literal corporation but the concept of a man's becoming a function of production or distribution to the point where his personality becomes divorced from the actions it propels.

This passage is only a brief quotation from a long discussion (pp. 12–22) in which the author follows *All My Sons* from inception to production, compares it to an earlier play, *The Man Who Had All the Luck*, and considers the influence his reading of Ibsen may have had on the writing of it. Not that what an author says need be taken as the last word about his play— particularly, as in this case, when the remarks were written ten years after the play.

28

All My Sons†

The Characters

JOE KELLER	DR. JIM BAYLISS
KATE KELLER	SUE BAYLISS
CHRIS KELLER	FRANK LUBEY
ANN DEEVER	LYDIA LUBEY
GEORGE DEEVER	BERT

Act One

The back yard of the Keller home in the outskirts of an American town. August of our era.

The stage is hedged on right and left by tall, closely planted poplars which lend the yard a secluded atmosphere. Upstage is filled with the back of the house and its open, unroofed porch which extends into the yard some six feet. The house is two stories high and has seven rooms. It would have cost perhaps fifteen thousand in the early twenties when it was built. Now it is nicely painted, looks tight and comfortable, and the yard is green with sod, here and there plants whose season is gone. At the right, beside the house, the entrance of the driveway can be seen, but the poplars cut off view of its continuation downstage. In the left corner, downstage, stands the four-foot-high stump of a slender apple tree whose upper trunk and branches lie toppled beside it, fruit still clinging to its branches.

Downstage right is a small, trellised arbor, shaped like a sea shell, with a decorative bulb hanging from its forward-curving roof. Garden chairs and a table are scattered about. A garbage pail on the ground next to the porch steps, a wire leaf-burner near it.

On the rise: It is early Sunday morning. JOE KELLER is sitting in the sun reading the want ads of the Sunday paper, the other sections of which lie neatly on the ground beside him. Behind his back, inside the arbor, DOCTOR JIM BAYLISS is reading part of the paper at the table.

KELLER is nearing sixty. A heavy man of stolid mind and build, a business man these many years, but with the imprint of the machine-shop worker and boss still upon him. When he reads, when he speaks, when he listens, it is with the terrible concentration of the uneducated man for whom there is still wonder in many commonly known things, a man whose judgments must be dredged out of experience and a peasant-like common sense. A man among men.

DOCTOR BAYLISS *is nearly forty. A wry self-controlled man, an easy talker, but with a wisp of sadness that clings even to his self-effacing humor.*

At curtain, JIM *is standing at left, staring at the broken tree. He taps a pipe on it, blows through the pipe, feels in his pockets for tobacco, then speaks.*

JIM. Where's your tobacco?

KELLER. I think I left it on the table. [JIM *goes slowly to table on the arbor, finds a pouch, and sits there on the bench, filling his pipe.*] Gonna rain tonight.

JIM. Paper says so?

KELLER. Yeah, right here.

JIM. Then it can't rain.

[FRANK LUBEY *enters, through a small space between the poplars.* FRANK *is thirty-two but balding. A pleasant, opinionated man, uncertain of himself, with a tendency toward peevishness when crossed, but always wanting it pleasant and neighborly. He rather saunters in, leisurely, nothing to do. He does not notice* JIM *in the arbor. On his greeting,* JIM *does not bother looking up.*]

FRANK. Hya.

KELLER. Hello, Frank. What's doin'?

FRANK. Nothin'. Walking off my breakfast. [*looks up at the sky*] That beautiful? Not a cloud.

KELLER. [*looking up*] Yeah, nice.

FRANK. Every Sunday ought to be like this.

KELLER. [*indicating the sections beside him*] Want the paper?

FRANK. What's the difference, it's all bad news. What's today's calamity?

KELLER. I don't know, I don't read the news part any more. It's more interesting in the want ads.

FRANK. Why, you trying to buy something?

KELLER. No, I'm just interested. To see what people want, y'know? For instance, here's a guy is lookin' for two Newfoundland dogs. Now what's he want with two Newfoundland dogs?

FRANK. That is funny.

KELLER. Here's another one. Wanted—old dictionaries. High prices paid. Now what's a man going to do with an old dictionary?

FRANK. Why not? Probably a book collector.

KELLER. You mean he'll make a living out of that?

FRANK. Sure, there's a lot of them.

KELLER. [*shaking his head*] All the kind of business goin' on. In my day, either you were a lawyer, or a doctor, or you worked in a shop. Now—

FRANK. Well, I was going to be a forester once.

KELLER. Well, that shows you; in my day, there was no such thing.

[*scanning the page, sweeping it with his hand*] You look at a page like this you realize how ignorant you are. [*softly, with wonder, as he scans page*] Psss!

FRANK. [*noticing tree*] Hey, what happened to your tree?

KELLER. Ain't that awful? The wind must've got it last night. You heard the wind, didn't you?

FRANK. Yeah, I got a mess in my yard, too. [*goes to tree*] What a pity. [*turning to* KELLER] What'd Kate say?

KELLER. They're all asleep yet. I'm just waiting for her to see it.

FRANK. [*struck*] You know?—it's funny.

KELLER. What?

FRANK. Larry was born in August. He'd been twenty-seven this month. And his tree blows down.

KELLER. [*touched*] I'm surprised you remember his birthday, Frank. That's nice.

FRANK. Well, I'm working on his horoscope.

KELLER. How can you make him a horoscope? That's for the future, ain't it?

FRANK. Well, what I'm doing is this, see. Larry was reported missing on November twenty-fifth, right?

KELLER. Yeah?

FRANK. Well, then, we assume that if he was killed it was on November twenty-fifth. Now, what Kate wants—

KELLER. Oh, Kate asked you to make a horoscope?

FRANK. Yeah, what she wants to find out is whether November twenty-fifth was a favorable day for Larry.

KELLER. What is that, favorable day?

FRANK. Well, a favorable day for a person is a fortunate day, according to his stars. In other words it would be practically impossible for him to have died on his favorable day.

KELLER. Well, was that his favorable day?—November twenty-fifth?

FRANK. That's what I'm working on to find out. It takes time! See, the point is, if November twenty-fifth was his favorable day, then it's completely possible he's alive somewhere, because—I mean it's possible. [*He notices* JIM *now.* JIM *is looking at him as though at an idiot. To* JIM—*with an uncertain laugh*] I didn't even see you.

KELLER. [*to* JIM] Is he talkin' sense?

JIM. Him? He's all right. He's just completely out of his mind, that's all.

FRANK. [*peeved*] The trouble with you is, you don't *believe* in anything.

JIM. And your trouble is that you believe in *anything*. You didn't see my kid this morning, did you?

FRANK. No.

KELLER. Imagine? He walked off with his thermometer. Right out of his bag.

JIM. [*getting up*] What a problem. One look at a girl and he takes her temperature. [*goes to driveway, looks upstage toward street*]

FRANK. That boy's going to be a real doctor; he's smart.

JIM. Over my dead body he'll be a doctor. A good beginning, too.

FRANK. Why? It's an honorable profession.

JIM. [*looking at him tiredly*] Frank, will you stop talking like a civics book? [KELLER *laughs.*]

FRANK. Why, I saw a movie a couple of weeks ago, reminded me of you. There was a doctor in that picture—

KELLER. Don Ameche!

FRANK. I think it was, yeah. And he worked in his basement discovering things. That's what you ought to do; you could help humanity, instead of—

JIM. I would love to help humanity on a Warner Brothers salary.

KELLER. [*pointing at him, laughing*] That's very good, Jim.

JIM. [*looking toward house*] Well, where's the beautiful girl was supposed to be here?

FRANK. [*excited*] Annie came?

KELLER. Sure, sleepin' upstairs. We picked her up on the one o'clock train last night. Wonderful thing. Girl leaves here, a scrawny kid. Couple of years go by, she's a regular woman. Hardly recognized her, and she was running in and out of this yard all her life. That was a very happy family used to live in your house, Jim.

JIM. Like to meet her. The block can use a pretty girl. In the whole neighborhood there's not a damned thing to look at. [SUE, JIM's *wife, enters. She is rounding forty, an overweight woman who fears it. On seeing her* JIM *wryly adds*] Except my wife, of course.

SUE. [*in same spirit*] Mrs. Adams is on the phone, you dog.

JIM. [*to* KELLER] Such is the condition which prevails—[*going to his wife*] my love, my light.

SUE. Don't sniff around me. [*pointing to their house*] And give her a nasty answer. I can smell her perfume over the phone.

JIM. What's the matter with her now?

SUE. I don't know, dear. She sounds like she's in terrible pain—unless her mouth is full of candy.

JIM. Why don't you just tell her to lay down?

SUE. She enjoys it more when you tell her to lay down. And when are you going to see Mr. Hubbard?

JIM. My dear; Mr. Hubbard is not sick; and I have better things to do than to sit there and hold his hand.

SUE. It seems to me that for ten dollars you could hold his hand.

JIM. [*to* KELLER] If your son wants to play golf tell him I'm ready. Or if he'd like to take a trip around the world for about thirty years. [*He exits.*]

KELLER. Why do you needle him? He's a doctor, women are supposed to call him up.

SUE. All I said was Mrs. Adams is on the phone. Can I have some of your parsley?

KELLER. Yeah, sure. [*She goes to parsley box and pulls some parsley.*] You were a nurse too long, Susie. You're too . . . too . . . realistic.

SUE. [*laughing, pointing at him*] Now you said it!

[LYDIA LUBEY *enters. She is a robust, laughing girl of twenty-seven.*]

LYDIA. Frank, the toaster—[*sees the others*] Hya.

KELLER. Hello!

LYDIA. [*to* FRANK] The toaster is off again.

FRANK. Well, plug it in, I just fixed it.

LYDIA. [*kindly, but insistently*] Please, dear, fix it back like it was before.

FRANK. I don't know why you can't learn to turn on a simple thing like a toaster! [*He exits.*]

SUE. [*laughing*] Thomas Edison.

LYDIA. [*apologetically*] He's really very handy. [*She sees broken tree.*] Oh, did the wind get your tree?

KELLER. Yeah, last night.

LYDIA. Oh, what a pity. Annie get in?

KELLER. She'll be down soon. Wait'll you meet her, Sue, she's a knockout.

SUE. I should've been a man. People are always introducing me to beautiful women. [*to* JOE] Tell her to come over later: I imagine she'd like to see what we did with her house. And thanks. [*She exits.*]

LYDIA. Is she still unhappy, Joe?

KELLER. Annie? I don't suppose she goes around dancing on her toes, but she seems to be over it.

LYDIA. She going to get married? Is there anybody—?

KELLER. I suppose—say, it's a couple years already. She can't mourn a boy forever.

LYDIA. It's so strange—Annie's here and not even married. And I've got three babies. I always thought it'd be the other way around.

KELLER. Well, that's what a war does. I had two sons, now I got one. It changed all the tallies. In my day when you had sons it was an honor. Today a doctor could make a million dollars if he could figure out a way to bring a boy into the world without a trigger finger.

LYDIA. You know, I was just reading—

[*Enter* CHRIS KELLER *from house, stands in doorway.*]

LYDIA. Hya, Chris.

[FRANK *shouts from offstage.*]

FRANK. Lydia, come in here! If you want the toaster to work don't plug in the malted mixer.

LYDIA. [*embarrassed, laughing*] Did I?

FRANK. And the next time I fix something don't tell me I'm crazy! Now come in here!

LYDIA. [*to* KELLER] I'll never hear the end of this one.

KELLER. [*calling to* FRANK] So what's the difference? Instead of toast have a malted!

LYDIA. Sh! sh! [*She exits, laughing.*]

[CHRIS *watches her off. He is thirty-two; like his father, sol-*

idly built, a listener. A man capable of immense affection and loyalty. He has a cup of coffee in one hand, part of a doughnut in the other.]

KELLER. You want the paper?

CHRIS. That's all right, just the book section. [*He bends down and pulls out part of paper on porch floor.*]

KELLER. You're always reading the book section and you never buy a book.

CHRIS. [*coming down to settee*] I like to keep abreast of my ignorance. [*He sits on settee.*]

KELLER. What is that, every week a new book comes out?

CHRIS. Lot of new books.

KELLER. All different.

CHRIS. All different.

[KELLER *shakes his head, puts knife down on bench, takes oilstone up to the cabinet.*]

KELLER. Psss! Annie up yet?

CHRIS. Mother's giving her breakfast in the dining room.

KELLER. [*looking at broken tree*] See what happened to the tree?

CHRIS. [*without looking up*] Yeah.

KELLER. What's Mother going to say?

[BERT *runs on from driveway. He is about eight. He jumps on stool, then on* KELLER's *back.*]

BERT. You're finally up.

KELLER. [*swinging him around and putting him down*] Ha! Bert's here! Where's Tommy? He's got his father's thermometer again.

BERT. He's taking a reading.

CHRIS. What!

BERT. But it's only oral.

KELLER. Oh, well, there's no harm in oral. So what's new this morning, Bert?

BERT. Nothin'. [*He goes to broken tree, walks around it.*]

KELLER. Then you couldn't've made a complete inspection of the block. In the beginning, when I first made you a policeman you used to come in every morning with something new. Now, nothin's ever new.

BERT. Except some kids from Thirtieth Street. They started kicking a can down the block, and I made them go away because you were sleeping.

KELLER. Now you're talkin', Bert. Now you're on the ball. First thing you know I'm liable to make you a detective.

BERT. [*pulling him down by the lapel and whispering in his ear*] Can I see the jail now?

KELLER. Seein' the jail ain't allowed, Bert. You know that.

BERT. Aw, I betcha there isn't even a jail. I don't see any bars on the cellar windows.

KELLER. Bert, on my word of honor there's a jail in the basement. I showed you my gun, didn't I?

BERT. But that's a hunting gun.

KELLER. That's an arresting gun!

BERT. Then why don't you ever arrest anybody? Tommy said an-

other dirty word to Doris yesterday, and you didn't even demote
him.

[KELLER *chuckles and winks at* CHRIS, *who is enjoying all
this.*]

KELLER. Yeah, that's a dangerous character, that Tommy. [*beckons
him closer*] What word does he say?

BERT. [*backing away quickly in great embarrassment*] Oh, I can't
say that.

KELLER. [*grabbing him by the shirt and pulling him back*] Well,
gimme an idea.

BERT. I can't. It's not a nice word.

KELLER. Just whisper it in my ear. I'll close my eyes. Maybe I won't
even hear it.

[BERT, *on tiptoe, puts his lips to* KELLER'S *ear, then in unbearable embarrassment steps back.*]

BERT. I can't, Mr. Keller.

CHRIS. [*laughing*] Don't make him do that.

KELLER. Okay, Bert. I take your word. Now go out, and keep both
eyes peeled.

BERT. [*interested*] For what?

KELLER. For what! Bert, the whole neighborhood is depending on
you. A policeman don't ask questions. Now peel them eyes!

BERT. [*mystified, but willing*] Okay. [*He runs off stage back of arbor.*]

KELLER. [*calling after him*] And mum's the word, Bert.

[BERT *stops and sticks his head through the arbor.*]

BERT. About what?

KELLER. Just in general. Be v-e-r-y careful.

BERT. [*nodding in bewilderment*] Okay. [*He exits.*]

KELLER. [*laughing*] I got all the kids crazy!

CHRIS. One of these days, they'll all come in here and beat your
brains out.

KELLER. What's she going to say? Maybe we ought to tell her before
she sees it.

CHRIS. She saw it.

KELLER. How could she see it? I was the first one up. She was still
in bed.

CHRIS. She was out here when it broke.

KELLER. When?

CHRIS. About four this morning. [*indicating window above them*]
I heard it cracking and I woke up and looked out. She was standing right here when it cracked.

KELLER. What was she doing out here four in the morning?

CHRIS. I don't know. When it cracked she ran back into the house
and cried in the kitchen.

KELLER. Did you talk to her?

CHRIS. No, I—I figured the best thing was to leave her alone.

[*Pause.*]

KELLER. [*deeply touched*] She cried hard?

CHRIS. I could hear her right through the floor of my room.

KELLER. [*after slight pause*] What was she doing out here at that hour? [CHRIS *silent. With an undertone of anger showing*] She's dreaming about him again. She's walking around at night.

CHRIS. I guess she is.

KELLER. She's getting just like after he died. [*slight pause*] What's the meaning of that?

CHRIS. I don't know the meaning of it. [*slight pause*] But I know one thing, Dad. We've made a terrible mistake with Mother.

KELLER. What?

CHRIS. Being dishonest with her. That kind of thing always pays off, and now it's paying off.

KELLER. What do you mean, dishonest?

CHRIS. You know Larry's not coming back and I know it. Why do we allow her to go on thinking that we believe with her?

KELLER. What do you want to do, argue with her?

CHRIS. I don't want to argue with her, but it's time she realized that nobody believes Larry is alive any more. [KELLER *simply moves away, thinking, looking at the ground.*] Why shouldn't she dream of him, walk the nights waiting for him? Do we contradict her? Do we say straight out that we have no hope any more? That we haven't had any hope for years now?

KELLER. [*frightened at the thought*] You can't say that to her.

CHRIS. We've got to say it to her.

KELLER. How're you going to prove it? Can you prove it?

CHRIS. For God's sake, three years! Nobody comes back after three years. It's insane.

KELLER. To you it is, and to me. But not to her. You can talk yourself blue in the face, but there's no body and there's no grave, so where are you?

CHRIS. Sit down, Dad. I want to talk to you.

[KELLER *looks at him searchingly a moment.*]

KELLER. The trouble is the Goddam newspapers. Every month some boy turns up from nowhere, so the next one is going to be Larry, so—

CHRIS. All right, all right, listen to me. [*Slight pause.* KELLER *sits on settee.*] You know why I asked Annie here, don't you?

KELLER. [*He knows, but—*] Why?

CHRIS. You know.

KELLER. Well, I got an idea, but— What's the story?

CHRIS. I'm going to ask her to marry me. [*slight pause*]
[KELLER *nods.*]

KELLER. Well, that's only your business, Chris.

CHRIS. You know it's not only my business.

KELLER. What do you want me to do? You're old enough to know your own mind.

CHRIS. [*asking, annoyed*] Then it's all right, I'll go ahead with it?

KELLER. Well, you want to be sure Mother isn't going to—

CHRIS. Then it isn't just my business.

KELLER. I'm just sayin'—

CHRIS. Sometimes you infuriate me, you know that? Isn't it your business, too, if I tell this to Mother and she throws a fit about it?

You have such a talent for ignoring things.

KELLER. I ignore what I gotta ignore. The girl is Larry's girl.

CHRIS. She's not Larry's girl.

KELLER. From Mother's point of view he is not dead and you have no right to take his girl. [*slight pause*] Now you can go on from there if you know where to go, but I'm tellin' you I don't know where to go. See? I don't know. Now what can I do for you?

CHRIS. I don't know why it is, but every time I reach out for something I want, I have to pull back because other people will suffer. My whole bloody life, time after time after time.

KELLER. You're a considerate fella, there's nothing wrong in that.

CHRIS. To hell with that.

KELLER. Did you ask Annie yet?

CHRIS. I wanted to get this settled first.

KELLER. How do you know she'll marry you? Maybe she feels the same way Mother does?

CHRIS. Well, if she does, then that's the end of it. From her letters I think she's forgotten him. I'll find out. And then we'll thrash it out with Mother? Right? Dad, don't avoid me.

KELLER. The trouble is, you don't see enough women. You never did.

CHRIS. So what? I'm not fast with women.

KELLER. I don't see why it has to be Annie.

CHRIS. Because it is.

KELLER. That's a good answer, but it don't answer anything. You haven't seen her since you went to war. It's five years.

CHRIS. I can't help it. I know her best. I was brought up next door to her. These years when I think of someone for my wife, I think of Annie. What do you want, a diagram?

KELLER. I don't want a diagram . . . I—I'm— She thinks he's coming back, Chris. You marry that girl and you're pronouncing him dead. Now what's going to happen to Mother? Do you know? I don't! [*pause*]

CHRIS. All right, then, Dad.

KELLER. [*thinking* CHRIS *has retreated*] Give it some more thought.

CHRIS. I've given it three years of thought. I'd hoped that if I waited, Mother would forget Larry and then we'd have a regular wedding and everything happy. But if that can't happen here, then I'll have to get out.

KELLER. What the hell is *this*?

CHRIS. I'll get out. I'll get married and live some place else. Maybe in New York.

KELLER. Are you crazy?

CHRIS. I've been a good son too long, a good sucker. I'm through with it.

KELLER. You've got a business here, what the hell is this?

CHRIS. The business! The business doesn't inspire me.

KELLER. Must you be inspired?

CHRIS. Yes. I like it an hour a day. If I have to grub for money all day long at least at evening I want it beautiful. I want a family,

I want some kids, I want to build something I can give myself to. Annie is in the middle of that. Now . . . where do I find it?

KELLER. You mean— [*goes to him*] Tell me something, you mean you'd leave the business?

CHRIS. Yes. On this I would.

KELLER. [*after a pause*] Well . . . you don't want to think like that.

CHRIS. Then help me stay here.

KELLER. All right, but—but don't think like that. Because what the hell did I work for? That's only for you, Chris, the whole shootin' match is for you!

CHRIS. I know that, Dad. Just you help me stay here.

KELLER. [*putting a fist up to* CHRIS's *jaw*] But don't think that way, you hear me?

CHRIS. I am thinking that way.

KELLER. [*lowering his hand*] I don't understand you, do I?

CHRIS. No, you don't. I'm a pretty tough guy.

KELLER. Yeah. I can see that.

[MOTHER *appears on porch. She is in her early fifties, a woman of uncontrolled inspirations and an overwhelming capacity for love.*]

MOTHER. Joe?

CHRIS. [*going toward porch*] Hello, Mom.

MOTHER. [*indicating house behind her; to* KELLER] Did you take a bag from under the sink?

KELLER. Yeah, I put it in the pail.

MOTHER. Well, get it out of the pail. That's my potatoes.

[CHRIS *bursts out laughing—goes up into alley.*]

KELLER. [*laughing*] I thought it was garbage.

MOTHER. Will you do me a favor, Joe? Don't be helpful.

KELLER. I can afford another bag of potatoes.

MOTHER. Minnie scoured that pail in boiling water last night. It's cleaner than your teeth.

KELLER. And I don't understand why, after I worked forty years and I got a maid, why I have to take out the garbage.

MOTHER. If you would make up your mind that every bag in the kitchen isn't full of garbage you wouldn't be throwing out my vegetables. Last time it was the onions.

[CHRIS *comes on, hands her bag.*]

KELLER. I don't like garbage in the house.

MOTHER. Then don't eat. [*She goes into the kitchen with bag.*]

CHRIS. That settles you for today.

KELLER. Yeah, I'm in last place again. I don't know, once upon a time I used to think that when I got money again I would have a maid and my wife would take it easy. Now I got money, and I got a maid, and my wife is workin' for the maid. [*He sits in one of the chairs.*]

[MOTHER *comes out on last line. She carries a pot of string beans.*]

MOTHER. It's her day off, what are you crabbing about?

CHRIS. [*to* MOTHER] Isn't Annie finished eating?

MOTHER. [*looking around preoccupiedly at yard*] She'll be right out. [*moves*] That wind did some job on this place. [*of the tree*] So much for that, thank God.

KELLER. [*indicating chair beside him*] Sit down, take it easy.

MOTHER. [*pressing her hand to top of her head*] I've got such a funny pain on the top of my head.

CHRIS. Can I get you an aspirin?

> [MOTHER *picks a few petals off ground, stands there smelling them in her hand, then sprinkles them over plants.*]

MOTHER. No more roses. It's so funny . . . everything decides to happen at the same time. This month is his birthday; his tree blows down, Annie comes. Everything that happened seems to be coming back. I was just down the cellar, and what do I stumble over? His baseball glove. I haven't seen it in a century.

CHRIS. Don't you think Annie looks well?

MOTHER. Fine. There's no question about it. She's a beauty . . . I still don't know what brought her here. Not that I'm not glad to see her, but—

CHRIS. I just thought we'd all like to see each other again. [MOTHER *just looks at him, nodding ever so slightly—almost as though admitting something.*] And I wanted to see her myself.

MOTHER. [*as her nods halt, to* KELLER] The only thing is I think her nose got longer. But I'll always love that girl. She's one that didn't jump into bed with somebody else as soon as it happened with her fella.

KELLER. [*as though that were impossible for* ANNIE] Oh, what're you—?

MOTHER. Never mind. Most of them didn't wait till the telegrams were opened. I'm just glad she came, so you can see I'm not *completely* out of my mind. [*sits, and rapidly breaks string beans in the pot*]

CHRIS. Just because she isn't married doesn't mean she's been mourning Larry.

MOTHER. [*with an undercurrent of observation*] Why then isn't she?

CHRIS. [*a little flustered*] Well . . . it could've been any number of things.

MOTHER. [*directly at him*] Like what, for instance?

CHRIS. [*embarrassed, but standing his ground*] I don't know. Whatever it is. Can I get you an aspirin?

> [MOTHER *puts her hand to her head. She gets up and goes aimlessly toward the trees on rising.*]

MOTHER. It's not like a headache.

KELLER. You don't sleep, that's why. She's wearing out more bedroom slippers than shoes.

MOTHER. I had a terrible night. [*She stops moving.*] I never had a night like that.

CHRIS. [*looking at* KELLER] What was it, Mom? Did you dream?

MOTHER. More, more than a dream.

CHRIS. [*hesitantly*] About Larry?

MOTHER. I was fast asleep, and— [*raising her arm over the audience*] Remember the way he used to fly low past the house when he was in training? When we used to see his face in the cockpit going by? That's the way I saw him. Only high up. Way, way up, where the clouds are. He was so real I could reach out and touch him. And suddenly he started to fall. And crying, crying to me . . . Mom, Mom! I could hear him like he was in the room. Mom! . . . it was his voice! If I could touch him I knew I could stop him, if I could only— [*breaks off, allowing her outstretched hand to fall*] I woke up and it was so funny— The wind . . . it was like the roaring of his engine. I came out here . . . I must've still been half asleep. I could hear that roaring like he was going by. The tree snapped right in front of me—and I like—came awake. [*She is looking at tree. She suddenly realizes something, turns with a reprimanding finger shaking slightly at* KELLER.] See? We should never have planted that tree. I said so in the first place; it was too soon to plant a tree for him.

CHRIS. [*alarmed*] Too soon!

MOTHER. [*angering*] We rushed into it. Everybody was in such a hurry to bury him. I *said* not to plant it yet. [*to* KELLER] I *told* you to—!

CHRIS. Mother, Mother! [*She looks into his face.*] The wind blew it down. What significance has that got? What are you talking about? Mother, please . . . Don't go through it all again, will you? It's no good, it doesn't accomplish anything. I've been thinking, y'know?—maybe we ought to put our minds to forgetting him?

MOTHER. That's the third time you've said that this week.

CHRIS. Because it's not right; we never took up our lives again. We're like at a railroad station waiting for a train that never comes in.

MOTHER. [*pressing top of her head*] Get me an aspirin, heh?

CHRIS. Sure, and let's break out of this, heh, Mom? I thought the four of us might go out to dinner a couple of nights, maybe go dancing out at the shore.

MOTHER. Fine. [*to* KELLER] We can do it tonight.

KELLER. Swell with me!

CHRIS. Sure, let's have some fun. [*to* MOTHER] You'll start with this aspirin. [*He goes up and into house with new spirit. Her smile vanishes.*]

MOTHER. [*with an accusing undertone*] Why did he invite her here?

KELLER. Why does that bother you?

MOTHER. She's been in New York three and a half years, why all of a sudden—?

KELLER. Well, maybe—maybe he just wanted to see her.

MOTHER. Nobody comes seven hundred miles "just to see."

KELLER. What do you mean? He lived next door to the girl all his life, why shouldn't he want to see her again? [MOTHER *looks at him critically.*] Don't look at me like that, he didn't tell me any more than he told you.

MOTHER. [*a warning and a question*] He's not going to marry her.

KELLER. How do you know he's even thinking of it?

MOTHER. It's got that about it.

KELLER. [*sharply watching her reaction*] Well? So what?

MOTHER. [*alarmed*] What's going on here, Joe?

KELLER. Now listen, kid—

MOTHER. [*avoiding contact with him*] She's not his girl, Joe; she knows she's not.

KELLER. You can't read her mind.

MOTHER. Then why is she still single? New York is full of men, why isn't she married? [*pause*] Probably a hundred people told her she's foolish, but she's waited.

KELLER. How do you know why she waited?

MOTHER. She knows what I know, that's why. She's faithful as a rock. In my worst moments, I think of her waiting, and I know again that I'm right.

KELLER. Look, it's a nice day. What are we arguing for?

MOTHER. [*warningly*] Nobody in this house dast take her faith away, Joe. Strangers might. But not his father, not his brother.

KELLER. [*exasperated*] What do you want me to do? What do you want?

MOTHER. I want you to act like he's coming back. Both of you. Don't think I haven't noticed you since Chris invited her. I won't stand for any nonsense.

KELLER. But, Kate—

MOTHER. Because if he's not coming back, then I'll kill myself! Laugh. Laugh at me. [*She points to tree.*] But why did that happen the very night she came back? Laugh, but there are meanings in such things. She goes to sleep in his room and his memorial breaks in pieces. Look at it; look. [*She sits on bench.*] Joe—

KELLER. Calm yourself.

MOTHER. Believe with me, Joe. I can't stand all alone.

KELLER. Calm yourself.

MOTHER. Only last week a man turned up in Detroit, missing longer than Larry. You read it yourself.

KELLER. All right, all right, calm yourself.

MOTHER. You above all have got to believe, you—

KELLER. [*rising*] Why me above all?

MOTHER. Just don't stop believing.

KELLER. What does that mean, me above all?

[BERT *comes rushing on.*]

BERT. Mr. Keller! Say, Mr. Keller . . . [*pointing up driveway*] Tommy just said it again!

KELLER. [*not remembering any of it*] Said what? Who?

BERT. The dirty word.

KELLER. Oh. Well—

BERT. Gee, aren't you going to arrest him? I warned him.

MOTHER. [*with suddenness*] Stop that, Bert. Go home. [BERT *backs up, as she advances.*] There's no jail here.

KELLER. [*as though to say, "Oh-what-the-hell-let-him-believe-there-is"*] Kate—

MOTHER. [*turning on* KELLER *furiously*] There's no jail here! I want you to stop that jail business! [*He turns, shamed, but peeved.*]

BERT. [*past her to* KELLER] He's right across the street.

MOTHER. Go home, Bert. [BERT *turns around and goes up driveway. She is shaken. Her speech is bitten off, extremely urgent.*] I want you to stop that, Joe. That whole jail business!

KELLER. [*alarmed, therefore angered*] Look at you, look at you shaking.

MOTHER. [*trying to control herself, moving about clasping her hands*] I can't help it.

KELLER. What have I got to hide? What the hell is the matter with you, Kate?

MOTHER. I didn't say you had anything to hide, I'm just telling you to stop it! Now stop it! [*As* ANN *and* CHRIS *appear on porch.* ANN *is twenty-six, gentle but despite herself capable of holding fast to what she knows.* CHRIS *opens door for her.*]

ANN. Hya, Joe! [*She leads off a general laugh that is not self-conscious because they know one another too well.*]

CHRIS. [*bringing* ANN *down, with an outstretched, chivalric arm*] Take a breath of that air, kid. You never get air like that in New York.

MOTHER. [*genuinely overcome with it*] Annie, where did you get that dress!

ANN. I couldn't resist. I'm taking it right off before I ruin it. [*swings around*] How's that for three weeks' salary?

MOTHER. [*to* KELLER] Isn't she the most—? [*to* ANN] It's gorgeous, simply gor—

CHRIS. [*to* MOTHER] No kidding, now, isn't she the prettiest gal you ever saw?

MOTHER. [*Caught short by his obvious admiration, she finds herself reaching out for a glass of water and aspirin in his hand, and—*] You gained a little weight, didn't you, darling? [*She gulps pill and drinks.*]

ANN. It comes and goes.

KELLER. Look how nice her legs turned out!

ANN. [*as she runs to fence*] Boy, the poplars got thick, didn't they?
[KELLER *moves to settee and sits.*]

KELLER. Well, it's three years, Annie. We're gettin' old, kid.

MOTHER. How does Mom like New York? [ANN *keeps looking through trees.*]

ANN. [*a little hurt*] Why'd they take our hammock away?

KELLER. Oh, no, it broke. Couple of years ago.

MOTHER. What broke? He had one of his light lunches and flopped into it.

ANN. [*laughs and turns back toward* JIM's *yard*] Oh, excuse me!
[JIM *has come to fence and is looking over it. He is smoking a cigar. As she cries out, he comes on around on stage.*]

JIM. How do you do. [*to* CHRIS] She looks very intelligent!

CHRIS. Ann, this is Jim—Doctor Bayliss.

ANN. [*shaking* JIM's *hand*] Oh, sure, he writes a lot about you.

JIM. Don't you believe it. He likes everybody. In the battalion he was known as Mother McKeller.

ANN. I can believe it. You know—? [*to* MOTHER] It's so strange seeing him come out of that yard. [*to* CHRIS] I guess I never grew up. It almost seems that Mom and Pop are in there now. And you and my brother doing algebra, and Larry trying to copy my homework. Gosh, those dear dead days beyond recall.

JIM. Well, I hope that doesn't mean you want me to move out?

SUE. [*calling from offstage*] Jim, come in here! Mr. Hubbard is on the phone!

JIM. I told you I don't want—

SUE. [*commandingly sweet*] Please, dear! Please!

JIM. [*resigned*] All right, Susie. [*trailing off*] All right, all right . . . [*to* ANN] I've only just met you, Ann, but if I may offer you a piece of advice— When you marry, never—even in your mind—never count your husband's money.

SUE. [*from offstage*] Jim?

JIM. At once! [*turns and goes off*] At once. [*He exits.*]

MOTHER. [ANN *is looking at her. She speaks meaningfully.*] I told her to take up the guitar. It'd be a common interest for them. [*They laugh.*] Well, he loves the guitar!

[ANN, *as though to overcome* MOTHER, *becomes suddenly lively, crosses to* KELLER *on settee, sits on his lap.*]

ANN. Let's eat at the shore tonight! Raise some hell around here, like we used to before Larry went!

MOTHER. [*emotionally*] You think of him! You see? [*triumphantly*] She thinks of him!

ANN. [*with an uncomprehending smile*] What do you mean, Kate?

MOTHER. Nothing. Just that you—remember him, he's in your thoughts.

ANN. That's a funny thing to say; how could I help remembering him?

MOTHER. [*It is drawing to a head the wrong way for her; she starts anew. She rises and comes to* ANN.] Did you hang up your things?

ANN. Yeah . . . [*to* CHRIS] Say, you've sure gone in for clothes. I could hardly find room in the closet.

MOTHER. No, don't you remember? That's Larry's room.

ANN. You mean . . . they're Larry's?

MOTHER. Didn't you recognize them?

ANN. [*slowly rising, a little embarrassed*] Well, it never occurred to me that you'd—I mean the shoes are all shined.

MOTHER. Yes, dear. [*Slight pause.* ANN *can't stop staring at her.* MOTHER *breaks it by speaking with the relish of gossip, putting her arm around* ANN *and walking with her.*] For so long I've been aching for a nice conversation with you, Annie. Tell me something.

ANN. What?

MOTHER. I don't know. Something nice.

CHRIS. [*wryly*] She means do you go out much?

MOTHER. Oh, shut up.

KELLER. And are any of them serious?

MOTHER. [*laughing, sits in her chair*] Why don't you both choke?

KELLER. Annie, you can't go into a restaurant with that woman any more. In five minutes thirty-nine strange people are sitting at the table telling her their life story.

MOTHER. If I can't ask Annie a personal question—

KELLER. Askin' is all right, but don't beat her over the head. You're beatin' her, you're beatin' her. [*They are laughing.*]

[ANN *takes pan of beans off stool, puts them on floor under chair and sits.*]

ANN. [*to* MOTHER] Don't let them bulldoze you. Ask me anything you like. What do you want to know, Kate? Come on, let's gossip.

MOTHER. [*to* CHRIS *and* KELLER] She's the only one got any sense. [*to* ANN] Your mother—she's not getting a divorce, heh?

ANN. No, she's calmed down about it now. I think when he gets out they'll probably live together. In New York, of course.

MOTHER. That's fine. Because your father is still—I mean he's a decent man after all is said and done.

ANN. I don't care. She can take him back if she likes.

MOTHER. And you? You—[*shakes her head negatively*]—go out much? [*slight pause*]

ANN. [*delicately*] You mean am I still waiting for him?

MOTHER. Well, no. I don't expect you to wait for him but—

ANN. [*kindly*] But that's what you mean, isn't it?

MOTHER. Well . . . yes.

ANN. Well, I'm not, Kate.

MOTHER. [*faintly*] You're not?

ANN. Isn't it ridiculous? You don't really imagine he's—?

MOTHER. I know, dear, but don't say it's ridiculous, because the papers were full of it; I don't know about New York, but there was half a page about a man missing even longer than Larry, and he turned up from Burma.

CHRIS. [*coming to* ANN] He couldn't have wanted to come home very badly, Mom.

MOTHER. Don't be so smart.

CHRIS. You can have a helluva time in Burma.

ANN. [*rises and swings around in back of* CHRIS] So I've heard.

CHRIS. Mother, I'll bet you money that you're the only woman in the country who after three years is still—

MOTHER. You're sure?

CHRIS. Yes, I am.

MOTHER. Well, if you're sure then you're sure. [*She turns her head away an instant.*] They don't say it on the radio but I'm sure that in the dark at night they're still waiting for their sons.

CHRIS. Mother, you're absolutely—

MOTHER. [*waving him off*] Don't be so damned smart! Now stop it! [*slight pause*] There are just a few things you *don't* know. All of you. And I'll tell you one of them, Annie. Deep, deep in your heart you've always been waiting for him.

ANN. [*resolutely*] No, Kate.

MOTHER. [*with increasing demand*] But deep in your heart, Annie!

CHRIS. She ought to know, shouldn't she?

MOTHER. Don't let them tell you what to think. Listen to your heart. Only your heart.

ANN. Why does your heart tell you he's alive?

MOTHER. Because he has to be.

ANN. But why, Kate?

MOTHER. [*going to her*] Because certain things have to be, and certain things can never be. Like the sun has to rise, it has to be. That's why there's God. Otherwise anything could happen. But there's God, so certain things can never happen. I would know, Annie—just like I knew the day he—[*indicates* CHRIS]—went into that terrible battle. Did he write me? Was it in the papers? No, but that morning I couldn't raise my head off the pillow. Ask Joe. Suddenly, I knew. I knew! And he was nearly killed that day. Ann, you *know* I'm right!

[ANN *stands there in silence, then turns trembling, going upstage.*]

ANN. No, Kate.

MOTHER. I have to have some tea.

[FRANK *appears, carrying ladder.*]

FRANK. Annie! [*coming down*] How are you, gee whiz!

ANN. [*taking his hand*] Why, Frank, you're losing your hair.

KELLER. He's got responsibility.

FRANK. Gee whiz!

KELLER. Without Frank the stars wouldn't know when to come out.

FRANK. [*laughs; to* ANN] You look more womanly. You've matured. You—

KELLER. Take it easy, Frank, you're a married man.

ANN. [*as they laugh*] You still haberdashering?

FRANK. Why not? Maybe I too can get to be president. How's your brother? Got his degree, I hear.

ANN. Oh, George has his own office now!

FRANK. Don't say! [*funereally*] And your dad? Is he—?

ANN. [*abruptly*] Fine. I'll be in to see Lydia.

FRANK [*sympathetically*] How about it, does Dad expect a parole soon?

ANN. [*with growing ill-ease*] I really don't know, I—

FRANK. [*staunchly defending her father for her sake*] I mean because I feel, y'know, that if an intelligent man like your father is put in prison, there ought to be a law that says either you execute him, or let him go after a year.

CHRIS. [*interrupting*] Want a hand with that ladder, Frank?

FRANK. [*taking cue*] That's all right, I'll— [*picks up ladder*] I'll finish the horoscope tonight, Kate. [*embarrassed*] See you later, Ann, you look wonderful. [*He exits. They look at* ANN.]

ANN. [*to* CHRIS, *as she sits slowly on stool*] Haven't they stopped talking about Dad?

CHRIS. [*comes down and sits on arm of chair*] Nobody talks about him any more.

KELLER. [*rises and comes to her*] Gone and forgotten, kid.

ANN. Tell me. Because I don't want to meet anybody on the block if they're going to—

CHRIS. I don't want you to worry about it.

ANN. [*to* KELLER] Do they still remember the case, Joe? Do they talk about you?

KELLER. The only one still talks about it is my wife.

MOTHER. That's because you keep on playing policeman with the kids. All their parents hear out of you is jail, jail, jail.

KELLER. Actually what happened was that when I got home from the penitentiary the kids got very interested in me. You know kids. I was—[*laughs*]—like the expert on the jail situation. And as time passed they got it confused and . . . I ended up a detective. [*laughs*]

MOTHER. Except that *they* didn't get it confused. [*to* ANN] He hands out police badges from the Post Toasties boxes. [*They laugh.*]

[ANN *rises and comes to* KELLER, *putting her arm around his shoulder.*]

ANN. [*wondrously at them, happy*] Gosh, it's wonderful to hear you laughing about it.

CHRIS. Why, what'd you expect?

ANN. The last thing I remember on this block was one word— "Murderers!" Remember that, Kate?—Mrs. Hammond standing in front of our house and yelling that word? She's still around, I suppose?

MOTHER. They're all still around.

KELLER. Don't listen to her. Every Saturday night the whole gang is playin' poker in this arbor. All the ones who yelled murderer takin' my money now.

MOTHER. Don't, Joe; she's a sensitive girl, don't fool her. [*to* ANN] They still remember about Dad. It's different with him. [*indicates* JOE] He was exonerated, your father's still there. That's why I wasn't so enthusiastic about your coming. Honestly, I know how sensitive you are, and I told Chris, I said—

KELLER. Listen, you do like I did and you'll be all right. The day I come home, I got out of my car—but not in front of the house . . . on the corner. You should've been here, Annie, and you too, Chris; you'd-a seen something. Everybody knew I was getting out that day; the porches were loaded. Picture it now; none of them believed I was innocent. The story was, I pulled a fast one getting myself exonerated. So I get out of my car, and I walk down the street. But very slow. And with a smile. The beast! I was the beast; the guy who sold cracked cylinder heads to the Army Air Force; the guy who made twenty-one P-40s crash in Australia. Kid, walkin' down the street that day I was guilty as hell. Except I wasn't, and there was a court paper in my pocket to prove I wasn't, and I walked . . . past . . . the porches. Result? Fourteen months later I had one of the best shops in the state again, a respected man again; bigger than ever.

CHRIS. [*with admiration*] Joe McGuts.

KELLER. [*now with great force*] That's the only way you lick 'em is guts! [*to* ANN] The worst thing you did was to move away from here. You made it tough for your father when he gets out. That's why I tell you, I like to see him move back right on this block.

MOTHER. [*pained*] How could they move back?

KELLER. It ain't gonna end *till* they move back! [*to* ANN] Till people play cards with him again, and talk with him, and smile with him—you play cards with a man you know he can't be a murderer. And the next time you write him I like you to tell him just what I said. [ANN *simply stares at him.*] You hear me?

ANN. [*surprised*] Don't you hold anything against him?

KELLER. Annie, I never believed in crucifying people.

ANN. [*mystified*] But he was your partner, he dragged you through the mud.

KELLER. Well, he ain't my sweetheart, but you gotta forgive, don't you?

ANN. You, either, Kate? Don't you feel any—?

KELLER. [*to* ANN] The next time you write Dad—

ANN. I don't write him.

KELLER. [*struck*] Well, every now and then you—

ANN. [*a little shamed, but determined*] No, I've *never* written to him. Neither has my brother. [*to* CHRIS] Say, do you feel this way, too?

CHRIS. He murdered twenty-one pilots.

KELLER. What the hell kinda talk is that?

MOTHER. That's not a thing to say about a man.

ANN. What else can you say? When they took him away I followed him, went to him every visiting day. I was crying all the time. Until the news came about Larry. Then I realized. It's wrong to pity a man like that. Father or no father, there's only one way to look at him. He knowingly shipped out parts that would crash an airplane. And how do you know Larry wasn't one of them?

MOTHER. I was waiting for that. [*going to her*] As long as you're here, Annie, I want to ask you never to say that again.

ANN. You surprise me. I thought you'd be mad at him.

MOTHER. What your father did had nothing to do with Larry. Nothing.

ANN. But we can't know that.

MOTHER. [*striving for control*] As long as you're here!

ANN. [*perplexed*] But, Kate—

MOTHER. Put that out of your head!

KELLER. Because—

MOTHER. [*quickly to* KELLER] That's all, that's enough. [*places her hand on her head*] Come inside now, and have some tea with me. [*She turns and goes up steps.*]

KELLER. [*to* ANN] The one thing you—

MOTHER. [*sharply*] He's not dead, so there's no argument! Now come!

KELLER. [*angrily*] In a minute! [MOTHER *turns and goes into house.*] Now look, Annie—

CHRIS. All right, Dad, forget it.

KELLER. No, she dasn't feel that way. Annie—

CHRIS. I'm sick of the whole subject, now cut it out.

KELLER. You want her to go on like this? [*to* ANN] Those cylinder heads went into P-40s only. What's the matter with you? You know Larry never flew a P-40.

CHRIS. So who flew those P-40s, pigs?

KELLER. The man was a fool, but don't make a murderer out of him. You got no sense? Look what it does to her! [*to* ANN] Listen, you gotta appreciate what was doin' in that shop in the war. The both of you! It was a madhouse. Every half hour the Major callin' for cylinder heads, they were whippin' us with the telephone. The trucks were hauling them away hot, damn near. I mean just try to see it human, see it human. All of a sudden a batch comes out with a crack. That happens, that's the business. A fine, hairline crack. All right, so—so he's a little man, your father, always scared of loud voices. What'll the Major say?—Half a day's production shot. . . . What'll I say? You know what I mean? Human. [*He pauses.*] So he takes out his tools and he—covers over the cracks. All right—that's bad, it's wrong, but that's what a little man does. If I could have gone in that day I'd a told him —junk 'em, Steve, we can afford it. But alone he was afraid. But I know he meant no harm. He believed they'd hold up a hundred per cent. That's a mistake, but it ain't murder. You mustn't feel that way about him. You understand me? It ain't right.

ANN. [*She regards him a moment.*] Joe, let's forget it.

KELLER. Annie, the day the news came about Larry he was in the next cell to mine—Dad. And he cried, Annie—he cried half the night.

ANN. [*touched*] He shoulda cried all night. [*slight pause*]

KELLER. [*almost angered*] Annie, I do not understand why you—!

CHRIS. [*breaking in—with nervous urgency*] Are you going to stop it?

ANN. Don't yell at him. He just wants everybody happy.

KELLER. [*clasps her around waist, smiling*] That's my sentiments. Can you stand steak?

CHRIS. And champagne!

KELLER. Now you're operatin'! I'll call Swanson's for a table! Big time tonight, Annie!

ANN. Can't scare me.

KELLER. [*to* CHRIS, *pointing at* ANN] I like that girl. Wrap her up. [*They laugh; goes up porch*] You got nice legs, Annie! . . . I want to see everybody drunk tonight. [*pointing to* CHRIS] Look at him, he's blushin'! [*He exits, laughing, into house.*]

CHRIS. [*calling after him*] Drink your tea, Casanova. [*He turns to* ANN.] Isn't he a great guy?

ANN. You're the only one I know who loves his parents.

CHRIS. I know. It went out of style, didn't it?

ANN. [*with a sudden touch of sadness*] It's all right. It's a good thing. [*She looks about.*] You know? It's lovely here. The air is sweet.

CHRIS. [*hopefully*] You're not sorry you came?

ANN. Not sorry, no. But I'm—not going to stay.

CHRIS. Why?

ANN. In the first place, your mother as much as told me to go.

CHRIS. Well—

ANN. You saw that—and then you—you've been kind of—

CHRIS. What?

ANN. Well . . . kind of embarrassed ever since I got here.

CHRIS. The trouble is I planned on kind of sneaking up on you over a period of a week or so. But they take it for granted that we're all set.

ANN. I knew they would. Your mother anyway.

CHRIS. How did you know?

ANN. From *her* point of view, why else would I come?

CHRIS. Well . . . would you want to? [ANN *still studies him.*] I guess you know this is why I asked you to come.

ANN. I guess this is why I came.

CHRIS. Ann, I love you. I love you a great deal. [*finally*] I love you. [*Pause. She waits.*] I have no imagination . . . that's all I know to tell you. [ANN *is waiting, ready.*] I'm embarrassing you. I didn't want to tell it to you here. I wanted some place we'd never been; a place where we'd be brand new to each other. . . . You feel it's wrong here, don't you? This yard, this chair? I want you to be ready for me. I don't want to win you away from anything.

ANN. [*putting her arms around him*] Oh, Chris, I've been ready a long, long time!

CHRIS. Then he's gone forever. You're sure.

ANN. I almost got married two years ago.

CHRIS. Why didn't you?

ANN. You started to write to me— [*slight pause*]

CHRIS. You felt something that far back?

ANN. Every day since!

CHRIS. Ann, why didn't you let me know?

ANN. I was waiting for you, Chris. Till then you never wrote. And when you did, what did you say? You sure can be ambiguous, you know.

CHRIS. [*looks toward house, then at her, trembling*] Give me a kiss, Ann. Give me a— [*They kiss.*] God, I kissed you, Annie, I kissed Annie. How long, how long I've been waiting to kiss you!

ANN. I'll never forgive you. Why did you wait all these years? All I've done is sit and wonder if I was crazy for thinking of you.

CHRIS. Annie, we're going to live now! I'm going to make you so happy. [*He kisses her, but without their bodies touching.*]

ANN. [*a little embarrassed*] Not like that you're not.

CHRIS. I kissed you . . .

ANN. Like Larry's brother. Do it like you, Chris. [*He breaks away from her abruptly.*] What is it, Chris?

CHRIS. Let's drive some place . . . I want to be alone with you.

ANN. No . . . what is it, Chris, your mother?

CHRIS. No—nothing like that.

ANN. Then what's wrong? Even in your letters, there was something ashamed.

CHRIS. Yes. I suppose I have been. But it's going from me.

ANN. You've got to tell me—

CHRIS. I don't know how to start. [*He takes her hand.*]

ANN. It wouldn't work this way. [*slight pause*]

CHRIS. [*speaks quietly, factually at first*] It's all mixed up with so many other things. . . . You remember, overseas, I was in command of a company?

ANN. Yeah, sure.

CHRIS. Well, I lost them.

ANN. How many?

CHRIS. Just about all.

ANN. Oh, gee!

CHRIS. It takes a little time to toss that off. Because they weren't just men. For instance, one time it'd been raining several days and this kid came to me, and gave me his last pair of dry socks. Put them in my pocket. That's only a little thing—but . . . that's the kind of guys I had. They didn't die; they killed themselves for each other. I mean that exactly; a little more selfish and they'd 've been here today. And I got an idea—watching them go down. Everything was being destroyed, see, but it seemed to me that one new thing was made. A kind of—responsibility. Man for man. You understand me?—To show that, to bring that onto the earth again like some kind of a monument and everyone would feel it standing there, behind him, and it would make a difference to him. [*pause*] And then I came home and it was incredible. I—there was no meaning in it here; the whole thing to them was a kind of a—bus accident. I went to work with Dad, and that rat-race again. I felt—what you said—ashamed somehow. Because nobody was changed at all. It seemed to make suckers out of a lot of guys. I felt wrong to be alive, to open the bank-book, to drive the new car, to see the new refrigerator. I mean you can take those things out of a war, but when you drive that car you've got to know that it came out of the love a man can have for a man, you've got to be a little better because of that. Otherwise what you have is really loot, and there's blood on it. I didn't want to take any of it. And I guess that included you.

ANN. And you still feel that way?

CHRIS. I want you now, Annie.

ANN. Because you mustn't feel that way any more. Because you have a right to whatever you have. Everything, Chris, understand that? To me, too . . . And the money, there's nothing wrong in your money. Your father put hundreds of planes in the air, you should be proud. A man should be paid for that . . .

CHRIS. Oh Annie, Annie . . . I'm going to make a fortune for you!

KELLER. [*offstage*] Hello . . . Yes. Sure.

ANN. [*laughing softly*] What'll I do with a fortune?
  [*They kiss.* KELLER *enters from house.*]

KELLER. [*thumbing toward house*] Hey, Ann, your brother— [*They step apart shyly.* KELLER *comes down, and wryly*] What is this, Labor Day?

CHRIS. [*waving him away, knowing the kidding will be endless*] All right, all right.

ANN. You shouldn't burst out like that.

KELLER. Well, nobody told me it was Labor Day. [*looks around*] Where's the hot dogs?

CHRIS. [*loving it*] All right. You said it once.

KELLER. Well, as long as I know it's Labor Day from now on, I'll wear a bell around my neck.

ANN. [*affectionately*] He's so subtle!

CHRIS. George Bernard Shaw as an elephant.

KELLER. George!—hey, you kissed it out of my head—your brother's on the phone.

ANN. [*surprised*] My brother?

KELLER. Yeah, George. Long distance.

ANN. What's the matter, is anything wrong?

KELLER. I don't know, Kate's talking to him. Hurry up, she'll cost him five dollars.

ANN. [*takes a step upstage, then comes down toward* CHRIS] I wonder if we ought to tell your mother yet? I mean I'm not very good in an argument.

CHRIS. We'll wait till tonight. After dinner. Now don't get tense, just leave it to me.

KELLER. What're you telling her?

CHRIS. Go ahead, Ann. [*With misgivings,* ANN *goes up and into house.*] We're getting married, Dad. [KELLER *nods indecisively.*] Well, don't you say anything?

KELLER. [*distracted*] I'm glad, Chris, I'm just—George is calling from Columbus.

CHRIS. Columbus!

KELLER. Did Annie tell you he was going to see his father today?

CHRIS. No, I don't think she knew anything about it.

KELLER. [*asking uncomfortably*] Chris! You—you think you know her pretty good?

CHRIS. [*hurt and apprehensive*] What kind of a question?

KELLER. I'm just wondering. All these years George don't go to see his father. Suddenly he goes . . . and she comes here.

CHRIS. Well, what about it?

KELLER. It's crazy, but it comes to my mind. She don't hold nothin' against me, does she?

CHRIS. [*angry*] I don't know what you're talking about.

KELLER. [*a little more combatively*] I'm just talkin'. To his last day in court the man blamed it all on me; and this is his daughter. I mean if she was sent here to find out something?

CHRIS. [*angered*] Why? What is there to find out?

ANN. [*on phone, offstage*] Why are you so excited, George? What happened there?

KELLER. I mean if they want to open up the case again, for the nuisance value, to hurt us?

CHRIS. Dad . . . how could you think that of her?

ANN. [*still on phone*] But what did he say to you, for God's sake? [*together*]

KELLER. It couldn't be, heh. You know.

CHRIS. Dad, you amaze me . . .

KELLER. [*breaking in*] All right, forget it, forget it. [*with great force, moving about*] I want a clean start for you, Chris. I want a new sign over the plant—Christopher Keller, Incorporated.

CHRIS. [*a little uneasily*] J. O. Keller is good enough.

KELLER. We'll talk about it. I'm going to build you a house, stone, with a driveway from the road. I want you to spread out, Chris, I want you to use what I made for you. [*He is close to him now.*] I mean, with joy, Chris, without shame . . . with joy.

CHRIS. [*touched*] I will, Dad.

KELLER. [*with deep emotion*] Say it to me.

CHRIS. Why?

KELLER. Because sometimes I think you're . . . ashamed of the money.

CHRIS. No, don't feel that.

KELLER. Because it's good money, there's nothing wrong with that money.

CHRIS. [*a little frightened*] Dad, you don't have to tell me this.

KELLER. [*with overriding affection and self-confidence now. He grips Chris by the back of the neck, and with laughter between his determined jaws*] Look, Chris, I'll go to work on Mother for you. We'll get her so drunk tonight we'll all get married! [*steps away, with a wide gesture of his arm*] There's gonna be a wedding, kid, like there never was seen! Champagne, tuxedos—!

[*He breaks off as* ANN's *voice comes out loud from the house where she is still talking on phone.*]

ANN. Simply because when you get excited you don't control yourself. . . . [MOTHER *comes out of house.*] Well, what did he tell you for God's sake? [*pause*] All right, come then. [*pause*] Yes, they'll all be here. Nobody's running away from you. And try to get hold of yourself, will you? [*pause*] All right, all right. Good-by.

[*There is a brief pause as* ANN *hangs up receiver, then comes out of kitchen.*]

CHRIS. Something happen?

KELLER. He's coming here?

ANN. On the seven o'clock. He's in Columbus. [*to* MOTHER] I told him it would be all right.

KELLER. Sure, fine! Your father took sick?

ANN. [*mystified*] No, George didn't say he was sick. I— [*shaking it off*] I don't know, I suppose it's something stupid, you know my brother— [*She comes to* CHRIS.] Let's go for a drive, or something . . .

CHRIS. Sure. Give me the keys, Dad.

MOTHER. Drive through the park. It's beautiful now.

CHRIS. Come on, Ann. [*to them*] Be back right away.

ANN. [*as she and* CHRIS *exit up driveway*] See you.

[MOTHER *comes down toward* KELLER, *her eyes fixed on him.*]

KELLER. Take your time. [*to* MOTHER.] What does George want?

MOTHER. He's been in Columbus since this morning with Steve. He's gotta see Annie right away, he says.

KELLER. What for?

MOTHER. I don't know. [*She speaks with warning.*] He's a lawyer now, Joe. George is a lawyer. All these years he never even sent a postcard to Steve. Since he got back from the war, not a postcard.

KELLER. So what?

MOTHER. [*her tension breaking out*] Suddenly he takes an airplane from New York to see him. An airplane!

KELLER. Well? So?

MOTHER. [*trembling*] Why?

KELLER. I don't read minds. Do you?

MOTHER. Why, Joe? What has Steve suddenly got to tell him that he takes an airplane to see him?

KELLER. What do I care what Steve's got to tell him?

MOTHER. You're sure, Joe?

KELLER. [*frightened, but angry*] Yes, I'm sure.

MOTHER. [*sits stiffly in a chair*] Be smart now, Joe. The boy is coming. Be smart.

KELLER. [*desperately*] Once and for all, did you hear what I said? I said I'm sure!

MOTHER. [*nods weakly*] All right, Joe. [*He straightens up.*] Just . . . be smart.

[KELLER, *in hopeless fury, looks at her, turns around, goes up to porch and into house, slamming screen door violently behind him.* MOTHER *sits in chair downstage, stiffly, staring, seeing.*]

CURTAIN

Act Two

As twilight falls, that evening.

On the rise, CHRIS *is discovered sawing the broken-off tree, leaving stump standing alone. He is dressed in good pants, white shoes, but without a shirt. He disappears with tree up the alley when* MOTHER *appears on porch. She comes down and stands watching him. She has on a dressing gown, carries a tray of grape-juice drink in a pitcher, and glasses with sprigs of mint in them.*

MOTHER. [*calling up alley*] Did you have to put on good pants to do that? [*She comes downstage and puts tray on table in the arbor. Then looks around uneasily, then feels pitcher for coolness.* CHRIS *enters from alley brushing off his hands.*] You notice there's more light with that thing gone?

CHRIS. Why aren't you dressing?

MOTHER. It's suffocating upstairs. I made a grape drink for Georgie.

He always liked grape. Come and have some.

CHRIS. [*impatiently*] Well, come on, get dressed. And what's Dad sleeping so much for? [*He goes to table and pours a glass of juice.*]

MOTHER. He's worried. When he's worried he sleeps. [*pauses, looks into his eyes*] We're dumb, Chris. Dad and I are stupid people. We don't know anything. You've got to protect us.

CHRIS. You're silly; what's there to be afraid of?

MOTHER. To his last day in court Steve never gave up the idea that Dad made him do it. If they're going to open the case again I won't live through it.

CHRIS. George is just a damn fool, Mother. How can you take him seriously?

MOTHER. That family hates us. Maybe even Annie—

CHRIS. Oh, now, Mother . . .

MOTHER. You think just because you like everybody, they like you!

CHRIS. All right, stop working yourself up. Just leave everything to me.

MOTHER. When George goes home tell her to go with him.

CHRIS. [*noncommittally*] Don't worry about Annie.

MOTHER. Steve is her father, too.

CHRIS. Are you going to cut it out? Now, come.

MOTHER. [*going upstage with him*] You don't realize how people can hate, Chris, they can hate so much they'll tear the world to pieces.

[ANN, *dressed up, appears on porch.*]

CHRIS. Look! She's dressed already. [*as he and* MOTHER *mount porch*] I've just got to put on a shirt.

ANN. [*in a preoccupied way*] Are you feeling well, Kate?

MOTHER. What's the difference, dear. There are certain people, y'know, the sicker they get the longer they live. [*She goes into house.*]

CHRIS. You look nice.

ANN. We're going to tell her tonight.

CHRIS. Absolutely, don't worry about it.

ANN. I wish we could tell her now. I can't stand scheming. My stomach gets hard.

CHRIS. It's not scheming, we'll just get her in a better mood.

MOTHER. [*offstage, in the house*] Joe, are you going to sleep all day!

ANN. [*laughing*] The only one who's relaxed is your father. He's fast asleep.

CHRIS. I'm relaxed.

ANN. Are you?

CHRIS. Look. [*He holds out his hand and makes it shake.*] Let me know when George gets here.

[*He goes into the house.* ANN *moves aimlessly, and then is drawn toward tree stump. She goes to it, hesitantly touches broken top in the hush of her thoughts. Offstage* LYDIA *calls,* "Johnny! Come get your supper!" SUE *enters, and halts, seeing* ANN.]

SUE. Is my husband—?

ANN. [*turns, startled*] Oh!

SUE. I'm terribly sorry.

ANN. It's all right, I—I'm a little silly about the dark.

SUE. [*looks about*] It is getting dark.

ANN. Are you looking for your husband?

SUE. As usual. [*laughs tiredly*] He spends so much time here, they'll be charging him rent.

ANN. Nobody was dressed so he drove over to the depot to pick up my brother.

SUE. Oh, your brother's in?

ANN. Yeah, they ought to be here any minute now. Will you have a cold drink?

SUE. I will, thanks. [ANN *goes to table and pours.*] My husband. Too hot to drive me to beach. Men are like little boys; for the neighbors they'll always cut the grass.

ANN. People like to do things for the Kellers. Been that way since I can remember.

SUE. It's amazing. I guess your brother's coming to give you away, heh?

ANN. [*giving her drink*] I don't know. I suppose.

SUE. You must be all nerved up.

ANN. It's always a problem getting yourself married, isn't it?

SUE. That depends on your shape, of course. I don't see why you should have had a problem.

ANN. I've had chances—

SUE. I'll bet. It's romantic . . . it's very unusual to me, marrying the brother of your sweetheart.

ANN. I don't know. I think it's mostly that whenever I need somebody to tell me the truth I've always thought of Chris. When he tells you something you know it's so. He relaxes me.

SUE. And he's got money. That's important, you know.

ANN. It wouldn't matter to me.

SUE. You'd be surprised. It makes all the difference. I married an intern. On my salary. And that was bad, because as soon as a woman supports a man he owes her something. You can never owe somebody without resenting them. [ANN *laughs.*] That's true, you know.

ANN. Underneath, I think the doctor is very devoted.

SUE. Oh, certainly. But it's bad when a man always sees the bars in front of him. Jim thinks he's in jail all the time.

ANN. Oh . . .

SUE. That's why I've been intending to ask you a small favor, Ann. It's something very important to me.

ANN. Certainly, if I can do it.

SUE. You can. When you take up housekeeping, try to find a place away from here.

ANN. Are you fooling?

SUE. I'm very serious. My husband is unhappy with Chris around.

ANN. How is that?

SUE. Jim's a successful doctor. But he's got an idea he'd like to do medical research. Discover things. You see?

ANN. Well, isn't that good?

SUE. Research pays twenty-five dollars a week minus laundering the hair shirt. You've got to give up your life to go into it.

ANN. How does Chris—

SUE. [with growing feeling] Chris makes people want to be better than it's possible to be. He does that to people.

ANN. Is that bad?

SUE. My husband has a family, dear. Every time he has a session with Chris he feels as though he's compromising by not giving up everything for research. As though Chris or anybody else isn't compromising. It happens with Jim every couple of years. He meets a man and makes a statue out of him.

ANN. Maybe he's right. I don't mean that Chris is a statue, but—

SUE. Now darling, you know he's not right.

ANN. I don't agree with you. Chris—

SUE. Let's face it, dear. Chris is working with his father, isn't he? He's taking money out of that business every week in the year.

ANN. What of it?

SUE. You ask me what of it?

ANN. I certainly do. [She seems about to burst out.] You oughtn't cast aspersions like that, I'm surprised at you.

SUE. You're surprised at me!

ANN. He'd never take five cents out of that plant if there was anything wrong with it.

SUE. You know that.

ANN. I know it. I resent everything you've said.

SUE. [moving toward her] You know what I resent, dear?

ANN. Please, I don't want to argue.

SUE. I resent living next door to the Holy Family. It makes me look like a bum, you understand?

ANN. I can't do anything about that.

SUE. Who is he to ruin a man's life? Everybody knows Joe pulled a fast one to get out of jail.

ANN. That's not true!

SUE. Then why don't you go out and talk to people? Go on, talk to them. There's not a person on the block who doesn't know the truth.

ANN. That's a lie. People come here all the time for cards and—

SUE. So what? They give him credit for being smart. I do, too, I've got nothing against Joe. But if Chris wants people to put on the hair shirt let him take off his broadcloth. He's driving my husband crazy with that phony idealism of his, and I'm at the end of my rope on it! [CHRIS enters on porch, wearing shirt and tie now. She turns quickly, hearing. With a smile] Hello, darling. How's Mother?

CHRIS. I thought George came.

SUE. No, it was just us.

CHRIS. [coming down to them] Susie, do me a favor, heh? Go up to Mother and see if you can calm her. She's all worked up.

SUE. She still doesn't know about you two?

CHRIS. [*laughs a little*] Well, she senses it, I guess. You know my mother.

SUE. [*going up to porch*] Oh, yeah, she's psychic.

CHRIS. Maybe there's something in the medicine chest.

SUE. I'll give her one of everything. [*on porch*] Don't worry about Kate; couple of drinks, dance her around a little . . . She'll love Ann. [*to* ANN] Because you're the female version of him. [CHRIS *laughs.*] Don't be alarmed, I said version. [*She goes into house.*]

CHRIS. Interesting woman, isn't she?

ANN. Yeah, she's very interesting.

CHRIS. She's a great nurse, you know, she—

ANN. [*in tension, but trying to control it*] Are you still doing that?

CHRIS. [*sensing something wrong, but still smiling*] Doing what?

ANN. As soon as you get to know somebody you find a distinction for them. How do you know she's a great nurse?

CHRIS. What's the matter, Ann?

ANN. The woman hates you. She despises you!

CHRIS. Hey . . . What's hit you?

ANN. Gee, Chris—

CHRIS. What happened here?

ANN. You never— Why didn't you tell me?

CHRIS. Tell you what?

ANN. She says they think Joe is guilty.

CHRIS. What difference does it make what they think?

ANN. I don't care what they think, I just don't understand why you took the trouble to deny it. You said it was all forgotten.

CHRIS. I didn't want you to feel there was anything wrong in you coming here, that's all. I know a lot of people think my father was guilty, and I assumed there might be some question in your mind.

ANN. But I never once said I suspected him.

CHRIS. Nobody says it.

ANN. Chris, I know how much you love him, but it could never—

CHRIS. Do you think I could forgive him if he'd done that thing?

ANN. I'm not here out of a blue sky, Chris. I turned my back on my father, if there's anything wrong here now—

CHRIS. I know that, Ann.

ANN. George is coming from Dad, and I don't think it's with a blessing.

CHRIS. He's welcome here. You've got nothing to fear from George.

ANN. Tell me that . . . Just tell me that.

CHRIS. The man is innocent, Ann. Remember he was falsely accused once and it put him through hell. How would you behave if you were faced with the same thing again? Annie, believe me, there's nothing wrong for you here, believe me, kid.

ANN. All right, Chris, all right. [*They embrace as* KELLER *appears quietly on porch.* ANN *simply studies him.*]

KELLER. Every time I come out here it looks like Playland! [*They break and laugh in embarrassment.*]

CHRIS. I thought you were going to shave?

KELLER. [*sitting on bench*] In a minute. I just woke up, I can't see nothin'.

ANN. You look shaved.

KELLER. Oh, no. [*massages his jaw*] Gotta be extra special tonight. Big night, Annie. So how's it feel to be a married woman?

ANN [*laughs*] I don't know, yet.

KELLER. [*to* CHRIS] What's the matter, you slippin'? [*He takes a little box of apples from under the bench as they talk.*]

CHRIS. The great roué!

KELLER. What is that, roué?

CHRIS. It's French.

KELLER. Don't talk dirty. [*They laugh.*]

CHRIS. [*to* ANN] You ever meet a bigger ignoramus?

KELLER. Well, somebody's got to make a living.

ANN. [*as they laugh*] That's telling him.

KELLER. I don't know, everybody's gettin' so Goddam educated in this country there'll be nobody to take away the garbage. [*They laugh.*] It's gettin' so the only dumb ones left are the bosses.

ANN. You're not so dumb, Joe.

KELLER. I know, but you go into our plant, for instance. I got so many lieutenants, majors and colonels that I'm ashamed to ask somebody to sweep the floor. I gotta be careful I'll insult somebody. No kiddin'. It's a tragedy: you stand on the street today and spit, you're gonna hit a college man.

CHRIS. Well, don't spit.

KELLER. [*breaks apple in half, passing it to* ANN *and* CHRIS] I mean to say, it's comin' to a pass. [*He takes a breath.*] I been thinkin', Annie . . . your brother, George. I been thinkin' about your brother George. When he comes I like you to *brooch* something to him.

CHRIS. Broach.

KELLER. What's the matter with brooch?

CHRIS. [*smiling*] It's not English.

KELLER. When I went to night school it was brooch.

ANN. [*laughing*] Well, in day school it's broach.

KELLER. Don't surround me, will you? Seriously, Ann . . . You say he's not well. George, I been thinkin', why should he knock himself out in New York with that cut-throat competition, when I got so many friends here; I'm very friendly with some big lawyers in town. I could set George up here.

ANN. That's awfully nice of you, Joe.

KELLER. No, kid, it ain't nice of me. I want you to understand me. I'm thinking of Chris. [*slight pause*] See . . . this is what I mean. You get older, you want to feel that you—accomplished something. My only accomplishment is my son. I ain't brainy. That's all I accomplished. Now, a year, eighteen months, your father'll be a free man. Who is he going to come to, Annie? His baby. You. He'll come, old, mad, into your house.

ANN. That can't matter any more, Joe.

KELLER. I don't want that to come between us. [*gestures between* CHRIS *and himself*]

ANN. I can only tell you that that could never happen.

KELLER. You're in love now, Annie, but believe me, I'm older than you and I know—a daughter is a daughter, and a father is a father. And it could happen. [*He pauses.*] I like you and George to go to him in prison and tell him . . . "Dad, Joe wants to bring you into the business when you get out."

ANN. [*surprised, even shocked*] You'd have him as a partner?

KELLER. No, no partner. A good job. [*Pause. He sees she is shocked, a little mystified. He gets up, speaks more nervously.*] I want him to know, Annie . . . while he's sitting there I want him to know that when he gets out he's got a place waitin' for him. It'll take his bitterness away. To know you got a place . . . it sweetens you.

ANN. Joe, you owe him nothing.

KELLER. I owe him a good kick in the teeth, but he's your father.

CHRIS. Then kick him in the teeth! I don't want him in the plant, so that's that! You understand? And besides, don't talk about him like that. People misunderstand you!

KELLER. And I don't understand why she has to crucify the man.

CHRIS. Well, it's her father, if she feels—

KELLER. No, no.

CHRIS. [*almost angrily*] What's it to you? Why—?

KELLER. [*a commanding outburst in high nervousness*] A father is a father! [*As though the outburst had revealed him, he looks about, wanting to retract it. His hand goes to his cheek.*] I better —I better shave. [*He turns and a smile is on his face. To* ANN] I didn't mean to yell at you, Annie.

ANN. Let's forget the whole thing, Joe.

KELLER. Right. [*to* CHRIS] She's likeable.

CHRIS. [*a little peeved at the man's stupidity*] Shave, will you?

KELLER. Right again.

[*As he turns to porch* LYDIA *comes hurrying from her house.*]

LYDIA. I forgot all about it. [*seeing* CHRIS *and* ANN] Hya. [*to* JOE] I promised to fix Kate's hair for tonight. Did she comb it yet?

KELLER. Always a smile, hey Lydia?

LYDIA. Sure, why not?

KELLER. [*going up on porch*] Come on up and comb my Katie's hair. [LYDIA *goes up on porch*] She's got a big night, make her beautiful.

LYDIA. I will.

KELLER. [*holds door open for her and she goes into kitchen; to* CHRIS *and* ANN] Hey, that could be a song. [*He sings softly.*]

"Come on up and comb my Katie's hair . . .
Oh, come on up, 'cause she's my lady fair—"

[*to* ANN] How's that for one year of night school? [*He continues singing as he goes into kitchen.*]

"Oh come on up, come on up, and comb my lady's hair—"

[JIM BAYLISS *rounds corner of driveway, walking rapidly.* JIM *crosses to* CHRIS, *motions him and pulls him down excitedly.* KELLER *stands just inside kitchen door, watching them.*]

CHRIS. What's the matter? Where is he?

JIM. Where's your mother?

CHRIS. Upstairs, dressing.

ANN. [*crossing to them rapidly*] What happened to George?

JIM. I asked him to wait in the car. Listen to me now. Can you take some advice? [*They wait.*] Don't bring him in here.

ANN. Why?

JIM. Kate is in bad shape, you can't explode this in front of her.

ANN. Explode what?

JIM. You know why he's here, don't try to kid it away. There's blood in his eye; drive him somewhere and talk to him alone.

[ANN *turns to go up drive, takes a couple of steps, sees* KELLER, *and stops. He goes quietly on into house.*]

CHRIS. [*shaken, and therefore angered*] Don't be an old lady.

JIM. He's come to take her home. What does that mean? [*to* ANN] You know what that means. Fight it out with him some place else.

ANN. [*comes back down toward* CHRIS] I'll drive . . . him somewhere.

CHRIS. [*goes to her*] No.

JIM. Will you stop being an idiot?

CHRIS. Nobody's afraid of him here. Cut that out!

[*He starts for driveway, but is brought up short by* GEORGE, *who enters there.* GEORGE *is* CHRIS'S *age, but a paler man, now on the edge of his self-restraint. He speaks quietly, as though afraid to find himself screaming. An instant's hesitation and* CHRIS *steps up to him, hand extended, smiling.*]

CHRIS. Helluva way to do; what're you sitting out there for?

GEORGE. Doctor said your mother isn't well, I—

CHRIS. So what? She'd want to see you, wouldn't she? We've been waiting for you all afternoon. [*He puts his hand on* GEORGE'S *arm, but* GEORGE *pulls away, coming across toward* ANN.]

ANN. [*touching his collar*] This is filthy, didn't you bring another shirt?

[GEORGE *breaks away from her, and moves down, examining the yard. Door opens, and he turns rapidly, thinking it is* KATE, *but it's* SUE. *She looks at him; he turns away and moves to fence. He looks over it at his former home.* SUE *comes downstage.*]

SUE. [*annoyed*] How about the beach, Jim?

JIM. Oh, it's too hot to drive.

SUE. How'd you get to the station—Zeppelin?

CHRIS. This is Mrs. Bayliss, George. [*calling, as* GEORGE *pays no attention, staring at house*] George! [GEORGE *turns.*] Mrs. Bayliss.

SUE. How do you do.

GEORGE. [*removing his hat*] You're the people who bought our house, aren't you?

SUE. That's right. Come and see what we did with it before you leave.

GEORGE. [*walks down and away from her*] I liked it the way it was.

SUE. [*after a brief pause*] He's frank, isn't he?

JIM. [*pulling her off*] See you later. . . . Take it easy, fella. [*They exit.*]

CHRIS. [*calling after them*] Thanks for driving him! [*turning to* GEORGE] How about some grape juice? Mother made it especially for you.

GEORGE. [*with forced appreciation*] Good old Kate, remembered my grape juice.

CHRIS. You drank enough of it in this house. How've you been, George?—Sit down.

GEORGE. [*keeps moving*] It takes me a minute. [*looking around*] It seems impossible.

CHRIS. What?

GEORGE. I'm back here.

CHRIS. Say, you've gotten a little nervous, haven't you?

GEORGE. Yeah, toward the end of the day. What're you, big executive now?

CHRIS. Just kind of medium. How's the law?

GEORGE. I don't know. When I was studying in the hospital it seemed sensible, but outside there doesn't seem to be much of a law. The trees got thick, didn't they? [*points to stump*] What's that?

CHRIS. Blew down last night. We had it there for Larry. You know.

GEORGE. Why, afraid you'll forget him?

CHRIS. [*starts for* GEORGE] Kind of a remark is that?

ANN. [*breaking in, putting a restraining hand on* CHRIS] When did you start wearing a hat?

GEORGE. [*discovers hat in his hand*] Today. From now on I decided to look like a lawyer, anyway. [*He holds it up to her.*] Don't you recognize it?

ANN. Why? Where—?

GEORGE. Your father's— He asked me to wear it.

ANN. How is he?

GEORGE. He got smaller.

ANN. Smaller?

GEORGE. Yeah, little. [*holds out his hand to measure*] He's a little man. That's what happens to suckers, you know. It's good I went to him in time—another year there'd be nothing left but his smell.

CHRIS. What's the matter, George, what's the trouble?

GEORGE. The trouble? The trouble is when you make suckers out of people once, you shouldn't try to do it twice.

CHRIS. What does that mean?

GEORGE. [*to* ANN] You're not married yet, are you?

ANN. George, will you sit down and stop—?

GEORGE. Are you married yet?

ANN. No, I'm not married yet.

GEORGE. You're not going to marry him.

ANN. Why am I not going to marry him?

GEORGE. Because his father destroyed your family.

CHRIS. Now look, George . . .

GEORGE. Cut it short, Chris. Tell her to come home with me. Let's not argue, you know what I've got to say.

CHRIS. George, you don't want to be the voice of God, do you?

GEORGE. I'm—

CHRIS. That's been your trouble all your life, George, you dive into things. What kind of a statement is that to make? You're a big boy now.

GEORGE. I'm a big boy now.

CHRIS. Don't come bulling in here. If you've got something to say, be civilized about it.

GEORGE. Don't civilize me!

ANN. Shhh!

CHRIS. [*ready to hit him*] Are you going to talk like a grown man or aren't you?

ANN. [*quickly, to forestall an outburst*] Sit down, dear. Don't be angry, what's the matter? [*He allows her to seat him, looking at her.*] Now what happened? You kissed me when I left, now you—

GEORGE. [*breathlessly*] My life turned upside down since then. I couldn't go back to work when you left. I wanted to go to Dad and tell him you were going to be married. It seemed impossible not to tell him. He loved you so much. [*He pauses.*] Annie—we did a terrible thing. We can never be forgiven. Not even to send him a card at Christmas. I didn't see him once since I got home from the war! Annie, you don't know what was done to that man. You don't know what happened.

ANN. [*afraid*] Of course I know.

GEORGE. You can't know, you wouldn't be here. Dad came to work that day. The night foreman came to him and showed him the cylinder heads . . . they were coming out of the process with defects. There was something wrong with the process. So Dad went directly to the phone and called here and told Joe to come down right away. But the morning passed. No sign of Joe. So Dad called again. By this time he had over a hundred defectives. The Army was screaming for stuff and Dad didn't have anything to ship. So Joe told him . . . on the phone he told him to weld, cover up the cracks in any way he could, and ship them out.

CHRIS. Are you through now?

GEORGE. [*surging up at him*] I'm not through now! [*back to* ANN] Dad was afraid. He wanted Joe there if he was going to do it. But Joe can't come down . . . He's sick. Sick! He suddenly gets the flu! Suddenly! But he promised to take responsibility. Do you understand what I'm saying? On the telephone you can't have responsibility! In a court you can always deny a phone call and that's exactly what he did. They knew he was a liar the first time, but in the appeal they believed that rotten lie and now Joe is a big shot and your father is the patsy. [*He gets up.*] Now what're you going to do? Eat his food, sleep in his bed? Answer me; what're you going to do?

CHRIS. What're you going to do, George?

GEORGE. He's too smart for me, I can't prove a phone call.

CHRIS. Then how dare you come in here with that rot?

ANN. George, the court—

GEORGE. The court didn't know your father! But you know him. You know in your heart Joe did it.

CHRIS. [*whirling him around*] Lower your voice or I'll throw you out of here!

GEORGE. She knows. She knows.

CHRIS. [*to* ANN] Get him out of here, Ann. Get him out of here.

ANN. George, I know everything you've said. Dad told that whole thing in court, and they—

GEORGE. [*almost a scream*] The court did not know him, Annie!

ANN. Shhh!—But he'll say anything, George. You know how quick he can lie.

GEORGE. [*turning to* CHRIS, *with deliberation*] I'll ask you something, and look me in the eye when you answer me.

CHRIS. I'll look you in the eye.

GEORGE. You know your father—

CHRIS. I know him well.

GEORGE. And he's the kind of boss to let a hundred and twenty-one cylinder heads be repaired and shipped out of his shop without even knowing about it?

CHRIS. He's that kind of boss.

GEORGE. And that's the same Joe Keller who never left his shop without first going around to see that all the lights were out.

CHRIS. [*with growing anger*] The same Joe Keller.

GEORGE. The same man who knows how many minutes a day his workers spend in the toilet.

CHRIS. The same man.

GEORGE. And my father, that frightened mouse who'd never buy a shirt without somebody along—that man would dare do such a thing on his own?

CHRIS. On his own. And because he's a frightened mouse this is another thing he'd do—throw the blame on somebody else because he's not man enough to take it himself. He tried it in court but it didn't work, but with a fool like you it works!

GEORGE. Oh, Chris, you're a liar to yourself!

ANN. [*deeply shaken*] Don't talk like that!

CHRIS. [*sits facing* GEORGE] Tell me, George. What happened? The court record was good enough for you all these years, why isn't it good now? Why did you believe it all these years?

GEORGE. [*after a slight pause*] Because you believed it. . . . That's the truth, Chris. I believed everything, because I thought you did. But today I heard it from his mouth. From his mouth it's altogether different than the record. Anyone who knows him, and knows your father, will believe it from his mouth. Your Dad took everything we have. I can't beat that. But she's one item he's not going to grab. [*He turns to* ANN.] Get your things. Everything they have is covered with blood. You're not the kind of a girl who can live with that. Get your things.

CHRIS. Ann . . . you're not going to believe that, are you?

ANN. [*goes to him*] You know it's not true, don't you?

GEORGE. How can he tell you? It's his father. [*to* CHRIS] None of these things ever even cross your mind?

CHRIS. Yes, they crossed my mind. Anything can cross your mind!

GEORGE. *He knows*, Annie. He knows!

CHRIS. The voice of God!

GEORGE. Then why isn't your name on the business? Explain that to her!

CHRIS. What the hell has that got to do with—?

GEORGE. Annie, why isn't his name on it?

CHRIS. Even when I don't own it!

GEORGE. Who're you kidding? Who gets it when he dies? [*to* ANN] Open your eyes, you know the both of them, isn't that the first thing they'd do, the way they love each other?—J. O. Keller and Son? [*Pause.* ANN *looks from him to* CHRIS.] I'll settle it. Do you want to settle it, or are you afraid to?

CHRIS. What do you mean?

GEORGE. Let me go up and talk to your father. In ten minutes you'll have the answer. Or are you afraid of the answer?

CHRIS. I'm not afraid of the answer. I know the answer. But my mother isn't well and I don't want a fight here now.

GEORGE. Let me go to him.

CHRIS. You're not going to start a fight here now.

GEORGE. [*to* ANN] What more do you want!

[*There is a sound of footsteps in the house.*]

ANN. [*turns her head suddenly toward house*] Someone's coming.

CHRIS. [*to* GEORGE, *quietly*] You won't say anything now.

ANN. You'll go soon. I'll call a cab.

GEORGE. You're coming with me.

ANN. And don't mention marriage, because we haven't told her yet.

GEORGE. You're coming with me.

ANN. You understand? Don't— George, you're not going to start anything now! [*She hears footsteps.*] Shsh!

[MOTHER *enters on porch. She is dressed almost formally; her hair is fixed. They are all turned toward her. On seeing* GEORGE *she raises both hands, comes down toward him.*]

MOTHER. Georgie, Georgie.

GEORGE. [*He has always liked her.*] Hello, Kate.

MOTHER. [*cups his face in her hands*] They made an old man out of you. [*touches his hair*] Look, you're gray.

GEORGE. [*Her pity, open and unabashed, reaches into him, and he smiles sadly.*] I know, I—

MOTHER. I told you when you went away, don't try for medals.

GEORGE. [*laughs tiredly*] I didn't try, Kate. They made it very easy for me.

MOTHER. [*actually angry*] Go on. You're all alike. [*to* ANN] Look at him, why did you say he's fine? He looks like a ghost.

GEORGE. [*relishing her solicitude*] I feel all right.

MOTHER. I'm sick to look at you. What's the matter with your mother, why don't she feed you?

ANN. He just hasn't any appetite.

MOTHER. If he ate in my house he'd have an appetite. [*to* ANN] I pity your husband! [*to* GEORGE] Sit down. I'll make you a sand-wich.

GEORGE. [*sits with an embarrassed laugh*] I'm really not hungry.

MOTHER. Honest to God, it breaks my heart to see what happened to all the children. How we worked and planned for you, and you end up no better than us.

GEORGE. [*with deep feeling for her*] You . . . you haven't changed at all, you know that, Kate?

MOTHER. None of us changed, Georgie. We all love you. Joe was just talking about the day you were born and the water got shut off. People were carrying basins from a block away—a stranger would have thought the whole neighborhood was on fire! [*They laugh. She sees the juice. To* ANN] Why didn't you give him some juice!

ANN. [*defensively*] I offered it to him.

MOTHER. [*scoffingly*] You offered it to him! [*thrusting glass into* GEORGE's *hand*] Give it to him! [*to* GEORGE, *who is laughing*] And now you're going to sit here and drink some juice . . . and look like something!

GEORGE. [*sitting*] Kate, I feel hungry already.

CHRIS. [*proudly*] She could turn Mahatma Ghandi into a heavy-weight!

MOTHER. [*to* CHRIS, *with great energy*] Listen, to hell with the res-taurant! I got a ham in the icebox, and frozen strawberries, and avocados, and—

ANN. Swell, I'll help you!

GEORGE. The train leaves at eight-thirty, Ann.

MOTHER. [*to* ANN] You're leaving?

CHRIS. No, Mother, she's not—

ANN. [*breaking through it, going to* GEORGE] You hardly got here; give yourself a chance to get acquainted again.

CHRIS. Sure, you don't even know us any more.

MOTHER. Well, Chris, if they can't stay, don't—

CHRIS. No, it's just a question of George, Mother, he planned on—

GEORGE. [*gets up politely, nicely, for* KATE's *sake*] Now wait a min-ute, Chris . . .

CHRIS. [*smiling and full of command, cutting him off*] If you want to go, I'll drive you to the station now, but if you're staying, no arguments while you're here.

MOTHER. [*at last confessing the tension*] Why should he argue? [*She goes to him. With desperation and compassion, stroking his hair*] Georgie and us have no argument. How could we have an argument, Georgie? We all got hit by the same lightning, how can you—? Did you see what happened to Larry's tree, Georgie? [*She has taken his arm, and unwillingly he moves across stage with her.*] Imagine? While I was dreaming of him in the middle of the night, the wind came along and—

[LYDIA *enters on porch. As soon as she sees him:*]

LYDIA. Hey, Georgie! Georgie! Georgie! Georgie! Georgie! [*She comes down to him eagerly. She has a flowered hat in her hand, which* KATE *takes from her as she goes to* GEORGE.]

GEORGE. [*as they shake hands eagerly, warmly*] Hello, Laughy. What'd you do, grow?

LYDIA. I'm a big girl now.

MOTHER. Look what she can do to a hat!

ANN. [*to* LYDIA, *admiring the hat*] Did you make that?

MOTHER. In ten minutes! [*She puts it on.*]

LYDIA. [*fixing it on her head*] I only rearranged it.

GEORGE. You still make your own clothes?

CHRIS. [*of* MOTHER] Ain't she classy! All she needs now is a Russian wolfhound.

MOTHER. [*moving her head*] It feels like somebody is sitting on my head.

ANN. No, it's beautiful, Kate.

MOTHER. [*kisses* LYDIA; *to* GEORGE] She's a genius! You should've married her. [*They laugh.*] This one can feed you!

LYDIA. [*strangely embarrassed*] Oh, stop that, Kate.

GEORGE. [*to* LYDIA] Didn't I hear you had a baby?

MOTHER. You don't hear so good. She's got three babies.

GEORGE. [*a little hurt by it—to* LYDIA] No kidding, three?

LYDIA. Yeah, it was one, two, three— You've been away a long time, Georgie.

GEORGE. I'm beginning to realize.

MOTHER. [*to* CHRIS *and* GEORGE] The trouble with you kids is you *think* too much.

LYDIA. Well, we think, too.

MOTHER. Yes, but not all the time.

GEORGE. [*with almost obvious envy*] They never took Frank, heh?

LYDIA. [*a little apologetically*] No, he was always one year ahead of the draft.

MOTHER. It's amazing. When they were calling boys twenty-seven Frank was just twenty-eight, when they made it twenty-eight he was just twenty-nine. That's why he took up astrology. It's all in when you were born, it just goes to show.

CHRIS. What does it go to show?

MOTHER. [*to* CHRIS] Don't be so intelligent. Some superstitions are very nice! [*to* LYDIA] Did he finish Larry's horoscope?

LYDIA. I'll ask him now, I'm going in. [*to* GEORGE, *a little sadly, almost embarrassed*] Would you like to see my babies? Come on.

GEORGE. I don't think so, Lydia.

LYDIA. [*understanding*] All right. Good luck to you, George.

GEORGE. Thanks. And to you . . . And Frank. [*She smiles at him, turns and goes off to her house.* GEORGE *stands staring after her.*]

LYDIA. [*as she runs off*] Oh, Frank!

MOTHER. [*reading his thoughts*] She got pretty, heh?

GEORGE. [*sadly*] Very pretty.

MOTHER. [*as a reprimand*] She's beautiful, you damned fool!

GEORGE. [*looks around longingly; and softly, with a catch in his throat*] She makes it seem so nice around here.

MOTHER. [*shaking her finger at him*] Look what happened to you because you wouldn't listen to me! I told you to marry that girl and stay out of the war!

GEORGE. [*laughs at himself*] She used to laugh too much.

MOTHER. And you didn't laugh enough. While you were getting mad about Fascism Frank was getting into her bed.

GEORGE. [*to* CHRIS] He won the war, Frank.

CHRIS. All the battles.

MOTHER. [*in pursuit of this mood*] The day they started the draft, Georgie, I told you you loved that girl.

CHRIS. [*laughs*] And truer love hath no man!

MOTHER. I'm smarter than any of you.

GEORGE. [*laughing*] She's wonderful!

MOTHER. And now you're going to listen to me, George. You had big principles, Eagle Scouts the three of you; so now I got a tree, and this one—[*indicating* CHRIS]—when the weather gets bad he can't stand on his feet; and that big dope—[*pointing to* LYDIA's *house*]—next door who never reads anything but Andy Gump has three children and his house paid off. Stop being a philosopher, and look after yourself. Like Joe was just saying—you move back here, he'll help you get set, and I'll find you a girl and put a smile on your face.

GEORGE. Joe? Joe wants me here?

ANN. [*eagerly*] He asked me to tell you, and I think it's a good idea.

MOTHER. Certainly. Why must you make believe you hate us? Is that another principle?—that you have to hate us? You don't hate us, George, I know you, you can't fool me, I diapered you. [*suddenly, to* ANN] You remember Mr. Marcy's daughter?

ANN. [*laughing, to* GEORGE] She's got you hooked already! [GEORGE *laughs, is excited.*]

MOTHER. You look her over, George; you'll see she's the most beautiful—

CHRIS. She's got warts, George.

MOTHER. [*to* CHRIS] She hasn't got warts! [*to* GEORGE] So the girl has a little beauty mark on her chin—

CHRIS. And two on her nose.

MOTHER. You remember. Her father's the retired police inspector.

CHRIS. Sergeant, George.

MOTHER. He's a very kind man!

CHRIS. He looks like a gorilla.

MOTHER. [*to* GEORGE] He never shot anybody.

> [*They all burst out laughing, as* KELLER *appears in doorway.* GEORGE *rises abruptly and stares at* KELLER, *who comes rapidly down to him.*]

KELLER. [*The laughter stops. With strained joviality*] Well! Look who's here! [*extending his hand*] Georgie, good to see ya.

GEORGE. [*shaking hands—somberly*] How're you, Joe?

KELLER. So-so. Gettin' old. You comin' out to dinner with us?

GEORGE. No, got to be back in New York.

ANN. I'll call a cab for you. [*She goes up into the house.*]

KELLER. Too bad you can't stay, George. Sit down. [*to* MOTHER] He looks fine.

MOTHER. He looks terrible.

KELLER. That's what I said, you look terrible, George. [*They laugh.*] I wear the pants and she beats me with the belt.

GEORGE. I saw your factory on the way from the station. It looks like General Motors.

KELLER. I wish it was General Motors, but it ain't. Sit down, George. Sit down. [*takes cigar out of his pocket*] So you finally went to see your father, I hear?

GEORGE. Yes, this morning. What kind of stuff do you make now?

KELLER. Oh, little of everything. Pressure cookers, an assembly for washing machines. Got a nice, flexible plant now. So how'd you find Dad? Feel all right?

GEORGE. [*searching* KELLER, *speaking indecisively*] No, he's not well, Joe.

KELLER. [*lighting his cigar*] Not his heart again, is it?

GEORGE. It's everything, Joe. It's his soul.

KELLER. [*blowing out smoke*] Uh huh—

CHRIS. How about seeing what they did with your house?

KELLER. Leave him be.

GEORGE. [*to* CHRIS, *indicating* KELLER] I'd like to talk to him.

KELLER. Sure, he just got here. That's the way they do, George. A little man makes a mistake and they hang him by the thumbs; the big ones become ambassadors. I wish you'd-a told me you were going to see Dad.

GEORGE. [*studying him*] I didn't know you were interested.

KELLER. In a way, I am. I would like him to know, George, that as far as I'm concerned, any time he wants, he's got a place with me. I would like him to know that.

GEORGE. He hates your guts, Joe. Don't you know that?

KELLER. I imagined it. But that can change, too.

MOTHER. Steve was never like that.

GEORGE. He's like that now. He'd like to take every man who made money in the war and put him up against a wall.

CHRIS. He'll need a lot of bullets.

GEORGE. And he'd better not get any.

KELLER. That's a sad thing to hear.

GEORGE. [*with bitterness dominant*] Why? What'd you expect him to think of you?

KELLER. [*the force of his nature rising, but under control*] I'm sad to see he hasn't changed. As long as I know him, twenty-five years, the man never learned how to take the blame. You know that, George.

GEORGE. [*He does.*] Well, I—

KELLER. But you do know it. Because the way you come in here you don't look like you remember it. I mean like in nineteen thirty-seven when we had the shop on Flood Street. And he damn near blew us all up with that heater he left burning for two days without water. He wouldn't admit that was his fault, either. I had to fire a mechanic to save his face. You remember that.

GEORGE. Yes, but—

KELLER. I'm just mentioning it, George. Because this is just another one of a lot of things. Like when he gave Frank that money to invest in oil stock.

GEORGE. [*distressed*] I know that, I—

KELLER. [*driving in, but restrained*] But it's good to remember those things, kid. The way he cursed Frank because the stock went down. Was that Frank's fault? To listen to him Frank was a swindler. And all the man did was give him a bad tip.

GEORGE. [*gets up, moves away*] I know those things . . .

KELLER. Then remember them, remember them. [ANN *comes out of house.*] There are certain men in the world who rather see everybody hung before they'll take blame. You understand me, George?

[*They stand facing each other,* GEORGE *trying to judge him.*]

ANN. [*coming downstage*] The cab's on its way. Would you like to wash?

MOTHER. [*with the thrust of hope*] Why must he go? Make the midnight, George.

KELLER. Sure, you'll have dinner with us!

ANN. How about it? Why not? We're eating at the lake, we could have a swell time.

[*A long pause, as* GEORGE *looks at* ANN, CHRIS, KELLER, *then back to her.*]

GEORGE. All right.

MOTHER. Now you're talking.

CHRIS. I've got a shirt that'll go right with that suit.

MOTHER. Size fifteen and a half, right, George?

GEORGE. Is Lydia—? I mean—Frank and Lydia coming?

MOTHER. I'll get you a date that'll make her look like a— [*She starts upstage.*]

GEORGE. [*laughing*] No, I don't want a date.

CHRIS. I know somebody just for you! Charlotte Tanner! [*He starts for the house.*]

KELLER. Call Charlotte, that's right.

MOTHER. Sure, call her up. [CHRIS *goes into house.*]

ANN. You go up and pick out a shirt and tie.

GEORGE. [*stops, looks around at them and the place*] I never felt at home anywhere but here. I feel so— [*He nearly laughs, and turns away from them.*] Kate, you look so young, you know? You didn't change at all. It . . . rings an old bell. [*turns to* KELLER] You too, Joe, you're amazingly the same. The whole atmosphere is.

KELLER. Say, I ain't got time to get sick.

MOTHER. He hasn't been laid up in fifteen years.

KELLER. Except my flu during the war.

MOTHER. Huhh?

KELLER. My flu, when I was sick during . . . the war.

MOTHER. Well, sure . . . [*to* GEORGE] I mean except for that flu. [GEORGE *stands perfectly still.*] Well, it slipped my mind, don't look at me that way. He wanted to go to the shop but he couldn't lift himself off the bed. I thought he had pneumonia.

GEORGE. Why did you say he's never—?

KELLER. I know how you feel, kid, I'll never forgive myself. If I could've gone in that day I'd never allow Dad to touch those heads.

GEORGE. She said you've never been sick.

MOTHER. I said he was sick, George.

GEORGE. [*going to* ANN] Ann, didn't you hear her say—?

MOTHER. Do you remember every time you were sick?

GEORGE. I'd remember pneumonia. Especially if I got it just the day my partner was going to patch up cylinder heads . . . What happened that day, Joe?

[FRANK *enters briskly from driveway, holding Larry's horoscope in his hand. He comes to* KATE.]

FRANK. Kate! Kate!

MOTHER. Frank, did you see George?

FRANK. [*extending his hand*] Lydia told me, I'm glad to . . . you'll have to pardon me. [*pulling* MOTHER *over*] I've got something amazing for you, Kate, I finished Larry's horoscope.

MOTHER. You'd be interested in this, George. It's wonderful the way he can understand the—

CHRIS. [*entering from house*] George, the girl's on the phone—

MOTHER. [*desperately*] He finished Larry's horoscope!

CHRIS. Frank, can't you pick a better time than this?

FRANK. The greatest men who ever lived believed in the stars!

CHRIS. Stop filling her head with that junk!

FRANK. Is it junk to feel that there's a greater power than ourselves? I've studied the stars of his life! I won't argue with you, I'm telling you. Somewhere in this world your brother is alive!

MOTHER. [*instantly to* CHRIS] Why isn't it possible?

CHRIS. Because it's insane.

FRANK. Just a minute now. I'll tell you something and you can do as you please, just let me say it. He was supposed to have died on November twenty-fifth. But November twenty-fifth was his favorable day.

CHRIS. Mother!

MOTHER. Listen to him!

FRANK. It was a day when everything good was shining on him, the kind of day he should've married on. You can laugh at a lot of it, I can understand you laughing. But the odds are a million to one that a man won't die on his favorable day. That's known, that's known, Chris!

MOTHER. Why isn't it possible, why isn't it possible, Chris!

GEORGE. [*to* ANN] Don't you understand what she's saying? She just told you to go. What are you waiting for now?

CHRIS. Nobody can tell her to go. [*A car horn is heard.*]

MOTHER. [*to* FRANK] Thank you, darling, for your trouble. Will you tell him to wait, Frank?

FRANK. [*as he goes*] Sure thing.

MOTHER. [*calling out*] They'll be right out, driver!

CHRIS. She's not leaving, Mother.

GEORGE. You heard her say it, he's never been sick!

MOTHER. He misunderstood me, Chris! [CHRIS *looks at her, struck.*]

GEORGE. [*to* ANN] He simply told your father to kill pilots, and covered himself in bed!

CHRIS. You'd better answer him, Annie. Answer him.

MOTHER. I packed your bag, darling.

CHRIS. What?

MOTHER. I packed your bag. All you've got to do is close it.

ANN. I'm not closing anything. He asked me here and I'm staying till he tells me to go. [*to* GEORGE] Till Chris tells me!

CHRIS. That's all! Now get out of here, George!

MOTHER. [*to* CHRIS] But if that's how he feels—

CHRIS. That's all, nothing more till Christ comes, about the case or Larry as long as I'm here! [*to* GEORGE] Now get out of here, George!

GEORGE. [*to* ANN] You tell me. I want to hear you tell me.

ANN. Go, George!

[*They disappear up the driveway,* ANN *saying, "Don't take it that way, Georgie! Please don't take it that way."*]

CHRIS. [*turning to his mother*] What do you mean, you packed her bag? How dare you pack her bag?

MOTHER. Chris—

CHRIS. How dare you pack her bag?

MOTHER. She doesn't belong here.

CHRIS. Then I don't belong here.

MOTHER. She's Larry's girl.

CHRIS. And I'm his brother and he's dead, and I'm marrying his girl.

MOTHER. Never, never in this world!

KELLER. You lost your mind?

MOTHER. You have nothing to say!

KELLER. [*cruelly*] I got plenty to say. Three and a half years you been talking like a maniac—

[MOTHER *smashes him across the face.*]

MOTHER. Nothing. You have nothing to say. Now I say. He's coming back, and everybody has got to wait.

CHRIS. Mother, Mother—

MOTHER. Wait, wait—

CHRIS. How long? How long?

MOTHER. [*rolling out of her*] Till he comes; forever and ever till he comes!

CHRIS. [*as an ultimatum*] Mother, I'm going ahead with it.

MOTHER. Chris, I've never said no to you in my life, now I say no!

CHRIS. You'll never let him go till I do it.

MOTHER. I'll never let him go and you'll never let him go!

CHRIS. I've let him go. I've let him go a long—

MOTHER. [*with no less force, but turning from him*] Then let your father go. [*Pause.* CHRIS *stands transfixed.*]

KELLER. She's out of her mind.

MOTHER. Altogether! [*to* CHRIS, *but not facing them*] Your brother's alive, darling, because if he's dead, your father killed him. Do you understand me now? As long as you live, that boy is alive. God does not let a son be killed by his father. Now you see, don't you? Now you see. [*Beyond control, she hurries up and into house.*]

KELLER. [CHRIS *has not moved. He speaks insinuatingly, questioningly*] She's out of her mind.

CHRIS. [*in a broken whisper*] Then . . . you did it?

KELLER. [*with the beginning of plea in his voice*] He never flew a P-40—

CHRIS. [*struck; deadly*] But the others.

KELLER. [*insistently*] She's out of her mind. [*He takes a step toward* CHRIS, *pleadingly.*]

CHRIS. [*unyielding*] Dad . . . you did it?

KELLER. He never flew a P-40, what's the matter with you?

CHRIS. [*still asking, and saying*] Then you did it. To the others.
[*Both hold their voices down.*]

KELLER. [*afraid of him, his deadly insistence*] What's the matter with you? What the hell is the matter with you?

CHRIS. [*quietly, incredibly*] How could you do that? How?

KELLER. What's the matter with you!

CHRIS. Dad . . . Dad, you killed twenty-one men!

KELLER. What, killed?

CHRIS. You killed them, you murdered them.

KELLER. [*as though throwing his whole nature open before* CHRIS] How could I kill anybody?

CHRIS. Dad! Dad!

KELLER. [*trying to hush him*] I didn't kill anybody!

CHRIS. Then explain it to me. What did you do? Explain it to me or I'll tear you to pieces!

KELLER. [*horrified at his overwhelming fury*] Don't, Chris, don't—

CHRIS. I want to know what you did, now what did you do? You had a hundred and twenty cracked engine-heads, now what did you do?

KELLER. If you're going to hang me then I—

CHRIS. I'm listening. God Almighty, I'm listening!

KELLER. [*Their movements now are those of subtle pursuit and escape.* KELLER *keeps a step out of* CHRIS's *range as he talks.*] You're a boy, what could I do! I'm in business, a man is in business; a hundred and twenty cracked, you're out of business; you got a process, the process don't work you're out of business; you don't know how to operate, your stuff is no good; they close you up, they tear up your contracts, what the hell's it to them? You lay forty years into a business and they knock you out in five minutes, what could I do, let them take forty years, let them take my life away? [*his voice cracking*] I never thought they'd install them. I swear to God. I thought they'd stop 'em before anybody took off.

CHRIS. Then why'd you ship them out?

KELLER. By the time they could spot them I thought I'd have the process going again, and I could show them they needed me and they'd let it go by. But weeks passed and I got no kick-back, so I was going to tell them.

CHRIS. Then why didn't you tell them?

KELLER. It was too late. The paper, it was all over the front page, twenty-one went down, it was too late. They came with handcuffs into the shop, what could I do? [*He sits on bench.*] Chris . . . Chris, I did it for you, it was a chance and I took it for you. I'm sixty-one years old, when would I have another chance to make something for you? Sixty-one years old you don't get another chance, do ya?

CHRIS. You even knew they wouldn't hold up in the air.

KELLER. I didn't say that.

CHRIS. But you were going to warn them not to use them—

KELLER. But that don't mean—

CHRIS. It means you knew they'd crash.

KELLER. It don't mean that.

CHRIS. Then you *thought* they'd crash.

KELLER. I was afraid maybe—

CHRIS. You were afraid maybe! God in heaven, what kind of a man are you? Kids were hanging in the air by those heads. You knew that!

KELLER. For you, a business for you!

CHRIS. [*with burning fury*] For me! Where do you live, where have you come from? For me!—I was dying every day and you were killing my boys and you did it for me? What the hell do you think I was thinking of, the Goddam business? Is that as far as your mind can see, the business? What is that, the world—the business? What the hell do you mean, you did it for me? Don't you have a country? Don't you live in the world? What the hell are you? You're not even an animal, no animal kills his own, what are you? What must I do to you? I ought to tear the tongue out of your mouth, what must I do? [*With his fist he pounds down upon his father's shoulder. He stumbles away, covering his face as he weeps.*] What must I do, Jesus God, what must I do?

KELLER. Chris . . . My Chris . . .

CURTAIN

Act Three

Two o'clock the following morning, MOTHER *is discovered on the rise, rocking ceaselessly in a chair, staring at her thoughts. It is an intense, slight, sort of rocking. A light shows from upstairs bedroom, lower floor windows being dark. The moon is strong and casts its bluish light.*

   Presently JIM, *dressed in jacket and hat, appears, and seeing her, goes up beside her.*

JIM. Any news?

MOTHER. No news.

JIM. [*gently*] You can't sit up all night, dear, why don't you go to bed?

MOTHER. I'm waiting for Chris. Don't worry about me, Jim, I'm perfectly all right.

JIM. But it's almost two o'clock.

MOTHER. I can't sleep. [*slight pause*] You had an emergency?

JIM. [*tiredly*] Somebody had a headache and thought he was dying. [*slight pause*] Half of my patients are quite mad. Nobody realizes how many people are walking around loose, and they're cracked as coconuts. Money. Money-money-money-money. You say it long enough it doesn't mean anything. [*She smiles, makes a silent laugh.*] Oh, how I'd love to be around when that happens!

MOTHER. [*shaking her head*] You're so childish, Jim! Sometimes you are.

JIM. [*looks at her a moment*] Kate. [*pause*] What happened?

MOTHER. I told you. He had an argument with Joe. Then he got in the car and drove away.

JIM. What kind of an argument?

MOTHER. An argument, Joe . . . He was crying like a child, before.

JIM. They argued about Ann?

MOTHER. [*after slight hesitation*] No, not Ann. Imagine? [*indicates lighted window above*] She hasn't come out of that room since he left. All night in that room.

JIM. [*looks at window, then at her*] What'd Joe do, tell him?

MOTHER. [*stops rocking*] Tell him what?

JIM. Don't be afraid, Kate, I know. I've always known.

MOTHER. How?

JIM. It occurred to me a long time ago.

MOTHER. I always had the feeling that in the back of his head, Chris . . . almost knew. I didn't think it would be such a shock.

JIM. [*gets up*] Chris would never know how to live with a thing like that. It takes a certain talent—for lying. You have it, and I do. But not him.

MOTHER. What do you mean . . . He's not coming back?

JIM. Oh, no, he'll come back. We all come back, Kate. These private little revolutions always die. The compromise is always made. In a peculiar way. Frank is right—every man does have a star. The star of one's honesty. And you spend your life groping for it, but once it's out it never lights again. I don't think he went very far. He probably just wanted to be alone to watch his star go out.

MOTHER. Just as long as he comes back.

JIM. I wish he wouldn't, Kate. One year I simply took off, went to New Orleans; for two months I lived on bananas and milk, and studied a certain disease. It was beautiful. And then she came, and she cried. And I went back home with her. And now I live

in the usual darkness; I can't find myself; it's even hard sometimes to remember the kind of man I wanted to be. I'm a good
husband; Chris is a good son—he'll come back.

[KELLER *comes out on porch in dressing gown and slippers.
He goes upstage—to alley.* JIM *goes to him.*]

JIM. I have a feeling he's in the park. I'll look around for him. Put
her to bed, Joe; this is no good for what she's got. [JIM *exits up
driveway.*]

KELLER. [*coming down*] What does he want here?

MOTHER. His friend is not home.

KELLER. [*comes down to her; his voice is husky*] I don't like him
mixing in so much.

MOTHER. It's too late, Joe. He knows.

KELLER. [*apprehensively*] How does he know?

MOTHER. He guessed a long time ago.

KELLER. I don't like that.

MOTHER. [*laughs dangerously, quietly into the line*] What you
don't like.

KELLER. Yeah, what I don't like.

MOTHER. You can't bull yourself through this one, Joe, you better
be smart now. This thing—this thing is not over yet.

KELLER. [*indicating lighted window above*] And what is she doing
up there? She don't come out of the room.

MOTHER. I don't know, what is she doing? Sit down, stop being mad.
You want to live? You better figure out your life.

KELLER. She don't know, does she?

MOTHER. She saw Chris storming out of here. It's one and one—
she knows how to add.

KELLER. Maybe I ought to talk to her?

MOTHER. Don't ask me, Joe.

KELLER. [*almost an outburst*] Then who do I ask? But I don't think
she'll do anything about it.

MOTHER. You're asking me again.

KELLER. I'm askin' you. What am I, a stranger? I thought I had a
family here. What happened to my family?

MOTHER. You've got a family. I'm simply telling you that I have no
strength to think any more.

KELLER. You have no strength. The minute there's trouble you have
no strength.

MOTHER. Joe, you're doing the same thing again; all your life whenever there's trouble you yell at me and you think that settles it.

KELLER. Then what do I do? Tell me, talk to me, what do I do?

MOTHER. Joe . . . I've been thinking this way. If he comes back—

KELLER. What do you mean "if"? He's comin' back!

MOTHER. I think if you sit him down and you—explain yourself. I
mean you ought to make it clear to him that you know you did
a terrible thing. [*not looking into his eyes*] I mean if he saw that
you realize what you did. You see?

KELLER. What ice does that cut?

MOTHER. [*a little fearfully*] I mean if you told him that you want to pay for what you did.

KELLER. [*sensing . . . quietly*] How can I pay?

MOTHER. Tell him—you're willing to go to prison. [*pause*]

KELLER. [*struck, amazed*] I'm willing to—?

MOTHER. [*quickly*] You wouldn't go, he wouldn't ask you to go. But if you told him you wanted to, if he could feel that you wanted to pay, maybe he would forgive you.

KELLER. He would forgive me! For what?

MOTHER. Joe, you know what I mean.

KELLER. I don't know what you mean! You wanted money, so I made money. What must I be forgiven? You wanted money, didn't you?

MOTHER. I didn't want it that way.

KELLER. I didn't want it that way, either! What difference is it what you want? I spoiled the both of you. I should've put him out when he was ten like I was put out, and make him earn his keep. Then he'd know how a buck is made in this world. Forgiven! I could live on a quarter a day myself, but I got a family so I—

MOTHER. Joe, Joe . . . It don't excuse it that you did it for the family.

KELLER. It's got to excuse it!

MOTHER. There's something bigger than the family to him.

KELLER. Nothin' is bigger!

MOTHER. There is to him.

KELLER. There's nothin' he could do that I wouldn't forgive. Because he's my son. Because I'm his father and he's my son.

MOTHER. Joe, I tell you—

KELLER. Nothin's bigger than that. And you're goin' to tell him, you understand? I'm his father and he's my son, and if there's something bigger than that I'll put a bullet in my head!

MOTHER. You stop that!

KELLER. You heard me. Now you know what to tell him. [*Pause. He moves from her—halts.*] But he wouldn't put me away though . . . He wouldn't do that . . . Would he?

MOTHER. He loved you, Joe, you broke his heart.

KELLER. But to put me away . . .

MOTHER. I don't know. I'm beginning to think we don't really know him. They say in the war he was such a killer. Here he was always afraid of mice. I don't know him. I don't know what he'll do.

KELLER. Goddam, if Larry was alive he wouldn't act like this. He understood the way the world is made. He listened to me. To him the world had a forty-foot front, it ended at the building line. This one, everything bothers him. You make a deal, overcharge two cents, and his hair falls out. He don't understand money. Too easy, it came too easy. Yes, sir. Larry. That was a boy we lost. Larry. Larry. [*He slumps on chair in front of her.*] What am I gonna do, Kate?

MOTHER. Joe, Joe, please . . . You'll be all right, nothing is going to happen.

KELLER. [*desperately, lost*] For you, Kate, for both of you, that's all I ever lived for . . .

MOTHER. I know, darling, I know. [ANN *enters from house. They say nothing, waiting for her to speak.*]

ANN. Why do you stay up? I'll tell you when he comes.

KELLER. [*rises, goes to her*] You didn't eat supper, did you? [*to* MOTHER] Why don't you make her something?

MOTHER. Sure, I'll—

ANN. Never mind, Kate, I'm all right. [*They are unable to speak to each other.*] There's something I want to tell you. [*She starts, then halts.*] I'm not going to do anything about it.

MOTHER. She's a good girl! [*to* KELLER] You see? She's a—

ANN. I'll do nothing about Joe, but you're going to do something for me. [*directly to* MOTHER] You made Chris feel guilty with me. Whether you wanted to or not, you've crippled him in front of me. I'd like you to tell him that Larry is dead and that you know it. You understand me? I'm not going out of here alone. There's no life for me that way. I want you to set him free. And then I promise you, everything will end, and we'll go away, and that's all.

KELLER. You'll do that. You'll tell him.

ANN. I know what I'm asking, Kate. You had two sons. But you've only got one now.

KELLER. You'll tell him.

ANN. And you've got to say it to him so he knows you mean it.

MOTHER. My dear, if the boy was dead, it wouldn't depend on my words to make Chris know it. . . The night he gets into your bed, his heart will dry up. Because he knows and you know. To his dying day he'll wait for his brother! No, my dear, no such thing. You're going in the morning, and you're going alone. That's your life, that's your lonely life. [*She goes to porch, and starts in.*]

ANN. Larry is dead, Kate.

MOTHER. [*She stops.*] Don't speak to me.

ANN. I said he's dead. I know! He crashed off the coast of China November twenty-fifth! His engine didn't fail him. But he died. I know . . .

MOTHER. How did he die? You're lying to me. If you know, how did he die?

ANN. I loved him. You know I loved him. Would I have looked at anyone else if I wasn't sure? That's enough for you.

MOTHER. [*moving on her*] What's enough for me? What're you talking about? [*She grasps* ANN's *wrists.*]

ANN. You're hurting my wrists.

MOTHER. What are you talking about! [*Pause. She stares at* ANN *a moment, then turns and goes to* KELLER.]

ANN. Joe, go in the house.

KELLER. Why should I—

ANN. Please go.

KELLER. Lemme know when he comes. [KELLER *goes into house.*]

MOTHER. [*as she sees* ANN *taking a letter from her pocket*] What's that?

ANN. Sit down. [MOTHER *moves left to chair, but does not sit.*] First you've got to understand. When I came, I didn't have any idea that Joe—I had nothing against him or you. I came to get married. I hoped . . . So I didn't bring this to hurt you. I thought I'd show it to you only if there was no other way to settle Larry in your mind.

MOTHER. Larry? [*snatches letter from* ANN's *hand*]

ANN. He wrote it to me just before he— [MOTHER *opens and begins to read letter.*] I'm not trying to hurt you, Kate. You're making me do this, now remember you're— Remember. I've been so lonely, Kate . . . I can't leave here alone again. [*A long, low moan comes from* MOTHER's *throat as she reads.*] You made me show it to you. You wouldn't believe me. I told you a hundred times, why wouldn't you believe me!

MOTHER. Oh, my God . . .

ANN. [*with pity and fear*] Kate, please, please . . .

MOTHER. My God, my God . . .

ANN. Kate, dear, I'm so sorry . . . I'm so sorry.

[CHRIS *enters from driveway. He seems exhausted.*]

CHRIS. What's the matter—?

ANN. Where were you? . . . You're all perspired. [MOTHER *doesn't move.*] Where were you?

CHRIS. Just drove around a little. I thought you'd be gone.

ANN. Where do I go? I have nowhere to go.

CHRIS. [*to* MOTHER] Where's Dad?

ANN. Inside lying down.

CHRIS. Sit down, both of you. I'll say what there is to say.

MOTHER. I didn't hear the car . . .

CHRIS. I left it in the garage.

MOTHER. Jim is out looking for you.

CHRIS. Mother . . . I'm going away. There are a couple of firms in Cleveland, I think I can get a place. I mean, I'm going away for good. [*to* ANN *alone*] I know what you're thinking, Annie. It's true. I'm yellow. I was made yellow in this house because I suspected my father and I did nothing about it, but if I knew that night when I came home what I know now, he'd be in the district attorney's office by this time, and I'd have brought him there. Now if I look at him, all I'm able to do is cry.

MOTHER. What are you talking about? What else can you do?

CHRIS. I could jail him! I could jail him, if I were human any more. But I'm like everybody else now. I'm practical now. You made me practical.

MOTHER. But you have to be.

CHRIS. The cats in that alley are practical, the bums who ran away when we were fighting were practical. Only the dead ones weren't practical. But now I'm practical, and I spit on myself. I'm going away. I'm going now.

ANN. [*going up to him*] I'm coming with you.

CHRIS. No, Ann.

ANN. Chris, I don't ask you to do anything about Joe.

CHRIS. You do, you do.

ANN. I swear I never will.

CHRIS. In your heart you always will.

ANN. Then do what you have to do!

CHRIS. Do what? What is there to do? I've looked all night for a reason to make him suffer.

ANN. There's reason, there's reason!

CHRIS. What? Do I raise the dead when I put him behind bars? Then what'll I do it for? We used to shoot a man who acted like a dog, but honor was real there, you were protecting something. But here? This is the land of the great big dogs, you don't love a man here, you eat him! That's the principle; the only one we live by—it just happened to kill a few people this time, that's all. The world's that way, how can I take it out on him? What sense does that make? This is a zoo, a zoo!

ANN. [*to* MOTHER] You know what he's got to do! Tell him!

MOTHER. Let him go.

ANN. I won't let him go. You'll tell him what he's got to do . . .

MOTHER. Annie!

ANN. Then I will!

> [KELLER *enters from house.* CHRIS *sees him, goes down near arbor.*]

KELLER. What's the matter with you? I want to talk to you.

CHRIS. I've got nothing to say to you.

KELLER. [*taking his arm*] I want to talk to you!

CHRIS. [*pulling violently away from him*] Don't do that, Dad. I'm going to hurt you if you do that. There's nothing to say, so say it quick.

KELLER. Exactly what's the matter? What's the matter? You got too much money? Is that what bothers you?

CHRIS. [*with an edge of sarcasm*] It bothers me.

KELLER. If you can't get used to it, then throw it away. You hear me? Take every cent and give it to charity, throw it in the sewer. Does that settle it? In the sewer, that's all. You think I'm kidding? I'm tellin' you what to do, if it's dirty then burn it. It's your money, that's not my money. I'm a dead man, I'm an old dead man, nothing's mine. Well, talk to me! What do you want to do?

CHRIS. It's not what I want to do. It's what you want to do.

KELLER. What should I want to do? [CHRIS *is silent.*] Jail? You want me to go to jail? If you want me to go, say so! Is that where I belong? Then tell me so! [*slight pause*] What's the matter, why can't you tell me? [*furiously*] You say everything else to me, say that! [*slight pause*] I'll tell you why you can't say it. Because you know I don't belong there. Because you know! [*with growing emphasis and passion, and a persistent tone of desperation*] Who worked for nothin' in that war? When they work for nothin', I'll work for nothin'. Did they ship a gun or a truck outa Detroit before they got their price? Is that clean? It's dollars and cents, nickels and dimes; war and peace, it's nickels and dimes, what's clean? Half the Goddam country is gotta go if I go! That's why you can't tell me.

CHRIS. That's exactly why.

KELLER. Then . . . why am *I* bad?

CHRIS. *I* know you're no worse than most men but I thought you were better. I never saw you as a man. I saw you as my father. [*almost breaking*] I can't look at you this way, I can't look at myself!

[*He turns away, unable to face* KELLER. ANN *goes quickly to* MOTHER, *takes letter from her and starts for* CHRIS. MOTHER *instantly rushes to intercept her.*]

MOTHER. Give me that!

ANN. He's going to read it! [*She thrusts letter into* CHRIS's *hand.*] Larry. He wrote it to me the day he died.

KELLER. Larry!

MOTHER. Chris, it's not for you. [*He starts to read.*] Joe . . . go away . . .

KELLER. [*mystified, frightened*] Why'd she say, Larry, what—?

MOTHER. [*desperately pushes him toward alley, glancing at* CHRIS] Go to the street, Joe, go to the street! [*She comes down beside* KELLER.] Don't, Chris . . . [*pleading from her whole soul*] Don't tell him.

CHRIS. [*quietly*] Three and one half years . . . talking, talking. Now you tell me what you must do. . . . This is how he died, now tell me where you belong.

KELLER. [*pleading*] Chris, a man can't be a Jesus in this world!

CHRIS. I know all about the world. I know the whole crap story. Now listen to this, and tell me what a man's got to be! [*reads*] "My dear Ann: . . ." You listening? He wrote this the day he died. Listen, don't cry. . . . Listen! "My dear Ann: It is impossible to put down the things I feel. But I've got to tell you something. Yesterday they flew in a load of papers from the States and I read about Dad and your father being convicted. I can't express myself. I can't tell you how I feel—I can't bear to live any more. Last night I circled the base for twenty minutes before I could bring myself in. How could he have done that? Every day three or four men never come back and he sits back there doing business. . . . I don't know how to tell you what I feel. . . . I can't face anybody. . . . I'm going out on a mission in a few minutes. They'll probably report me missing. If they do, I want you to know that you mustn't wait for me. I tell you, Ann, if I had him there now I could kill him—" [KELLER *grabs letter from* CHRIS's *hand and reads it. After a long pause*] Now blame the world. Do you understand that letter?

KELLER. [*speaking almost inaudibly*] I think I do. Get the car. I'll put on my jacket. [*He turns and starts slowly for the house.* MOTHER *rushes to intercept him.*]

MOTHER. Why are you going? You'll sleep, why are you going?

KELLER. I can't sleep here. I'll feel better if I go.

MOTHER. You're so foolish. Larry was your son too, wasn't he? You know he'd never tell you to do this.

KELLER. [*looking at letter in his hand*] Then what is this if it isn't telling me? Sure, he was my son. But I think to him they were all my sons. And I guess they were, I guess they were. I'll be right down. [*exits into house*]

MOTHER. [*to* CHRIS, *with determination*] You're not going to take him!

CHRIS. I'm taking him.

MOTHER. It's up to you, if you tell him to stay he'll stay. Go and tell him!

CHRIS. Nobody could stop him now.

MOTHER. You'll stop him! How long will he live in prison? Are you trying to kill him?

CHRIS. [*holding out letter*] I thought you read this!

MOTHER. [*of Larry, the letter*] The war is over! Didn't you hear? It's over!

CHRIS. Then what was Larry to you? A stone that fell into the water? It's not enough for him to be sorry. Larry didn't kill himself to make you and Dad sorry.

MOTHER. What more can we be!

CHRIS. You can be better! Once and for all you can know there's a universe of people outside and you're responsible to it, and unless you know that, you threw away your son because that's why he died.

[*A shot is heard in the house. They stand frozen for a brief second.* CHRIS *starts for porch, pauses at step, turns to* ANN.]

CHRIS. Find Jim! [*He goes on into the house and* ANN *runs up driveway.* MOTHER *stands alone, transfixed.*]

MOTHER. [*softly, almost moaning*] Joe . . . Joe . . . Joe . . . Joe . . . [CHRIS *comes out of house, down to* MOTHER'S *arms.*]

CHRIS. [*almost crying*] Mother, I didn't mean to—

MOTHER. Don't dear. Don't take it on yourself. Forget now. Live. [CHRIS *stirs as if to answer.*] Shhh . . . [*She puts his arms down gently and moves toward porch.*] Shhh . . . [*As she reaches porch steps she begins sobbing.*]

CURTAIN

The Wild Duck

HENRIK IBSEN

The Wild Duck was first published on November 11, 1884; it was first performed, at Bergen, on January 8, 1885. Although the first edition sold out within a month of publication and although the play was performed all over Europe within ten years of its first appearance, it was slow to receive the approbation it deserves. Now considered one of Henrik Ibsen's best plays—although he perhaps overworks that wild-duck metaphor—it was greeted at first with baffled amazement, occasionally with anger. In the eighty years since then, the obscurity has dropped away. In fact, at first look, the play may seem a little old-fashioned, an impression that is probably heightened by the stilted English into which Mrs. Archer has translated Ibsen's Norwegian. It would be a mistake to stop at that first look—as, eighty years ago, it was a critical error to give in to any initial confusion—for in *The Wild Duck* Ibsen has created one of his finest characters. In approaching Hialmar—and the whole play—it might be well to remember two comments on it. The first, from Ibsen himself, in a letter to a theater manager who was about to stage the play: "This part must definitely not be played with any kind of parody of expression; there must be no trace that the actor is conscious of there being any kind of comic element in the lines at all." The second, from Bernard Shaw, reviewing a London production of the play in 1897: "Where shall I find an epithet magnificent enough for The Wild Duck! . . . to look on with horror and pity at a profound tragedy, shaking with laughter all the time at an irresistible comedy."

The Wild Duck †

Characters

WERLE, *a merchant, manufacturer, etc.*

GREGERS WERLE, *his son*

OLD EKDAL

HIALMAR EKDAL, *his son, a photographer*

GINA EKDAL, *Hialmar's wife*

HEDVIG, *their daughter, a girl of fourteen*

MRS. SÖRBY, *Werle's housekeeper*

RELLING, *a doctor*

MOLVIK, *student of theology*

GRÅBERG, *Werle's bookkeeper*

PETTERSEN, *Werle's servant*

† Translated by Frances Archer.

JENSEN, *a hired waiter*
FLABBY GENTLEMAN
THIN-HAIRED GENTLEMAN
SHORT-SIGHTED GENTLEMAN

SIX OTHER GENTLEMEN, *guests at*
Werle's dinner-party
SEVERAL HIRED WAITERS

The first act passes in WERLE'S *house, the remaining acts at* HIALMAR EKDAL'S.

Act I

SCENE—*At* WERLE'S *house. A richly and comfortably furnished study; bookcases and upholstered furniture; a writing-table, with papers and documents, in the centre of the room; lighted lamps with green shades, giving a subdued light. At the back, open folding-doors with curtains drawn back. Within is seen a large and hand-some room, brilliantly lighted with lamps and branching candle-sticks. In front, on the right (in the study), a small baize door leads into* WERLE'S *office. On the left, in front, a fireplace with a glowing coal fire, and farther back a double door leading into the dining-room.*

WERLE'S *servant,* PETTERSEN, *in livery, and* JENSEN, *the hired waiter, in black, are putting the study in order. In the large room, two or three other hired waiters are moving about, arranging things and lighting more candles. From the dining-room, the hum of con-versation and laughter of many voices are heard; a glass is tapped with a knife; silence follows, and a toast is proposed; shouts of "Bravo!" and then again a buzz of conversation.*

PETTERSEN. [*lights a lamp on the chimney-place and places a shade over it*] Listen to them, Jensen! Now the old man's on his legs holding a long palaver about Mrs. Sörby.

JENSEN. [*pushing forward an armchair*] Is it true, what folks say, that they're—very good friends, eh?

PETTERSEN. Lord knows.

JENSEN. I've heard tell as he's been a lively customer in his day.

PETTERSEN. May be.

JENSEN. And he's giving this spread in honor of his son, they say.

PETTERSEN. Yes. His son came home yesterday.

JENSEN. This is the first time I ever heard as Mr. Werle had a son.

PETTERSEN. Oh, yes, he has a son, right enough. But he's a fixture, as you might say, up at the Höidal works. He's never once come to town all the years I've been in service here.

A WAITER. [*in the doorway of the other room*] Pettersen, here's an old fellow wanting——

PETTERSEN. [*mutters*] The devil—who's this now?

[OLD EKDAL *appears from the right, in the inner room. He is dressed in a threadbare overcoat with a high collar; he wears woollen mittens and carries in his hand a stick and a fur cap. Under his arm, a brown paper parcel. Dirty red-brown wig and small grey moustache.*]

PETTERSEN. [goes towards him] Good Lord—what do you want here?

EKDAL. [in the doorway] Must get into the office, Pettersen.

PETTERSEN. The office was closed an hour ago, and——

EKDAL. So they told me at the front door. But Gråberg's in there still. Let me slip in this way, Pettersen; there's a good fellow. [points towards the baize door] It's not the first time I've come this way.

PETTERSEN. Well, you may pass. [opens the door] But mind you go out again the proper way, for we've got company.

EKDAL. I know, I know—h'm! Thanks, Pettersen, good old friend! Thanks! [mutters softly] Ass!

[He goes into the office; PETTERSEN shuts the door after him.]

JENSEN. Is he one of the office people?

PETTERSEN. No he's only an outside hand that does odd jobs of copying. But he's been a tip-topper in his day, has old Ekdal.

JENSEN. You can see he's been through a lot.

PETTERSEN. Yes; he was an army officer, you know.

JENSEN. You don't say so?

PETTERSEN. No mistake about it. But then he went into the timber trade or something of the sort. They say he once played Mr. Werle a very nasty trick. They were partners in the Höidal works at the time. Oh, I know old Ekdal well, I do. Many a nip of bitters and bottle of ale we two have drunk at Madame Eriksen's.

JENSEN. He don't look as if he'd much to stand treat with.

PETTERSEN. Why, bless you, Jensen, it's me that stands treat. I always think there's no harm in being a bit civil to folks that have seen better days.

JENSEN. Did he go bankrupt, then?

PETTERSEN. Worse than that. He went to prison.

JENSEN. To prison!

PETTERSEN. Or perhaps it was the Penitentiary.[1] [listens] Sh! They're leaving the table.

[The dining-room door is thrown open from within by a couple of waiters. MRS. SÖRBY comes out conversing with two GENTLEMEN. Gradually the whole company follows, amongst them WERLE. Last come HIALMAR EKDAL and GREGERS WERLE.]

MRS. SÖRBY. [in passing, to the servant] Tell them to serve the coffee in the music-room, Pettersen.

PETTERSEN. Very well, Madam.

[She goes with the two GENTLEMEN into the inner room and thence out to the right. PETTERSEN and JENSEN go out the same way.]

FLABBY GENTLEMAN. [to THIN-HAIRED GENTLEMAN] Whew! What a dinner!—It was no joke to do it justice!

THIN-HAIRED GENTLEMAN. Oh, with a little good-will one can get

1. "Penitentiary" implies a less severe sentence than "prison." Like any good gossip, Pettersen opens with the shocker and backtracks toward the truth.

through a lot in three hours.

FLABBY GENTLEMAN. Yes, but afterwards, afterwards, my dear Chamberlain![2]

THIRD GENTLEMAN. I hear the coffee and maraschino are to be served in the music-room.

FLABBY GENTLEMAN. Bravo! Then perhaps Mrs. Sörby will play us something.

THIN-HAIRED GENTLEMAN. [*in a low voice*] I hope Mrs. Sörby mayn't play us a tune we don't like, one of these days!

FLABBY GENTLEMAN. Oh, no, not she! Bertha will never turn against her old friends.

[*They laugh and pass into the inner room.*]

WERLE. [*in a low voice, dejectedly*] I don't think anybody noticed it, Gregers.

GREGERS. [*looks at him*] Noticed what?

WERLE. Did you not notice it either?

GREGERS. What do you mean?

WERLE. We were thirteen at table.

GREGERS. Indeed? Were there thirteen of us?

WERLE. [*glances towards* HIALMAR EKDAL] Our usual party is twelve. [*to the others*] This way, gentlemen!

[WERLE *and the others, all except* HIALMAR *and* GREGERS, *go out by the back, to the right.*]

HIALMAR. [*who has overheard the conversation*] You ought not to have invited me, Gregers.

GREGERS. What! Not ask my best and only friend to a party supposed to be in my honor——?

HIALMAR. But I don't think your father likes it. You see I am quite outside his circle.

GREGERS. So I hear. But I wanted to see you and have a talk with you, and I certainly shan't be staying long.—Ah, we two old schoolfellows have drifted far apart from each other. It must be sixteen or seventeen years since we met.

HIALMAR. Is it so long?

GREGERS. It is indeed. Well, how goes it with you? You look well. You have put on flesh and grown almost stout.

HIALMAR. Well, "stout" is scarcely the word; but I daresay I look a little more of a man than I used to.

GREGERS. Yes, you do; your outer man is in first-rate condition.

HIALMAR. [*in a tone of gloom*] Ah, but the inner man! That is a very different matter, I can tell you! Of course you know of the terrible catastrophe that has befallen me and mine since last we met.

GREGERS. [*more softly*] How are things going with your father now?

HIALMAR. Don't let us talk of it, old fellow. Of course my poor unhappy father lives with me. He hasn't another soul in the world to care for him. But you can understand that this is a miserable subject for me.—Tell me, rather, how you have been getting on

2. "Chamberlain" was the nonhereditary honorary title conferred by the King upon men of wealth and position. [Translator's note.]

up at the works.

GREGERS. I have had a delightfully lonely time of it—plenty of leisure to think and think about things. Come over here; we may as well make ourselves comfortable.

[*He seats himself in an armchair by the fire and draws* HIALMAR *down into another alongside of it.*]

HIALMAR. [*sentimentally*] After all, Gregers, I thank you for inviting me to your father's table, for I take it as a sign that you have got over your feeling against me.

GREGERS. [*surprised*] How could you imagine I had any feeling against you?

HIALMAR. You had at first, you know.

GREGERS. How at first?

HIALMAR. After the great misfortune. It was natural enough that you should. Your father was within an ace of being drawn into that—well, that terrible business.

GREGERS. Why should that give me any feeling against you? Who can have put that into your head?

HIALMAR. I know it did, Gregers; your father told me so himself.

GREGERS. [*starts*] My father! Oh, indeed. H'm.—Was that why you never let me hear from you?—not a single word.

HIALMAR. Yes.

GREGERS. Not even when you made up your mind to become a photographer?

HIALMAR. Your father said I had better not write to you at all, about anything.

GREGERS. [*looking straight before him*] Well, well, perhaps he was right.—But tell me now, Hialmar: are you pretty well satisfied with your present position?

HIALMAR. [*with a little sigh*] Oh, yes, I am; I have really no cause to complain. At first, as you may guess, I felt it a little strange. It was such a totally new state of things for me. But of course my whole circumstances were totally changed. Father's utter, irretrievable ruin,—the shame and disgrace of it, Gregers——

GREGERS. [*affected*] Yes, yes; I understand.

HIALMAR. I couldn't think of remaining at college; there wasn't a shilling to spare; on the contrary, there were debts—mainly to your father, I believe——

GREGERS. H'm——

HIALMAR. In short, I thought it best to break, once for all, with my old surroundings and associations. It was your father that specially urged me to it; and since he interested himself so much in me——

GREGERS. My father did?

HIALMAR. Yes, you surely knew that, didn't you? Where do you suppose I found the money to learn photography, and to furnish a studio and make a start? All that cost a pretty penny, I can tell you.

GREGERS. And my father provided the money?

HIALMAR. Yes, my dear fellow, didn't you know? I understood him to say he had written to you about it.

GREGERS. Not a word about his part in the business. He must have forgotten it. Our correspondence has always been purely a business one. So it was my father that——!

HIALMAR. Yes, certainly. He didn't wish it to be generally known; but he it was. And of course it was he, too, that put me in a position to marry. Don't you—don't you know about that either?

GREGERS. No, I haven't heard a word of it. [*shakes him by the arm*] But, my dear Hialmar, I can't tell you what pleasure all this gives me—pleasure, and self-reproach. I have perhaps done my father injustice after all—in some things. This proves that he has a heart. It shows a sort of compunction——

HIALMAR. Compunction——?

GREGERS. Yes, yes—whatever you like to call it. Oh, I can't tell you how glad I am to hear this of father.—So you are a married man, Hialmar! That is further than I shall ever get. Well, I hope you are happy in your married life?

HIALMAR. Yes, thoroughly happy. She is as good and capable a wife as any man could wish for. And she is by no means without culture.

GREGERS. [*rather surprised*] No, of course not.

HIALMAR. You see, life is itself an education. Her daily intercourse with me—— And then we know one or two rather remarkable men, who come a good deal about us. I assure you, you would hardly know Gina again.

GREGERS. Gina?

HIALMAR. Yes; had you forgotten that her name was Gina?

GREGERS. Whose name? I haven't the slightest idea——

HIALMAR. Don't you remember that she used to be in service here?

GREGERS. [*looks at him*] Is it Gina Hansen——?

HIALMAR. Yes, of course it is Gina Hansen.

GREGERS. ——who kept house for us during the last year of my mother's illness?

HIALMAR. Yes, exactly. But, my dear friend, I'm quite sure your father told you that I was married.

GREGERS. [*who has risen*] Oh, yes, he mentioned it; but not that—— [*walking about the room*] Stay—perhaps he did—now that I think of it. My father always writes such short letters. [*half seats himself on the arm of the chair*] Now tell me, Hialmar—this is interesting—how did you come to know Gina—your wife?

HIALMAR. The simplest thing in the world. You know Gina did not stay here long; everything was so much upset at that time, owing to your mother's illness and so forth, that Gina was not equal to it all; so she gave notice and left. That was the year before your mother died—or it may have been the same year.

GREGERS. It was the same year. I was up at the works then. But afterwards——?

HIALMAR. Well, Gina lived at home with her mother, Madame

Hansen, an excellent hard-working woman, who kept a little eating-house. She had a room to let, too, a very nice comfortable room.

GREGERS. And I suppose you were lucky enough to secure it?

HIALMAR. Yes; in fact, it was your father that recommended it to me. So it was there, you see, that I really came to know Gina.

GREGERS. And then you got engaged?

HIALMAR. Yes. It doesn't take young people long to fall in love——; h'm——

GREGERS. [*rises and moves about a little*] Tell me: was it after your engagement—was it then that my father—I mean was it then that you began to take up photography?

HIALMAR. Yes, precisely. I wanted to make a start and to set up house as soon as possible; and your father and I agreed that this photography business was the readiest way. Gina thought so, too. Oh, and there was another thing in its favor, by-the-bye: it happened, luckily, that Gina had learnt to retouch.

GREGERS. That chimed in marvellously.

HIALMAR. [*pleased, rises*] Yes, didn't it? Don't you think it was a marvellous piece of luck?

GREGERS. Oh, unquestionably. My father seems to have been almost a kind of providence for you.

HIALMAR. [*with emotion*] He did not forsake his old friend's son in the hour of his need. For he has a heart, you see.

MRS. SÖRBY. [*enters, arm-in-arm with* WERLE] Nonsense, my dear Mr. Werle; you mustn't stop there any longer staring at all the lights. It's very bad for you.

WERLE. [*lets go her arm and passes his hand over his eyes*] I daresay you are right.

[PETTERSEN *and* JENSEN *carry round refreshment trays.*]

MRS. SÖRBY. [*to the guests in the other room*] This way, if you please, gentlemen. Whoever wants a glass of punch must be so good as to come in here.

FLABBY GENTLEMAN. [*comes up to* MRS. SÖRBY] Surely, it isn't possible that you have suspended our cherished right to smoke?

MRS. SÖRBY. Yes. No smoking here, in Mr. Werle's sanctum, Chamberlain.

THIN-HAIRED GENTLEMAN. When did you enact these stringent amendments to the cigar law, Mrs. Sörby?

MRS. SÖRBY. After the last dinner, Chamberlain, when certain persons permitted themselves to overstep the mark.

THIN-HAIRED GENTLEMAN. And may one never overstep the mark a little bit, Madame Bertha? Not the least little bit?

MRS. SÖRBY. Not in any respect whatsoever, Mr. Balle.

[*Most of the guests have assembled in the study; servants hand round glasses of punch.*]

WERLE. [*to* HIALMAR, *who is standing beside a table*] What are you studying so intently, Ekdal?

HIALMAR. Only an album, Mr. Werle.

THIN-HAIRED GENTLEMAN. [*who is wandering about*] Ah, photographs! They are quite in your line, of course.

FLABBY GENTLEMAN. [*in an armchair*] Haven't you brought any of
your own with you?

HIALMAR. No, I haven't.

FLABBY GENTLEMAN. You ought to have; it's very good for the digestion to sit and look at pictures.

THIN-HAIRED GENTLEMAN. And it contributes to the entertainment,
you know.

SHORT-SIGHTED GENTLEMAN. And all contributions are thankfully
received.

MRS. SÖRBY. The Chamberlains think that when one is invited out
to dinner, one ought to exert oneself a little in return, Mr. Ekdal.

FLABBY GENTLEMAN. Where one dines so well, that duty becomes a
pleasure.

THIN-HAIRED GENTLEMAN. And when it's a case of the struggle for
existence, you know——

MRS. SÖRBY. I quite agree with you!

[*They continue the conversation, with laughter and joking.*]

GREGERS. [*softly*] You must join in, Hialmar.

HIALMAR. [*writhing*] What am I to talk about?

FLABBY GENTLEMAN. Don't you think, Mr. Werle, that Tokay may
be considered one of the more wholesome sorts of wine?

WERLE. [*by the fire*] I can answer for the Tokay you had today, at
any rate; it's one of the very finest seasons. Of course you would
notice that.

FLABBY GENTLEMAN. Yes, it had a remarkably delicate flavor.

HIALMAR. [*shyly*] Is there any difference between the seasons?

FLABBY GENTLEMAN. [*laughs*] Come! That's good!

WERLE. [*smiles*] It really doesn't pay to set fine wine before you.

THIN-HAIRED GENTLEMAN. Tokay is like photographs, Mr. Ekdal:
they both need sunshine. Am I not right?

HIALMAR. Yes, light is important, no doubt.

MRS. SÖRBY. And it's exactly the same with Chamberlains—they,
too, depend very much on sunshine,[3] as the saying is.

THIN-HAIRED GENTLEMAN. Oh, fie! That's a very threadbare sarcasm!

SHORT-SIGHTED GENTLEMAN. Mrs. Sörby is coming out——

FLABBY GENTLEMAN. ——and at our expense, too. [*holds up his
finger reprovingly*] Oh, Madame Bertha, Madame Bertha!

MRS. SÖRBY. Yes, and there's not the least doubt that the seasons
differ greatly. The old vintages are the finest.

SHORT-SIGHTED GENTLEMAN. Do you reckon me among the old
vintages?

MRS. SÖRBY. Oh, far from it.

THIN-HAIRED GENTLEMAN. There now! But me, dear Mrs. Sörby——?

FLABBY GENTLEMAN. Yes, and me? What vintage should you say
that we belong to?

MRS. SÖRBY. Why, to the sweet vintages, gentlemen.

[*She sips a glass of punch. The GENTLEMEN laugh and flirt
with her.*]

WERLE. Mrs. Sörby can always find a loop-hole—when she wants

3. The "sunshine" of court favor. [Translator's note.]

to. Fill your glasses, gentlemen! Pettersen, will you see to it——!
Gregers, suppose we have a glass together. [GREGERS *does not
move.*] Won't you join us, Ekdal? I found no opportunity of
drinking with you at table.

[GRÅBERG, *the bookkeeper, looks in at the baize door.*]

GRÅBERG. Excuse me, sir, but I can't get out.

WERLE. Have you been locked in again?

GRÅBERG. Yes, and Flakstad has carried off the keys.

WERLE. Well, you can pass out this way.

GRÅBERG. But there's some one else——

WERLE. All right; come through, both of you. Don't be afraid.

[GRÅBERG *and* OLD EKDAL *come out of the office.*]

WERLE. [*involuntarily*] Ugh!

[*The laughter and talk among the guests cease.* HIALMAR
*starts at the sight of his father, puts down his glass and turns
towards the fireplace.*]

EKDAL. [*does not look up, but makes little bows to both sides as
he passes, murmuring*] Beg pardon, come the wrong way. Door
locked—door locked. Beg pardon.

[*He and* GRÅBERG *go out by the back, to the right.*]

WERLE. [*between his teeth*] That idiot Gråberg.

GREGERS. [*opened-mouthed and staring, to* HIALMAR] Why surely
that wasn't——!

FLABBY GENTLEMAN. What's the matter? Who was it?

GREGERS. Oh, nobody; only the bookkeeper and some one with him.

SHORT-SIGHTED GENTLEMAN. [*to* HIALMAR] Did you know that man?

HIALMAR. I don't know—I didn't notice——

FLABBY GENTLEMAN. What the deuce has come over every one?

[*He joins another group who are talking softly.*]

MRS. SÖRBY. [*whispers to the servant*] Give him something to take
with him;—something good, mind.

PETTERSEN. [*nods*] I'll see to it. [*goes out*]

GREGERS. [*softly and with emotion, to* HIALMAR] So that was really
he!

HIALMAR. Yes.

GREGERS. And you could stand there and deny that you knew him!

HIALMAR. [*whispers vehemently*] But how could I——!

GREGERS. ——acknowledge your own father?

HIALMAR. [*with pain*] Oh, if you were in my place——

[*The conversation amongst the guests, which has been carried on in a low tone, now swells into constrained joviality.*]

THIN-HAIRED GENTLEMAN. [*approaching* HIALMAR *and* GREGERS *in
a friendly manner*] Aha! Reviving old college memories, eh? Don't
you smoke, Mr. Ekdal? May I give you a light? Oh, by-the-bye,
we mustn't——

HIALMAR. No, thank you, I won't——

FLABBY GENTLEMAN. Haven't you a nice little poem you could recite to us, Mr. Ekdal? You used to recite so charmingly.

HIALMAR. I am sorry I can't remember anything.

FLABBY GENTLEMAN. Oh, that's a pity. Well, what shall we do,

Balle?

[*Both* GENTLEMEN *move away and pass into the other room.*]

HIALMAR. [*gloomily*] Gregers—I am going! When a man has felt the crushing hand of Fate, you see—— Say good-bye to your father for me.

GREGERS. Yes, yes. Are you going straight home?

HIALMAR. Yes. Why?

GREGERS. Oh, because I may perhaps look in on you later.

HIALMAR. No, you mustn't do that. You must not come to my home. Mine is a melancholy abode, Gregers, especially after a splendid banquet like this. We can always arrange to meet somewhere in the town.

MRS. SÖRBY. [*who has quietly approached*] Are you going, Ekdal?

HIALMAR. Yes.

MRS. SÖRBY. Remember me to Gina.

HIALMAR. Thanks.

MRS. SÖRBY. And say I am coming up to see her one of these days.

HIALMAR. Yes, thank you. [*to* GREGERS] Stay here; I will slip out unobserved.

[*He saunters away, then into the other room, and so out to the right.*]

MRS. SÖRBY. [*softly to the servant, who has come back*] Well, did you give the old man something?

PETTERSEN. Yes; I sent him off with a bottle of cognac.

MRS. SÖRBY. Oh, you might have thought of something better than that.

PETTERSEN. Oh, no, Mrs. Sörby; cognac is what he likes best in the world.

FLABBY GENTLEMAN. [*in the doorway with a sheet of music in his hand*] Shall we play a duet, Mrs. Sörby?

MRS. SÖRBY. Yes, suppose we do.

THE GUESTS. Bravo, bravo!

[*She goes with all the guests through the back room, out to the right.* GREGERS *remains standing by the fire.* WERLE *is looking for something on the writing-table and appears to wish that* GREGERS *would go; as* GREGERS *does not move,* WERLE *goes towards the door.*]

GREGERS. Father, won't you stay a moment?

WERLE. [*stops*] What is it?

GREGERS. I must have a word with you.

WERLE. Can it not wait till we are alone?

GREGERS. No, it cannot; for perhaps we shall never be alone together.

WERLE. [*drawing nearer*] What do you mean by that?

[*During what follows, the pianoforte is faintly heard from the distant music-room.*]

GREGERS. How has that family been allowed to go so miserably to the wall?

WERLE. You mean the Ekdals, I suppose.

GREGERS. Yes, I mean the Ekdals. Lieutenant Ekdal was once so closely associated with you.

WERLE. Much too closely; I have felt that to my cost for many a year. It is thanks to him that I—yes *I*—have had a kind of slur cast upon my reputation.

GREGERS. [*softly*] Are you sure that he alone was to blame?

WERLE. Who else do you suppose——?

GREGERS. You ard he acted together in that affair of the forests——

WERLE. But was it not Ekdal that drew the map of the tracts we had bought—that fraudulent map! It was he who felled all that timber illegally on Government ground. In fact, the whole management was in his hands. I was quite in the dark as to what Lieutenant Ekdal was doing.

GREGERS. Lieutenant Ekdal himself seems to have been very much in the dark as to what he was doing.

WERLE. That may be. But the fact remains that he was found guilty and I acquitted.

GREGERS. Yes, I know that nothing was proved against you.

WERLE. Acquittal is acquittal. Why do you rake up these old miseries that turned my hair grey before its time? Is that the sort of thing you have been brooding over up there, all these years? I can assure you, Gregers, here in the town the whole story has been forgotten long ago—so far as *I* am concerned.

GREGERS. But that unhappy Ekdal family——

WERLE. What would you have had me do for the people? When Ekdal came out of prison he was a broken-down being, past all help. There are people in the world who dive to the bottom the moment they get a couple of slugs in their body and never come to the surface again. You may take my word for it, Gregers, I have done all I could without positively laying myself open to all sorts of suspicion and gossip——

GREGERS. Suspicion——? Oh, I see.

WERLE. I have given Ekdal copying to do for the office, and I pay him far, far more for it than his work is worth——

GREGERS. [*without looking at him*] H'm; that I don't doubt.

WERLE. You laugh? Do you think I am not telling you the truth? Well, I certainly can't refer you to my books, for I never enter payments of that sort.

GREGERS. [*smiles coldly*] No, there are certain payments it is best to keep no account of.

WERLE. [*taken aback*] What do you mean by that?

GREGERS. [*mustering up courage*] Have you entered what it cost you to have Hialmar Ekdal taught photography?

WERLE. I? How "entered" it?

GREGERS. I have learnt that it was you who paid for his training. And I have learnt, too, that it was you who enabled him to set up house so comfortably.

WERLE. Well, and yet you talk as though I had done nothing for the Ekdals! I can assure you these people have cost me enough in all conscience.

GREGERS. Have you entered any of these expenses in your books?

WERLE. Why do you ask?

GREGERS. Oh, I have my reasons. Now tell me: when you interested yourself so warmly in your old friend's son—it was just before his marriage, was it not?

WERLE. Why, deuce take it—after all these years, how can I——?

GREGERS. You wrote me a letter about that time—a business letter, of course; and in a postscript you mentioned—quite briefly—that Hialmar Ekdal had married a Miss Hansen.

WERLE. Yes, that was quite right. That was her name.

GREGERS. But you did not mention that this Miss Hansen was Gina Hansen—our former housekeeper.

WERLE. [*with a forced laugh of derision*] No; to tell the truth, it didn't occur to me that you were so particularly interested in our former housekeeper.

GREGERS. No more I was. But [*lowers his voice*] there were others in this house who were particularly interested in her.

WERLE. What do you mean by that? [*flaring up*] You are not alluding to me, I hope?

GREGERS. [*softly but firmly*] Yes, I am alluding to you.

WERLE. And you dare——! You presume to——! How can that ungrateful hound—that photographer fellow—how dare he go making such insinuations!

GREGERS. Hialmar has never breathed a word about this. I don't believe he has the faintest suspicion of such a thing.

WERLE. Then where have you got it from? Who can have put such notions in your head?

GREGERS. My poor unhappy mother told me; and that the very last time I saw her.

WERLE. Your mother! I might have known as much! You and she—you always held together. It was she who turned you against me, from the first.

GREGERS. No, it was all that she had to suffer and submit to, until she broke down and came to such a pitiful end.

WERLE. Oh, she had nothing to suffer or submit to; not more than most people, at all events. But there's no getting on with morbid, overstrained creatures—that I have learnt to my cost.—And you could go on nursing such a suspicion—burrowing into all sorts of old rumors and slanders against your own father! I must say, Gregers, I really think that at your age you might find something more useful to do.

GREGERS. Yes, it is high time.

WERLE. Then perhaps your mind would be easier than it seems to be now. What can be your object in remaining up at the works, year out and year in, drudging away like a common clerk, and not drawing a farthing more than the ordinary monthly wage? It is downright folly.

GREGERS. Ah, if I were only sure of that.

WERLE. I understand you well enough. You want to be independent; you won't be beholden to me for anything. Well, now there happens to be an opportunity for you to become independent, your own master in everything.

GREGERS. Indeed? In what way——?

WERLE. When I wrote you insisting on your coming to town at once—h'm——

GREGERS. Yes, what is it you really want of me? I have been waiting all day to know.

WERLE. I want to propose that you should enter the firm, as partner.

GREGERS. I! Join your firm? As partner?

WERLE. Yes. It would not involve our being constantly together. You could take over the business here in town, and I should move up to the works.

GREGERS. You would?

WERLE. The fact is, I am not so fit for work as I once was. I am obliged to spare my eyes, Gregers; they have begun to trouble me.

GREGERS. They have always been weak.

WERLE. Not as they are now. And, besides, circumstances might possibly make it desirable for me to live up there—for a time, at any rate.

GREGERS. That is certainly quite a new idea to me.

WERLE. Listen, Gregers: there are many things that stand between us; but we are father and son after all. We ought surely to be able to come to some sort of understanding with each other.

GREGERS. Outwardly, you mean, of course?

WERLE. Well, even that would be something. Think it over, Gregers. Don't you think it ought to be possible? Eh?

GREGERS. [*looking at him coldly*] There is something behind all this.

WERLE. How so?

GREGERS. You want to make use of me in some way.

WERLE. In such a close relationship as ours, the one can always be useful to the other.

GREGERS. Yes, so people say.

WERLE. I want very much to have you at home with me for a time. I am a lonely man, Gregers; I have always felt lonely, all my life through; but most of all now that I am getting up in years. I feel the need of some one about me——

GREGERS. You have Mrs. Sörby.

WERLE. Yes, I have her; and she has become, I may say, almost indispensable to me. She is lively and even-tempered; she brightens up the house; and that is a very great thing for me.

GREGERS. Well, then, you have everything just as you wish it.

WERLE. Yes, but I am afraid it can't last. A woman so situated may easily find herself in a false position, in the eyes of the world. For that matter it does a man no good, either.

GREGERS. Oh, when a man gives such dinners as you give, he can risk a great deal.

WERLE. Yes, but how about the woman, Gregers? I fear she won't accept the situation much longer; and even if she did—even if, out of attachment to me, she were to take her chance of gossip and scandal and all that——? Do you think, Gregers—you with your strong sense of justice——

GREGERS. [*interrupts him*] Tell me in one word: are you thinking of marrying her?

WERLE. Suppose I were thinking of it? What then?

GREGERS. That's what I say: what then?

WERLE. Should you be inflexibly opposed to it!

GREGERS. Not at all. Not by any means.

WERLE. I was not sure whether your devotion to your mother's memory——

GREGERS. I am not overstrained.

WERLE. Well, whatever you may or may not be, at all events you have lifted a great weight from my mind. I am extremely pleased that I can reckon on your concurrence in this matter.

GREGERS. [*looking intently at him*] Now I see the use you want to put me to.

WERLE. Use to put you to? What an expression!

GREGERS. Oh, don't let us be nice in our choice of words—not when we are alone together, at any rate. [*with a short laugh*] Well, well. So this is what made it absolutely essential that I should come to town in person. For the sake of Mrs. Sörby, we are to get up a pretence at family life in the house—a tableau of filial affection! That will be something new indeed.

WERLE. How dare you speak in that tone!

GREGERS. Was there ever any family life here? Never since I can remember. But now, forsooth, your plans demand something of the sort. No doubt it will have an excellent effect when it is reported that the son has hastened home, on the wings of filial piety, to the grey-haired father's wedding-feast. What will then remain of all the rumors as to the wrongs the poor dead mother had to submit to? Not a vestige. Her son annihilates them at one stroke.

WERLE. Gregers—I believe there is no one in the world you detest as you do me.

GREGERS. [*softly*] I have seen you at too close quarters.

WERLE. You have seen me with your mother's eyes. [*lowers his voice a little*] But you should remember that her eyes were—clouded now and then.

GREGERS. [*quivering*] I see what you are hinting at. But who was to blame for mother's unfortunate weakness? Why, you, and all those——! The last of them was this woman that you palmed off upon Hialmar Ekdal, when you were—— Ugh!

WERLE. [*shrugs his shoulders*] Word for word as if it were your mother speaking!

GREGERS. [*without heeding*] And there he is now, with his great, confiding, childlike mind, compassed about with all this treachery —living under the same roof with such a creature and never dreaming that what he calls his home is built upon a lie! [*comes a step nearer*] When I look back upon your past, I seem to see a battle-field with shattered lives on every hand.

WERLE. I begin to think the chasm that divides us is too wide.

GREGERS. [*bowing, with self-command*] So I have observed; and therefore I take my hat and go.

WERLE. You are going! Out of the house?

GREGERS. Yes. For at last I see my mission in life.

WERLE. What mission?

GREGERS. You would only laugh if I told you.

WERLE. A lonely man doesn't laugh so easily, Gregers.

GREGERS. [pointing towards the background] Look, father,—the Chamberlains are playing blind-man's-buff with Mrs. Sörby.— Good-night and good-bye.

> [He goes out by the back to the right. Sounds of laughter and merriment from the company, who are now visible in the outer room.]

WERLE. [muttering contemptuously after GREGERS] Ha——! Poor wretch—and he says he is not overstrained!

Act II

SCENE—HIALMAR EKDAL'S studio, a good-sized room, evidently in the top story of the building. On the right, a sloping roof of large panes of glass, half-covered by a blue curtain. In the right-hand corner, at the back, the entrance door; farther forward, on the same side, a door leading to the sitting-room. Two doors on the opposite side, and between them an iron stove. At back, a wide double sliding-door. The studio is plainly but comfortably fitted up and furnished. Between the doors on the right, standing out a little from the wall, a sofa with a table and some chairs; on the table a lighted lamp with a shade; beside the stove an old arm-chair. Photographic instruments and apparatus of different kinds lying about the room. Against the back wall, to the left of the double door, stands a bookcase containing a few books, boxes, and bottles of chemicals, instruments, tools, and other objects. Photographs and small articles, such as camel's-hair pencils, paper, and so forth, lie on the table.

GINA EKDAL sits on a chair by the table, sewing. HEDVIG is sitting on the sofa, with her hands shading her eyes and her thumbs in her ears, reading a book.

GINA. [glances once or twice at HEDVIG, as if with secret anxiety; then says] Hedvig!

> [HEDVIG does not hear.]

GINA. [repeats more loudly] Hedvig!

HEDVIG. [takes away her hands and looks up] Yes, mother?

GINA. Hedvig dear, you mustn't sit reading any longer now.

HEDVIG. Oh, mother, mayn't I read a little more? Just a little bit?

GINA. No, no, you must put away your book now. Father doesn't like it; he never reads hisself in the evening.

HEDVIG. [shuts the book] No, father doesn't care much about reading.

GINA. [puts aside her sewing and takes up a lead pencil and a little account-book from the table] Can you remember how much we paid for the butter today?

HEDVIG. It was one crown sixty-five.

GINA. That's right. [*puts it down*] It's terrible what a lot of butter we get through in this house. Then there was the smoked sausage, and the cheese—let me see—[*writes*]—and the ham—[*adds up*] Yes, that makes just——

HEDVIG. And then the beer.

GINA. Yes, to be sure. [*writes*] How it do mount up! But we can't manage with no less.

HEDVIG. And then you and I didn't need anything hot for dinner, as father was out.

GINA. No; that was so much to the good. And then I took eight crowns fifty for the photographs.

HEDVIG. Really! So much as that?

GINA. Exactly eight crowns fifty.

[*Silence.* GINA *takes up her sewing again;* HEDVIG *takes paper and pencil and begins to draw, shading her eyes with her left hand.*]

HEDVIG. Isn't it jolly to think that father is at Mr. Werle's big dinner-party?

GINA. You know he's not really Mr. Werle's guest. It was the son invited him. [*after a pause*] We have nothing to do with that Mr. Werle.

HEDVIG. I'm longing for father to come home. He promised to ask Mrs. Sörby for something nice for me.

GINA. Yes, there's plenty of good things in that house, I can tell you.

HEDVIG. [*goes on drawing*] And I believe I'm a little hungry, too.

[OLD EKDAL, *with the paper parcel under his arm and another parcel in his coat pocket, comes in by the entrance door.*]

GINA. How late you are today, grandfather!

EKDAL. They had locked the office door. Had to wait in Gråberg's room. And then they let me through—h'm.

HEDVIG. Did you get some more copying to do, grandfather?

EKDAL. This whole packet. Just look.

GINA. That's capital.

HEDVIG. And you have another parcel in your pocket.

EKDAL. Eh? Oh, never mind, that's nothing. [*puts his stick away in a corner*] This work will keep me going a long time, Gina. [*opens one of the sliding-doors in the back wall a little*] Hush! [*peeps into the room for a moment, then pushes the door carefully to again*] Hee-hee! They're fast asleep, all the lot of them. And she's gone into the basket herself. Hee-hee!

HEDVIG. Are you sure she isn't cold in that basket, grandfather?

EKDAL. Not a bit of it! Cold? With all that straw? [*goes towards the farther door on the left*] There are matches in here, I suppose.

GINA. The matches is on the drawers.

[EKDAL *goes into his room.*]

HEDVIG. It's nice that grandfather has got all that copying.

GINA. Yes, poor old father; it means a bit of pocket-money for him.

HEDVIG. And he won't be able to sit the whole forenoon down at that horrid Madame Eriksen's.

GINA. No more he won't.

[*Short silence.*]

HEDVIG. Do you suppose they are still at the dinner-table?

GINA. Goodness knows; as like as not.

HEDVIG. Think of all the delicious things father is having to eat! I'm certain he'll be in splendid spirits when he comes. Don't you think so, mother?

GINA. Yes; and if only we could tell him that we'd got the room let——

HEDVIG. But we don't need that this evening.

GINA. Oh, we'd be none the worst of it, I can tell you. It's no use to us as it is.

HEDVIG. I mean we don't need it this evening, for father will be in a good humor at any rate. It is best to keep the letting of the room for another time.

GINA. [*looks across at her*] You like having some good news to tell father when he comes home in the evening?

HEDVIG. Yes; for then things are pleasanter somehow.

GINA. [*thinking to herself*] Yes, yes, there's something in that.

[OLD EKDAL *comes in again and is going out by the foremost door to the left.*]

GINA. [*half turning in her chair*] Do you want something out of the kitchen, grandfather?

EKDAL. Yes, yes, I do. Don't you trouble. [*goes out*]

GINA. He's not poking away at the fire, is he? [*waits a moment*] Hedvig, go and see what he's about.

[EKDAL *comes in again with a small jug of steaming hot water.*]

HEDVIG. Have you been getting some hot water, grandfather?

EKDAL. Yes, hot water. Want it for something. Want to write, and the ink has got as thick as porridge—h'm.

GINA. But you'd best have your supper first, grandfather. It's laid in there.

EKDAL. Can't be bothered with supper, Gina. Very busy, I tell you. No one's to come to my room. No one—h'm.

[*He goes into his room;* GINA *and* HEDVIG *look at each other.*]

GINA. [*softly*] Can you imagine where he's got money from?

HEDVIG. From Gråberg, perhaps.

GINA. Not a bit of it. Gråberg always send money to me.

HEDVIG. Then he must have got a bottle on credit somewhere.

GINA. Poor grandfather, who'd give him credit?

[HIALMAR EKDAL, *in an overcoat and grey felt hat, comes in from the right.*]

GINA. [*throws down her sewing and rises*] Why, Ekdal, is that you already?

HEDVIG. [*at the same time, jumping up*] Fancy your coming so soon, father!

HIALMAR. [*taking off his hat*] Yes, most of the people were coming away.

HEDVIG. So early?

HIALMAR. Yes, it was a dinner-party, you know. [*taking off his over-coat*]

GINA. Let me help you.

HEDVIG. Me, too.

[*They draw off his coat;* GINA *hangs it up on the back wall.*]

HEDVIG. Were there many people there, father?

HIALMAR. Oh, no, not many. We were about twelve or fourteen at table.

GINA. And you had some talk with them all?

HIALMAR. Oh, yes, a little; but Gregers took up most of my time.

GINA. Is Gregers as ugly as ever?

HIALMAR. Well, he's not very much to look at. Hasn't the old man come home?

HEDVIG. Yes, grandfather is in his room, writing.

HIALMAR. Did he say anything?

GINA. No, what should he say?

HIALMAR. Didn't he say anything about——? I heard something about his having been with Gråberg. I'll go in and see him for a moment.

GINA. No, no, better not.

HIALMAR. Why not? Did he say he didn't want me to go in?

GINA. I don't think he wants to see nobody this evening——

HEDVIG. [*making signs*] H'm—h'm!

GINA. [*not noticing*]——he has been in to fetch hot water——

HIALMAR. Aha! Then he's——

GINA. Yes, I suppose so.

HIALMAR. Oh, God! my poor old white-haired father!—— Well, well; there let him sit and get all the enjoyment he can.

[OLD EKDAL, *in an indoor coat and with a lighted pipe, comes from his room.*]

EKDAL. Got home? Thought it was you I heard talking.

HIALMAR. Yes, I have just come.

EKDAL. You didn't see me, did you?

HIALMAR. No, but they told me you had passed through—so I thought I would follow you.

EKDAL. H'm, good of you, Hialmar.—Who were they, all those fellows?

HIALMAR.—Oh, all sorts of people. There was Chamberlain Flor, and Chamberlain Balle, and Chamberlain Kaspersen and Chamberlain—this, that, and the other—I don't know who all——

EKDAL. [*nodding*] Hear that, Gina! Chamberlains every one of them!

GINA. Yes, I hear as they're terrible genteel in that house nowadays.

HEDVIG. Did the Chamberlains sing, father? Or did they read aloud?

HIALMAR. No, they only talked nonsense. They wanted me to recite something for them; but I knew better than that.

EKDAL. You weren't to be persuaded, eh?

GINA. Oh, you might have done it.

HIALMAR. No; one mustn't be at everybody's beck and call. [*walks about the room*] That's not my way, at any rate.

EKDAL. No, no; Hialmar's not to be had for the asking, he isn't.

HIALMAR. I don't see why *I* should bother myself to entertain people on the rare occasions when I go into society. Let the others exert themselves. These fellows go from one great dinner-table to the next and gorge and guzzle day out and day in. It's for them to bestir themselves and do something in return for all the good feeding they get.

GINA. But you didn't say that?

HIALMAR. [*humming*] Ho-ho-ho——; faith, I gave them a bit of my mind.

EKDAL. Not the Chamberlains?

HIALMAR. Oh, why not? [*lightly*] After that, we had a little discussion about Tokay.

EKDAL. Tokay! There's a fine wine for you!

HIALMAR. [*comes to a standstill*] It may be a fine wine. But of course you know the vintages differ; it all depends on how much sunshine the grapes have had.

GINA. Why, you know everything, Ekdal.

EKDAL. And did they dispute that?

HIALMAR. They tried to; but they were requested to observe that it was just the same with Chamberlains—that with them, too, different batches were of different qualities.

GINA. What things you do think of!

EKDAL. Hee-hee! So they got that in their pipes, too?

HIALMAR. Right in their teeth.

EKDAL. Do you hear that, Gina? He said it right in the very teeth of all the Chamberlains.

GINA. Fancy——! Right in their teeth!

HIALMAR. Yes, but I don't want it talked about. One doesn't speak of such things. The whole affair passed off quite amicably of course. They were nice, genial fellows; I didn't want to wound them—not I!

EKDAL. Right in their teeth, though——!

HEDVIG. [*caressingly*] How nice it is to see you in a dress-coat! It suits you so well, father.

HIALMAR. Yes, don't you think so? And this one really sits to perfection. It fits almost as if it had been made for me;—a little tight in the arm-holes perhaps;—help me, Hedvig. [*takes off the coat*] I think I'll put on my jacket. Where is my jacket, Gina?

GINA. Here it is. [*brings the jacket and helps him*]

HIALMAR. That's it! Don't forget to send the coat back to Molvik first thing tomorrow morning.

GINA. [*laying it away*] I'll be sure and see to it.

HIALMAR. [*stretching himself*] After all, there's a more homely feeling about this. A free-and-easy indoor costume suits my whole personality better. Don't you think so, Hedvig?

HEDVIG. Yes, father.

HIALMAR. When I loosen my necktie into a pair of flowing ends—like this—eh?

HEDVIG. Yes, that goes so well with your moustache and the sweep of your curls.

HIALMAR. I should not call them curls exactly; I should rather say locks.

HEDVIG. Yes, they are too big for curls.

HIALMAR. Locks describes them better.

HEDVIG. [*after a pause, twitching his jacket*] Father!

HIALMAR. Well, what is it?

HEDVIG. Oh, you know very well.

HIALMAR. No, really I don't——

HEDVIG. [*half laughing, half whispering*] Oh, yes, father; now don't tease me any longer!

HIALMAR. Why, what do you mean?

HEDVIG. [*shaking him*] Oh, what nonsense; come, where are they, father? All the good things you promised me, you know?

HIALMAR. Oh—if I haven't forgotten all about them!

HEDVIG. Now you're only teasing me, father! Oh, it's too bad of you! Where have you put them?

HIALMAR. No, I positively forgot to get anything. But wait a little! I have something else for you, Hedvig. [*goes and searches in the pockets of the coat*]

HEDVIG. [*skipping and clapping her hands*] Oh, mother, mother!

GINA. There, you see; if you only give him time——

HIALMAR. [*with a paper*] Look, here it is.

HEDVIG. That? Why, that's only a paper.

HIALMAR. That is the bill of fare, my dear; the whole bill of fare. Here you see: "Menu"—that means bill of fare.

HEDVIG. Haven't you anything else?

HIALMAR. I forgot the other things, I tell you. But you may take my word for it, these dainties are very unsatisfying. Sit down at the table and read the bill of fare, and then I'll describe to you how the dishes taste. Here you are, Hedvig.

HEDVIG. [*gulping down her tears*] Thank you. [*She seats herself, but does not read;* GINA *makes signs to her;* HIALMAR *notices it.*]

HIALMAR. [*pacing up and down the room*] It's monstrous what absurd things the father of a family is expected to think of; and if he forgets the smallest trifle, he is treated to sour faces at once. Well, well, one gets used to that, too. [*stops near the stove, by the old man's chair*] Have you peeped in there this evening, father?

EKDAL. Yes, to be sure I have. She's gone into the basket.

HIALMAR. Ah, she has gone into the basket. Then she's beginning to get used to it.

EKDAL. Yes; just as I prophesied. But you know there are still a few little things—

HIALMAR. A few improvements, yes.

EKDAL. They've got to be made, you know.

HIALMAR. Yes, let us have a talk about the improvements, father. Come, let us sit on the sofa.

EKDAL. All right. H'm—think I'll just fill my pipe first. Must clean it out, too. H'm.

[*He goes into his room.*]

GINA. [*smiling to* HIALMAR] His pipe!

HIALMAR. Oh, yes, yes, Gina; let him alone—the poor shipwrecked old man.—Yes, these improvements—we had better get them out of hand tomorrow.

GINA. You'll hardly have time tomorrow, Ekdal.

HEDVIG. [*interposing*] Oh, yes he will, mother!

GINA. ——for remember them prints that has to be retouched; they've sent for them time after time.

HIALMAR. There now! those prints again! I shall get them finished all right! Have any new orders come in?

GINA. No, worse luck; tomorrow I have nothing but those two sittings, you know.

HIALMAR. Nothing else? Oh, no, if people won't set about things with a will——

GINA. But what more can I do? Don't I advertise in the papers as much as we can afford?

HIALMAR. Yes, the papers, the papers; you see how much good they do. And I suppose no one has been to look at the room either?

GINA. No, not yet.

HIALMAR. That was only to be expected. If people won't keep their eyes open——. Nothing can be done without a real effort, Gina!

HEDVIG. [*going towards him*] Shall I fetch you the flute, father?

HIALMAR. No; no flute for me; *I* want no pleasures in this world. [*pacing about*] Yes, indeed I will work tomorrow; you shall see if I don't. You may be sure I shall work as long as my strength holds out.

GINA. But my dear, good Ekdal, I didn't mean it in that way.

HEDVIG. Father, mayn't I bring in a bottle of beer?

HIALMAR. No, certainly not. I require nothing, nothing——[*comes to a standstill*] Beer? Was it beer you were talking about?

HEDVIG. [*cheerfully*] Yes, father; beautiful, fresh beer.

HIALMAR. Well—since you insist upon it, you may bring in a bottle.

GINA. Yes, do; and we'll be nice and cosy.

[HEDVIG *runs towards the kitchen door.*]

HIALMAR. [*by the stove, stops her, looks at her, puts his arm round her neck and presses her to him*] Hedvig, Hedvig!

HEDVIG. [*with tears of joy*] My dear, kind father!

HIALMAR. No, don't call me that. Here have I been feasting at the rich man's table,—battening at the groaning board——! And I couldn't even——!

GINA. [*sitting at the table*] Oh, nonsense, nonsense, Ekdal.

HIALMAR. It's not nonsense! And yet you mustn't be too hard upon me. You know that I love you for all that.

HEDVIG. [*throwing her arms round him*] And we love you, oh, so dearly, father!

HIALMAR. And if I am unreasonable once in a while,—why then—you must remember that I am a man beset by a host of cares. There, there! [*dries his eyes*] No beer at such a moment as this. Give me the flute.

[HEDVIG *runs to the bookcase and fetches it.*]

HIALMAR. Thanks! That's right. With my flute in my hand and you two at my side——ah——!

[HEDVIG *seats herself at the table near* GINA; HIALMAR *paces backwards and forwards, pipes up vigorously and plays a Bohemian peasant dance, but in a slow plaintive tempo, and with sentimental expression.*]

HIALMAR. [*breaking off the melody, holds out his left hand to* GINA *and says with emotion*] Our roof may be poor and humble, Gina, but it is home. And with all my heart I say: here dwells my happiness.

[*He begins to play again; almost immediately after, a knocking is heard at the entrance door.*]

GINA. [*rising*] Hush, Ekdal,—I think there's some one at the door.

HIALMAR. [*laying the flute on the bookcase*] There! Again!

[GINA *goes and opens the door.*]

GREGERS WERLE. [*in the passage*] Excuse me——

GINA. [*starting back slightly*] Oh!

GREGERS. ——does not Mr. Ekdal, the photographer, live here?

GINA. Yes, he does.

HIALMAR. [*going towards the door*] Gregers! You here after all? Well, come in then.

GREGERS. [*coming in*] I told you I would come and look you up.

HIALMAR. But this evening——? Have you left the party?

GREGERS. I have left both the party and my father's house.—Good evening, Mrs. Ekdal. I don't know whether you recognize me?

GINA. Oh, yes; it's not difficult to know young Mr. Werle again.

GREGERS. No, I am like my mother; and no doubt you remember her.

HIALMAR. Left your father's house, did you say?

GREGERS. Yes, I have gone to a hotel.

HIALMAR. Indeed. Well, since you're here, take off your coat and sit down.

GREGERS. Thanks.

[*He takes off his overcoat. He is now dressed in a plain grey suit of a countrified cut.*]

HIALMAR. Here, on the sofa. Make yourself comfortable.

[GREGERS *seats himself on the sofa;* HIALMAR *takes a chair at the table.*]

GREGERS. [*looking around him*] So these are your quarters, Hialmar —this is your home.

HIALMAR. This is the studio, as you see——

GINA. But it's the largest of our rooms, so we generally sit here.

HIALMAR. We used to live in a better place; but this flat has one great advantage; there are such capital outer rooms——

GINA. And we have a room on the other side of the passage that we can let.

GREGERS. [*to* HIALMAR] Ah—so you have lodgers, too?

HIALMAR. No, not yet. They're not so easy to find, you see; you have to keep your eyes open. [*to* HEDVIG] What about the beer, eh?

[HEDVIG *nods and goes out into the kitchen.*]

GREGERS. So that is your daughter?

HIALMAR. Yes, that is Hedvig.

GREGERS. And she is your only child?

HIALMAR. Yes, the only one. She is the joy of our lives, and—[*lowering his voice*]—at the same time our deepest sorrow, Gregers.

GREGERS. What do you mean?

HIALMAR. She is in serious danger of losing her eyesight.

GREGERS. Becoming blind?

HIALMAR. Yes. Only the first symptoms have appeared as yet, and she may not feel it much for some time. But the doctor has warned us. It is coming, inexorably.

GREGERS. What a terrible misfortune! How do you account for it?

HIALMAR. [*sighs*] Hereditary, no doubt.

GREGERS. [*starting*] Hereditary?

GINA. Ekdal's mother had weak eyes.

HIALMAR. Yes, so my father says; I can't remember her.

GREGERS. Poor child! And how does she take it?

HIALMAR. Oh, you can imagine we haven't the heart to tell her of it. She dreams of no danger. Gay and careless and chirping like a little bird, she flutters onward into a life of endless night. [*overcome*] Oh, it is cruelly hard on me, Gregers.

[HEDVIG *brings a tray with beer and glasses, which she sets upon the table.*]

HIALMAR. [*stroking her hair*] Thanks, thanks, Hedvig.

[HEDVIG *puts her arm around his neck and whispers in his ear.*]

HIALMAR. No, no bread and butter just now. [*looks up*] But perhaps you would like some, Gregers.

GREGERS. [*with a gesture of refusal*] No, no, thank you.

HIALMAR. [*still melancholy*] Well, you can bring in a little all the same. If you have a crust, that is all I want. And plenty of butter on it, mind.

[HEDVIG *nods gaily and goes out into the kitchen again.*]

GREGERS. [*who has been following her with his eyes*] She seems quite strong and healthy otherwise.

GINA. Yes. In other ways there's nothing amiss with her, thank goodness.

GREGERS. She promises to be very like you, Mrs. Ekdal. How old is she now?

GINA. Hedvig is close on fourteen; her birthday is the day after tomorrow.

GREGERS. She is pretty tall for her age, then.

GINA. Yes, she's shot up wonderful this last year.

GREGERS. It makes one realize one's own age to see these young people growing up.—How long is it now since you were married?

GINA. We've been married—let me see—just on fifteen years.

GREGERS. Is it so long as that?

GINA. [*becomes attentive; looks at him*] Yes, it is indeed.

HIALMAR. Yes, so it is. Fifteen years all but a few months. [*changing his tone*] They must have been long years for you, up at the works, Gregers.

GREGERS. They seemed long while I was living them; now they are over, I hardly know how the time has gone.

[OLD EKDAL *comes from his room without his pipe, but with his old-fashioned uniform cap on his head; his gait is somewhat unsteady.*]

EKDAL. Come now, Hialmar, let's sit down and have a good talk about this—h'm—what was it again?

HIALMAR. [*going towards him*] Father, we have a visitor here— Gregers Werle.—I don't know if you remember him.

EKDAL. [*looking at* GREGERS, *who has risen*] Werle? Is that the son? What does he want with me?

HIALMAR. Nothing; it's me he has come to see.

EKDAL. Oh! Then there's nothing wrong?

HIALMAR. No, no, of course not.

EKDAL. [*with a large gesture*] Not that I'm afraid, you know; but——

GREGERS. [*goes over to him*] I bring you a greeting from your old hunting-grounds, Lieutenant Ekdal.

EKDAL. Hunting-grounds?

GREGERS. Yes, up in Höidal, about the works, you know.

EKDAL. Oh, up there. Yes, I knew all those places well in the old days.

GREGERS. You were a great sportsman then.

EKDAL. So I was, I don't deny it. You're looking at my uniform cap. I don't ask anybody's leave to wear it in the house. So long as I don't go out in the streets with it——

[HEDVIG *brings a plate of bread and butter, which she puts upon the table.*]

HIALMAR. Sit down, father, and have a glass of beer. Help yourself, Gregers.

[EKDAL *mutters and stumbles over to the sofa.* GREGERS *seats himself on the chair nearest to him,* HIALMAR *on the other side of* GREGERS. GINA *sits a little way from the table, sewing;* HEDVIG *stands beside her father.*]

GREGERS. Can you remember, Lieutenant Ekdal, how Hialmar and I used to come up and visit you in the summer and at Christmas?

EKDAL. Did you? No, no, no; I don't remember it. But sure enough I've been a tidy bit of a sportsman in my day. I've shot bears, too. I've shot nine of 'em, no less.

GREGERS. [*looking sympathetically at him*] And now you never get any shooting?

EKDAL. Can't just say that, sir. Get a shot now and then perhaps. Of course not in the old way. For the woods, you see—the woods, the woods——! [*drinks*] Are the woods fine up there now?

GREGERS. Not so fine as in your time. They have been thinned a good deal.

EKDAL. Thinned? [*more softly, and as if afraid*] It's dangerous work that. Bad things come of it. The woods revenge themselves.

HIALMAR. [*filling up his glass*] Come—a little more, father.

GREGERS. How can a man like you—such a man for the open air— live in the midst of a stuffy town, boxed within four walls?

EKDAL. [*laughs quietly and glances at* HIALMAR] Oh, it's not so bad here. Not at all so bad.

GREGERS. But don't you miss all the things that used to be a part of your very being—the cool sweeping breezes, the free life in the woods and on the uplands, among beasts and birds——?

EKDAL. [*smiling*] Hialmar, shall we let him see it?

HIALMAR. [*hastily and a little embarrassed*] Oh, no, no, father; not this evening.

GREGERS. What does he want to show me?

HIALMAR. Oh, it's only something—you can see it another time.

GREGERS. [*continues, to the old man*] You see I have been thinking, Lieutenant Ekdal, that you should come up with me to the works; I am sure to be going back soon. No doubt you could get some copying there, too. And here, you have nothing on earth to interest you—nothing to liven you up.

EKDAL. [*stares in astonishment at him*] Have *I* nothing on earth to——!

GREGERS. Of course you have Hialmar; but then he has his own family. And a man like you, who has always had such a passion for what is free and wild——

EKDAL. [*thumps the table*] Hialmar, he shall see it!

HIALMAR. Oh, do you think it's worth while, father? It's all dark.

EKDAL. Nonsense; it's moonlight. [*rises*] He shall see it, I tell you. Let me pass! Come and help me, Hialmar.

HEDVIG. Oh, yes, do, father!

HIALMAR. [*rising*] Very well then.

GREGERS. [*to* GINA] What is it?

GINA. Oh, nothing so very wonderful, after all.

[EKDAL *and* HIALMAR *have gone to the back wall and are each pushing back a side of the sliding door;* HEDVIG *helps the old man;* GREGERS *remains standing by the sofa;* GINA *sits still and sews. Through the open doorway a large, deep irregular garret is seen with odd nooks and corners; a couple of stove-pipes running through it, from rooms below. There are skylights through which clear moonbeams shine in on some parts of the great room; others lie in deep shadow.*]

EKDAL. [*to* GREGERS] You may come close up if you like.

GREGERS. [*going over to them*] Why, what is it?

EKDAL. Look for yourself. H'm.

HIALMAR. [*somewhat embarrassed*] This belongs to father, you understand.

GREGERS. [*at the door, looks into the garret*] Why, you keep poultry, Lieutenant Ekdal.

EKDAL. Should think we did keep poultry. They've gone to roost now. But you should just see our fowls by daylight, sir!

HEDVIG. And there's a——

EKDAL. Sh—sh! don't say anything about it yet.

GREGERS. And you have pigeons, too, I see.

EKDAL. Oh, yes, haven't we just got pigeons! They have their nest-boxes up there under the roof-tree; for pigeons like to roost high, you see.

HIALMAR. They aren't all common pigeons.

EKDAL. Common! Should think not indeed! We have tumblers and a pair of pouters, too. But come here! Can you see that hutch down there by the wall?

GREGERS. Yes; what do you use it for?

EKDAL. That's where the rabbits sleep, sir.

GREGERS. Dear me; so you have rabbits, too?

EKDAL. Yes, you may take my word for it, we have rabbits! He wants to know if we have rabbits, Hialmar! H'm! But now comes the thing, let me tell you! Here we have it! Move away, Hedvig. Stand here; that's right,—and now look down there.—Don't you see a basket with straw in it?

GREGERS. Yes. And I can see a fowl lying in the basket.

EKDAL. H'm—"a fowl"——

GREGERS. Isn't it a duck?

EKDAL. [hurt] Why, of course it's a duck.

HIALMAR. But what kind of duck, do you think?

HEDVIG. It's not just a common duck——

EKDAL. Sh!

GREGERS. And it's not a Muscovy duck either.

EKDAL. No, Mr.—Werle; it's not a Muscovy duck; for it's a wild duck!

GREGERS. Is it really? A wild duck?

EKDAL. Yes, that's what it is. That "fowl" as you call it—is the wild duck. It's our wild duck, sir.

HEDVIG. My wild duck. It belongs to me.

GREGERS. And can it live up here in the garret? Does it thrive?

EKDAL. Of course it has a trough of water to splash about in, you know.

HIALMAR. Fresh water every other day.

GINA. [turning towards HIALMAR] But my dear Ekdal, it's getting icy cold here.

EKDAL. H'm, we had better shut up then. It's as well not to disturb their night's rest, too. Close up, Hedvig.

[HIALMAR and HEDVIG push the garret doors together.]

EKDAL. Another time you shall see her properly. [seats himself in the armchair by the stove] Oh, they're curious things, these wild ducks, I can tell you.

GREGERS. How did you manage to catch it, Lieutenant Ekdal?

EKDAL. I didn't catch it. There's a certain man in this town whom we have to thank for it.

GREGERS. [starts slightly] That man was not my father, was he?

EKDAL. You've hit it. Your father and no one else. H'm.

HIALMAR. Strange that you should guess that, Gregers.

GREGERS. You were telling me that you owed so many things to my father; and so I thought perhaps——

GINA. But we didn't get the duck from Mr. Werle himself——

EKDAL. It's Håkon Werle we have to thank for her, all the same, Gina. [to GREGERS] He was shooting from a boat, you see, and he brought her down. But your father's sight is not very good now. H'm; she was only wounded.

GREGERS. Ah! She got a couple of slugs in her body, I suppose.

HIALMAR. Yes, two or three.

HEDVIG. She was hit under the wing, so that she couldn't fly.

GREGERS. And I suppose she dived to the bottom, eh?

EKDAL. [*sleepily, in a thick voice*] Of course. Always do that, wild ducks do. They shoot to the bottom as deep as they can get, sir —and bite themselves fast in the tangle and seaweed—and all the devil's own mess that grows down there. And they never come up again.

GREGERS. But your wild duck came up again, Lieutenant Ekdal.

EKDAL. He had such an amazingly clever dog, your father had. And that dog—he dived in after the duck and fetched her up again.

GREGERS. [*who has turned to* HIALMAR] And then she was sent to you here?

HIALMAR. Not at once; at first your father took her home. But she wouldn't thrive there; so Pettersen was told to put an end to her——

EKDAL. [*half asleep*] H'm—yes—Pettersen—that ass——

HIALMAR. [*speaking more softly*] That was how we got her, you see; for father knows Pettersen a little; and when he heard about the wild duck he got him to hand her over to us.

GREGERS. And now she thrives as well as possible in the garret there?

HIALMAR. Yes, wonderfully well. She has got fat. You see, she has lived in there so long now that she has forgotten her natural wild life; and it all depends on that.

GREGERS. You are right there, Hialmar. Be sure you never let her get a glimpse of the sky and the sea——. But I mustn't stay any longer; I think your father is asleep.

HIALMAR. Oh, as for that——

GREGERS. But, by-the-bye—you said you had a room to let—a spare room?

HIALMAR. Yes; what then? Do you know of anybody——?

GREGERS. Can I have that room?

HIALMAR. You?

GINA. Oh, no, Mr. Werle, you——

GREGERS. May I have the room? If so, I'll take possession first thing tomorrow morning.

HIALMAR. Yes, with the greatest pleasure——

GINA. But, Mr. Werle, I'm sure it's not at all the sort of room for you.

HIALMAR. Why, Gina! how can you say that?

GINA. Why, because the room's neither large enough nor light enough, and——

GREGERS. That really doesn't matter, Mrs. Ekdal.

HIALMAR. I call it quite a nice room, and not at all badly furnished, either.

GINA. But remember the pair of them underneath.

GREGERS. What pair?

GINA. Well, there's one as has been a tutor——

HIALMAR. That's Molvik—Mr. Molvik, B.A.

GINA. And then there's a doctor, by the name of Relling.

GREGERS. Relling? I know him a little; he practised for a time up in Höidal.

GINA. They're a regular rackety pair, they are. As often as not, they're out on the loose in the evenings; and then they come home at all hours, and they're not always just——

GREGERS. One soon gets used to that sort of thing. I daresay I shall be like the wild duck——

GINA. H'm; I think you ought to sleep upon it first, anyway.

GREGERS. You seem very unwilling to have me in the house, Mrs. Ekdal.

GINA. Oh, no! What makes you think that?

HIALMAR. Well, you really behave strangely about it, Gina. [*to* GREGERS] Then I suppose you intend to remain in the town for the present?

GREGERS. [*putting on his overcoat*] Yes, now I intend to remain here.

HIALMAR. And yet not at your father's? What do you propose to do, then?

GREGERS. Ah, if I only knew that, Hialmar, I shouldn't be so badly off! But when one has the misfortune to be called Gregers—! "Gregers"—and then "Werle" after it; did you ever hear anything so hideous?

HIALMAR. Oh, I don't think so at all.

GREGERS. Ugh! Bah! I feel I should like to spit upon the fellow that answers to such a name. But when a man is once for all doomed to be Gregers—Werle in this world, as I am——

HIALMAR. [*laughs*] Ha, ha! If you weren't Gregers Werle, what would you like to be?

GREGERS. If I should choose, I should like best to be a clever dog.

GINA. A dog!

HEDVIG. [*involuntarily*] Oh, no!

GREGERS. Yes, an amazingly clever dog; one that goes to the bottom after wild ducks when they dive and bite themselves fast in tangle and seaweed, down among the ooze.

HIALMAR. Upon my word now, Gregers—I don't in the least know what you're driving at.

GREGERS. Oh, well, you might not be much the wiser if you did. It's understood, then, that I move in early tomorrow morning. [*to* GINA] I won't give you any trouble; I do everything for myself. [*to* HIALMAR] We can talk about the rest tomorrow.—Goodnight, Mrs. Ekdal. [*nods to* HEDVIG] Goodnight.

GINA. Goodnight, Mr. Werle.

HEDVIG. Goodnight.

HIALMAR. [*who has lighted a candle*] Wait a moment; I must show you a light; the stairs are sure to be dark.

[GREGERS *and* HIALMAR *go out by the passage door.*]

GINA. [*looking straight before her, with her sewing in her lap*]

Wasn't that queer-like talk about wanting to be a dog?

HEDVIG. Do you know, mother—I believe he meant something quite different by that.

GINA. Why, what should he mean?

HEDVIG. Oh, I don't know; but it seemed to me he meant something different from what he said—all the time.

GINA. Do you think so? Yes, it was sort of queer.

HIALMAR. [comes back] The lamp was still burning. [puts out the candle and sets it down] Ah, now one can get a mouthful of food at last. [begins to eat the bread and butter] Well, you see, Gina—if only you keep your eyes open——

GINA. How, keep your eyes open——?

HIALMAR. Why, haven't we at last had the luck to get the room let? And just think—to a person like Gregers—a good old friend.

GINA. Well, I don't know what to say about it.

HEDVIG. Oh, mother, you'll see; it'll be such fun!

HIALMAR. You're very strange. You were so bent upon getting the room let before; and now you don't like it.

GINA. Yes, I do, Ekdal; if it had only been to some one else—— But what do you suppose Mr. Werle will say?

HIALMAR. Old Werle? It doesn't concern him.

GINA. But surely you can see that there's something amiss between them again, or the young man wouldn't be leaving home. You know very well those two can't get on with each other.

HIALMAR. Very likely not, but——

GINA. And now Mr. Werle may fancy it's you that has egged him on——

HIALMAR. Let him fancy so, then! Mr. Werle has done a great deal for me; far be it from me to deny it. But that doesn't make me everlastingly dependent upon him.

GINA. But, my dear Ekdal, maybe grandfather'll suffer for it. He may lose the little bit of work he gets from Gråberg.

HIALMAR. I could almost say: so much the better! Is it not humiliating for a man like me to see his grey-haired father treated as a pariah? But now I believe the fulness of time is at hand. [takes a fresh piece of bread and butter] As sure as I have a mission in life, I mean to fulfil it now!

HEDVIG. Oh, yes, father, do!

GINA. Hush! Don't wake him!

HIALMAR. [more softly] I will fulfil it, I say. The day shall come when—— And that is why I say it's a good thing we have let the room; for that makes me more independent. The man who has a mission in life must be independent. [by the armchair, with emotion] Poor old white-haired father! Rely on your Hialmar. He has broad shoulders—strong shoulders, at any rate. You shall yet wake up some fine day and—— [to GINA] Do you not believe it?

GINA. [rising] Yes, of course I do; but in the meantime suppose we see about getting him to bed.

HIALMAR. Yes, come.

[They take hold of the old man carefully.]

Act III

SCENE—HIALMAR EKDAL'S *studio. It is morning: the daylight shines through the large window in the slanting roof; the curtain is drawn back.*

HIALMAR *is sitting at the table, busy retouching a photograph; several others lie before him. Presently* GINA, *wearing her hat and cloak, enters by the passage door; she has a covered basket on her arm.*

HIALMAR. Back already, Gina?

GINA. Oh, yes, one can't let the grass grow under one's feet. [*sets her basket on a chair and takes off her things*]

HIALMAR. Did you look in at Gregers' room?

GINA. Yes, that I did. It's a rare sight, I can tell you; he's made a pretty mess to start off with.

HIALMAR. How so?

GINA. He was determined to do everything for himself, he said; so he sets to work to light the stove, and what must he do but screw down the damper till the whole room is full of smoke. Ugh! There was a smell fit to——

HIALMAR. Well, really!

GINA. But that's not the worst of it; for then he thinks he'll put out the fire, and goes and empties his water-jug into the stove and so makes the whole floor one filthy puddle.

HIALMAR. How annoying!

GINA. I've got the porter's wife to clear up after him, pig that he is! But the room won't be fit to live in till the afternoon.

HIALMAR. What's he doing with himself in the meantime?

GINA. He said he was going out for a little while.

HIALMAR. I looked in upon him, too, for a moment—after you had gone.

GINA. So I heard. You've asked him to lunch.

HIALMAR. Just to a little bit of early lunch, you know. It's his first day—we can hardly do less. You've got something in the house, I suppose?

GINA. I shall have to find something or other.

HIALMAR. And don't cut it too fine, for I fancy Relling and Molvik are coming up, too. I just happened to meet Relling on the stairs, you see; so I had to——

GINA. Oh, are we to have those two as well?

HIALMAR. Good Lord—couple more or less can't make any difference.

OLD EKDAL. [*opens his door and looks in*] I say, Hialmar—— [*sees* GINA] Oh!

GINA. Do you want anything, grandfather?

EKDAL. Oh, no, it doesn't matter. H'm! [*retires again*]

GINA. [*takes up the basket*] Be sure you see that he doesn't go out.

HIALMAR. All right, all right. And, Gina, a little herring-salad wouldn't be a bad idea; Relling and Molvik were out on the loose again last night.

GINA. If only they don't come before I'm ready for them——

HIALMAR. No, of course they won't; take your own time.

GINA. Very well; and meanwhile you can be working a bit.

HIALMAR. Well, I am working! I am working as hard as I can!

GINA. Then you'll have that job off your hands, you see.

[*She goes out to the kitchen with her basket.* HIALMAR *sits for a time penciling away at the photograph in an indolent and listless manner.*]

EKDAL. [*peeps in, looks round the studio and says softly*] Are you busy?

HIALMAR. Yes, I'm toiling at these wretched pictures——

EKDAL. Well, well, never mind,—since you're so busy—h'm!

[*He goes out again; the door stands open.*]

HIALMAR. [*continues for some time in silence; then he lays down his brush and goes over to the door*] Are you busy, father?

EKDAL. [*in a grumbling tone, within*] If you're busy, I'm busy, too. H'm!

HIALMAR. Oh, very well, then. [*goes to his work again*]

EKDAL. [*presently, coming to the door again*] H'm; I say, Hialmar, I'm not so very busy, you know.

HIALMAR. I thought you were writing.

EKDAL. Oh, the devil take it! can't Gråberg wait a day or two? After all, it's not a matter of life and death.

HIALMAR. No; and you're not his slave either.

EKDAL. And about that other business in there——

HIALMAR. Just what I was thinking of. Do you want to go in? Shall I open the door for you?

EKDAL. Well, it wouldn't be a bad notion.

HIALMAR. [*rises*] Then we'd have that off our hands.

EKDAL. Yes, exactly. It's got to be ready first thing tomorrow. It is tomorrow, isn't it? H'm?

HIALMAR. Yes, of course it's tomorrow.

[HIALMAR *and* EKDAL *push aside each his half of the sliding door. The morning sun is shining in through the skylights: some doves are flying about; others sit cooing upon the perches; the hens are heard clucking now and then, further back in the garret.*]

HIALMAR. There; now you can get to work, father.

EKDAL. [*goes in*] Aren't you coming, too?

HIALMAR. Well, really, do you know——; I almost think—— [*sees* GINA *at the kitchen door*] I? No; I haven't time; I must work.— But now for our new contrivance——

[*He pulls a cord, a curtain slips down inside, the lower part consisting of a piece of old sailcloth, the upper part of a stretched fishing net. The floor of the garret is thus no longer visible.*]

HIALMAR. [*goes to the table*] So! Now, perhaps I can sit in peace for a little while.

GINA. Is he rampaging in there again?

HIALMAR. Would you rather have had him slip down to Madame Eriksen's? [*seats himself*] Do you want anything? You know you said——

GINA. I only wanted to ask if you think we can lay the table for lunch here?

HIALMAR. Yes; we have no early appointment, I suppose?

GINA. No, I expect no one today except those two sweethearts that are to be taken together.

HIALMAR. Why the deuce couldn't they be taken together another day?

GINA. Don't you know I told them to come in the afternoon, when you are having your nap?

HIALMAR. Oh, that's capital. Very well, let us have lunch here then.

GINA. All right; but there's no hurry about laying the cloth; you can have the table for a good while yet.

HIALMAR. Do you think I am not sticking at my work? I'm at it as hard as I can!

GINA. Then you'll be free later on, you know. [*goes out into the kitchen again*]

[*Short pause.*]

EKDAL. [*in the garret doorway, behind the net*] Hialmar!

HIALMAR. Well?

EKDAL. Afraid we shall have to move the water-trough, after all.

HIALMAR. What else have I been saying all along?

EKDAL. H'm——h'm——h'm.

[*Goes away from the door again.* HIALMAR *goes on working a little; glances towards the garret and half rises.* HEDVIG *comes in from the kitchen.*]

HIALMAR. [*sits down again hurriedly*] What do you want?

HEDVIG. I only wanted to come in beside you, father.

HIALMAR. [*after a pause*] what makes you go prying around like that? Perhaps you are told off to watch me?

HEDVIG. No, no.

HIALMAR. What is your mother doing out there?

HEDVIG. Oh, mother's in the middle of making the herring-salad. [*goes to the table*] Isn't there any little thing I could help you with, father?

HIALMAR. Oh, no. It is right that I should bear the whole burden—so long as my strength holds out. Set your mind at rest, Hedvig; if only your father keeps his health——

HEDVIG. Oh, no, father! You mustn't talk in that horrid way.

[*She wanders about a little, stops by the doorway and looks into the garret.*]

HIALMAR. Tell me, what is he doing?

HEDVIG. I think he's making a new path to the water-trough.

HIALMAR. He can never manage that by himself! And here am I doomed to sit——!

HEDVIG. [*goes to him*] Let me take the brush, father; I can do it, quite well.

HIALMAR. Oh, nonsense; you will only hurt your eyes.

HEDVIG. Not a bit. Give me the brush.

HIALMAR. [rising] Well, it won't take more than a minute or two.

HEDVIG. Pooh, what harm can it do then? [takes the brush] There! [seats herself] I can begin upon this one.

HIALMAR. But mind you don't hurt your eyes! Do you hear? I won't be answerable; you do it on your own responsibility—understand that.

HEDVIG. [retouching] Yes, yes, I understand.

HIALMAR. You are quite clever at it, Hedvig. Only a minute or two, you know.

[He slips through by the edge of the curtain into the garret. HEDVIG sits at her work. HIALMAR and EKDAL are heard disputing inside.]

HIALMAR. [appears behind the net] I say, Hedvig—give me those pincers that are lying on the shelf. And the chisel. [turns away inside] Now you shall see, father. Just let me show you first what I mean!

[HEDVIG has fetched the required tools from the shelf and hands them to him through the net.]

HIALMAR. Ah, thanks. I didn't come a moment too soon.

[Goes back from the curtain again; they are heard carpentering and talking inside. HEDVIG stands looking in at them. A moment later there is a knock at the passage door; she does not notice it.]

GREGERS WERLE. [bareheaded, in indoor dress, enters and stops near the door] H'm——!

HEDVIG. [turns and goes towards him] Good morning. Please come in.

GREGERS. Thank you. [looking towards the garret] You seem to have workpeople in the house.

HEDVIG. No, it is only father and grandfather. I'll tell them you are here.

GREGERS. No, no, don't do that; I would rather wait a little. [seats himself on the sofa]

HEDVIG. It looks so untidy here—— [begins to clear away the photographs]

GREGERS. Oh, don't take them away. Are those prints that have to be finished off?

HEDVIG. Yes, they are a few I was helping father with.

GREGERS. Please don't let me disturb you.

HEDVIG. Oh, no.

[She gathers the things to her and sits down to work; GREGERS looks at her, meanwhile, in silence.]

GREGERS. Did the wild duck sleep well last night?

HEDVIG. Yes, I think so, thanks.

GREGERS. [turning towards the garret] It looks quite different by day from what it did last night in the moonlight.

HEDVIG. Yes, it changes ever so much. It looks different in the morning and in the afternoon; and it's different on rainy days from what it is in fine weather.

GREGERS. Have you noticed that?

HEDVIG. Yes, how could I help it?

GREGERS. Are you, too, fond of being in there with the wild duck?

HEDVIG. Yes, when I can manage it——

GREGERS. But I suppose you haven't much spare time; you go to school, no doubt.

HEDVIG. No, not now; father is afraid of my hurting my eyes.

GREGERS. Oh; then he reads with you himself?

HEDVIG. Father has promised to read with me; but he has never had time yet.

GREGERS. Then is there nobody else to give you a little help?

HEDVIG. Yes, there is Mr. Molvik; but he is not always exactly— quite——

GREGERS. Sober?

HEDVIG. Yes, I suppose that's it!

GREGERS. Why, then you must have any amount of time on your hands. And in there I suppose it is a sort of world by itself?

HEDVIG. Oh, yes, quite. And there are such lots of wonderful things.

GREGERS. Indeed?

HEDVIG. Yes, there are big cupboards full of books; and a great many of the books have pictures in them.

GREGERS. Aha!

HEDVIG. And there's an old bureau with drawers and flaps, and a big clock with figures that go out and in. But the clock isn't going now.

GREGERS. So time has come to a standstill in there—in the wild duck's domain.

HEDVIG. Yes. And then there's an old paint-box and things of that sort, and all the books.

GREGERS. And you read the books, I suppose?

HEDVIG. Oh, yes, when I get the chance. Most of them are English though, and I don't understand English. But then I look at the pictures.—There is one great big book called "Harrison's History of London." It must be a hundred years old; and there are such heaps of pictures in it. At the beginning there is Death with an hour-glass and a woman. I think that is horrid. But then there are all the other pictures of churches, and castles, and streets, and great ships sailing on the sea.

GREGERS. But tell me, where did all those wonderful things come from?

HEDVIG. Oh, an old sea captain once lived here, and he brought them home with him. They used to call him "The Flying Dutchman." That was curious, because he wasn't a Dutchman at all.

GREGERS. Was he not?

HEDVIG. No. But at last he was drowned at sea, and so he left all those things behind him.

GREGERS. Tell me now—when you are sitting in there looking at the pictures, don't you wish you could travel and see the real world for yourself?

HEDVIG. Oh, no! I mean always to stay at home and help father and mother.

GREGERS. To retouch photographs?

HEDVIG. No, not only that. I should love above everything to learn to engrave pictures like those in the English books.

GREGERS. H'm. What does your father say to that?

HEDVIG. I don't think father likes it; father is strange about such things. Only think, he talks of my learning basket-making and straw-plaiting! But I don't think that would be much good.

GREGERS. Oh, no, I don't think so either.

HEDVIG. But father was right in saying that if I had learnt basket-making I could have made the new basket for the wild duck.

GREGERS. So you could; and it was you that ought to have done it, wasn't it?

HEDVIG. Yes, for it's my wild duck.

GREGERS. Of course it is.

HEDVIG. Yes, it belongs to me. But I lend it to father and grandfather as often as they please.

GREGERS. Indeed? What do they do with it?

HEDVIG. Oh, they look after it, and build places for it, and so on.

GREGERS. I see; for no doubt the wild duck is by far the most distinguished inhabitant of the garret?

HEDVIG. Yes, indeed she is; for she is a real wild fowl, you know. And then she is so much to be pitied; she has no one to care for, poor thing.

GREGERS. She has no family, as the rabbits have—

HEDVIG. No. The hens, too, many of them, were chickens together; but she has been taken right away from all her friends. And then there is so much that is strange about the wild duck. Nobody knows her, and nobody knows where she came from either.

GREGERS. And she has been down in the depths of the sea.

HEDVIG. [*with a quick glance at him, represses a smile and asks*] Why do you say "depths of the sea"?

GREGERS. What else should I say?

HEDVIG. You could say "the bottom of the sea."[4]

GREGERS. Oh, mayn't I just as well say the depths of the sea?

HEDVIG. Yes; but it sounds so strange to me when other people speak of the depths of the sea.

GREGERS. Why so? Tell me why?

HEDVIG. No, I won't; it's so stupid.

GREGERS. Oh, no, I am sure it's not. Do tell me why you smiled.

HEDVIG. Well, this is the reason: whenever I come to realize suddenly—in a flash—what is in there, it always seems to me that the whole room and everything in it should be called "the depths of the sea."—But that is so stupid.

GREGERS. You mustn't say that.

HEDVIG. Oh, yes, for you know it is only a garret.

4. Gregers here uses the old-fashioned expression "havsens bund," while Hedvig would have him use the more commonplace "havets bund" or "havbunden." [Translator's note.]

GREGERS. [*looks fixedly at her*] Are you so sure of that?

HEDVIG. [*astonished*] That it's a garret?

GREGERS. Are you quite certain of it?

[HEDVIG *is silent, and looks at him open-mouthed.* GINA *comes in from the kitchen with the table things.*]

GREGERS. [*rising*] I have come in upon you too early.

GINA. Oh, you must be somewhere; and we're nearly ready now, anyway. Clear the table, Hedvig.

[HEDVIG *clears away her things; she and* GINA *lay the cloth during what follows.* GREGERS *seats himself in the armchair and turns over an album.*]

GREGERS. I hear you can retouch, Mrs. Ekdal.

GINA. [*with a side glance*] Yes, I can.

GREGERS. That was exceedingly lucky.

GINA. How—lucky?

GREGERS. Since Ekdal took to photography, I mean.

HEDVIG. Mother can take photographs, too.

GINA. Oh, yes; I was bound to learn that.

GREGERS. So it is really you that carry on the business, I suppose?

GINA. Yes, when Ekdal hasn't time himself——

GREGERS. He is a great deal taken up with his old father, I daresay.

GINA. Yes; and then you can't expect a man like Ekdal to do nothing but take pictures of Dick, Tom, and Harry.

GREGERS. I quite agree with you; but having once gone in for the thing——

GINA. You can surely understand, Mr. Werle, that Ekdal's not like one of your common photographers.

GREGERS. Of course not; but still——

[*A shot is fired within the garret.*]

GREGERS. [*starting up*] What's that?

GINA. Ugh! now they're firing again!

GREGERS. Have they firearms in there?

HEDVIG. They are out shooting.

GREGERS. What! [*at the door of the garret*] Are you shooting, Hialmar?

HIALMAR. [*inside the net*] Are you there? I didn't know; I was so taken up—— [*to* HEDVIG] Why did you not let us know? [*comes into the studio*]

GREGERS. Do you go shooting in the garret?

HIALMAR. [*showing a double-barrelled pistol*] Oh, only with this thing.

GINA. Yes, you and grandfather will do yourselves a mischief some day with that there pigstol.

HIALMAR. [*with irritation*] I believe I have told you that this kind of firearm is called a pistol.

GINA. Oh, that doesn't make it much better, that I can see.

GREGERS. So you have become a sportsman, too, Hialmar?

HIALMAR. Only a little rabbit-shooting now and then. Mostly to please father, you understand.

GINA. Men are strange beings; they must always have something to pervert theirselves with.

HIALMAR. [*snappishly*] Just so; we must always have something to divert ourselves with.

GINA. Yes, that's just what I say.

HIALMAR. H'm. [*to* GREGERS] You see the garret is fortunately so situated that no one can hear us shooting. [*lays the pistol on the top shelf of the bookcase*] Don't touch the pistol, Hedvig! One of the barrels is loaded; remember that.

GREGERS. [*looking through the net*] You have a fowling-piece, too, I see.

HIALMAR. That is father's old gun. It's no use now; something has gone wrong with the lock. But it's fun to have it all the same; for we can take it to pieces now and then, and clean and grease it, and screw it together again.—Of course, it's mostly father that fiddle-faddles with all that sort of thing.

HEDVIG. [*beside* GREGERS] Now you can see the wild duck properly.

GREGERS. I was just looking at her. One of her wings seems to me to droop a bit.

HEDVIG. Well, no wonder; her wing was broken, you know.

GREGERS. And she trails one foot a little. Isn't that so?

HIALMAR. Perhaps a very little bit.

HEDVIG. Yes, it was by that foot the dog took hold of her.

HIALMAR. But otherwise she hasn't the least thing the matter with her; and that is simply marvellous for a creature that has a charge of shot in her body and has been between a dog's teeth——

GREGERS. [*with a glance at* HEDVIG] ——and that has lain in the depths of the sea—so long.

HEDVIG. [*smiling*] Yes.

GINA. [*laying the table*] That blessed wild duck! What a lot of fuss you do make over her.

HIALMAR. H'm;—will lunch soon be ready?

GINA. Yes, directly. Hedvig, you must come and help me now.

[GINA *and* HEDVIG *go out into the kitchen.*]

HIALMAR. [*in a low voice*] I think you had better not stand there looking in at father; he doesn't like it. [GREGERS *moves away from the garret door.*] Besides, I may as well shut up before the others come. [*claps his hands to drive the fowls back*] Shh—shh, in with you! [*draws up the curtain and pulls the doors together*] All the contrivances are my own invention. It's really quite amusing to have things of this sort to potter with and to put to rights when they get out of order. And it's absolutely necessary, too; for Gina objects to having rabbits and fowls in the studio.

GREGERS. To be sure; and I suppose the studio is your wife's special department?

HIALMAR. As a rule, I leave the everyday details of business to her; for then I can take refuge in the parlor and give my mind to more important things.

GREGERS. What things may they be, Hialmar?

HIALMAR. I wonder you have not asked that question sooner. But perhaps you haven't heard of the invention?

GREGERS. The invention? No.

HIALMAR. Really? Have you not? Ah, no, out there in the wilds——

GREGERS. So you have invented something, have you?

HIALMAR. It is not quite completed yet; but I am working at it. You can easily imagine that when I resolved to devote myself to photography, it wasn't simply with the idea of taking likenesses of all sorts of commonplace people.

GREGERS. No; your wife was saying the same thing just now.

HIALMAR. I swore that if I consecrated my powers to this handicraft, I would so exalt it that it should become both an art and a science. And to that end I determined to make this great invention.

GREGERS. And what is the nature of the invention? What purpose does it serve?

HIALMAR. Oh, my dear fellow, you mustn't ask for details yet. It takes time, you see. And you must not think that my motive is vanity. It is not for my own sake that I am working. Oh, no; it is my life's mission that stands before me night and day.

GREGERS. What is your life's mission?

HIALMAR. Do you forget the old man with the silver hair?

GREGERS. Your poor father? Well, but what can you do for him?

HIALMAR. I can raise up his self-respect from the dead, by restoring the name of Ekdal to honor and dignity.

GREGERS. Then that is your life's mission?

HIALMAR. Yes. I will rescue the shipwrecked man. For shipwrecked he was, by the very first blast of the storm. Even while those terrible investigations were going on, he was no longer himself. That pistol there—the one we use to shoot rabbits with—has played its part in the tragedy of the house of Ekdal.

GREGERS. The pistol? Indeed?

HIALMAR. When the sentence of imprisonment was passed—he had the pistol in his hand——

GREGERS. Had he——?

HIALMAR. Yes; but he dared not use it. His courage failed him. So broken, so demoralized was he even then! Oh, can you understand it? He, a soldier; he, who had shot nine bears, and who was descended from two lieutenant-colonels—one after the other, of course. Can you understand it, Gregers?

GREGERS. Yes, I understand it well enough.

HIALMAR. I cannot. And once more the pistol played a part in the history of our house. When he had put on the grey clothes and was under lock and key—oh, that was a terrible time for me, I can tell you. I kept the blinds drawn down over both my windows. When I peeped out, I saw the sun shining as if nothing had happened. I could not understand it. I saw people going along the street, laughing and talking about indifferent things. I could not understand it. It seemed to me that the whole of existence must be at a standstill—as if under an eclipse.

GREGERS. I felt that, too, when my mother died.

HIALMAR. It was in such an hour that Hialmar Ekdal pointed the pistol at his own breast.

GREGERS. You, too, thought of——!

HIALMAR. Yes.

GREGERS. But you did not fire?

HIALMAR. No. At the decisive moment I won the victory over myself. I remained in life. But I can assure you it takes some courage to choose life under circumstances like those.

GREGERS. Well, that depends on how you look at it.

HIALMAR. Yes, indeed, it takes courage. But I am glad I was firm: for now I shall soon perfect my invention; and Dr. Relling thinks, as I do myself, that father may be allowed to wear his uniform again. I will demand that as my sole reward.

GREGERS. So that is what he meant about his uniform——?

HIALMAR. Yes, that is what he most yearns for. You can't think how my heart bleeds for him. Every time we celebrate any little family festival—Gina's and my wedding-day, or whatever it may be—in comes the old man in the lieutenant's uniform of happier days. But if he only hears a knock at the door—for he daren't show himself to strangers, you know—he hurries back to his room again as fast as his old legs can carry him. Oh, it's heart-rending for a son to see such things!

GREGERS. How long do you think it will take you to finish your invention?

HIALMAR. Come now, you mustn't expect me to enter into particulars like that. An invention is not a thing completely under one's own control. It depends largely on inspiration—on intuition—and it is almost impossible to predict when the inspiration may come.

GREGERS. But it's advancing?

HIALMAR. Yes, certainly, it is advancing. I turn it over in my mind every day; I am full of it. Every afternoon, when I have had my dinner, I shut myself up in the parlor, where I can ponder undisturbed. But I can't be goaded to it; it's not a bit of good; Relling says so, too.

GREGERS. And you don't think that all that business in the garret draws you off and distracts you too much?

HIALMAR. No, no, no; quite the contrary. You mustn't say that. I cannot be everlastingly absorbed in the same laborious train of thought. I must have something alongside of it to fill up the time of waiting. The inspiration, the intuition, you see—when it comes, it comes, and there's an end of it.

GREGERS. My dear Hialmar, I almost think you have something of the wild duck in you.

HIALMAR. Something of the wild duck? How do you mean?

GREGERS. You have dived down and bitten yourself fast in the undergrowth.

HIALMAR. Are you alluding to the well-nigh fatal shot that has broken my father's wing—and mine, too?

GREGERS. Not exactly to that. I don't say that your wing has been broken; but you have strayed into a poisonous marsh, Hialmar;

an insidious disease has taken hold of you, and you have sunk down to die in the dark.

HIALMAR. I? To die in the dark? Look here, Gregers, you must really leave off talking such nonsense.

GREGERS. Don't be afraid; I shall find a way to help you up again. I, too, have a mission in life now; I found it yesterday.

HIALMAR. That's all very well; but you will please leave me out of it. I can assure you that—apart from my very natural melancholy, of course—I am as contented as any one can wish to be.

GREGERS. Your contentment is an effect of the marsh poison.

HIALMAR. Now, my dear Gregers, pray do not go on about disease and poison; I am not used to that sort of talk. In my house nobody ever speaks to me about unpleasant things.

GREGERS. Ah, that I can easily believe.

HIALMAR. It's not good for me, you see. And there are no marsh poisons here, as you express it. The poor photographer's roof is lowly, I know—and my circumstances are narrow. But I am an inventor, and I am the breadwinner of a family. That exalts me above my mean surroundings.—Ah, here comes lunch!

[GINA *and* HEDVIG *bring bottles of ale, a decanter of brandy, glasses, etc. At the same time,* RELLING *and* MOLVIK *enter from the passage; they are both without hat or overcoat.* MOLVIK *is dressed in black.*]

GINA. [*placing the things upon the table*] Ah, you two have come in the nick of time.

RELLING. Molvik got it into his head that he could smell herring-salad, and then there was no holding him.—Good morning again, Ekdal.

HIALMAR. Gregers, let me introduce you to Mr. Molvik. Doctor—— Oh, you know Relling, don't you?

GREGERS. Yes, slightly.

RELLING. Oh, Mr. Werle, junior! Yes, we two have had one or two little skirmishes up at the Höidal works. You've just moved in?

GREGERS. I moved in this morning.

RELLING. Molvik and I live right under you, so you haven't far to go for the doctor and the clergyman, if you should need anything in that line.

GREGERS. Thanks, it's not quite unlikely, for yesterday we were thirteen at table.

HIALMAR. Oh, come now, don't let us get upon unpleasant subjects again!

RELLING. You may make your mind easy, Ekdal; I'll be hanged if the finger of fate points to you.

HIALMAR. I should hope not, for the sake of my family. But let us sit down now, and eat and drink and be merry.

GREGERS. Shall we not wait for your father?

HIALMAR. No, his lunch will be taken in to him later. Come along!

[*The men seat themselves at table, and eat and drink.* GINA *and* HEDVIG *go in and out and wait upon them.*]

RELLING. Molvik was frightfully stewed yesterday, Mrs. Ekdal.

GINA. Really? Yesterday again?

RELLING. Didn't you hear him when I brought him home last night?

GINA. No, I can't say I did.

RELLING. That was a good thing, for Molvik was disgusting last night.

GINA. Is that true, Molvik?

MOLVIK. Let us draw a veil over last night's proceedings. That sort of thing is totally foreign to my better self.

RELLING. [to GREGERS] It comes over him like a sort of possession, and then I have to go out on the loose with him. Mr. Molvik is dæmonic, you see.

GREGERS. Dæmonic?

RELLING. Molvik is dæmonic, yes.

GREGERS. H'm.

RELLING. And dæmonic natures are not made to walk straight through the world; they must meander a little now and then.— Well, so you still stick up there at those horrible grimy works?

GREGERS. I have stuck there until now.

RELLING. And did you ever manage to collect that claim you went about presenting?

GREGERS. Claim? [understands him] Ah. I see.

HIALMAR. Have you been presenting claims, Gregers?

GREGERS. Oh, nonsense.

RELLING. Faith, but he has, though! He went around to all the cotters' cabins presenting something he called "the claim of the ideal."

GREGERS. I was young then.

RELLING. You're right; you were very young. And as for the claim of the ideal—you never got it honored while I was up there.

GREGERS. Nor since either.

RELLING. Ah, then you've learnt to knock a little discount off, I expect.

GREGERS. Never, when I have a true man to deal with.

HIALMAR. No, I should think not, indeed. A little butter, Gina.

RELLING. And a slice of bacon for Molvik.

MOLVIK. Ugh; not bacon!

[A knock at the garret door.]

HIALMAR. Open the door, Hedvig; father wants to come out.

[HEDVIG goes over and opens the door a little way; EKDAL enters with a fresh rabbit-skin; she closes the door after him.]

EKDAL. Good morning, gentlemen! Good sport today. Shot a big one.

HIALMAR. And you've gone and skinned it without waiting for me——!

EKDAL. Salted it, too. It's good tender meat, is rabbit; it's sweet; it tastes like sugar. Good appetite to you, gentlemen! [goes into his room]

MOLVIK. [rising] Excuse me——; I can't——; I must get downstairs immediately——

RELLING. Drink some soda water, man!

MOLVIK. [*hurrying away*] Ugh—ugh! [*goes out by the passage door*]

RELLING. [*to* HIALMAR] Let us drain a glass to the old hunter.

HIALMAR. [*clinks glasses with him*] To the undaunted sportsman who has looked death in the face!

RELLING. To the grey-haired—— [*drinks*] By-the-bye, is his hair grey or white?

HIALMAR. Something between the two, I fancy; for that matter, he has very few hairs left of any color.

RELLING. Well, well, one can get through the world with a wig. After all, you are a happy man, Ekdal; you have your noble mission to labor for——

HIALMAR. And I do labor, I can tell you.

RELLING. And then you have your excellent wife, shuffling quietly in and out in her felt slippers, and that seesaw walk of hers, and making everything cosy and comfortable about you.

HIALMAR. Yes, Gina—[*nods to her*]—you were a good helpmate on the path of life.

GINA. Oh, don't sit there cricketizing me.

RELLING. And your Hedvig, too, Ekdal!

HIALMAR. [*affected*] The child, yes! The child before everything! Hedvig, come here to me. [*strokes her hair*] What day is it to-morrow, eh?

HEDVIG. [*shaking him*] Oh, no, you're not to say anything, father.

HIALMAR. It cuts me to the heart when I think what a poor affair it will be; only a little festivity in the garret——

HEDVIG. Oh, but that's just what I like!

RELLING. Just you wait till the wonderful invention sees the light, Hedvig!

HIALMAR. Yes, indeed—then you shall see——! Hedvig, I have resolved to make your future secure. You shall live in comfort all your days. I will demand—something or other—on your behalf. That shall be the poor inventor's sole reward.

HEDVIG. [*whispering, with her arms round his neck*] Oh, you dear, kind father!

RELLING. [*to* GREGERS] Come now, don't you find it pleasant, for once in a way, to sit at a well-spread table in a happy family circle?

HIALMAR. Ah, yes, I really prize these social hours.

GREGERS. For my part, I don't thrive in marsh vapors.

RELLING. Marsh vapors?

HIALMAR. Oh, don't begin with that stuff again!

GINA. Goodness knows there's no vapors in this house, Mr. Werle; I give the place a good airing every blessed day.

GREGERS. [*leaves the table*] No airing you can give will drive out the taint I mean.

HIALMAR. Taint!

GINA. Yes, what do you say to that, Ekdal?

RELLING. Excuse me—may it not be you yourself that have brought the taint from those mines up there?

GREGERS. It is like you to call what I bring into this house a taint.

RELLING. [goes up to him] Look here, Mr. Werle, junior: I have a strong suspicion that you are still carrying about that "claim of the ideal," large as life, in your coat-tail pocket.

GREGERS. I carry it in my breast.

RELLING. Well, wherever you carry it, I advise you not to come dunning us with it here, so long as I am on the premises.

GREGERS. And if I do so nonetheless?

RELLING. Then you'll go head-foremost down the stairs; now I've warned you.

HIALMAR. [rising] Oh, but Relling——!

GREGERS. Yes, you may turn me out——

GINA. [interposing between them] We can't have that, Relling. But I must say, Mr. Werle, it ill becomes you to talk about vapors and taints, after all the mess you made with your stove.

[A knock at the passage door.]

HEDVIG. Mother, there's somebody knocking.

HIALMAR. There now, we're going to have a whole lot of people!

GINA. I'll go—— [goes over and opens the door, starts, and draws back] Oh—oh, dear!

[WERLE, in a fur coat, advances one step into the room.]

WERLE. Excuse me, but I think my son is staying here.

GINA. [with a gulp] Yes.

HIALMAR. [approaching him] Won't you do us the honor to——?

WERLE. Thank you, I merely wish to speak to my son.

GREGERS. What is it? Here I am.

WERLE. I want a few words with you, in your room.

GREGERS. In my room? Very well—— [about to go]

GINA. No, no, your room's not in a fit state——

WERLE. Well then, out in the passage here; I want to have a few words with you alone.

HIALMAR. You can have them here, sir. Come into the parlor, Relling.

[HIALMAR and RELLING go off to the right. GINA takes HEDVIG with her into the kitchen.]

GREGERS. [after a short pause] Well, now we are alone.

WERLE. From something you let fall last evening, and from your coming to lodge with the Ekdals, I can't help inferring that you intend to make yourself unpleasant to me in one way or another.

GREGERS. I intend to open Hialmar Ekdal's eyes. He shall see his position as it really is—that is all.

WERLE. Is that the mission in life you spoke of yesterday?

GREGERS. Yes. You have left me no other.

WERLE. Is it I, then, that have crippled your mind, Gregers?

GREGERS. You have crippled my whole life. I am not thinking of all that about mother—— But it's thanks to you that I am continually haunted and harassed by a guilty conscience.

WERLE. Indeed! It is your conscience that troubles you, is it?

GREGERS. I ought to have taken a stand against you when the trap was set for Lieutenant Ekdal. I ought to have cautioned him, for I had a misgiving as to what was in the wind.

WERLE. Yes, that was the time to have spoken.

GREGERS. I did not dare to, I was so cowed and spiritless. I was mortally afraid of you—not only then, but long afterwards.

WERLE. You have got over that fear now, it appears.

GREGERS. Yes, fortunately. The wrong done to old Ekdal, both by me and by—others, can never be undone; but Hialmar I can rescue from all the falsehood and deception that are bringing him to ruin.

WERLE. Do you think that will be doing him a kindness?

GREGERS. I have not the least doubt of it.

WERLE. You think our worthy photographer is the sort of man to appreciate such friendly offices?

GREGERS. Yes, I do.

WERLE. H'm—we shall see.

GREGERS. Besides, if I am to go on living, I must try to find some cure for my sick conscience.

WERLE. It will never be sound. Your conscience has been sickly from childhood. That is a legacy from your mother, Gregers— the only one she left you.

GREGERS. [with a scornful half-smile] Have you not yet forgiven her for the mistake you made in supposing she would bring you a fortune?

WERLE. Don't let us wander from the point.—Then you hold to your purpose of setting young Ekdal upon what you imagine to be the right scent?

GREGERS. Yes, that is my fixed resolve.

WERLE. Well, in that case I might have spared myself this visit; for, of course, it is useless to ask whether you will return home with me?

GREGERS. Quite useless.

WERLE. And I suppose you won't enter the firm either?

GREGERS. No.

WERLE. Very good. But as I am thinking of marrying again, your share in the property will fall to you at once.[5]

GREGERS. [quickly] No, I do not want that.

WERLE. You don't want it?

GREGERS. No, I dare not take it, for conscience' sake.

WERLE. [after a pause] Are you going up to the works again?

GREGERS. No; I consider myself released from your service.

WERLE. But what are you going to do?

GREGERS. Only to fulfil my mission; nothing more.

WERLE. Well, but afterwards? What are you going to live upon?

GREGERS. I have laid by a little out of my salary.

WERLE. How long will that last?

GREGERS. I think it will last my time.

WERLE. What do you mean?

GREGERS. I shall answer no more questions.

5. By Norwegian law, before a widower can marry again, a certain proportion of his property must be settled on his children by his former marriage. [Translator's note.]

WERLE. Good-bye then, Gregers.

GREGERS. Good-bye.

[WERLE goes.]

HIALMAR. [peeping in] He's gone, isn't he?

GREGERS. Yes.

[HIALMAR and RELLING enter; also GINA and HEDVIG from the kitchen.]

RELLING. That luncheon-party was a failure.

GREGERS. Put on your coat, Hialmar; I want you to come for a long walk with me.

HIALMAR. With pleasure. What was it your father wanted? Had it anything to do with me?

GREGERS. Come along. We must have a talk. I'll go and put on my overcoat. [goes out by the passage door]

GINA. You shouldn't go out with him, Ekdal.

RELLING. No, don't you do it. Stay where you are.

HIALMAR. [gets his hat and overcoat] Oh, nonsense! When a friend of my youth feels impelled to open his mind to me in private——

RELLING. But devil take it—don't you see that the fellow's mad, cracked, demented?

GINA. There, what did I tell you? His mother before him had crazy fits like that sometimes.

HIALMAR. The more need for a friend's watchful eye. [to GINA] Be sure you have dinner ready in good time. Good-bye for the present. [goes out by the passage door]

RELLING. It's a thousand pities the fellow didn't go to hell through one of the Höidal mines.

GINA. Good Lord! what makes you say that?

RELLING. [muttering] Oh, I have my own reasons.

GINA. Do you think young Werle is really mad?

RELLING. No, worse luck; he's no madder than most other people. But one disease he has certainly got in his system.

GINA. What's the matter with him?

RELLING. Well, I'll tell you, Mrs. Ekdal. He is suffering from an acute attack of integrity.

GINA. Integrity?

HEDVIG. Is that a kind of disease?

RELLING. Yes, it's a national disease; but it only appears sporadically. [nods to GINA] Thanks for your hospitality.

[He goes out by the passage door.]

GINA. [moving restlessly to and fro] Ugh, that Gregers Werle—he was always a wretched creature.

HEDVIG. [standing by the table and looking searchingly at her] I think all this is very strange.

Act IV

SCENE—HIALMAR EKDAL's studio. A photograph has just been taken; a camera with the cloth over it, a pedestal, two chairs, a folding table, etc., are standing out in the room. Afternoon light; the *sun is going down; a little later it begins to grow dusk.*

    GINA *stands in the passage doorway, with a little box and a wet glass plate in her hand, and is speaking to somebody outside.*

GINA. Yes, certainly. When I make a promise I keep it. The first dozen shall be ready on Monday. Good afternoon.

    [*Someone is heard going downstairs.* GINA *shuts the door, slips the plate into the box and puts it into the covered camera.*]

HEDVIG. [*comes in from the kitchen*] Are they gone?

GINA. [*tidying up*] Yes, thank goodness, I've got rid of them at last.

HEDVIG. But can you imagine why father hasn't come home yet?

GINA. Are you sure he's not down in Relling's room?

HEDVIG. No, he's not; I ran down the kitchen stair just now and asked.

GINA. And his dinner standing and getting cold, too.

HEDVIG. Yes, I can't understand it. Father's always so careful to be home to dinner!

GINA. Oh, he'll be here directly, you'll see.

HEDVIG. I wish he would come; everything seems so queer today.

GINA. [*calls out*] There he is!

    [HIALMAR EKDAL *comes in at the passage door.*]

HEDVIG. [*going to him*] Father! Oh, what a time we've been waiting for you!

GINA. [*glancing sidelong at him*] You've been out a long time, Ekdal.

HIALMAR. [*without looking at her*] Rather long, yes.

    [*He takes off his overcoat;* GINA *and* HEDVIG *go to help him; he motions them away.*]

GINA. Perhaps you've had dinner with Werle?

HIALMAR. [*hanging up his coat*] No.

GINA. [*going towards the kitchen door*] Then I'll bring some in for you.

HIALMAR. No; let the dinner alone. I want nothing to eat.

HEDVIG. [*going nearer to him*] Are you not well, father?

HIALMAR. Well? Oh, yes, well enough. We have had a tiring walk, Gregers and I.

GINA. You didn't ought to have gone so far, Ekdal; you're not used to it.

HIALMAR. H'm; there's many a thing a man must get used to in this world. [*wanders about the room*] Has any one been here whilst I was out?

GINA. Nobody but the two sweethearts.

HIALMAR. No new orders?

GINA. No, not today.

HEDVIG. There will be some tomorrow, father; you'll see.

HIALMAR. I hope there will, for tomorrow I am going to set to work in real earnest.

HEDVIG. Tomorrow! Don't you remember what day it is tomorrow?

HIALMAR. Oh, yes, by-the-bye——. Well, the day after, then. Henceforth I mean to do everything myself; I shall take all the work into my own hands.

GINA. Why, what can be the good of that, Ekdal? It'll only make your life a burden to you. I can manage the photography all right, and you can go on working at your invention.

HEDVIG. And think of the wild duck, father,—and all the hens and rabbits and——!

HIALMAR. Don't talk to me of all that trash! From tomorrow I will never set foot in the garret again.

HEDVIG. Oh, but father, you promised that we should have a little party——

HIALMAR. H'm, true. Well, then, from the day after tomorrow. I should almost like to wring that cursed wild duck's neck!

HEDVIG. [*shrieks*] The wild duck!

GINA. Well, I never!

HEDVIG. [*shaking him*] Oh, no, father; you know it's my wild duck!

HIALMAR. That is why I don't do it. I haven't the heart to—for your sake, Hedvig. But in my inmost soul I feel that I ought to do it. I ought not to tolerate under my roof a creature that has been through those hands.

GINA. Why, good gracious, even if grandfather did get it from that poor creature, Pettersen——

HIALMAR. [*wandering about*] There are certain claims—what shall I call them?—let me say claims of the ideal—certain obligations, which a man cannot disregard without injury to his soul.

HEDVIG. [*going after him*] But think of the wild duck,—the poor wild duck!

HIALMAR. [*stops*] I tell you I will spare it—for your sake. Not a hair of its head shall be—I mean, it shall be spared. There are greater problems than that to be dealt with. But you should go out a little now, Hedvig, as usual; it is getting dusk enough for you now.

HEDVIG. No, I don't care about going out now.

HIALMAR. Yes, do; it seems to me your eyes are blinking a great deal; all these vapors in here are bad for you. The air is heavy under this roof.

HEDVIG. Very well, then, I'll run down the kitchen stair and go for a little walk. My cloak and hat?—oh, they're in my own room. Father—be sure you don't do the wild duck any harm while I'm out.

HIALMAR. Not a feather of its head shall be touched. [*draws her to him*] You and I, Hedvig—we two——! Well, go along.

[HEDVIG *nods to her parents and goes out through the kitchen.*]

HIALMAR. [*walks about without looking up*] Gina.

GINA. Yes?

HIALMAR. From tomorrow—or, say, from the day after tomorrow— I should like to keep the household account-book myself.

GINA. Do you want to keep the accounts, too, now?

HIALMAR. Yes; or to check the receipts at any rate.

GINA. Lord help us! that's soon done.

HIALMAR. One would hardly think so; at any rate, you seem to make the money go a very long way. [*stops and looks at her*] How do you manage it?

GINA. It's because me and Hedvig, we need so little.

HIALMAR. Is it the case that father is very liberally paid for the copying he does for Mr. Werle?

GINA. I don't know as he gets anything out of the way. I don't know the rates for that sort of work.

HIALMAR. Well, what does he get, about? Let me hear!

GINA. Oh, it varies; I daresay it'll come to about as much as he costs us, with a little pocket-money over.

HIALMAR. As much as he costs us! And you have never told me this before!

GINA. No, how could I tell you? It pleased you so much to think he got everything from you.

HIALMAR. And he gets it from Mr. Werle.

GINA. Oh, well, he has plenty and to spare, he has.

HIALMAR. Light the lamp for me, please!

GINA. [*lighting the lamp*] And, of course, we don't know as it's Mr. Werle himself; it may be Gråberg——

HIALMAR. Why attempt such an evasion?

GINA. I don't know; I only thought——

HIALMAR. H'm.

GINA. It wasn't me that got grandfather that copying. It was Bertha, when she used to come about us.

HIALMAR. It seems to me your voice is trembling.

GINA. [*putting the lamp-shade on*] Is it?

HIALMAR. And your hands are shaking, are they not?

GINA. [*firmly*] Come right out with it, Ekdal. What has he been saying about me?

HIALMAR. Is it true—can it be true that—that there was an—an understanding between you and Mr. Werle, while you were in service there?

GINA. That's not true. Not at that time. Mr. Werle did come after me, that's a fact. And his wife thought there was something in it, and then she made such a hocus-pocus and hurly-burly, and she hustled me and bustled me about so that I left her service.

HIALMAR. But afterwards, then?

GINA. Well, then I went home. And mother—well, she wasn't the woman you took her for, Ekdal; she kept on worrying and worrying at me about one thing and another—for Mr. Werle was a widower by that time.

HIALMAR. Well, and then?

GINA. I suppose you've got to know it. He gave me no peace until he'd had his way.

HIALMAR. [*striking his hands together*] And this is the mother of my child! How could you hide this from me?

GINA. Yes, it was wrong of me; I ought certainly to have told you long ago.

HIALMAR. You should have told me at the very first;—then I should have known the sort of woman you were.

GINA. But would you have married me all the same?

HIALMAR. How can you dream that I would?

GINA. That's just why I didn't dare tell you anything, then. For I'd come to care for you so much, you see; and I couldn't go and make myself utterly miserable——

HIALMAR. [walks about] And this is my Hedvig's mother. And to know that all I see before me—[kicks a chair]—all that I call my home—I owe to a favored predecessor! Oh, that scoundrel Werle!

GINA. Do you repent of the fourteen—the fifteen years we've lived together?

HIALMAR. [placing himself in front of her] Have you not every day, every hour, repented of the spider's-web of deceit you have spun around me? Answer me that! How could you help writhing with penitence and remorse?

GINA. Oh, my dear Ekdal, I've had all I could do to look after the house and get through the day's work——

HIALMAR. Then you never think of reviewing your past?

GINA. No; Heaven knows I'd almost forgotten those old stories.

HIALMAR. Oh, this dull, callous contentment! To me there is something revolting about it. Think of it—never so much as a twinge of remorse!

GINA. But tell me, Ekdal—what would have become of you if you hadn't had a wife like me?

HIALMAR. Like you——!

GINA. Yes; for you know I've always been a bit more practical and wide-awake than you. Of course I'm a year or two older.

HIALMAR. What would have become of me!

GINA. You'd got into all sorts of bad ways when first you met me; that you can't deny.

HIALMAR. "Bad ways" do you call them? Little do you know what a man goes through when he is in grief and despair—especially a man of my fiery temperament.

GINA. Well, well, that may be so. And I've no reason to crow over you, neither; for you turned a moral of a husband, that you did, as soon as ever you had a house and home of your own.—And now we've got everything so nice and cosy about us; and me and Hedvig was just thinking we'd soon be able to let ourselves go a bit, in the way of both food and clothes.

HIALMAR. In the swamp of deceit, yes.

GINA. I wish to goodness that detestable thing had never set his foot inside our doors!

HIALMAR. And I, too, thought my home such a pleasant one. That was a delusion. Where shall I now find the elasticity of spirit to bring my invention into the world of reality? Perhaps it will die with me; and then it will be your past, Gina, that will have killed it.

GINA. [nearly crying] You mustn't say such things, Ekdal. Me, that has only wanted to do the best I could for you, all my days!

HIALMAR. I ask you, what becomes of the breadwinner's dream? When I used to lie in there on the sofa and brood over my invention, I had a clear enough presentiment that it would sap my vitality to the last drop. I felt ever. then that the day when I held the patent in my hand—that day—would bring my—release. And then it was my dream that you should live on after me, the dead inventor's well-to-do widow.

GINA. [*drying her tears*] No, you mustn't talk like that, Ekdal. May the Lord never let me see the day I am left a widow!

HIALMAR. Oh, the whole dream has vanished. It is all over now. All over!

[GREGERS WERLE *opens the passage door cautiously and looks in.*]

GREGERS. May I come in?

HIALMAR. Yes, come in.

GREGERS. [*comes forward, his face beaming with satisfaction, and holds out both his hands to them*] Well, dear friends——! [*looks from one to the other and whispers to* HIALMAR] Have you not done it yet?

HIALMAR. [*aloud*] It is done.

GREGERS. It is?

HIALMAR. I have passed through the bitterest moments of my life.

GREGERS. But also, I trust, the most ennobling.

HIALMAR. Well, at any rate, we have got through it for the present.

GINA. God forgive you, Mr. Werle.

GREGERS. [*in great surprise*] But I don't understand this.

HIALMAR. What don't you understand?

GREGERS. After so great a crisis—a crisis that is to be the starting-point of an entirely new life—of a communion founded on truth, and free from all taint of deception——

HIALMAR. Yes, yes, I know; I know that quite well.

GREGERS. I confidently expected, when I entered the room, to find the light of transfiguration shining upon me from both husband and wife. And now I see nothing but dulness, oppression, gloom——

GINA. Oh, is that it? [*takes off the lamp-shade*]

GREGERS. You will not understand me, Mrs. Ekdal. Ah, well, you, I suppose, need time to——. But you, Hialmar? Surely you feel a new consecration after the great crisis.

HIALMAR. Yes, of course I do. That is—in a sort of way.

GREGERS. For surely nothing in the world can compare with the joy of forgiving one who has erred and raising her up to oneself in love.

HIALMAR. Do you think a man can so easily throw off the bitter cup I have drained?

GREGERS. No, not a common man, perhaps. But a man like you——!

HIALMAR. Good God! I know that well enough. But you must keep me up to it, Gregers. It takes time, you know.

GREGERS. You have much of the wild duck in you, Hialmar.

[RELLING *has come in at the passage door.*]

RELLING. Oho! is the wild duck to the fore again?

HIALMAR. Yes; Mr. Werle's wing-broken victim.

RELLING. Mr. Werle's——? So it's him you are talking about?

HIALMAR. Him and—ourselves.

RELLING. [*in an undertone to* GREGERS] May the devil fly away with you!

HIALMAR. What is that you are saying?

RELLING. Only uttering a heartfelt wish that this quack-salver would take himself off. If he stays here, he is quite equal to making an utter mess of life, for both of you.

GREGERS. These two will not make a mess of life, Mr. Relling. Of course I won't speak of Hialmar—him we know. But she, too, in her innermost heart, has certainly something loyal and sincere——

GINA. [*almost crying*] You might have let me alone for what I was, then.

RELLING. [*to* GREGERS] Is it rude to ask what you really want in this house?

GREGERS. To lay the foundations of a true marriage.

RELLING. So you don't think Ekdal's marriage is good enough as it is?

GREGERS. No doubt it is as good a marriage as most others, worse luck. But a true marriage it has yet to become.

HIALMAR. You have never had eyes for the claims of the ideal, Relling.

RELLING. Rubbish, my boy!—but excuse me, Mr. Werle: how many —in round numbers—how many true marriages have you seen in the course of your life?

GREGERS. Scarcely a single one.

RELLING. Nor I either.

GREGERS. But I have seen innumerable marriages of the opposite kind. And it has been my fate to see at close quarters what ruin such a marriage can work in two human souls.

HIALMAR. A man's whole moral basis may give away beneath his feet; that is the terrible part of it.

RELLING. Well, I can't say I've ever been exactly married, so I don't pretend to speak with authority. But this I know, that the child enters into the marriage problem. And you must leave the child in peace.

HIALMAR. Oh—Hedvig! my poor Hedvig!

RELLING. Yes, you must be good enough to keep Hedvig outside of all this. You two are grown-up people; you are free, in God's name, to make what mess and muddle you please of your life. But you must deal cautiously with Hedvig, I tell you; else you may do her a great injury.

HIALMAR. An injury!

RELLING. Yes, or she may do herself an injury—and perhaps others, too.

GINA. How can you know that, Relling?

HIALMAR. Her sight is in no immediate danger, is it?

RELLING. I am not talking about her sight. Hedvig is at a critical age. She may be getting all sorts of mischief into her head.

GINA. That's true—I've noticed it already! She's taken to carrying on with the fire, out in the kitchen. She calls it playing at house-on-fire. I'm often scared for fear she really sets fire to the house.

RELLING. You see; I thought as much.

GREGERS. [*to* RELLING] But how do you account for that?

RELLING. [*sullenly*] Her constitution's changing, sir.

HIALMAR. So long as the child has me——! So long as *I* am above ground——!

[*A knock at the door.*]

GINA. Hush, Ekdal; there's some one in the passage. [*calls out*] Come in!

[MRS. SÖRBY, *in walking dress, comes in.*]

MRS. SÖRBY. Good evening.

GINA. [*going towards her*] Is it really you, Bertha?

MRS. SÖRBY. Yes, of course it is. But I'm disturbing you, I'm afraid?

HIALMAR. No, not at all; an emissary from that house——

MRS. SÖRBY. [*to* GINA] To tell the truth, I hoped your men-folk would be out at this time. I just ran up to have a little chat with you, and to say good-bye.

GINA. Good-bye? Are you going away, then?

MRS. SÖRBY. Yes, tomorrow morning,—up to Höidal. Mr. Werle started this afternoon. [*lightly to* GREGERS] He asked me to say good-bye for him.

GINA. Only fancy——!

HIALMAR. So Mr. Werle has gone? And now you are going after him?

MRS. SÖRBY. Yes, what do you say to that, Ekdal?

HIALMAR. I say: beware!

GREGERS. I must explain the situation. My father and Mrs. Sörby are going to be married.

HIALMAR. Going to be married!

GINA. Oh, Bertha! So it's come to that at last!

RELLING. [*his voice quivering a little*] This is surely not true?

MRS. SÖRBY. Yes, my dear Relling, it's true enough.

RELLING. You are going to marry again?

MRS. SÖRBY. Yes, it looks like it. Werle has got a special licence, and we are going to be married quite quietly, up at the works.

GREGERS. Then I must wish you all happiness, like a dutiful stepson.

MRS. SÖRBY. Thank you very much—if you mean what you say. I certainly hope it will lead to happiness, both for Werle and for me.

RELLING. You have every reason to hope that. Mr. Werle never gets drunk—so far as I know; and I don't suppose he's in the habit of thrashing his wives, like the late lamented horse-doctor.

MRS. SÖRBY. Come now, let Sörby rest in peace. He had his good points, too.

RELLING. Mr. Werle has better ones, I have no doubt.

MRS. SÖRBY. He hasn't frittered away all that was good in him, at any rate. The man who does that must take the consequences.

RELLING. I shall go out with Molvik this evening.

MRS. SÖRBY. You mustn't do that, Relling. Don't do it—for my sake.

RELLING. There's nothing else for it. [*to* HIALMAR] If you're going with us, come along.

GINA. No, thank you. Ekdal doesn't go in for that sort of dissertation.

HIALMAR. [*half aloud, in vexation*] Oh, do hold your tongue!

RELLING. Good-bye, Mrs.—Werle. [*goes out through the passage door*]

GREGERS. [*to* MRS. SÖRBY] You seem to know Dr. Relling pretty intimately.

MRS. SÖRBY. Yes, we have known each other for many years. At one time it seemed as if things might have gone further between us.

GREGERS. It was surely lucky for you that they did not.

MRS. SÖRBY. You may well say that. But I have always been wary of acting on impulse. A woman can't afford absolutely to throw herself away.

GREGERS. Are you not in the least afraid that I may let my father know about this old friendship?

MRS. SÖRBY. Why, of course, I have told him all about it myself.

GREGERS. Indeed?

MRS. SÖRBY. Your father knows every single thing that can, with any truth, be said about me. I have told him all; it was the first thing I did when I saw what was in his mind.

GREGERS. Then you have been franker than most people, I think.

MRS. SÖRBY. I have always been frank. We women find that the best policy.

HIALMAR. What do you say to that, Gina?

GINA. Oh, we're not all alike, us women aren't. Some are made one way, some another.

MRS. SÖRBY. Well, for my part, Gina, I believe it's wisest to do as I've done. And Werle has no secrets either, on his side. That's really the great bond between us, you see. Now he can talk to me as openly as a child. He has never had the chance to do that before. Fancy a man like him, full of health and vigor, passing his whole youth and the best years of his life in listening to nothing but penitential sermons! And very often the sermons had for their text the most imaginary offences—at least so I understand.

GINA. That's true enough.

GREGERS. If you ladies are going to follow up this topic, I had better withdraw.

MRS. SÖRBY. You can stay as far as that's concerned. I shan't say a word more. But I wanted you to know that I had done nothing secretly or in an underhand way. I may seem to have come in for a great piece of luck; and so I have, in a sense. But after all, I don't think I am getting any more than I am giving. I shall stand by him always, and I can tend and care for him as no one else can, now that he is getting helpless.

HIALMAR. Getting helpless?

GREGERS. [*to* MRS. SÖRBY] Hush, don't speak of that here.

MRS. SÖRBY. There is no disguising it any longer, however much he would like to. He is going blind.

HIALMAR. [*starts*] Going blind? That's strange. He, too, going blind!

GINA. Lots of people do.

MRS. SÖRBY. And you can imagine what that means to a business man. Well, I shall try as well as I can to make my eyes take the place of his. But I mustn't stay any longer; I have heaps of things to do.—Oh, by-the-bye, Ekdal, I was to tell you that if there is anything Werle can do for you, you must just apply to Gråberg.

GREGERS. That offer I am sure Hialmar Ekdal will decline with thanks.

MRS. SÖRBY. Indeed? I don't think he used to be so——

GINA. No, Bertha, Ekdal doesn't need anything from Mr. Werle now.

HIALMAR. [*slowly, and with emphasis*] Will you present my compliments to your future husband and say that I intend very shortly to call upon Mr. Gråberg——

GREGERS. What! You don't really mean that?

HIALMAR. To call upon Mr. Gråberg, I say, and obtain an account of the sum I owe his principal. I will pay that debt of honor— ha ha ha! a debt of honor, let us call it! In any case, I will pay the whole with five per cent interest.

GINA. But, my dear Ekdal, God knows we haven't got the money to do it.

HIALMAR. Be good enough to tell your future husband that I am working assiduously at my invention. Please tell him that what sustains me in this laborious task is the wish to free myself from a torturing burden of debt. That is my reason for proceeding with the invention. The entire profits shall be devoted to releasing me from my pecuniary obligations to your future husband.

MRS. SÖRBY. Something has happened here.

HIALMAR. Yes, you are right.

MRS. SÖRBY. Well, good-bye. I had something else to speak to you about, Gina; but it must keep till another time. Good-bye.

[HIALMAR *and* GREGERS *bow silently.* GINA *follows* MRS. SÖRBY *to the door.*]

HIALMAR. Not beyond the threshold, Gina!

[MRS. SÖRBY *goes;* GINA *shuts the door after her.*]

HIALMAR. There now, Gregers; I have got that burden of debt off my mind.

GREGERS. You soon will, at all events.

HIALMAR. I think my attitude may be called correct.

GREGERS. You are the man I have always taken you for.

HIALMAR. In certain cases, it is impossible to disregard the claim of the ideal. Yet, as the breadwinner of a family, I cannot but writhe and groan under it. I can tell you it is no joke for a man without capital to attempt the repayment of a long-standing obligation, over which, so to speak, the dust of oblivion had gathered. But it cannot be helped: the Man in me demands his rights.

GREGERS. [laying his hand on HIALMAR's shoulder] My dear Hial-mar—was it not a good thing I came?

HIALMAR. Yes.

GREGERS. Are you not glad to have had your true position made clear to you?

HIALMAR. [somewhat impatiently] Yes, of course I am. But there is one thing that is revolting to my sense of justice.

GREGERS. And what is that?

HIALMAR. It is that—but I don't know whether I ought to express myself so unreservedly about your father.

GREGERS. Say what you please, so far as I am concerned.

HIALMAR. Well, then, is it not exasperating to think that it is not I, but he, who will realize the true marriage?

GREGERS. How can you say such a thing?

HIAMAR. Because it is clearly the case. Isn't the marriage between your father and Mrs. Sörby founded upon complete confidence, upon entire and unreserved candor on both sides? They hide nothing from each other; they keep no secrets in the background; their relation is based, if I may put it so, on mutual confession and absolution.

GREGERS. Well, what then?

HIALMAR. Well, is not that the whole thing? Did you not yourself say this was precisely the difficulty that had to be overcome in order to found a true marriage?

GREGERS. But this is a totally different matter, Hialmar. You surely don't compare either yourself or your wife with those two——? Oh, you understand me well enough.

HIALMAR. Say what you like, there is something in all this that hurts and offends my sense of justice. It really looks as if there were no just providence to rule the world.

GINA. Oh, no, Ekdal; for God's sake don't say such things.

GREGERS. H'm; don't let us get upon those questions.

HIALMAR. And yet, after all, I cannot but recognize the guiding finger of fate. He is going blind.

GINA. Oh, you can't be sure of that.

HIALMAR. There is no doubt about it. At all events there ought not to be; for in that very fact lies the righteous retribution. He has hoodwinked a confiding fellow-creature in days gone by——

GREGERS. I fear he has hoodwinked many.

HIALMAR. And now comes inexorable, mysterious Fate and demands Werle's own eyes.

GINA. Oh, how dare you say such dreadful things! You make me quite scared.

HIALMAR. It is profitable, now and then, to plunge deep into the night side of existence.

[HEDVIG, in her hat and cloak, comes in by the passage door. She is pleasurably excited and out of breath.]

GINA. Are you back already?

HEDVIG. Yes, I didn't care to go any farther. It was a good thing, too; for I've just met some one at the door.

HIALMAR. It must have been that Mrs. Sörby.

HEDVIG. Yes.

HIALMAR. [*walks up and down*] I hope you have seen her for the last time.

[*Silence.* HEDVIG, *discouraged, looks first at one and then at the other, trying to divine their frame of mind.*]

HEDVIG. [*approaching, coaxingly*] Father.

HIALMAR. Well—what is it, Hedvig?

HEDVIG. Mrs. Sörby had something with her for me.

HIALMAR. [*stops*] For you?

HEDVIG. Yes. Something for tomorrow.

GINA. Bertha has always given you some little thing on your birthday.

HIALMAR. What is it?

HEDVIG. Oh, you mustn't see it now. Mother is to give it to me tomorrow morning before I'm up.

HIALMAR. What is all this hocus-pocus that I am to be in the dark about?

HEDVIG. [*quickly*] Oh, no, you may see it if you like. It's a big letter. [*takes the letter out of her cloak pocket*]

HIALMAR. A letter, too?

HEDVIG. Yes, it is only a letter. The rest will come afterwards, I suppose. But fancy—a letter! I've never had a letter before. And there's "Miss" written upon it. [*reads*] "Miss Hedvig Ekdal." Only fancy—that's me!

HIALMAR. Let me see that letter.

HEDVIG. [*hands it to him*] There it is.

HIALMAR. That is Mr. Werle's hand.

GINA. Are you sure of that, Ekdal?

HIALMAR. Look for yourself.

GINA. Oh, what do I know about such-like things?

HIALMAR. Hedvig, may I open the letter—and read it?

HEDVIG. Yes, of course you may, if you want to.

GINA. No, not tonight, Ekdal; it's to be kept till tomorrow.

HEDVIG. [*softly*] Oh, can't you let him read it? It's sure to be something good; and then father will be glad, and everything will be nice again.

HIALMAR. I may open it, then?

HEDVIG. Yes, do, father. I'm so anxious to know what it is.

HIALMAR. Well and good. [*opens the letter, takes out a paper, reads it through and appears bewildered*] What is this——?

GINA. What does it say?

HEDVIG. Oh, yes, father—tell us!

HIALMAR. Be quiet. [*reads it through again; he has turned pale, but says with self-control*] It is a deed of gift, Hedvig.

HEDVIG. Is it? What sort of gift am I to have?

HIALMAR. Read for yourself.

[HEDVIG *goes over and reads for a time by the lamp.*]

HIALMAR. [*half-aloud, clenching his hands*] The eyes! The eyes—and then that letter!

HEDVIG. [*leaves off reading*] Yes, but it seems to me that it's grandfather that's to have it.

HIALMAR. [*takes letter from her*] Gina—can you understand this?

GINA. I know nothing whatever about it; tell me what's the matter.

HIALMAR. Mr. Werle writes to Hedvig that her old grandfather need not trouble himself any longer with the copying, but that he can henceforth draw on the office for a hundred crowns a month——

GREGERS. Aha!

HEDVIG. A hundred crowns, mother! I read that.

GINA. What a good thing for grandfather!

HIALMAR. ——a hundred crowns a month so long as he needs it— that means, of course, so long as he lives.

GINA. Well, so he's provided for, poor dear.

HIALMAR. But there is more to come. You didn't read that, Hedvig. Afterwards this gift is to pass on to you.

HEDVIG. To me! The whole of it?

HIALMAR. He says that the same amount is assured to you for the whole of your life. Do you hear that, Gina?

GINA. Yes, I hear.

HEDVIG. Fancy—all that money for me! [*shakes him*] Father, father, aren't you glad——?

HIALMAR. [*eluding her*] Glad! [*walks about*] Oh, what vistas—what perspectives open up before me! It is Hedvig, Hedvig that he showers these benefactions upon!

GINA. Yes, because it's Hedvig's birthday——

HEDVIG. And you'll get it all the same, father! You know quite well I shall give all the money to you and mother.

HIALMAR. To mother, yes! There we have it.

GREGERS. Hialmar, this is a trap he is setting for you.

HIALMAR. Do you think it's another trap?

GREGERS. When he was here this morning he said: Hialmar Ekdal is not the man you imagine him to be.

HIALMAR. Not the man——!

GREGERS. That you shall see, he said.

HIALMAR. He meant you should see that I would let myself be bought off——!

HEDVIG. Oh, mother, what does all this mean?

GINA. Go and take off your things.

[HEDVIG *goes out by the kitchen door, half-crying.*]

GREGERS. Yes, Hialmar—now is the time to show who was right, he or I.

HIALMAR. [*slowly tears the paper across, lays both pieces on the table and says*] Here is my answer.

GREGERS. Just what I expected.

HIALMAR. [*goes over to* GINA, *who stands by the stove, and says in a low voice*] Now please make a clean breast of it. If the connection between you and him was quite over when you—came to care for me, as you call it—why did he place us in a position to marry?

GINA. I suppose he thought as he could come and go in our house.

HIALMAR. Only that? Was not he afraid of a possible contingency?

GINA. I don't know what you mean.

HIALMAR. I want to know whether—your child has the right to live under my roof.

GINA. [*draws herself up; her eyes flash*] You ask that?

HIALMAR. You shall answer me this one question: Does Hedvig belong to me—or——? Well?

GINA. [*looking at him with cold defiance*] I don't know.

HIALMAR. [*quivering a little*] You don't know!

GINA. How should *I* know? A creature like me——

HIALMAR. [*quietly turning away from her*] Then I have nothing more to do in this house.

GREGERS. Take care, Hialmar! Think what you are doing!

HIALMAR. [*puts on his overcoat*] In this case, there is nothing for a man like me to think twice about.

GREGERS. Yes, indeed, there are endless things to be considered. You three must be together if you are to attain the true frame of mind for self-sacrifice and forgiveness.

HIALMAR. I don't want to attain it. Never, never! My hat! [*takes his hat*] My home has fallen in ruins about me. [*bursts into tears*] Gregers, I have no child!

HEDVIG. [*who has opened the kitchen door*] What is that you're saying? [*coming to him*] Father, father!

GINA. There, you see!

HIALMAR. Don't come near me, Hedvig! Keep far away. I cannot bear to see you! Oh! those eyes——! Good-bye. [*makes for the door*]

HEDVIG. [*clinging close to him and screaming loudly*] No! no! Don't leave me!

GINA. [*cries out*] Look at the child, Ekdal! Look at the child!

HIALMAR. I will not! I cannot! I must get out—away from all this!

[*He tears himself away from* HEDVIG *and goes out by the passage door.*]

HEDVIG. [*with despairing eyes*] He is going away from us, mother! He is going away from us! He will never come back again!

GINA. Don't cry, Hedvig. Father's sure to come back again.

HEDVIG. [*throws herself sobbing on the sofa*] No, no, he'll never come home to us any more.

GREGERS. Do you believe I meant all for the best, Mrs. Ekdal?

GINA. Yes, I daresay you did; but God forgive you, all the same.

HEDVIG. [*lying on the sofa*] Oh, this will kill me! What have I done to him? Mother, you must fetch him home again!

GINA. Yes, yes, yes; only be quiet, and I'll go out and look for him. [*puts on her outdoor things*] Perhaps he's gone in to Relling's. But you mustn't lie there and cry. Promise me!

HEDVIG. [*weeping convulsively*] Yes, I'll stop, I'll stop; if only father comes back!

GREGERS. [*to* GINA, *who is going*] After all, had you not better leave him to fight out his bitter fight to the end?

GINA. Oh, he can do that afterwards. First of all, we must get the child quieted. [goes out by the passage door]

HEDVIG. [sits up and dries her tears] Now you must tell me what all this means? Why doesn't father want me any more?

GREGERS. You mustn't ask that till you are a big girl—quite grown-up.

HEDVIG. [sobs] But I can't go on being as miserable as this till I'm grown-up.—I think I know what it is.—Perhaps I'm not really father's child.

GREGERS. [uneasily] How could that be?

HEDVIG. Mother might have found me. And perhaps father has just got to know it; I've read of such things.

GREGERS. Well, but if it were so——

HEDVIG. I think he might be just as fond of me for all that. Yes, fonder almost. We got the wild duck in a present, you know, and I love it so dearly all the same.

GREGERS. [turning the conversation] Ah, the wild duck, by-the-bye! Let us talk about the wild duck a little, Hedvig.

HEDVIG. The poor wild duck! He doesn't want to see it any more either. Only think, he wanted to wring its neck!

GREGERS. Oh, he won't do that.

HEDVIG. No; but he said he would like to. And I think it was horrid of father to say it, for I pray for the wild duck every night and ask that it may be preserved from death and all that is evil.

GREGERS. [looking at her] Do you say your prayers every night?

HEDVIG. Yes.

GREGERS. Who taught you to do that?

HEDVIG. I myself, one time when father was very ill, and had leeches on his neck and said that death was staring him in the face.

GREGERS. Well?

HEDVIG. Then I prayed for him as I lay in bed, and since then I have always kept it up.

GREGERS. And now you pray for the wild duck, too?

HEDVIG. I thought it was best to bring in the wild duck, for she was so weakly at first.

GREGERS. Do you pray in the morning, too?

HEDVIG. No, of course not.

GREGERS. Why not in the morning as well?

HEDVIG. In the morning it's light, you know, and there's nothing in particular to be afraid of.

GREGERS. And your father was going to wring the neck of the wild duck that you love so dearly?

HEDVIG. No; he said he ought to wring its neck, but he would spare it for my sake; and that was kind of father.

GREGERS. [coming a little nearer] But suppose you were to sacrifice the wild duck of your own free will for his sake.

HEDVIG. [rising] The wild duck!

GREGERS. Suppose you were to make a free-will offering, for his sake, of the dearest treasure you have in the world!

HEDVIG. Do you think that would do any good?

GREGERS. Try it, Hedvig.

HEDVIG. [*softly, with flashing eyes*] Yes, I will try it.

GREGERS. Have you really the courage for it, do you think?

HEDVIG. I'll ask grandfather to shoot the wild duck for me.

GREGERS. Yes, do. But not a word to your mother about it.

HEDVIG. Why not?

GREGERS. She doesn't understand us.

HEDVIG. The wild duck! I'll try it tomorrow morning.

> [GINA *comes in by the passage door.*]

HEDVIG. [*going towards her*] Did you find him, mother?

GINA. No, but I heard as he had called and taken Relling with him.

GREGERS. Are you sure of that?

GINA. Yes, the porter's wife said so. Molvik went with them, too, she said.

GREGERS. This evening, when his mind so sorely needs to wrestle in solitude——!

GINA. [*takes off her things*] Yes, men are strange creatures, so they are. The Lord only knows where Relling has dragged him to! I ran over to Madame Eriksen's, but they weren't there.

HEDVIG. [*struggling to keep back her tears*] Oh, if he should never come home any more!

GREGERS. He will come home again. I shall have news to give him tomorrow; and then you shall see how he comes home. You may rely upon that, Hedvig, and sleep in peace. Good-night!

> [*He goes out by the passage door.*]

HEDVIG. [*throws herself sobbing on* GINA's *neck*] Mother, mother!

GINA. [*pats her shoulder and sighs*] Ah, yes; Relling was right, he was. That's what comes of it when crazy creatures go about presenting the claims of the—what-you-may-call-it.

Act V

SCENE—HIALMAR EKDAL's *studio. Cold, grey morning light. Wet snow lies upon the large panes of the sloping roof-window.*

GINA *comes from the kitchen with an apron and bib on, and carrying a dusting-brush and a duster; she goes towards the sitting-room door. At the same moment* HEDVIG *comes hurriedly in from the passage.*

GINA. [*stops*] Well?

HEDVIG. Oh, mother, I almost think he's down at Relling's——

GINA. There, you see!

HEDVIG. ——because the porter's wife says she could hear that Relling had two people with him when he came home last night.

GINA. That's just what I thought.

HEDVIG. But it's no use his being there, if he won't come up to us.

GINA. I'll go down and speak to him at all events.

> [OLD EKDAL, *in dressing-gown and slippers, and with a lighted pipe, appears at the door of his room.*]

EKDAL. Hialmar—— Isn't Hialmar at home?

GINA. No, he's gone out.

EKDAL. So early? And in such a tearing snowstorm? Well, well; just as he pleases; I can take my morning walk alone.

[*He slides the garret door aside;* HEDVIG *helps him; he goes in; she closes it after him.*]

HEDVIG. [*in an undertone*] Only think, mother, when poor grandfather hears that father is going to leave us.

GINA. Oh, nonsense; grandfather mustn't hear anything about it. It was a heaven's mercy he wasn't at home yesterday in all that hurly-burly.

HEDVIG. Yes, but——

[GREGERS *comes in by the passage door.*]

GREGERS. Well, have you any news of him?

GINA. They say he's down at Relling's.

GREGERS. At Relling's! Has he really been out with those creatures?

GINA. Yes, like enough.

GREGERS. When he ought to have been yearning for solitude, to collect and clear his thoughts——

GINA. Yes, you may well say so.

[RELLING *enters from the passage.*]

HEDVIG. [*going to him*] Is father in your room?

GINA. [*at the same time*] Is he there?

RELLING. Yes, to be sure he is.

HEDVIG. And you never let us know!

RELLING. Yes, I'm a brute. But in the first place I had to look after the other brute; I mean our dæmonic friend, of course; and then I fell so dead asleep that——

GINA. What does Ekdal say today?

RELLING. He says nothing whatever.

HEDVIG. Doesn't he speak?

RELLING. Not a blessed word.

GREGERS. No, no; I can understand that very well.

GINA. But what's he doing then?

RELLING. He's lying on the sofa, snoring.

GINA. Oh, is he? Yes, Ekdal's a rare one to snore.

HEDVIG. Asleep? Can he sleep?

RELLING. Well, it certainly looks like it.

GREGERS. No wonder, after the spiritual conflict that has rent him——

GINA. And then he's never been used to gadding about out of doors at night.

HEDVIG. Perhaps it's a good thing that he's getting sleep, mother.

GINA. Of course it is; and we must take care we don't wake him up too early. Thank you, Relling. I must get the house cleaned up a bit now, and then—— Come and help me, Hedvig.

[GINA *and* HEDVIG *go into the sitting-room.*]

GREGERS. [*turning to* RELLING] What is your explanation of the spiritual tumult that is now going on in Hialmar Ekdal?

RELLING. Devil a bit of a spiritual tumult have *I* noticed in him.

GREGERS. What! Not at such a crisis, when his whole life has been placed on a new foundation——? How can you think that such an individuality as Hialmar's——?

RELLING. Oh, individuality—he! If he ever had any tendency to the abnormal development you call individuality, I can assure you it was rooted out of him while he was still in his teens.

GREGERS. That would be strange indeed,—considering the loving care with which he was brought up.

RELLING. By those two high-flown, hysterical maiden aunts, you mean?

GREGERS. Let me tell you that they were women who never forgot the claim of the ideal—but of course you will only jeer at me again.

RELLING. No, I'm in no humor for that. I know all about those ladies; for he has ladled out no end of rhetoric on the subject of his "two soul-mothers." But I don't think he has much to thank them for. Ekdal's misfortune is that in his own circle he has always been looked upon as a shining light——

GREGERS. Not without reason, surely. Look at the depth of his mind!

RELLING. *I* have never discovered it. That his father believed in it I don't so much wonder; the old lieutenant has been an ass all his days.

GREGERS. He has had a child-like mind all his days; that is what you cannot understand.

RELLING. Well, so be it. But then, when our dear, sweet Hialmar went to college, he at once passed for the great light of the future amongst his comrades, too! He was handsome, the rascal— red and white—a shop-girl's dream of manly beauty; and with his superficially emotional temperament, and his sympathetic voice and his talent for declaiming other people's verses and other people's thoughts——

GREGERS. [*indignantly*] Is it Hialmar Ekdal you are talking about in this strain?

RELLING. Yes, with your permission; I am simply giving you an inside view of the idol you are grovelling before.

GREGERS. I should hardly have thought I was quite stone blind.

RELLING. Yes, you are—or not far from it. You are a sick man, too, you see.

GREGERS. You are right there.

RELLING. Yes. Yours is a complicated case. First of all there is that plaguy integrity-fever; and then—what's worse—you are always in a delirium of hero-worship; you must always have something to adore, outside yourself.

GREGERS. Yes, I must certainly seek it outside myself.

RELLING. But you make such shocking mistakes about every new phœnix you think you have discovered. Here again you have come to a cotter's cabin with your claim of the ideal; and the people of the house are insolvent.

GREGERS. If you don't think better than that of Hialmar Ekdal, what pleasure can you find in being everlastingly with him?

RELLING. Well, you see, I'm supposed to be a sort of doctor—save the mark! I can't but give a hand to the poor sick folk who live under the same roof with me.

GREGERS. Oh, indeed! Hialmar Ekdal is sick, too, is he?

RELLING. Most people are, worse luck.

GREGERS. And what remedy are you applying in Hialmar's case?

RELLING. My usual one. I am cultivating the life-illusion[6] in him.

GREGERS. Life-illusion? I didn't catch what you said.

RELLING. Yes, I said illusion. For illusion, you know, is the stimulating principle.

GREGERS. May I ask with what illusion Hialmar is inoculated?

RELLING. No, thank you; I don't betray professional secrets to quack-salvers. You would probably go and muddle his case still more than you have already. But my method is infallible. I have applied it to Molvik as well. I have made him "dæmonic." That's the blister I have to put on his neck.

GREGERS. Is he not really dæmonic, then?

RELLING. What the devil do you mean by dæmonic? It's only a piece of gibberish I've invented to keep up a spark of life in him. But for that, the poor harmless creature would have succumbed to self-contempt and despair many a long year ago. And then the old lieutenant! But he has hit upon his own cure, you see.

GREGERS. Lieutenant Ekdal? What of him?

RELLING. Just think of the old bear-hunter shutting himself up in that dark garret to shoot rabbits! I tell you there is not a happier sportsman in the world than that old man pottering about in there among all that rubbish. The four or five withered Christmas trees he has saved up are the same to him as the whole great fresh Höidal forest; the cock and the hens are big game-birds in the fir-tops; and the rabbits that flop about the garret floor are the bears he has to battle with—the mighty hunter of the mountains!

GREGERS. Poor unfortunate old man! Yes; he has indeed had to narrow the ideals of his youth.

RELLING. While I think of it, Mr. Werle, junior—don't use that foreign word: ideals. We have the excellent native word: lies.

GREGERS. Do you think the two things are related?

RELLING. Yes, just about as closely as typhus and putrid fever.

GREGERS. Dr. Relling, I shall not give up the struggle until I have rescued Hialmar from your clutches!

RELLING. So much the worse for him. Rob the average man of his life-illusion, and you rob him of his happiness at the same stroke. [to HEDVIG, who comes in from the sitting-room] Well, little wild-duck-mother, I'm just going down to see whether papa is still lying meditating upon that wonderful invention of his. [goes out by passage door]

GREGERS. [approaches HEDVIG] I can see by your face that you have not yet done it.

HEDVIG. What? Oh, that about the wild duck! No.

GREGERS. I suppose your courage failed when the time came.

HEDVIG. No, that wasn't it. But when I awoke this morning and

6. "Livslögnen," literally "the life-lie." [Translator's note.]

remembered what we had been talking about, it seemed so strange.

GREGERS. Strange?

HEDVIG. Yes, I don't know—— Yesterday evening, at the moment, I thought there was something so delightful about it; but since I have slept and thought of it again, it somehow doesn't seem worth while.

GREGERS. Ah, I thought you could not have grown up quite unharmed in this house.

HEDVIG. I don't care about that, if only father would come up——

GREGERS. Oh, if only your eyes had been opened to that which gives life its value—if you possessed the true, joyous, fearless spirit of sacrifice, you would soon see how he would come up to you.—But I believe in you still, Hedvig.

[*He goes out by the passage door.* HEDVIG *wanders about the room for a time; she is on the point of going into the kitchen when a knock is heard at the garret door.* HEDVIG *goes over and opens it a little;* OLD EKDAL *comes out; she pushes the door to again.*]

EKDAL. H'm, it's not much fun to take one's morning walk alone.

HEDVIG. Wouldn't you like to go shooting, grandfather?

EKDAL. It's not the weather for it today. It's so dark there, you can scarcely see where you're going.

HEDVIG. Do you never want to shoot anything besides the rabbits?

EKDAL. Do you think the rabbits aren't good enough?

HEDVIG. Yes, but what about the wild duck?

EKDAL. Ho-ho! are you afraid I shall shoot your wild duck? Never in the world. Never.

HEDVIG. No, I suppose you couldn't; they say it's very difficult to shoot wild ducks.

EKDAL. Couldn't! Should rather think I could.

HEDVIG. How would you set about it, grandfather?—I don't mean with my wild duck, but with others?

EKDAL. I should take care to shoot them in the breast, you know; that's the surest place. And then you must shoot against the feathers, you see—not the way of the feathers.

HEDVIG. Do they die then, grandfather?

EKDAL. Yes, they die right enough—when you shoot properly. Well, I must go and brush up a bit. H'm—understand—h'm. [*goes into his room*]

[HEDVIG *waits a little, glances towards the sitting-room door, goes over to the book-case, stands on tip-toe, takes the double-barrelled pistol down from the shelf and looks at it.* GINA, *with brush and duster, comes from the sitting-room.* HEDVIG *hastily lays down the pistol, unobserved.*]

GINA. Don't stand raking amongst father's things, Hedvig.

HEDVIG. [*goes away from the bookcase*] I was only going to tidy up a little.

GINA. You'd better go into the kitchen and see if the coffee's keeping hot; I'll take his breakfast on a tray, when I go down to him.

[HEDVIG *goes out.* GINA *begins to sweep and clean up the studio. Presently the passage door is opened with hesitation, and* HIALMAR EKDAL *looks in. He has on his overcoat, but not his hat; he is unwashed, and his hair is dishevelled and unkempt. His eyes are dull and heavy.*]

GINA. [*standing with the brush in her hand and looking at him*] Oh, there now, Ekdal—so you've come after all!

HIALMAR. [*comes in and answers in a toneless voice*] I come—only to depart again immediately.

GINA. Yes, yes, I suppose so. But, Lord help us! what a sight you are!

HIALMAR. A sight?

GINA. And your nice winter coat, too! Well, that's done for.

HEDVIG. [*at the kitchen door*] Mother, hadn't I better——? [*sees* HIALMAR, *gives a loud scream of joy and runs to him*] Oh, father, father!

HIALMAR. [*turns away and makes a gesture of repulsion*] Away, away, away! [*to* GINA] Keep her away from me, I say!

GINA. [*in a low tone*] Go into the sitting-room, Hedvig.

[HEDVIG *does so without a word.*]

HIALMAR. [*fussily pulls out the table-drawer*] I must have my books with me. Where are my books?

GINA. Which books?

HIALMAR. My scientific books, of course; the technical magazines I require for my invention.

GINA. [*searches in the bookcase*] Is it these here paper-covered ones?

HIALMAR. Yes, of course.

GINA. [*lays a heap of magazines on the table*] Shan't I get Hedvig to cut them for you?

HIALMAR. I don't require to have them cut for me.

[*Short silence.*]

GINA. Then you're still set on leaving us, Ekdal?

HIALMAR. [*rummaging amongst the books*] Yes, that is a matter of course, I should think.

GINA. Well, well.

HIALMAR. [*vehemently*] How can I live here, to be stabbed to the heart every hour of the day?

GINA. God forgive you for thinking such vile things of me.

HIALMAR. Prove——!

GINA. I think it's you as has got to prove.

HIALMAR. After a past like yours? There are certain claims—I may almost call them claims of the ideal——

GINA. But what about grandfather? What's to become of him, poor dear?

HIALMAR. I know my duty; my helpless father will come with me. I am going out into the town to make arrangements—— H'm— [*hesitatingly*]—has any one found my hat on the stairs?

GINA. No. Have you lost your hat?

HIALMAR. Of course I had it on when I came in last night; there's no doubt about that; but I couldn't find it this morning.

GINA. Lord help us! where have you been to with those two ne'er-do-wells?

HIALMAR. Oh, don't bother me about trifles. Do you suppose I am in the mood to remember details?

GINA. If only you haven't caught cold, Ekdal—— [*goes out into the kitchen*]

HIALMAR. [*talks to himself in a low tone of irritation, while he empties the table-drawer*] You're a scoundrel, Relling!—You're a low fellow!—Ah, you shameless tempter!—I wish I could get some one to stick a knife into you!

[*He lays some old letters on one side, finds the torn document of yesterday, takes it up and looks at the pieces; puts it down hurriedly as* GINA *enters.*]

GINA. [*sets a tray with coffee, etc., on the table*] Here's a drop of something hot, if you'd fancy it. And there's some bread and butter and a snack of salt meat.

HIALMAR. [*glancing at the tray*] Salt meat? Never under this roof! It's true I have not had a mouthful of solid food for nearly twenty-four hours; but no matter.—My memoranda! The commencement of my autobiography! What has become of my diary, and all my important papers? [*opens the sitting-room door but draws back*] She is there, too!

GINA. Good Lord! the child must be somewhere!

HIALMAR. Come out.

[*He makes room;* HEDVIG *comes, scared, into the studio.*]

HIALMAR. [*with his hand upon the door-handle, says to* GINA] In these, the last moments I spend in my former home, I wish to be spared from interlopers—— [*goes into the room*]

HEDVIG. [*with a bound towards her mother, asks softly, trembling*] Does that mean me?

GINA. Stay out in the kitchen, Hedvig; or, no—you'd best go into your own room. [*speaks to* HIALMAR *as she goes in to him*] Wait a bit, Ekdal; don't rummage so in the drawers; *I* know where everything is.

HEDVIG. [*stands a moment immovable, in terror and perplexity, biting her lips to keep back the tears; then she clenches her hands convulsively and says softly*] The wild duck.

[*She steals over and takes the pistol from the shelf, opens the garret door a little way, creeps in and draws the door to after her.* HIALMAR *and* GINA *can be heard disputing in the sitting-room.*]

HIALMAR. [*comes in with some manuscript books and old loose papers, which he lays upon the table*] That portmanteau is of no use! There are a thousand and one things I must drag with me.

GINA. [*following with the portmanteau*] Why not leave all the rest for the present and only take a shirt and a pair of woollen drawers with you?

HIALMAR. Whew!—all these exhausting preparations——! [*pulls off his overcoat and throws it upon the sofa*]

GINA. And there's the coffee getting cold.

HIALMAR. H'm. [*drinks a mouthful without thinking of it and then another*]

GINA. [*dusting the backs of the chairs*] A nice job you'll have to find such another big garret for the rabbits.

HIALMAR. What! Am I to drag all those rabbits with me, too?

GINA. You don't suppose grandfather can get on without his rabbits.

HIALMAR. He must just get used to doing without them. Have not I to sacrifice very much greater things than rabbits?

GINA. [*dusting the bookcase*] Shall I put the flute in the portmanteau for you?

HIALMAR. No. No flute for me. But give me the pistol!

GINA. Do you want to take the pistol with you?

HIALMAR. Yes My loaded pistol.

GINA. [*searching for it*] It's gone. He must have taken it in with him.

HIALMAR. Is he in the garret?

GINA. Yes, of course he's in the garret.

HIALMAR. H'm—poor lonely old man.

[*He takes a piece of bread and butter, eats it, and finishes his cup of coffee.*]

GINA. If we hadn't have let that room, you could have moved in there.

HIALMAR. And continued to live under the same roof with——! Never,—never!

GINA. But couldn't you put up with the sitting-room for a day or two? You could have it all to yourself.

HIALMAR. Never within these walls!

GINA. Well, then, down with Relling and Molvik.

HIALMAR. Don't mention those wretches' names to me! The very thought of them almost takes away my appetite.—Oh, no, I must go out into the storm and the snow-drift,—go from house to house and seek shelter for my father and myself.

GINA. But you've got no hat, Ekdal! You've been and lost your hat, you know.

HIALMAR. Oh, those two brutes, those slaves of all the vices! A hat must be procured. [*takes another piece of bread and butter*] Some arrangements must be made. For I have no mind to throw away my life, either. [*looks for something on the tray*]

GINA. What are you looking for?

HIALMAR. Butter.

GINA. I'll get some at once. [*goes out into the kitchen*]

HIALMAR. [*calls after her*] Oh, it doesn't matter; dry bread is good enough for me.

GINA. [*brings a dish of butter*] Look here; this is fresh churned.

[*She pours out another cup of coffee for him; he seats himself on the sofa, spreads more butter on the already buttered bread and eats and drinks awhile in silence.*]

HIALMAR. Could I, without being subject to intrusion—intrusion of any sort—could I live in the sitting-room there for a day or two?

GINA. Yes, to be sure you could, if you only would.

HIALMAR. For I see no possibility of getting all father's things out in such a hurry.

GINA. And, besides, you've surely got to tell him first as you don't mean to live with us others no more.

HIALMAR. [*pushes away his coffee cup*] Yes, there is that, too; I shall have to lay bare the whole tangled story to him—— I must turn matters over; I must have breathing-time; I cannot take all these burdens on my shoulders in a single day.

GINA. No, especially in such horrible weather as it is outside.

HIALMAR. [*touching* WERLE'S *letter*] I see that paper is still lying about here.

GINA. Yes, I haven't touched it.

HIALMAR. So far as I am concerned it is mere waste paper——

GINA. Well, I have certainly no notion of making any use of it.

HIALMAR. ——but we had better not let it get lost all the same;—in all the upset when I move, it might easily——

GINA. I'll take good care of it, Ekdal.

HIALMAR. The donation is in the first instance made to father, and it rests with him to accept or decline it.

GINA. [*sighs*] Yes, poor old father——

HIALMAR. To make quite safe—— Where shall I find some gum?

GINA. [*goes to the bookcase*] Here's the gum-pot.

HIALMAR. And a brush?

GINA. The brush is here, too. [*brings him the things*]

HIALMAR. [*takes a pair of scissors*] Just a strip of paper at the back——[*clips and gums*] Far be it from me to lay hands upon what is not my own—and least of all upon what belongs to a destitute old man—and to—the other as well.—There now. Let it lie there for a time; and when it is dry, take it away. I wish never to see that document again. Never!

[GREGERS WERLE *enters from the passage.*]

GREGERS. [*somewhat surprised*] What,—are you sitting here, Hialmar?

HIALMAR. [*rises hurriedly*] I had sunk down from fatigue.

GREGERS. You have been having breakfast, I see.

HIALMAR. The body sometimes makes its claims felt, too.

GREGERS. What have you decided to do?

HIALMAR. For a man like me, there is only one course possible. I am just putting my most important things together. But it takes time, you know.

GINA. [*with a touch of impatience*] Am I to get the room ready for you, or am I to pack your portmanteau?

HIALMAR. [*after a glance of annoyance at* GREGERS] Pack—and get the room ready!

GINA. [*takes the portmanteau*] Very well; then I'll put in the shirt and the other things. [*goes into the sitting-room and draws the door to after her*]

GREGERS. [*after a short silence*] I never dreamed that this would be the end of it. Do you really feel it a necessity to leave house and home?

HIALMAR. [*wanders about restlessly*] What would you have me do?

—I am not fitted to bear unhappiness, Gregers. I must feel secure and at peace in my surroundings.

GREGERS. But can you not feel that here? Just try it. I should have thought you had firm ground to build upon now—if only you start afresh. And, remember, you have your invention to live for.

HIALMAR. Oh, don't talk about my invention. It's perhaps still in the dim distance.

GREGERS. Indeed!

HIALMAR. Why, great heavens, what would you have me invent? Other people have invented almost everything already. It becomes more and more difficult every day——

GREGERS. And you have devoted so much labor to it.

HIALMAR. It was that blackguard Relling that urged me to it.

GREGERS. Relling?

HIALMAR. Yes, it was he that first made me realize my aptitude for making some notable discovery in photography.

GREGERS. Aha—it was Relling!

HIALMAR. Oh, I have been so truly happy over it! Not so much for the sake of the invention itself, as because Hedvig believed in it— believed in it with a child's whole eagerness of faith.—At least, I have been fool enough to go and imagine that she believed in it.

GREGERS. Can you really think Hedvig has been false towards you?

HIALMAR. I can think anything now. It is Hedvig that stands in my way. She will blot out the sunlight from my whole life.

GREGERS. Hedvig! Is it Hedvig you are talking of? How should she blot out your sunlight?

HIALMAR. [without answering] How unutterably I have loved that child! How unutterably happy I have felt every time I came home to my humble room, and she flew to meet me, with her sweet little blinking eyes. Oh, confiding fool that I have been! I loved her unutterably;—and I yielded myself up to the dream, the delusion, that she loved me unutterably in return.

GREGERS. Do you call that a delusion?

HIALMAR. How should I know? I can get nothing out of Gina; and besides, she is totally blind to the ideal side of these complications. But to you I feel impelled to open my mind, Gregers. I cannot shake off this frightful doubt—perhaps Hedvig has never really and honestly loved me.

GREGERS. What would you say if she were to give you a proof of her love? [listens] What's that? I thought I heard the wild duck——?

HIALMAR. It's the wild duck quacking. Father's in the garret.

GREGERS. Is he? [His face lights up with joy.] I say, you may yet have proof that your poor misunderstood Hedvig loves you!

HIALMAR. Oh, what proof can she give me? I dare not believe in any assurance from that quarter.

GREGERS. Hedvig does not know what deceit means.

HIALMAR. Oh, Gregers, that is just what I cannot be sure of. Who knows what Gina and that Mrs. Sörby may many a time have sat here whispering and tattling about? And Hedvig usually has her ears open, I can tell you. Perhaps the deed of gift was not such a surprise to her, after all. In fact, I'm not sure but that I noticed something of the sort.

GREGERS. What spirit is this that has taken possession of you?

HIALMAR. I have had my eyes opened. Just you notice;—you'll see, the deed of gift is only a beginning. Mrs. Sörby has always been a good deal taken up with Hedvig, and now she has the power to do whatever she likes for the child. They can take her from me whenever they please.

GREGERS. Hedvig will never, never leave you.

HIALMAR. Don't be so sure of that. If only they beckon to her and throw out a golden bait——! And, oh! I have loved her so unspeakably! I would have counted it my highest happiness to take her tenderly by the hand and lead her, as one leads a timid child through a great dark empty room!—I am cruelly certain now that the poor photographer in his humble attic has never really and truly been anything to her. She has only cunningly contrived to keep on a good footing with him until the time came.

GREGERS. You don't believe that yourself, Hialmar.

HIALMAR. That is just the terrible part of it—I don't know what to believe,—I never can know it. But can you really doubt that it must be as I say? Ho-ho, you have far too much faith in the claim of the ideal, my good Gregers! If those others came, with the glamour of wealth about them, and called to the child:—"Leave him: come to us: here life awaits you——!"

GREGERS. [*quickly*] Well, what then?

HIALMAR. If I then asked her: Hedvig, are you willing to renounce that life for me? [*laughs scornfully*] No thank you! You would soon hear what answer I should get.

[*A pistol shot is heard from within the garret.*]

GREGERS. [*loudly and joyfully*] Hialmar!

HIALMAR. There now; he must needs go shooting, too.

GINA. [*comes in*] Oh, Ekdal, I can hear grandfather blazing away in the garret by hisself.

HIALMAR. I'll look in——

GREGERS. [*eagerly, with emotion*] Wait a moment! Do you know what that was?

HIALMAR. Yes, of course I know.

GREGERS. No, you don't know. But *I* do. That was the proof!

HIALMAR. What proof?

GREGERS. It was a child's free-will offering. She has got your father to shoot the wild duck.

HIALMAR. To shoot the wild duck!

GINA. Oh, think of that——!

HIALMAR. What was that for?

GREGERS. She wanted to sacrifice to you her most cherished possession; for then she thought you would surely come to love her again.

HIALMAR. [*tenderly, with emotion*] Oh, poor child!

GINA. What things she does think of!

GREGERS. She only wanted your love again, Hialmar. She could not live without it.

GINA. [struggling with her tears] There, you can see for yourself, Ekdal.

HIALMAR. Gina, where is she?

GINA. [sniffs] Poor dear, she's sitting out in the kitchen, I dare say.

HIALMAR. [goes over, tears open the kitchen door and says] Hedvig, come, come in to me! [looks around] No, she's not here.

GINA. Then she must be in her own little room.

HIALMAR. [without] No, she's not here either. [comes in] She must have gone out.

GINA. Yes, you wouldn't have her anywheres in the house.

HIALMAR. Oh, if she would only come home quickly, so that I can tell her—— Everything will come right now, Gregers; now I believe we can begin life afresh.

GREGERS. [quietly] I knew it; I knew the child would make amends.

[OLD EKDAL appears at the door of his room; he is in full uniform and is busy buckling on his sword.]

HIALMAR. [astonished] Father! Are you there?

GINA. Have you been firing in your room?

EKDAL. [resentfully, approaching] So you go shooting alone, do you, Hialmar?

HIALMAR. [excited and confused] Then it wasn't you that fired that shot in the garret?

EKDAL. Me that fired? H'm.

GREGERS. [calls out to HIALMAR] She has shot the wild duck herself!

HIALMAR. What can it mean? [hastens to the garret door, tears it aside, looks in and calls loudly] Hedvig!

GINA. [runs to the door] Good God, what's that?

HIALMAR. [goes in] She's lying on the floor!

GREGERS. Hedvig! lying on the floor? [goes in to HIALMAR]

GINA. [at the same time] Hedvig! [inside the garret] No, no, no!

EKDAL. Ho-ho! does she go shooting, too, now?

[HIALMAR, GINA, and GREGERS carry HEDVIG into the studio; in her dangling right hand she holds the pistol fast clasped in her fingers.]

HIALMAR. [distracted] The pistol has gone off. She has wounded herself. Call for help! Help!

GINA. [runs into the passage and calls down] Relling! Relling! Doctor Relling; come up as quick as you can!

[HIALMAR and GREGERS lay HEDVIG down on the sofa.]

EKDAL. [quietly] The woods avenge themselves.

HIALMAR. [on his knees beside HEDVIG] She'll soon come to now. She's coming to——; yes, yes, yes.

GINA. [who has come in again] Where has she hurt herself? I can't see anything——

[RELLING comes hurriedly, and immediately after him MOL-VIK; the latter without his waistcoat and necktie, and with his coat open.]

RELLING. What's the matter here?

GINA. They say Hedvig has shot herself.

HIALMAR. Come and help us!

RELLING. Shot herself!

[*He pushes the table aside and begins to examine her.*]

HIALMAR. [*kneeling and looking anxiously up at him*] It can't be dangerous? Speak, Relling! She is scarcely bleeding at all. It can't be dangerous?

RELLING. How did it happen?

HIALMAR. Oh, we don't know——

GINA. She wanted to shoot the wild duck.

RELLING. The wild duck?

HIALMAR. The pistol must have gone off.

RELLING. H'm. Indeed.

EKDAL. The woods avenge themselves. But I'm not afraid, all the same. [*goes into the garret and closes the door after him*]

HIALMAR. Well, Relling,—why don't you say something?

RELLING. The ball has entered the breast.

HIALMAR. Yes, but she's coming to!

RELLING. Surely you can see that Hedvig is dead.

GINA. [*bursts into tears*] Oh, my child, my child——

GREGERS. [*huskily*] In the depths of the sea——

HIALMAR. [*jumps up*] No, no, she must live! Oh, for God's sake, Relling—only a moment—only just till I can tell her how unspeakably I loved her all the time!

RELLING. The bullet has gone through her heart. Internal hemorrhage. Death must have been instantaneous.

HIALMAR. And I! I hunted her from me like an animal! And she crept terrified into the garret and died for love of me! [*sobbing*] I can never atone to her! I can never tell her——! [*clenches his hands and cries, upwards*] O thou above——! If thou be indeed! Why hast thou done this thing to me?

GINA. Hush, hush, you mustn't go on that awful way. We had no right to keep her, I suppose.

MOLVIK. The child is not dead, but sleepeth.

RELLING. Bosh.

HIALMAR. [*becomes calm, goes over to the sofa, folds his arms and looks at* HEDVIG] There she lies so stiff and still.

RELLING. [*tries to loosen the pistol*] She's holding it so tight, so tight.

GINA. No, no, Relling, don't break her fingers; let the pistol be.

HIALMAR. She shall take it with her.

GINA. Yes, let her. But the child mustn't lie here for a show. She shall go to her own room, so she shall. Help me, Ekdal.

[HIALMAR *and* GINA *take* HEDVIG *between them.*]

HIALMAR. [*as they are carrying her*] Oh, Gina, Gina, can you survive this?

GINA. We must help each other to bear it. For now at least she belongs to both of us.

MOLVIK. [*stretches out his arms and mumbles*] Blessed be the Lord; to earth thou shalt return; to earth thou shalt return——

RELLING. [*whispers*] Hold your tongue, you fool; you're drunk.

[HIALMAR *and* GINA *carry the body out through the kitchen door.* RELLING *shuts it after them.* MOLVIK *slinks out into the passage.*]

RELLING. [*goes over to* GREGERS *and says*] No one shall ever convince me that the pistol went off by accident.

GREGERS. [*who has stood terrified, with convulsive twitchings*] Who can say how the dreadful thing happened?

RELLING. The powder has burnt the body of her dress. She must have pressed the pistol right against her breast and fired.

GREGERS. Hedvig has not died in vain. Did you not see how sorrow set free what is noble in him?

RELLING. Most people are ennobled by the actual presence of death. But how long do you suppose this nobility will last in him?

GREGERS. Why should it not endure and increase throughout his life?

RELLING. Before a year is over, little Hedvig will be nothing to him but a pretty theme for declamation.

GREGERS. How dare you say that of Hialmar Ekdal?

RELLING. We will talk of this again, when the grass has first withered on her grave. Then you'll hear him spouting about "the child too early torn from her father's heart;" then you'll see him steep himself in a syrup of sentiment and self-admiration and self-pity. Just you wait!

GREGERS. If you are right and I am wrong, then life is not worth living.

RELLING. Oh, life would be quite tolerable, after all, if only we could be rid of the confounded duns that keep on pestering us, in our poverty, with the claim of the ideal.

GREGERS. [*looking straight before him*] In that case, I am glad that my destiny is what it is.

RELLING. May I inquire,—what is your destiny?

GREGERS. [*going*] To be the thirteenth at table.

RELLING. The devil it is.

ROCOCO

GRANVILLE BARKER

Rococo was first produced on October 3, 1911. It was one of a bill of three one-act plays which Barker directed as the last of a series of productions presented by him and his wife, Lillah McCarthy, who acted in it, in a season at the Little Theatre in London. Barker's stage-direction comment on Mr. Uglow's praise of the Germans ("This was before the war. What he says of them now is unprintable") indicates that he must have touched up the play before its publication in 1917. In any case, Barker, who published as many as three versions of his play *The Voysey Inheritance*, was a compulsive reviser. In reading *Rococo*, it is well to remember that Barker's excessive stage directions, whether they amuse or offend you, are interrupting the rhythm of his farce; the production in your head must move from shambles to calm to shambles with all deliberate speed. There is method in the novelistic open and close, for Barker, who was both an actor and director, wants to give you an idea of a kind of chaos on stage; he knows that individual lines will be lost in the melée.

Rococo†

CHARACTERS

THE VICAR
REGINALD, *his nephew*
MRS. REGINALD
MRS. UNDERWOOD, *the Vicar's wife*

MISS UNDERWOOD, *the Vicar's sister*
MORTIMER UGLOW, *Reginald's father*

Do you know how ugly the drawing-room of an English vicarage can be? Yes, I am aware of all that there should be about it; the old-world grace and charm of Jane-Austenism. One should sit upon Chippendale and glimpse the grey Norman church-tower through the casement. But what of the pious foundations of a more industrial age, churches built in mid-nineteenth century and rather scamped in the building, dedicated to the Glory of God and the soul's health of some sweating and sweated urban district?

† Reprinted by permission of the Trustees of the Granville-Barker Estates and Field Roscoe & Co.

155

The Bishop would have a vicarage added, grumbled the church-donor. Well, then, consider his comfort a little, but to the glory of the Vicar nothing need be done. And nothing was. The architect (this an added labour of but little love to him) would give an ecclesiastical touch to the front porch, a pointed top to the front door, add some stained glass to the staircase window. But a mean house, a stuffy house, and the Vicar must indeed have fresh air in his soul if mean and stuffy doctrine was not to be generated there.

The drawing-room would be the best room, and not a bad room in its way, if it weren't that its proportions were vile, as though it felt it wanted to be larger than it was, and if the window and the fireplace and the door didn't seem to be quarrelling as to which should be the most conspicuous. The fireplace wins.

This particular one in this particular drawing-room is of yellow wood, stained and grained. It reaches not quite to the ceiling. It has a West Front air, if looking-glass may stand for windows; it is fretted, moreover, here and there, with little trefoil holes. It bears a full assault of THE VICAR'S *wife's ideas of how to make the place "look nice." There is the clock, of course, which won't keep time; there are the vases which won't hold water; framed photographs, as many as can be crowded on the shelves; in every other crevice knick-knacks. Then, if you stand, as* THE VICAR *often stands, at this point of vantage you are conscious of the wall-paper of amber and blue with a frieze above it measuring off yard by yard a sort of desert scene, a mountain, a lake, three palm trees, two camels; and again; and again; until by the corner a camel and a palm tree are cut out. On the walls there are pictures, of course. Two of them convey to you in a vague and water-colour sort of way that an English countryside is pretty. There is "Christ among the Doctors", with a presentation brass plate on its frame; there is "Simply to Thy Cross I Cling." And there is an illuminated testimonial to* THE VICAR, *a mark of affection and esteem from the flock he ministered to as senior curate.*

The furniture is either very heavy, stuffed, sprung, and tapestry-covered, or very light. There are quite a number of small tables (occasional-tables they are called), which should have four legs but have only three. There are several chairs, too, on which it would be unwise to sit down.

In the centre of the room, beneath the hanging, pink-shaded, electric chandelier, is a mahogany monument, a large round table of the "pedestal" variety, and on it tower to a climax the vicarage symbols of gentility and culture. In the centre of this table, beneath a glass shade, an elaborate reproduction of some sixteenth-century Pietà (a little High Church, it is thought; but Art, for some reason, runs that way). It stands on a Chinese silk mat, sent home by some exiled uncle. It is symmetrically surrounded by gift books, a photograph album, a tray of painted Indian figures (very jolly! another gift from the exiled uncle), and a whale's tooth. The whole affair is draped with a red embroidered cloth.

The window of the room, with so many sorts of curtains and blinds to it that one would think THE VICAR *hatched conspiracies here by night, admits but a blurring light, which the carpet (Brussels) reflects, toned to an ugly yellow.*

You really would not expect such a thing to be happening in such a place, but this carpet is at the moment the base of an apparently mortal struggle. THE VICAR *is undermost, his baldish head, when he tries to raise it, falls back and bumps. Kneeling on him, throttling his collar, is a hefty young man conscientiously out of temper, with scarlet face glowing against carrotty hair. His name is* REGINALD *and he is (one regrets to add)* THE VICAR'S *nephew, though it be only by marriage.* THE VICAR'S *wife, fragile and fifty, is making pathetic attempts to pull him off.*

"Have you had enough?" *asks* REGINALD *and grips* THE VICAR *hard.*

"Oh, Reginald . . . be good," *is all* THE VICAR'S *wife's appeal.*

Not two yards off a minor battle rages. MRS. REGINALD, *coming up to reinforce, was intercepted by* MISS UNDERWOOD, THE VICAR'S *sister, on the same errand. The elder lady now has the younger pinned by the elbows and she emphasises this very handsome control of the situation by teeth-rattling shakes.*

"Cat . . . cat . . . cat!" *gasps* MRS. REGINALD, *who is plump and flaxen and easily disarranged.*

MISS UNDERWOOD *only shakes her again.* "I'll teach you manners, miss."

"Oh, Reginald . . . do drop him," *moans poor* MRS. UNDERWOOD. *For this is really very bad for* THE VICAR.

"Stick a pin into him, Mary," *advises her sister-in-law. Whereat* MRS. REGINALD *yelps in her iron grasp,*

"Don't you dare . . . it's poisonous," *and then,* "Oh . . . if you weren't an old woman I'd have boxed your ears."

Three violent shakes. "Would you? Would you? Would you?"

"I haven't got a pin, Carinthia," *says* MRS. UNDERWOOD. *She has conscientiously searched.*

"Pull his hair, then," *commands* CARINTHIA.

At intervals, like a signal gun, REGINALD *repeats his query:* "Have you had enough?" *And* THE VICAR, *though it is evident that he has, still, with some unsurrendering school-days' echo answering in his mind, will only gasp,* "Most undignified . . . clergyman of the Church of England . . . your host, sir . . . ashamed of you . . . let me up at once."

MRS. UNDERWOOD *has failed at the hair; she flaps her hands in despair.* "It's too short, Carinthia," *she moans.*

MRS. REGINALD *begins to sob pitifully. It is very painful to be tightly held by the elbows from behind. So* MISS UNDERWOOD, *with the neatest of twists and pushes, lodges her in a chair, and thus released herself, folds her arms and surveys the situation.* "Box my ears, would you?" *is her postscript.*

MRS. REGINALD. Well . . . you boxed father's.

MISS UNDERWOOD. Where is your wretched father-in-law? [*Her hawk-*

like eye surveys the room for this unknown in vain.]

REGINALD. [*the proper interval having apparently elapsed*] Have you had enough?

> [*Dignified he cannot look, thus outstretched.* THE VICAR, *therefore, assumes a mixed expression of saintliness and obstinacy, his next best resource. His poor wife moans again.*]

MRS. UNDERWOOD. Oh, please, Reginald . . . the floor's so hard for him!

REGINALD. [*a little anxious to have done with it himself*] Have you had enough?

THE VICAR. [*quite supine*] Do you consider this conduct becoming a gentleman?

MRS. UNDERWOOD. And . . . Simon! . . . if the servants have heard . . . they must have heard. What will they think?

> [*No, even this heart-breaking appeal falls flat.*]

REGINALD. Say you've had enough and I'll let you up.

THE VICAR. [*reduced to casuistry*] It's not at all the sort of thing I ought to say.

MRS. UNDERWOOD. [*so helpless*] Oh . . . I think you might say it, Simon, just for once.

MISS UNDERWOOD. [*grim with the pride of her own victory*] Say nothing of the sort, Simon!

> [THE VICAR *has a burst of exasperation; for, after all, he is on the floor and being knelt on.*]

THE VICAR. Confound it all, then, Carinthia, why don't you do something?

> [CARINTHIA *casts a tactical eye over* REGINALD. THE VICAR *adds in parenthesis . . . a human touch! . . .*]

THE VICAR. Don't kneel there, you young fool, you'll break my watch!

MISS UNDERWOOD. Wait till I get my breath.

> [*But this prospect raises in* MRS. UNDERWOOD *a perfect dithyramb of despair.*]

MRS. UNDERWOOD. Oh, please, Carinthia . . . No . . . don't start again. Such a scandal! I wonder everything's not broken. [*so coaxingy to* REGINALD] Shall I say it for him?

MRS. REGINALD. [*fat little bantam, as she smooths her feathers in the armchair*] You make him say it, Reggie.

> [*But now the servants are on poor* MRS. UNDERWOOD's *brain. Almost down to her knees she goes.*]

MRS. UNDERWOOD. They'll be coming up to see what the noise is. Oh . . . Simon!

> [*It does strike* THE VICAR *that this would occasion considerable scandal in the parish. There are so few good excuses for being found lying on the carpet, your nephew kneeling threateningly on the top of you. So he makes up his mind to it and enunciates with musical charm; it might be a benediction.*]

THE VICAR. I have had enough.

REGINALD. [*in some relief*] That's all right.

[*He rises from the prostrate church militant; he even helps it rise. This pleasant family party then look at each other, and, truth to tell, they are all a little ashamed.*]

MRS. UNDERWOOD. [*walking round the re-erected pillar of righteousness*] Oh, how dusty you are!

MISS UNDERWOOD. Yes! [*the normal self uprising*] Room's not been swept this morning.

[THE VICAR, *dusted, feels that a reign of moral law can now be resumed. He draws himself up to fully five foot six.*]

THE VICAR. Now, sir, you will please apologise.

REGINALD. [*looking very muscular*] I shall not.

[THE VICAR *drops the subject.* MRS. REGINALD *mutters and crows from the armchair.*]

MRS. REGINALD. Ha . . . who began it? Black and blue I am! Miss Underwood can apologise . . . your precious sister can apologise.

MISS UNDERWOOD. [*crushing if inconsequent*] You're running to fat, Gladys. Where's my embroidery?

MRS. UNDERWOOD. I put it safe, Carinthia. [*She discloses it and then begins to pat and smooth the dishevelled room.*] Among relations too! One expects to quarrel sometimes . . . it can't be helped. But not fighting! Oh, I never did . . . I feel so ashamed!

MISS UNDERWOOD. [*Britannia-like*] Nonsense, Mary.

MRS. REGINALD. Nobody touched you, Aunt Mary.

THE VICAR. [*after his eyes have wandered vaguely round*] Where's your father, Reginald?

REGINALD. [*quite uninterested; he is straightening his own tie and collar*] I don't know.

[*In the little silence that follows there comes a voice from under the mahogany monument. It is a voice at once dignified and pained, and the property of Reginald's father, whose name is* MORTIMER UGLOW. *And it says . . .*]

THE VOICE. I am here.

MRS. UNDERWOOD. [*who may be forgiven nerves*] Oh, how uncanny!

REGINALD. [*still at his tie*] Well, you can come out, father, it's quite safe.

THE VOICE. [*most unexpectedly*] I shall not. [*and then more unexpectedly still*] You can all leave the room.

THE VICAR. [*who is generally resentful*] Leave the room! whose room is it, mine or yours? Come out, Mortimer, and don't be a fool.

[*But there is only silence. Why will not* MR. UGLOW *come out? Must he be ratted for? Then* MRS. UNDERWOOD *sees why. She points to an object on the floor.*]

MRS. UNDERWOOD. Simon!

THE VICAR. What is it?

[*Again, and this time as if to indicate some mystery,* MRS. UNDERWOOD *points.* THE VICAR *picks up the object, some disjection of the fight he thinks, and waves it mildly.*]

THE VICAR. Well, where does it go? I wonder everything in the room's not been upset!

MRS. UNDERWOOD. No, Simon, it's not a mat, it's his . . .

[*She concludes with an undeniable gesture, even a smile.* THE VICAR, *sniffing a little, hands over the trophy.*]

REGINALD. [*as he views it*] Oh, of course.

MRS. REGINALD. Reggie, am I tidy at the back?

[*He tidies her at the back—a meticulous matter of hooks and eyes and oh, his fingers are so big.* MRS. UNDERWOOD *has taken a little hand-painted mirror from the mantelpiece, and this and the thing in question she places just without the screen of the falling tablecloth much as a devotee might place an offering at a shrine. But in* MISS UNDERWOOD *dwells no respect for persons.*]

MISS UNDERWOOD. Now, sir, for Heaven's sake put on your wig and come out.

[*There emerges a hand that trembles with wrath; it retrieves the offerings; there follow bumpings into the tablecloth as of a head and elbows.*]

THE VICAR. I must go and brush myself.

MRS. UNDERWOOD. Simon, d'you think you could tell the maids that something fell over . . . they are such tattlers. It wouldn't be untrue. [*It wouldn't.*]

THE VICAR. I should scorn to do so, Mary. If they ask me, I must make the best explanation I can.

[THE VICAR *swims out.* MR. MORTIMER UGLOW, *his wig assumed and hardly awry at all, emerges from beneath the table. He is a vindictive-looking little man.*]

MRS. UNDERWOOD. You're not hurt, Mortimer, are you?

[MR. UGLOW'S *only wound is in the dignity. That he cures by taking the situation oratorically in hand.*]

MR. UGLOW. If we are to continue this family discussion and if Miss Underwood, whom it does not in the least concern, has not the decency to leave the room and if you, Mary, cannot request your sister-in-law to leave it, I must at least demand that she does not speak to me again.

[*Whoever else might be impressed,* MISS UNDERWOOD *is not. She does not even glance up from her embroidery.*]

MISS UNDERWOOD. A good thing for you I hadn't my thimble on when I did it.

MRS. UNDERWOOD. Carinthia, I don't think you should have boxed Mortimer's ears . . . you know him so slightly.

MISS UNDERWOOD. He called me a Futile Female. I considered it a suitable reply.

[*The echo of that epigram brings compensation to* MR. UGLOW. *He puffs his chest.*]

MR. UGLOW. Your wife rallied to me, Reginald. I am much obliged to her . . . which is more than can be said of you.

REGINALD. Well, you can't hit a woman.

MR. UGLOW. [*bitingly*] And she knows it.

MISS UNDERWOOD. Pf!

[*The sound conveys that she would tackle a regiment of men with her umbrella: and she would.*]

REGINALD. [*apoplectic, but he has worked down to the waist*] There's a hook gone.

MRS. REGINALD. I thought so! Lace torn?

REGINALD. It doesn't show much. But I tackled Uncle Simon the minute he touched Gladys . . . that got my blood up all right. Don't you worry. We won.

> [*This callously sporting summary is too much for* MRS. UNDERWOOD: *she dissolves.*]

MRS. UNDERWOOD. Oh, that such a thing should ever have happened in our house! . . . in my drawing-room! ! . . . real blows! ! ! . . .

MRS. REGINALD. Don't cry, Aunt Mary . . . it wasn't your fault.

> [THE VICAR *returns, his hair and his countenance smoother. He adds his patting consolations to his poor wife's comfort.*]

MRS. UNDERWOOD. And I was kicked on the shin.

MRS. REGINALD. Say you're sorry, Reggie.

THE VICAR. My dear Mary . . . don't cry.

MRS. UNDERWOOD. [*clasping her beloved's arm*] Simon did it . . . Reggie was throttling him black . . . he couldn't help it.

THE VICAR. I suggest that we show a more or less Christian spirit in letting bygones be bygones and endeavour to resume the discussion at the point where it ceased to be an amicable one. [*His wife, her clasp on his coat, through her drying tears has found more trouble.*] Yes, there is a slight rent . . . never mind.

> [*The family party now settles itself into what may have been more or less the situations from which they were roused to physical combat.* MR. UGLOW *secures a central place.*]

MR. UGLOW. My sister-in-law Jane had no right to bequeath the Vase . . . it was not hers to bequeath.

> [*That is the gage of battle. A legacy! What English family has not at some time shattered its mutual regard upon this iron rock. One notices now that all these good folk are in deepest mourning, on which the dust of combat stands up the more distinctly, as indeed it should.*]

MRS. UNDERWOOD. Oh, Mortimer, think if you'd been able to come to the funeral and this had all happened then . . . it might have done!

MISS UNDERWOOD. But it didn't, Mary . . . control yourself.

MR. UGLOW. My brother George wrote to me on his deathbed . . . [*and then fiercely to* THE VICAR, *as if this concerned his calling*] . . . on his death-bed, sir. I have the letter here. . . .

THE VICAR. Yes, we've heard it.

REGINALD. And you sent them a copy.

> [MR. UGLOW's *hand always seems to tremble; this time it is with excitement as he has pulled the letter from his pocketbook.*]

MR. UGLOW. Quiet, Reginald! Hear it again and pay attention. [*They settle to a strained boredom.*] "The Rococo Vase presented to me by the Emperor of Germany" . . . Now there he's wrong. [*The sound of his own reading has uplifted him: he condescends to them.*] They're German Emperors, not Emperors of Germany. But George was an inaccurate fellow. Reggie has the same trick . . . it's in the family. I haven't it.

[*He is returning to the letter. But* THE VICAR *interposes, lamblike, ominous though.*]

THE VICAR. I have not suggested on Mary's behalf . . . I wish you would remember, Mortimer, that the position I take up in this matter, I take up purely on my wife's behalf. What have I to gain?

REGINALD. [*clodhopping*] Well, you're her husband, aren't you? She'll leave things to you. And she's older than you are.

THE VICAR. Reginald, you are most indelicate. [*and then, really thinking it is true*] I have forborne to demand an apology from you. . . .

REGINALD. Because you wouldn't get it.

MRS. UNDERWOOD. [*genuinely and generously accommodating*] Oh, I don't want the vase . . . I don't want anything!

THE VICAR. [*He is gradually mounting the pulpit.*] Don't think of the vase, Mary. Think of the principle involved.

MRS. UNDERWOOD. And you may die first, Simon. You're not strong, though you look it . . . all the colds you get . . . and nothing's ever the matter with me.

MR. UGLOW. [*ignored . . . ignored!*] Mary, how much longer am I to wait to read this letter?

THE VICAR. [*ominously, ironically lamblike now*] Quite so. Your brother is waiting patiently . . . and politely. Come, come; a Christian and a businesslike spirit!

[MR. UGLOW's *very breath has been taken to resume the reading of the letter, when on him . . . worse, on that tender topknot of his . . . he finds* MISS UNDERWOOD's *hawklike eye. Its look passes through him, piercing Infinity as she says . . .*]

MISS UNDERWOOD. Why not a skull-cap . . . a sanitary skull cap?

MR. UGLOW. [*with a minatory though fearful gasp*] What's that?

THE VICAR. Nothing, Mortimer.

REGINALD. Some people look for trouble!

MISS UNDERWOOD. [*addressing the Infinite still*] And those that it fits can wear it.

THE VICAR. [*a little fearful himself. He is terrified of his sister, that's the truth. And well he may be.*] Let's have the letter, Mortimer.

MISS UNDERWOOD. Or at least a little gum . . . a little glue . . . a little stickphast for decency's sake.

[*She swings it to a beautiful rhythm. No, on the whole,* MR. UGLOW *will not join issue.*]

MR. UGLOW. I trust that my dignity requires no vindication. Never mind . . . I say nothing. [*and with a forgiving air he returns at last to the letter*] "The Rococo Vase presented to me by the Emperor of Germany" . . . or German Emperor.

THE VICAR. Agreed. Don't cry, Mary. Well, here's a clean one. [*Benevolently he hands her a handkerchief.*]

MR. UGLOW. "On the occasion of my accompanying the mission."

MISS UNDERWOOD. Mission! [*The word has touched a spot.*]

THE VICAR. Not a real mission, Carinthia.

MR. UGLOW. A perfectly real mission. A mission from the Chamber of Commerce at . . . Don't go on as if the world were made up of low church parsons and . . . and . . . their sisters! [*As a convinced secularist behold him a perfect fighting cock.*]

REGINALD. [*bored, but oh, so bored!*] Do get ahead, father.

MR. UGLOW. [*with a flourish*] "Mission et cetera." Here we are. "My dear wife must have the enjoyment" . . . [*Again he condescends to them.*] Why he called her his dear wife I don't know. They hated each other like poison. But that was George all over . . . soft . . . never would face the truth. It's a family trait. You show signs of it, Mary.

THE VICAR. [*soft and low*] He was on his death-bed.

REGINALD. Get on . . . father.

MR. UGLOW. "My wife" . . . She wasn't his dear wife. What's the good of pretending it? . . . "must have the enjoyment of it while she lives. At her death I desire it to be an heirloom for the family." [*And he makes the last sentence tell, every word.*] There you are!

THE VICAR. [*lamblike, ominous, ironic, persistent*] You sit looking at Mary. His sister and yours. Is she a member of the family or not?

MR. UGLOW. [*cocksure*] Boys before girls . . . men before women. Don't argue that . . . it's the law. Titles and heirlooms . . . all the same thing.

MRS. UNDERWOOD. [*worm-womanlike, turning ever so little*] Mortimer, it isn't as if we weren't giving you all the family things . . . the miniature and the bust of John Bright and grandmother's china and the big Shakespeare . . .

MR. UGLOW. Giving them, Mary, giving them?

THE VICAR. Surrendering them willingly, Mortimer. They have ornamented our house for years.

MRS. REGINALD. It isn't as if you hadn't done pretty well out of Aunt Jane while she was alive!

THE VICAR. Oh, delicacy, Gladys! And some regard for the truth!

MRS. REGINALD. [*no nonsense about her*] No, if we're talking business let's talk business. Her fifty pounds a year more than paid you for keeping her, didn't it? Did it or didn't it?

REGINALD. [*gloomily*] She never ate anything that I could see.

THE VICAR. She had a delicate appetite. It needed teasing . . . I mean coaxing. Oh, dear, this is most unpleasant!

REGINALD. Fifty pound a year is nearly a pound a week, you know.

THE VICAR. What about her clothes . . . what about her little holidays . . . what about the doctor . . . what about her temper to the last? [*He summons the classics to clear the sordid air.*] Oh: *De mortuis nil nisi bonum!*

MRS. UNDERWOOD. She was a great trouble with her meals, Reginald.

MR. UGLOW. [*letting rip*] She was a horrible woman. I disliked her more than any woman I've ever met. She brought George to bankruptcy. When he was trying to arrange with his creditors and she came into the room, her face would sour them . . . I tell you, sour them.

MRS. REGINALD. [*She sums it up.*] Well, Uncle Simon's a clergyman and can put up with unpleasant people. It suited them well enough to have her. You had the room, Aunt Mary, you can't deny that. And anyway she's dead now . . . poor Aunt Jane! [*She throws this conventional verbal bone to Cerberus.*] And what with the things she has left you . . . ! What's to be done with her clothes?

[GLADYS *and* MRS. UNDERWOOD *suddenly face each other like two ladylike ghouls.*]

MRS. UNDERWOOD. Well, you remember the mauve silk . . .

THE VICAR. Mary, pray allow me. [*Somehow his delicacy is shocked.*] The Poor.

MRS. REGINALD. [*in violent protest*] Not the mauve silk! Not her black lace shawl!

MISS UNDERWOOD. [*shooting it out*] They will make soup.

[*It makes* MR. UGLOW *jump, physically and mentally too.*]

MR. UGLOW. What!

MISS UNDERWOOD. The proceeds of their sale will make much needed soup . . . and blankets. [*Again her gaze transfixes that wig and she addresses Eternity.*] No brain under it! . . . No wonder it's loose! No brain.

[MR. UGLOW *just manages to ignore it.*]

REGINALD. Where is the beastly vase? I don't know that I want to inherit it.

MR. UGLOW. Yes, may I ask for the second or third time to-day?

MISS UNDERWOOD. The third.

MR. UGLOW. [*He screws a baleful glance at her.*] May I ask for the second or third time . . .

REGINALD. It is the third time, father.

MR. UGLOW. [*his own son, too!*] Reginald, you have no tact. May I ask why the vase is not to be seen?

MISS UNDERWOOD. [*sharply*] It's put away.

MRS. REGINALD. [*As sharp as she. Never any nonsense about* GLADYS.] Why?

MR. UGLOW. Gladys . . . ignore that, please, Mary?

MRS. UNDERWOOD. Yes, Mortimer.

MR. UGLOW. It has been chipped.

THE VICAR. It has not been chipped.

MR. UGLOW. If it has been chipped . . .

THE VICAR. I say it has not been chipped.

MR. UGLOW. If it had been chipped, sir . . . I should have held you responsible! Produce it.

[*He is indeed very much of a man. A little more and he'll slap his chest. But* THE VICAR, *lamblike, etc. . . . we can now add dangerous.*]

THE VICAR. Oh, no, we must not be ordered to produce it.

MR. UGLOW. [*trumpet-toned*] Produce it, Simon.

THE VICAR. Neither must we be shouted at.

MISS UNDERWOOD. . . . or bawled at. Bald at! Ha, ha!

> [*And she taps her grey-haired parting with a thimbled finger to emphasize the pun.* MR. UGLOW *rises, too intent on his next impressive stroke even to notice it, or seem to.*]

MR. UGLOW. Simon, if you do not instantly produce the vase I shall refuse to treat this any longer in a friendly way. I shall place the matter in the hands of my solicitors.

> [*This, in any family—is it not the final threat?* MRS. UNDER-WOOD *is genuinely shocked.*]

MRS. UNDERWOOD. Oh, Simon!

THE VICAR. As a matter of principle, Mary. . . .

REGINALD. [*impartially*] What rot!

MRS. UNDERWOOD. It was put away, I think, so that the sight of it might not rouse discussion . . . wasn't it, Simon?

REGINALD. Well, we've had the discussion. Now get it out.

THE VICAR. [*lamblike . . . etc.; add obstinate now*] It is my principle not to submit to dictation. If I were asked politely to produce it. . . .

REGINALD. Ask him politely, father.

MR. UGLOW. [*Why shouldn't he have principles, too?*] I don't think I can. To ask politely might be an admission of some right of his to detain the property. This matter will go further. I shall commit myself in nothing without legal advice.

MRS. REGINALD. You get it out, Aunt Mary.

MRS. UNDERWOOD. [*almost thankful to be helpless in the matter*] I can't. I don't know where it is.

MR. UGLOW. [*all the instinct for Law in him blazing*] You don't . . . ! This is important. He has no right to keep it from you, Mary. I venture to think . . .

THE VICAR. Husband and wife are one, Mortimer.

MR. UGLOW. Not in Law. Don't you cram your religion down my throat. Not in Law any longer. We've improved all that. The married woman's property act! I venture to think. . . .

> [MISS UNDERWOOD *has disappeared. Her comment is to slam the door.*]

MRS. UNDERWOOD. I think perhaps Carinthia has gone for it, Mortimer.

MR. UGLOW. [*The case given him, he asks for costs, as it were.*] Then I object. . . . I object most strongly to this woman knowing the whereabouts of a vase which you, Mary. . . .

THE VICAR. [*a little of the mere layman peeping now*] Mortimer, do not refer to my sister as "this woman."

MR. UGLOW. Then treat my sister with the respect that is due to her, Simon.

> [*They are face to face.*]

THE VICAR. I hope I do, Mortimer.

MR. UGLOW. And will you request Miss Underwood not to return to this room with or without the vase?

THE VICAR. Why should I?

MR. UGLOW. What has she to do with a family matter of mine? I make no comment, Mary, upon the way you allow yourself to be ousted from authority in your own house. It is not my place to comment upon it and I make none. I make no reference to the insults . . . the unwomanly insults that have been hurled at me by this Futile Female. . . .

REGINALD. [*a remembered schoolmaster joke. He feels not unlike one as he watches his two elders squared to each other.*] Apt alliteration's artful aid . . . what?

MR. UGLOW. Don't interrupt.

MRS. REGINALD. You're getting excited again, father.

MR. UGLOW. I am not.

MRS. REGINALD. Father!

[*There is one sure way to touch* MR. UGLOW. *She takes it. She points to his wig.*]

MR. UGLOW. What? Well . . . where's a glass . . . where's a glass?

[*He goes to the mantelpiece mirror. His sister follows him.*]

MRS. UNDERWOOD. We talked it over this morning, Mortimer, and we agreed that I am of a yielding disposition and I said I should feel much safer if I did not even know where it was while you were in the house.

MR. UGLOW. [*with every appropriate bitterness*] And I your loving brother!

THE VICAR. [*not to be outdone by* REGINALD *in quotations*] A little more than kin and less than kind.

MR. UGLOW. [*His wig is straight.*] How dare you, Simon? A little more than ten minutes ago I was struck . . . here in your house. How dare you quote poetry at me?

[THE VICAR *feels he must pronounce on this.*]

THE VICAR. I regret that Carinthia has a masterful nature. She is apt to take the law into her own hands. And I fear there is something about you, Mortimer, that invites violence. I can usually tell when she is going to be unruly; there's a peculiar twitching of her hands. If you had not been aggravating us all with your so-called arguments, I should have noticed it in time and . . . taken steps.

MRS. UNDERWOOD. We're really very sorry, Mortimer. We can always . . . take steps. But . . . dear me! . . . I was never so surprised in my life. You all seemed to go mad at once. It makes me hot now to think of it.

[*The truth about* CARINTHIA *is that she is sometimes thought to be a little off her head. It's a form of genius.*]

THE VICAR. I shall have a headache to-morrow . . . my sermon day.

[MR. UGLOW *now begins to glow with a sense of coming victory. And he's not bad-natured, give him what he wants.*]

MR. UGLOW. Oh, no, you won't. More frightened than hurt! These things will happen . . . the normal gross-feeding man sees red, you know, sees red. Reggie as a small boy . . . quite uncontrollable!

REGINALD. Well, I like that! You howled out for help.

THE VICAR. [*lamblike and only lamblike*] I am willing to obliterate the memory.

MRS. REGINALD. I'm sure I'm black and blue . . . and more torn than I can see.

MR. UGLOW. But what can you do when a woman forgets herself? I simply stepped aside . . . I happen to value my dignity.

> [*The door opens.* MISS UNDERWOOD *with the vase. She deposits it on the mahogany table. It is two feet in height. It is lavishly blotched with gold and white and red. It has curves and crinkles. Its handles are bossy. My God, it is a Vase!*]

MISS UNDERWOOD. There it is.

MR. UGLOW. [*with a victor's dignity*] Thank you, Miss Underwood. [*He puts up gold-rimmed glasses.*] Ah . . . pure Rococo!

REGINALD. The Vi-Cocoa vase![1]

MR. UGLOW. That's not funny, Reginald.

REGINALD. Well . . . I think it is.

> [*The trophy before him,* MR. UGLOW *mellows.*]

MR. UGLOW. Mary, you've often heard George tell us. The Emperor welcoming 'em . . . fine old fellow . . . speech in German . . . none of them understood it. Then at the end . . . Gentlemen, I raise my glass. Hock . . . hock . . . hock!

REGINALD. [*who knows a German accent when he hears it*] A little more spit in it.

MR. UGLOW. Reginald, you're very vulgar.

REGINALD. Is that Potsdam?

> [*The monstrosity has coloured views on it, one back, one front.*]

MR. UGLOW. Yes . . . home of Friedrich der Grosse! A great nation. We can learn a lot from 'em!

> [*This was before the war. What he says of them now is unprintable.*]

REGINALD. Yes. I suppose it's a jolly handsome piece of goods. Cost a lot.

MR. UGLOW. Royal factory . . . built to imitate Sèvres!

> [*Apparently he would contemplate it for hours. But* THE VICAR . . . *Lamblike, etc.; add insinuating now.*]

THE VICAR. Well, Mortimer, here is the vase. Now where are we?

MRS. REGINALD. [*really protesting for the first time*] Oh . . . are we going to begin all over again! Why don't you sell it and share up?

MRS. UNDERWOOD. Gladys, I don't think that would be quite nice.

MRS. REGINALD. I can't see why not.

MR. UGLOW. Sell an heirloom . . . it can't be done.

---

1. For a line like this to elicit a response—a laugh or a shudder, depending on one's reaction to bad puns —the product mentioned has to be a familiar one. My English informants tell me that Vi-Cocoa is a fortified cocoa that was very popular and widely advertised, particularly in the years right before World War I.

REGINALD. Oh, yes, it can. You and I together . . . cut off the entail . . . that's what it's called. It'd fetch twenty pounds at Christie's.

MR. UGLOW. [*The sight of it has exalted him beyond reason.*] More . . . more! First class rococo. I shouldn't dream of it.

> [MISS UNDERWOOD *has resumed her embroidery. She pulls a determined needle as she says* . . .]

MISS UNDERWOOD. I think Mary would have a share in the proceeds, wouldn't she?

MR. UGLOW. I think not.

THE VICAR. Why not, Mortimer?

MR. UGLOW. [*with fine detachment*] Well, it's a point of law. I'm not quite sure . . . but let's consider it in Equity. [*Not that he knows what on earth he means!*] If I died . . . and Reginald died childless and Mary survived us . . . and it came to her? Then there would be our cousins the Bamfords as next inheritors. Could she by arrangement with them sell and . . . ?

MRS. UNDERWOOD. I shouldn't like to sell it. It would seem like a slight on George . . . because he went bankrupt perhaps. And Jane always had it in her bedroom.

MISS UNDERWOOD. [*thimbling the determined needle through*] Most unsuitable for a bedroom.

MRS. UNDERWOOD. [*anxious to please*] Didn't you suggest, Simon, that I might undertake not to leave it out of the family?

THE VICAR. [*covering a weak spot*] In private conversation with you, Mary . . .

MR. UGLOW. [*most high and mighty, oh most!*] I don't accept the suggestion. I don't accept it at all.

THE VICAR. [*and now taking the legal line in his turn*] Let me point out to you, Mortimer, that there is nothing to prevent Mary's selling the vase for her own exclusive benefit.

MR. UGLOW. [*his guard down*] Simon!

THE VICAR. [*satisfied to have touched him*] Once again, I merely insist upon a point of principle.

MR. UGLOW. [*but now flourishing his verbal sword*] And I insist . . . let everybody understand it . . . I insist that all thought of selling an heirloom is given up! Reginald . . . Gladys, you are letting me be exceedingly upset.

REGINALD. Well . . . shall I walk off with it? They couldn't stop me.

> [*He lifts it up; and this simplest of solutions strikes them all stupent; except* MISS UNDERWOOD, *who glances under her bushy eyebrows.*]

MISS UNDERWOOD. You'll drop it if you're not careful.

MRS. UNDERWOOD. Oh, Reggie, you couldn't carry that to the station . . . everyone would stare at you.

THE VICAR. I hope you would not be guilty of such an unprincipled act.

MRS. REGINALD. I won't have it at home, Reg, so I tell you. One of the servants'd be sure to . . . ! [*She sighs desperately.*] Why not sell the thing?

MR. UGLOW. Gladys, be silent.

REGINALD. [*as he puts the vase down, a little nearer the edge of the table*] It is a weight.

    [*So they have argued high and argued low and also argued round about it; they have argued in a full circle. And now there is a deadly calm.* MR. UGLOW *breaks it; his voice trembles a little as does his hand with its signet ring rattling on the table.*]

MR. UGLOW. Then we are just where we started half an hour ago . . . are we, Simon?

THE VICAR. [*lamblike in excelsis*] Precisely, Mortimer.

MR. UGLOW. I'm sorry. I'm very sorry. [*He gazes at them with cool ferocity.*] Now let us all keep our tempers.

THE VICAR. I hope I shall have no occasion to lose mine.

MR. UGLOW. Nor I mine.

    [*He seems not to move a muscle, but in some mysterious way his wig shifts: a sure sign.*]

MRS. UNDERWOOD. Oh, Mortimer, you're going to get excited.

MR. UGLOW. I think not, Mary. I trust not.

REGINALD. [*proffering real temptation*] Father . . . come away and write a letter about it.

MR. UGLOW. [*as his wrath swells*] If I write a letter . . . if my solicitors have to write a letter . . . there are people here who will regret this day.

MRS. UNDERWOOD. [*trembling at the coming storm*] Simon, I'd much sooner he took it . . . I'd much rather he took everything Jane left me.

MR. UGLOW. Jane did not leave it to you, Mary.

MRS. UNDERWOOD. Oh, Mortimer, she did try to leave it to me.

MR. UGLOW. [*running up the scale of indignation*] She may have tried . . . but she did not succeed . . . because she could not . . . because she had no right to do so. [*and reaching the summit*] I am not in the least excited.

    [*Suddenly* MISS UNDERWOOD *takes a shrewd hand in the game.*]

MISS UNDERWOOD. Have you been to your lawyer?

MR. UGLOW. [*swivelling round*] What's that?

MISS UNDERWOOD. Have you asked your lawyer?

    [*He has not.*]

MR. UGLOW. Gladys, I will not answer her. I refuse to answer the . . . the . . . the female.

    [*But he has funked the "futile."*]

MRS. REGINALD. [*soothing him*] All right, father.

MISS UNDERWOOD. He hasn't because he knows what his lawyer would say. Rot's what his lawyer would say!

MR. UGLOW. [*calling on the gods to protect this woman from him*] Heaven knows I wish to discuss this calmly!

REGINALD. Aunt Mary, might I smoke?

MISS UNDERWOOD. Not in the drawing-room.

MRS. UNDERWOOD. No . . . not in the drawing-room, please, Reginald.

MR. UGLOW. You're not to go away, Reginald.

REGINALD. Oh, well . . . hurry up.

> [MR. UGLOW *looks at* THE VICAR. THE VICAR *is actually smiling. Can this mean defeat for the house of Uglow? Never.*]

MR. UGLOW. Do I understand that on your wife's behalf you entirely refuse to own the validity of my brother George's letter . . . where is it? . . . I read you the passage written on his death-bed.

THE VICAR. [*Measured and confident. Victory gleams for him now.*] Why did he not mention the vase in his will?

MR. UGLOW. There were a great many things he did not mention in his will.

THE VICAR. Was his widow aware of the letter?

MR. UGLOW. You know she was.

THE VICAR. Why did she not carry out what you think to have been her husband's intention?

MR. UGLOW. Because she was a beast of a woman.

> [MR. UGLOW *is getting the worst of it, his temper is slipping.*]

MRS. UNDERWOOD. Mortimer, what language about the newly dead!

THE VICAR. An heirloom in the family?

MR. UGLOW. Quite so.

THE VICAR. On what grounds do you maintain that George's intentions are not carried out when it is left to my wife?

> [*And indeed,* "MR. UGLOW *is against the ropes," so to speak.*]

MISS UNDERWOOD. The man hasn't a wig to stand on. . . . I mean a leg.

MR. UGLOW. [*pale with fury, hoarse with it, even pathetic in it*] Don't you speak to me . . . I request you not to speak to me.

> [REGINALD *and* GLADYS *quite seriously think this is bad for him.*]

REGINALD. Look here, father, Aunt Mary will undertake not to let it go out of the family. Leave it at that.

MRS. REGINALD. We don't want the thing, father . . . the drawing-room's full already.

MR. UGLOW. [*the pathos in him growing; he might flood the best Brussels with tears at any moment*] It's not the vase. It's no longer the vase. It's the principle.

MRS. UNDERWOOD. Oh, don't, Mortimer . . . don't be like Simon. That's why I mustn't give in. It'll make it much more difficult if you start thinking of it like that.

MISS UNDERWOOD. [*pulling and pushing that embroidery needle more grimly than ever*] It's a principle in our family not to be bullied.

MRS. REGINALD. [*in almost a vulgar tone, really*] If she'd go and mind her own family's business!

> [THE VICAR *knows that he has his Uglows on the run. Suavely he presses the advantage.*]

THE VICAR. I am sorry to repeat myself, Mortimer, but the vase was left to Jane absolutely. It has been specifically left to Mary. She is under no obligation to keep it in the family.

MR. UGLOW. [*control breaking*] You'll get it, will you . . . you and your precious female sister?

THE VICAR. [*quieter and quieter; the superior quietude*] Oh, this is so unpleasant.

MR. UGLOW. [*control broken*] Never! Never! ! . . . not if I beggar myself in law-suits.

MISS UNDERWOOD. [*a sudden and vicious jab*] Who wants the hideous thing?

MR. UGLOW. [*broken, all of him. In sheer hysterics. Tears starting from his eyes.*] Hideous! You hear her? They'd sell it for what it would fetch. My brother George's rococo vase! An *objet d'art et vertu* . . . an heirloom . . . a family record of public service! Have you no feelings, Mary?

MRS. UNDERWOOD. [*dissolved*] Oh, I'm very unhappy.

[*Again are* MR. UGLOW *and* THE VICAR *breast to breast.*]

THE VICAR. Don't make your sister cry, sir.

MR. UGLOW. Make your sister hold her tongue, sir. She has no right in this discussion at all. Am I to be provoked and badgered by a Futile Female?

[THE VICAR *and* MR. UGLOW *are intent on each other, the others are intent on them. No one notices that* MISS UNDERWOOD'S *embroidery is very decidedly laid down and that her fingers begin to twitch.*]

THE VICAR. How dare you suppose, Mortimer, that Mary and I would not respect the wishes of the dead?

MR. UGLOW. It's nothing to do with you, either.

[MISS UNDERWOOD *has risen from her chair. This* GLADYS *does notice.*]

MRS. REGINALD. I say . . . Uncle Simon.

THE VICAR. What is it?

REGINALD. Look here, Uncle Simon, let Aunt Mary write a letter undertaking. . . . There's no need for all this row . . .

MRS. UNDERWOOD. I will! I'll undertake anything!

THE VICAR. [*the Church on its militant dignity now*] Keep calm, Mary. I am being much provoked, too. Keep calm.

MR. UGLOW. [*stamping it out*] He won't let her . . . he and his sister . . . he won't give way in anything. Why should I be reasonable?

REGINALD. If she will undertake it, will you . . . ?

MRS. REGINALD. Oh, Aunt Mary, stop her!

[*In the precisest manner possible, judging her distance with care, aiming well and true,* MISS UNDERWOOD *has for the second time to-day, soundly boxed* MR. UGLOW'S *ear. He yells.*]

MR. UGLOW. I say . . . I'm hurt.

REGINALD. Look here now . . . not again!

THE VICAR. [*He gets flustered. No wonder.*] Carinthia! I should have taken steps! It is almost excusable.

MR. UGLOW. I'm seriously hurt.

MRS. REGINALD. You ought to be ashamed of yourself.

MISS UNDERWOOD. Did you feel the thimble ?

MRS. UNDERWOOD. Oh, Carinthia, this is dreadful!

MR. UGLOW. I wish to preserve my dignity.

[*He backs out of her reach that he may the better do so.*]

MISS UNDERWOOD. Your wig's crooked.

MRS. REGINALD. [*rousing: though her well-pinched arms have lively recollections of half an hour ago*] Don't you insult my father.

MISS UNDERWOOD. Shall I put it straight? It'll be off again.

[*She advances, her eyes gleaming. To do . . . Heaven knows what!*]

MR. UGLOW. [*still backing*] Go away.

REGINALD. [*who really doesn't fancy tackling the lady either*] Why don't you keep her in hand?

MR. UGLOW. [*backed as far as he can, and in terror*] Simon, you're a cad and your sister's a mad cad. Take her away.

But this THE VICAR *will not endure. He has been called a cad, and that no English gentleman will stand, and a clergyman is a gentleman, sir. In ringing tones and with his finest gesture you hear him.* "Get out of my house!" MR. UGLOW *doubtless could reply more fittingly were it not that* MISS UNDERWOOD *still approaches. He is feebly forcible merely.* "Don't you order me about," *he quavers. What is he but a fascinated rabbit before the terrible woman? The gentlemanly* VICAR *advances*—"Get out before I put you out," *he vociferates*—*Englishman to the backbone. But that is* REGINALD'S *waited-for excuse.* "Oh, no, you don't," *he says and bears down on* THE VICAR. MRS. UNDERWOOD *yelps in soft but agonized apprehension:* "Oh, Simon, be careful." MR. UGLOW *has his hands up, not indeed in token of surrender,—though surrender to the virago poised at him he would,—but to shield his precious wig.*

"Mind my head, do," *he yells; he will have it that it is his head.* "Come away from my father," *calls out* MRS. REGINALD, *stoutly clasping* MISS UNDERWOOD *from behind round that iron-corseted waist.* MISS UNDERWOOD *swivels round.* "Don't you touch me, Miss," *she snaps. But* GLADYS *has weight and the two are toppling ground-ward while* REGINALD, *one hand on* THE VICAR, *one grabbing at* MISS UNDERWOOD *to protect his wife (*"Stop it, do!" *he shouts), is outbalanced. And* THE VICAR *making still determinedly for* MR. UGLOW, *and* MR. UGLOW, *his wig securer, preparing to defy* THE VICAR, *the mêlée is joined once more. Only* MRS. UNDERWOOD *is so far safe.*

The fighters breathe hard and sway. They sway against the great mahogany table. The Rococo Vase totters; it falls; it is smashed to pieces. By a supreme effort the immediate authors of its destruction—linked together—contrive not to sit down among them. MRS. UNDERWOOD *is heard to breathe,* "Oh . . . Thank goodness."

Arms and the Man

BERNARD SHAW

Paradox was once the fashionable word to use in any discussion of Shaw and his work. It came to suggest a kind of intellectual perversity, however, and so passed out of currency. Still, it might be possible to revive the word if we use it to describe Shaw's favorite dramatic technique—the introduction of a situation or a character which appears to be one thing and turns out to be something quite different. *Arms and the Man*, for instance, opens as though it might be a standard romantic melodrama, but how long does Shaw allow that audience expectation to stay alive?

The play was written (or at least finished quickly) so that Florence Farr might offer a new Shaw play—instead of *Widowers' Houses* which she had wanted to revive—in a season of "New Dramatists" (Shaw's phrase) at the Avenue Theatre in London. The play, with Miss Farr as Louka, opened on April 21, 1894, on a double bill with William Butler Yeats's *The Land of Heart's Desire*. It was Shaw's first production in the commercial theater. "It passed for a success, the applause on the first night being as promising as could be wished," Shaw later wrote in the Preface to *Plays Pleasant*, but he went on to indicate that the success was not financial. *Arms* was the first Shaw play to be acted in America; Richard Mansfield, who played Bluntschli, presented it at the Herald Square Theatre in New York on September 17, 1894. Bluntschli is said to have been modeled on Sidney Webb, Shaw's old friend and fellow Fabian.

Arms and the Man

Act I

Night: A lady's bedchamber in Bulgaria, in a small town near the Dragoman Pass, late in November in the year 1885. Through an open window with a little balcony a peak of the Balkans, wonderfully white and beautiful in the starlit snow, seems quite close at hand, though it is really miles away. The interior of the room is not like anything to be seen in the west of Europe. It is half rich Bulgarian, half cheap Viennese. Above the head of the bed, which stands against a little wall cutting off the left-hand corner of the room, is a painted wooden shrine, blue and gold, with an ivory image of Christ, and a light hanging before it in a pierced metal ball suspended by three chains. The principal seat, placed towards the other side of the room and opposite the window, is a Turkish ottoman. The counterpane and hangings of the bed, the window curtains, the little carpet, and all the ornamental textile fabrics in the room are oriental and gorgeous; the paper on the walls is oc-cidental and paltry. The washstand, against the wall on the side nearest the ottoman and window, consists of an enamelled iron basin with a pail beneath it in a painted metal frame, and a single towel on the rail at the side. The dressing table, between the bed and the window, is a common pine table, covered with a cloth of many colours, with an expensive toilet mirror on it. The door is on the side nearest the bed; and there is a chest of drawers between. This chest of drawers is also covered by a variegated native cloth; and on it there is a pile of paper-backed novels, a box of chocolate creams, and a miniature easel with a large photograph of an ex-tremely handsome officer, whose lofty bearing and magnetic glance can be felt even from the portrait. The room is lighted by a candle on the chest of drawers, and another on the dressing table with a box of matches beside it.

The window is hinged doorwise and stands wide open. Outside, a pair of wooden shutters, opening outwards, also stand open. On the balcony a young lady, intensely conscious of the romantic beauty of the night, and of the fact that her own youth and beauty are part of it, is gazing at the snowy Balkans. She is in her night-gown, well covered by a long mantle of furs, worth, on a moderate estimate, about three times the furniture of the room.

Her reverie is interrupted by her mother, CATHERINE PETKOFF, a woman over forty, imperiously energetic, with magnificent black hair and eyes, who might be a very splendid specimen of the wife of a mountain farmer, but is determined to be a Viennese lady, and to that end wears a fashionable tea gown on all occasions.

CATHERINE. *[entering hastily, full of good news]* Raina! *[She pro-nounces it Rah-eena, with the stress on the ee.]* Raina! *[She goes to the bed, expecting to find RAINA there.]* Why, where—? *[RAINA looks into the room.]* Heavens, child! are you out in the night air instead of in your bed? Youll catch your death. Louka told me you were asleep.

RAINA. *[dreamily]* I sent her away. I wanted to be alone. The stars are so beautiful! What is the matter?

CATHERINE. Such news! There has been a battle.

RAINA. *[her eyes dilating]* Ah! *[She comes eagerly to CATHERINE.]*

CATHERINE. A great battle at Slivnitza! A victory! And it was won by Sergius.

RAINA. *[with a cry of delight]* Ah! *[They embrace rapturously.]* Oh, mother! *[then, with sudden anxiety]* Is father safe?

CATHERINE. Of course: he sends me the news. Sergius is the hero of the hour, the idol of the regiment.

RAINA. Tell me, tell me. How was it? *[ecstatically]* Oh, mother! mother! mother! *[She pulls her mother down on the ottoman; and they kiss one another frantically.]*

CATHERINE. [*with surging enthusiasm*] You cant guess how splendid it is. A cavalry charge! think of that! He defied our Russian commanders—acted without orders—led a charge on his own responsibility—headed it himself—was the first man to sweep through their guns. Cant you see it, Raina: our gallant splendid Bulgarians with their swords and eyes flashing, thundering down like an avalanche and scattering the wretched Serbs and their dandified Austrian officers like chaff. And you! you kept Sergius waiting a year before you would be betrothed to him. Oh, if you have a drop of Bulgarian blood in your veins, you will worship him when he comes back.

RAINA. What will he care for my poor little worship after the acclamations of a whole army of heroes? But no matter: I am so happy! so proud! [*She rises and walks about excitedly*.] It proves that all our ideas were real after all.

CATHERINE. [*indignantly*] Our ideas real! What do you mean?

RAINA. Our ideas of what Sergius would do. Our patriotism. Our heroic ideals. I sometimes used to doubt whether they were anything but dreams. Oh, what faithless little creatures girls are! When I buckled on Sergius's sword he looked so noble: it was treason to think of disillusion or humiliation or failure. And yet —and yet—[*She sits down again suddenly*.] Promise me youll never tell him.

CATHERINE. Dont ask me for promises until I know what I'm promising.

RAINA. Well, it came into my head just as he was holding me in his arms and looking into my eyes, that perhaps we only had our heroic ideas because we are so fond of reading Byron and Pushkin,[1] and because we were so delighted with the opera that season at Bucharest. Real life is so seldom like that! indeed never, as far as I knew it then. [*remorsefully*] Only think, mother: I doubted him: I wondered whether all his heroic qualities and his soldiership might not prove mere imagination when he went into a real battle. I had an uneasy fear that he might cut a poor figure there beside all those clever officers from the Tsar's court.

CATHERINE. A poor figure! Shame on you! The Serbs have Austrian officers who are just as clever as the Russians; but we have beaten them in every battle for all that.[2]

RAINA. [*laughing and snuggling against her mother*] Yes: I was only a prosaic little coward. Oh, to think that it was all true! that Sergius is just as splendid and noble as he looks! that the world is really a glorious world for women who can see its glory and men who can act its romance! What happiness! what unspeakable fulfilment!

[*They are interrupted by the entry of* LOUKA, *a handsome*

1. Alexander Pushkin is generally recognized as the great Russian Romantic poet; he was influenced by Byron.
2. The reference here and elsewhere in the play to the Austrian officers serving with the Serbs, the Russians with the Bulgarians is an indication of how the great powers kept their fingers in even the smallest of Balkan wars. The details of this particular war are hardly necessary to an understanding of Shaw's play.

proud girl in a pretty Bulgarian peasant's dress with double apron, so defiant that her servility to RAINA *is almost insolent. She is afraid of* CATHERINE, *but even with her goes as far as she dares.*]

LOUKA. If you please, madam, all the windows are to be closed and the shutters made fast. They say there may be shooting in the streets. [RAINA *and* CATHERINE *rise together, alarmed.*] The Serbs are being chased right back through the pass; and they say they may run into the town. Our cavalry will be after them; and our people will be ready for them, you may be sure, now theyre running away. [*She goes out on the balcony, and pulls the outside shutters to; then steps back into the room.*]

CATHERINE. [*businesslike, housekeeping instincts aroused*] I must see that everything is made safe downstairs.

RAINA. I wish our people were not so cruel. What glory is there in killing wretched fugitives?

CATHERINE. Cruel! Do you suppose they would hesitate to kill you —or worse?

RAINA. [*to* LOUKA] Leave the shutters so that I can just close them if I hear any noise.

CATHERINE. [*authoritatively, turning on her way to the door*] Oh no, dear: you must keep them fastened. You would be sure to drop off to sleep and leave them open. Make them fast, Louka.

LOUKA. Yes, madam. [*She fastens them.*]

RAINA. Dont be anxious about me. The moment I hear a shot, I shall blow out the candles and roll myself up in bed with my ears well covered.

CATHERINE. Quite the wisest thing you can do, my love. Goodnight.

RAINA. Goodnight. [*Her emotion comes back for a moment.*] Wish me joy. [*They kiss.*] This is the happiest night of my life—if only there are no fugitives.

CATHERINE. Go to bed, dear; and dont think of them. [*She goes out.*]

LOUKA. [*secretly to* RAINA] If you would like the shutters open, just give them a push like this [*She pushes them: they open: she pulls them to again.*] One of them ought to be bolted at the bottom; but the bolt's gone.

RAINA. [*with dignity, reproving her*] Thanks, Louka; but we must do what we are told. [LOUKA *makes a grimace.*] Goodnight.

LOUKA. [*carelessly*] Goodnight. [*She goes out, swaggering.*]

[RAINA, *left alone, takes off her fur cloak and throws it on the ottoman. Then she goes to the chest of drawers, and adores the portrait there with feelings that are beyond all expression. She does not kiss it or press it to her breast, or shew it any mark of bodily affection; but she takes it in her hands and elevates it, like a priestess.*]

RAINA. [*looking up at the picture*] Oh, I shall never be unworthy of you any more, my soul's hero: never, never, never. [*She replaces it reverently. Then she selects a novel from the little pile of books. She turns over the leaves dreamily; finds her page; turns*

*the book inside out at it; and, with a happy sigh, gets into bed
and prepares to read herself to sleep. But before abandoning herself to fiction, she raises her eyes once more, thinking of the
blessed reality, and murmurs]* My hero! my hero!

[*A distant shot breaks the quiet of the night. She starts,
listening; and two more shots, much nearer, follow, startling
her so that she scrambles out of bed, and hastily blows out
the candle on the chest of drawers. Then, putting her fingers
in her ears, she runs to the dressing table, blows out the light
there, and hurries back to bed in the dark, nothing being
visible but the glimmer of the light in the pierced ball before the image, and the starlight seen through the slits at
the top of the shutters. The firing breaks out again: there
is a startling fusillade quite close at hand. Whilst it is still
echoing, the shutters disappear, pulled open from without;
and for an instant the rectangle of snowy starlight flashes
out with the figure of a man silhouetted in black upon it.
The shutters close immediately; and the room is dark again.
But the silence is now broken by the sound of panting. Then
there is a scratch; and the flame of a match is seen in the
middle of the room.*]

RAINA. [*crouching on the bed*] Who's there? [*The match is out instantly.*]Who's there? Who is that?

A MAN'S VOICE. [*in the darkness, subduedly, but threateningly*] Sh
—sh! Dont call out; or youll be shot. Be good; and no harm will
happen to you. [*She is heard leaving her bed, and making for the
door.*] Take care: it's no use trying to run away.

RAINA. But who—

THE VOICE. [*warning*] Remember: if you raise your voice my revolver will go off. [*commandingly*] Strike a light and let me see
you. Do you hear. [*Another moment of silence and darkness as
she retreats to the chest of drawers. Then she lights a candle; and
the mystery is at an end. He is a man of about 35, in a deplorable
plight, bespattered with mud and blood and snow, his belt and
the strap of his revolver case keeping together the torn ruins of
the blue tunic of a Serbian artillery officer. All that the candle-
light and his unwashed unkempt condition make it possible to
discern is that he is of middling stature and undistinguished appearance, with strong neck and shoulders, roundish obstinate
looking head covered with short crisp bronze curls, clear quick
eyes and good brows and mouth, hopelessly prosaic nose like that
of a strong minded baby, trim soldierlike carriage and energetic
manner, and with all his wits about him in spite of his desperate
predicament: even with a sense of the humor of it, without, however, the least intention of trifling with it or throwing away a
chance. Reckoning up what he can guess about* RAINA: *her age,
her social position, her character, and the extent to which she is
frightened, he continues, more politely but still most determinedly.*] Excuse my disturbing you; but you recognize my uniform? Serb! If I'm caught I shall be killed. [*menacingly*] Do you

understand that?

RAINA. Yes.

THE MAN. Well, I dont intend to get killed if I can help it. [*still more formidably*] Do you understand that? [*He locks the door quickly but quietly.*]

RAINA. [*disdainfully*] I suppose not. [*She draws herself up superbly, and looks him straight in the face, adding, with cutting emphasis*] Some soldiers, I know, are afraid to die.

THE MAN. [*with grim goodhumor*] All of them, dear lady, all of them, believe me. It is our duty to live as long as we can. Now, if you raise an alarm—

RAINA. [*cutting him short*] You will shoot me. How do you know that *I* am afraid to die?

THE MAN. [*cunningly*] Ah; but suppose I dont shoot you, what will happen then? A lot of your cavalry will burst into this pretty room of yours and slaughter me here like a pig; for I'll fight like a demon: they shant get me into the street to amuse themselves with: I know what they are. Are you prepared to receive that sort of company in your present undress? [RAINA, *suddenly conscious of her nightgown, instinctively shrinks and gathers it more closely about her neck. He watches her and adds pitilessly*] Hardly presentable, eh? [*She turns to the ottoman. He raises his pistol instantly, and cries*] Stop! [*She stops.*] Where are you going?

RAINA. [*with dignified patience*] Only to get my cloak.

THE MAN. [*passing swiftly to the ottoman and snatching the cloak*] A good idea! I'll keep the cloak; and youll take care that nobody comes in and sees you without it. This is a better weapon than the revolver: eh? [*He throws the pistol down on the ottoman.*]

RAINA. [*revolted*] It is not the weapon of a gentleman!

THE MAN. It's good enough for a man with only you to stand between him and death. [*As they look at one another for a moment,* RAINA *hardly able to believe that even a Serbian officer can be so cynically and selfishly unchivalrous, they are startled by a sharp fusillade in the street. The chill of imminent death hushes the man's voice as he adds*] Do you hear? If you are going to bring those blackguards in on me you shall receive them as you are.

[*Clamor and disturbance. The pursuers in the street batter at the house door, shouting* Open the door! Open the door! Wake up, will you! *A man servant's voice calls to them angrily from within* This is Major Petkoff's house: you cant come in here; *but a renewal of the clamor, and a torrent of blows on the door, end with his letting a chain down with a clank, followed by a rush of heavy footsteps and a din of triumphant yells, dominated at last by the voice of* CATHERINE, *indignantly addressing an officer with* What does this mean, sir? Do you know where you are? *The noise subsides suddenly.*]

LOUKA. [*outside, knocking at the bedroom door*] My lady! my lady! get up quick and open the door. If you dont they will break it down.

[*The fugitive throws up his head with the gesture of a man who sees that it is all over with him, and drops the manner he has been assuming to intimidate* RAINA.]

THE MAN. [*sincerely and kindly*] No use, dear: I'm done for. [*flinging the cloak to her*] Quick! wrap yourself up: theyre coming.

RAINA. Oh, thank you. [*She wraps herself up with intense relief.*]

THE MAN. [*between his teeth*] Dont mention it.

RAINA. [*anxiously*] What will you do?

THE MAN. [*grimly*] The first man in will find out. Keep out of the way; and dont look. It wont last long; but it will not be nice. [*He draws his sabre and faces the door, waiting.*]

RAINA. [*impulsively*] I'll help you. I'll save you.

THE MAN. You cant.

RAINA. I can. I'll hide you. [*She drags him towards the window.*] Here! behind the curtains.

THE MAN. [*yielding to her*] Theres just half a chance, if you keep your head.

RAINA. [*drawing the curtain before him*] S-sh! [*She makes for the ottoman.*]

THE MAN. [*putting out his head*] Remember—

RAINA. [*running back to him*] Yes?

THE MAN.—nine soldiers out of ten are born fools.

RAINA. Oh! [*She draws the curtain angrily before him.*]

THE MAN. [*looking out at the other side*] If they find me, I promise you a fight: a devil of a fight.

[*She stamps at him. He disappears hastily. She takes off her cloak, and throws it across the foot of the bed. Then, with a sleepy, disturbed air, she opens the door.* LOUKA *enters excitedly.*]

LOUKA. One of those beasts of Serbs has been seen climbing up the waterpipe to your balcony. Our men went to search for him; and they are so wild and drunk and furious. [*She makes for the other side of the room to get as far from the door as possible.*] My lady says you are to dress at once and to—[*She sees the revolver lying on the ottoman, and stops, petrified.*]

RAINA. [*as if annoyed at being disturbed*] They shall not search here. Why have they been let in?

CATHERINE. [*coming in hastily*] Raina, darling, are you safe? Have you seen anyone or heard anything?

RAINA. I heard the shooting. Surely the soldiers will not dare come in here?

CATHERINE. I have found a Russian officer, thank Heaven: he knows Sergius. [*speaking through the door to someone outside*] Sir: will you come in now. My daughter will receive you.

[*A young Russian officer, in Bulgarian uniform, enters, sword in hand.*]

OFFICER. [*with soft feline politeness and stiff military carriage*] Good evening, gracious lady. I am sorry to intrude; but there is a Serb hiding on the balcony. Will you and the gracious lady your mother please to withdraw whilst we search?

RAINA. [*petulantly*] Nonsense, sir: you can see that there is no one on the balcony. [*She throws the shutters wide open and stands with her back to the curtain where the man is hidden, pointing to the moonlit balcony. A couple of shots are fired right under the window; and a bullet shatters the glass opposite* RAINA, *who winks and gasps, but stands her ground; whilst* CATHERINE *screams, and the officer, with a cry of* Take care! *rushes to the balcony.*]

THE OFFICER. [*on the balcony, shouting savagely down to the street*] Cease firing there, you fools: do you hear? Cease firing, damn you! [*He glares down for a moment; then turns to* RAINA, *trying to resume his polite manner.*] Could anyone have got in without your knowledge? Were you asleep?

RAINA. No: I have not been to bed.

THE OFFICER. [*impatiently, coming back into the room*] Your neighbors have their heads so full of runaway Serbs that they see them everywhere. [*politely*] Gracious lady: a thousand pardons. Goodnight. [*Military bow, which* RAINA *returns coldly. Another to* CATHERINE, *who follows him out.*]

[RAINA *closes the shutters. She turns and sees* LOUKA, *who has been watching the scene curiously.*]

RAINA. Dont leave my mother, Louka, until the soldiers go away.

[LOUKA *glances at* RAINA, *at the ottoman, at the curtain; then purses her lips secretively, laughs insolently, and goes out.* RAINA, *highly offended by this demonstration, follows her to the door, and shuts it behind her with a slam, locking it violently. The man immediately steps out from behind the curtain, sheathing his sabre. Then, dismissing the danger from his mind in a businesslike way, he comes affably to* RAINA.]

THE MAN. A narrow shave; but a miss is as good as a mile. Dear young lady: your servant to the death. I wish for your sake I had joined the Bulgarian army instead of the other one. I am not a native Serb.

RAINA. [*haughtily*] No: you are one of the Austrians who set the Serbs on to rob us of our national liberty, and who officer their army for them. We hate them!

THE MAN. Austrian! not I. Dont hate me, dear young lady. I am a Swiss, fighting merely as a professional soldier. I joined the Serbs because they came first on the road from Switzerland. Be generous: youve beaten us hollow.

RAINA. Have I not been generous?

THE MAN. Noble! Heroic! But I'm not saved yet. This particular rush will soon pass through; but the pursuit will go on all night by fits and starts. I must take my chance to get off in a quiet interval. [*pleasantly*] You dont mind my waiting just a minute or two, do you?

RAINA. [*putting on her most genteel society manner*] Oh, not at all. Wont you sit down?

THE MAN. Thanks. [*He sits on the foot of the bed.*]

[RAINA *walks with studied elegance to the ottoman and sits down. Unfortunately she sits on the pistol, and jumps up with a shriek. The man, all nerves, shies like a frightened horse to the other side of the room.*]

THE MAN. [*irritably*] Dont frighten me like that. What is it?

RAINA. Your revolver! It was staring that officer in the face all the time. What an escape!

THE MAN. [*vexed at being unnecessarily terrified*] Oh, is that all?

RAINA. [*staring at him rather superciliously as she conceives a poorer and poorer opinion of him, and feels proportionately more and more at her ease*] I am sorry I frightened you. [*She takes up the pistol and hands it to him.*] Pray take it to protect yourself against me.

THE MAN. [*grinning wearily at the sarcasm as he takes the pistol*] No use, dear young lady: theres nothing in it. It's not loaded. [*He makes a grimace at it, and drops it disparagingly into his revolver case.*]

RAINA. Load it by all means.

THE MAN. Ive no ammunition. What use are cartridges in battle? I always carry chocolate instead; and I finished the last cake of that hours ago.

RAINA. [*outraged in her most cherished ideals of manhood*] Chocolate! Do you stuff your pockets with sweets—like a schoolboy—even in the field?

THE MAN. [*grinning*] Yes: isnt it contemptible? [*hungrily*] I wish I had some now.

RAINA. Allow me. [*She sails away scornfully to the chest of drawers, and returns with the box of confectionery in her hand.*] I am sorry I have eaten them all except these. [*She offers him the box.*]

THE MAN. [*ravenously*] Youre an angel! [*He gobbles the contents.*] Creams! Delicious! [*He looks anxiously to see whether there are any more. There are none: he can only scrape the box with his fingers and suck them. When that nourishment is exhausted he accepts the inevitable with pathetic goodhumor, and says, with grateful emotion*] Bless you, dear young lady! You can always tell an old soldier by the inside of his holsters and cartridge boxes. The young ones carry pistols and cartridges: the old ones, grub. Thank you. [*He hands back the box. She snatches it contemptuously from him and throws it away. He shies again, as if she had meant to strike him.*] Ugh! Dont do things so suddenly, gracious lady. It's mean to revenge yourself because I frightened you just now.

RAINA. [*loftily*] Frighten me! Do you know, sir, that though I am only a woman, I think I am at heart as brave as you.

THE MAN. I should think so. You havnt been under fire for three days as I have. I can stand two days without shewing it much; but no man can stand three days: I'm as nervous as a mouse. [*He sits down on the ottoman, and takes his head in his hands.*] Would you like to see me cry?

RAINA. [*alarmed*] No.

THE MAN. If you would, all you have to do is to scold me just as if

I were a little boy and you my nurse. If I were in camp now, theyd play all sorts of tricks on me.

RAINA. [*a little moved*] I'm sorry. I wont scold you. [*Touched by the sympathy in her tone, he raises his head and looks gratefully at her: she immediately draws back and says stiffly*] You must excuse me: our soldiers are not like that. [*She moves away from the ottoman.*]

THE MAN. Oh yes they are. There are only two sorts of soldiers: old ones and young ones. Ive served fourteen years: half of your fellows never smelt powder before. Why, how is it that youve just beaten us? Sheer ignorance of the art of war, nothing else. [*indignantly*] I never saw anything so unprofessional.

RAINA. [*ironically*] Oh! was it unprofessional to beat you?

THE MAN. Well, come! is it professional to throw a regiment of cavalry on a battery of machine guns, with the dead certainty that if the guns go off not a horse or man will ever get within fifty yards of the fire? I couldnt believe my eyes when I saw it.

RAINA. [*eagerly turning to him, as all her enthusiasm and her dreams of glory rush back on her*] Did you see the great cavalry charge? Oh, tell me about it. Describe it to me.

THE MAN. You never saw a cavalry charge, did you?

RAINA. How could I?

THE MAN. Ah, perhaps not. No: of course not! Well, it's a funny sight. It's like slinging a handful of peas against a window pane: first one comes; then two or three close behind him; and then all the rest in a lump.

RAINA. [*her eyes dilating as she raises her clasped hands ecstatically*] Yes, first One! the bravest of the brave!

THE MAN. [*prosaically*] Hm! you should see the poor devil pulling at his horse.

RAINA. Why should he pull at his horse?

THE MAN. [*impatient of so stupid a question*] It's running away with him, of course: do you suppose the fellow wants to get there before the others and be killed? Then they all come. You can tell the young ones by their wildness and their slashing. The old ones come bunched up under the number one guard: they know that theyre mere projectiles, and that it's no use trying to fight. The wounds are mostly broken knees, from the horses cannoning together.

RAINA. Ugh! But I dont believe the first man is a coward. I know he is a hero!

THE MAN. [*goodhumoredly*] Thats what youd have said if youd seen the first man in the charge today.

RAINA. [*breathless, forgiving him everything*] Ah, I knew it! Tell me. Tell me about him.

THE MAN. He did it like an operatic tenor. A regular handsome fellow, with flashing eyes and lovely moustache, shouting his warcry and charging like Don Quixote at the windmills. We did laugh.

RAINA. You dared to laugh!

THE MAN. Yes; but when the sergeant ran up as white as a sheet, and told us theyd sent us the wrong ammunition, and that we couldnt fire a round for the next ten minutes, we laughed at the other side of our mouths. I never felt so sick in my life; though Ive been in one or two very tight places. And I hadnt even a revolver cartridge: only chocolate. We'd no bayonets: nothing. Of course, they just cut us to bits. And there was Don Quixote flourishing like a drum major, thinking he'd done the cleverest thing ever known, whereas he ought to be courtmartialled for it. Of all the fools ever let loose on a field of battle, that man must be the very maddest. He and his regiment simply committed suicide; only the pistol missed fire: thats all.

RAINA. [*deeply wounded, but steadfastly loyal to her ideals*] Indeed! Would you know him again if you saw him?

THE MAN. Shall I ever forget him!

[*She again goes to the chest of drawers. He watches her with a vague hope that she may have something more for him to eat. She takes the portrait from its stand and brings it to him.*]

RAINA. That is a photograph of the gentleman—the patriot and hero—to whom I am betrothed.

THE MAN. [*recognizing it with a shock*] I'm really very sorry. [*looking at her*] Was it fair to lead me on? [*He looks at the portrait again.*] Yes: thats Don Quixote: not a doubt of it. [*He stifles a laugh.*]

RAINA. [*quickly*] Why do you laugh?

THE MAN. [*apologetic, but still greatly tickled*] I didnt laugh, I assure you. At least I didnt mean to. But when I think of him charging the windmills and imagining he was doing the finest thing—[*He chokes with suppressed laughter.*]

RAINA. [*sternly*] Give me back the portrait, sir.

THE MAN. [*with sincere remorse*] Of course. Certainly. I'm really very sorry. [*He hands her the picture. She deliberately kisses it and looks him straight in the face before returning to the chest of drawers to replace it. He follows her, apologizing.*] Perhaps I'm quite wrong, you know: no doubt I am. Most likely he had got wind of the cartridge business somehow, and knew it was a safe job.

RAINA. That is to say, he was a pretender and a coward! You did not dare say that before.

THE MAN. [*with a comic gesture of despair*] It's no use, dear lady: I cant make you see it from the professional point of view. [*As he turns away to get back to the ottoman, a couple of distant shots threaten renewed trouble.*]

RAINA. [*sternly, as she sees him listening to the shots*] So much the better for you!

THE MAN. [*turning*] How?

RAINA. You are my enemy; and you are at my mercy. What would I do if I were a professional soldier?

THE MAN. Ah, true, dear young lady: youre always right. I know how good youve been to me: to my last hour I shall remember those three chocolate creams. It was unsoldierly; but it was angelic.

RAINA. [*coldly*] Thank you. And now I will do a soldierly thing. You cannot stay here after what you have just said about my future husband; but I will go out on the balcony and see whether it is safe for you to climb down into the street. [*She turns to the window.*]

THE MAN. [*changing countenance*] Down that waterpipe! Stop! Wait! I cant! I darent! The very thought of it makes me giddy. I came up it fast enough with death behind me. But to face it now in cold blood—! [*He sinks on the ottoman.*] It's no use: I give up: I'm beaten. Give the alarm. [*He drops his head on his hands in the deepest dejection.*]

RAINA. [*disarmed by pity*] Come: dont be disheartened. [*She stoops over him almost maternally: he shakes his head.*] Oh, you are a very poor soldier: a chocolate cream soldier! Come, cheer up! it takes less courage to climb down than to face capture: remember that.

THE MAN. [*dreamily, lulled by her voice*] No: capture only means death; and death is sleep: oh, sleep, sleep, sleep, undisturbed sleep! Climbing down the pipe means doing something—exerting myself—thinking! Death ten times over first.

RAINA. [*softly and wonderingly, catching the rhythm of his weariness*] Are you as sleepy as that?

THE MAN. Ive not had two hours undisturbed sleep since I joined. I havnt closed my eyes for forty-eight hours.

RAINA. [*at her wit's end*] But what am I to do with you?

THE MAN. [*staggering up, roused by her desperation*] Of course. I must do something. [*He shakes himself; pulls himself together; and speaks with rallied vigor and courage.*] You see, sleep or no sleep, hunger or no hunger, tired or not tired, you can always do a thing when you know it must be done. Well, that pipe must be got down: [*He hits himself on the chest.*] do you hear that, you chocolate cream soldier? [*He turns to the window.*]

RAINA. [*anxiously*] But if you fall?

THE MAN. I shall sleep as if the stones were a feather bed. Goodbye. [*He makes boldly for the window; and his hand is on the shutter when there is a terrible burst of firing in the street beneath.*]

RAINA. [*rushing to him*] Stop! [*She seizes him recklessly, and pulls him quite round.*] Theyll kill you.

THE MAN. [*coolly, but attentively*] Never mind: this sort of thing is all in my day's work. I'm bound to take my chance. [*decisively*] Now do what I tell you. Put out the candle; so that they shant see the light when I open the shutters. And keep away from the window, whatever you do. If they see me theyre sure to have a shot at me.

RAINA. [*clinging to him*] Theyre sure to see you: it's bright moonlight. I'll save you. Oh, how can you be so indifferent! You want me to save you, dont you?

THE MAN. I really dont want to be troublesome. [*She shakes him in her impatience.*] I am not indifferent, dear young lady, I assure you. But how is it to be done?

RAINA. Come away from the window. [*She takes him firmly back to the middle of the room. The moment she releases him he turns mechanically towards the window again. She seizes him and turns him back, exclaiming*] Please! [*He becomes motionless, like a hypnotized rabbit, his fatigue gaining fast on him. She releases him, and addresses him patronizingly.*] Now listen. You must trust to our hospitality. You do not yet know in whose house you are. I am a Petkoff.

THE MAN. A pet what?

RAINA. [*rather indignantly*] I mean that I belong to the family of the Petkoffs, the richest and best known in our country.

THE MAN. Oh yes, of course. I beg your pardon. The Petkoffs, to be sure. How stupid of me!

RAINA. You know how you never heard of them until this moment. How can you stoop to pretend!

THE MAN. Forgive me: I'm too tired to think; and the change of subject was too much for me. Dont scold me.

RAINA. I forgot. It might make you cry. [*He nods, quite seriously. She pouts and then resumes her patronizing tone.*] I must tell you that my father holds the highest command of any Bulgarian in our army. He is [*proudly*] a Major.

THE MAN. [*pretending to be deeply impressed*] A Major! Bless me! Think of that!

RAINA. You shewed great ignorance in thinking that it was necessary to climb up the balcony because ours is the only private house that has two rows of windows. There is a flight of stairs inside to get up and down by.

THE MAN. Stairs! How grand! You live in great luxury indeed, dear young lady.

RAINA. Do you know what a library is?

THE MAN. A library? A roomful of books?

RAINA. Yes. We have one, the only one in Bulgaria.

THE MAN. Actually a real library! I should like to see that.

RAINA. [*affectedly*] I tell you these things to shew you that you are not in the house of ignorant country folk who would kill you the moment they saw your Serbian uniform, but among civilized people. We go to Bucharest every year for the opera season; and I have spent a whole month in Vienna.

THE MAN. I saw that, dear young lady. I saw at once that you knew the world.

RAINA. Have you ever seen the opera of Ernani?

THE MAN. Is that the one with the devil in it in red velvet, and a soldiers' chorus?

RAINA. [*contemptuously*] No!

THE MAN. [*stifling a heavy sigh of weariness*] Then I dont know it.

RAINA. I thought you might have remembered the great scene where Ernani, flying from his foes just as you are tonight, takes refuge in the castle of his bitterest enemy, an old Castilian noble. The noble refuses to give him up. His guest is sacred to him.

THE MAN. [*quickly, waking up a little*] Have your people got that notion?

RAINA. [*with dignity*] My mother and I can understand that notion, as you call it. And if instead of threatening me with your pistol as you did you had simply thrown yourself as a fugitive on our hospitality, you would have been as safe as in your father's house.

THE MAN. Quite sure?

RAINA. [*turning her back on him in disgust*] Oh, it is useless to try to make you understand.

THE MAN. Dont be angry: you see how awkward it would be for me if there was any mistake. My father is a very hospitable man: he keeps six hotels; but I couldnt trust him as far as that. What about your father?

RAINA. He is away at Slivnitza fighting for his country. I answer for your safety. There is my hand in pledge of it. Will that reassure you? [*She offers him her hand.*]

THE MAN. [*looking dubiously at his own hand*] Better not touch my hand, dear young lady. I must have a wash first.

RAINA. [*touched*] That is very nice of you. I see that you are a gentleman.

THE MAN. [*puzzled*] Eh?

RAINA. You must not think I am surprised. Bulgarians of really good standing—people in our position—wash their hands nearly every day. So you see I can appreciate your delicacy. You may take my hand. [*She offers it again.*]

THE MAN. [*kissing it with his hands behind his back*] Thanks, gracious young lady: I feel safe at last. And now would you mind breaking the news to your mother? I had better not stay here secretly longer than is necessary.

RAINA. If you will be so good as to keep perfectly still whilst I am away.

THE MAN. Certainly. [*He sits down on the ottoman.*]

[RAINA *goes to the bed and wraps herself in the fur cloak. His eyes close. She goes to the door. Turning for a last look at him, she sees that he is dropping off to sleep.*]

RAINA. [*at the door*] You are not going asleep, are you? [*He murmurs inarticulately: she runs to him and shakes him.*] Do you hear? Wake up: you are falling asleep.

THE MAN. Eh? Falling aslee—? Oh no: not the least in the world: I was only thinking. It's all right: I'm wide awake.

RAINA. [*severely*] Will you please stand up while I am away. [*He rises reluctantly.*] All the time, mind.

THE MAN. [*standing unsteadily*] Certainly. Certainly: you may depend on me.

[RAINA *looks doubtfully at him. He smiles weakly. She goes reluctantly, turning again at the door, and almost catching him in the act of yawning. She goes out.*]

THE MAN. [*drowsily*] Sleep, sleep, sleep, sleep, slee—[*The words trail off into a murmur. He wakes again with a shock on the point of falling.*] Where am I? Thats what I want to know: where am I? Must keep awake. Nothing keeps me awake except danger: remember that: [*intently*] danger, danger, danger, dan—[*trailing off again: another shock*] Wheres danger? Mus' find it. [*He starts off vaguely round the room in search of it.*] What am I looking for? Sleep—danger—dont know. [*He stumbles against the bed.*] Ah yes: now I know. All right now. I'm to go to bed, but not to sleep. Be sure not to sleep, because of danger. Not to lie down either, only sit down. [*He sits on the bed. A blissful expression comes into his face.*] Ah! [*With a happy sigh he sinks back at full length; lifts his boots into the bed with a final effort; and falls fast asleep instantly.*]

[CATHERINE *comes in, followed by* RAINA.]

RAINA. [*looking at the ottoman*] He's gone! I left him here.

CATHERINE. Here! Then he must have climbed down from the—

RAINA. [*seeing him*] Oh! [*She points.*]

CATHERINE. [*scandalized*] Well! [*She strides to the bed,* RAINA *following until she is opposite her on the other side.*] He's fast asleep. The brute!

RAINA. [*anxiously*] Sh!

CATHERINE. [*shaking him*] Sir! [*shaking him again, harder*] Sir!! [*vehemently, shaking very hard*] Sir!!!

RAINA. [*catching her arm*] Dont, mamma; the poor darling is worn out. Let him sleep.

CATHERINE. [*letting him go, and turning amazed to* RAINA] The poor darling! Raina!!! [*She looks sternly at her daughter.*]

[THE MAN *sleeps profoundly.*]

Act II

The sixth of March, 1886. In the garden of MAJOR PETKOFF'S house. It is a fine spring morning: the garden looks fresh and pretty. Beyond the paling the tops of a couple of minarets can be seen, shewing that there is a valley there, with the little town in it. A few miles further the Balkan mountains rise and shut in the landscape. Looking towards them from within the garden, the side of the house is seen on the left, with a garden door reached by a little flight of steps. On the right the stable yard, with its gateway, encroaches on the garden. There are fruit bushes along the paling and house, covered with washing spread out to dry. A path runs by the house, and rises by two steps at the corner, where it turns out of sight. In the middle, a small table, with two bent wood chairs at it, is laid for breakfast with Turkish coffee pot, cups, rolls, etc.; but the cups have been used and the bread broken. There is a wooden garden seat against the wall on the right.

LOUKA, smoking a cigaret, is standing between the table and the house, turning her back with angry disdain on a man servant who is lecturing her. He is a middle-aged man of cool temperament and low but clear and keen intelligence, with the complacency of the

servant who values himself on his rank in servitude, and the im-
perturbability of the accurate calculator who has no illusions. He
wears a white Bulgarian costume: jacket with embroidered border,
sash, wide knickerbockers, and decorated gaiters. His head is shaved
up to the crown, giving him a high Japanese forehead. His name is
NICOLA.

NICOLA. Be warned in time, Louka: mend your manners. I know the
mistress. She is so grand that she never dreams that any servant
could dare be disrespectful to her; but if she once suspects that
you are defying her, out you go.

LOUKA. I do defy her. I will defy her. What do I care for her?

NICOLA. If you quarrel with the family, I never can marry you. It's
the same as if you quarrelled with me!

LOUKA. You take her part against me, do you?

NICOLA. [*sedately*] I shall always be dependent on the good will of
the family. When I leave their service and start a shop in Sofia,
their custom will be half my capital: their bad word would ruin
me.

LOUKA. You have no spirit. I should like to catch them saying a word
against me!

NICOLA. [*pityingly*] I should have expected more sense from you,
Louka. But youre young: youre young!

LOUKA. Yes; and you like me the better for it, dont you? But I
know some family secrets they wouldnt care to have told, young
as I am. Let them quarrel with me if they dare!

NICOLA. [*with compassionate superiority*] Do you know what they
would do if they heard you talk like that?

LOUKA. What could they do?

NICOLA. Discharge you for untruthfulness. Who would believe any
stories you told after that? Who would give you another situation? Who in this house would dare be seen speaking to you ever
again? How long would your father be left on his little farm?
[*She impatiently throws away the end of her cigaret, and stamps
on it.*] Child: you dont know the power such high people have
over the like of you and me when we try to rise out of our poverty
against them. [*He goes close to her and lowers his voice.*] Look
at me, ten years in their service. Do you think I know no secrets?
I know things about the mistress that she wouldnt have the
master know for a thousand levas.[3] I know things about him that
she wouldnt let him hear the last of for six months if I blabbed
them to her. I know things about Raina that would break off her
match with Sergius if—

LOUKA. [*turning on him quickly*] How do you know? I never told
you!

NICOLA. [*opening his eyes cunningly*] So thats your little secret, is
it? I thought it might be something like that. Well, you take my
advice and be respectful; and make the mistress feel that no matter what you know or dont know, she can depend on you to hold

3. The *lev* was the Bulgarian monetary   parently thought the plural, *leva*, was
unit, equal to about a cent; Shaw ap-   the singular.

your tongue and serve the family faithfully. Thats what they like; and thats how youll make most out of them.

LOUKA. [*with searching scorn*] You have the soul of a servant, Nicola.

NICOLA. [*complacently*] Yes: thats the secret of success in service.

[*A loud knocking with a whip handle on a wooden door is heard from the stable yard.*]

MALE VOICE OUTSIDE. Hollo! Hollo there! Nicola!

LOUKA. Master! back from the war!

NICOLA. [*quickly*] My word for it, Louka, the war's over. Off with you and get some fresh coffee. [*He runs out into the stable yard.*]

LOUKA. [*as she collects the coffee pot and cups on the tray, and carries it into the house*] You'll never put the soul of a servant into me.

[MAJOR PETKOFF *comes from the stable yard, followed by* NICOLA. *He is a cheerful, excitable, insignificant, unpolished man of about 50, naturally unambitious except as to his income and his importance in local society, but just now greatly pleased with the military rank which the war has thrust on him as a man of consequence in his town. The fever of plucky patriotism which the Serbian attack roused in all the Bulgarians has pulled him through the war; but he is obviously glad to be home again.*]

PETKOFF. [*pointing to the table with his whip*] Breakfast out here, eh?

NICOLA. Yes, sir. The mistress and Miss Raina have just gone in.

PETKOFF. [*sitting down and taking a roll*] Go in and say Ive come; and get me some fresh coffee.

NICOLA. It's coming, sir. [*He goes to the house door.* LOUKA, *with fresh coffee, a clean cup, and a brandy bottle on her tray, meets him.*] Have you told the mistress?

LOUKA. Yes: she's coming.

[NICOLA *goes into the house.* LOUKA *brings the coffee to the table.*]

PETKOFF. Well: the Serbs havnt run away with you, have they?

LOUKA. No, sir.

PETKOFF. Thats right. Have you brought me some cognac?

LOUKA. [*putting the bottle on the table*] Here, sir.

PETKOFF. Thats right. [*He pours some into his coffee.*]

[CATHERINE, *who, having at this early hour made only a very perfunctory toilet, wears a Bulgarian apron over a once brilliant but now half worn-out dressing gown, and a colored handkerchief tied over her thick black hair, comes from the house with Turkish slippers on her bare feet, looking astonishingly handsome and stately under all the circumstances.* LOUKA *goes into the house.*]

CATHERINE. My dear Paul: what a surprise for us! [*She stoops over the back of his chair to kiss him.*] Have they brought you fresh coffee?

PETKOFF. Yes: Louka's been looking after me. The war's over. The treaty was signed three days ago at Bucharest; and the decree for our army to demobilize was issued yesterday.

CATHERINE. [*springing erect, with flashing eyes*] Paul: have you let the Austrians force you to make peace?

PETKOFF. [*submissively*] My dear: they didnt consult me. What could I do? [*She sits down and turns away from him.*] But of course we saw to it that the treaty was an honorable one. It declares peace—

CATHERINE. [*outraged*] Peace!

PETKOFF. [*appeasing her*]—but not friendly relations: remember that. They wanted to put that in; but I insisted on its being struck out. What more could I do?

CATHERINE. You could have annexed Serbia and made Prince Alexander[4] Emperor of the Balkans. Thats what I would have done.

PETKOFF. I dont doubt it in the least, my dear. But I should have had to subdue the whole Austrian Empire first; and that would have kept me too long away from you. I missed you greatly.

CATHERINE. [*relenting*] Ah! [*She stretches her hand affectionately across the table to squeeze his.*]

PETKOFF. And how have you been, my dear?

CATHERINE. Oh, my usual sore throats: thats all.

PETKOFF. [*with conviction*] That comes from washing your neck every day. Ive often told you so.

CATHERINE. Nonsense, Paul!

PETKOFF. [*over his coffee and cigaret*] I dont believe in going too far with these modern customs. All this washing cant be good for the health: it's not natural. There was an Englishman at Philippopolis who used to wet himself all over with cold water every morning when he got up. Disgusting! It all comes from the English: their climate makes them so dirty that they have to be perpetually washing themselves. Look at my father! he never had a bath in his life; and he lived to be ninety-eight, the healthiest man in Bulgaria. I dont mind a good wash once a week to keep up my position; but once a day is carrying the thing to a ridiculous extreme.

CATHERINE. You are a barbarian at heart still, Paul. I hope you behaved yourself before all those Russian officers.

PETKOFF. I did my best. I took care to let them know that we have a library.

CATHERINE. Ah; but you didnt tell them that we have an electric bell in it? I have had one put up.

PETKOFF. Whats an electric bell?

CATHERINE. You touch a button; something tinkles in the kitchen; and then Nicola comes up.

PETKOFF. Why not shout for him?

CATHERINE. Civilized people never shout for their servants. Ive learnt that while you were away.

PETKOFF. Well, I'll tell you something Ive learnt too. Civilized people dont hang out their washing to dry where visitors can see it; so youd better have all that [*indicating the clothes on the*

4. Prince Alexander of Battenberg, then ruler of Bulgaria.

bushes] put somewhere else.

CATHERINE. Oh, thats absurd, Paul: I dont believe really refined people notice such things.

SERGIUS. [*knocking at the stable gates*] Gate, Nicola!

PETKOFF. Theres Sergius. [*shouting*] Hollo, Nicola!

CATHERINE. Oh, dont shout, Paul: it really isnt nice.

PETKOFF. Bosh! [*He shouts louder than before.*] Nicola!

NICOLA. [*appearing at the house door*] Yes, sir.

PETKOFF. Are you deaf? Dont you hear Major Saranoff knocking? Bring him round this way. [*He pronounces the name with the stress on the second syllable: Sarahnoff.*]

PETKOFF. You must talk to him, my dear, until Raina takes him off our hands. He bores my life out about our not promoting him. Over my head, if you please.

CATHERINE. He certainly ought to be promoted when he marries Raina. Besides, the country should insist on having at least one native general.

PETKOFF. Yes; so that he could throw away whole brigades instead of regiments. It's no use, my dear: he hasnt the slightest chance of promotion until we're quite sure that the peace will be a lasting one.

NICOLA. [*at the gate, announcing*] Major Sergius Saranoff! [*He goes into the house and returns presently with a third chair, which he places at the table. He then withdraws.*]

[MAJOR SERGIUS SARANOFF, *the original of the portrait in* RAINA'S *room, is a tall romantically handsome man, with the physical hardihood, the high spirit, and the susceptible imagination of an untamed mountaineer chieftain. But his remarkable personal distinction is of a characteristically civilized type. The ridges of his eyebrows, curving with an interrogative twist round the projections at the outer corners; his jealously observant eye; his nose, thin, keen, and apprehensive in spite of the pugnacious high bridge and large nostril; his assertive chin would not be out of place in a Parisian salon, shewing that the clever imaginative barbarian has an acute critical faculty which has been thrown into intense activity by the arrival of western civilization in the Balkans. The result is precisely what the advent of nineteenth century thought first produced in England: to wit, Byronism. By his brooding on the perpetual failure, not only of others, but of himself, to live up to his ideals; by his consequent cynical scorn for humanity; by his jejune credulity as to the absolute validity of his concepts and the unworthiness of the world in disregarding them; by his wincings and mockeries under the sting of the petty disillusions which every hour spent among men brings to his sensitive observation, he has acquired the half tragic, half ironic air, the mysterious moodiness, the suggestion of a strange and terrible history that has left nothing but undying remorse, by which Childe Harold fascinated the grandmothers of his English*] *contemporaries. It is clear that here or nowhere is* RAINA'S *ideal hero.* CATHERINE *is hardly less enthusiastic about him than her daughter, and much less reserved in shewing her enthusiasm. As he enters from the stable gate, she rises effusively to greet him.* PETKOFF *is distinctly less disposed to make a fuss about him.*]

PETKOFF. Here already, Sergius! Glad to see you.

CATHERINE. My dear Sergius! [*She holds out both her hands.*]

SERGIUS. [*kissing them with scrupulous gallantry*] My dear mother, if I may call you so.

PETKOFF. [*drily*] Mother-in-law, Sergius: mother-in-law! Sit down; and have some coffee.

SERGIUS. Thank you: none for me. [*He gets away from the table with a certain distaste for* PETKOFF's *enjoyment of it, and posts himself with conscious dignity against the rail of the steps leading to the house.*]

CATHERINE. You look superb. The campaign has improved you, Sergius. Everybody here is mad about you. We were all wild with enthusiasm about that magnificent cavalry charge.

SERGIUS. [*with grave irony*] Madam: it was the cradle and the grave of my military reputation.

CATHERINE. How so?

SERGIUS. I won the battle the wrong way when our worthy Russian generals were losing it the right way. In short, I upset their plans, and wounded their self-esteem. Two Cossack colonels had their regiments routed on the most correct principles of scientific warfare. Two major-generals got killed strictly according to military etiquette. The two colonels are now major-generals; and I am still a simple major.

CATHERINE. You shall not remain so, Sergius. The women are on your side; and they will see that justice is done you.

SERGIUS. It is too late. I have only waited for the peace to send in my resignation.

PETKOFF. [*dropping his cup in his amazement*] Your resignation!

CATHERINE. Oh, you must withdraw it!

SERGIUS. [*with resolute measured emphasis, folding his arms*] I never withdraw.

PETKOFF. [*vexed*] Now who could have supposed you were going to do such a thing?

SERGIUS. [*with fire*] Everyone that knew me. But enough of myself and my affairs. How is Raina; and where is Raina?

RAINA. [*suddenly coming round the corner of the house and standing at the top of the steps in the path*] Raina is here.

[*She makes a charming picture as they turn to look at her. She wears an underdress of pale green silk, draped with an overdress of thin ecru canvas embroidered with gold. She is crowned with a dainty eastern cap of gold tinsel.* SERGIUS *goes impulsively to meet her. Posing regally, she presents her hand: he drops chivalrously on one knee and kisses it.*]

PETKOFF. [*aside to* CATHERINE, *beaming with parental pride*] Pretty, isn't it? She always appears at the right moment.

CATHERINE. [*impatiently*] Yes; she listens for it. It is an abominable habit.

[SERGIUS *leads* RAINA *forward with splendid gallantry. When they arrive at the table, she turns to him with a bend of the head: he bows; and thus they separate, he coming to his place and she going behind her father's chair.*]

RAINA. [*stooping and kissing her father*] Dear father! Welcome home!

PETKOFF. [*patting her cheek*] My little pet girl. [*He kisses her. She goes to the chair left by* NICOLA *for* SERGIUS, *and sits down.*]

CATHERINE. And so you are no longer a soldier, Sergius.

SERGIUS. I am no longer a soldier. Soldiering, my dear madam, is the coward's art of attacking mercilessly when you are strong, and keeping out of harm's way when you are weak. That is the whole secret of successful fighting. Get your enemy at a disadvantage; and never, on any account, fight him on equal terms.

PETKOFF. They wouldnt let us make a fair stand-up fight of it. However, I suppose soldiering has to be a trade like any other trade.

SERGIUS. Precisely. But I have no ambition to shine as a tradesman; so I have taken the advice of that bagman of a captain that settled the exchange of prisoners with us at Pirot, and given it up.

PETKOFF. What! that Swiss fellow? Sergius: Ive often thought of that exchange since. He over-reached us about those horses.

SERGIUS. Of course he over-reached us. His father was a hotel and livery stable keeper; and he owed his first step to his knowledge of horse-dealing. [*with mock enthusiasm*] Ah, he was a soldier: every inch a soldier! If only I had bought the horses for my regiment instead of foolishly leading it into danger, I should have been a field-marshal now!

CATHERINE. A Swiss? What was he doing in the Serbian army?

PETKOFF. A volunteer, of course: keen on picking up his profession. [*chuckling*] We shouldnt have been able to begin fighting if these foreigners hadnt shewn us how to do it: we knew nothing about it; and neither did the Serbs. Egad, thered have been no war without them!

RAINA. Are there many Swiss officers in the Serbian Army?

PETKOFF. No. All Austrians, just as our officers were all Russians. This was the only Swiss I came across. I'll never trust a Swiss again. He humbugged us into giving him fifty ablebodied men for two hundred worn out chargers. They werent even eatable!

SERGIUS. We were two children in the hands of that consummate soldier, major: simply two innocent little children.

RAINA. What was he like?

CATHERINE. Oh, Raina, what a silly question!

SERGIUS. He was like a commercial traveller in uniform. Bourgeois to his boots!

PETKOFF. [*grinning*] Sergius: tell Catherine that queer story his friend told us about how he escaped after Slivnitza. You remember. About his being hid by two women.

SERGIUS. [*with bitter irony*] Oh yes: quite a romance! He was serving in the very battery I so unprofessionally charged. Being a thorough soldier, he ran away like the rest of them, with our cavalry at his heels. To escape their sabres he climbed a waterpipe and made his way into the bedroom of a young Bulgarian lady. The young lady was enchanted by his persuasive commercial traveller's manners. She very modestly entertained him for an hour or so, and then called in her mother lest her conduct should appear unmaidenly. The old lady was equally fascinated; and the fugitive was sent on his way in the morning, disguised in an old coat belonging to the master of the house, who was away at the war.

RAINA. [*rising with marked stateliness*] Your life in the camp has made you coarse, Sergius. I did not think you would have repeated such a story before me. [*She turns away coldly.*]

CATHERINE. [*also rising*] She is right, Sergius. If such women exist, we should be spared the knowledge of them.

PETKOFF. Pooh! nonsense! what does it matter?

SERGIUS. [*ashamed*] No, Petkoff: I was wrong. [*to* RAINA, *with earnest humility*] I beg your pardon. I have behaved abominably. Forgive me, Raina. [*She bows reservedly.*] And you too, madam. [CATHERINE *bows graciously and sits down. He proceeds solemnly, again addressing* RAINA.] The glimpses I have had of the seamy side of life during the last few months have made me cynical; but I should not have brought my cynicism here: least of all into your presence, Raina. I— [*Here, turning to the others, he is evidently going to begin a long speech when the* MAJOR *interrupts him.*]

PETKOFF. Stuff and nonsense, Sergius! Thats quite enough fuss about nothing: a soldier's daughter should be able to stand up without flinching to a little strong conversation. [*He rises.*] Come: it's time for us to get to business. We have to make up our minds how those three regiments are to get back to Philippopolis: theres no forage for them on the Sofia route. [*He goes towards the house.*] Come along. [SERGIUS *is about to follow him when* CATHERINE *rises and intervenes.*]

CATHERINE. Oh, Paul, cant you spare Sergius for a few moments? Raina has hardly seen him yet. Perhaps I can help you to settle about the regiments.

SERGIUS. [*protesting*] My dear madam, impossible: you—

CATHERINE. [*stopping him playfully*] You stay here, my dear Sergius: theres no hurry. I have a word or two to say to Paul. [SERGIUS *instantly bows and steps back.*] Now, dear [*taking* PETKOFF's *arm*]: come and see the electric bell.

PETKOFF. Oh, very well, very well.

[*They go into the house together affectionately.* SERGIUS, *left alone with* RAINA, *looks anxiously at her, fearing that she is still offended. She smiles, and stretches out her arms to him.*]

SERGIUS. [*hastening to her*] Am I forgiven?

RAINA. [*placing her hands on his shoulders as she looks up at him with admiration and worship*] My hero! My king!

SERGIUS. My queen! [*He kisses her on the forehead.*]

RAINA. How I have envied you, Sergius! You have been out in the world, on the field of battle, able to prove yourself there worthy of any woman in the world; whilst I have had to sit at home inactive—dreaming—useless—doing nothing that could give me the right to call myself worthy of any man.

SERGIUS. Dearest: all my deeds have been yours. You inspired me. I have gone through the war like a knight in a tournament with his lady looking down at him!

RAINA. And you have never been absent from my thoughts for a moment. [*very solemnly*] Sergius: I think we two have found the higher love. When I think of you, I feel that I could never do a base deed, or think an ignoble thought.

SERGIUS. My lady and my saint! [*He clasps her reverently.*]

RAINA. [*returning his embrace*] My lord and my—

SERGIUS. Sh—sh! Let me be the worshipper, dear. You little know how unworthy even the best man is of a girl's pure passion!

RAINA. I trust you. I love you. You will never disappoint me, Sergius. [LOUKA *is heard singing within the house. They quickly release each other.*] I cant pretend to talk indifferently before her: my heart is too full. [LOUKA *comes from the house with her tray. She goes to the table, and begins to clear it, with her back turned to them.*] I will get my hat; and then we can go out until lunch time. Wouldnt you like that?

SERGIUS. Be quick. If you are away five minutes, it will seem five hours. [RAINA *runs to the top of the steps, and turns there to exchange looks with him and wave him a kiss with both hands. He looks after her with emotion for a moment; then turns slowly away, his face radiant with the loftiest exaltation. The movement shifts his field of vision, into the corner of which there now comes the tail of* LOUKA's *double apron. His attention is arrested at once. He takes a stealthy look at her, and begins to twirl his moustache mischievously, with his left hand akimbo on his hip. Finally, striking the ground with his heels in something of a cavalry swagger, he strolls over to the other side of the table, opposite her, and says*] Louka: do you know what the higher love is?

LOUKA. [*astonished*] No, sir.

SERGIUS. Very fatiguing thing to keep up for any length of time, Louka. One feels the need of some relief after it.

LOUKA. [*innocently*] Perhaps you would like some coffee, sir? [*She stretches her hand across the table for the coffee pot.*]

SERGIUS. [*taking her hand*] Thank you, Louka.

LOUKA. [*pretending to pull*] Oh, sir, you know I didnt mean that. I'm surprised at you!

SERGIUS. [*coming clear of the table and drawing her with him*] I am surprised at myself, Louka. What would Sergius, the hero of Slivnitza, say if he saw me now? What would Sergius, the apostle of the higher love, say if he saw me now? What would the half

dozen Sergiuses who keep popping in and out of this handsome
figure of mine say if they caught us here? [*letting go her hand
and slipping his arm dexterously round her waist*] Do you consider my figure handsome, Louka?

LOUKA. Let me go, sir. I shall be disgraced. [*She struggles: he holds
her inexorably.*] Oh, will you let go?

SERGIUS. [*looking straight into her eyes*] No.

LOUKA. Then stand back where we cant be seen. Have you no common sense?

SERGIUS. Ah! thats reasonable. [*He takes her into the stableyard
gateway, where they are hidden from the house.*]

LOUKA. [*plaintively*] I may have been seen from the windows: Miss
Raina is sure to be spying about after you.

SERGIUS. [*stung: letting her go*] Take care, Louka. I may be worthless enough to betray the higher love; but do not you insult it.

LOUKA. [*demurely*] Not for the world, sir, I'm sure. May I go on
with my work, please, now?

SERGIUS. [*again putting his arm round her*] You are a provoking
little witch, Louka. If you were in love with me, would you spy
out of windows on me?

LOUKA. Well, you see, sir, since you say you are half a dozen different gentlemen all at once, I should have a great deal to look
after.

SERGIUS. [*charmed*] Witty as well as pretty. [*He tries to kiss her.*]

LOUKA. [*avoiding him*] No: I dont want your kisses. Gentlefolk are
all alike: you making love to me behind Miss Raina's back; and
she doing the same behind yours.

SERGIUS. [*recoiling a step*] Louka!

LOUKA. It shews how little you really care.

SERGIUS. [*dropping his familiarity, and speaking with freezing politeness*] If our conversation is to continue, Louka, you will please
remember that a gentleman does not discuss the conduct of the
lady he is engaged to with her maid.

LOUKA. It's so hard to know what a gentleman considers right. I
thought from your trying to kiss me that you had given up being
so particular.

SERGIUS. [*turning from her and striking his forehead as he comes
back into the garden from the gateway*] Devil! devil!

LOUKA. Ha! ha! I expect one of the six of you is very like me, sir;
though I am only Miss Raina's maid. [*She goes back to her work
at the table, taking no further notice of him.*]

SERGIUS. [*speaking to himself*] Which of the six is the real man?
thats the question that torments me. One of them is a hero, another a buffoon, another a humbug, another perhaps a bit of a
blackguard. [*He pauses, and looks furtively at* LOUKA *as he adds,
with deep bitterness*] And one, at least, is a coward: jealous, like
all cowards. [*He goes to the table.*] Louka.

LOUKA. Yes?

SERGIUS. Who is my rival?

LOUKA. You shall never get that out of me, for love or money.

SERGIUS. Why?

LOUKA. Never mind why. Besides, you would tell that I told you; and I should lose my place.

SERGIUS. [*holding out his right hand in affirmation*] No! on the honor of a—[*He checks himself; and his hand drops, nerveless, as he concludes sardonically*]—of a man capable of behaving as I have been behaving for the last five minutes. Who is he?

LOUKA. I dont know. I never saw him. I only heard his voice through the door of her room.

SERGIUS. Damnation! How dare you?

LOUKA. [*retreating*] Oh, I mean no harm: youve no right to take up my words like that. The mistress knows all about it. And I tell you that if that gentleman ever comes here again, Miss Raina will marry him, whether he likes it or not. I know the difference between the sort of manner you and she put on before one another and the real manner.

[SERGIUS *shivers as if she had stabbed him. Then, setting his face like iron, he strides grimly to her, and grips her above the elbows with both hands.*]

SERGIUS. Now listen you to me.

LOUKA. [*wincing*] Not so tight: youre hurting me.

SERGIUS. That doesn't matter. You have stained my honor by making me a party to your eavesdropping. And you have betrayed your mistress.

LOUKA. [*writhing*] Please—

SERGIUS. That shews that you are an abominable little clod of common clay, with the soul of a servant. [*He lets her go as if she were an unclean thing, and turns away, dusting his hands of her, to the bench by the wall, where he sits down with averted head, meditating gloomily.*]

LOUKA. [*whimpering angrily with her hands up her sleeves, feeling her bruised arms*] You know how to hurt with your tongue as well as with your hands. But I dont care, now Ive found out that whatever clay I'm made of, youre made of the same. As for her, she's a liar; and her fine airs are a cheat; and I'm worth six of her. [*She shakes the pain off hardily; tosses her head; and sets to work to put the things on the tray.*]

[*He looks doubtfully at her. She finishes packing the tray, and laps the cloth over the edges, so as to carry all out together. As she stoops to lift it, he rises.*]

SERGIUS. Louka! [*She stops and looks defiantly at him.*] A gentleman has no right to hurt a woman under any circumstances. [*with profound humility, uncovering his head*] I beg your pardon.

LOUKA. That sort of apology may satisfy a lady. Of what use is it to a servant?

SERGIUS. [*rudely crossed in his chivalry, throws it off with a bitter laugh, and says slightingly*] Oh! you wish to be paid for the hurt! [*He puts on his shako, and takes some money from his pocket.*]

LOUKA. [*her eyes filling with tears in spite of herself*] No: I want my hurt made well.

SERGIUS. [*sobered by her tone*] How?

> [*She rolls up her left sleeve; clasps her arm with the thumb and fingers of her right hand; and looks down at the bruise. Then she raises her head and looks straight at him. Finally, with a superb gesture, she presents her arm to be kissed. Amazed, he looks at her; at the arm; at her again; hesitates; and then, with shuddering intensity, exclaims* Never! *and gets away as far as possible from her.*
>
> *Her arm drops. Without a word, and with unaffected dignity, she takes her tray, and is approaching the house when* RAINA *returns, wearing a hat and jacket in the height of the Vienna fashion of the previous year,* 1885. LOUKA *makes way proudly for her, and then goes into the house.*]

RAINA. I'm ready. Whats the matter? [*gaily*] Have you been flirting with Louka?

SERGIUS. [*hastily*] No, no. How can you think such a thing?

RAINA. [*ashamed of herself*] Forgive me, dear: it was only a jest. I am so happy today.

> [*He goes quickly to her, and kisses her hand remorsefully.* CATHERINE *comes out and calls to them from the top of the steps.*]

CATHERINE. [*coming down to them*] I am sorry to disturb you, children; but Paul is distracted over those three regiments. He doesnt know how to send them to Philippopolis; and he objects to every suggestion of mine. You must go and help him, Sergius. He is in the library.

RAINA. [*disappointed*] But we are just going out for a walk.

SERGIUS. I shall not be long. Wait for me just five minutes. [*He runs up the steps to the door.*]

RAINA. [*following him to the foot of the steps and looking up at him with timid coquetry*] I shall go round and wait in full view of the library windows. Be sure you draw father's attention to me. If you are a moment longer than five minutes, I shall go in and fetch you, regiments or no regiments.

SERGIUS. [*laughing*] Very well. [*He goes in.*]

> [RAINA *watches him until he is out of her sight. Then, with a perceptible relaxation of manner, she begins to pace up and down the garden in a brown study.*]

CATHERINE. Imagine their meeting that Swiss and hearing the whole story! The very first thing your father asked for was the old coat we sent him off in. A nice mess you have got us into!

RAINA. [*gazing thoughtfully at the gravel as she walks*] The little beast!

CATHERINE. Little beast! What little beast?

RAINA. To go and tell! Oh, if I had him here, I'd cram him with chocolate creams til he couldnt ever speak again!

CATHERINE. Dont talk such stuff. Tell me the truth, Raina. How long was he in your room before you came to me?

RAINA. [*whisking round and recommencing her march in the op-*

posite direction] Oh, I forget.

CATHERINE. You cannot forget! Did he really climb up after the soldiers were gone; or was he there when that officer searched the room?

RAINA. No. Yes: I think he must have been there then.

CATHERINE. You think! Oh, Raina! Raina! Will anything ever make you straightforward? If Sergius finds out, it will be all over between you.

RAINA. [*with cool impertinence*] Oh, I know Sergius is your pet. I sometimes wish you could marry him instead of me. You would just suit him. You would pet him, and spoil him, and mother him to perfection.

CATHERINE. [*opening her eyes very widely indeed*] Well, upon my word!

RAINA. [*capriciously: half to herself*] I always feel a longing to do or say something dreadful to him—to shock his propriety—to scandalize the five senses out of him. [*to* CATHERINE, *perversely*] I dont care whether he finds out about the chocolate cream soldier or not. I half hope he may. [*She again turns and strolls flippantly away up the path to the corner of the house.*]

CATHERINE. And what should I be able to say to your father, pray?

RAINA. [*over her shoulder, from the top of the two steps*] Oh, poor father! As if he could help himself! [*She turns the corner and passes out of sight.*]

CATHERINE. [*looking after her, her fingers itching*] Oh, if you were only ten years younger! [LOUKA *comes from the house with a salver, which she carries hanging down by her side.*] Well?

LOUKA. Theres a gentleman just called, madam. A Serbian officer.

CATHERINE. [*flaming*] A Serb! And how dare he—[*checking herself bitterly*] Oh, I forgot. We are at peace now. I suppose we shall have them calling every day to pay their compliments. Well: if he is an officer why dont you tell your master? He is in the library with Major Saranoff. Why do you come to me?

LOUKA. But he asks for you, madam. And I dont think he knows who you are: he said the lady of the house. He gave me this little ticket for you. [*She takes a card out of her bosom; puts it on the salver; and offers it to* CATHERINE.]

CATHERINE. [*reading*] "Captain Bluntschli"? Thats a German name.

LOUKA. Swiss, madam, I think.

CATHERINE. [*with a bound that makes* LOUKA *jump back*] Swiss! What is he like?

LOUKA. [*timidly*] He has a big carpet bag, madam.

CATHERINE. Oh Heavens! he's come to return the coat. Send him away: say we're not at home: ask him to leave his address and I'll write to him. Oh stop: that will never do. Wait! [*She throws herself into a chair to think it out.* LOUKA *waits.*] The master and Major Saranoff are busy in the library, arnt they?

LOUKA. Yes, madam.

CATHERINE. [*decisively*] Bring the gentleman out here at once. [*peremptorily*] And be very polite to him. Dont delay. Here [*im-*

patiently snatching the salver from her]: leave that here; and go straight back to him.

LOUKA. Yes, madam [*going*].

CATHERINE. Louka!

LOUKA. [*stopping*] Yes, madam.

CATHERINE. Is the library door shut?

LOUKA. I think so, madam.

CATHERINE. If not, shut it as you pass through.

LOUKA. Yes, madam [*going*].

CATHERINE. Stop. [LOUKA *stops*.] He will have to go that way [*indicating the gate of the stable yard*]. Tell Nicola to bring his bag here after him. Dont forget.

LOUKA. [*surprised*] His bag?

CATHERINE. Yes: here: as soon as possible. [*vehemently*] Be quick! [LOUKA *runs into the house.* CATHERINE *snatches her apron off and throws it behind a bush. She then takes up the salver and uses it as a mirror, with the result that the handkerchief tied round her head follows the apron. A touch to her hair and a shake to her dressing gown make her presentable.*] Oh, how? how? how can a man be such a fool! Such a moment to select! [LOUKA *appears at the door of the house, announcing* Captain Bluntschli. *She stands aside at the top of the steps to let him pass before she goes in again. He is the man of the midnight adventure in* RAINA'S *room, clean, well brushed, smartly uniformed, and out of trouble, but still unmistakably the same man. The moment* LOUKA'S *back is turned,* CATHERINE *swoops on him with impetuous, urgent, coaxing appeal.*] Captain Bluntschli: I am very glad to see you; but you must leave this house at once. [*He raises his eyebrows.*] My husband has just returned with my future son-in-law; and they know nothing. If they did, the consequences would be terrible. You are a foreigner: you do not feel our national animosities as we do. We still hate the Serbs: the effect of the peace on my husband has been to make him feel like a lion baulked of his prey. If he discovers our secret, he will never forgive me; and my daughter's life will hardly be safe. Will you, like the chivalrous gentleman and soldier you are, leave at once before he finds you here?

BLUNTSCHLI. [*disappointed, but philosophical*] At once, gracious lady. I only came to thank you and return the coat you lent me. If you will allow me to take it out of my bag and leave it with your servant as I pass out, I need detain you no further. [*He turns to go into the house.*]

CATHERINE. [*catching him by the sleeve*] Oh, you must not think of going back that way. [*coaxing him across to the stable gates*] This is the shortest way out. Many thanks. So glad to have been of service to you. Good-bye.

BLUNTSCHLI. But my bag?

CATHERINE. It shall be sent on. You will leave me your address.

BLUNTSCHLI. True. Allow me. [*He takes out his cardcase, and stops to write his address, keeping* CATHERINE *in an agony of im-*

patience. As he hands her the card, PETKOFF, *hatless, rushes from the house in a *fluster of hospitality, followed by* SERGIUS.]

PETKOFF. [*as he hurries down the steps*] My dear Captain Bluntschli—

CATHERINE. Oh Heavens! [*She sinks on the seat against the wall.*]

PETKOFF. [*too preoccupied to notice her as he shakes* BLUNTSCHLI'S *hand heartily*] Those stupid people of mine thought I was out here, instead of in the—haw!—library [*he cannot mention the library without betraying how proud he is of it*]. I saw you through the window. I was wondering why you didnt come in. Saranoff is with me: you remember him, dont you?

SERGIUS. [*saluting humorously, and then offering his hand with great charm of manner*] Welcome, our friend the enemy!

PETKOFF. No longer the enemy, happily. [*rather anxiously*] I hope youve called as a friend, and not about horses or prisoners.

CATHERINE. Oh, quite as a friend, Paul. I was just asking Captain Bluntschli to stay to lunch; but he declares he must go at once.

SERGIUS. [*sardonically*] Impossible, Bluntschli. We want you here badly. We have to send on three cavalry regiments to Philippopolis; and we dont in the least know how to do it.

BLUNTSCHLI. [*suddenly attentive and businesslike*] Philippopolis? The forage is the trouble, I suppose.

PETKOFF. [*eagerly*] Yes: thats it. [*to* SERGIUS] He sees the whole thing at once.

BLUNTSCHLI. I think I can shew you how to manage that.

SERGIUS. Invaluable man! Come along! [*Towering over* BLUNTSCHLI, *he puts his hand on his shoulder and takes him to the steps,* PETKOFF *following.*]

[RAINA *comes from the house as* BLUNTSCHLI *puts his foot on the first step.*]

RAINA. Oh! The chocolate cream soldier!

[BLUNTSCHLI *stands rigid.* SERGIUS, *amazed, looks at* RAINA, *then at* PETKOFF, *who looks back at him and then at his wife.*]

CATHERINE. [*with commanding presence of mind*] My dear Raina, dont you see that we have a guest here? Captain Bluntschli: one of our new Serbian friends.

[RAINA *bows:* BLUNTSCHLI *bows.*]

RAINA. How silly of me! [*She comes down into the centre of the group, between* BLUNTSCHLI *and* PETKOFF.] I made a beautiful ornament this morning for the ice pudding; and that stupid Nicola has just put down a pile of plates on it and spoilt it. [*to* BLUNTSCHLI, *winningly*] I hope you didn't think that you were the chocolate cream soldier, Captain Bluntschli.

BLUNTSCHLI. [*laughing*] I assure you I did. [*stealing a whimsical glance at her*] Your explanation was a relief.

PETKOFF. [*suspiciously, to* RAINA] And since when, pray, have you taken to cooking?

CATHERINE. Oh, whilst you were away. It is her latest fancy.

PETKOFF. [*testily*] And has Nicola taken to drinking? He used to

be careful enough. First he shews Captain Bluntschli out here
when he knew quite well I was in the library; and then he goes
downstairs and breaks Raina's chocolate soldier. He must—
[NICOLA *appears at the top of the steps with the bag. He de-
scends; places it respectfully before* BLUNTSCHLI; *and waits for
further orders. General amazement.* NICOLA, *unconscious of the
effect he is producing, looks perfectly satisfied with himself.
When* PETKOFF *recovers his power of speech, he breaks out at
him with*] Are you mad, Nicola?

NICOLA. [*taken aback*] Sir?

PETKOFF. What have you brought that for?

NICOLA. My lady's orders, major. Louka told me that—

CATHERINE. [*interrupting him*] My orders! Why should I order you
to bring Captain Bluntschli's luggage out here? What are you
thinking of, Nicola?

NICOLA. [*after a moment's bewilderment, picking up the bag as he
addresses* BLUNTSCHLI *with the very perfection of servile discretion*] I beg your pardon, captain, I am sure. [*to* CATHERINE] My
fault, madam: I hope youll overlook it. [*He bows, and is going
to the steps with the bag, when* PETKOFF *addresses him angrily.*]

PETKOFF. Youd better go and slam that bag, too, down on Miss
Raina's ice pudding! [*This is too much for* NICOLA. *The bag drops
from his hand almost on his master's toes, eliciting a roar of*]
Begone, you butter-fingered donkey.

NICOLA. [*snatching up the bag, and escaping into the house*] Yes,
major.

CATHERINE. Oh, never mind. Paul: dont be angry.

PETKOFF. [*blustering*] Scoundrel! He's got out of hand while I was
away. I'll teach him. Infernal blackguard! The sack next Saturday! I'll clear out the whole establishment—[*He is stifled by the
caresses of his wife and daughter, who hang round his neck, pet-
ting him*].

CATHERINE. ⎱ [*together*] ⎰ Now, now, now, it mustnt be angry. He
RAINA.   ⎰   ⎱ Wow, wow, wow: not on your first day at
                        ⎧ meant no harm. Be good to please me, dear.
                        ⎨ home. I'll make another ice pudding. Tch-
                        ⎩ Sh-sh-sh-sh!
                          ch-ch!

PETKOFF. [*yielding*] Oh well, never mind. Come, Bluntschli: lets
have no more nonsense about going away. You know very well
youre not going back to Switzerland yet. Until you do go back
youll stay with us.

RAINA. Oh, do, Captain Bluntschli.

PETKOFF. [*to* CATHERINE] Now, Catherine: it's of you he's afraid.
Press him: and he'll stay.

CATHERINE. Of course I shall be only too delighted if [*appealingly*]
Captain Bluntschli really wishes to stay. He knows my wishes.

BLUNTSCHLI. [*in his driest military manner*] I am at madam's orders.

SERGIUS. [*cordially*] That settles it!

PETKOFF. [*heartily*] Of course!

RAINA. You see you must stay.

BLUNTSCHLI. [*smiling*] Well, if I must, I must.

[*Gesture of despair from* CATHERINE.]

Act III

In the library after lunch. It is not much of a library. Its literary equipment consists of a single fixed shelf stocked with old paper covered novels, broken backed, coffee stained, torn and thumbed; and a couple of little hanging shelves with a few gift books on them: the rest of the wall space being occupied by trophies of war and the chase. But it is a most comfortable sitting room. A row of three large windows shews a mountain panorama, just now seen in one of its friendliest aspects in the mellowing afternoon light. In the corner next the right-hand window a square earthenware stove, a perfect tower of glistening pottery, rises nearly to the ceiling and guarantees plenty of warmth. The ottoman is like that in RAINA's *room, and similarly placed; and the window seats are luxurious with decorated cushions. There is one object, however, hopelessly out of keeping with its surroundings. This is a small kitchen table, much the worse for wear, fitted as a writing table with an old canister full of pens, an eggcup filled with ink, and a deplorable scrap of heavily used pink blotting paper.*

At the side of this table, which stands to the left of anyone facing the window, BLUNTSCHLI *is hard at work with a couple of maps before him, writing orders. At the head of it sits* SERGIUS, *who is supposed to be also at work, but is actually gnawing the feather of a pen, and contemplating* BLUNTSCHLI's *quick, sure, businesslike progress with a mixture of envious irritation at his own incapacity and awestruck wonder at an ability which seems to him almost miraculous, though its prosaic character forbids him to esteem it. The* MAJOR *is comfortably established on the ottoman, with a newspaper in his hand and the tube of his hookah within easy reach.* CATHERINE *sits at the stove, with her back to them, embroidering.* RAINA, *reclining on the divan, is gazing in a daydream out at the Balkan landscape, with a neglected novel in her lap.*

The door is on the same side as the stove, farther from the window. The button of the electric bell is at the opposite side, behind BLUNTSCHLI.

PETKOFF. [*looking up from his paper to watch how they are getting on at the table*] Are you sure I cant help in any way, Bluntschli?

BLUNTSCHLI. [*without interrupting his writing or looking up*] Quite sure, thank you. Saranoff and I will manage it.

SERGIUS. [*grimly*] Yes: we'll manage it. He finds out what to do; draws up the orders; and I sign em. Division of labor! [BLUNTSCHLI *passes him a paper.*] Another one? Thank you. [*He plants the paper squarely before him; sets his chair carefully parallel to it; and signs with his cheek on his elbow and his protruded tongue following the movements of his pen.*] This hand is more accustomed to the sword than to the pen.

PETKOFF. It's very good of you, Bluntschli: it is indeed, to let yourself be put upon in this way. Now are you quite sure I can do nothing?

CATHERINE. [in a low warning tone] You can stop interrupting, Paul.

PETKOFF. [starting and looking round at her] Eh? Oh! Quite right, my love: quite right. [He takes his newspaper up again, but presently lets it drop.] Ah, you havnt been campaigning, Catherine: you dont know how pleasant it is for us to sit here, after a good lunch, with nothing to do but enjoy ourselves. Theres only one thing I want to make me thoroughly comfortable.

CATHERINE. What is that?

PETKOFF. My old coat. I'm not at home in this one: I feel as if I were on parade.

CATHERINE. My dear Paul, how absurd you are about that old coat! It must be hanging in the blue closet where you left it.

PETKOFF. My dear Catherine, I tell you Ive looked there. Am I to believe my own eyes or not? [CATHERINE rises and crosses the room to press the button of the electric bell.] What are you shewing off that bell for? [She looks at him majestically, and silently resumes her chair and her needlework.] My dear: if you think the obstinacy of your sex can make a coat out of two old dressing gowns of Raina's, your waterproof, and my mackintosh, youre mistaken. Thats exactly what the blue closet contains at present. [NICOLA presents himself.]

CATHERINE. Nicola: go to the blue closet and bring your master's old coat here: the braided one he wears in the house.

NICOLA. Yes, madame. [He goes out.]

PETKOFF. Catherine.

CATHERINE. Yes, Paul.

PETKOFF. I bet you any piece of jewellery you like to order from Sofia against a week's housekeeping money that the coat isnt there.

CATHERINE. Done, Paul!

PETKOFF. [excited by the prospect of a gamble] Come: heres an opportunity for some sport. Wholl bet on it? Bluntschli: I'll give you six to one.

BLUNTSCHLI. [imperturbably] It would be robbing you, major. Madame is sure to be right. [Without looking up, he passes another batch of papers to SERGIUS.]

SERGIUS. [also excited] Bravo, Switzerland! Major: I bet my best charger against an Arab mare for Raina that Nicola finds the coat in the blue closet.

PETKOFF. [eagerly] Your best char—

CATHERINE. [hastily interrupting him] Dont be foolish, Paul. An Arabian mare will cost you 50,000 levas.

RAINA. [suddenly coming out of her picturesque revery] Really, mother, if you are going to take the jewellery, I dont see why you should grudge me my Arab.

[NICOLA comes back with the coat, and brings it to PETKOFF,

who can hardly believe his eyes.]

CATHERINE. Where was it, Nicola?

NICOLA. Hanging in the blue closet, madame.

PETKOFF. Well, I am d—

CATHERINE. [*stopping him*] Paul!

PETKOFF. I could have sworn it wasnt there. Age is beginning to tell on me. I'm getting hallucinations. [*to* NICOLA] Here: help me to change. Excuse me, Bluntschli. [*He begins changing coats,* NICOLA *acting as valet.*] Remember: I didnt take that bet of yours, Sergius. Youd better give Raina that Arab steed yourself, since youve roused her expectations. Eh, Raina? [*He looks round at her; but she is again rapt in the landscape. With a little gush of parental affection and pride, he points her out to them, and says*] She's dreaming, as usual.

SERGIUS. Assuredly she shall not be the loser.

PETKOFF. So much the better for her. I shant come off so cheaply, I expect. [*The change is now complete.* NICOLA *goes out with the discarded coat.*] Ah, now I feel at home at last. [*He sits down and takes his newspaper with a grunt of relief.*]

BLUNTSCHLI. [*to* SERGIUS, *handing a paper*] Thats the last order.

PETKOFF. [*jumping up*] What! Finished?

BLUNTSCHLI. Finished.

PETKOFF. [*with childlike envy*] Havnt you anything for me to sign?

BLUNTSCHLI. Not necessary. His signature will do.

PETKOFF. [*inflating his chest and thumping it*] Ah well, I think weve done a thundering good day's work. Can I do anything more?

BLUNTSCHLI. You had better both see the fellows that are to take these. [SERGIUS *rises.*] Pack them off at once; and shew them that Ive marked on the orders the time they should hand them in by. Tell them that if they stop to drink or tell stories—if theyre five minutes late, theyll have the skin taken off their backs.

SERGIUS. [*stiffening indignantly*] I'll say so. [*He strides to the door.*] And if one of them is man enough to spit in my face for insulting him, I'll buy his discharge and give him a pension. [*He goes out.*]

BLUNTSCHLI. [*confidentially*] Just see that he talks to them properly, major, will you?

PETKOFF. [*officiously*] Quite right, Bluntschli, quite right. I'll see to it. [*He goes to the door importantly, but hesitates on the threshold.*] By the bye, Catherine, you may as well come too. Theyll be far more frightened of you than of me.

CATHERINE. [*putting down her embroidery*] I daresay I had better. You would only splutter at them. [*She goes out,* PETKOFF *holding the door for her and following her.*]

BLUNTSCHLI. What an army! They make cannons out of cherry trees, and the officers send for their wives to keep discipline! [*He begins to fold and docket the papers.*]

[RAINA, *who has risen from the divan, marches slowly down the room with her hands clasped behind her, and looks mischievously at him.*]

RAINA. You look ever so much nicer than when we last met. [*He looks up, surprised.*] What have you done to yourself?

BLUNTSCHLI. Washed; brushed; good night's sleep and breakfast. Thats all.

RAINA. Did you get back safely that morning?

BLUNTSCHLI. Quite, thanks.

RAINA. Were they angry with you for running away from Sergius's charge?

BLUNTSCHLI. [*grinning*] No: they were glad; because theyd all just run away themselves.

RAINA. [*going to the table, and leaning over it towards him*] It must have made a lovely story for them: all that about me and my room.

BLUNTSCHLI. Capital story. But I only told it to one of them: a particular friend.

RAINA. On whose discretion you could absolutely rely?

BLUNTSCHLI. Absolutely.

RAINA. Hm! He told it all to my father and Sergius the day you exchanged the prisoners. [*She turns away and strolls carelessly across to the other side of the room.*]

BLUNTSCHLI. [*deeply concerned, and half incredulous*] No! You dont mean that, do you?

RAINA. [*turning, with sudden earnestness*] I do indeed. But they dont know that it was in this house you took refuge. If Sergius knew, he would challenge you and kill you in a duel.

BLUNTSCHLI. Bless me! then dont tell him.

RAINA. Please be serious, Captain Bluntschli. Can you not realize what it is to me to deceive him? I want to be quite perfect with Sergius: no meanness, no smallness, no deceit. My relation to him is the one really beautiful and noble part of my life. I hope you can understand that.

BLUNTSCHLI. [*sceptically*] You mean that you wouldnt like him to find out that the story about the ice pudding was a—a—a—You know.

RAINA. [*wincing*] Ah, dont talk of it in that flippant way. I lied: I know it. But I did it to save your life. He would have killed you. That was the second time I ever uttered a falsehood. [BLUNTSCHLI *rises quickly and looks doubtfully and somewhat severely at her.*] Do you remember the first time?

BLUNTSCHLI. I! No. Was I present?

RAINA. Yes; and I told the officer who was searching for you that you were not present.

BLUNTSCHLI. True. I should have remembered it.

RAINA. [*greatly encouraged*] Ah, it is natural that you should forget it first. It cost you nothing: it cost me a lie! A lie!

[*She sits down on the ottoman, looking straight before her with her hands clasped around her knee.* BLUNTSCHLI, *quite touched, goes to the ottoman with a particularly reassuring and considerate air, and sits down beside her.*]

BLUNTSCHLI. My dear young lady, dont let this worry you. Remember: I'm a soldier. Now what are the two things that happen to a soldier so often that he comes to think nothing of them? One is hearing people tell lies: [RAINA *recoils*.] the other is getting his life saved in all sorts of ways by all sorts of people.

RAINA. [*rising in indignant protest*] And so he becomes a creature incapable of faith and of gratitude.

BLUNTSCHLI. [*making a wry face*] Do you like gratitude? I dont. If pity is akin to love, gratitude is akin to the other thing.

RAINA. Gratitude! [*turning on him*] If you are incapable of gratitude you are incapable of any noble sentiment. Even animals are grateful. Oh, I see now exactly what you think of me! You were not surprised to hear me lie. To you it was something I probably did every day! every hour! That is how men think of women. [*She paces the room tragically.*]

BLUNTSCHLI. [*dubiously*] Theres reason in everything. You said youd told only two lies in your whole life. Dear young lady: isnt that rather a short allowance? I'm quite a straightforward man myself; but it wouldnt last me a whole morning.

RAINA. [*staring haughtily at him*] Do you know, sir, that you are insulting me?

BLUNTSCHLI. I cant help it. When you strike that noble attitude and speak in that thrilling voice, I admire you; but I find it impossible to believe a single word you say.

RAINA. [*superbly*] Captain Bluntschli!

BLUNTSCHLI. [*unmoved*] Yes?

RAINA. [*standing over him, as if she could not believe her senses*] Do you mean what you said just now? Do you know what you said just now?

BLUNTSCHLI. I do.

RAINA. [*gasping*] I! I!!! [*She points to herself incredulously, meaning "I, Raina Petkoff, tell lies!" He meets her gaze unflinchingly. She suddenly sits down beside him, and adds, with a complete change of manner from the heroic to a babyish familiarity*] How did you find me out?

BLUNTSCHLI. [*promptly*] Instinct, dear young lady. Instinct, and experience of the world.

RAINA. [*wonderingly*] Do you know, you are the first man I ever met who did not take me seriously?

BLUNTSCHLI. You mean, dont you, that I am the first man that has ever taken you quite seriously?

RAINA. Yes: I suppose I do mean that. [*cosily, quite at her ease with him*] How strange it is to be talked to in such a way! You know, Ive always gone on like that.

BLUNTSCHLI. You mean the—?

RAINA. I mean the noble attitude and the thrilling voice. [*They laugh together.*] I did it when I was a tiny child to my nurse. She believed in it. I do it before my parents. They believe in it. I do it before Sergius. He believes in it.

BLUNTSCHLI. Yes: he's a little in that line himself, isnt he?

RAINA. [startled] Oh! Do you think so?

BLUNTSCHLI. You know him better than I do.

RAINA. I wonder—I wonder is he? If I thought that—! [discouraged] Ah, well: what does it matter? I suppose, now youve found me out, you despise me.

BLUNTSCHLI. [warmly, rising] No, my dear young lady, no, no, no a thousand times. It's part of your youth: part of your charm. I'm like all the rest of them: the nurse, your parents, Sergius: I'm your infatuated admirer.

RAINA. [pleased] Really?

BLUNTSCHLI. [slapping his breast smartly with his hand, German fashion] Hand aufs Herz! Really and truly.

RAINA. [very happy] But what did you think of me for giving you my portrait?

BLUNTSCHLI. [astonished] Your portrait! You never gave me your portrait.

RAINA. [quickly] Do you mean to say you never got it?

BLUNTSCHLI. No. [He sits down beside her, with renewed interest, and says, with some complacency] When did you send it to me?

RAINA. [indignantly] I did not send it to you. [She turns her head away, and adds, reluctantly] It was in the pocket of that coat.

BLUNTSCHLI. [pursing his lips and rounding his eyes] Oh-o-oh! I never found it. It must be there still.

RAINA. [springing up] There still! for my father to find the first time he puts his hand in his pocket! Oh, how could you be so stupid?

BLUNTSCHLI. [rising also] It doesnt matter: I suppose it's only a photograph: how can he tell who it was intended for? Tell him he put it there himself.

RAINA. [bitterly] Yes: that is so clever! isnt it? [distractedly] Oh! what shall I do?

BLUNTSCHLI. Ah, I see. You wrote something on it. That was rash.

RAINA. [vexed almost to tears] Oh, to have done such a thing for you, who care no more—except to laugh at me—oh! Are you sure nobody has touched it?

BLUNTSCHLI. Well, I cant be quite sure. You see, I couldnt carry it about with me all the time: one cant take much luggage on active service.

RAINA. What did you do with it?

BLUNTSCHLI. When I got through to Pirot I had to put it in safe keeping somehow. I thought of the railway cloak room; but thats the surest place to get looted in modern warfare. So I pawned it.

RAINA. Pawned it!!!

BLUNTSCHLI. I know it doesn't sound nice; but it was much the safest plan. I redeemed it the day before yesterday. Heaven only knows whether the pawnbroker cleared out the pockets or not.

RAINA. [furious: throwing the words right into his face] You have a low shopkeeping mind. You think of things that would never come into a gentleman's head.

BLUNTSCHLI. [phlegmatically] Thats the Swiss national character, dear lady. [*He returns to the table.*]

RAINA. Oh, I wish I had never met you. [*She flounces away, and sits at the window fuming.*]

> [LOUKA *comes in with a heap of letters and telegrams on her salver, and crosses, with her bold free gait, to the table. Her left sleeve is looped up to the shoulder with a brooch, shewing her naked arm, with a broad gilt bracelet covering the bruise.*]

LOUKA. [*to* BLUNTSCHLI] For you. [*She empties the salver with a fling on to the table.*] The messenger is waiting. [*She is determined not to be civil to an enemy, even if she must bring him his letters.*]

BLUNTSCHLI. [*to* RAINA] Will you excuse me: the last postal delivery that reached me was three weeks ago. These are the subsequent accumulations. Four telegrams: a week old. [*He opens one.*] Oho! Bad news!

RAINA. [*rising and advancing a little remorsefully*] Bad news?

BLUNTSCHLI. My father's dead. [*He looks at the telegram with his lips pursed, musing on the unexpected change in his arrangements.* LOUKA *crosses herself hastily.*]

RAINA. Oh, how very sad!

BLUNTSCHLI. Yes: I shall have to start for home in an hour. He has left a lot of big hotels behind him to be looked after. [*He takes up a fat letter in a long blue envelope.*] Here's a whacking letter from the family solicitor. [*He puts out the enclosures and glances over them.*] Great Heavens! Seventy! Two hundred! [*in a crescendo of dismay*] Four hundred! Four thousand! Nine thousand six hundred!!! What on earth am I to do with them all?

RAINA. [*timidly*] Nine thousand hotels?

BLUNTSCHLI. Hotels! nonsense. If you only knew! Oh, it's too ridiculous! Excuse me: I must give my fellow orders about starting. [*He leaves the room hastily, with the documents in his hand.*]

LOUKA. [*knowing instinctively that she can annoy* RAINA *by disparaging* BLUNTSCHLI] He has not much heart, that Swiss. He has not a word of grief for his poor father.

RAINA. [*bitterly*] Grief! A man who has been doing nothing but killing people for years! What does he care? What does any soldier care? [*She goes to the door, restraining her tears with difficulty.*]

LOUKA. Major Saranoff has been fighting too; and he has plenty of heart left. [RAINA, *at the door, draws herself up haughtily and goes out.*] Aha! I thought you wouldnt get much feeling out of your soldier. [*She is following* RAINA *when* NICOLA *enters with an armful of logs for the stove.*]

NICOLA. [*grinning amorously at her*] Ive been trying all the afternoon to get a minute alone with you, my girl. [*His countenance changes as he notices her arm.*] Why, what fashion is that of wearing your sleeve, child?

LOUKA. [*proudly*] My own fashion.

NICOLA. Indeed! If the mistress catches you, she'll talk to you. [*He puts the logs down, and seats himself comfortably on the ottoman.*]

LOUKA. Is that any reason why you should take it on yourself to talk to me?

NICOLA. Come! dont be so contrary with me. Ive some good news for you. [*She sits down beside him. He takes out some paper money.* LOUKA, *with an eager gleam in her eyes, tries to snatch it; but he shifts it quickly to his left hand, out of her reach.*] See! a twenty leva bill! Sergius gave me that, out of pure swagger. A fool and his money are soon parted. Theres ten levas more. The Swiss gave me that for backing up the mistress's and Raina's lies about him. He's no fool, he isnt. You should have heard old Catherine downstairs as polite as you please to me, telling me not to mind the Major being a little impatient; for they knew what a good servant I was—after making a fool and a liar of me before them all! The twenty will go to our savings; and you shall have the ten to spend if youll only talk to me so as to remind me I'm a human being. I get tired of being a servant occasionally.

LOUKA. Yes: sell your manhood for 30 levas, and buy me for 10! [*rising scornfully*] Keep your money. You were born to be a servant. I was not. When you set up your shop you will only be everybody's servant instead of somebody's servant. [*She goes moodily to the table and seats herself regally in* SERGIUS'S *chair.*]

NICOLA. [*picking up his logs, and going to the stove*] Ah, wait til you see. We shall have our evenings to ourselves; and I shall be master in my own house, I promise you. [*He throws the logs down and kneels at the stove.*]

LOUKA. You shall never be master in mine.

NICOLA. [*turning, still on his knees, and squatting down rather forlornly on his calves, daunted by her implacable disdain*] You have a great ambition in you, Louka. Remember: if any luck comes to you, it was I that made a woman of you.

LOUKA. You!

NICOLA. [*scrambling up and going to her*] Yes, me. Who was it made you give up wearing a couple of pounds of false black hair on your head and reddening your lips and cheeks like any other Bulgarian girl! I did. Who taught you to trim your nails, and keep your hands clean, and be dainty about yourself, like a fine Russian lady! Me: do you hear that? me! [*She tosses her head defiantly; and he turns away, adding more coolly*] Ive often thought that if Raina were out of the way, and you just a little less of a fool and Sergius just a little more of one, you might come to be one of my grandest customers, instead of only being my wife and costing me money.

LOUKA. I believe you would rather be my servant than my husband. You would make more out of me. Oh, I know that soul of yours.

NICOLA. [*going closer to her for greater emphasis*] Never you mind my soul; but just listen to my advice. If you want to be a lady, your present behavior to me wont do at all, unless when we're alone. It's too sharp and impudent; and impudence is a sort of familiarity: it shews affection for me. And don't you try being high and mighty with me, either. Youre like all country girls: you think it's genteel to treat a servant the way I treat a stableboy. Thats only your ignorance; and dont you forget it. And dont be so ready to defy everybody. Act as if you expected to have your own way, not as if you expected to be ordered about. The way to get on as a lady is the same as the way to get on as a servant: youve got to know your place: thats the secret of it. And you may depend on me to know my place if you get promoted. Think over it, my girl. I'll stand by you: one servant should always stand by another.

LOUKA. [*rising impatiently*] Oh, I must behave in my own way. You take all the courage out of me with your cold-blooded wisdom. Go and put those logs in the fire: thats the sort of thing you understand.

> [*Before* NICOLA *can retort,* SERGIUS *comes in. He checks himself a moment on seeing* LOUKA; *then goes to the stove.*]

SERGIUS. [*to* NICOLA] I am not in the way of your work, I hope.

NICOLA. [*in a smooth, elderly manner*] Oh no, sir: thank you kindly. I was only speaking to this foolish girl about her habit of running up here to the library whenever she gets a chance, to look at the books. Thats the worst of her education, sir: it gives her habits above her station. [*to* LOUKA] Make that table tidy, Louka, for the Major. [*He goes out sedately.*]

> [LOUKA, *without looking at* SERGIUS, *pretends to arrange the papers on the table. He crosses slowly to her, and studies the arrangement of her sleeve reflectively.*]

SERGIUS. Let me see: is there a mark there? [*He turns up the bracelet and sees the bruise made by his grasp. She stands motionless, not looking at him: fascinated, but on her guard.*] Ffff! Does it hurt?

LOUKA. Yes.

SERGIUS. Shall I cure it?

LOUKA. [*instanty withdrawing herself proudly, but still not looking at him*] No. You cannot cure it now.

SERGIUS. [*masterfully*] Quite sure? [*He makes a movement as if to take her in his arms.*]

LOUKA. Dont trifle with me, please. An officer should not trifle with a servant.

SERGIUS. [*indicating the bruise with a merciless stroke of his forefinger*] That was no trifle, Louka.

LOUKA. [*flinching; then looking at him for the first time*] Are you sorry?

SERGIUS. [*with measured emphasis, folding his arms*] I am never sorry.

LOUKA. [*wistfully*] I wish I could believe a man could be as unlike a woman as that. I wonder are you really a brave man?

SERGIUS. [*unaffectedly, relaxing his attitude*] Yes: I am a brave man. My heart jumped like a woman's at the first shot; but in the charge I found that I was brave. Yes: that at least is real about me.

LOUKA. Did you find in the charge that the men whose fathers are poor like mine were any less brave than the men who are rich like you?

SERGIUS. [*with bitter levity*] Not a bit. They all slashed and cursed and yelled like heroes. Psha! the courage to rage and kill is cheap. I have an English bull terrier who has as much of that sort of courage as the whole Bulgarian nation, and the whole Russian nation at its back. But he lets my groom thrash him, all the same. Thats your soldier all over! No, Louka: your poor men can cut throats; but they are afraid of their officers; they put up with insults and blows; they stand by and see one another punished like children: aye, and help to do it when they are ordered. And the officers!!! Well [*with a short harsh laugh*] I am an officer. Oh, [*fervently*] give me the man who will defy to the death any power on earth or in heaven that sets itself up against his own will and conscience: he alone is the brave man.

LOUKA. How easy it is to talk! Men never seem to me to grow up: they all have schoolboy's ideas. You dont know what true courage is.

SERGIUS. [*ironically*] Indeed! I am willing to be instructed. [*He sits on the ottoman, sprawling magnificently.*]

LOUKA. Look at me! How much am I allowed to have my own will? I have to get your room ready for you: to sweep and dust, to fetch and carry. How could that degrade me if it did not degrade you to have it done for you? But [*with subdued passion*] if I were Empress of Russia, above everyone in the world, then!! Ah then, though according to you I could shew no courage at all, you should see, you should see.

SERGIUS. What would you do, most noble Empress?

LOUKA. I would marry the man I loved, which no other queen in Europe has the courage to do. If I loved you, though you would be as far beneath me as I am beneath you, I would dare to be the equal of my inferior. Would you dare as much if you loved me? No: if you felt the beginnings of love for me you would not let it grow. You would not dare: you would marry a rich man's daughter because you would be afraid of what other people would say of you.

SERGIUS. [*bounding up*] You lie: it is not so, by all the stars! If I loved you, and I were the Tsar himself, I would set you on the throne by my side. You know that I love another woman, a woman as high above you as heaven is above earth. And you are jealous of her.

LOUKA. I have no reason to be. She will never marry you now. The man I told you of has come back. She will marry the Swiss.

SERGIUS. [*recoiling*] The Swiss!

LOUKA. A man worth ten of you. Then you can come to me; and I will refuse you. You are not good enough for me. [*She turns to the door.*]

SERGIUS. [*springing after her and catching her fiercely in his arms*]

I will kill the Swiss; and afterwards I will do as I please with you.

LOUKA. [*in his arms, passive and steadfast*] The Swiss will kill you, perhaps. He has beaten you in love. He may beat you in war.

SERGIUS. [*tormentedly*] Do you think I believe that she—she! whose worst thoughts are higher than your best ones, is capable of trifling with another man behind my back?

LOUKA. Do you think she would believe the Swiss if he told her now that I am in your arms?

SERGIUS. [*releasing her in despair*] Damnation! Oh, damnation! Mockery! mockery everywhere! everything I think is mocked by everything I do. [*He strikes himself frantically on the breast.*] Coward! liar! fool! Shall I kill myself like a man, or live and pretend to laugh at myself? [*She again turns to go.*] Louka! [*She stops near the door.*] Remember: you belong to me.

LOUKA. [*turning*] What does that mean? an insult?

SERGIUS. [*commandingly*] It means that you love me, and that I have had you here in my arms, and will perhaps have you there again. Whether that is an insult I neither know nor care: take it as you please. But [*vehemently*] I will not be a coward and a trifler. If I choose to love you, I dare marry you, in spite of all Bulgaria. If these hands ever touch you again, they shall touch my affianced bride.

LOUKA. We shall see whether you dare keep your word. And take care. I will not wait long.

SERGIUS. [*again folding his arms and standing motionless in the middle of the room*] Yes: we shall see. And you shall wait my pleasure.

[BLUNTSCHLI, *much preoccupied, with his papers still in his hand, enters, leaving the door open for* LOUKA *to go out. He goes across to the table, glancing at her as he passes.* SERGIUS, *without altering his resolute attitude, watches him steadily.* LOUKA *goes out, leaving the door open.*]

BLUNTSCHLI. [*absently, sitting at the table as before, and putting down his papers*] Thats a remarkable looking young woman.

SERGIUS. [*gravely, without moving*] Captain Bluntschli.

BLUNTSCHLI. Eh?

SERGIUS. You have deceived me. You are my rival. I brook no rivals. At six o'clock I shall be in the drilling-ground on the Klissoura road, alone, on horseback, with my sabre. Do you understand?

BLUNTSCHLI. [*staring, but sitting quite at his ease*] Oh, thank you: thats a cavalry man's proposal. I'm in the artillery; and I have the choice of weapons. If I go, I shall take a machine gun. And there shall be no mistake about the cartridges this time.

SERGIUS. [*flushing, but with deadly coldness*] Take care, sir. It is not our custom in Bulgaria to allow invitations of that kind to be trifled with.

BLUNTSCHLI. [*warmly*] Pooh! dont talk to me about Bulgaria. You dont know what fighting is. But have it your own way. Bring your sabre along. I'll meet you.

SERGIUS. [*fiercely delighted to find his opponent a man of spirit*] Well said, Switzer. Shall I lend you my best horse?

BLUNTSCHLI. No: damn your horse! thank you all the same, my dear fellow. [RAINA *comes in, and hears the next sentence.*] I shall fight you on foot. Horseback's too dangerous; I dont want to kill you if I can help it.

RAINA. [*hurrying forward anxiously*] I have heard what Captain Bluntschli said, Sergius. You are going to fight. Why? [SERGIUS *turns away in silence, and goes to the stove, where he stands watching her as she continues, to* BLUNTSCHLI] What about?

BLUNTSCHLI. I dont know: he hasnt told me. Better not interfere, dear young lady. No harm will be done: Ive often acted as sword instructor. He wont be able to touch me; and I'll not hurt him. It will save explanations. In the morning I shall be off home; and youll never see me or hear of me again. You and he will then make it up and live happily ever after.

RAINA. [*turning away deeply hurt, almost with a sob in her voice*] I never said I wanted to see you again.

SERGIUS. [*striding forward*] Ha! That is a confession.

RAINA. [*haughtily*] What do you mean?

SERGIUS. You love that man!

RAINA. [*scandalized*] Sergius!

SERGIUS. You allow him to make love to you behind my back, just as you treat me as your affianced husband behind his. Bluntschli: you knew our relations; and you deceived me. It is for that that I call you to account, not for having received favors I never enjoyed.

BLUNTSCHLI. [*jumping up indignantly*] Stuff! Rubbish! I have received no favors. Why, the young lady doesnt even know whether I'm married or not.

RAINA. [*forgetting herself*] Oh! [*collapsing on the ottoman*] Are you?

SERGIUS. You see the young lady's concern, Captain Bluntschli. Denial is useless. You have enjoyed the privilege of being received in her own room, late at night—

BLUNTSCHLI. [*interrupting him pepperily*] Yes, you blockhead! she received me with a pistol at her head. Your cavalry were at my heels. I'd have blown out her brains if she'd uttered a cry.

SERGIUS. [*taken aback*] Bluntschli! Raina: is this true?

RAINA. [*rising in wrathful majesty*] Oh, how dare you, how dare you?

BLUNTSCHLI. Apologize, man: apologize. [*He resumes his seat at the table.*]

SERGIUS. [*with the old measured emphasis, folding his arms*] I never apologize!

RAINA. [*passionately*] This is the doing of that friend of yours, Captain Bluntschli. It is he who is spreading this horrible story about me. [*She walks about excitedly.*]

BLUNTSCHLI. No: he's dead. Burnt alive!

RAINA. [*stopping, shocked*] Burnt alive!

BLUNTSCHLI. Shot in the hip in a woodyard. Couldnt drag himself out. Your fellows' shells set the timber on fire and burnt him, with half a dozen other poor devils in the same predicament.

RAINA. How horrible!

SERGIUS. And how ridiculous! Oh, war! war! the dream of patriots and heroes! A fraud, Bluntschli. A hollow sham, like love.

RAINA. [*outraged*] Like love! You say that before me!

BLUNTSCHLI. Come, Saranoff: that matter is explained.

SERGIUS. A hollow sham, I say. Would you have come back here if nothing had passed between you except at the muzzle of your pistol? Raina is mistaken about your friend who was burnt. He was not my informant.

RAINA. Who then? [*suddenly guessing the truth*] Ah, Louka! my maid! my servant! You were with her this morning all that time after—after—Oh, what sort of god is this I have been worshipping! [*He meets her gaze with sardonic enjoyment of her disenchantment. Angered all the more, she goes closer to him, and says, in a lower, intenser tone*] Do you know that I looked out of the window as I went upstairs, to have another sight of my hero; and I saw something I did not understand then. I know now that you were making love to her.

SERGIUS. [*with grim humor*] You saw that?

RAINA. Only too well. [*She turns away, and throws herself on the divan under the centre window, quite overcome.*]

SERGIUS. [*cynically*] Raina: our romance is shattered. Life's a farce.

BLUNTSCHLI. [*to* RAINA, *whimsically*] You see: he's found himself out now.

SERGIUS. [*going to him*] Bluntschli: I have allowed you to call me a blockhead. You may now call me a coward as well. I refuse to fight you. Do you know why?

BLUNTSCHLI. No; but it doesnt matter. I didnt ask the reason when you cried on; and I dont ask the reason now that you cry off. I'm a professional soldier! I fight when I have to, and am very glad to get out of it when I havnt to. Youre only an amateur: you think fighting's an amusement.

SERGIUS. [*sitting down at the table, nose to nose with him*] You shall hear the reason all the same, my professional. The reason is that it takes two men—real men—men of heart, blood and honor—to make a genuine combat. I could no more fight with you than I could make love to an ugly woman. Youve no magnetism: youre not a man: youre a machine.

BLUNTSCHLI. [*apologetically*] Quite true, quite true. I always was that sort of chap. I'm very sorry.

SERGIUS. Psha!

BLUNTSCHLI. But now that youve found that life isnt a farce, but something quite sensible and serious, what further obstacle is there to your happiness?

RAINA. [*rising*] You are very solicitous about my happiness and his. Do you forget his new love—Louka? It is not you that he must fight now, but his rival, Nicola.

SERGIUS. Rival!! [*bounding half across the room*]

RAINA. Dont you know that theyre engaged?

SERGIUS. Nicola! Are fresh abysses opening? Nicola!!

RAINA. [*sarcastically*] A shocking sacrifice, isnt it? Such beauty! such intellect! such modesty! wasted on a middle-aged servant man. Really, Sergius, you cannot stand by and allow such a thing. It would be unworthy of your chivalry.

SERGIUS. [*losing all self-control*] Viper! Viper! [*He rushes to and fro, raging.*]

BLUNTSCHLI. Look here, Saranoff: youre getting the worst of this.

RAINA. [*getting angrier*] Do you realize what he has done, Captain Bluntschli? He has set this girl as a spy on us; and her reward is that he makes love to her.

SERGIUS. False! Monstrous!

RAINA. Monstrous! [*confronting him*] Do you deny that she told you about Captain Bluntschli being in my room?

SERGIUS. No; but—

RAINA. [*interrupting*] Do you deny that you were making love to her when she told you?

SERGIUS. No; but I tell you—

RAINA. [*cutting him short contemptuously*] It is unnecessary to tell us anything more. That is quite enough for us. [*She turns away from him and sweeps majestically back to the window.*]

BLUNTSCHLI. [*quietly, as* SERGIUS, *in an agony of mortification, sinks on the ottoman, clutching his averted head between his fists*] I told you you were getting the worst of it, Saranoff.

SERGIUS. Tiger cat!

RAINA. [*running excitedly to* BLUNTSCHLI] You hear this man calling me names, Captain Bluntschli?

BLUNTSCHLI. What else can he do, dear lady? He must defend himself somehow. Come [*very persuasively*]: dont quarrel. What good does it do?

> [RAINA, *with a gasp, sits down on the ottoman, and after a vain effort to look vexedly at* BLUNTSCHLI, *falls a victim to her sense of humor, and actually leans back babyishly against the writhing shoulder of* SERGIUS.]

SERGIUS. Engaged to Nicola! Ha! ha! Ah well, Bluntschli, you are right to take this huge imposture of a world coolly.

RAINA. [*quaintly to* BLUNTSCHLI, *with an intuitive guess at his state of mind*] I daresay you think us a couple of grown-up babies, dont you?

SERGIUS. [*grinning savagely*] He does: he does. Swiss civilization nursetending Bulgarian barbarism, eh?

BLUNTSCHLI. [*blushing*] Not at all, I assure you. I'm only very glad to get you two quieted. There! there! let's be pleasant and talk it over in a friendly way. Where is this other young lady?

RAINA. Listening at the door, probably.

SERGIUS. [*shivering as if a bullet had struck him, and speaking with quiet but deep indignation*] I will prove that that, at least, is a calumny. [*He goes with dignity to the door and opens it. A yell of fury bursts from him as he looks out. He darts into the passage, and returns dragging in* LOUKA, *whom he flings violently against the table, exclaiming*] Judge her, Bluntschli. You, the cool impartial man: judge the eavesdropper.

[LOUKA *stands her ground, proud and silent.*]

BLUNTSCHLI. [*shaking his head*] I mustnt judge her. I once listened myself outside a tent when there was a mutiny brewing. It's all a question of the degree of provocation. My life was at stake.

LOUKA. My love was at stake. I am not ashamed.

RAINA. [*contemptuously*] Your love! Your curiosity, you mean.

LOUKA. [*facing her and returning her contempt with interest*] My love, stronger than anything you can feel, even for your chocolate cream soldier.

SERGIUS. [*with quick suspicion, to* LOUKA] What does that mean?

LOUKA. [*fiercely*] I mean—

SERGIUS. [*interrupting her slightingly*] Oh, I remember: the ice pudding. A paltry taunt, girl!

[MAJOR PETKOFF *enters, in his shirtsleeves.*]

PETKOFF. Excuse my shirtsleeves, gentlemen. Raina: somebody has been wearing that coat of mine: I'll swear it. Somebody with a differently shaped back. It's all burst open at the sleeve. Your mother is mending it. I wish she'd make haste: I shall catch cold. [*He looks more attentively at them.*] Is anything the matter?

RAINA. No. [*She sits down at the stove, with a tranquil air.*]

SERGIUS. Oh no. [*He sits down at the end of the table, as at first.*]

BLUNTSCHLI. [*who is already seated*] Nothing. Nothing.

PETKOFF. [*sitting down on the ottoman in his old place*] Thats all right. [*He notices* LOUKA.] Anything the matter, Louka?

LOUKA. No, sir.

PETKOFF. [*genially*] Thats all right. [*He sneezes.*] Go and ask your mistress for my coat, like a good girl, will you?

[NICOLA *enters with the coat.* LOUKA *makes a pretence of having business in the room by taking the little table with the hookah away to the wall near the windows.*]

RAINA. [*rising quickly as she sees the coat on* NICOLA's *arm*] Here it is, papa. Give it to me, Nicola; and do you put some more wood on the fire. [*She takes the coat, and brings it to the* MAJOR, *who stands up to put it on.* NICOLA *attends to the fire.*]

PETKOFF. [*to* RAINA, *teasing her affectionately*] Aha! Going to be very good to poor old papa just for one day after his return from the wars, eh?

RAINA. [*with solemn reproach*] Ah, how can you say that to me, father?

PETKOFF. Well, well, only a joke, little one. Come: give me a kiss. [*She kisses him.*] Now give me the coat.

RAINA. No: I am going to put it on for you. Turn your back. [*He turns his back and feels behind him with his arms for the sleeves. She dexterously takes the photograph from the pocket and throws it on the table before* BLUNTSCHLI, *who covers it with a sheet of paper under the very nose of Sergius, who looks on amazed, with his suspicions roused in the highest degree. She then helps* PETKOFF *on with his coat.*] There, dear! Now are you comfortable?

PETKOFF. Quite, little love. Thanks. [*He sits down; and* RAINA *re-*

turns to her seat near the stove.] Oh, by the bye, Ive found something funny. Whats the meaning of this? [*He puts his hand into
the picked pocket.*] Eh? Hallo! [*He tries the other pocket.*] Well,
I could have sworn—! [*Much puzzled, he tries the breast pocket.*]
I wonder—[*trying the original pocket*] Where can it—? [*he rises,
exclaiming*] Your mother's taken it!

RAINA. [*very red*] Taken what?

PETKOFF. Your photograph, with the inscription: "Raina, to her
Chocolate Cream Soldier: a Souvenir." Now you know theres
something more in this than meets the eye; and I'm going to find
it out. [*shouting*] Nicola!

NIKOLA. [*coming to him*] Sir!

PETKOFF. Did you spoil any pastry of Miss Raina's this morning?

NICOLA. You heard Miss Raina say that I did, sir.

PETKOFF. I know that, you idiot. Was it true?

NICOLA. I am sure Miss Raina is incapable of saying anything that is
not true, sir.

PETKOFF. Are you? Then I'm not. [*turning to the others*] Come:
do you think I dont see it all? [*He goes to* SERGIUS, *and slaps him
on the shoulder.*] Sergius: youre the chocolate cream soldier, arnt
you?

SERGIUS. [*starting up*] I! A chocolate cream soldier! Certainly not.

PETKOFF. Not! [*He looks at them. They are all very serious and very
conscious.*] Do you mean to tell me that Raina sends things like
that to other men?

SERGIUS. [*enigmatically*] The world is not such an innocent place as
we used to think, Petkoff.

BLUNTSCHLI. [*rising*] It's all right, major. I'm the chocolate cream
soldier. [PETKOFF *and* SERGIUS *are equally astonished.*] The gracious young lady saved my life by giving me chocolate creams
when I was starving: shall I ever forget their flavour! My late
friend Stolz told you the story at Pirot. I was the fugitive.

PETKOFF. You! [*He gasps.*] Sergius: do you remember how those
two women went on this morning when we mentioned it?
[SERGIUS *smiles cynically.* PETKOFF *confronts* RAINA *severely.*]
Youre a nice young woman, arnt you?

RAINA. [*bitterly*] Major Saranoff has changed his mind. And when
I wrote that on the photograph, I did not know that Captain
Bluntschli was married.

BLUNTSCHLI. [*startled into vehement protest*] I'm not married.

RAINA. [*with deep reproach*] You said you were.

BLUNTSCHLI. I did not. I positively did not. I never was married in
my life.

PETKOFF. [*exasperated*] Raina: will you kindly inform me, if I am
not asking too much, which of these gentlemen you are engaged
to?

RAINA. To neither of them. This young lady [*introducing* LOUKA,
who faces them all proudly] is the object of Major Saranoff's affections at present.

PETKOFF. Louka! Are you mad, Sergius? Why, this girl's engaged to

Nicola.

NICOLA. I beg your pardon, sir. There is a mistake. Louka is not engaged to me.

PETKOFF. Not engaged to you, you scoundrel! Why, you had twenty-five levas from me on the day of your betrothal; and she had that gilt bracelet from Miss Raina.

NICOLA. [*with cool unction*] We gave it out so, sir. But it was only to give Louka protection. She had a soul above her station; and I have been no more than her confidential servant. I intend, as you know, sir, to set up a shop later on in Sofia; and I look forward to her custom and recommendation should she marry into the nobility. [*He goes out with impressive discretion, leaving them all staring after him.*]

PETKOFF. [*breaking the silence*] Well, I am—hm!

SERGIUS. This is either the finest heroism or the most crawling baseness. Which is it, Bluntschli?

BLUNTSCHLI. Never mind whether it's heroism or baseness. Nicola's the ablest man Ive met in Bulgaria. I'll make him manager of a hotel if he can speak French and German.

LOUKA. [*suddenly breaking out at* SERGIUS] I have been insulted by everyone here. You set them the example. You owe me an apology.

[SERGIUS, *like a repeating clock of which the spring has been touched, immediately begins to fold his arms.*]

BLUNTSCHLI. [*before he can speak*] It's no use. He never apologizes.

LOUKA. Not to you, his equal and his enemy. To me, his poor servant, he will not refuse to apologize.

SERGIUS. [*approvingly*] You are right. [*He bends his knee in his grandest manner.*] Forgive me.

LOUKA. I forgive you. [*She timidly gives him her hand, which he kisses.*] That touch makes me your affianced wife.

SERGIUS. [*springing up*] Ah! I forgot that.

LOUKA. [*coldly*] You can withdraw if you like.

SERGIUS. Withdraw! Never! You belong to me. [*He puts his arm about her.*]

[CATHERINE *comes in and finds* LOUKA *in* SERGIUS'S *arms, with all the rest gazing at them in bewildered astonishment.*]

CATHERINE. What does this mean?

[SERGIUS *releases* LOUKA.]

PETKOFF. Well, my dear, it appears that Sergius is going to marry Louka instead of Raina. [*She is about to break out indignantly at him: he stops her by exclaiming testily*] Dont blame me: Ive nothing to do with it. [*He retreats to the stove.*]

CATHERINE. Marry Louka! Sergius: you are bound by your word to us!

SERGIUS. [*folding his arms*] Nothing binds me.

BLUNTSCHLI. [*much pleased by this piece of common sense*] Saranoff: your hand. My congratulations. These heroics of yours have their practical side after all. [*to* LOUKA] Gracious young lady: the best wishes of a good Republican! [*He kisses her hand, to* RAINA'S *great disgust, and returns to his seat.*]

CATHERINE. Louka: you have been telling stories.

LOUKA. I have done Raina no harm.

CATHERINE. [*haughtily*] Raina!

[RAINA, *equally indignant, almost snorts at the liberty.*]

LOUKA. I have a right to call her Raina: she calls me Louka. I told Major Saranoff she would never marry him if the Swiss gentleman came back.

BLUNTSCHLI. [*rising, much surprised*] Hallo!

LOUKA. [*turning to* RAINA] I thought you were fonder of him than of Sergius. You know best whether I was right.

BLUNTSCHLI. What nonsense! I assure you, my dear major, my dear madame, the gracious young lady simply saved my life, nothing else. She never cared two straws for me. Why, bless my heart and soul, look at the young lady and look at me. She, rich, young, beautiful, with her imagination full of fairy princes and noble natures and cavalry charges and goodness knows what! And I, a commonplace Swiss soldier who hardly knows what a decent life is after fifteen years of barracks and battles: a vagabond, a man who has spoiled all his chances in life through an incurably romantic disposition, a man—

SERGIUS. [*starting as if a needle had pricked him and interrupting* BLUNTSCHLI *in incredulous amazement*] Excuse me, Bluntschli: what did you say had spoiled your chances in life?

BLUNTSCHLI. [*promptly*] An incurably romantic disposition. I ran away from home twice when I was a boy. I went into the army instead of into my father's business. I climbed the balcony of this house when a man of sense would have dived into the nearest cellar. I came sneaking back here to have another look at the young lady when any other man of my age would have sent the coat back—

PETKOFF. My coat!

BLUNTSCHLI.—yes: thats the coat I mean—would have sent it back and gone quietly home. Do you suppose I am the sort of fellow a young girl falls in love with? Why, look at our ages! I'm thirty-four: I dont suppose the young lady is much over seventeen. [*This estimate produces a marked sensation, all the rest turning and staring at one another. He proceeds innocently.*] All that adventure which was life or death to me, was only a schoolgirl's game to her—chocolate creams and hide and seek. Heres the proof! [*He takes the photograph from the table.*] Now, I ask you, would a woman who took the affair seriously have sent me this and written on it "Raina, to her Chocolate Cream Soldier: a Souvenir"? [*He exhibits the photograph triumphantly, as if it settled the matter beyond all possibility of refutation.*]

PETKOFF. Thats what I was looking for. How the deuce did it get there? [*He comes from the stove to look at it, and sits down on the ottoman.*]

BLUNTSCHLI. [*to* RAINA, *complacently*] I have put everything right, I hope, gracious young lady.

RAINA. [*going to the table to face him*] I quite agree with your account of yourself. You are a romantic idiot. [BLUNTSCHLI *is unspeakably taken aback.*] Next time, I hope you will know the difference between a schoolgirl of seventeen and a woman of twenty-three.

BLUNTSCHLI. [*stupefied*] Twenty-three!

[RAINA *snaps the photograph contemptuously from his hand; tears it up; throws the pieces in his face; and sweeps back to her former place.*]

SERGIUS. [*with grim enjoyment of his rival's discomfiture*] Bluntschli: my one last belief is gone. Your sagacity is a fraud, like everything else. You have less sense than even I!

BLUNTSCHLI. [*overwhelmed*] Twenty-three! Twenty-three! [*He considers.*] Hm! [*swiftly making up his mind and coming to his host*] In that case, Major Petkoff, I beg to propose formally to become a suitor for your daughter's hand, in place of Major Saranoff retired.

RAINA. You dare!

BLUNTSCHLI. If you were twenty-three when you said those things to me this afternoon, I shall take them seriously.

CATHERINE. [*loftily polite*] I doubt, sir, whether you quite realize either my daughter's position or that of Major Sergius Saranoff, whose place you propose to take. The Petkoffs and the Saranoffs are known as the richest and most important families in the country. Our position is almost historical: we can go back for twenty years.

PETKOFF. Oh, never mind that, Catherine. [*to BLUNTSCHLI*] We should be most happy, Bluntschli, if it were only a question of your position; but hang it, you know, Raina is accustomed to a very comfortable establishment. Sergius keeps twenty horses.

BLUNTSCHLI. But who wants twenty horses? We're not going to keep a circus.

CATHERINE. [*severely*] My daughter, sir, is accustomed to a first-rate stable.

RAINA. Hush, mother: youre making me ridiculous.

BLUNTSCHLI. Oh well, if it comes to a question of an establishment, here goes! [*He darts impetuously to the table; seizes the papers in the blue envelope; and turns to* SERGIUS.] How many horses did you say?

SERGIUS. Twenty, noble Switzer.

BLUNTSCHLI. I have two hundred horses. [*They are amazed.*] How many carriages?

SERGIUS. Three.

BLUNTSCHLI. I have seventy. Twenty-four of them will hold twelve inside, besides two on the box, without counting the driver and conductor. How many tablecloths have you?

SERGIUS. How the deuce do I know?

BLUNTSCHLI. Have you four thousand?

SERGIUS. No.

BLUNTSCHLI. I have. I have nine thousand six hundred pairs of sheets and blankets, with two thousand four hundred eider-down quilts. I have ten thousand knives and forks, and the same quantity of dessert spoons. I have three hundred servants. I have six palatial establishments, besides two livery stables, a tea garden, and a private house. I have four medals for distinguished services; I have the rank of an officer and the standing of a gentleman; and I have three native languages. Shew me any man in Bulgaria that can offer as much!

PETKOFF. [*with childish awe*] Are you Emperor of Switzerland?

BLUNTSCHLI. My rank is the highest known in Switzerland: I am a free citizen.

CATHERINE. Then, Captain Bluntschli, since you are my daughter's choice—

RAINA. [*mutinously*] He's not.

CATHERINE. [*ignoring her*]—I shall not stand in the way of her happiness. [PETKOFF *is about to speak*.] That is Major Petkoff's feeling also.

PETKOFF. Oh, I shall be only too glad. Two hundred horses! Whew!

SERGIUS. What says the lady?

RAINA. [*pretending to sulk*] The lady says that he can keep his table-cloths and his omnibuses. I am not here to be sold to the highest bidder. [*She turns her back on him.*]

BLUNTSCHLI. I wont take that answer. I appealed to you as a fugitive, a beggar, and a starving man. You accepted me. You gave me your hand to kiss, your bed to sleep in, and your roof to shelter me.

RAINA. I did not give them to the Emperor of Switzerland.

BLUNTSCHLI. Thats just what I say. [*He catches her by the shoulders and turns her face-to-face with him.*] Now tell us whom you did give them to.

RAINA. [*succumbing with a shy smile*] To my chocolate cream soldier.

BLUNTSCHLI. [*with a boyish laugh of delight*] Thatll do. Thank you. [*He looks at his watch and suddenly becomes businesslike.*] Time's up, major. Youve managed those regiments so well that youre sure to be asked to get rid of some of the infantry of the Timok division. Send them home by way of Lom Palanka. Saranoff: dont get married until I come back: I shall be here punctually at five in the evening on Tuesday fortnight. Gracious ladies [*his heels click*] good evening. [*He makes them a military bow, and goes.*]

SERGIUS. What a man! Is he a man?

The Matchmaker

THORNTON WILDER

The Matchmaker, after playing at the Edinburgh Festival and in London in 1954, opened its long run in New York in December, 1955. It was already an old play by then, a slight revision of *The Merchant of Yonkers*, which had played unsuccessfully (39 performances) in New York in 1938. As Thornton Wilder's note on sources indicates, however, the play's ancestry goes back much earlier than 1938. John Oxenford's *A Day Well Spent* (1835), the original source, is a one-act farce which uses most of the material—the elopement, the day on the town, the shop as refuge, the restaurant scene, the disguise, the mistaken identity, the multiple marriages—that goes into *The Matchmaker*; it has into the bargain, a burglary, the foiling of which reconciles the merchant to his wayward clerks. With so much happening in so short a space, Oxenford cannot savor his incidents as Wilder does; all that he offers his audience aside from the fantastic accidents of the plot is a number of rather horrifying puns of which one example ought to be enough: Cutaway says of the absent Mr. Cotton: "for though a *father*, he is not yet *apparent*." In *Einen Jux will er sich machen* (1842), Johann Nestroy, the Austrian farceur whose work influenced so many later German playwrights, took over the events in Oxenford's short play, expanded them to four acts, added songs, and gave the mixture the satiric color that Nestroy always found in the juxtaposition of marriage and money. Perhaps Thornton Wilder's own words, from his Preface to *Three Plays* (New York: Harper, 1957), can show best the difference in tone between his work and that of Nestroy, his immediate source:

> There is most of the plot (except that our friend Dolly Levi is not in Nestroy's play); there are some of the tags; but it's all "about" quite different matters. My play is about the aspirations of the young (and not only of the young) for a fuller, freer participation in life. Imagine an Austrian pharmacist going to the shelf to draw from a bottle which he knows to contain a stinging corrosive liquid, guaranteed to remove warts and wens; and imagine his surprise when he discovers that it has been filled overnight with very American birch-bark beer.

Dolly Levi's description of the cooking talents of the mythical Ernestina Simple in Act I shows, by Wilder's admission, that Molière's *L'Avare* is also one of *The Matchmaker*'s ancestors and another statement from the Preface quoted above indicates still more of the play's relatives: "This play parodies the stock-company plays that I used to see at Ye Liberty

223

Theatre, Oakland, California, when I was a boy." Thornton Wilder is the American playwright who knows best something that Shakespeare also knew: that you can borrow ingredients from anyone and everyone if you have the wit to bake your own cake and make it a good one.

The Matchmaker†

This play is a rewritten version of The Merchant of Yonkers, *which was directed in 1938 by Max Reinhardt and is again dedicated to Max Reinhardt with deep admiration and indebtedness*

Characters

HORACE VANDERGELDER, *a merchant of Yonkers, New York*

CORNELIUS HACKL
BARNABY TUCKER } *clerks in his store*
MALACHI STACK

AMBROSE KEMPER, *an artist*

JOE SCANLON, *a barber*

RUDOLPH
AUGUST } *waiters*

A CABMAN

MRS. DOLLY LEVI
MISS FLORA VAN HUYSEN } *friends of Vandergelder's late wife*

MRS. IRENE MOLLOY, *a milliner*

MINNIE FAY, *her assistant*

ERMENGARDE, *Vandergelder's niece*

GERTRUDE, *Vandergelder's housekeeper*

MISS VAN HUYSEN'S COOK

TIME: *The early 80's.*

Act I.   Vandergelder's house in Yonkers, New York.
Act II.   Mrs. Molloy's hat shop, New York.
Act III.   The Harmonia Gardens Restaurant on the Battery, New York.
Act IV.   Miss Van Huysen's house, New York.

This play is based upon a comedy by Johann Nestroy, *Einen Jux will er sich machen* (Vienna, 1842), which was in turn based upon an English original, *A Day Well Spent* (London, 1835) by John Oxenford.

Act I

Living room of MR. VANDERGELDER'S *house, over his hay, feed and provision store in Yonkers, fifteen miles north of New York City. Articles from the store have overflowed into this room; it has not been cleaned for a long time and is in some disorder, but it is not sordid or gloomy.*

There are three entrances. One at the center back leads into the principal rooms of the house. One on the back right (all the directions are from the point of view of the actors) opens on steps which descend to the street door. One on the left leads to ERMENGARDE'S *room.*

In the center of the room is a trap door; below it is a ladder descending to the store below.

Behind the trap door and to the left of it is a tall accountant's desk; to the left of it is an old-fashioned stove with a stovepipe going up into the ceiling. Before the desk is a tall stool. On the right of the stage is a table with some chairs about it.

MR. VANDERGELDER'S *Gladstone bag, packed for a journey, is beside the desk.*

It is early morning.

VANDERGELDER, *sixty, choleric, vain and sly, wears a soiled dressing gown. He is seated with a towel about his neck, in a chair beside the desk, being shaved by* JOE SCANLON. VANDERGELDER *is smoking a cigar and holding a hand mirror.* AMBROSE KEMPER *is angrily striding about the room.*

VANDERGELDER. [*loudly*] I tell you for the hundredth time you will never marry my niece.

AMBROSE. [*thirty; dressed as an "artist"*] And I tell you for the thousandth time that I will marry your niece; and right soon, too.

VANDERGELDER. Never!

AMBROSE. Your niece is of age, Mr. Vandergelder. Your niece has consented to marry me. This is a free country, Mr. Vandergelder —not a private kingdom of your own.

VANDERGELDER. There are no free countries for fools, Mr. Kemper. Thank you for the honor of your visit—good morning.

JOE. [*fifty; lanky, mass of gray hair falling into his eyes*] Mr. Vandergelder, will you please sit still one minute? If I cut your throat it'll be practically unintentional.

VANDERGELDER. Ermengarde is not for you, nor for anybody else who can't support her.

AMBROSE. I tell you I can support her. I make a very good living.

VANDERGELDER. No, sir! A living is made, Mr. Kemper, by selling something that everybody needs at least once a year. Yes, sir! And a million is made by producing something that everybody needs every day. You artists produce something that nobody needs at any time. You may sell a picture once in a while, but

226 · Thornton Wilder

you'll make no living. Joe, go over there and stamp three times. I want to talk to Cornelius.

[JOE *crosses to trap door and stamps three times.*]

AMBROSE. Not only can I support her now, but I have considerable expectations.

VANDERGELDER. *Expectations!* We merchants don't do business with them. I don't keep accounts with people who promise somehow to pay something someday, and I don't allow my niece to marry such people.

AMBROSE. Very well, from now on you might as well know that I regard any way we can find to get married is right and fair. Ermengarde is of age, and there's no law . . .

[VANDERGELDER *rises and crosses toward* AMBROSE. JOE SCANLON *follows him complainingly and tries to find a chance to cut his hair even while he is standing.*][1]

VANDERGELDER. Law? Let me tell you something, Mr. Kemper: most of the people in the world are fools. The law is there to prevent crime; we men of sense are there to prevent foolishness. It's I, and not the law, that will prevent Ermengarde from marrying you, and I've taken some steps already. I've sent her away to get this nonsense out of her head.

AMBROSE. Ermengarde's . . . not here?

VANDERGELDER. She's gone—east, west, north, south. I thank you for the honor of your visit.

[Enter GERTRUDE—*eighty; deaf; half blind; and very pleased with herself.*]

GERTRUDE. Everything's ready, Mr. Vandergelder. Ermengarde and I have just finished packing the trunk.

VANDERGELDER. Hold your tongue! [JOE *is shaving* VANDERGELDER'S *throat, so he can only wave his hands vainly.*]

GERTRUDE. Yes, Mr. Vandergelder, Ermengarde's ready to leave. Her trunk's all marked. Care Miss Van Huysen, 8 Jackson Street, New York.

VANDERGELDER. [*breaking away from* JOE] Hell and damnation! Didn't I tell you it was a secret?

AMBROSE. [*picks up hat and coat—kisses* GERTRUDE] Care Miss Van Huysen, 8 Jackson Street, New York. Thank you very much. Good morning, Mr. Vandergelder. [*Exit* AMBROSE, *to the street.*]

VANDERGELDER. It won't help you, Mr. Kemper— [*to* GERTRUDE] Deaf! And blind! At least you can do me the favor of being dumb!

GERTRUDE. Chk—chk! Such a temper! Lord save us!

[CORNELIUS *puts his head up through the trap door. He is thirty-three; mock-deferential—he wears a green apron and is in his shirt-sleeves.*]

CORNELIUS. Yes, Mr. Vandergelder?

VANDERGELDER. Go in and get my niece's trunk and carry it over to the station. Wait! Gertrude, has Mrs. Levi arrived yet?

1. I have always wondered why Joe is trying to cut Vandergelder's hair in this stage direction when he is shaving him everywhere else in the act.

[CORNELIUS *comes up the trap door, steps into the room and closes the trap door behind him.*]

GERTRUDE. Don't shout. I can hear perfectly well. Everything's clearly marked. [*Exit left.*]

VANDERGELDER. Have the buggy brought round to the front of the store in half an hour.

CORNELIUS. Yes, Mr. Vandergelder.

VANDERGELDER. This morning I'm joining my lodge parade and this afternoon I'm going to New York. Before I go, I have something important to say to you and Barnaby. Good news. Fact is—I'm going to promote you. How old are you?

CORNELIUS. Thirty-three, Mr. Vandergelder.

VANDERGELDER. What?

CORNELIUS. Thirty-three.

VANDERGELDER. That all? That's a foolish age to be at. I thought you were forty.

CORNELIUS. Thirty-three.

VANDERGELDER. A man's not worth a cent until he's forty. We just pay 'em wages to make mistakes—don't we, Joe?

JOE. You almost lost an ear on it, Mr. Vandergelder.

VANDERGELDER. I was thinking of promoting you to chief clerk.

CORNELIUS. What am I now, Mr. Vandergelder?

VANDERGELDER. You're an impertinent fool, that's what you are. Now, if you behave yourself, I'll promote you from impertinent fool to chief clerk, with a raise in your wages. And Barnaby may be promoted from idiot apprentice to incompetent clerk.

CORNELIUS. Thank you, Mr. Vandergelder.

VANDERGELDER. However, I want to see you again before I go. Go in and get my niece's trunk.

CORNELIUS. Yes, Mr. Vandergelder. [*Exit* CORNELIUS, *left.*]

VANDERGELDER. Joe—the world's getting crazier every minute. Like my father used to say: the horses'll be taking over the world soon.

JOE. [*presenting mirror*] I did what I could, Mr. Vandergelder, what with you flying in and out of the chair. [*He wipes last of the soap from* VANDERGELDER's *face.*]

VANDERGELDER. Fine, fine. Joe, you do a fine job, the same fine job you've done me for twenty years. Joe . . . I've got special reasons for looking my best today . . . isn't there something a little extry you could do, something a little special? I'll pay you right up to fifty cents—see what I mean? Do some of those things you do to the young fellas. Touch me up; smarten me up a bit.

JOE. All I know is fifteen cents' worth, like usual, Mr. Vandergelder; and that includes everything that's decent to do to a man.

VANDERGELDER. Now hold your horses, Joe—all I meant was . . .

JOE. I've shaved you for twenty years and you never asked me no such question before.

VANDERGELDER. Hold your horses, I say, Joe! I'm going to tell you a secret. But I don't want you telling it to that riffraff down to the barbershop what I'm going to tell you now. All I ask of you is a little extry because I'm thinking of getting married again; and this very afternoon I'm going to New York to call on my intended, a very refined lady.

JOE. Your gettin' married is none of my business, Mr. Vandergelder. I done everything to you I know, and the charge is fifteen cents like it always was, and . . .

[CORNELIUS *crosses, left to right, and exit, carrying a trunk on his shoulder.* ERMENGARDE *and* GERTRUDE *enter from left.*]

I don't dye no hair, not even for fifty cents I don't!

VANDERGELDER. Joe Scanlon, get out!

JOE. And lastly, it looks to me like you're pretty rash to judge which is fools and which isn't fools, Mr. Vandergelder. People that's et onions is bad judges of who's et onions and who ain't. Good morning, ladies; good morning, Mr. Vandergelder. [*Exit* JOE.]

VANDERGELDER. Well, what do you want?

ERMENGARDE. [*twenty-four; pretty, sentimental*] Uncle! You said you wanted to talk to us.

VANDERGELDER. Oh yes. Gertrude, go and get my parade regalia— the uniform for my lodge parade.

GERTRUDE. What? Oh yes. Lord have mercy! [*Exit* GERTRUDE, *back center.*]

VANDERGELDER. I had a talk with that artist of yours. He's a fool. [ERMENGARDE *starts to cry.*] Weeping! Weeping! You can go down and weep for a while in New York where it won't be noticed. [*He sits on desk chair, puts tie round neck and calls her over to tie it for him.*] Ermengarde! I told him that when you were old enough to marry you'd marry someone who could support you. I've done you a good turn. You'll come and thank me when you're fifty.

ERMENGARDE. But Uncle, I love him!

VANDERGELDER. I tell you you don't.

ERMENGARDE. But I *do!*

VANDERGELDER. And I tell you you don't. Leave those things to me.

ERMENGARDE. If I don't marry Ambrose I know I'll die.

VANDERGELDER. What of?

ERMENGARDE. A broken heart.

VANDERGELDER. Never heard of it. Mrs. Levi is coming in a moment to take you to New York. You are going to stay two or three weeks with Miss Van Huysen, an old friend of your mother's.

[GERTRUDE *re-enters with coat, sash and sword. Enter from the street, right,* MALACHI STACK.]

You're not to receive any letters except from me. I'm coming to New York myself today and I'll call on you tomorrow. [*to* MALACHI] Who are you?

MALACHI. [*Fifty. Sardonic. Apparently innocent smile; pretense of humility*] Malachi Stack, your honor. I heard you wanted an apprentice in the hay, feed, provision and hardware business.

VANDERGELDER. An apprentice at your age?

MALACHI. Yes. your honor; I bring a lot of experience to it.

VANDERGELDER. Have you any letters of recommendation?

MALACHI. [*extending a sheaf of soiled papers*] Yes, indeed, your honor! First-class recommendation.

VANDERGELDER. Ermengarde! Are you ready to start?

ERMENGARDE. Yes.

VANDERGELDER. Well, go and get ready some more. Ermengarde! Let me know the minute Mrs. Levi gets here.

ERMENGARDE. Yes, Uncle Horace.

[ERMENGARDE *and* GERTRUDE *exit.* VANDERGELDER *examines the letters, putting them down one by one.*]

VANDERGELDER. I don't want an able seaman. Nor a typesetter. And I don't want a hospital cook.

MALACHI. No, your honor, but it's all experience. Excuse me! [*selects a letter*] This one is from your former partner, Joshua Van Tuyl, in Albany. [*He puts letters from table back into pocket.*]

VANDERGELDER. ". . . for the most part honest and reliable . . . occasionally willing and diligent." There seems to be a certain amount of hesitation about these recommendations.

MALACHI. Businessmen aren't writers, your honor. There's only one businessman in a thousand that can write a good letter of recommendation, your honor. Mr. Van Tuyl sends his best wishes and wants to know if you can use me in the provision and hardware business.

VANDERGELDER. Not so fast, not so fast! What's this "your honor" you use so much?

MALACHI. Mr. Van Tuyl says you're President of the Hudson River Provision Dealers' Recreational, Musical and Burial Society.

VANDERGELDER. I am; but there's no "your honor" that goes with it. Why did you come to Yonkers?

MALACHI. I heard that you'd had an apprentice that was a good-for-nothing, and that you were at your wit's end for another.

VANDERGELDER. Wit's end, wit's end! There's no dearth of good-for-nothing apprentices.

MALACHI. That's right, Mr. Vandergelder. It's employers there's a dearth of. Seems like you hear of a new one dying every day.

VANDERGELDER. What's that? Hold your tongue. I see you've been a barber, and a valet too. Why have you changed your place so often?

MALACHI. Changed my place, Mr. Vandergelder? When a man's interested in experience . . .

VANDERGELDER. Do you drink?

MALACHI. No, thanks. I've just had breakfast.

VANDERGELDER. I didn't ask you whether—Idiot! I asked you if you were a drunkard.

MALACHI. No, sir! No! Why, looking at it from all sides I don't even like liquor.

VANDERGELDER. Well, if you keep on looking at it from all sides, out you go. Remember that. Here. [*gives him remaining letters*] With all your faults, I'm going to give you a try.

MALACHI. You'll never regret it, Mr. Vandergelder. You'll never regret it.

VANDERGELDER. Now today I want to use you in New York. I judge you know your way around New York?

MALACHI. Do I know New York? Mr. Vandergelder, I know every hole and corner in New York.

VANDERGELDER. Here's a dollar. A train leaves in a minute. Take that bag to the Central Hotel on Water Street, have them save me a room. Wait for me. I'll be there about four o'clock.

MALACHI. Yes, Mr. Vandergelder. [*picks up the bag, starts out, then comes back*] Oh, but first, I'd like to meet the other clerks I'm to work with.

VANDERGELDER. You haven't time. Hurry now. The station's across the street.

MALACHI. Yes, sir. [*away—then back once more*] You'll see, sir, you'll never regret it. . . .

VANDERGELDER. I regret it already. Go on. Off with you.

[*Exit* MALACHI, *right.*]

[*The following speech is addressed to the audience. During it* MR. VANDERGELDER *takes off his dressing gown, puts on his scarlet sash, his sword and his bright-colored coat. He is already wearing light blue trousers with a red stripe down the sides.*]

VANDERGELDER. Ninety-nine per cent of the people in the world are fools and the rest of us are in great danger of contagion. But I wasn't always free of foolishness as I am now. I was once young, which was foolish; I fell in love, which was foolish; and I got married, which was foolish; and for a while I was poor, which was more foolish than all the other things put together. Then my wife died, which was foolish of her; I grew older, which was sensible of me; then I became a rich man, which is as sensible as it is rare. Since you see I'm a man of sense, I guess you were surprised to hear that I'm planning to get married again. Well, I've two reasons for it. In the first place, I like my house run with order, comfort and economy. That's a woman's work; but even a woman can't do it well if she's merely being paid for it. In order to run a house well, a woman must have the feeling that she owns it. Marriage is a bribe to make a housekeeper think she's a householder. Did you ever watch an ant carry a burden twice its size? What excitement! What patience! What will! Well, that's what I think of when I see a woman running a house. What giant passions in those little bodies—what quarrels with the butcher for the best cut—what fury at discovering a moth in a cupboard! Believe me!—if women could harness their natures to something bigger than a house and a baby carriage—tck! tck!—they'd change the world. And the second reason, ladies and gentlemen? Well, I see by your faces you've guessed it already. There's nothing like mixing with women to bring out all the foolishness in a man of sense. And that's a risk I'm willing to take. I've just turned sixty, and I've just laid side by side the last dollar of my first half million. So if I should lose my head a little, I still have enough money to buy it back. After many years' caution and hard work, I have a right to a little risk and adventure, and I'm thinking of getting married. Yes, like all you other fools, I'm willing to risk a little security for a certain amount of adventure. Think it over. [*Exit back center.*]

[AMBROSE *enters from the street, crosses left, and whistles softly.* ERMENGARDE *enters from left.*]

ERMENGARDE. Ambrose! If my uncle saw you!

AMBROSE. Sh! Get your hat.

ERMENGARDE. My hat!

AMBROSE. Quick! Your trunk's at the station. Now quick! We're running away.

ERMENGARDE. Running away!

AMBROSE. Sh!

ERMENGARDE. Where?

AMBROSE. To New York. To get married.

ERMENGARDE. Oh, Ambrose, I can't do that. Ambrose dear—it wouldn't be proper!

AMBROSE. Listen. I'm taking you to my friend's house. His wife will take care of you.

ERMENGARDE. But, Ambrose, a girl can't go on a train with a man. I can see you don't know anything about girls.

AMBROSE. But I'm telling you we're going to get married!

ERMENGARDE. Married! But what would *Uncle* say?

AMBROSE. We don't care what Uncle'd say—we're eloping.

ERMENGARDE. Ambrose Kemper! How can you use such an awful word!

AMBROSE. Ermengarde, you have the soul of a field mouse.

ERMENGARDE. [*crying*] Ambrose, why do you say such cruel things to me?

[*Enter* MRS. LEVI, *from the street, right. She stands listening.*]

AMBROSE. For the last time I beg you—get your hat and coat. The train leaves in a few minutes. Ermengarde, we'll get married tomorrow. . . .

ERMENGARDE. Oh, Ambrose! I see you don't understand anything about weddings. Ambrose, don't you *respect* me? . . .

MRS LEVI. [*uncertain age; mass of sandy hair; impoverished elegance; large, shrewd but generous nature, an assumption of worldly cynicism conceals a tireless amused enjoyment of life. She carries a handbag and a small brown paper bag.*] Good morning, darling girl—how are you? [*They kiss.*]

ERMENGARDE. Oh, good morning, Mrs. Levi.

MRS. LEVI. And who is this gentleman who is so devoted to you?

ERMENGARDE. This is Mr. Kemper, Mrs. Levi. Ambrose, this is . . . Mrs. Levi . . . she's an old friend. . . .

MRS. LEVI. Mrs. Levi, born Gallagher. Very happy to meet you, Mr. Kemper.

AMBROSE. Good morning, Mrs. Levi.

MRS. LEVI. Mr. Kemper, *the artist!* Delighted! Mr. Kemper, may I say something very frankly?

AMBROSE. Yes, Mrs. Levi.

MRS. LEVI. This thing you were planning to do is a very great mistake.

ERMENGARDE. Oh, Mrs. Levi, please explain to Ambrose—of *course!* I want to marry him, but to *elope!* . . . How . . .

MRS. LEVI. Now, my dear girl, you go in and keep one eye on your uncle. I wish to talk to Mr. Kemper for a moment. You give us a warning when you hear your Uncle Horace coming. . . .

ERMENGARDE. Ye-es, Mrs. Levi. [*Exit* ERMENGARDE, *back center.*]

MRS. LEVI. Mr. Kemper, I was this dear girl's mother's oldest friend. Believe me, I am on your side. I hope you two will be married very soon, and I think I can be of real service to you. Mr. Kemper, I always go right to the point.

AMBROSE. What is the point, Mrs. Levi?

MRS. LEVI. Mr. Vandergelder is a very rich man, Mr. Kemper, and Ermengarde is his only relative.

AMBROSE. But I am not interested in Mr. Vandergelder's money. I have enough to support a wife and family.

MRS. LEVI. Enough? How much is enough when one is thinking about children and the future? The future is the most expensive luxury in the world, Mr. Kemper.

AMBROSE. Mrs. Levi, what is the point.

MRS. LEVI. Believe me, Mr. Vandergelder wishes to get rid of Ermengarde, and if you follow my suggestions he will even permit her to marry you. You see, Mr. Vandergelder is planning to get married himself.

AMBROSE. What? That monster!

MRS. LEVI. Mr. Kemper!

AMBROSE. Married! To you, Mrs. Levi?

MRS. LEVI. [*taken aback*] Oh, no, no . . . NO! I am merely arranging it. I am helping him find a suitable bride.

AMBROSE. For Mr. Vandergelder there are no suitable brides.

MRS. LEVI. I think we can safely say that Mr. Vandergelder will be married to someone by the end of next week.

AMBROSE. What are you suggesting, Mrs. Levi?

MRS. LEVI. I am taking Ermengarde to New York on the next train. I shall not take her to Miss Van Huysen's, as is planned; I shall take her to my house. I wish you to call for her at my house at five thirty. Here is my card.

AMBROSE. "Mrs. Dolly Gallagher Levi. Varicose veins reduced."

MRS. LEVI. [*trying to take back card*] I beg your pardon . . .

AMBROSE. [*holding card*] I beg *your* pardon. "Consultations free."

MRS. LEVI. I meant to give you my other card. Here.

AMBROSE. "Mrs. Dolly Gallagher Levi. Aurora Hosiery. Instruction in the guitar and mandolin." You do all these things, Mrs. Levi?

MRS. LEVI. Two and two make four, Mr. Kemper—always did. So you will come to my house at five thirty. At about six I shall take you both with me to the Harmonia Gardens Restaurant on the Battery; Mr. Vandergelder will be there and everything will be arranged.

AMBROSE. How?

MRS. LEVI. Oh, I don't know. One thing will lead to another.

AMBROSE. How do I know that I can trust you, Mrs. Levi? You could easily make our situation worse.

MRS. LEVI. Mr. Kemper, your situation could not possibly be worse.

AMBROSE. I wish I knew what you get out of this, Mrs. Levi.

MRS. LEVI. That is a very proper question. I get two things: profit and pleasure.

AMBROSE. How?

MRS. LEVI. Mr. Kemper, I am a woman who arranges things. At present I am arranging Mr. Vandergelder's domestic affairs. Out of it I get—shall we call it: little pickings? I need little pickings, Mr. Kemper, and especially just now, when I haven't got my train fare back to New York. You see: I am frank with you.

AMBROSE. That's your profit, Mrs. Levi; but where do you get your pleasure?

MRS. LEVI. My pleasure? Mr. Kemper, when you artists paint a hill-side or a river you change everything a little, you make thousands of little changes, don't you? Nature is never completely satisfactory and must be corrected. Well, I'm like you artists. Life as it is is never quite interesting enough for me—I'm bored, Mr. Kemper, with life as it is—and so I do things. I put my hand in here, and I put my hand in there, and I watch and I listen—and often I'm very much amused.

AMBROSE. [*rises*] Not in my affairs, Mrs. Levi.

MRS. LEVI. Wait, I haven't finished. There's another thing. I'm very interested in this household here—in Mr. Vandergelder and all that idle, frozen money of his. I don't like the thought of it lying in great piles, useless, motionless, in the bank, Mr. Kemper. Money should circulate like rain water. It should be flowing down among the people, through dressmakers and restaurants and cab-men, setting up a little business here, and furnishing a good time there. Do you see what I mean?

AMBROSE. Yes, I do.

MRS. LEVI. New York should be a very happy city, Mr. Kemper, but it isn't. My late husband came from Vienna; now there's a city that understands this. I want New York to be more like Vienna and less like a collection of nervous and tired ants. And if you and Ermengarde get a good deal of Mr. Vandergelder's money, I want you to see that it starts flowing in and around a lot of people's lives. And for that reason I want you to come with me to the Harmonia Gardens Restaurant tonight.

[*Enter* ERMENGARDE.]

ERMENGARDE. Mrs. Levi, Uncle Horace is coming.

MRS. LEVI. Mr. Kemper, I think you'd better be going. . . .

[AMBROSE *crosses to trap door and disappears down the lad-der, closing trap as he goes.*]

Darling girl, Mr. Kemper and I have had a very good talk. You'll see: Mr. Vandergelder and I will be dancing at your wedding very soon—

> [*Enter* VANDERGELDER *at back. He has now added a splendid plumed hat to his costume and is carrying a standard or small flag bearing the initials of his lodge.*]

Oh, Mr. Vandergelder, how handsome you look! You take my breath away. Yes, my dear girl, I'll see you soon.

> [*Exit* ERMENGARDE *back center.*]

Oh, Mr. Vandergelder, I wish Irene Molloy could see you now. But then! I don't know what's come over you lately. You seem to be growing younger every day.

VANDERGELDER. Allowing for exaggeration, Mrs. Levi. If a man eats careful there's no reason why he should look old.

MRS. LEVI. You never said a truer word.

VANDERGELDER. I'll never see fifty-five again.

MRS. LEVI. Fifty-five! Why, I can see at a glance that you're the sort that will be stamping about at a hundred—and eating five meals a day, like my Uncle Harry. At fifty-five my Uncle Harry was a mere boy. I'm a judge of hands, Mr. Vandergelder—show me your hand. [*looks at it*] Lord in heaven! What a life line!

VANDERGELDER. Where?

MRS. LEVI. From *here* to *here.* It runs right off your hand. I don't know where it goes. They'll have to hit you on the head with a mallet. They'll have to stifle you with a sofa pillow. You'll bury us all! However, to return to our business—Mr. Vandergelder, I suppose you've changed your mind again. I suppose you've given up all idea of getting married.

VANDERGELDER. [*complacently*] Not at all, Mrs. Levi. I have news for you.

MRS. LEVI. News?

VANDERGELDER. Mrs. Levi, I've practically decided to ask Mrs. Molloy to be my wife.

MRS. LEVI. [*taken aback*] You have?

VANDERGELDER. Yes, I have.

MRS. LEVI. Oh, you have! Well, I guess that's just about the best news I ever heard. So there's nothing more for me to do but wish you every happiness under the sun and say good-by. [*crosses as if to leave*]

VANDERGELDER. [*stopping her*] Well—Mrs. Levi—Surely I thought—

MRS. LEVI. Well, I did have a little suggestion to make—but I won't. You're going to marry Irene Molloy, and that closes the matter.

VANDERGELDER. What suggestion was that, Mrs. Levi?

MRS. LEVI. Well—I *had* found *another* girl for you.

VANDERGELDER. Another?

MRS. LEVI. The most wonderful girl, the ideal wife.

VANDERGELDER. Another, eh? What's her name?

MRS. LEVI. Her name?

VANDERGELDER. Yes!

MRS. LEVI. [*groping for it*] Err . . . er . . . her *name?*—Ernestina
—Simple. *Miss* Ernestina Simple. But now of course all that's
too late. After all, you're engaged—you're practically engaged to
marry Irene Molloy.

VANDERGELDER. Oh, I ain't engaged to Mrs. Molloy!

MRS. LEVI. Nonsense! You can't break poor Irene's heart now and
change to another girl. . . . When a man at your time of life
calls four times on an attractive widow like that—and sends her
a pot of geraniums—that's practically an engagement!

VANDERGELDER. That ain't an engagement!

MRS. LEVI. And yet—! If only you were free! I've found this treasure
of a girl. Every moment I felt like a traitor to Irene Molloy—but
let me tell you: I couldn't help it. I told this girl all about you,
just as though you were a free man. Isn't that dreadful? The fact
is: she has fallen in love with you already.

VANDERGELDER. Ernestina?

MRS. LEVI. Ernestina Simple.

VANDERGELDER. Ernestina Simple.

MRS. LEVI. Of course she's a very different idea from Mrs. Molloy,
Ernestina is. Like her name—simple, domestic, practical.

VANDERGELDER. Can she cook?

MRS. LEVI. Cook, Mr. Vandergelder? I've had two meals from her
hands, and—as I live—I don't know what I've done that God
should reward me with such meals.

[*The following passage—adapted from a scene in Molière's
L'Avare—has been cut in recent performances:*]

MRS. LEVI. [*continues*] Her duck! Her steak!

VANDERGELDER. Eh! Eh! In this house we don't eat duck and steak
every day, Mrs. Levi.

MRS. LEVI. But didn't I tell you?—that's the wonderful part about
it. Her duck—what was it? Pigeon! I'm alive to tell you. I don't
know how she does it. It's a secret that's come down in her
family. The greatest chefs would give their right hands to know
it. And the steaks? Shoulder of beef—four cents a pound. Dogs
wouldn't eat. But when Ernestina passes her hands over it—! !

VANDERGELDER. Allowing for exaggeration, Mrs. Levi.

MRS. LEVI. No exaggeration.

I'm the best cook in the world myself, and I *know* what's good.

VANDERGELDER. Hm. How old is she, Mrs. Levi?

MRS. LEVI. Nineteen, well—say twenty.

VANDERGELDER. Twenty, Mrs. Levi? Girls of twenty are apt to favor
young fellows of their own age.

MRS. LEVI. But you don't listen to me. And you don't know the
girl. Mr. Vandergelder, she has a positive horror of flighty, brainless young men. A fine head of gray hair, she says, is worth twenty
shined up with goose grease. No, sir. "I like a man that's *settled*"
—in so many words she said it.

236 · *Thornton Wilder*

VANDERGELDER. That's . . . that's not usual, Mrs. Levi.

MRS. LEVI. Usual? I'm not wearing myself to the bone hunting up *usual* girls to interest you, Mr. Vandergelder. Usual, indeed. Listen to me. Do you know the sort of pictures she has on her wall? Is it any of these young Romeos and Lochinvars? No!—it's Moses on the Mountain—that's what she's got. If you want to make her happy, you give her a picture of Methuselah surrounded by his grandchildren. That's my advice to you.

[*Following passage—also based on Molière—has generally been cut in performance:*]

VANDERGELDER. I hope . . . hm . . . that she has some means, Mrs. Levi. I have a large household to run.

MRS. LEVI. Ernestina? She'll bring you five thousand dollars a year.

VANDERGELDER. Eh! Eh!

MRS. LEVI. Listen to me, Mr. Vandergelder. You're a man of sense, I hope. A man that can reckon. In the first place, she's an orphan. She's been brought up with a great saving of food. What does she eat herself? Apples and lettuce. It's what she's been used to eat and what she likes best. She saves you two thousand a year right there. Secondly, she makes her own clothes—out of old tablecloths and window curtains. And she's the best-dressed woman in Brooklyn this minute. She saves you a thousand dollars right there. Thirdly, her health is of iron—

VANDERGELDER. But, Mrs. Levi, that's not money in the pocket.

MRS. LEVI. We're talking about marriage, aren't we, Mr. Vandergelder? The money she saves while she's in Brooklyn is none of your affair—but if she were your wife that would be *money*. Yes, sir, that's money.

VANDERGELDER. What's her family?

MRS. LEVI. Her father?—God be good to him! He was the best—what am I trying to say?—the best undertaker in Brooklyn, respected, esteemed. He knew all the best people—knew them well, even before they died. So—well, that's the way it is. [*lowering her voice, intimately*] Now let me tell you a little more of her appearance. Can you hear me: as I say, a beautiful girl, beautiful, I've seen her go down the street—you know what I mean?—the young men get dizzy. They have to lean against lampposts. And she? Modest, eyes on the ground—I'm not going to tell you any more. . . . Couldn't you come to New York today?

VANDERGELDER. I was thinking of coming to New York this afternoon. . . .

MRS. LEVI. You were? Well now, I wonder if something could be arranged—oh, she's so eager to see you! Let me see . . .

VANDERGELDER. Could I . . . Mrs. Levi, could I give you a little dinner, maybe?

MRS. LEVI. Really, come to think of it, I don't see where I could get the time. I'm so busy over that wretched lawsuit of mine.

Yes. If I win it, I don't mind telling you, I'll be what's called a very rich woman. I'll own half of Long Island, that's a fact. But just now I'm at my wit's end for a little help, just enough money to finish it off. My wit's end!

[*She looks in her handbag. In order not to hear this,* VAN-DERGELDER *has a series of coughs, sneezes and minor convulsions.*]

But perhaps I could arrange a little dinner; I'll see. Yes, for that lawsuit all I need is fifty dollars, and Staten Island's as good as mine. I've been trotting all over New York for you, trying to find you a suitable wife.

VANDERGELDER. Fifty dollars! !

MRS. LEVI. Two whole months I've been . . .

VANDERGELDER. Fifty dollars, Mrs. Levi . . . is no joke. [*producing purse*] I don't know where money's gone to these days. It's in hiding. . . . There's twenty . . . well, there's twenty-five. I can't spare no more, not now I can't.

MRS. LEVI. Well, this will help—will help somewhat. Now let me tell you what we'll do. I'll bring Ernestina to that restaurant on the Battery. You know it: the Harmonia Gardens. It's good, but it's not flashy. Now, Mr. Vandergelder, I think it'd be nice if just this once you'd order a real nice dinner. I guess you can afford it.

VANDERGELDER. Well, just this once.

MRS. LEVI. A chicken wouldn't hurt.

VANDERGELDER. Chicken! !—Well, just this once.

MRS. LEVI. And a little wine.

VANDERGELDER. Wine? Well, just this once.

MRS. LEVI. Now about Mrs. Molloy—what do you think? Shall we call that subject closed?

VANDERGELDER. No, not at all, Mrs. Levi, I want to have dinner with Miss . . . with Miss . . .

MRS. LEVI. Simple.

VANDERGELDER. With Miss Simple; but first I want to make another call on Mrs. Molloy.

MRS. LEVI. Dear, dear, dear! And Miss Simple? What races you make me run! Very well; I'll meet you on one of those benches in front of Mrs. Molloy's hat store at four thirty, as usual.

[*Trap door rises, and* CORNELIUS' *head appears.*]

CORNELIUS. The buggy's here, ready for the parade, Mr. Vandergelder.

VANDERGELDER. Call Barnaby. I want to talk to both of you.

CORNELIUS. Yes, Mr. Vandergelder. [*Exit* CORNELIUS *down trap door. Leaves trap open.*]

MRS. LEVI. Now do put your thoughts in order, Mr. Vandergelder. I can't keep upsetting and disturbing the finest women in New York City unless you mean business.

VANDERGELDER. Oh, I mean business all right!

MRS. LEVI. I hope so. Because, you know, you're playing a very dangerous game.

VANDERGELDER. Dangerous?—Dangerous, Mrs. Levi?

MRS. LEVI. Of course, it's dangerous—and there's a name for it! You're tampering with these women's affections, aren't you? And the only way you can save yourself now is to be married to *someone* by the end of next week. So think that over! [*Exit center back.*]

[*Enter* CORNELIUS *and* BARNABY, *by the trap door.*]

VANDERGELDER. This morning I'm joining my lodge parade, and this afternoon I'm going to New York. When I come back, there are going to be some changes in the house here. I'll tell you what the change is, but I don't want you discussing it amongst yourselves: you're going to have a mistress.

BARNABY. [*seventeen; round-faced, wide-eyed innocence; wearing a green apron*] I'm too young, Mr. Vandergelder! !

VANDERGELDER. Not yours! Death and damnation! Not yours, idiot —mine! [*then, realizing*] Hey! Hold your tongue until you're spoken to! I'm thinking of getting married.

CORNELIUS. [*crosses, hand outstretched*] Many congratulations, Mr. Vandergelder, and my compliments to the lady.

VANDERGELDER. That's none of your business. Now go back to the store.

[*The boys start down the ladder,* BARNABY *first.*]

Have you got any questions you want to ask before I go?

CORNELIUS. Mr. Vandergelder—er—Mr. Vandergelder, does the chief clerk get one evening off every week?

VANDERGELDER. So that's the way you begin being chief clerk, is it? When I was your age I got up at five; I didn't close the shop until ten at night, and then I put in a good hour at the account books. The world's going to pieces. You elegant ladies lie in bed until six and at nine o'clock at night you rush to close the door so fast the line of customers bark their noses. No, sir—you'll attend to the store as usual, and on Friday and Saturday nights you'll remain open until ten—now hear what I say! This is the first time I've been away from the store overnight. When I come back I want to hear that you've run the place perfectly in my absence. If I hear of any foolishness, I'll discharge you. An evening free! Do you suppose that *I* had evenings free? [*at the top of his complacency*] If I'd had evenings free I wouldn't be what I am now! [*He marches out, right.*]

BARNABY. [*watching him go*] The horses nearly ran away when they saw him. What's the matter, Cornelius?

CORNELIUS. [*sits in dejected thought*] Chief clerk! Promoted from chief clerk to chief clerk.

BARNABY. Don't you like it?

CORNELIUS. Chief clerk!—and if I'm good, in ten years I'll be promoted to chief clerk again. Thirty-three years old and I still don't get an evening free? When am I going to begin to live?

BARNABY. Well—ah . . . you can begin to live on Sundays, Cornelius.

CORNELIUS. That's not living. Twice to church, and old Wolf-trap's eyes on the back of my head the whole time. And as for holidays! What did we do last Christmas? All those canned tomatoes went bad and exploded. We had to clean up the mess all afternoon. Was that living?

BARNABY. [*holding his nose at the memory of the bad smell*] No! ! !

CORNELIUS. [*rising with sudden resolution*] Barnaby, how much money have you got—where you can get at it?

BARNABY. Oh—three dollars. Why, Cornelius?

CORNELIUS. You and I are going to New York.

BARNABY. Cornelius! ! ! We can't! Close the store?

CORNELIUS. Some more rotten-tomato cans are going to explode.

BARNABY. Holy cabooses! How do you know?

CORNELIUS. I know they're rotten. All you have to do is to light a match under them. They'll make such a smell that customers can't come into the place for twenty-four hours. That'll get us an evening free. We're going to New York too, Barnaby, we're going to live! I'm going to have enough adventures to last me until I'm *partner*. So go and get your Sunday clothes on.

BARNABY. Wha-a-a-t?

CORNELIUS. Yes, I mean it. We're going to have a good meal; and we're going to be in danger; and we're going to get almost arrested; and we're going to spend all our money.

BARNABY. Holy cabooses! !

CORNELIUS. And one more thing: we're not coming back to Yonkers until we've kissed a girl.

BARNABY. Kissed a girl! Cornelius, you can't do that. You don't know any girls.

CORNELIUS. I'm thirty-three. I've got to begin sometime.

BARNABY. I'm only seventeen, Cornelius. It isn't so urgent for me.

CORNELIUS. Don't start backing down now—if the worst comes to the worst and we get discharged from here we can always join the Army.

BARNABY. Uh—did I hear you say that you'd be old Wolf-trap's partner?

CORNELIUS. How can I help it? He's growing old. If you go to bed at nine and open the store at six, you get promoted upward whether you like it or not.

BARNABY. My! Partner.

CORNELIUS. Oh, there's no way of getting away from it. You and I will be Vandergelders.

BARNABY. I? Oh, no—I may rise a little, but I'll never be a Vandergelder.

CORNELIUS. Listen—everybody thinks when he gets rich he'll be a different kind of rich person from the rich people he sees around him; later on he finds out there's only one kind of rich person, and he's it.

BARNABY. Oh, but I'll—

CORNELIUS. No. The best of all would be a person who has all the good things a poor person has, and all the good meals a rich person has, but that's never been known. No, you and I are go-

ing to be Vandergelders; all the more reason, then, for us to try
and get some living and some adventure into us now—will you
come, Barnaby?

BARNABY. [*in a struggle with his fears, a whirlwind of words*] But
Wolf-trap—KRR-pt, Gertrude-KRR-pt—[*with a sudden cry of
agreement*] Yes, Cornelius!

> [*Enter* MRS. LEVI, ERMENGARDE *and* GERTRUDE *from back
> center. The* BOYS *start down the ladder,* CORNELIUS *last.*]

MRS. LEVI. Mr. Hackl, is the trunk waiting at the station?

CORNELIUS. Yes, Mrs. Levi. [*closes the trap door*]

MRS. LEVI. Take a last look, Ermengarde.

ERMENGARDE. What?

MRS. LEVI. Take a last look at your girlhood home, dear. I remember
when I left my home. I gave a whinny like a young colt, and off
I went.

> [ERMENGARDE *and* GERTRUDE *exit.*]

ERMENGARDE. [*as they go*] Oh, Gertrude, do you think I ought to
get married this way? A young girl has to be so careful!

> [MRS. LEVI *is alone. She addresses the audience.*]

MRS. LEVI. You know, I think I'm going to have this room with
blue wallpaper,—yes, in blue! [*hurries out after the others*]

> [BARNABY *comes up trap door, looks off right, then lies on
> floor, gazing down through the trap door.*]

BARNABY. All clear up here, Cornelius! Cornelius—hold the candle
steady a minute—the bottom row's all right—but try the top
now . . . they're swelled up like they are ready to bust!

> [*BANG.*]

Holy CABOOSES!

> [*BANG, BANG.*]

Cornelius! I can smell it up here! [*rises and dances about, holding his nose*]

CORNELIUS. [*rushing up the trap door*] Get into your Sunday clothes,
Barnaby. We're going to New York!

> [*As they run out . . . there is a big explosion. A shower
> of tomato cans comes up from below, as—*]

THE

CURTAIN

FALLS

Act II

MRS. MOLLOY'S *hat shop, New York City.*

*There are two entrances. One door at the extreme right of the
back wall, to* MRS. MOLLOY'S *workroom; one at the back left corner,
to the street. The whole left wall is taken up with the show windows, filled with hats. It is separated from the shop by a low brass
rail, hung with net; during the act both* MRS. MOLLOY *and* BARNABY
*stoop under the rail and go into the shop window. By the street
door stands a large cheval glass. In the middle of the back wall is*

a large wardrobe or clothes cupboard, filled with ladies' coats, large enough for CORNELIUS *to hide in. At the left, beginning at the back wall, between the wardrobe and the workroom door, a long counter extends toward the audience, almost to the footlights. In the center of the room is a large round table with a low-hanging red cloth. There are a small gilt chair by the wardrobe and two chairs in front of the counter. Over the street door and the workroom door are bells which ring when the doors are opened.*

As the curtain rises, MRS. MOLLOY *is in the window, standing on a box, reaching up to put hats on the stand.* MINNIE FAY *is sewing by the counter.* MRS. MOLLOY *has a pair of felt overshoes, to be removed later.*

MRS. MOLLOY. Minnie, you're a fool. Of course I shall marry Horace Vandergelder.

MINNIE. Oh, Mrs. Molloy! I didn't ask you. I wouldn't dream of asking you such a personal question.

MRS. MOLLOY. Well, it's what you meant, isn't it? And there's your answer. I shall certainly marry Horace Vandergelder if he asks me. [*crawls under window rail, into the room, singing loudly*]

MINNIE. I know it's none of my business . . .

MRS. MOLLOY. Speak up, Minnie, I can't hear you.

MINNIE. . . . but do you . . . do you . . . ?

MRS. MOLLOY. [*having crossed the room, is busy at the counter*] Minnie, you're a fool. Say it: Do I love him? Of course, I don't love him. But I have two good reasons for marrying him just the same. Minnie, put something on that hat. It's not ugly enough. [*throws hat over counter*]

MINNIE. [*catching and taking hat to table*] Not ugly enough!

MRS. MOLLOY. I couldn't sell it. Put a . . . put a sponge on it.

MINNIE. Why, Mrs. Molloy, you're in such a *mood* today.

MRS. MOLLOY. In the first place I shall marry Mr. Vandergelder to get away from the millinery business. I've hated it from the first day I had anything to do with it. Minnie, I hate hats. [*sings loudly again*]

MINNIE. Why, what's the matter with the millinery business?

MRS. MOLLOY. [*crossing to window with two hats*] I can no longer stand being suspected of being a wicked woman, while I have nothing to show for it. I can't stand it. [*She crawls under rail into window.*]

MINNIE. Why, no one would dream of suspecting you—

MRS. MOLLOY. [*On her knees, she looks over the rail.*] Minnie, you're a fool. All millineresses are suspected of being wicked women. Why, half the time all those women come into the shop merely to look at me.

MINNIE. Oh!

MRS. MOLLOY. They enjoy the suspicion. But they aren't certain. If they were *certain* I was a wicked woman, they wouldn't put foot in this place again. Do I go to restaurants? No, it would be bad for business. Do I go to balls, or theatres, or operas? No, it would be bad for business. The only men I ever meet are feather merchants. [*crawls out of window, but gazes intently into the street*] What are those two young men doing out there on that park bench? Take my word for it, Minnie, either I marry Horace Vandergelder, or I break out of this place like a fire engine. I'll go to every theatre and ball and opera in New York City. [*returns to counter, singing again*]

MINNIE. But Mr. Vandergelder's not . . .

MRS. MOLLOY. Speak up, Minnie, I can't hear you.

MINNIE. . . . I don't think he's attractive.

MRS. MOLLOY. But what I think he is—and it's very important—I think he'd make a good fighter.

MINNIE. Mrs. Molloy!

MRS. MOLLOY. Take my word for it, Minnie: the best part of married life is the fights. The rest is merely so-so.

MINNIE. [*fingers in ears*] I won't listen.

MRS. MOLLOY. Peter Molloy—God rest him!—was a fine arguing man. I pity the woman whose husband slams the door and walks out of the house at the beginning of an argument. Peter Molloy would stand up and fight for hours on end. He'd even throw things, Minnie, and there's no pleasure to equal that. When I felt tired I'd start a good bloodwarming fight and it'd take ten years off my age; now Horace Vandergelder would put up a good fight; I know it. I've a mind to marry him.

MINNIE. I think they're just awful, the things you're saying today.

MRS. MOLLOY. Well, I'm enjoying them myself, too.

MINNIE. [*at the window*] Mrs. Molloy, those two men out in the street—

MRS. MOLLOY. What?

MINNIE. Those men. It looks as if they meant to come in here.

MRS. MOLLOY. Well now, it's time some men came into this place. I give you the younger one, Minnie.

MINNIE. Aren't you terrible!

[MRS. MOLLOY *sits on center table, while* MINNIE *takes off her felt overshoes.*]

MRS. MOLLOY. Wait till I get my hands on that older one! Mark my words, Minnie, we'll get an adventure out of this yet. Adventure, adventure! Why does everybody have adventures except me, Minnie? Because I have no spirit, I have no gumption. Minnie, they're coming in here. Let's go into the workroom and make them wait for us for a minute.

MINNIE. Oh, but Mrs. Molloy . . . my work! . . .

MRS. MOLLOY. [*running to workroom*] Hurry up, be quick now, Minnie! [*They go out to workroom.*]

[BARNABY *and* CORNELIUS *run in from street, leaving front door open. They are dressed in the stiff discomfort of their Sunday clothes.* CORNELIUS *wears a bowler hat,* BARNABY *a straw hat too large for him.*]

BARNABY. No one's here.

CORNELIUS. Some women were here a minute ago. I saw them.

[*They jump back to the street door and peer down the street.*]

That's Wolf-trap all right! [*coming back*] Well, we've got to hide here until he passes by.

BARNABY. He's sitting down on that bench. It may be quite a while.

CORNELIUS. When these women come in, we'll have to make conversation until he's gone away. We'll pretend we're buying a hat. How much money have you got now?

BARNABY. [*counting his money*] Forty cents for the train—seventy cents for dinner—twenty cents to see the whale—and a dollar I lost—I have seventy cents.

CORNELIUS. And I have a dollar seventy-five. I wish I knew how much hats cost!

BARNABY. Is this an adventure, Cornelius?

CORNELIUS. No, but it may be.

BARNABY. I think it is. There we wander around New York all day and nothing happens; and then we come to the quietest street in the whole city and suddenly Mr. Vandergelder turns the corner. [*going to door*] I think that's an adventure. I think . . . Cornelius! That Mrs. Levi is there now. She's sitting down on the bench with him.

CORNELIUS. What do you know about that! We know only one person in all New York City, and there she is!

BARNABY. Even if our adventure came along now I'd be too tired to enjoy it. Cornelius, why isn't this an adventure?

CORNELIUS. Don't be asking that. When you're in an adventure, you'll know it all right.

BARNABY. Maybe I wouldn't. Cornelius, let's arrange a signal for you to give me when an adventure's really going on. For instance, Cornelius, you say . . . uh . . . uh . . . *pudding*; you say *pudding* to me if it's an adventure we're in.

CORNELIUS. I wonder where the lady who runs this store is? What's her name again?

BARNABY. "Mrs. Molloy, hats for ladies."

CORNELIUS. Oh yes. I must think over what I'm going to say when she comes in. [*to counter*] "Good afternoon, Mrs. Molloy, wonderful weather we're having. We've been looking everywhere for some beautiful hats."

BARNABY. That's fine, Cornelius!

CORNELIUS. "Good afternoon, Mrs. Molloy; wonderful weather . . ." We'll make her think we're very rich. [*one hand in trouser pocket, the other on back of chair*] "Good afternoon, Mrs. Molloy . . ." You keep one eye on the door the whole time. "We've been looking everywhere for . . ."

[*Enter* MRS. MOLLOY *from the workroom.*]

MRS. MOLLOY. [*behind the counter*] Oh, I'm sorry. Have I kept you waiting? Good afternoon, gentlemen.

CORNELIUS. [*hat off*] Here, Cornelius Hackl.

BARNABY. [*hat off*] Here, Barnaby Tucker.

MRS. MOLLOY. I'm very happy to meet you. Perhaps I can help you. Won't you sit down?

CORNELIUS. Thank you, we will. [*The* BOYS *place their hats on the table, then sit down at the counter facing* MRS. MOLLOY.] You see, Mrs. Molloy, we're looking for hats. We've looked everywhere. Do you know what we heard? Go to Mrs. Molloy's, they said. So we came here. Only place we *could* go . . .

MRS. MOLLOY. Well now, that's *very* complimentary.

CORNELIUS. . . . and we were right. Everybody was right.

MRS. MOLLOY. You wish to choose some hats for a friend?

CORNELIUS. Yes, exactly. [*kicks* BARNABY]

BARNABY. Yes, exactly.

CORNELIUS. We were thinking of five or six, weren't we, Barnaby?

BARNABY. Er—five.

CORNELIUS. You see, Mrs. Molloy, money's no object with us. None at all.

MRS. MOLLOY. Why, Mr. Hackl . . .

CORNELIUS. [*rises and goes toward street door*] . . . I beg your pardon, what an interesting street! Something happening every minute. Passers-by, and . . . [BARNABY *runs to join him.*]

MRS. MOLLOY. You're from out of town, Mr. Hackl?

CORNELIUS. [*coming back*] Yes, ma'am—Barnaby, just keep your eye on the street, will you? You won't see that in Yonkers every day.

[BARNABY *remains kneeling at street door.*]

BARNABY. Oh yes, I will.

CORNELIUS. Not all of it.

MRS. MOLLOY. Now this friend of yours—couldn't she come in with you someday and choose her hats herself?

CORNELIUS. [*sits at counter*] No. Oh no. It's a surprise for her.

MRS. MOLLOY. Indeed? That may be a little difficult, Mr. Hackl. It's not entirely customary.—Your friend's very interested in the street, Mr. Hackl.

CORNELIUS. Oh yes. Yes. He has reason to be.

MRS. MOLLOY. You said you were from out of town?

CORNELIUS. Yes, we're from Yonkers.

MRS. MOLLOY. Yonkers?

CORNELIUS. Yonkers . . . yes, Yonkers. [*He gazes rapt into her eyes.*] You should know Yonkers, Mrs. Molloy. Hudson River; Palisades; drives; some say it's the most beautiful town in the world; that's what they say.

MRS. MOLLOY. Is that so!

CORNELIUS. [*rises*] Mrs. Molloy, if you ever had a Sunday free, I'd . . . we'd like to show you Yonkers. Y'know, it's very historic, too.

MRS. MOLLOY. That's very kind of you. Well, perhaps . . . now about those hats. [*takes two hats from under counter, and crosses to back center of the room*]

CORNELIUS. [*following*] Is there . . . Have you a . . . Maybe Mr. Molloy would like to see Yonkers too?

MRS. MOLLOY. Oh, I'm a widow, Mr. Hackl.

CORNELIUS. [*joyfully*] You are! [*with sudden gravity*] Oh, that's too bad. Mr. Molloy would have enjoyed Yonkers.

MRS. MOLLOY. Very likely. Now about these hats. Is your friend dark or light?

CORNELIUS. Don't think about that for a minute. Any hat you'd like would be perfectly all right with her.

MRS. MOLLOY. Really! [*She puts one on.*] Do you like this one?

CORNELIUS. [*in awe-struck admiration*] Barnaby! [*in sudden anger*] Barnaby! Look! [BARNABY *turns; unimpressed, he laughs vaguely, and turns to door again.*] Mrs. Molloy, that's the most beautiful hat I ever saw. [BARNABY *now crawls under the rail into the window.*]

MRS. MOLLOY. Your friend is acting very strangely, Mr. Hackl.

CORNELIUS. Barnaby, stop acting strangely. When the street's quiet and empty, come back and talk to us. What was I saying? Oh yes: Mrs. Molloy, you should know Yonkers.

MRS. MOLLOY. [*hat off*] The fact is, I have a friend in Yonkers. Perhaps you know him. It's always so foolish to ask in cases like that, isn't it?

[*They both laugh over this with increasing congeniality.* MRS. MOLLOY *goes to counter with hats from table.* COR-NELIUS *follows.*]

It's a Mr. Vandergelder.

CORNELIUS. [*stops abruptly*] What was that you said?

MRS. MOLLOY. Then you do know him?

CORNELIUS. Horace Vandergelder?

MRS. MOLLOY. Yes, that's right.

CORNELIUS. Know him! [*look to* BARNABY] Why, no. No!

BARNABY. No! No!

CORNELIUS. [*starting to glide about the room, in search of a hiding place*] I beg your pardon, Mrs. Molloy—what an attractive shop you have! [*smiling fixedly at her he moves to the workshop door*] And where does this door lead to? [*opens it, and is alarmed by the bell which rings above it*]

MRS. MOLLOY. Why, Mr. Hackl, that's my workroom.

CORNELIUS. Everything here is so interesting. [*looks under counter*] Every corner. Every door, Mrs. Molloy. Barnaby, notice the interesting door and cupboards. [*He opens the cupboard door.*] Deeply interesting. Coats for ladies. [*laughs*] Barnaby, make a note of the table. Precious piece of furniture, with a low-hanging cloth, I see. [*stretches his leg under table*]

MRS. MOLLOY. [*taking a hat from box left of wardrobe*] Perhaps your friend might like some of this new Italian straw. Mr. Vandergelder's a substantial man and very well liked, they tell me.

CORNELIUS. A lovely man, Mrs. Molloy.

MRS. MOLLOY. Oh yes—charming, charming!

CORNELIUS. [*smiling sweetly*] Has only one fault, as far as I know; he's hard as nails; but apart from that, as you say, a charming nature, ma'am.

MRS. MOLLOY. And a large circle of friends—?

CORNELIUS. Yes, indeed, yes indeed—five or six.

BARNABY. Five!

CORNELIUS. He comes and calls on you here from time to time, I suppose.

MRS. MOLLOY. [*turns from mirror where she has been putting a hat on*] This summer we'll be wearing ribbons down our back. Yes, as a matter of fact I am expecting a call from him this afternoon. [*hat off*]

BARNABY. I think . . . Cornelius! I think . . . !!

MRS. MOLLOY. Now to show you some more hats—

BARNABY. Look out! [*He takes a flying leap over the rail and flings himself under the table.*]

CORNELIUS. Begging your pardon, Mrs. Molloy. [*He jumps into the cupboard.*]

MRS. MOLLOY. Gentlemen! Mr. Hackl! Come right out of there this minute!

CORNELIUS. [*sticking his head out of the wardrobe door*] Help us just this once, Mrs. Molloy! We'll explain later!

MRS. MOLLOY. Mr. Hackl!

BARNABY. We're as innocent as can be, Mrs. Molloy.

MRS. MOLLOY. But really! Gentlemen! I can't have this! *What are you doing?*

BARNABY. Cornelius! Cornelius! Pudding?

CORNELIUS. [*a shout*] Pudding!

[*They disappear. Enter from the street* MRS. LEVI, *followed by* MR. VANDERGELDER. VANDERGELDER *is dressed in a too-bright checked suit, and wears a green derby—or bowler—hat. He is carrying a large ornate box of chocolates in one hand, and a cane in the other.*]

MRS. LEVI. Irene, my darling child, how *are* you? Heaven be good to us, how well you look! [*They kiss.*]

MRS. MOLLOY. But what a surprise! And Mr. Vandergelder in New York—what a pleasure!

VANDERGELDER. [*swaying back and forth on his heels complacently*] Good afternoon, Mrs. Molloy.

[*They shake hands.* MRS. MOLLOY *brings chair from counter for him. He sits at left of table.*]

MRS. LEVI. Yes, Mr. Vandergelder's in New York. Yonkers lies up there—*decimated* today. Irene, we thought we'd pay you a very short call. Now you'll tell us if it's inconvenient, won't you?

MRS. MOLLOY. [*placing a chair for* MRS. LEVI *at right of table.*] Inconvenient, Dolly! The idea! Why, it's sweet of you to come. [*She notices the boys' hats on the table—sticks a spray of flowers into crown of* CORNELIUS' *bowler and winds a piece of chiffon round* BARNABY'S *panama.*]

VANDERGELDER. We waited outside a moment.

MRS. LEVI. Mr. Vandergelder thought he saw two customers coming in—two men.

MRS. MOLLOY. Men! Men, Mr. Vandergelder? Why, what will you be saying next?

MRS. LEVI. Then we'll sit down for a minute or two. . . .

MRS. MOLLOY. [*wishing to get them out of the shop into the work-*

room] Before you sit down— [*She pushes them both.*] Before you sit down, there's something I want to show you. I want to show Mr. Vandergelder my workroom, too.

MRS. LEVI. I've seen the workroom a hundred times. I'll stay right here and try on some of these hats.

MRS. MOLLOY. No, Dolly, you come too. I have something for you. Come along, everybody.

[*Exit* MRS. LEVI *to workroom.*]

Mr. Vandergelder, I want your advice. You don't know how helpless a woman in business is. Oh, I feel I need advice every minute from a fine business head like yours.

[*Exit* VANDERGELDER *to workroom.* MRS. MOLLOY *shouts this line and then slams the workroom door.*]

Now I shut the door!!

[*Exit* MRS. MOLLOY.]

[CORNELIUS *puts his head out of the wardrobe door and gradually comes out into the room, leaving door open.*]

CORNELIUS. Hsst!

BARNABY. [*pokes his head out from under the table*] Maybe she wants us to go, Cornelius?

CORNELIUS. Certainly I won't go. Mrs. Molloy would think we were just thoughtless fellows. No, all I want is to stretch a minute.

BARNABY. What are you going to do when he's gone, Cornelius? Are we just going to run away?

CORNELIUS. Well . . . I don't know yet. I like Mrs. Molloy a lot. I wouldn't like her to think badly of me. I think I'll buy a hat. We can walk home to Yonkers, even if it takes us all night. I wonder how much hats cost. Barnaby, give me all the money you've got. [*As he leans over to take the money, he sneezes. Both return to their hiding places in alarm; then emerge again.*] My, all those perfumes in that cupboard tickle my nose! But I like it in there . . . it's a woman's world, and very different.

BARNABY. I like it where I am, too; only I'd like it better if I had a pillow.

CORNELIUS. [*taking coat from wardrobe*] Here, take one of these coats. I'll roll it up for you so it won't get mussed. Ladies don't like to have their coats mussed.

BARNABY. That's fine. Now I can just lie here and hear Mr. Vandergelder talk.

[CORNELIUS *goes slowly above table towards cheval mirror, repeating* MRS. MOLLOY's *line dreamily.*]

CORNELIUS. This summer we'll be wearing ribbons down our back. . . .

BARNABY. Can I take off my shoes, Cornelius?

[CORNELIUS *does not reply. He comes to the footlights and addresses the audience, in completely simple naïve sincerity.*]

CORNELIUS. Isn't the world full of wonderful things. There we sit cooped up in Yonkers for years and years and all the time wonderful people like Mrs. Molloy are walking around in New York and we don't know them at all. I don't know whether—from where you're sitting—you can see—well, for instance, the way [*He points to the edge of his right eye.*] her eye and forehead and cheek come together, up here. Can you? And the kind of fireworks that shoot out of her eyes all the time. I tell you right now: a fine woman is the greatest work of God. You can talk all you like about Niagara Falls and the Pyramids; they aren't in it at all. Of course, up there at Yonkers they came into the store all the time, and bought this and that, and I said, "Yes, ma'am," and "That'll be seventy-five cents, ma'am"; and I *watched* them. But today I've talked to one, equal to equal, equal to equal, and to the finest one that ever existed, in my opinion. They're so different from men! Everything that they say and do is so different that you feel like laughing all the time. [*He laughs.*] Golly, they're different from men. And they're awfully mysterious, too. You never can be really sure what's going on in their heads. They have a kind of wall around them all the time—of pride and a sort of play-acting: I bet you could know a woman a hundred years without ever being really sure whether she liked you or not. This minute I'm in danger. I'm in danger of losing my job and my future and everything that people think is important; but I don't care. Even if I have to dig ditches for the rest of my life, I'll be a ditch digger who once had a wonderful day. Barnaby!

BARNABY. Oh, you woke me up!

CORNELIUS. [*kneels*] Barnaby, we can't go back to Yonkers yet and you know why.

BARNABY. Why not?

CORNELIUS. We've had a good meal. We've had an adventure. We've been in danger of getting arrested. There's only one more thing we've got to do before we go back to be successes in Yonkers.

BARNABY. Cornelius! You're never going to kiss Mrs. Molloy!

CORNELIUS. Maybe.

BARNABY. But she'll scream.

CORNELIUS. Barnaby, you don't know anything at all. You might as well know right now that everybody except us goes through life kissing right and left all the time.

BARNABY. [*pauses for reflection; humbly:*] Well, thanks for telling me, Cornelius. I often wondered.

[*Enter* MRS. LEVI *from workroom.*]

MRS. LEVI. Just a minute, Irene. I must find my handkerchief.

[CORNELIUS, *caught by the arrival of* MRS. LEVI, *drops to his hands and knees, and starts very slowly to crawl back to the wardrobe, as though the slowness rendered him invisible.* MRS. LEVI, *leaning over the counter, watches him. From the cupboard he puts his head out of it and looks pleadingly at her.*]

Why, Mr. Hackl, I thought you were up in Yonkers.

CORNELIUS. I almost always am, Mrs. Levi. Oh, Mrs. Levi, don't tell Mr. Vandergelder! I'll explain everything later.

BARNABY. [*puts head out*] We're terribly innocent, Mrs. Levi.

MRS. LEVI. Why, who's that?

BARNABY. Barnaby Tucker—just paying a call.

MRS. LEVI. [*looking under counter and even shaking out her skirts*] Well, who else is here?

CORNELIUS. Just the two of us, Mrs. Levi, that's all.

MRS. LEVI. Old friends of Mrs. Molloy's, is that it?

CORNELIUS. We never knew her before a few minutes ago, but we like her a lot—don't we, Barnaby? In fact, I think she's . . . I think she's the finest person in the world. I'm ready to tell that to anybody.

MRS. LEVI. And does she think *you're* the finest person in the world?

CORNELIUS. Oh, no. I don't suppose she even notices that I'm alive.

MRS. LEVI. Well, I think she must notice that you're alive in that cupboard, Mr. Hackl. Well, if I were you, I'd get back into it right away. Somebody could be coming in any minute.

[CORNELIUS *disappears. She sits unconcernedly in chair right. Enter* MRS. MOLLOY.]

MRS. MOLLOY. [*leaving door open and looking about in concealed alarm*] Can I help you, Dolly?

MRS. LEVI. No, no, no. I was just blowing my nose.

[*Enter* VANDERGELDER *from workroom.*]

VANDERGELDER. Mrs. Molloy, I've got some advice to give you about your business.

[MRS. MOLLOY *comes to the center of the room and puts* BARNABY'S *hat on floor in window, then* CORNELIUS' *hat on the counter.*]

MRS. LEVI. Oh, advice from Mr. Vandergelder! The whole city should hear this.

VANDERGELDER. [*standing in the workroom door, pompously:*] In the first place, the aim of business is to make profit.

MRS. MOLLOY. Is that so?

MRS. LEVI. I never heard it put so clearly before. Did you hear it?

VANDERGELDER. [*crossing the room to the left*] You pay those girls of yours too much. You pay them as much as men. Girls like that enjoy their work. Wages, Mrs. Molloy, are paid to make people do work they don't want to do.

MRS. LEVI. Mr. Vandergelder thinks so ably. And that's exactly the way his business is run up in Yonkers.

VANDERGELDER. [*patting her hand*] Mrs. Molloy, I'd like for you to come up to Yonkers.

MRS. MOLLOY. That would be very nice. [*He hands her the box of chocolates.*] Oh, thank you. As a matter of fact, I know someone from Yonkers, someone else.

VANDERGELDER. [*hangs hat on the cheval mirror*] Oh? Who's that?

[MRS. MOLLOY *puts chocolates on table and brings gilt chair forward and sits center at table facing the audience.*]

MRS. MOLLOY. Someone quite well-to-do, I believe, though a little free and easy in his behavior. Mr. Vandergelder, do you know Mr. Cornelius Hackl in Yonkers?

VANDERGELDER. I know him like I know my own boot. He's my

head clerk.

MRS. MOLLOY. Is that so?

VANDERGELDER. He's been in my store for ten years.

MRS. MOLLOY. Well, I never!

VANDERGELDER. Where would you have known him?

[MRS. MOLLOY *is in silent confusion. She looks for help to* MRS. LEVI, *seated at right end of table.*]

MRS. LEVI. [*groping for means to help* MRS. MOLLOY] Err . . . blah err . . . bl . . . er . . . Oh, just one of those chance meetings, I suppose.

MRS. MOLLOY. Yes, oh yes! One of those chance meetings.

VANDERGELDER. What? Chance meetings? Cornelius Hackl has no right to chance meetings. Where was it?

MRS. MOLLOY. Really, Mr. Vandergelder, it's very unlike you to question me in such a way. I think Mr. Hackl is better known than you think he is.

VANDERGELDER. Nonsense.

MRS. MOLLOY. He's in New York often, and he's very well liked.

MRS. LEVI. [*having found her idea, with decision*] Well, the truth might as well come out now as later. Mr. Vandergelder, Irene is quite right. Your head clerk is often in New York. Goes everywhere; has an army of friends. Everybody knows Cornelius Hackl.

VANDERGELDER. [*laughs blandly and sits in chair at left of table*] He never comes to New York. He works all day in my store and at nine o'clock at night he goes to sleep in the bran room.

MRS. LEVI. So you think. But it's not true.

VANDERGELDER. Dolly Gallagher, you're crazy.

MRS. LEVI. Listen to me. You keep your nose so deep in your account books you don't know what goes on. Yes, by day, Cornelius Hackl is your faithful trusted clerk—that's true; but by night! Well, he leads a double life, that's all! He's here at the opera; at the great restaurants; in all the fashionable homes . . . why, he's at the Harmonia Gardens Restaurant three nights a week. The fact is, he's the wittiest, gayest, naughtiest, most delightful man in New York. Well, he's just *the* famous Cornelius Hackl!

VANDERGELDER. [*sure of himself*] It ain't the same man. If I ever thought Cornelius Hackl came to New York, I'd discharge him.

MRS. LEVI. Who took the horses out of Jenny Lind's carriage and pulled her through the streets?

MRS. MOLLOY. Who?

MRS. LEVI. Cornelius Hackl! Who dressed up as a waiter at the Fifth Avenue Hotel the other night and took an oyster and dropped it right down Mrs. . . . [*rises*] No, it's too wicked to tell you!

MRS. MOLLOY. Oh yes, Dolly, tell it! Go on!

MRS. LEVI. No. But it *was* Cornelius Hackl.

VANDERGELDER. [*loud*] It ain't the same man. Where'd he get the money?

MRS. LEVI. But he's very rich.

VANDERGELDER. [*rises*] Rich! I keep his money in my own safe. He has a hundred and forty-six dollars and thirty-five cents.

MRS. LEVI. Oh, Mr. Vandergelder, you're killing me! Do come to your senses. He's one of *the* Hackls.

[MRS. MOLLOY *sits at chair right of table where* MRS. LEVI *has been sitting.*]

VANDERGELDER. *The* Hackls?

MRS. LEVI. They built the Raritan Canal.

VANDERGELDER. Then why should he work in my store?

MRS. LEVI. Well, I'll tell you. [*sits at the center of the table, facing the audience*]

VANDERGELDER. [*striding about*] I don't want to hear! I've got a headache! I'm going home. *It ain't the same man!!* He sleeps in my bran room. You can't get away from facts. I just made him my chief clerk.

MRS. LEVI. If you had any sense you'd make him partner. [*rises, crosses to* MRS. MOLLOY] Now Irene, I can see you were as taken with him as everybody else is.

MRS. MOLLOY. Why, I only met him once, very hastily.

MRS. LEVI. Yes, but I can see that you were taken with him. Now don't you be thinking of marrying him!

MRS. MOLLOY. [*her hands on her cheeks*] Dolly! What are you saying! Oh!

MRS. LEVI. Maybe it'd be fine. But think it over carefully. He breaks hearts like hickory nuts.

VANDERGELDER. Who?

MRS. LEVI. Cornelius Hackl!

VANDERGELDER. Mrs. Molloy, how often has he called on you?

MRS. MOLLOY. Oh, I'm telling the truth. I've only seen him once in my life. Dolly Levi's been exaggerating so. I don't know where to look!

[*Enter* MINNIE *from workroom and crosses to window.*]

MINNIE. Excuse me, Mrs. Molloy. I must get together that order for Mrs. Parkinson.

MRS. MOLLOY. Yes, we must get that off before closing.

MINNIE. I want to send it off by the errand girl. [*having taken a hat from the window*] Oh, I almost forgot the coat. [*She starts for the wardrobe.*]

MRS. MOLLOY. [*running to the wardrobe to prevent her*] Oh, oh! I'll do that, Minnie!

[*But she is too late.* MINNIE *opens the right-hand cupboard door and falls back in terror, and screams.*]

MINNIE. Oh, Mrs. Molloy! Help! There's a man!

[MRS. MOLLOY *with the following speech pushes her back to the workroom door.* MINNIE *walks with one arm pointing at the cupboard. At the end of each of* MRS. MOLLOY's *sentences she repeats—at the same pitch and degree—the words: "There's a man!"*]

MRS. MOLLOY. [*slamming cupboard door*] Minnie, you imagined it. You're tired, dear. You go back in the workroom and lie down. Minnie, you're a fool; hold your tongue!

MINNIE. There's a man! [*Exit* MINNIE *to workroom.*]

> [MRS. MOLLOY *returns to the front of the stage.* VANDER-GELDER *raises his stick threateningly.*]

VANDERGELDER. If there's a man there, we'll get him out. Whoever you are, come out of there! [*strikes table with his stick*]

MRS. LEVI. [*goes masterfully to the cupboard—sweeps her umbrella around among the coats and closes each door as she does so*] Nonsense! There's no man there. See! Miss Fay's nerves have been playing tricks on her. Come now, let's sit down again. What were you saying, Mr. Vandergelder? [*They sit,* MRS. MOLLOY *right,* MRS. LEVI *center,* VANDERGELDER *left. A sneeze is heard from the cupboard. They all rise, look towards cupboard, then sit again.*] Well now . . . [*Another tremendous sneeze. With a gesture that says, "I can do no more."*] God bless you!

> [*They all rise.* MRS. MOLLOY *stands with her back to the cupboard.*]

MRS. MOLLOY. [*to* VANDERGELDER] Yes, there is a man in there. I'll explain it all to you another time. Thank you very much for coming to see me. Good afternoon, Dolly. Good afternoon, Mr. Vandergelder.

VANDERGELDER. You're protecting a man in there!

MRS. MOLLOY. [*with back to cupboard*] There's a very simple explanation, but for the present, good afternoon.

> [BARNABY *now sneezes twice, lifting the table each time.* VANDERGELDER, *right of table, jerks off the tablecloth.* BARNABY *pulls cloth under table and rolls himself up in it.* MRS. MOLLOY *picks up the box of chocolates, which has rolled on to the floor.*]

MRS. LEVI. Lord, the whole room's *crawling* with men! I'll never get over it.

VANDERGELDER. The world is going to pieces! I can't believe my own eyes!

MRS. LEVI. Come, Mr. Vandergelder. Ernestina Simple is waiting for us.

VANDERGELDER. [*finds his hat and puts it on*] Mrs. Molloy, I shan't trouble you again, and *vice versa.*

> [MRS. MOLLOY *is standing transfixed in front of cupboard, clasping the box of chocolates.* VANDERGELDER *snatches the box from her and goes out.*]

MRS. LEVI. [*crosses to her*] Irene, when I think of all the interesting things you have in this room! [*kisses her*] Make the most of it, dear. [*raps cupboard*] Good-by! [*raps on table with umbrella*] Good-by! [*Exit* MRS. LEVI.]

> [MRS. MOLLOY *opens door of cupboard.* CORNELIUS *steps out.*]

MRS. MOLLOY. So that was one of your practical jokes, Mr. Hackl?

CORNELIUS. No, no, Mrs. Molloy!

MRS. MOLLOY. Come out from under that, Barnaby Tucker, you troublemaker! [*She snatches the cloth and spreads it back on table.* MINNIE *enters.*] There's nothing to be afraid of, Minnie, I know all about these gentlemen.

CORNELIUS. Mrs. Molloy, we realize that what happened here—

MRS. MOLLOY. You think because you're rich you can make up for all the harm you do, is that it?

CORNELIUS. No, no!

BARNABY. [*on the floor putting shoes on*] No, no!

MRS. MOLLOY. Minnie, this is the famous Cornelius Hackl who goes round New York tying people into knots; and that's Barnaby Tucker, another troublemaker.

BARNABY. How d'you do?

MRS. MOLLOY. Minnie, choose yourself any hat and coat in the store. We're going out to dinner. If this Mr. Hackl is so rich and gay and charming, he's going to be rich and gay and charming to us. He dines three nights a week at the Harmonia Gardens Restaurant, does he? Well, he's taking us there now.

MINNIE. Mrs. Molloy, are you sure it's safe?

MRS. MOLLOY. Minnie, hold your tongue. We're in a position to put these men into jail if they so much as squeak.

CORNELIUS. Jail, Mrs. Molloy?

MRS. MOLLOY. Jail, Mr. Hackl. Officer Cogarty does everything I tell him to do. Minnie, you and I have been respectable for years; now we're in disgrace, we might as well make the most of it. Come into the workroom with me; I know some ways we can perk up our appearances. Gentlemen, we'll be back in a minute.

CORNELIUS. Uh—Mrs. Molloy, I hear there's an awfully good restaurant at the railway station.

MRS. MOLLOY. [*high indignation*] Railway station? Railway station? Certainly not! No, sir! You're going to give us a good dinner in the heart of the fashionable world. Go on in, Minnie! Don't you boys forget that you've made us lose our reputations, and now the fashionable world's the only place we *can* eat. [MRS. MOLLOY *exits to workroom.*]

BARNABY. She's angry at us, Cornelius. Maybe we'd better run away now.

CORNELIUS. No, I'm going to go through with this if it kills me. Barnaby, for a woman like that a man could consent to go back to Yonkers and be a success.

BARNABY. All I know is no woman's going to make a success out of me.

CORNELIUS. Jail or no jail, we're going to take those ladies out to dinner. So grit your teeth.

[*Enter* MRS. MOLLOY *and* MINNIE *from workroom dressed for the street.*]

MRS. MOLLOY. Gentlemen, the cabs are at the corner, so forward march! [*She takes a hat—which will be* BARNABY's *at the end of Act III—and gives it to* MINNIE.]

CORNELIUS. Yes, ma'am.

[BARNABY *stands shaking his empty pockets warningly.*]
Oh, Mrs. Molloy . . . is it far to the restaurant? Couldn't we walk?

MRS. MOLLOY. [*pauses a moment, then*] Minnie, take off your things. We're not going.

OTHERS. Mrs. Molloy!

MRS. MOLLOY. Mr. Hackl, I don't go anywhere I'm not wanted. Good night. I'm not very happy to have met you. [*She crosses the stage as though going to the workroom door.*]

OTHERS. Mrs. Molloy!

MRS. MOLLOY. I suppose you think we're not fashionable enough for you? Well, I won't be a burden to you. Goodnight, Mr. Tucker.

> [*The others follow her behind counter:* CORNELIUS, BARNABY, *then* MINNIE.]

CORNELIUS. We want you to come with us more than anything in the world, Mrs. Molloy.

> [MRS. MOLLOY *turns and pushes the three back. They are now near the center of the stage, to the right of the table,* MRS. MOLLOY *facing the audience.*]

MRS. MOLLOY. No, you don't! Look at you! Look at the pair of them, Minnie! Scowling, both of them!

CORNELIUS. Please, Mrs. Molloy!

MRS. MOLLOY. Then smile. [*to* BARNABY] Go on, smile! No, that's not enough. Minnie, you come with me and we'll get our own supper.

CORNELIUS. Smile, Barnaby, you lout!

BARNABY. My face can't smile any stronger than that.

MRS. MOLLOY. Then do something! Show some interest. Do something lively: sing!

CORNELIUS. I can't sing, really I can't.

MRS. MOLLOY. We're wasting our time, Minnie. They don't want us.

CORNELIUS. Barnaby, what can you sing? Mrs. Molloy, all we know are sad songs.

MRS. MOLLOY. That doesn't matter. If you want us to go out with you, you've got to sing something.

> [*All this has been very rapid; the boys turn up to counter, put their heads together, confer and abruptly turn, stand stiffly and sing "Tenting tonight; tenting tonight; tenting on the old camp ground." The four of them now repeat the refrain, softly harmonizing. At the end of the song, after a pause,* MRS. MOLLOY, *moved, says*]

We'll come!

> [*The boys shout joyfully.*]

You boys go ahead.

> [CORNELIUS *gets his hat from counter; as he puts it on he discovers the flowers on it.* BARNABY *gets his hat from window. They go out whistling.* MINNIE *turns and puts her hat on at the mirror.*]

Minnie, get the front door key—I'll lock the workroom.

> [MRS. MOLLOY *goes to workroom.* MINNIE *takes key from hook left of wardrobe and goes to* MRS. MOLLOY, *at the workroom door. She turns her around.*]

MINNIE. Why, Mrs. Molloy, you're crying! [MRS. MOLLOY *flings her arms round* MINNIE.]

MRS. MOLLOY. Oh, Minnie, the world is full of wonderful things. Watch me, dear, and tell me if my petticoat's showing. [*She crosses to door, followed by* MINNIE, *as*—]

THE
CURTAIN
FALLS

Act III

Veranda at the Harmonia Gardens Restaurant on the Battery, New York.

This room is informal and rustic. The main restaurant is indicated to be off stage back right.

There are three entrances: swinging double doors at the center of the back wall leading to the kitchen; one on the right wall (perhaps up a few steps and flanked by potted palms) to the street; one on the left wall to the staircase leading to the rooms above.

On the stage are two tables, left and right, each with four chairs. It is now afternoon and they are not yet set for dinner.

Against the back wall is a large folding screen. Also against the back wall are hat and coat racks.

As the curtain rises, VANDERGELDER *is standing, giving orders to* RUDOLPH, *a waiter.* MALACHI STACK *sits at table left.*

VANDERGELDER. Now, hear what I say. I don't want you to make any mistakes. I want a table for three.

RUDOLPH. [*tall "snob" waiter, alternating between cold superiority and rage; German accent*] For three.

VANDERGELDER. There'll be two ladies and myself.

MALACHI. It's a bad combination, Mr. Vandergelder. You'll regret it.

VANDERGELDER. And I want a chicken.

MALACHI. A chicken! You'll regret it.

VANDERGELDER. Hold your tongue. Write it down: chicken.

RUDOLPH. Yes, sir. Chicken Esterhazy? Chicken cacciatore? Chicken à la crème—?

VANDERGELDER. [*exploding*] A chicken! A chicken like everybody else has. And with the chicken I want a bottle of wine.

RUDOLPH. Moselle? Chablis? Vouvray?

MALACHI. He doesn't understand you, Mr. Vandergelder. You'd better speak louder.

VANDERGELDER. [*spelling*] W-I-N-E.

RUDOLPH. Wine.

VANDERGELDER. Wine! And I want this table removed. We'll eat at that table alone.

[*Exit* RUDOLPH *through service door at back.*]

MALACHI. There are some people coming in here now, Mr. Vandergelder.

[VANDERGELDER *goes to back right to look at the newcomers.*]

VANDERGELDER. What! Thunder and damnation! It's my niece Ermengarde! What's she doing here?!—Wait till I get my hands on her.

MALACHI. [*running up to him*] Mr. Vandergelder! You must keep your temper!

VANDERGELDER. And there's that rascal artist with her. Why, it's a plot. I'll throw them in jail.

MALACHI. Mr. Vandergelder! They're old enough to come to New York. You can't throw people into jail for coming to New York.

VANDERGELDER. And there's Mrs. Levi! What's she doing with them? It's a plot. It's a conspiracy! What's she saying to the cabman? Go up and hear what she's saying.

MALACHI. [*listening at entrance, right*] She's telling the cabman to wait, Mr. Vandergelder. She's telling the young people to come in and have a good dinner, Mr. Vandergelder.

VANDERGELDER. I'll put an end to this.

MALACHI. Now, Mr. Vandergelder, if you lose your temper, you'll make matters worse. Mr. Vandergelder, come here and take my advice.

VANDERGELDER. Stop pulling my coat. What's your advice?

MALACHI. Hide, Mr. Vandergelder. Hide behind this screen, and listen to what they're saying.

VANDERGELDER. [*being pulled behind the screen*] Stop pulling at me.

> [*They hide behind the screen as* MRS. LEVI, ERMENGARDE *and* AMBROSE *enter from the right.* AMBROSE *is carrying* ERMENGARDE'S *luggage.*]

ERMENGARDE. But I don't want to eat in a restaurant. It's not proper.

MRS. LEVI. Now, Ermengarde, dear, there's nothing wicked about eating in a restaurant. There's nothing wicked, even, about being in New York. Clergymen just make those things up to fill out their sermons.

ERMENGARDE. Oh, I wish I were in Yonkers, where *nothing* ever happens!

MRS. LEVI. Ermengarde, you're hungry. That's what's troubling you.

ERMENGARDE. Anyway, after dinner you must promise to take me to Aunt Flora's. She's been waiting for me all day and she must be half dead of fright.

MRS. LEVI. All right, but of course you know at Miss Van Huysen's you'll be back in your uncle's hands.

AMBROSE. [*hands raised to heaven*] I can't stand it.

MRS. LEVI. [*to* AMBROSE] Just keep telling yourself how pretty she is. Pretty girls have very little opportunity to improve their other advantages.

AMBROSE. Listen, Ermengarde! You don't want to go back to your uncle. Stop and think! That old man with one foot in the grave!

MRS. LEVI. And the other three in the cashbox.

AMBROSE. Smelling of oats—

MRS. LEVI. And axle grease.

MALACHI. That's not true. It's only partly true.

VANDERGELDER. [*loudly*] Hold your tongue! I'm going to teach them a lesson.

MALACHI. [*whisper*] Keep your temper, Mr. Vandergelder. Listen to what they say.

MRS. LEVI. [*hears this; throws a quick glance toward the screen; her whole manner changes*] Oh dear, what was I saying? The Lord be praised, how glad I am that I found you two dreadful children just as you were about to break poor dear Mr. Vandergelder's heart.

AMBROSE. He's got no heart to break!

MRS. LEVI. [*vainly signaling*] Mr. Vandergelder's a much kinder man than you think.

AMBROSE. Kinder? He's a wolf.

MRS. LEVI. Remember that he leads a very lonely life. Now you're going to have dinner upstairs. There are some private rooms up there,—just meant for shy timid girls like Ermengarde. Come with me. [*She pushes the young people out left,* AMBROSE *carrying the luggage.*]

VANDERGELDER. [*coming forward*] I'll show them! [*He sits at table right.*]

MALACHI. Everybody should eavesdrop once in a while, I always say. There's nothing like eavesdropping to show you that the world outside your head is different from the world inside your head.

VANDERGELDER. [*producing a pencil and paper*] I want to write a note. Go and call that cabman in here. I want to talk to him.

MALACHI. No one asks advice of a cabman, Mr. Vandergelder. They see so much of life that they have no ideas left.

VANDERGELDER. Do as I tell you.

MALACHI. Yes, sir. Advice of a cabman! [*Exit right.*]

[VANDERGELDER *writes his letter.*]

VANDERGELDER. "My dear Miss Van Huysen"—[*to audience*] Everybody's dear in a letter. It's enough to make you give up writing 'em. "My dear Miss Van Huysen. This is Ermengarde and that rascal Ambrose Kemper. They are trying to run away. Keep them in your house until I come."

[MALACHI *returns with an enormous* CABMAN *in a high hat and a long coat. He carries a whip.*]

CABMAN. [*entering*] What's he want?

VANDERGELDER. I want to talk to you.

CABMAN. I'm engaged. I'm waiting for my parties.

VANDERGELDER. [*folding letter and writing address*] I know you are. Do you want to earn five dollars?

CABMAN. Eh?

VANDERGELDER. I asked you, do you want to earn five dollars?

CABMAN. I don't know. I never tried.

VANDERGELDER. When those parties of yours come downstairs, I want you to drive them to this address. Never mind what they say, drive them to this address. Ring the bell: give this letter to the lady of the house: see that they get in the door and keep them there.

CABMAN. I can't make people go into a house if they don't want to.

VANDERGELDER. [*producing purse*] Can you for ten dollars?

CABMAN. Even for ten dollars, I can't do it alone.

VANDERGELDER. This fellow here will help you.

MALACHI. [*sitting at table left*] Now I'm pushing people into houses.

VANDERGELDER. There's the address: Miss Flora Van Huysen, 8 Jackson Street.

CABMAN. Even if I get them in the door I can't be sure they'll stay there.

VANDERGELDER. For fifteen dollars you can.

MALACHI. Murder begins at twenty-five.

VANDERGELDER. Hold your tongue! [*to* CABMAN] The lady of the house will help you. All you have to do is to sit in the front hall and see that the man doesn't run off with the girl. I'll be at Miss Van Huysen's in an hour or two and I'll pay you then.

CABMAN. If they call the police, I can't do anything.

VANDERGELDER. It's perfectly honest business. Perfectly honest.

MALACHI. Every man's the best judge of his own honesty.

VANDERGELDER. The young lady is my niece.

[*The* CABMAN *laughs, skeptically.*]

The young lady is my niece! !

[*The* CABMAN *looks at* MALACHI *and shrugs.*]

She's trying to run away with a good-for-nothing and we're preventing it.

CABMAN. Oh, I know them, sir. They'll win in the end. Rivers don't run uphill.

MALACHI. What did I tell you, Mr. Vandergelder? Advice of a cabman.

VANDERGELDER. [*hits table with his stick*] Stack! I'll be back in half an hour. See that the table's set for three. See that nobody else eats here. Then go and join the cabman on the box.

MALACHI. Yes, sir.

[*Exit* VANDERGELDER *right.*]

CABMAN. Who's your friend?

MALACHI. Friend! ! That's not a friend; that's an employer I'm trying out for a few days.

CABMAN. You won't like him.

MALACHI. I can see you're in business for yourself because you talk about liking employers. No one's ever liked an employer since business began.

CABMAN. AW—!

MALACHI. No, sir. I suppose you think *your horse* likes you?

CABMAN. My old Clementine? She'd give her right feet for me.

MALACHI. That's what all employers think. You imagine it. The streets of New York are full of cab horses winking at one another. Let's go in the kitchen and get some whiskey. I can't push people into houses when I'm sober. No, I've had about fifty employers in my life, but this is the most employer of them all.

He talks to everybody as though he were paying them.

CABMAN. I had an employer once. He watched me from eight in the morning until six at night—just sat there and watched me. Oh, dear! Even my mother didn't think I was as interesting as that. [CABMAN *exits through service door.*]

MALACHI. [*following him off*] Yes, being employed is like being loved: you know that somebody's thinking about you the whole time. [*Exits.*]

[*Enter right,* MRS. MOLLOY, MINNIE, BARNABY *and* CORNELIUS.]

MRS. MOLLOY. See! Here's the place I meant! Isn't it fine? Minnie, take off your things; we'll be here for hours.

CORNELIUS. [*stopping at door*] Mrs. Molloy, are you sure you'll like it here? I think I feel a draught.

MRS. MOLLOY. Indeed, I do like it. We're going to have a fine dinner right in this room; it's private, and it's elegant. Now we're all going to forget our troubles and call each other by our first names. Cornelius! Call the waiter.

CORNELIUS. Wait—wait—I can't make a sound. I must have caught a cold on that ride. Wai—No! It won't come.

MRS. MOLLOY. I don't believe you. Barnaby, you call him.

BARNABY. [*boldly*] Waiter! Waiter!

[CORNELIUS *threatens him.* BARNABY *runs left.*]

MINNIE. I never thought I'd be in such a place in my whole life. Mrs. Molloy, is this what they call a "café"?

MRS. MOLLOY. [*sits at table left, facing audience*] Yes, this a café. Sit down, Minnie. Cornelius, Mrs. Levi gave us to understand that every waiter in New York knew you.

CORNELIUS. They will.

[BARNABY *sits at chair left;* MINNIE *in chair back to audience. Enter* RUDOLPH *from service door.*]

RUDOLPH. Good evening, ladies and gentlemen.

CORNELIUS. [*shaking his hand*] How are you, Fritz? How are you, my friend?

RUDOLPH. I am Rudolph.

CORNELIUS. Of course. Rudolph, of course. Well, Rudolph, these ladies want a little something to eat—you know what I mean? Just if you can find the time—we know how busy you are.

MRS. MOLLOY. Cornelius, there's no need to be so familiar with the waiter. [*takes menu from* RUDOLPH]

CORNELIUS. Oh, yes, there is.

MRS. MOLLOY. [*passing menu across*] Minnie, what do you want to eat?

MINNIE. Just anything, Irene.

MRS. MOLLOY. No, speak up, Minnie. What do you want?

MINNIE. No, really, I have no appetite at all. [*swings round in her chair and studies the menu, horrified at the prices*] Oh . . . Oh . . . I'd like some sardines on toast and a glass of milk.

CORNELIUS. [*takes menu from her*] Great grindstones! What a sensible girl. Barnaby, shake Minnie's hand. She's the most sensible girl in the world. Rudolph, bring us gentlemen two glasses of beer, a loaf of bread and some cheese.

MRS. MOLLOY. [*takes menu*] I never heard such nonsense. Cornelius, we've come here for a good dinner and a good time. Minnie, have you ever eaten pheasant?

MINNIE. Pheasant? No-o-o-o!

MRS. MOLLOY. Rudolph, have you any pheasant?

RUDOLPH. Yes, ma'am. Just in from New Jersey today.

MRS. MOLLOY. Even the pheasants are leaving New Jersey. [*She laughs loudly, pushing* CORNELIUS, *then* RUDOLPH; *not from menu.*] Now, Rudolph, write this down: mock turtle soup; pheasant; mashed chestnuts; green salad; and some nice red wine.

[RUDOLPH *repeats each item after her.*]

CORNELIUS. [*losing all his fears, boldly*] All right, Barnaby, you watch me. [*He reads from the bill of fare.*] Rudolph, write this down: Neapolitan ice cream; hothouse peaches; champagne . . .

ALL. Champagne!

[BARNABY *spins round in his chair.*]

CORNELIUS. [*holds up a finger*] . . . and a German band. Have you got a German band?

MRS. MOLLOY. No, Cornelius, I won't let you be extravagant. Champagne, but no band. Now, Rudolph, be quick about this. We're hungry.

[*Exit* RUDOLPH *to kitchen.* MRS. MOLLOY *crosses to right.*] Minnie, come upstairs. I have an idea about your hair. I think it'd be nice in two wee horns—

MINNIE. [*hurrying after her, turns and looks at the boys*] Oh! Horns!

[*They go out right. There is a long pause.* CORNELIUS *sits staring after them.*]

BARNABY. Cornelius, in the Army, you have to peel potatoes all the time.

CORNELIUS. [*not turning*] Oh, that doesn't matter. By the time we get out of jail we can move right over to the Old Men's Home.

[*Another waiter,* AUGUST, *enters from service door bearing a bottle of champagne in cooler, and five glasses.* MRS. MOLLOY *re-enters right, followed by* MINNIE, *and stops* AUGUST.]

MRS. MOLLOY. Waiter! What's that? What's that you have?

AUGUST. [*young waiter; baby face; is continually bursting into tears*] It's some champagne, ma'am.

MRS. MOLLOY. Cornelius; it's our champagne.

[ALL *gather round* AUGUST.]

AUGUST. No, no. It's for His Honor the Mayor of New York and he's very impatient.

MRS. MOLLOY. Shame on him! The Mayor of New York has more important things to be impatient about. Cornelius, open it.

[CORNELIUS *takes the bottle, opens it and fills the glasses.*]

AUGUST. Ma'am, he'll kill me.

MRS. MOLLOY. Well, have a glass first and die happy.

AUGUST. [*sits at table right, weeping*] He'll kill me.

[RUDOLPH *lays the cloth on the table, left.*]

MRS. MOLLOY. I go to a public restaurant for the first time in ten years and all the waiters burst into tears. There, take that and stop crying, love. [*She takes a glass to* AUGUST *and pats his head, then comes back.*] Barnaby, make a toast!

BARNABY. [*center of the group, with naïve sincerity*] I? . . . uh . . . To all the ladies in the world . . . may I get to know more of them . . . and . . . may I get to know them better.

[*There is a hushed pause.*]

CORNELIUS. [*softly*] To the ladies!

MRS. MOLLOY. That's *very* sweet and *very* refined. Minnie, for that I'm going to give Barnaby a kiss.

MINNIE. Oh!

MRS. MOLLOY. Hold your tongue, Minnie. I'm old enough to be his mother, and—[*indicating a height three feet from the floor*] a dear wee mother I would have been too. Barnaby, this is for you from all the ladies in the world.

[*She kisses him.* BARNABY *is at first silent and dazed, then—*]

BARNABY. Now I can go back to Yonkers, Cornelius. Pudding. Pudding. Pudding! [*He spins round and falls on his knees.*]

MRS. MOLLOY. Look at Barnaby. He's not strong enough for a kiss. His head can't stand it.

[*Exit* AUGUST, *right service door, with tray and cooler. The sound of "Les Patineurs" waltz comes from off left.* CORNELIUS *sits in chair facing audience, top of table.* MINNIE *at left.* BARNABY *at right and* MRS. MOLLOY *back to audience.*]

Minnie, I'm enjoying myself. To think that this goes on in hundreds of places every night, while I sit at home darning my stockings. [MRS. MOLLOY *rises and dances, alone, slowly about the stage.*] Cornelius, dance with me.

CORNELIUS. [*rises*] Irene, the Hackls don't dance. We're Presbyterian.

MRS. MOLLOY. Minnie, you dance with me.

[MINNIE *joins her.* CORNELIUS *sits again.*]

MINNIE. Lovely music.

MRS. MOLLOY. Why, Minnie, you dance beautifully.

MINNIE. We girls dance in the workroom when you're not looking, Irene.

MRS. MOLLOY. You thought I'd be angry! Oh dear, no one in the world understands anyone else in the world.

[*The girls separate.* MINNIE *dances off to her place at the table.* MRS. MOLLOY *sits thoughtfully at table right. The music fades away.*]

Cornelius! Jenny Lind and all those other ladies—do you see them all the time?

CORNELIUS. [*rises and joins her at table right*] Irene, I've put them right out of my head. I'm interested in . . .

[RUDOLPH *has entered by the service door. He now flings a tablecloth between them on table.*]

MRS. MOLLOY. Rudolph, what are you doing?

RUDOLPH. A table's been reserved here. Special orders.

MRS. MOLLOY. Stop right where you are. That party can eat inside. This veranda's ours.

RUDOLPH. I'm very sorry. This veranda is open to anybody who wants it. Ah, there comes the man who brought the order.

[*Enter* MALACHI *from the kitchen, drunk.*]

MRS. MOLLOY. [*to* MALACHI] Take your table away from here. We got here first, Cornelius, throw him out.

MALACHI. Ma'am, my employer reserved this room at four o'clock this afternoon. You can go and eat in the restaurant. My employer said it was very important that he have a table alone.

MRS. MOLLOY. No, sir. We got here first and we're going to stay here—alone, too.

[MINNIE *and* BARNABY *come forward.*]

RUDOLPH. Ladies and gentlemen!

MRS. MOLLOY. Shut up, you! [*to* MALACHI] You're an impertinent, idiotic kill-joy.

MALACHI. [*very pleased*] That's an insult!

MRS. MOLLOY. All the facts about you are insults. [*to* CORNELIUS] Cornelius, do something. Knock it over! The table.

CORNELIUS. Knock it over.

[*After a shocked struggle with himself* CORNELIUS *calmly overturns the table.* AUGUST *rights the table and picks up cutlery, weeping copiously.*]

RUDOLPH. [*in cold fury*] I'm sorry, but this room can't be reserved for anyone. If you want to eat alone, you must go upstairs. I'm sorry, but that's the rule.

MRS. MOLLOY. We're having a nice dinner alone and we're going to stay here. Cornelius, knock it over.

[CORNELIUS *overturns the table again. The girls squeal with pleasure. The waiter* AUGUST *again scrambles for the silver.*]

MALACHI. Wait till you see my employer!

RUDOLPH. [*bringing screen down*] Ladies and gentlemen! I tell you what we'll do. There's a big screen here. We'll put the screen up between the tables. August, come and help me.

MRS. MOLLOY. I won't eat behind a screen. I won't. Minnie, make a noise. We're not animals in a menagerie. Cornelius, no screen. Minnie, there's a fight. I feel ten years younger. No screen! No screen!

[*During the struggle with the screen all talk at once.*]

MALACHI. [*loud and clear and pointing to entrance right*] Now you'll learn something. There comes my employer now, getting out of that cab.

CORNELIUS. [*coming to him, taking off his coat*] Where? I'll knock him down too.

[BARNABY *has gone up to right entrance. He turns and shouts clearly:*]

BARNABY. Cornelius, it's Wolf-trap. Yes, it is!

CORNELIUS. Wolf-trap! Listen, everybody. I think the screen's a good idea. Have you got any more screens, Rudolph? We could use three or four.[*He pulls the screen forward again.*]

MRS. MOLLOY. Quiet down, Cornelius, and stop changing your mind. Hurry up, Rudolph, we're ready for the soup.

[*During the following scene* RUDOLPH *serves the meal at the table left, as unobtrusively as possible. The stage is now divided in half. The quartet's table is at the left. Enter* VANDERGELDER *from the right. Now wears overcoat and carries the box of chocolates.*]

VANDERGELDER. Stack! What's the meaning of this? I told you I wanted a table alone. What's that?

[VANDERGELDER *hits the screen twice with his stick.* MRS. MOLLOY *hits back twice with a spoon. The four young people sit:* BARNABY *facing audience;* MRS. MOLLOY *right,* MINNIE *left, and* CORNELIUS *back to audience.*]

MALACHI. Mr. Vandergelder, I did what I could. Mr. Vandergelder, you wouldn't believe what wild savages the people of New York are. There's a woman over there, Mr. Vandergelder—civilization hasn't touched her.

VANDERGELDER. Everything's wrong. You can't even manage a thing like that. Help me off with my coat. Don't kill me. Don't kill me.

[*During the struggle with the overcoat* MR. VANDERGELDER'S *purse flies out of his pocket and falls by the screen.* VANDERGELDER *goes to the coat tree and hangs his coat up.*]

MRS. MOLLOY. Speak up! I can't hear you.

CORNELIUS. My voice again. Barnaby, how's your throat? Can you speak?

BARNABY. Can't make a sound.

MRS. MOLLOY. Oh, all right. Bring your heads together, and we'll whisper.

VANDERGELDER. Who are those people over there?

MALACHI. Some city sparks and their girls, Mr. Vandergelder. What goes on in big cities, Mr. Vandergelder—best not think of it.

VANDERGELDER. Has that couple come down from upstairs yet? I hope they haven't gone off without your seeing them.

MALACHI. No, sir. Myself and the cabman have kept our eyes on everything.

VANDERGELDER. [*sits at right of table right, profile to the audience*] I'll sit here and wait for my guests. You go out to the cab.

MALACHI. Yes, sir.

[VANDERGELDER *unfurls newspaper and starts to read.* MALACHI *sees the purse on the floor and picks it up.*] Eh? What's that? A purse. Did you drop something, Mr. Vandergelder?

VANDERGELDER. No. Don't bother me any more. Do as I tell you.

MALACHI. [*stooping over; coming center*] A purse. That fellow over there must have let it fall during the misunderstanding about the screen. No, I won't look inside. Twenty-dollar bills, dozens of them. I'll go over and give it to him. [*starts towards* CORNELIUS, *then turns and says to audience*] You're surprised? You're surprised to see me getting rid of this money so quickly, eh? I'll explain it to you. There was a time in my life when my chief interest was picking up money that didn't belong to me. The law is there to protect property, but—sure, the law doesn't care whether a property owner deserves his property or not, and the law has to be corrected. There are several thousands of people in this country engaged in correcting the law. For a while, I too was engaged in the redistribution of superfluities. A man works all his life and leaves a million to his widow. She sits in hotels and eats great meals and plays cards all afternoon and evening, with ten diamonds on her fingers. Call in the robbers! Call in the robbers! Or a man leaves it to his son who stands leaning against bars all night boring a bartender. Call in the robbers! Stealing's a weakness. There are some people who say you shouldn't have any weaknesses at all—no vices. But if a man has no vices, he's in great danger of making vices out of his virtues, and there's a spectacle. We've all seen them: men who were monsters of philanthropy and women who were dragons of purity. We've seen people who told the truth, though the Heavens fall,—and the Heavens fell. No, no—nurse one vice in your bosom. Give it the attention it deserves and let your virtues spring up modestly around it. Then you'll have the miser who's no liar; and the drunkard who's the benefactor of a whole city. Well, after I'd had that weakness of stealing for a while, I found another: I took to whisky—whisky took to me. And then I discovered an important rule that I'm going to pass on to you: Never support two weaknesses at the same time. It's your combination sinners—your lecherous liars and your miserly drunkards—who dishonor the vices and bring them into bad repute. So now you see why I want to get rid of this money: I want to keep my mind free to do the credit to whisky that it deserves. And my last word to you, ladies and gentlemen, is this: one vice at a time. [*goes over to* CORNELIUS] Can I speak to you for a minute?

CORNELIUS. [*rises*] You certainly can. We all want to apologize to you about that screen—that little misunderstanding.

[*They all rise, with exclamations of apology.*]

What's your name, sir?

MALACHI. Stack, sir. Malachi Stack. If the ladies will excuse you, I'd like to speak to you for a minute. [*draws* CORNELIUS *down to front of stage*] Listen, boy, have you lost . . . ? Come here . . . [*LEADS him further down, out of* VANDERGELDER's *hearing*] Have you lost something?

CORNELIUS. Mr. Stack, in this one day I've lost everything I own.

MALACHI. There it is. [*gives him purse*] Don't mention it.

CORNELIUS. Why, Mr. Stack . . . you know what it is? It's a miracle. [*looks toward the ceiling*]

MALACHI. Don't mention it.

CORNELIUS. Barnaby, come here a minute. I want you to shake hands with Mr. Stack. [BARNABY, *napkin tucked into his collar, joins them.*] Mr. Stack's just found the purse I lost, Barnaby. You know—the purse full of money.

BARNABY. [*shaking his hand vigorously*] You're a wonderful man, Mr. Stack.

MALACHI. Oh, it's nothing—nothing.

CORNELIUS. I'm certainly glad I went to church all these years. You're a good person to know, Mr. Stack. In a way. Mr. Stack, where do you work?

MALACHI. Well, I've just begun. I work for a Mr. Vandergelder in Yonkers.

[CORNELIUS *is thunderstruck. He glances at* BARNABY *and turns to* MALACHI *with awe. All three are swaying slightly, back and forth.*]

CORNELIUS. You do? It's a miracle. [*He points to the ceiling.*] Mr. Stack, I know you don't need it—but can I give you something for . . . for the good work?

MALACHI. [*putting out his hand*] Don't mention it. It's nothing. [*starts to go left*]

CORNELIUS. Take that. [*hands him a note*]

MALACHI. [*taking note*] Don't mention it.

CORNELIUS. And that. [*another note*]

MALACHI [*takes it and moves away*] I'd better be going.

CORNELIUS. Oh, here. And that.

MALACHI. [*hands third note back*] No . . . I might get to like them. [*Exit left.*]

[CORNELIUS *bounds exultantly back to table.*]

CORNELIUS. Irene, I feel a lot better about everything. Irene, I feel so well that I'm going to tell the truth.

MRS. MOLLOY. I'd forgotten that, Minnie. Men get drunk so differently from women. All right, what is the truth?

CORNELIUS. If I tell the truth, will you let me . . . will you let me put my arm around your waist?

[MINNIE *screams and flings her napkin over her face.*]

MRS. MOLLOY. Hold your tongue, Minnie. All right, you can put your arm around my waist just to show it can be done in a gentlemanly way; but I might as well warn you: a corset is a corset.

CORNELIUS. [*his arm around her; softly*] You're a wonderful person, Mrs. Molloy.

MRS. MOLLOY. Thank you. [*She removes his hand from around her waist.*] All right, now that's enough. What is the truth?

CORNELIUS. Irene, I'm not rich as Mrs. Levi said I was.

MRS. MOLLOY. Not rich!

CORNELIUS. I almost never came to New York. And I'm not like she said I was,—bad. And I think you ought to know that at this very minute Mr. Vandergelder's sitting on the other side of that screen.

MRS. MOLLOY. What!! Well, he's not going to spoil any party of mine. So *that's* why we've been whispering? Let's forget all about Mr. Vandergelder and have some more wine.

[*They start to sing softly: "The Sidewalks of New York." Enter* MRS. LEVI, *from the street, in an elaborate dress.* VANDERGELDER *rises.*]

MRS. LEVI. Good evening, Mr. Vandergelder.

VANDERGELDER. Where's—where's Miss Simple?

MRS. LEVI. Mr. Vandergelder, I'll never trust a woman again as long as I live.

VANDERGELDER. Well? What is it?

MRS. LEVI. She ran away this afternoon and got married!

VANDERGELDER. She did?

MRS. LEVI. Married, Mr. Vandergelder, to a young boy of fifty.

VANDERGELDER. She did?

MRS. LEVI. Oh, I'm as disappointed as you are. I-can't-eat-a-thing-what-have-you-ordered?

VANDERGELDER. I ordered what you told me to, a chicken.

[*Enter* AUGUST. *He goes to* VANDERGELDER's *table.*]

MRS. LEVI. I don't think I could face a chicken. Oh, waiter. How do you do? What's your name?

AUGUST. August, ma'am.

MRS. LEVI. August, this is Mr. Vandergelder of Yonkers—Yonkers' most influential citizen, in fact. I want you to see that he's served with the best you have and served promptly. And there'll only be the two of us. [MRS. LEVI *gives one set of cutlery to* AUGUST. VANDERGELDER *puts chocolate box under table.*] Mr. Vandergelder's been through some trying experiences today—what with men hidden all over Mrs. Molloy's store—like Indians in ambush.

VANDERGELDER. [*between his teeth*] Mrs. Levi, you don't have to tell him everything about me.

[*The quartet commences singing again very softly.*]

MRS. LEVI. Mr. Vandergelder, if you're thinking about getting married, you might as well learn right now you have to let women be women. Now, August, we want excellent service.

AUGUST. Yes, ma'am. [*Exits to kitchen.*]

VANDERGELDER. You've managed things very badly. When I plan a thing it takes place. [MRS. LEVI *rises.*] Where are you going?

MRS. LEVI. Oh, I'd just like to see who's on the other side of that screen.

[MRS. LEVI *crosses to the other side of the stage and sees the quartet. They are frightened and fall silent.*]

CORNELIUS. [*rising*] Good evening, Mrs. Levi.

[MRS. LEVI *takes no notice, but, taking up the refrain where they left off, returns to her place at the table right.*]

VANDERGELDER. Well, who was it?

MRS. LEVI. Oh, just some city sparks entertaining their girls, I guess.

VANDERGELDER. Always wanting to know everything; always curious about everything; always putting your nose into other people's affairs. Anybody who lived with you would get as nervous as a cat.

MRS. LEVI. What? What's that you're saying?

VANDERGELDER. I said anybody who lived with you would—

MRS. LEVI. Horace Vandergelder, get that idea right out of your head this minute. I'm surprised that you even mentioned such a thing. Understand once and for all that I have no intention of marrying you.

VANDERGELDER. I didn't mean that.

MRS. LEVI. You've been hinting around at such a thing for some time, but from now on put such ideas right out of your head.

VANDERGELDER. Stop talking that way. That's not what I meant at all.

MRS. LEVI. I hope not. I should hope not. Horace Vandergelder, you go your way [*points a finger*] and I'll go mine. [*points again in same direction*] I'm not some Irene Molloy, whose head can be turned by a pot of geraniums. Why, the idea of your even suggesting such a thing.

VANDERGELDER. Mrs. Levi, you misunderstood me.

MRS. LEVI. I certainly hope I did. If I had any intention of marrying again it would be to a far more pleasure-loving man than you. Why I'd marry Cornelius Hackl before I'd marry you.

[CORNELIUS *raises his head in alarm. The others stop eating and listen.*]

However, we won't discuss it any more.

[*Enter* AUGUST *with a tray.*]

Here's August with our food. I'll serve it, August.

AUGUST. Yes, ma'am. [*Exit* AUGUST.]

MRS. LEVI. Here's some white meat for you, and some giblets, very tender and very good for you. No, as I said before, you go your way and I'll go mine.—Start right in on the wine. I think you'll feel better at once. However, since you brought the matter up, there's one more thing I think I ought to say.

VANDERGELDER. [*rising in rage*] I didn't bring the matter up at all.

MRS. LEVI. We'll have forgotten all about it in a moment, but—sit down, sit down, we'll close the matter forever in just a moment, but there's one more thing I ought to say: [VANDERGELDER *sits down.*] It's true, I'm a woman who likes to know everything that's going on; who likes to manage things, you're perfectly right about that. But I wouldn't like to manage anything as disorderly as your household, as out of control, as untidy. You'll have to do that yourself, God helping you.

VANDERGELDER. It's not out of control.

MRS. LEVI. Very well, let's not say another word about it. Take some more of that squash, it's good. No, Horace, a complaining, quarrelsome, friendless soul like you is no sort of companion for me. You go your way [*peppers her own plate*] and I'll go mine. [*peppers his plate*]

VANDERGELDER. Stop saying that.

MRS. LEVI. I won't say another word.

VANDERGELDER. Besides . . . I'm not those things you said I am.

MRS. LEVI. What?—Well, I guess you're friendless, aren't you? Ermengarde told me this morning you'd even quarreled with your barber—a man who's held a razor to your throat for twenty years! Seems to me that that's sinking pretty low.

VANDERGELDER. Well, . . . but . . . my clerks, they . . .

MRS. LEVI. They like you? Cornelius Hackl and that Barnaby? Behind your back they call you Wolf-trap.

[*Quietly the quartet at the other table have moved up to the screens—bringing chairs for* MRS. MOLLOY *and* MINNIE. *Wine glasses in hand, they overhear this conversation.*]

VANDERGELDER. [*blanching*] They don't.

MRS. LEVI. No, Horace. It looks to me as though I were the last person in the world that liked you, and even I'm just so-so. No, for the rest of my life I intend to have a good time. You'll be able to find some housekeeper who can prepare you three meals for a dollar a day—it can be done, you know, if you like cold baked beans. You'll spend your last days listening at keyholes, for fear someone's cheating you. Take some more of that.

VANDERGELDER. Dolly, you're a damned exasperating woman.

MRS. LEVI. There! You see? That's the difference between us. I'd be nagging you all day to get some spirit into you. You could be a perfectly charming, witty, amiable man, if you wanted to.

VANDERGELDER. [*rising, bellowing*] I don't want to be charming.

MRS. LEVI. But you are. Look at you now. You can't hide it.

VANDERGELDER. [*sits*] Listening at keyholes! Dolly, you have no right to say such things to me.

MRS. LEVI. At your age you ought to enjoy hearing the honest truth.

VANDERGELDER. My age! My age! You're always talking about my age.

MRS. LEVI. I don't know what your age is, but I do know that up at Yonkers with bad food and bad temper you'll double it in six months. Let's talk of something else; but before we leave the subject there's one more thing I *am* going to say.

VANDERGELDER. Don't!

MRS. LEVI. Sometimes, just sometimes, I think I'd be tempted to marry you out of sheer pity; and if the confusion in your house gets any worse I may *have* to.

VANDERGELDER. I haven't asked you to marry me.

MRS. LEVI. Well, *please don't*.

VANDERGELDER. And my house is not in confusion.

MRS. LEVI. What? With your niece upstairs in the restaurant right now?

VANDERGELDER. I've fixed that better than you know.

MRS. LEVI. And your clerks skipping around New York behind your back?

VANDERGELDER. They're in Yonkers where they always are.

MRS. LEVI. Nonsense!

VANDERGELDER. What do you mean, nonsense?

MRS. LEVI. Cornelius Hackl's the other side of that screen this very minute.

VANDERGELDER. It ain't the same man!

MRS. LEVI. All right. Go on. Push it, knock it down. Go and see.

VANDERGELDER. [*goes to screen, pauses in doubt, then returns to his chair again*] I don't believe it.

MRS. LEVI. All right. All right. Eat your chicken. Of course, Horace, if your affairs went from bad to worse and you became actually miserable, I might feel that it was my duty to come up to Yonkers and be of some assistance to you. After all, I was your wife's oldest friend.

VANDERGELDER. I don't know how you ever got any such notion. Now understand, once and for all, I have *no intention of marrying anybody*. Now, I'm tired and I don't want to talk.

[CORNELIUS *crosses to extreme left*, MRS. MOLLOY *following him*.]

MRS. LEVI. I won't say another word, either.

CORNELIUS. Irene, I think we'd better go. You take this money and pay the bill. Oh, don't worry, it's not mine.

MRS. MOLLOY. No, no, I'll tell you what we'll do. You boys put on our coats and veils, and if he comes stamping over here, he'll think you're girls.

CORNELIUS. What! Those things!

MRS. MOLLOY. Yes. Come on.

[*She and* MINNIE *take the clothes from the stand*.]

VANDERGELDER. [*rises*] I've got a headache. I've had a bad day. I'm going to Flora Van Huysen's, and then I'm going back to my hotel. [*reaches for his purse*] So, here's the money to pay for the dinner. [*searching another pocket*] Here's the money to pay for the . . . [*going through all his pockets*] Here's the money . . . I've lost my purse!!

MRS. LEVI. Impossible! I can't imagine you without your purse.

VANDERGELDER. It's been stolen. [*searching overcoat*] Or I left it in the cab. What am I going to do? I'm new at the hotel; they don't know me. I've never been here before. . . . Stop eating the chicken, I can't pay for it!

MRS. LEVI. [*laughing gaily*] Horace, I'll be able to find some money. Sit down and calm yourself.

VANDERGELDER. Dolly Gallagher, I gave you twenty-five dollars this morning.

MRS. LEVI. I haven't a cent. I gave it to my lawyer. We can borrow it from Ambrose Kemper, upstairs.

VANDERGELDER. I wouldn't take it.

MRS. LEVI. Cornelius Hackl will lend it to us.

VANDERGELDER. He's in Yonkers.—Waiter!

[CORNELIUS *comes forward dressed in* MRS. MOLLOY'S *coat, thrown over his shoulder like a cape*. MRS. LEVI *is enjoying herself immensely*. VANDERGELDER *again goes to back wall to examine the pockets of his overcoat*.]

MRS. MOLLOY. Cornelius, is that Mr. Vandergelder's purse?

CORNELIUS. I didn't know it myself. I thought it was money just wandering around loose that didn't belong to anybody.

MRS. MOLLOY. Goodness! That's what politicians think!

VANDERGELDER. Waiter!

[*A band off left starts playing a polka*. BARNABY *comes forward dressed in* MINNIE'S *hat, coat and veil*.]

MINNIE. Irene, doesn't Barnaby make a lovely girl? He just ought to stay that way.

[MRS. LEVI *and* VANDERGELDER *move their table upstage*

while searching for the purse.]

MRS. MOLLOY. Why should we have our evening spoiled? Cornelius, I can teach you to dance in a few minutes. Oh, he won't recognize you.

MINNIE. Barnaby, it's the easiest thing in the world.

[*They move their table up against the back wall.*]

MRS. LEVI. Horace, you danced with me at your wedding and you danced with me at mine. Do you remember?

VANDERGELDER. No. Yes.

MRS. LEVI. Horace, you were a good dancer then. Don't confess to me that you're too old to dance.

VANDERGELDER. I'm not too old. I just don't want to dance.

MRS. LEVI. Listen to that music. Horace, do you remember the dances in the firehouse at Yonkers on Saturday nights? You gave me a fan. Come, come on!

[VANDERGELDER *and* MRS. LEVI *start to dance.* CORNELIUS, *dancing with* MRS. MOLLOY, *bumps into* VANDERGELDER, *back to back.* VANDERGELDER, *turning, fails at first to recognize him, then does and roars:*]

VANDERGELDER. You're discharged! Not a word! You're fired! Where's that idiot, Barnaby Tucker? He's fired, too.

[*The four young people, laughing, start rushing out the door to the street.* VANDERGELDER, *pointing at* MRS. MOLLOY, *shouts:*]

You're discharged!

MRS. MOLLOY. [*pointing at him*] You're discharged! [*Exit.*]

VANDERGELDER. You're discharged!

[*Enter from left,* AMBROSE *and* ERMENGARDE; *to* ERMENGARDE]

I'll lock you up for the rest of your life, young lady.

ERMENGARDE. Uncle! [*She faints in* AMBROSE'S *arms.*]

VANDERGELDER. [*to* AMBROSE] I'll have you arrested. Get out of my sight. I never want to see you again.

AMBROSE. [*carrying* ERMENGARDE *across to exit right*] You can't do anything to me, Mr. Vandergelder. [*Exit* AMBROSE *and* ERMENGARDE.]

MRS. LEVI. [*who has been laughing heartily, follows the distraught* VANDERGELDER *about the stage as he continues to hunt for his purse*] Well, there's your life, Mr. Vandergelder! Without niece —without clerks—without bride—and without your purse. Will you marry me now?

VANDERGELDER. No!

[*To get away from her, he dashes into the kitchen.* MRS. LEVI, *still laughing, exclaims to the audience:*]

MRS. LEVI. Damn!! [*and rushes off right*]

THE

CURTAIN

FALLS

Act IV

MISS FLORA VAN HUYSEN'S *house.*

This is a prosperous spinster's living room and is filled with knickknacks, all in bright colors, and hung with family portraits, bird cages, shawls, etc.

There is only one entrance—a large double door in the center of the back wall. Beyond it one sees the hall which leads left to the street door and right to the kitchen and the rest of the house. On the left are big windows hung with lace curtains on heavy draperies. Front left is MISS VAN HUYSEN'S *sofa, covered with bright-colored cushions, and behind it a table. On the right is another smaller sofa.* MISS VAN HUYSEN *is lying on the sofa. The* COOK *is at the window, left.* MISS VAN HUYSEN, *fifty, florid, stout and sentimental, is sniffing at smelling salts.* COOK (*enormous*) *holds a china mixing bowl.*

COOK. No, ma'am. I could swear I heard a cab drawing up to the door.

MISS VAN H. You imagined it. Imagination. Everything in life . . . like that . . . disappointment . . . illusion. Our plans . . . our hopes . . . what becomes of them? Nothing. The story of my life. [*She sings for a moment.*]

COOK. Pray God nothing's happened to the dear girl. Is it a long journey from Yonkers?

MISS VAN H. No; but long enough for a thousand things to happen.

COOK. Well, we've been waiting all day. Don't you think we ought to call the police about it?

MISS VAN H. The police! If it's God's will, the police can't prevent it. Oh, in three days, in a week, in a year, we'll know what's happened. . . . And if anything *has* happened to Ermengarde, it'll be a lesson to *him*—that's what it'll be.

COOK. To who?

MISS VAN H. To that cruel uncle of hers, of course,—to Horace Vandergelder, and to everyone else who tries to separate young lovers. Young lovers have enough to contend with as it is. Who should know that better than I? No one. The story of my life. [*sings for a moment, then:*] There! Now I hear a cab. Quick!

COOK. No. No, ma'am. I don't see anything.

MISS VAN H. There! What did I tell you? Everything's imagination—illusion.

COOK. But surely, if they'd changed their plans Mr. Vandergelder would have sent you a message.

MISS VAN H. Oh, I know what's the matter. That poor child probably thought she was coming to another prison—to another tyrant. If she'd known that I was her friend, and a friend of all young lovers, she'd be here by now. Oh, yes, she would. Her life shall not be crossed with obstacles and disappointments as . . . Cook, a minute ago my smelling salts were on this table. Now they've completely disappeared.

COOK. Why, there they are, ma'am, right there in your hand.

MISS VAN H. Goodness! How did they get there? I won't inquire. Stranger things have happened!

COOK. I suppose Mr. Vandergelder was sending her down with someone?

MISS VAN H. Two can go astray as easily as . . . [*She sneezes.*]

COOK. God bless you! [*runs to window*] Now, here's a carriage stopping.

[*The doorbell rings.*]

MISS VAN H. Well, open the door, Cook. [COOK *exits.*] It's probably some mistake . . . [*sneezes again*] God bless you!

[*Sounds of altercation off in hall.*]

It almost sounds as though I heard voices.

CORNELIUS. [*off*] I don't want to come in. This is a free country, I tell you.

CABMAN. [*off*] Forward march!

MALACHI. [*off*] In you go. We have orders.

CORNELIUS. [*off*] You can't make a person go where he doesn't want to go.

[*Enter* MALACHI, *followed by* COOK. *The* CABMAN *bundles* BARNABY *and* CORNELIUS *into the room, but they fight their way back into the hall.* CORNELIUS *has lost* MRS. MOLLOY'S *coat, but* BARNABY *is wearing* MINNIE'S *clothes.*]

MALACHI. Begging your pardon, ma'am, are you Miss Van Huysen?

MISS VAN H. Yes, I am, unfortunately. What's all this noise about?

MALACHI. There are two people here that Mr. Vandergelder said must be brought to this house and kept here until he comes. And here's his letter to you.

MISS VAN H. No one has any right to tell me whom I'm to keep in my house if they don't want to stay.

MALACHI. You're right, ma'am. Everybody's always talking about people breaking into houses, ma'am; but there are more people in the world who want to break out of houses, that's what I always say.— Bring them in, Joe.

[*Enter* CORNELIUS *and* BARNABY *being pushed by the* CABMAN.]

CORNELIUS. This young lady and I have no business here. We jumped into a cab and asked to be driven to the station and these men brought us to the house and forced us to come inside. There's been a mistake.

CABMAN. Is your name Miss Van Huysen?

MISS VAN H. Everybody's asking me if my name's Miss Van Huysen. I think that's a matter I can decide for myself. Now will you all be quiet while I read this letter? . . . "This is Ermengarde and that rascal Ambrose Kemper . . ." Now I know who you two are, anyway. "They are trying to run away . . ." Story of my life. "Keep them in your house until I come." Mr. Kemper, you have nothing to fear. [*to* CABMAN] Who are you?

CABMAN. I'm Joe. I stay here until the old man comes. He owes me fifteen dollars.

MALACHI. That's right, Miss Van Huysen, we must stay here to see they don't escape.

MISS VAN H. [*to* BARNABY] My dear child, take off your things. We'll all have some coffee. [*to* MALACHI *and* CABMAN] You two go out and wait in the hall. I'll send coffee out to you. Cook, take them.
[COOK *pushes* MALACHI *and* CABMAN *into the hall.*]

CORNELIUS. Ma'am, we're not the people you're expecting, and there's no reason . . .

MISS VAN H. Mr. Kemper, I'm not the tyrant you think I am. . . . You don't have to be afraid of me. . . . I know you're trying to run away with this innocent girl. . . . All my life I have suffered from the interference of others. You shall not suffer as I did. So put yourself entirely in my hands. [*She lifts* BARNABY'S *veil.*] Ermengarde! [*kisses him on both cheeks*] Where's your luggage?

BARNABY. It's—uh—uh—it's . . .

CORNELIUS. Oh, I'll find it in the morning. It's been mislaid.

MISS VAN H. Mislaid! How like life! Well, Ermengarde; you shall put on some of my clothes.

BARNABY. Oh, I know I wouldn't be happy, really.

MISS VAN H. She's a shy little thing, isn't she? Timid little darling! . . . Cook! Put some gingerbread in the oven and get the coffee ready . . .

COOK. Yes, ma'am. [*Exits to kitchen.*]

MISS VAN H. . . . while I go and draw a good hot bath for Ermengarde.

CORNELIUS. Oh, oh—Miss Van Huysen . . .

MISS VAN H. Believe me, Ermengarde, your troubles are at an end. You two will be married tomorrow. [*to* BARNABY] My dear, you look just like I did at your age, and your sufferings have been as mine. While you're bathing, I'll come and tell you the story of my life.

BARNABY. Oh, I don't want to take a bath. I always catch cold.

MISS VAN H. No, dear, you won't catch cold. I'll slap you all over. I'll be back in a minute. [*Exit.*]

CORNELIUS. [*looking out of window*] Barnaby, do you think we could jump down from this window?

BARNABY. Yes—we'd kill ourselves.

CORNELIUS. We'll just have to stay here and watch for something to happen. Barnaby, the situation's desperate.

BARNABY. It began getting desperate about half-past four and it's been getting worse ever since. Now I have to take a bath and get slapped all over.
[*Enter* MISS VAN HUYSEN *from kitchen.*]

MISS VAN H. Ermengarde, you've still got those wet things on. Your bath's nearly ready. Mr. Kemper, you come into the kitchen and put your feet in the oven.
[*The doorbell rings. Enter* COOK.]
What's that? It's the doorbell. I expect it's your uncle.

COOK. There's the doorbell. [*at window*] It's *another* man and a girl in a cab!

MISS VAN H. Well, go and let them in, Cook. Now, come with me, you two. Come, Ermengarde.

[*Exit* COOK. MISS VAN HUYSEN *drags* CORNELIUS *and the protesting* BARNABY *off into the kitchen.*]

COOK. [*off*] No, that's impossible. Come in, anyway.

[*Enter* ERMENGARDE, *followed by* AMBROSE, *carrying the two pieces of luggage.*]

There's some mistake. I'll tell Miss Van Huysen, but there's some mistake.

ERMENGARDE. But, I tell you, I *am* Mr. Vandergelder's niece; I'm Ermengarde.

COOK. Beg your pardon, Miss, but you *can't* be Miss Ermengarde.

ERMENGARDE. But—but—here I *am*. And that's my baggage.

COOK. Well, I'll tell Miss Van Huysen who you *think* you are, but she won't like it. [*Exits.*]

AMBROSE. You'll be all right now, Ermengarde. I'd better go before she sees me.

ERMENGARDE. Oh, no. You must stay. I feel so strange here.

AMBROSE. I know, but Mr. Vandergelder will be here in a minute. . . .

ERMENGARDE. Ambrose, you can't go. You can't leave me in this crazy house with those drunken men in the hall. Ambrose . . . Ambrose, let's say you're someone else that my uncle sent down to take care of me. Let's say you're—you're Cornelius Hackl!

AMBROSE. Who's Cornelius Hackl?

ERMENGARDE. You know. He's chief clerk in Uncle's store.

AMBROSE. I don't want to be Cornelius Hackl. No, no, Ermengarde, come away with me now. I'll take you to my friend's house. Or I'll take you to Mrs. Levi's house.

ERMENGARDE. Why, it was Mrs. Levi who threw us right at Uncle Horace's face. Oh, I wish I were back in Yonkers where nothing ever happens.

[*Enter* MISS VAN HUYSEN.]

MISS VAN H. What's all this I hear? Who do you say you are?

ERMENGARDE. Aunt Flora . . . don't you remember me? I'm Ermengarde.

MISS VAN H. And you're Mr. Vandergelder's niece?

ERMENGARDE. Yes, I am.

MISS VAN H. Well, that's very strange indeed, because he has just sent me another niece named Ermengarde. She came with a letter from him, explaining everything. Have you got a letter from him?

ERMENGARDE. No . . .

MISS VAN H. Really!—And who is this?

ERMENGARDE. This is Cornelius Hackl, Aunt Flora.

MISS VAN H. Never heard of him.

ERMENGARDE. He's chief clerk in Uncle's store.

MISS VAN H. Never heard of him. The other Ermengarde came with the man she's in love with, and that *proves* it. She came with

Mr. Ambrose Kemper.

AMBROSE. [*shouts*] Ambrose Kemper!

MISS VAN H. Yes, Mr. Hackl, and Mr. Ambrose Kemper is in the kitchen there now *with his feet in the oven.*

[ERMENGARDE *starts to cry.* MISS VAN HUYSEN *takes her to the sofa. They both sit.*]

Dear child, what is your trouble?

ERMENGARDE. Oh, dear. I don't know what to do.

MISS VAN H. [*in a low voice*] Are you in love with this man?

ERMENGARDE. Yes, I am.

MISS VAN H. I could see it—and are people trying to separate you?

ERMENGARDE. Yes, they are.

MISS VAN H. I could see it—who? Horace Vandergelder?

ERMENGARDE. Yes.

MISS VAN H. That's enough for me. I'll put a stop to Horace Vandergelder's goings on. [MISS VAN HUYSEN *draws* AMBROSE *down to sit on her other side.*] Mr. Hackl, think of me as your friend. Come in the kitchen and get warm. . . . [*She rises and starts to go out.*] We can decide later who everybody is. My dear, would you like a good hot bath?

ERMENGARDE. Yes, I would.

MISS VAN H. Well, when Ermengarde comes out you can go in.

[*Enter* CORNELIUS *from the kitchen.*]

CORNELIUS. Oh, Miss Van Huysen . . .

ERMENGARDE. Why, Mr. Hack—!!

CORNELIUS. [*sliding up to her, urgently*] Not yet! I'll explain. I'll explain everything.

MISS VAN H. Mr. Kemper!—Mr. Kemper! This is Mr. Cornelius Hackl. [*to* AMBROSE] Mr. Hackl, this is Mr. Ambrose Kemper. [*pause, while the men glare at one another*] Perhaps you two know one another?

AMBROSE. No!

CORNELIUS. No, we don't.

AMBROSE. [*hotly*] Miss Van Huysen, I know that man is not Ambrose Kemper.

CORNELIUS. [*ditto*] And he's not Cornelius Hackl.

MISS VAN H. My dear young men, what does it matter what your names are? The important thing is that you are you. [*to* AMBROSE] You are alive and breathing, aren't you, Mr. Hackl? [*pinches* AMBROSE's *left arm*]

AMBROSE. Ouch, Miss Van Huysen.

MISS VAN H. This dear child imagines she is Horace Vandergelder's niece Ermengarde.

ERMENGARDE. But I am.

MISS VAN H. The important thing is that you're all in love. Everything else is illusion. [*She pinches* CORNELIUS' *arm.*]

CORNELIUS. Ouch! Miss Van Huysen!

MISS VAN H. [*comes down and addresses the audience*] Everybody keeps asking me if I'm Miss Van Huys . . . [*She seems suddenly to be stricken with doubt as to who she is; her face shows bewildered alarm. She pinches herself on the upper arm and is abruptly and happily relieved.*] Now, you two gentlemen sit down and have a nice chat while this dear child has a good hot bath.

[*The doorbell rings.* ERMENGARDE *exits,* MISS VAN HUYSEN *about to follow her, but stops. Enter* COOK.]

COOK. There's the doorbell again.

MISS VAN H. Well, answer it. [*She and* ERMENGARDE *exit to kitchen.*]

COOK. [*at window, very happy about all these guests*] It's a cab and three ladies. I never saw such a night. [*Exit to front door.*]

MISS VAN H. Gentlemen, you can rest easy. I'll see that Mr. Vandergelder lets his nieces marry you both.

[*Enter* MRS. LEVI.]

MRS. LEVI. Flora, how are you?

MISS VAN H. Dolly Gallagher! What brings you here?

MRS. LEVI. Great Heavens, Flora, what are those two drunken men doing in your hall?

MISS VAN H. I don't know. Horace Vandergelder sent them to me.

MRS. LEVI. Well, I've brought you two girls in much the same condition. Otherwise they're the finest girls in the world. [*She goes up to the door and leads in* MRS. MOLLOY. MINNIE *follows.*] I want you to meet Irene Molloy and Minnie Fay.

MISS VAN H. Delighted to know you.

MRS. LEVI. Oh, I see you two gentlemen are here, too. Mr. Hackl, I was about to look for you [*pointing about the room*] somewhere here.

CORNELIUS. No, Mrs. Levi. I'm ready to face anything now.

MRS. LEVI. Mr. Vandergelder will be here in a minute. He's downstairs trying to pay for a cab without any money.

MRS. MOLLOY. [*holding* VANDERGELDER's *purse*] Oh, I'll help him.

MRS. LEVI. Yes, will you, dear? You had to pay the restaurant bills. You must have hundreds of dollars there it seems.

MRS. MOLLOY. This is his own purse he lost. I can't give it back to him without seeming . . .

MRS. LEVI. I'll give it back to him.—There, you help him with this now. [*She gives* MRS. MOLLOY *a bill and puts the purse airily under her arm.*]

VANDERGELDER. [*off*] Will somebody please pay for this cab?

[MRS. MOLLOY *exits to front door.*]

MRS. MOLLOY. [*off stage*] I'll take care of that, Mr. Vandergelder.

[*As* MR. VANDERGELDER *enters,* MALACHI *and the* CABMAN *follow him in.* VANDERGELDER *carries overcoat, stick and box of chocolates.*]

CABMAN. Fifteen dollars, Mr. Vandergelder.

MALACHI. Hello, Mr. Vandergelder.

VANDERGELDER. [*to* MALACHI] You're discharged! [*to* CABMAN] You too! [MALACHI *and* CABMAN *go out and wait in the hall.*] So I've caught up with you at last! [*to* AMBROSE] I never want to see you again! [*to* CORNELIUS] You're discharged! Get out of the house, both of you.

[*He strikes sofa with his stick; a second after,* MISS VAN HUYsen *strikes him on the shoulder with a folded newspaper or magazine.*]

MISS VAN H. [*forcefully*] Now then you. Stop ordering people out of my house. You can shout and carry on in Yonkers, but when you're in my house you'll behave yourself.

VANDERGELDER. They're both dishonest scoundrels.

MISS VAN H. Take your hat off. Gentlemen, you stay right where you are.

CORNELIUS. Mr. Vandergelder, I can explain—

MISS VAN H. There aren't going to be any explanations. Horace, stop scowling at Mr. Kemper and forgive him.

VANDERGELDER. That's not Kemper, that's a dishonest rogue named Cornelius Hackl.

MISS VAN H. You're crazy. [*points to* AMBROSE] That's Cornelius Hackl.

VANDERGELDER. I guess I know my own chief clerk.

MISS VAN H. I don't care what their names are. You shake hands with them both, or out you go.

VANDERGELDER. Shake hands with those dogs and scoundrels!

MRS. LEVI. Mr. Vandergelder, you've had a hard day. You don't want to go out in the rain now. Just for form's sake, you shake hands with them. You can start quarreling with them tomorrow.

VANDERGELDER. [*gives* CORNELIUS *one finger to shake*] There! Don't regard that as a handshake. [*He turns to* AMBROSE, *who mockingly offers him one finger.*] Hey! I never want to see you again.

[MRS. MOLLOY *enters from front door.*]

MRS. MOLLOY. Miss Van Huysen.

MISS VAN H. Yes, dear?

MRS. MOLLOY. Do I smell coffee?

MISS VAN H. Yes, dear.

MRS. MOLLOY. Can I have some, good and black?

MISS VAN H. Come along, everybody. We'll go into the kitchen and have some coffee. [*as they all go*] Horace, you'll be interested to know there are two Ermengardes in there. . . .

VANDERGELDER. Two!!

[*Last to go is* MINNIE, *who revolves about the room dreamily waltzing, a finger on her forehead.* MRS. LEVI *has been standing at one side. She now comes forward, in thoughtful mood.* MINNIE *continues her waltz round the left sofa and out to the kitchen.* MRS. LEVI, *left alone, comes to front, addressing an imaginary Ephraim.*]

MRS. LEVI. Ephraim Levi, I'm going to get married again. Ephraim, I'm marrying Horace Vandergelder for his money. I'm going to send his money out doing all the things you taught me. Oh, it won't be a marriage in the sense that we had one—but I shall certainly make him happy, and Ephraim—I'm tired. I'm tired of living from hand to mouth, and I'm asking your permission, Ephraim—will you give me away? [*Now addressing the audience, she holds up the purse.*] Money! Money!—it's like the sun we walk under; it can kill or cure.—Mr. Vandergelder's money!

Vandergelder's never tired of saying most of the people in the world are fools, and in a way he's right, isn't he? Himself, Irene, Cornelius, myself! But there comes a moment in everybody's life when he must decide whether he'll live among human beings or not—a fool among fools or a fool alone.

As for me, I've decided to live among them.

I wasn't always so. After my husband's death I retired into myself. Yes, in the evenings, I'd put out the cat, and I'd lock the door, and I'd make myself a little rum toddy; and before I went to bed I'd say a little prayer, thanking God that I was independent—that no one else's life was mixed up with mine. And when ten o'clock sounded from Trinity Church tower, I fell off to sleep and I was a perfectly contented woman. And one night, after two years of this, an oak leaf fell out of my Bible. I had placed it there on the day my husband asked me to marry him; a perfectly good oak leaf—but without color and without life. And suddenly I realized that for a long time I had not shed one tear; nor had I been filled with the wonderful hope that something or other would turn out well. I saw that I was like that oak leaf, and on that night I decided to rejoin the human race.

Yes, we're all fools and we're all in danger of destroying the world with our folly. But the surest way to keep us out of harm is to give us the four or five human pleasures that are our right in the world,—and that takes a little *money!*

The difference between a little money and no money at all is enormous—and can shatter the world. And the difference between a little money and an enoromus amount of money is very slight—and that, also, can shatter the world.

Money, I've always felt, money—pardon my expression—is like manure; it's not worth a thing unless it's spread about encouraging young things to grow.

Anyway,—that's the opinion of the second Mrs. Vandergelder.

[VANDERGELDER *enters with two cups of coffee. With his back, he closes both doors.*]

VANDERGELDER. Miss Van Huysen asked me to bring you this.

MRS. LEVI. Thank you both. Sit down and rest yourself. What's been going on in the kitchen?

VANDERGELDER. A lot of foolishness. Everybody falling in love with everybody. I forgave 'em; Ermengarde and that artist.

MRS. LEVI. I knew you would.

VANDERGELDER. I made Cornelius Hackl my partner.

MRS. LEVI. You won't regret it.

VANDERGELDER. Dolly, you said some mighty unpleasant things to me in the restaurant tonight . . . all that about my house . . . and everything.

MRS. LEVI. Let's not say another word about it.

VANDERGELDER. Dolly, you have a lot of faults—

MRS. LEVI. Oh, I know what you mean.

VANDERGELDER. You're bossy, scheming, inquisitive . . .

MRS. LEVI. Go on.

VANDERGELDER. But you're a wonderful woman. Dolly, marry me.

MRS. LEVI. Horace! [*rises*] Stop right there.

VANDERGELDER. I know I've been a fool about Mrs. Molloy, and that other woman. But, Dolly, forgive me and marry me. [*He goes on his knees.*]

MRS. LEVI. Horace, I don't dare. No. I don't dare.

VANDERGELDER. What do you mean?

MRS. LEVI. You know as well as I do that you're the first citizen of Yonkers. Naturally, you'd expect your wife to keep open house, to have scores of friends in and out all the time. Any wife of yours should be used to that kind of thing.

VANDERGELDER. [*after a brief struggle with himself*] Dolly, you can live any way you like.

MRS. LEVI. Horace, you can't deny it, your wife would have to be a *somebody*. Answer me: am I a somebody?

VANDERGELDER. You are . . . you are. Wonderful woman.

MRS. LEVI. Oh, you're partial. [*She crosses, giving a big wink at the audience, and sits on sofa right.* VANDERGELDER *follows her on his knees.*] Horace, it won't be enough for you to load your wife with money and jewels; to insist that she be a benefactress to half the town. [*He rises and, still struggling with himself, coughs so as not to hear this.*] No, she must be a somebody. Do you really think I have it in me to be a credit to you?

VANDERGELDER. Dolly, everybody knows that you could do anything you wanted to do.

MRS. LEVI. I'll try. With your help, I'll try—and by the way, I found your purse. [*holds it up*]

VANDERGELDER. Where did you—! Wonderful woman!

MRS. LEVI. It just walked into my hand. I don't know how I do it. Sometimes I frighten myself. Horace, take it. Money walks out of my hands, too.

VANDERGELDER. Keep it. Keep it.

MRS. LEVI. Horace! [*half laughing, half weeping, and with an air of real affection for him*] I never thought . . . I'd ever . . . hear you say a thing like that!

[BARNABY *dashes in from the kitchen in great excitement. He has discarded* MINNIE's *clothes.*]

BARNABY. Oh! Excuse me. I didn't know anybody was here.

VANDERGELDER. [*bellowing*] Didn't know anybody was here. Idiot!

MRS. LEVI. [*putting her hand on* VANDERGELDER's *arm; amiably*] Come in, Barnaby. Come in.

[VANDERGELDER *looks at her a minute; then says, imitating her tone:*]

VANDERGELDER. Come in, Barnaby. Come in.

BARNABY. Cornelius is going to marry Mrs. Molloy! !

MRS. LEVI. Isn't that fine! Horace! . . . [MRS. LEVI *rises, and indicates that he has an announcement to make.*]

VANDERGELDER. Barnaby, go in and tell the rest of them that Mrs. Levi has consented—

MRS. LEVI. *Finally* consented!

BARNABY. Holy cabooses. [*dashes back to the doorway*] Hey! Listen, everybody! Wolf-trap—I mean—Mr. Vandergelder is going to marry Mrs. Levi.

> [MISS VAN HUYSEN *enters followed by all the people in this act. She is now carrying the box of chocolates.*]

MISS VAN H. Dolly, that's the best news I ever heard. [*She addresses the audience.*] There isn't any more coffee; there isn't any more gingerbread; but there are three couples in my house and they're all going to get married. And do you know, one of those Ermengardes wasn't a dear little girl at all—she was a boy! Well, that's what life is: disappointment, illusion.

MRS. LEVI. [*to audience*] There isn't any more coffee; there isn't any more gingerbread, and there isn't any more play—but there is one more thing we have to do. . . . Barnaby, come here. [*She whispers to him, pointing to the audience. Then she says to the audience*] I think the youngest person here ought to tell us what the moral of the play is.

> [BARNABY *is reluctantly pushed forward to the footlights.*]

BARNABY. Oh, I think it's about . . . I think it's about adventure. The test of an adventure is that when you're in the middle of it, you say to yourself, "Oh, now I've got myself into an awful mess; I wish I were sitting quietly at home." And the sign that something's wrong with you is when you sit quietly at home wishing you were out having lots of adventure. What we would like for you is that you have just the right amount of sitting quietly at home, and just the right amount of—adventure! So that now we all want to thank you for coming tonight, and we all hope that in your lives you have just the right amount of—adventure!

THE

CURTAIN

FALLS

Camille and Perdican

ALFRED DE MUSSET

In 1830, Alfred de Musset's first play, *The Venetian Night*, was hooted off the Parisian stage. Already famous as a poet, the twenty-year-old Musset withdrew from the theater, decided to have nothing more to do with so unappreciative an audience. The plays he wrote over the next few years, so different from the romantic melodramas then popular, were offered to readers. Some of his plays were finally staged in the late 1840's, but *Camille and Perdican*, which was first published in 1834, was not performed until November 18, 1861, four years after his death. Musset called his play a *proverbe*, after a particular kind of eighteenth-century drama—a brief play in which a few actors, performing in a salon, used the simplest kind of plot to illustrate a proverb. Musset's play is, of course, much more complicated than a *proverbe*, but his title is a reminder that his play is related to that genre. Although Musset's working title was *Camille and Perdican*, which Peter Meyer reverts to in his translation, the play is more accurately known as *On ne badine pas avec l'amour*, which might be translated, roughly, *You Can't Kid Around with Love.*

Camille and Perdican†

Characters

THE BARON
PERDICAN, *his son, aged 21*
FATHER BLAZIUS, *Perdican's tutor*
FATHER BRIDAINE, *the village priest*
CAMILLE, *the Baron's niece, aged 18*

DAME PLUCHE, *her governess*
ROSETTE, *a village girl, Camille's foster sister*
CHORUS OF VILLAGE PEOPLE
PEASANT
SERVANTS

SCENE—*The action takes place in and near a small French village.*

281

Act One

SCENE I—*The village square in front of the castle.*

[CHORUS *enters.*]

CHORUS. Gently rocking on his sharp-eyed mule, Father Blazius approaches through the sunlit vineyards, his clothes all new, his inkhorn at his side. Like a baby on a cushion, he rolls upon his rounded stomach and with eyes half closed he mumbles a paternoster in his triple chin. [FATHER BLAZIUS *enters.*] Good morning, Father Blazius, you come in time for the grape harvest, like an antique amphora.

FATHER BLAZIUS. If you wish to hear news of great importance, first bring me here a glass of good cool wine.

CHORUS. Here is our largest pitcher. Drink up, Father Blazius. The wine is good. You can speak later.

FATHER BLAZIUS. You know, my children, that young Perdican, the Baron's son, has just reached his majority and taken his doctor's degree in Paris. He comes home here today, his mouth so full of fine and flowery phrases that half the time you don't know how to answer him. All his gracious person is a book of gold. If he but sees a blade of grass, he'll tell you what it's called in Latin. And if it blows, or pours with rain, he will explain quite clearly why. You will open your eyes as wide as these castle gates, when you see him unroll one of the parchments he has painted with inks of every color, with his own fair hands and without a word to anyone. He is, in short, from top to toe a sparkling jewel. And that is what I've come to tell the Baron. You realize this does me some honor, I've been his tutor from the age of four. Now, bring me a chair, so I may get off this mule without breaking my neck. The brute is rather stubborn and I should not be sorry to drink another mouthful before I go in.

CHORUS. Drink up, Father Blazius. It will do you good. We all knew Perdican as a child; there was no need to speak of him at such length. Let us hope we find that child again in the heart of the man.

FATHER BLAZIUS. Good lord, the pitcher's empty. I didn't think I'd drunk it all. Good-by, my friends. I prepared upon the road a few brief words, quite unpretentious, that will not, I think, displease the Baron. I shall go in to see him. [*goes out*]

CHORUS. Roughly jolted on a breathless ass, Dame Pluche climbs up the hill. Her groom, with all his might, cudgels the poor beast, which shakes its head, a thistle in its mouth. Her long, thin legs tremble with rage, as with her bony hands she scratches at a rosary. [DAME PLUCHE *enters.*] Good day to you, Dame Pluche. You come like influenza with the autumn wind which turns the leaves to yellow.

DAME PLUCHE. A glass of water, scoundrels that you are. A glass of water, with a little vinegar.

CHORUS. Where do you come from, Pluche my sweet? Even your

false hair is covered with dust. Your wig's awry and your chaste robe pulled up to your venerable garters.

DAME PLUCHE. Know then, you scum, that the lovely Camille, the Baron's niece, comes here today. She has left her convent at her uncle's strict command, to come, in proper time and place, to take, as well she should, the large estate bequeathed her by her mother. Her education, God be thanked, is finished. And those who see her have the joy of savoring a glorious flower of wisdom and devotion. Never has been seen a girl so pure and so angelic, so like a lamb, so like a dove, as this young novice. May the Lord God of Heaven watch over her. So be it. Out of the way, you rabble. I think my legs are swollen.

CHORUS. Calm yourself, good Pluche. And when you pray to God, ask Him for rain; our fields are as dry as your old shins.

DAME PLUCHE. You have brought me water in a pitcher that smells of garlic. Give me your hand to get down. You are ignorant, ill-mannered louts. [*goes out*]

CHORUS. Let us put on our best clothes and wait for the Baron to summon us. Unless I am much mistaken, there's a happy celebration in the air today.

SCENE II—*A room in the castle, immediately afterward.*

[*The* BARON, FATHER BRIDAINE, *and* FATHER BLAZIUS *enter.*]

BARON. Father Bridaine, you are my friend; let me present to you Father Blazius, tutor to my son. Yesterday at eight minutes past twelve noon my son was twenty-one years old. He has taken his doctor's degree in four separate subjects. Father Blazius, let me present to you Father Bridaine, our village priest. He is my friend.

FATHER BLAZIUS. [*bowing*] In four separate subjects, my lord. Literature, botany, Roman law, and canon law.

BARON. Go to your room, my dear Blazius, my son will soon be here. Get ready for dinner and come back when you hear the bell.

[FATHER BLAZIUS *goes out.*]

FATHER BRIDAINE. Shall I tell you what I think, my lord? Every breath of your son's tutor smells of wine.

BARON. Impossible.

FATHER BRIDAINE. I'm as certain as I'm standing here. He spoke to me from very close just now. The smell of wine was frightening.

BARON. That's enough. I tell you it's impossible. [DAME PLUCHE *enters.*] There you are, good Dame Pluche. My niece of course is with you?

DAME PLUCHE. She follows me, my lord. I came on a few yards ahead.

BARON. Father Bridaine, you are my friend, let me present to you Dame Pluche, governess to my niece. Yesterday evening at seven o'clock, my niece attained the age of eighteen. She has just left the best convent in France. Dame Pluche, let me present to you Father Bridaine, our village priest. He is my friend.

DAME PLUCHE. [*bowing*] The best convent in France, my lord. And, I might add, the best young Christian in the convent.

BARON. Dame Pluche, go and repair the ravages of your journey. My niece, I hope, will soon be here. Be ready in time for dnner.

[DAME PLUCHE *goes out.*]

FATHER BRIDAINE. The old lady seems a model of piety.

BARON. Of piety and propriety, Father Bridaine. Her virtue is unassailable.

FATHER BRIDAINE. But the tutor smells of wine, I'm sure of it.

BARON. Father Bridaine, there are times when I begin to doubt your friendship. Do you take it upon yourself to contradict me? Not another word about it. I have made a plan to marry my son to my niece. They are a well-matched couple. Their education cost me six thousand crowns.

FATHER BRIDAINE. You will have to obtain a papal dispensation.

BARON. I have it, Bridaine. It's on my table in my study. Oh, my dear fellow, now you realize how delighted I am. You know I have always had the most profound horror of solitude. However, the position I occupy forces me to spend three months here in winter and three in summer. It's impossible to please people in general, and one's tenants in particular, without sometimes giving the servants strict orders that no one is to enter. How austere and complicated is the life of a statesman! So what pleasure I should find in tempering, by the presence of my two united children, the heavy melancholy I must needs be a prey to, since I became the King's representative.

FATHER BRIDAINE. Will the wedding take place here or in Paris?

BARON. That's what I was waiting for, Bridaine, I was sure you would ask that question. Well, my dear friend, what would you say if these hands, yes, Bridaine, your own hands—don't look at them so piteously—were destined to give the solemn blessing to the happy confirmation of my dearest dreams? Eh?

FATHER BRIDAINE. I am silent. Gratitude seals my lips.

BARON. Come here to the window. Look, do you see my people crowding round the gate? My two children have arrived at the same time. What a happy chance! I have arranged for every contingency. My niece will be introduced by this door on the left and my son by the one on the right. What do you say to that? I'm so eager to see how they'll greet each other, what they'll say. Six thousand crowns is no trifle, there must be no mistakes. Besides, these children used to love each other very dearly when they were babies. Bridaine, I have an idea.

FATHER BRIDAINE. What is that?

BARON. During dinner, without appearing to stress it . . . you understand, my dear fellow . . . as you're drinking a happy toast or two . . . you know Latin, Bridaine?

FATHER BRIDAINE. Heavens above, do I know Latin!

BARON. I should be very pleased to see you dispute with the boy, discreetly of course, in front of his cousin. That can only produce a good effect. Make him speak a little Latin . . . not exactly during dinner, that would be too tedious and I of course don't understand a word . . . but during dessert . . . do you see?

FATHER BRIDAINE. If you don't understand a word, my lord, it's probable your niece doesn't either.

BARON. All the more reason. Surely you don't expect a woman to admire what she can understand. What are you thinking of, Bridaine? That's a ridiculous statement.

FATHER BRIDAINE. I know little about women. But it seems to me difficult to admire what you cannot understand.

BARON. I know them, Bridaine; I know those charming, unaccountable creatures. Take it from me, they love to have dust thrown in their eyes. And the more you throw, the wider they open them so they can take in even more.

[PERDICAN *enters on one side,* CAMILLE *on the other.*]

BARON. Good morning, children. My dear Perdican, my dear Camille! Come and kiss me; and kiss each other.

PERDICAN. Good morning, Father; and my dearest sister. How wonderful! I'm so happy!

CAMILLE. Father, cousin, I'm glad to see you.

PERDICAN. How tall you are, Camille! And lovely as the dawn!

BARON. When did you leave Paris, Perdican?

PERDICAN. Wednesday, I think, or Tuesday. So here you are, transformed into a woman! And I'm a man! It seems yesterday I saw you no taller than that.

BARON. You must both be tired. It's a long journey and the weather's hot.

PERDICAN. Good lord, no! Do look, Father, how pretty Camille is!

BARON. Now, Camille, kiss your cousin.

CAMILLE. Excuse me.

BARON. A compliment deserves a kiss. Take her in your arms, Perdican.

PERDICAN. If my cousin turns away when I stretch out my hand, it's my turn to say "Excuse me." Love can steal a kiss, but not friendship.

CAMILLE. Neither love nor friendship should receive what they cannot return.

BARON. [*to* FATHER BRIDAINE] That's an ill-omened beginning, eh?

FATHER BRIDAINE. [*to the* BARON] Too much modesty is no doubt a defect, but marriage removes many scruples.

BARON. [*to* FATHER BRIDAINE] I'm shocked, offended. That answer's upset me. "Excuse me!" Did you see she seemed to cross herself? Come here, I want to speak to you. This is extremely painful. This moment should have been so sweet to me, but now it's completely spoiled. I'm vexed, hurt. Damnation, this is very bad.

FATHER BRIDAINE. Say something to them. Look, they're turning their backs on each other.

BARON. Well, children, what are you thinking about? Camille, why are you looking at that picture?

CAMILLE. What a beautiful portrait, uncle! Isn't it our great-aunt?

BARON. Yes, my child, it's your great-grandmother, or rather your great-grandfather's sister, for the dear woman never contributed, other than in prayer, I think, on her part, to the enlargement of the family. She was, indeed she was, a saintly woman.

CAMILLE. Oh yes, a saint. It's my great-aunt Isabel. How well that nun's veil suits her.

BARON. Perdican, why are you looking at that vase of flowers?

PERDICAN. This is a charming flower, Father. It's a heliotrope.

BARON. What a long name for a flower that's no bigger than a fly.

PERDICAN. This little flower may be no bigger than a fly, but it certainly has its price.[1]

FATHER BRIDAINE. Of course! The doctor's right. Ask him its sex, its type, what elements it's made of, where it gets its sap and color. He'll whirl you into ecstasy by explaining all the phenomena of this tiny blade of grass, from its root up to its petals.

PERDICAN. I don't know as much as that, reverend Father. I know it smells sweet, that's all.

SCENE III—*The village square, later the same day.*

[CHORUS *enters.*]

CHORUS. A number of things amuse me and excite my curiosity. Come, my friends, let us sit down under this tree. Two formidable eaters are at this moment face to face in the castle, Father Bridaine and Father Blazius. Have you ever noticed something? When two men, almost identical, equally fat, equally foolish, with the same vices and the same passions, happen by chance to meet, then it follows inevitably that they either love or hate each other. For the same reason that opposites are attracted, that a tall, dried-up man will like one who is small and fat, or fair people make friends with dark, and conversely, I foresee a secret struggle between the tutor and our priest. Both of them are armed with equal impudence; both have a barrel of a stomach; not only are they gluttons, but gourmets too; both will argue at dinner, not only about the quantity but about the quality. If the fish is small, what will they do? And in any case they can't share the tongue of a carp and a carp can only have one tongue. Both of them love to talk; but if necessary they can talk at the same time without listening to each other. Father Bridaine has already tried to put several pedantic questions to Perdican and the tutor raised his eyebrows. He doesn't like anyone to seem to put his pupil to the test. Furthermore each is as ignorant as the other. Again, they are both of them priests: one will boast about his parish, the other will glory in his post as tutor. Blazius is confessor to the son, Bridaine to the father. I can see them already with their elbows on the table, cheeks aflame and eyes agoggle, shaking their triple chins with hatred. They look each other up and down, they open with a light skirmish; soon war will be declared: all kinds of pedantries will be crossed and parried; and, to crown it all, between these two drunkards flutters Dame Pluche, thrusting them off with her sharp elbows. Now dinner is finished

1. Although Meyer correctly translates the French *prix* as price, the line does not mean in English what it means in French. The English phrase "has its price" suggests that it can be bought; the line means that, little though it is, the flower has its worth.

and they are opening the castle gates. Here come the company.
Let us draw aside.

[CHORUS *goes out. The* BARON *and* DAME PLUCHE *enter.*]

BARON. Dame Pluche, I am pained.

DAME PLUCHE. Is that possible, my lord?

BARON. Yes, Pluche, it is possible. I have reckoned for a long time,
I had even written down, noted on my tablets, that today was to
be the happiest day of my life—yes, good woman, of my life. You
are not unaware that I had planned to marry my son to my niece;
it was decided, settled; I had mentioned it to Bridaine. And now
I see, I think I see, these children speaking coldly to each other.
At least they haven't said a word.

DAME PLUCHE. Here they come, my lord. Have they been told of
your plans?

BARON. I did say one or two words privately. I think it would be
wise, as they are here together, to sit down in that conveniently
shady place and leave them alone for a moment.

[*The* BARON *and* DAME PLUCHE *go out.* CAMILLE *and* PERDI-
CAN *enter.*]

PERDICAN. Camille, do you realize it was not at all kind to refuse to
kiss me?

CAMILLE. I am like that, it's my manner.

PERDICAN. Will you take my arm and walk around the village?

CAMILLE. No, I'm tired.

PERDICAN. Wouldn't you like to see the meadow again? Do you remember our parties in the boat? Let's go down to the mill. I'll
take the oars and you can steer.

CAMILLE. I have no desire to.

PERDICAN. You break my heart. What, have you no memories,
Camille? Not a quickening of your heart for our childhood, for
all that poor time past, so good and happy, so full of delightful
memories? Wouldn't you like to see the path we used to take to
the farm?

CAMILLE. No, not this evening.

PERDICAN. Not this evening! Well, when? Our whole life lies there.

CAMILLE. I'm not young enough to play with my dolls or old enough
to be in love with the past.

PERDICAN. What do you mean?

CAMILLE. I mean that childhood memories are not to my taste.

PERDICAN. They bore you?

CAMILLE. Yes, they bore me.

PERDICAN. Poor child. I am sincerely sorry for you.

[*They go out in different directions. The* BARON *and* DAME
PLUCHE *enter.*]

BARON. You saw them, my good Pluche, and you heard them. I was
expecting the sweetest harmony, but I seem to be listening to a
concert where the violin is playing a hymn tune and the flute a
country dance. Just think of the appalling discord such a combination would produce. Yet that is what is going on in my heart.

DAME PLUCHE. I agree. But I find it impossible to blame Camille. In my view, nothing could be in worse taste than boating parties.

BARON. Are you speaking seriously?

DAME PLUCHE. My lord, no young girl with any self-respect would venture out on rivers.

BARON. But do remember, Dame Pluche, her cousin is to marry her and besides. . . .

DAME PLUCHE. Decency forbids the holding of a tiller and it is unseemly to leave dry land alone with a young man.

BARON. But I repeat . . . I tell you. . . .

DAME PLUCHE. That is my opinion.

BARON. Are you mad? Really you'll make me say . . . there are some expressions I don't wish . . . I am loath to use. . . . You make me want to. . . . Really if I don't restrain myself. . . . You're a blithering fool, Pluche! I don't know what to think of you.

[*They go out.* PERDICAN *and* CHORUS *enter.*]

PERDICAN. Good evening, my old friends. Don't you recognize me?

CHORUS. My lord, you look like a child we once loved very dearly.

PERDICAN. Wasn't it you who used to carry me on your back to cross the streams in your meadows; you made me dance on your knees; you swung me up behind you on your sturdy horses; you sometimes used to squeeze up around your table to make room for me at supper on your farm.

CHORUS. We remember, my lord. You were quite the worst young scamp and the best young fellow we ever saw.

PERDICAN. Well then, why don't you take me in your arms, instead of bowing to me like a stranger?

CHORUS. God bless you, my dear boy! Every one of us wanted to take you in his arms. But we are old, my lord, and you're a man now.

PERDICAN. Yes, it's ten years since I saw you last and in a single day everything changes under the sun. I have grown up a few feet toward heaven and you have bent down a few inches toward the grave. Your heads are white and your steps are slower. You can't lift me up from the ground as you did when I was a child. So it's for me to be your father, as you were all once mine.

CHORUS. Your return is a happier day for us than your birth. It's better to find someone you love than to kiss an unknown baby.

PERDICAN. So here is my dear valley. My walnut trees, my green paths, my little woodland spring. Here are my days gone by, still so full of life; here is the mysterious world of my childhood dreams. Home! Home! Incomprehensible word! Is man born for only one particular place, where he must build his nest and live for just a single day?

CHORUS. They tell us you're a learned man now, my lord.

PERDICAN. Yes, they've told me that too. Science is a fine thing, my children. But these trees and meadows teach, for all the world to see, the finest thing of all, the way to forget all knowledge.

CHORUS. There has been more than a change or two, while you've been away. Girls have got married and boys gone off into the army.

PERDICAN. You must tell me everything. I am expecting so much news. But really I don't want it yet. How small this fountain is. In the old days I used to think it vast. I took away in my head the idea of an ocean and a forest, but now I find a drop of water and a few blades of grass. Who is that girl singing at her window behind those trees?

CHORUS. It's Rosette, your cousin's foster sister.

PERDICAN. [*approaching*] Rosette, come out quickly and join us.

[ROSETTE *enters.*]

ROSETTE. Yes, my lord.

PERDICAN. You saw me from the window, you wicked girl, and you didn't come? Quickly, give me your hand, and your cheeks. I must kiss you.

ROSETTE. Yes, my lord.

PERDICAN. Are you married, my dear? I was told you were.

ROSETTE. Oh, no.

PERDICAN. Why? There's not a prettier girl in the village. We'll find you a husband, my child.

CHORUS. My lord, she says she'll never marry.

PERDICAN. Is that true, Rosette?

ROSETTE. Oh, no.

PERDICAN. Your sister Camille is here. Have you seen her?

ROSETTE. No, not yet.

PERDICAN. Go and put on your best dress and come to supper at the castle.

SCENE IV—*A room in the castle.*

[*The* BARON *and* FATHER BLAZIUS *enter.*]

FATHER BLAZIUS. My lord, there is something I must tell you. The parish priest is a drunkard.

BARON. You should be ashamed of yourself. That's impossible.

FATHER BLAZIUS. I'm sure of it. He drank three bottles of wine at dinner.

BARON. That is excessive.

FATHER BLAZIUS. And when he left the castle, he began walking on the flowerbeds.

BARON. On the flowerbeds? I'm amazed. That's very odd. . . . Drinking three bottles of wine at dinner! Walking on the flowerbeds! I can't understand it. Why didn't he walk on the path?

FATHER BLAZIUS. Because he was staggering.

BARON. [*aside*] I'm beginning to believe Bridaine was right this morning. This fellow Blazius smells most horribly of wine.

FATHER BLAZIUS. Besides, he ate a great deal. And his speech was confused.

BARON. It's a fact. I noticed it too.

FATHER BLAZIUS. He let fall a few words of Latin. They were nothing but platitudes. My lord, he is a depraved man.

BARON. [*aside*] Pah! The smell of this fellow Blazius is intolerable. You must know, sir, I have other things to think about. I never bother myself with what people eat or with what they drink. I am not a butler.

FATHER BLAZIUS. May it please God that I should not displease you, my lord. Your wine is good.

BARON. There is good wine in my cellar.

[FATHER BRIDAINE *enters*.]

FATHER BRIDAINE. My lord, your son is down in the square, talking with all the rogues in the village.

BARON. Impossible.

FATHER BRIDAINE. I've seen him with my own eyes. He's picking up stones to play ducks and drakes.

BARON. Ducks and drakes? My head's in a whirl, my thoughts are all confused. Don't be ridiculous, Bridaine. No one's ever heard of a doctor of canon law playing ducks and drakes.

FATHER BRIDAINE. Look out of the window, my lord. You'll see him with your own eyes.

BARON. [*aside*] Heavens above, Blazius is right. Bridaine is staggering.

FATHER BRIDAINE. Look, my lord, there he is by the fountain. He's holding a young girl by the arm.

BARON. A young girl! Has my son come here to debauch my tenants? Holding her arm? And surrounded by all the rogues of the village! I'm going out of my mind.

FATHER BRIDAINE. This calls for vengeance.

BARON. Everything's ruined! Hopelessly ruined! I am ruined. Bridaine can't walk straight; Blazius smells most horribly of wine; and my son's playing ducks and drakes and seducing all the girls in the village.

Act Two

SCENE I—A *room in the castle, the next day.*

[FATHER BLAZIUS *and* PERDICAN *enter*.]

FATHER BLAZIUS. My lord, your father is in despair.

PERDICAN. Why is that?

FATHER BLAZIUS. You are not unaware that he had planned for you to marry your cousin.

PERDICAN. Well? There's nothing I should like better.

FATHER BLAZIUS. However the Baron thinks he's noticed that your characters are not well-matched.

PERDICAN. That's unfortunate. I can't alter mine.

FATHER BLAZIUS. You're not going to make this marriage impossible?

PERDICAN. I tell you once again there's nothing I'd like better than to marry Camille. Go and find the Baron and tell him that.

FATHER BLAZIUS. My lord, I'll leave you. Here is your cousin.

[FATHER BLAZIUS *goes out*. CAMILLE *enters*.]

PERDICAN. Up already, Camille? I still think what I told you yesterday. You're as lovely as the dawn.

CAMILLE. Let us talk seriously, Perdican. Your father wishes us to marry. I don't know what you think of it; but I believe I ought to tell you that as far as that is concerned my mind is made up.

PERDICAN. All the worse for me if you dislike me.

CAMILLE. No more than anyone else. I don't wish to marry. There is nothing in that to offend your pride.

PERDICAN. Pride is not one of my qualities. I care nothing for its joys or its pains.

CAMILLE. I have come here to receive my mother's estate. Tomorrow I return to the convent.

PERDICAN. You have behaved very frankly. Give me your hand, let us be friends.

CAMILLE. I don't like shaking hands.

PERDICAN. [*taking her hand*] Give me your hand, Camille, please. What have you to fear from me? You don't wish us to marry? Very well then; we won't. Is that any reason for us to hate each other? Aren't we brother and sister? When your mother prescribed this marriage in her will, she wished our friendship to last forever; that is all she wished. Why should we marry? Here is your hand and here is mine. For them to stay united till our last breath, we don't require a priest, do we? All we need is God.

CAMILLE. I'm glad that you don't mind my refusing.

PERDICAN. I do mind, Camille. Your love would have given me life, but your friendship will console me. Don't leave the castle tomorrow. Yesterday you refused to walk in the garden, because you saw in me a husband you didn't want. Stay here a few days. Let me hope our past life is not completely dead in your heart.

CAMILLE. I must go.

PERDICAN. Why?

CAMILLE. That is my secret.

PERDICAN. Do you love someone else?

CAMILLE. No. But I wish to go.

PERDICAN. Definitely?

CAMILLE. Yes, definitely.

PERDICAN. Well then, good-by. I should have liked to sit with you under the chestnut trees in the copse and talk as friends for an hour or two. But if you don't want to, let's say no more. Good-by, my dear.

[PERDICAN *goes out.* DAME PLUCHE *enters.*]

CAMILLE. Dame Pluche, is everything ready? Are we leaving tomorrow? Has my guardian finished the accounts?

DAME PLUCHE. Yes, my stainless dove. The Baron called me a blithering fool last night and I'm delighted to go.

CAMILLE. Wait. Here is a note I want you to take to Perdican before dinner.

DAME PLUCHE. Good lord above! I can't believe it! You're writing a note to a man?

CAMILLE. I'm to be his wife, aren't I? Surely I can write to the man I'm going to marry.

DAME PLUCHE. Perdican has just left you. What can you be writing to him? The man you're going to marry, for heaven's sake! You don't mean that you've forgotten Jesus?

CAMILLE. Do what I tell you, and get everything ready for our departure.

[*They go out.* FATHER BRIDAINE *enters with* SERVANTS *who start to lay the table.*]

FATHER BRIDAINE. Yes, it's certain he will be given the place of honor again today. This chair on the Baron's right which I have occupied for so long will be the tutor's prize. How miserable I am! An ignorant fool, a shameless drunkard, relegates me to the bottom of the table. The steward will serve him the first glass of Malaga, and when the dishes reach me they'll be half cold, with the choicest morsels already taken. Oh, holy Catholic Church! I can understand that he should be given the best place yesterday; he had just arrived; it was the first time for a number of years that he'd sat at this table. Heavens, how he ate! No, not a piece of chicken will be left for me but the bones and feet. I will not tolerate this insult. Farewell, beloved chair, where I have so often collapsed when gorged to the full with succulent dishes! Farewell, bottles of glorious vintage and scent of venison cooked to perfection! Farewell, splendid banquets, noble dining room where I shall never more say grace! I return to my own house. I shall never again be seen here mingling with the multitude of guests. Like Caesar I would rather be first in a village than second at Rome.

[*He goes out.*]

SCENE II—*The village square, immediately afterward.*

[ROSETTE *and* PERDICAN *enter.*]

PERDICAN. As your mother's not at home, come and take a walk with me.

ROSETTE. Do you think it's right to give me all these kisses?

PERDICAN. What harm is there in that? I'd kiss you in front of your mother. Aren't you Camille's sister? Aren't I your brother as much as hers?

ROSETTE. Words are words and kisses are kisses. I'm not very clever. I realize that as soon as I want to say something. Fine ladies know what it means if someone kisses their right hand or their left. Their fathers kiss them on the forehead, their brothers on the cheek, and their lovers on the lips. But everybody kisses me on both cheeks and that annoys me.

PERDICAN. How pretty you are, my dear.

ROSETTE. Now you mustn't start worrying about that. How unhappy you are this morning. Has your marriage been canceled?

PERDICAN. Everybody in the village remembers they once loved me. The dogs in the kennels and the trees in the woods remember too. But Camille remembers nothing. What about you, Rosette, when are you going to be married?

ROSETTE. Don't let's talk about that, please. Let's talk of the weather we're having, and those flowers over there, and your horses and my bonnets.

PERDICAN. Talk about anything you like, anything that can cross your lips without removing that lovely smile. I revere it more than anything on earth. [*He kisses her.*]

ROSETTE. You revere my smile, but you don't seem to revere my lips as far as I can see. Why look, a drop of rain has fallen on my hand, but the sky is clear.

PERDICAN. Forgive me.

ROSETTE. What have I done to make you weep?
[*They go out.*]

SCENE III—*Inside the castle, later the same day.*

[FATHER BLAZIUS *and the* BARON *enter.*]

FATHER BLAZIUS. My lord, I've something strange to tell you. Just now by chance I was in the kitchen, I mean the gallery; what would I be doing in the kitchen? Well, I was in the gallery. I'd found by accident a bottle of wine, I mean a glass of water; how could I have found a bottle of wine in the gallery? Well, I was in the act of drinking a glass of wine, I mean water, to pass the time, and I was looking out of the window between two vases of flowers which seemed to be in the modern style, although they were imitated from the Etruscan. . . .

BARON. What an insufferable way of talking you've adopted, Blazius. Your speech is most peculiar.

FATHER BLAZIUS. Listen to me, my lord, give me just a moment of your attention. As I say, I was looking out of the window. . . . Don't get impatient, for heaven's sake, the honor of the family is concerned in this.

BARON. The family? I don't understand a word. The honor of the family, Blazius? Do you realize we're thirty-seven males and almost as many females . . . that is, including Paris as well as the country?

FATHER BLAZIUS. Allow me to continue. While I was drinking a glass of wine, I mean water, to hasten my slow digestion, what do you think, I saw Dame Pluche pass in front of the window, out of breath.

BARON. Why out of breath, Blazius? This is most unusual.

FATHER BLAZIUS. And beside her, red with rage, your niece Camille.

BARON. Who was red with rage, my niece or Dame Pluche?

FATHER BLAZIUS. Your niece, my lord.

BARON. My niece red with rage! I've never heard of such a thing. And how do you know it was rage? She might have been red for dozens of reasons. She'd probably been chasing butterflies in the garden.

FATHER BLAZIUS. I can't say anything about that. You may be right. But she was shouting as loudly as she could, "Go on. Find him. Do what you're told. You're a fool. I insist." And she beat Dame Pluche on the neck with her fan, so that with every blow the old woman leapt into the shrubbery.

BARON. The shrubbery? Well, what did the governess reply to my niece's extravagances? For that's the only way I can describe her conduct.

FATHER BLAZIUS. The governess replied, "I won't go. I can't find him. He's chasing after village girls and shepherdesses. I'm too old to start carrying love letters. Thanks be to God I've lived a pure life till now." And as she spoke, she crumpled up a little piece of folded paper.

BARON. I don't understand a word. My thoughts are completely confused. What reason could Dame Pluche have to crumple up a piece of folded paper and start leaping into the shrubbery? I can't believe in such monstrous behavior.

FATHER BLAZIUS. But, my lord, don't you understand what that must mean?

BARON. No, my dear fellow, no. I understand absolutely nothing. It all seems most unruly behavior, it's true, but as pointless as it's inexcusable.

FATHER BLAZIUS. It means that your niece is conducting a secret correspondence.

BARON. What are you saying? Do you realize who you're talking to? Weigh your words well, sir.

FATHER BLAZIUS. If I weighed them in the celestial balance that's to weigh my soul at the last judgment, I should not find one word that rings false. Your niece is conducting a secret correspondence.

BARON. But just think, my dear fellow. That's impossible.

FATHER BLAZIUS. Why should she give the governess a letter? Why should she cry "Find him," while the old woman sulked and grumbled?

BARON. Who was this letter written to?

FATHER BLAZIUS. Precisely, my lord, there lies the whole kernel of the mystery. Who was this letter written to? A man who makes love to a shepherdess. Now if a man is publicly known to make love to girls who look after sheep, he may be strongly suspected of being born to look after them himself. However, it's impossible for your niece with her upbringing to be in love with such a man. That is what I say, and that is what I cannot understand, any more than you—with all respect, my lord.

BARON. Great heavens. Only this morning my niece told me she was refusing her cousin. She can't be in love with a shepherd! Let's go to my study. Since yesterday I've suffered such violent shocks, I can't collect my thoughts.

[*They go out.*]

SCENE IV—*A woodland spring, later the same day.*

[PERDICAN *enters, reading a note.*]

PERDICAN. "Be at the little spring at twelve o'clock." What can that mean? So very cold, so proud and hard, such a definite, cruel refusal, and after all this a rendezvous. If she wants to speak of business, why does she choose a place like this? Is it some feminine trick? This morning when I was walking with Rosette, I heard someone moving in the bushes, but I thought it was a deer. Is it a plot of some sort?

[CAMILLE *enters.*]

CAMILLE. Good morning, Perdican. Rightly or wrongly, I thought you seemed sad when you left me earlier. You took my hand against my will; I have come to ask you to give me yours. I refused you a kiss; here it is. [*She kisses him.*] Just now you told me you would like to talk as friends. Sit down, let us talk. [*She sits.*]

PERDICAN. Was that a dream, or is this?

CAMILLE. You thought it strange to receive a note from me, didn't you? My moods change. But this morning you said something very true. "As we're parting, let us part good friends." You don't know the reason why I'm leaving and I have come to tell you. I am going to take the veil.

PERDICAN. I can't believe it! Is this you, Camille, reflected in this pool, sitting here as you used to long ago?

CAMILLE. Yes, Perdican, it is. I have come here to relive ten minutes of our past life. I seemed to you abrupt and haughty. It's quite simple; I have renounced the world. However, before I leave it, I should like to have your opinion. Do you think I'm right to become a nun?

PERDICAN. Don't ask me about that. I'll never become a monk.

CAMILLE. In the ten years we have lived apart, you have begun to experience life. I know what sort of man you are; with a heart and mind like yours you must have learned a great deal in a short time. Tell me, have you had mistresses?

PERDICAN. Why do you ask that?

CAMILLE. Answer me, please, without modesty and without conceit.

PERDICAN. I have had them.

CAMILLE. Did you love them?

PERDICAN. With all my heart.

CAMILLE. Where are they now? Do you know?

PERDICAN. Really, these are strange questions. What do you want me to tell you? I'm not their husband or their brother. They went wherever they wanted to go.

CAMILLE. There must have been one of them you loved more than the others. How long did you love the one you loved the best?

PERDICAN. You're a strange girl. Do you want to be my confessor?

CAMILLE. It's a favor I'm asking you, to answer me sincerely. You are certainly not a rake and I think you have an honest heart. You must have inspired love; you deserve it, you wouldn't have given way to a passing fancy. Answer me, please.

PERDICAN. I must say, I don't remember.

CAMILLE. Do you know any man who has loved only one woman?

PERDICAN. There are such people, certainly.

CAMILLE. Do you know one? Tell me his name.

PERDICAN. There's no name I can tell you. But I believe there are men capable of loving only once in their life.

CAMILLE. How many times can an honorable man fall in love?

PERDICAN. Do you want to make me say a litany, or are you saying a catechism?

CAMILLE. I want to learn, to know if I am right or wrong to become a nun. If I married you, wouldn't you have to answer frankly all my questions and show me your heart quite bare? I respect you highly; through your education and your nature I believe you to be superior to many other men. I am sorry you can't remember what I ask you; perhaps if I got to know you better, I should grow bolder.

PERDICAN. What are you trying to say? Tell me: I shall answer.

CAMILLE. Then answer my first question. Am I right to stay in the convent?

PERDICAN. No.

CAMILLE. Then I should do better to marry you?

PERDICAN. Yes.

CAMILLE. If your village priest breathed on a glass of water and told you it was a glass of wine, would you drink it as if it were?

PERDICAN. No.

CAMILLE. If your village priest breathed on you and told me you'd love me all your life, would I be right to believe him?

PERDICAN. Yes and no.

CAMILLE. What would you advise me to do the day I saw you didn't love me any more?

PERDICAN. Take a lover.

CAMILLE. Then what shall I do the day my lover doesn't love me any more?

PERDICAN. You'll take another.

CAMILLE. How long will that last?

PERDICAN. Till your hair is gray; and then mine will be white.

CAMILLE. Do you know what the cloister is, Perdican? Have you ever sat there for a whole day?

PERDICAN. Yes, I have.

CAMILLE. I have a friend, a sister who is only thirty years old and had an income of five hundred thousand livres at the age of fifteen. She is the loveliest and noblest creature who ever walked on earth. She was a peeress of the realm and her husband was one of the most distinguished men in France. All the noblest human qualities had flowered in her; no one has ever been lovelier or happier. Her husband deceived her; she loved another man; now she is dying of despair.

PERDICAN. That is possible.

CAMILLE. We live in the same cell and I have spent whole nights talking of her misfortunes. They have almost become mine. That is strange, isn't it? I don't know how it happens. She told me of her marriage, she painted for me the ecstasy of the first days, then the peace of others, and how finally everything vanished; in the evening she would sit by the fire and he by the window, without exchanging a single word; their love had languished and every effort to come together only ended in quarrels; then little by little a strange face came to stand between them and glide into their sorrows. When she spoke, it was myself I saw. When she said: "Then, I was happy," my heart leapt; and when she added: "Then, I cried," my tears flowed. But do you know something even stranger? I finished by creating for myself an imaginary life. That has lasted for four years. There's no point in explaining all the meditations and heart searching that brought this about. What I wanted to tell you, as a curiosity, is that all Louise's stories, all the fictions of my dreams, bore your likeness.

PERDICAN. My likeness? Mine?

CAMILLE. Yes; it's natural. You were the only man I had known. It's a fact; I loved you, Perdican.

PERDICAN. How old are you, Camille?

CAMILLE. Eighteen.

PERDICAN. Go on, go on. I'm listening.

CAMILLE. There are two hundred women in our convent. A few of these women will never know life and all the rest are waiting for death. More than one of them has left the convent, as I leave it now, young and full of hope. They came back soon afterward, old and desolate. Every day one of them dies in our dormitories and every day a new one arrives to take the place of the dead on their horsehair mattress. When strangers visit us, they admire the calm and order of our house. They look with interest at the whiteness of our veils. But they ask why we lower them over our eyes. What do you think of these women, Perdican? Are they wrong or are they right?

PERDICAN. I have no idea.

CAMILLE. Some of them have advised me to remain unmarried. I'd like your opinion. Do you believe those women would have done better to take a lover and to advise me to do the same?

PERDICAN. I have no idea.

CAMILLE. You promised to answer.

PERDICAN. Obviously I'm excused. I don't believe it's you speaking.

CAMILLE. You may be right. In all these thoughts of mine there must be very silly things. It may be I've been learning a lesson and I'm only an ill-taught parrot. In the gallery there's a little picture of a monk bent over a missal; through the dark bars of his cell glides a feeble ray of sunshine; you can see an Italian inn and next to it a goatherd is dancing. Which of those men do you admire most?

PERDICAN. Neither and both. They're two men of flesh and blood. One of them's reading and the other's dancing. I see nothing else. You are right to become a nun.

CAMILLE. Just now you told me no.

PERDICAN. Did I say "No"? Perhaps I did.

CAMILLE. And so that is what you advise?

PERDICAN. And so you believe in nothing?

CAMILLE. Raise your head, Perdican. What kind of man believes in nothing?

PERDICAN. [*rising*] Here is one. I don't believe in immortal life. My dear, the nuns have given you their experience, but believe me it won't be yours. You won't die without loving.

CAMILLE. I want to love, but I don't want to suffer. I want to love with an eternal love and make vows that will not be broken. Here is my lover. [*She shows her crucifix.*]

PERDICAN. That lover does not exclude others.

CAMILLE. For me at least it will exclude them. Don't smile, Perdican. For ten years I haven't seen you and I leave tomorrow. After another ten years, if we meet, we'll talk of this again. I didn't want to remain in your memory as a cold statue, because lack of feeling can lead to the point I have reached. Listen to me. Return to life; and as long as you are happy, as long as you love, as one can love on earth, forget your sister Camille. But if it ever happens to you to be forgotten, or to forget, if the angel of hope abandons you, then when you're alone with a void in your heart, think of me. I shall pray for you.

PERDICAN. You are proud. Be careful.

CAMILLE. Why?

PERDICAN. You are eighteen and you don't believe in love?

CAMILLE. Do you believe in it? You? Here you are bent before me on knees that have worn themselves out on the carpets of mistresses whose names you don't even remember. You've wept tears of joy and tears of despair. But you knew the water in the springs is more constant than your tears and it would always be there to bathe your swollen eyelids. You behave as young men always do, you smile when you're told of women who are desolate. You don't think anyone can die of love, but you live, you have loved. Well, what is the world? I'd have thought you'd heartily despise the women who take you, such as you are, and chase away their last lover to welcome you in their arms with someone else's kisses on their lips. Just now I asked you if you'd ever loved and you answered like a traveler who's asked if he has ever been in Germany or Italy and says "Yes, I've been there"; then he thinks of going to Switzerland or the first country that comes into his mind. Is your love a coin to pass from hand to hand till death? No, it's not even a coin. The smallest piece of gold is worth more than you and keeps its likeness in whatever hands it passes.

PERDICAN. How beautiful you are, when your eyes flash.

CAMILLE. Yes, I am beautiful, I know. Flattery won't teach me anything. When the cold nun cuts off my hair, she may perhaps grow pale at the mutilation she is wreaking. But my hair will not be made into rings and chains to be sported in boudoirs. Not one hair will be missing from my head when the iron passes over it. I want a single stroke of the scissors. Then when the priest blesses me and puts on my finger the golden ring of my celestial husband, the lock of hair which I give him will serve him as a mantle.

PERDICAN. Yes, you are really angry.

CAMILLE. I was wrong to speak. My whole life is on my lips. Oh, Perdican, don't smile. It's so sad, it breaks my heart.

PERDICAN. Poor child, I've let you speak. Now I should like to say a word in reply. You told me of a nun who seems to have had a dismal influence on you. You say she was deceived, she herself deceived her husband, and she is in despair. Are you sure that if her husband or her lover came back to stretch out his hand through the convent grill, she would not stretch out her own to take it?

CAMILLE. What did you say? I didn't understand.

PERDICAN. Are you sure that if her husband or her lover came back to tell her to suffer once more, she would answer "No"?

CAMILLE. I believe so.

PERDICAN. There are two hundred women in your convent and the majority of them in the depths of their hearts have the deepest wounds. They have made you feel them, they have colored your girlish thoughts with drops of their blood. They have lived, haven't they? And they have shown you with horror the road they have traveled. You have crossed yourself before their scars as you would before the wounds of Christ. They have given you a place in their gloomy processions and you squeeze up against their skinny bodies with religious terror when you see a man go by. Are you sure that if that man was the one who deceived them, and made them weep and suffer, the man they're cursing as they pray to God, are you sure that at the sight of him they wouldn't break their chains to run toward their past miseries and press their bleeding breasts against the dagger that stabbed them? Oh, my child! Do you know the dreams of these women who tell you not to dream? Do you know what name they're murmuring as the sobs on their lips make the Host tremble when it's given to them? These women sit next to you with shaking heads to pour into your ear their withered old age, they sound the tocsin of their despair in the ruins of your youth and make your bright red blood feel the coldness of their tomb. But do you know what they are?

CAMILLE. You frighten me. You are angry too.

PERDICAN. Do you know what these nuns are, you wretched girl? These women represent to you the love of men as a lie, but do they know there is something still worse, the lie of divine love? Do they know what a sin they're committing to come and whisper these women's words into the ear of a young girl? Oh, how well they've taught you! Yes, this is what I expected when you stopped before our old aunt's portrait. You wanted to leave without shaking my hand. You didn't wish to see this little copse or this spring which looks at us and weeps. You were denying the days of your childhood and the plaster mask the nuns have placed on your cheeks refused me a brother's kiss. But your heart was beating. It couldn't read, it had forgotten its lesson, so you came back to sit on the grass and here we are. All right. Camille, these women have spoken well. They have put you on the right road. It will have cost me my life's happiness, but tell them from me, "Heaven is not for them."

CAMILLE. Nor for me, you mean?

PERDICAN. Good-by, Camille. Go back to your convent. And when they recall these dreadful stories that have poisoned your mind, tell them what I am going to say to you now. All men are liars, false, gossips, hypocrites; proud or cowardly, despicable and sensual. All women are faithless, artful, vain, inquisitive, and depraved. The world is just a bottomless sewer, where shapeless beasts writhe and crawl on mountains of mire. But in this world there is one thing holy and sublime; that is the union of two of these imperfect, frightful creatures. We are often deceived in love, often hurt, often unhappy. But we love. And when we are on the edge of the grave, we turn around to look back and say, "I have often suffered, sometimes made mistakes, but I have loved. It is I who have lived, not some artificial being created by my pride and my despair."

[*He goes out.*]

Act Three

SCENE I—*A room in the castle, the next day.*

[*The* BARON *and* FATHER BLAZIUS *enter.*]

BARON. Apart from your drunkenness, Father Blazius, you're a rogue. My servants saw you secretly enter the cellar, and when you're convicted of stealing my wine in the most pitiful manner, you think to justify yourself by accusing my niece of conducting a secret correspondence.

FATHER BLAZIUS. But, my lord, do please remember. . . .

BARON. Get out, sir, and never let me see you again. It's beyond all reason to behave as you have done, and my position forces me never to forgive you for the rest of my life.

[*The* BARON *goes out.* FATHER BLAZIUS *follows.* PERDICAN *enters.*]

PERDICAN. I should so like to know if I'm in love. First of all, this manner of asking questions is rather cavalier for a girl of eighteen. Then the ideas these nuns have planted in her head will be difficult to root out. Besides she's due to leave today. Devil take it, I love her, that's certain. After all, who knows? Perhaps she was repeating a lesson and anyway it's plain she doesn't care for me. And I don't mind if she is pretty, that doesn't prevent her being much too decided in her ways and sharp in her manner. All I have to do is to think no more about it. It's plain I don't love her. She certainly is pretty. But why can't I get yesterday's conversation out of my mind? It's a fact, I've been talking nonsense all night. Now where was I going? Ah yes, to the village. [*goes out*]

SCENE II—*The village square, immediately afterward.*

[FATHER BRIDAINE *enters.*]

FATHER BRIDAINE. What are they doing now? Ah me, it's twelve o'clock. They are sitting down to dinner. What are they eating? What are they not eating? I saw the cook crossing the square with an enormous turkey. The kitchen maid was carrying truffles and a basket of grapes.

[FATHER BLAZIUS *enters.*]

FATHER BLAZIUS. Who could have foreseen this disgrace? Here I am, turned out of the castle and of course the dining room. I shall never again drink wine from that cellar.

FATHER BRIDAINE. I shall never again smell those glorious dishes. I shall never again warm my ample stomach at the fire of that noble hearth.

FATHER BLAZIUS. Why did such fatal curiosity make me listen to Dame Pluche's conversation with his niece? Why did I report to the Baron everything I saw?

FATHER BRIDAINE. Why have pride and vanity made me quit that splendid table where I was so warmly welcomed? What did it matter if I was on the right or on the left?

FATHER BLAZIUS. Ah me, I was drunk, I must admit, when I behaved so foolishly.

FATHER BRIDAINE. Ah me, the wine had gone to my head, when I acted so imprudently.

FATHER BLAZIUS. I think I see the priest.

FATHER BRIDAINE. It's the tutor in person.

FATHER BLAZIUS. Oh, oh, my dear sir, what are you doing here?

FATHER BRIDAINE. I'm going to dinner. Aren't you coming?

FATHER BLAZIUS. Not today. Oh, Father Bridaine, intercede on my behalf. The Baron has turned me out. I falsely accused Camille of having a secret correspondence but, as God's my witness, I saw, or thought I saw, Dame Pluche in the shrubbery. My dear sir, I'm ruined.

FATHER BRIDAINE. What's that you're telling me?

FATHER BLAZIUS. The truth, the truth. I'm in complete disgrace for stealing a bottle of wine.

FATHER BRIDAINE. What are you saying, sir, about stolen bottles and correspondence in a shrubbery?

FATHER BLAZIUS. I beg you to plead my cause. I'm an honest man, my lord Bridaine. Oh, worthy lord Bridaine, I am your servant.

FATHER BRIDAINE. [*aside*] What good fortune! Am I dreaming? So I shall once again be sitting on you, happy, happy chair.

FATHER BLAZIUS. I'd be so grateful if you'd listen to my story. Do please excuse me, my worthy lord, my dear, dear sir.

FATHER BRIDAINE. That is impossible, sir. It has struck twelve and I am going to dinner. If the Baron complains about you, that is your business. I shall certainly not intercede for a drunkard. [*aside*] Quick, let us fly to the gate. Oh, my beloved stomach, extend yourself to capacity.

[FATHER BRIDAINE *goes out, running.*]

FATHER BLAZIUS. Wretched Pluche, I'll make you pay for this. Yes, you're the cause of my disgrace, shameless woman, vilest go-between, it's through you I'm ruined. Oh, holy University of Paris! I've been called a drunkard! I'm ruined if I can't seize a letter and prove to the Baron that his niece has a secret correspondence. I saw her this morning writing at her desk. Patience, here comes Pluche again. [DAME PLUCHE *enters, carrying a letter.*] Pluche, give me that letter.

DAME PLUCHE. What does this mean? It's a letter from my mistress. I'm going to send it off in the village.

FATHER BLAZIUS. Give it to me or I'll kill you.

DAME PLUCHE. Me? Kill me? Mary, Jesus, saints and martyrs!

FATHER BLAZIUS. Yes, Pluche, kill you. Give me that letter.

[*They fight.* PERDICAN *enters.*]

PERDICAN. What's happening? What are you doing, Blazius? Why are you assaulting this woman?

DAME PLUCHE. Give me back the letter. He took it from me, my lord. I demand justice.

FATHER BLAZIUS. She's a go-between, my lord. It's a love letter.

DAME PLUCHE. It's a letter from Camille, my lord, from your betrothed.

FATHER BLAZIUS. It's a love letter to a shepherd boy.

DAME PLUCHE. You're a liar, Father. And I'm happy to tell you so.

PERDICAN. Give me this letter. I don't understand a word you're saying, but as I'm going to marry Camille, I take upon myself the right to read it. [*He reads.*] "To Sister Louise, at the convent of. . . ."[*aside*] What dreadful curiosity seizes me in spite of myself? My heart beats so strongly, I don't know what I feel. You may go, Dame Pluche. You're a respectable woman and Father Blazius is a fool. Go to dinner. I will see that this letter's delivered. [DAME PLUCHE *and* FATHER BLAZIUS *go out.*] It's wrong to open a letter, I know that too well to do it. What can Camille be saying to this sister? Can I be in love? But what hold has this strange girl obtained over me to make my hand tremble at seeing this address? How odd! In fighting with Dame Pluche, Blazius has broken the seal. Is it wrong to unfold the paper? After all, I shan't change anything. [*He opens the letter and reads.*]

"I am leaving today, my dear, and everything has happened as I expected. It's a terrible thing, but this young man is heartbroken. He will never be consoled for losing me. But I have done everything I could to make him hate me. God will forgive me for reducing him to despair by my refusal. But, my dear, what could I do? Pray for me. We shall see each other again tomorrow and always. All my love to you, my dearest heart, Camille."

I can't believe it. Camille wrote this? It's me she's talking about! I am in despair at her refusal! By God, we'll see if that's true. What is there to be ashamed of in being in love? She has done everything she could to make me hate her, she says, and I'm heartbroken. What purpose can she have in inventing such a story? So it's true what I thought last night? Oh, women! This poor girl may be very pious. With the greatest joy she gives herself to God, but she resolved and decreed to leave me in despair. It was settled between these two good friends before she left the convent. It was decided that Camille would see her cousin, they would want to make him marry her, she'd refuse, and he'd be miserable. How very interesting, a young girl sacrifices her cousin's happiness to God! No, no, Camille, I don't love you, I'm not in despair, I'm not heartbroken, and I'll prove it to you. Yes, you'll know I love someone else before you leave here. Hey, there, fellow! [A PEASANT *enters.*] Go up to the castle and tell them in the kitchen to give this letter to Camille. [*He writes.*]

PEASANT. Yes, my lord. [*goes out*]

PERDICAN. Now then. I'm in despair, am I? Hey there, Rosette, Rosette! [*He knocks at her door.*]

[ROSETTE *opens the door.*]

ROSETTE. It's you, my lord! Come in, my mother's here.

PERDICAN. Put on your prettiest bonnet, Rosette, and come with me.

ROSETTE. Wherever to?

PERDICAN. I'm going to tell you. Ask your mother's permission; but hurry.

ROSETTE. Yes, my lord.

[ROSETTE *goes into the house.*]

PERDICAN. I've asked Camille for another rendezvous and I'm sure she'll come. But by heaven she won't find what she expects to find. I'm going to make love to Rosette in front of Camille herself.

SCENE III—*The woodland spring.*

[CAMILLE *and the* PEASANT *enter.*]

PEASANT. I was going to the castle with this letter for you. Should I give it to you now or leave it in the kitchen as Perdican told me?

CAMILLE. Give it to me.

PEASANT. If you'd rather I took it to the castle, it's no trouble.

CAMILLE. I tell you to give it me.

PEASANT. As you wish. [*He gives her the letter.*]

CAMILLE. Here. Take this for your pains.

PEASANT. Many thanks. I'll go, shall I?

CAMILLE. If you want to.

PEASANT. I'll go, I'll go. [*goes out*]

CAMILLE. [*reading*] Perdican asks me to say good-by to him, before I go, at the little spring where I made him come yesterday. What can he have to say to me? But here is the spring and I am ready. Should I grant him this second meeting? Oh! [*She hides behind a tree.*] Here he comes with Rosette. I suppose he'll leave her. I'm glad I shan't seem the first to arrive. [PERDICAN *and* ROSETTE *enter and sit down.* CAMILLE *is hidden.*] What does this mean? He makes her sit down next to him? Has he asked me to meet him here, so he can talk to someone else? I'm curious to know what he'll say to her.

PERDICAN. [*aloud, so that* CAMILLE *shall hear*] I love you, Rosette. You're the one person in the world who hasn't forgotten the lovely days gone by. Only you remember the life of long ago. Take part in my new life. Here is the pledge of our love. [*He puts his chain around her neck.*]

ROSETTE. You're giving me your gold chain?

PERDICAN. Now look at this ring. Get up, come to the pool. Do you see us both in the water, leaning on each other's arm? Do you see your lovely eyes next to mine, your hand in my hand? Watch it all disappear. [*He throws his ring in the water.*] See how our image has vanished? Here it is, coming slowly back. The troubled water resumes its calm. It still trembles. Great black circles rise to the surface. Be patient, we shall soon be there once more. I can already see your arms entwined again in mine. One more minute and not a single wrinkle will remain on your pretty face. Look. It was a ring Camille gave me.

CAMILLE. [*aside*] He threw my ring in the water.

PERDICAN. Do you know what love is, Rosette? Listen. The wind is silent. The morning rain rolls in pearls off the dry leaves. but the sun is giving them new life. By the light of heaven, by this sun you see above, I love you. You wish me well, don't you? Your youth has not been withered? The dregs of a faded blood have not been filtered into your pure, bright scarlet? You don't want to become a nun. Here you are, young and lovely, in the arms of a young man. Oh, Rosette, Rosette, do you know what love is?

ROSETTE. Oh, my lord, I'll love you as best I can.

PERDICAN. Yes, as best you can. And although you've never been to school, you'll love me better than these pale statues fashioned by the nuns, who have a head instead of a heart, and leave their cloisters to come and spread through life the damp atmosphere of their cells. You know nothing. You can't read in a book the prayer your mother teaches you, as her mother once taught it to her. You don't even understand the words you're repeating when you kneel at the foot of your bed. But you understand well enough that you're praying and that is all that God requires.

ROSETTE. The things you say, my lord.

PERDICAN. You can't read. But you know what these woods and meadows are saying, these warm streams, these lovely fields ripe with harvest, the whole of nature splendid in its youth. You recognize all these thousands of brothers and me as one of them. Get to your feet. You shall be my wife and we will take root together in the sap of the all-powerful world.

[PERDICAN *and* ROSETTE *go out.*]

SCENE IV—*The village square, later the same day.*

[CHORUS *enters.*]

CHORUS. Something strange is happening at the castle. Camille has refused to marry Perdican. She should return today to her convent. But I believe her noble cousin has been consoling himself with Rosette. I fear the poor girl doesn't know the danger she runs in listening to the speeches of a young and gallant gentleman.

[DAME PLUCHE *enters.*]

DAME PLUCHE. Quick, quick, saddle my mule.

CHORUS. Will you leave us like a passing dream, oh venerable dame? Are you going so soon to straddle once more that wretched beast which does so hate to carry you?

DAME PLUCHE. Thanks be to God, dear rabble, I shall not die here.

CHORUS. Die far away then, Pluche, my sweet. Die unknown in some insanitary cellar. We shall offer up prayers for your respected resurrection.

DAME PLUCHE. Here comes my mistress. [CAMILLE *enters.*] Camille dear, everything is ready for our departure. The Baron has finished the accounts and my mule is saddled.

CAMILLE. Go to the devil and take your mule with you. I shan't leave here today. [*goes out*]

CHORUS. What does this mean? Dame Pluche grows pale with fright. Her false hair tries hard to stand on end, her lungs whistle loudly, her fingers stretch and claw.

DAME PLUCHE. Beloved Jesus! She used bad language! [*goes out*]
[*The* BARON *enters, followed by* FATHER BRIDAINE.]

FATHER BRIDAINE. My lord, I must speak to you most urgently. Your son is making love to a girl from the village.

BARON. Don't be absurd, my dear fellow.

FATHER BRIDAINE. I distinctly saw him walking in the woods with her, arm in arm. He was whispering in her ear and promising to marry her.

BARON. This is monstrous.

FATHER BRIDAINE. Be convinced of it. He has given her a considerable present and the child has shown it to her mother.

BARON. Oh, great heavens! Considerable, Bridaine? In what way was it considerable?

FATHER BRIDAINE. In its value and its meaning. It's his gold chain.

BARON. Let us go to my study. I don't know what to think.
[*They go out.*]

SCENE v—*A room in the castle, later the same day.*

[CAMILLE *and* DAME PLUCHE *enter.*]

CAMILLE. He took my letter, you say?

DAME PLUCHE. Yes, my child. He undertook to have it delivered.

CAMILLE. Dame Pluche, be so good as to go and tell Perdican that I'm waiting for him here. [DAME PLUCHE *goes out.*] He read my letter, that's certain. The scene he staged in the wood was in revenge, like his love for Rosette. He wanted to show me he loved someone else and pretend not to care in spite of being angry. Would he by any chance be in love with me? [*She raises a curtain.*] Are you there, Rosette?
[ROSETTE *appears.*]

ROSETTE. Yes. May I come in?

CAMILLE. Listen to me, my child. Perdican has made love to you, hasn't he?

ROSETTE. [*sadly*] Yes, he has.

CAMILLE. What do you think of all he told you this morning?

ROSETTE. This morning? Why, where?

CAMILLE. Don't play the hypocrite. This morning, at the spring, in the copse.

ROSETTE. So you saw me?

CAMILLE. Poor little innocent! No, I didn't see you. He made fine speeches, didn't he? I'm sure he promised to marry you.

ROSETTE. How do you know that?

CAMILLE. What does it matter how I know? Do you believe in his promises, Rosette?

ROSETTE. Why shouldn't I? You mean he'd deceive me? Why should he do that?

CAMILLE. Perdican won't marry you, my dear.

ROSETTE. I don't know anything about that.

CAMILLE. You love him, poor child. He won't marry you. As for proof, I'm going to give it to you. Go back behind this curtain. You have only to listen and come when I call you. [ROSETTE *goes out.*] I thought I'd do an act of revenge; but will it be an act of kindness? The poor girl is deeply in love with him. [PERDICAN *enters.*] Good afternoon, Perdican. Sit down.

PERDICAN. What a lovely dress, Camille. Who are you angry with?

CAMILLE. You, perhaps. I'm sorry I couldn't come to the rendez-vous you gave me. Was there something you wanted to talk about?

PERDICAN. [*aside*] I must say that's a pretty big little lie for a stain-less lamb. I saw her behind a tree listening to our conversation. [*aloud*] All I have to say to you is good-by, Camille. I thought you had gone. But your horse is in the stable and you don't look as though you're dressed for travel.

CAMILLE. I like argument. I am not sure I wouldn't like to quarrel with you again.

PERDICAN. What's the point of quarreling when reconciliation is impossible? The pleasure of a dispute lies in making peace.

CAMILLE. Are you convinced I don't want to do that?

PERDICAN. Don't joke. I'm not feeling strong enough to answer you.

CAMILLE. I should like to be made love to. I don't know if it's be-cause I have a new dress, but I want to enjoy myself. You sug-gested we should go down to the village. Let us go, I should like to. Let's take the boat. I want to dine in the open air or walk in the forest. Will there be a moon this evening? How strange, you aren't wearing the ring I gave you.

PERDICAN. I've lost it.

CAMILLE. Then that is how I found it. Look, Perdican, here it is.

PERDICAN. I can't believe it. Where did you find it?

CAMILLE. You are looking to see if my hands are wet, aren't you? It's a fact, I spoiled my convent dress in taking this little chil-dren's plaything out of the spring. That is why I'm wearing another, and I tell you it has changed me. So put this on your finger.

PERDICAN. You took this ring from the water? Am I dreaming? You're here! You're putting it on my finger! Oh, Camille, why do you give me back this sad pledge of a happiness that no longer exists? Say something. Why are you going? Why are you staying? Why from one hour to the next do you change ap-pearance and color, like the stone of this ring at each ray of sunshine?

CAMILLE. Do you understand women, Perdican? Are you sure of

their inconstancy? Do you know if they really change their thoughts when they sometimes change their language? Some people say they do not. No doubt we must often play a part, often lie. You see I'm being frank. But are you sure that a woman lies with her whole being when she lies with her tongue? Have you considered the nature of this feeble, violent creature, how strictly she is judged, the principles that are imposed upon her? And who knows whether this little brainless being, forced by the world to deceive, can't take pleasure in so doing, and sometimes lie for amusement, as she lies for necessity?

PERDICAN. I don't understand any of this. I never lie. I love you, Camille, that's all I know.

CAMILLE. You say you love me and you never lie?

PERDICAN. Never.

CAMILLE. Yet here is someone who says it happens to you occasionally. [*She raises the curtain.* ROSETTE *can be seen on a chair, unconscious.*] How will you answer this child, Perdican, when she asks you to account for your words? If you never lie, how did she happen to faint when she heard you say you loved me? I leave you with her. Try to revive her. [*She wishes to go out.*]

PERDICAN. One moment, Camille, listen to me.

CAMILLE. What do you want to say? It's Rosette you must speak to. I don't love you. I didn't take this poor girl out of spite from her cottage to make her a bait, a plaything. I didn't recite to her ardent phrases addressed to someone else. I didn't pretend to throw away for her sake the souvenir of a cherished friendship. I didn't put my chain round her neck. I didn't tell her I'd marry her.

PERDICAN. Listen to me, listen to me.

CAMILLE. You smiled just now, didn't you, when I told you I couldn't go to the spring? Very well then. Yes, I was there and I heard everything. But God is my witness, I wouldn't wish to have spoken as you did. What will you do with this girl now, when she comes in tears with your burning kisses on her lips to show you how you've wounded her? You wanted to revenge yourself on me, didn't you, to punish me for the letter I wrote to the convent? At any price you wanted to deal some blow which could strike me, and you didn't care if your poisoned arrow pierced this girl, provided it hit me standing behind her. I prided myself I'd inspired in you some love, I'd leave you feeling some regret. And that wounded your noble pride? Very well then. Allow me to tell you, you love me, do you hear? But you shall marry this girl or you're nothing but a coward.

PERDICAN. Yes, I shall marry her.

CAMILLE. And you will do well to.

PERDICAN. Very well, and much better than marrying you. What is it that makes you so heated? This child has fainted. We must bring her to and all we need for that is a little vinegar. You wanted to prove I'd lied once in my life. That may be so, but I think it impudent of you to decide which time it was. Come and help me to revive Rosette.

[*They go out.*]

SCENE VI—*A room in the castle, a little later.*

[*The* BARON *and* CAMILLE *enter.*]

BARON. If that happens, I shall go out of my mind.

CAMILLE. Use your authority.

BARON. I shall go out of my mind and refuse my consent. That much is certain.

CAMILLE. You must speak to him and make him listen to reason.

BARON. This will throw me into despair for the whole season; I shan't be able to appear once at court. It's a marriage out of all proportion. No one's ever heard tell of marrying a cousin's foster sister. That passes every kind of bounds.

CAMILLE. Have him sent for, tell him clearly you don't like this marriage. Believe me, it's a sudden whim; he won't resist.

BARON. I shall wear black all winter, you may take that for granted.

CAMILLE. But speak to him, for heaven's sake. It's a desperate impulse. Perhaps it's too late already. If he's said he'll do it, he will.

BARON. I shall shut myself up to abandon myself to my grief. If he asks for me, tell him I have shut myself up and I'm abandoning myself to my grief at seeing him marry a nameless girl. [*goes out*]

CAMILLE. Shan't I ever find a man of courage? Really, when you look for one, it's frightening how alone you are. [PERDICAN *enters.*] Well, Perdican, when is the wedding to be?

PERDICAN. As soon as possible. I've already spoken to the notary, the priest, and all the village.

CAMILLE. Then you definitely intend to marry Rosette?

PERDICAN. Certainly.

CAMILLE. What will your father say?

PERDICAN. Whatever he likes. I want to marry this girl. It's an idea I owe to you and I'm keeping to it. Do I have to tell you again the ties that join her birth and mine? She is young and pretty and she loves me. That's more than we need, to be three times happy. Whether she's intelligent or whether she isn't, I could have found worse. Let people complain and laugh. I wash my hands of the matter.

CAMILLE. There's nothing to laugh at in that. You do well to marry her. But there is one thing that makes me sorry for you; people will say you have done it out of spite.

PERDICAN. You are sorry about that? Oh no, you're not.

CAMILLE. Yes, I am really sorry for you. It's bad for a young man, if he can't resist a moment of spite.

PERDICAN. Then be sorry. As far as I'm concerned, it's all the same to me.

CAMILLE. You can't be serious. She's a nobody.

PERDICAN. Then she'll be somebody, when she's my wife.

CAMILLE. She will bore you before the notary has put on his new coat and shoes to come here. You will lose all appetite at the wedding breakfast.

PERDICAN. You'll see I shan't. You don't know me. When a woman is sweet and sensitive, young and good and lovely, I'm capable of being content with that, yes, it's a fact, to the point of not caring whether she can speak Latin.

CAMILLE. It's a pity so much money has been spent in teaching it to you. That's three thousand crowns wasted.

PERDICAN. Yes. They'd have done better to give them to the poor.

CAMILLE. You will be doing that, at least to the poor in spirit.

PERDICAN. And they will give me in exchange the Kingdom of Heaven; for it is theirs.

CAMILLE. How long will this little joke last?

PERDICAN. What little joke?

CAMILLE. Your marriage to Rosette.

PERDICAN. Not very long. God didn't make man a very lasting work. Thirty or forty years at the most.

CAMILLE. I look forward to dancing at your wedding!

PERDICAN. Now listen, Camille, that bantering tone is quite unseasonable.

CAMILLE. I like it too much to leave it.

PERDICAN. Then I'll leave you. I've had enough of this just now.

CAMILLE. Are you going to see your bride?

PERDICAN. Yes, right away.

CAMILLE. Then give me your arm. I'll go with you.

[ROSETTE *enters*.]

PERDICAN. There you are, my dear. Come with me, I want you to meet my father.

ROSETTE. My lord, I've come to ask you a favor. Everyone I've spoken to in the village this morning tells me you're in love with your cousin and you only made love to me to amuse you both. They all make fun of me when I go by; I shall never be able to find a husband after being the laughingstock of the whole village. Allow me to give you back the chain you gave me and let me live in peace with my mother.

CAMILLE. You're a good girl, Rosette. Keep the chain. I give it to you and my cousin will take mine in its place. Don't worry about a husband, I undertake to find you one.

PERDICAN. That's not difficult, I must say. Come, Rosette, let me take you to my father.

CAMILLE. Why? There's no point.

PERDICAN. Yes, you're right. My father would receive us badly. This first moment of surprise he is feeling must be allowed to pass. Come with me, we'll go back to the village. I find it amusing they say I don't love you when I'm going to marry you. By God, we'll make them hold their tongues.

[*He goes out with* ROSETTE.]

CAMILLE. What's happening inside me? He took her away so calmly. How strange this is! I think I feel faint. Does he really mean to marry her? Hey, there! Dame Pluche! Dame Pluche! Is there no one here? [A servant *enters.*] Run after Perdican. Tell him to come back here. I want to talk to him. [*The* servant *goes out.*] But what is all this? I'm exhausted, my feet won't support me.

[perdican *enters.*]

PERDICAN. You sent for me, Camille?

CAMILLE. No. No.

PERDICAN. You are really very pale. What do you want to say? You called me back to speak to me?

CAMILLE. No, no. Oh God! [*goes out*]

SCENE VII—*The castle chapel, immediately afterward.*

[camille *enters and throws herself down at the foot of the altar.*]

CAMILLE. Oh God, have You abandoned me? When I came here, you know I swore to be faithful to You. When I refused to become the bride of another, I thought I was speaking sincerely before You and my conscience. You know that, Father, so why don't You want me any more? Oh, why do You make truth itself lie? Why am I so weak? Oh, I can't pray any more.

[perdican *enters.*]

PERDICAN. Oh, why did pride have to come between this girl and me? There she is, pale and frightened, pressing her heart and face on the unfeeling stones. She could have loved me; we were born for each other. Oh, what did pride do to our lips, when our hands were about to join?

CAMILLE. Who has followed me? Who is speaking over there? Is that you, Perdican?

PERDICAN. What fools we are! We love each other. What dream did we create, Camille? What vain words and miserable stupidities have passed like a blighted wind between us? Which of us wanted to deceive the other? Oh, this life itself is such a painful dream. Why should we mingle our own dreams with it? Oh, God, happiness is so rare a pearl in this ocean here on earth. But You gave it to us, You plucked this priceless jewel from the depths of the abyss, and we're such spoiled children, we made a plaything of it. Of course vanity and gossip and anger had to come between us. Of course we had to do wrong because we're men. Oh, what fools we are! We love each other. [*He takes her in his arms.*]

CAMILLE. Yes, Perdican, we love each other. Let me feel it on your heart. God is watching us, but He will not be offended. He wants me to love you; for fifteen years He has known it.

PERDICAN. My darling, you belong to me. [*He kisses her.*]

[*A great cry is heard from behind the altar.*]

CAMILLE. That is Rosette's voice.

PERDICAN. How can she be here? I left her on the stairs, when you sent for me. She must have followed me without my noticing.

CAMILLE. Come to the gallery. That is where the cry came from.

PERDICAN. I don't know what I feel. I think my hands are stained with blood.

CAMILLE. Poor child, she must have been watching us. She has fainted again. Let us go and help her. Oh, how cruel this all is!

PERDICAN. No, I will not go there. I feel a mortal cold that paralyzes me. Go and try to bring her round. [CAMILLE *goes out.*] I beseech you, God; do not make me a murderer. You see what is happening. We are two foolish children and we have played with life and death. But our hearts are pure. Do not kill Rosette! God, be just! I will find her a husband; I will redeem my fault. She is young; she shall be rich, she shall be happy. Do not do this thing, oh God! You can still bless four of your children. [CAMILLE *re-enters.*] Well, Camille, what is it?

CAMILLE. She is dead. Good-by, Perdican.

The Country Wife

WILLIAM WYCHERLEY

Written sometime in the early 1670's, *The Country Wife* was first performed in London in January, 1675. A success, it became a popular repertory play; its most recent professional production in New York was in 1957. William Wycherley, like Thornton Wilder in *The Matchmaker*, knew a good thing when he saw it; he made effective use of borrowings from Molière (for instance, the wife's tricking the husband into carrying a letter to her lover, from *L'École des Maris*) but Molière, like Terence (from whom he got the idea of the eunuch), was transmuted to unmistakably English Wycherley. There was a time when the fastidious shied away from Wycherley, finding his bluntness offensive, but today he is considered the toughest (in a complimentary sense) of the Restoration playwrights. Like his fellow dramatists, he writes mainly about sex and money, the chief status symbols of Restoration society—they have not exactly died out—but his satire is harsher than that of the others. In a dedicatory letter to *The Plain-Dealer*, his last play, he quotes a fictitious "some there are who say" to explain why some people dislike his work: " 'Tis the plain-dealing of the play, not the obscenity; 'tis taking off the ladies' masks, not offering at their petticoats, which offends 'em." It is typical of Wycherley that this very amusing letter—in an age when dedications were a kind of elegant fawning on the rich and the well-placed—should have been addressed "To My Lady B——," whom everyone recognized as Mother Bennett, a famous bawd of the day.

The Country Wife

Indignor quidquam reprehendi, non quia crasse
Compositum illepideve putetur, sed quia nuper:
Nec veniam antiquis, sed honorem et præmia posci.†
HORAT.

Dramatis Personae

MR. HORNER	MR. PINCHWIFE
MR. HARCOURT	MR. SPARKISH
MR. DORILANT	SIR JASPER FIDGET

† I am out of patience when anything is blamed, not because it is thought coarsely and inelegantly composed, but because it is new: when for the ancients not indulgence, but honour and rewards are demanded.—Horace, *Epistles*, II. i. 76–8.

A BOY	LADY FIDGET
A QUACK	MRS. DAINTY FIDGET, *Sister of*
WAITERS, SERVANTS, *and* ATTEND-	SIR JASPER
ANTS	MRS. SQUEAMISH
MRS. MARGERY PINCHWIFE	OLD LADY SQUEAMISH
ALITHEA, *Sister of* PINCHWIFE	LUCY, ALITHEA's *Maid*

SCENE—*London.*

Prologue

SPOKEN BY MR. HART[1]

Poets, like cudgelled bullies, never do
At first or second blow submit to you;
But will provoke you still, and ne'er have done,
Till you are weary first with laying on.
The late so baffled scribbler of this day,[2]
Though he stands trembling, bids me boldly say,
What we before most plays are used to do,
For poets out of fear first draw on you;
In a fierce prologue the still pit defy,
And, ere you speak, like Castril[3] give the lie.
But though our Bayes's[4] battles oft I've fought,
And with bruised knuckles their dear conquests bought;
Nay, never yet feared odds upon the stage,
In prologue dare not hector with the age;
But would take quarter from your saving hands,
Though Bayes within all yielding countermands,
Says, you confederate wits no quarter give,
Therefore his play shan't ask your leave to live.
Well, let the vain rash fop, by huffing so,
Think to obtain the better terms of you;
But we, the actors, humbly will submit,
Now, and at any time, to a full pit;
Nay, often we anticipate your rage,
And murder poets for you on our stage:
We set no guards upon our tiring-room,
But when with flying colours there you come,
We patiently, you see, give up to you
Our poets, virgins, nay, our matrons too.

1. The actor who played Horner in the first production of the play.
2. Wycherley was a "late so baffled scribbler" because *The Gentleman Dancing-Master*, the play of his that preceded *The Country Wife*, had been a failure three years before.
3. Castril is the angry boy in Ben Jonson's *The Alchemist*, who, before Subtle can begin to make excuses, shouts "You lie." The name is spelled Kastrill in most Jonson editions.

4. Bayes was the author in *The Rehearsal*, a play by George Villiers, second Duke of Buckingham. Here it apparently means simply the author, but since Bayes in Buckingham's play makes the playwright's usual complaints against both audience and actors (" 'Y gad, the town has used me as scurvily as the players have done."), the designation is particularly appropriate for this kind of needling Prologue.

· *William Wycherley*

Act I

HORNER's *Lodging.*

[*Enter* HORNER, *and* QUACK *following him at a distance.*]

HORNER. [*aside*] A quack is as fit for a pimp, as a midwife for a bawd; they are still but in their way, both helpers of nature.— [*aloud*] Well, my dear doctor, hast thou done what I desired?

QUACK. I have undone you for ever with the women, and reported you throughout the whole town as bad as an eunuch, with as much trouble as if I had made you one in earnest.

HORNER. But have you told all the midwives you know, the orange wenches at the playhouses, the city husbands, and old fumbling keepers of this end of the town? for they'll be the readiest to report it.

QUACK. I have told all the chambermaids, waiting-women, tire-women, and old women of my acqaintance; nay, and whispered it as a secret to 'em, and to the whisperers of Whitehall; so that you need not doubt 'twill spread, and you will be as odious to the handsome young women, as—

HORNER. As the small-pox. Well—

QUACK. And to the married women of this end of the town, as—

HORNER. As the great one; nay, as their own husbands.

QUACK. And to the city dames, as aniseed Robin,[5] of filthy and contemptible memory; and they will frighten their children with your name, especially their females.

HORNER. And cry, Horner's coming to carry you away. I am only afraid 'twill not be believed. You told 'em it was by an English-French disaster, and an English-French chirurgeon, who has given me at once not only a cure, but an antidote for the future against that damned malady, and that worse distemper, love, and all other women's evils?

QUACK. Your late journey into France has made it the more credible, and your being here a fortnight before you appeared in public, looks as if you apprehended the shame, which I wonder you do not. Well, I have been hired by young gallants to belie 'em t'other way; but you are the first would be thought a man unfit for women.

HORNER. Dear Mr. Doctor, let vain rogues be contented only to be thought abler men than they are, generally 'tis all the pleasure they have; but mine lies another way.

QUACK. You take, methinks, a very preposterous way to it, and as ridiculous as if we operators in physic should put forth bills to disparage our medicaments, with hopes to gain customers.

HORNER. Doctor, there are quacks in love as well as physic, who get but the fewer and worse patients for their boasting; a good name is seldom got by giving it one's self; and women, no more than honour, are compassed by bragging. Come, come, Doctor, the

5. Aniseed Robin was a famous hermaphrodite, the hero of a number of indecent stories.

wisest lawyer never discovers the merits of his cause till the trial; the wealthiest man conceals his riches, and the cunning gamester his play. Shy husbands and keepers, like old rooks, are not to be cheated but by a new unpractised trick: false friendship will pass now no more than false dice upon 'em; no, not in the city.

[*Enter* BOY.]

BOY. There are two ladies and a gentleman coming up. [*Exit.*]

HORNER. A pox! some unbelieving sisters of my former acquaintance, who, I am afraid, expect their sense should be satisfied of the falsity of the report. No—this formal fool and women!

[*Enter* SIR JASPER FIDGET, LADY FIDGET, *and* MRS. DAINTY FIDGET.]

QUACK. His wife and sister.

SIR JASPER. My coach breaking just now before your door, sir, I look upon as an occasional reprimand to me, sir, for not kissing your hands, sir, since your coming out of France, sir; and so my disaster, sir, has been my good fortune, sir; and this is my wife and sister, sir.

HORNER. What then, sir?

SIR JASPER. My lady, and sister, sir.—Wife, this is Master Horner.

LADY FIDGET. Master Horner, husband!

SIR JASPER. My lady, my Lady Fidget, sir.

HORNER. So, sir.

SIR JASPER. Won't you be acquainted with her, sir?—[*aside*] So, the report is true, I find, by his coldness or aversion to the sex; but I'll play the wag with him.—[*aloud*] Pray salute my wife, my lady, sir.

HORNER. I will kiss no man's wife, sir, for him, sir; I have taken my eternal leave, sir, of the sex already, sir.

SIR JASPER. [*aside*] Ha! ha! ha! I'll plague him yet.—[*aloud*] Not know my wife, sir?

HORNER. I do know your wife, sir; she's a woman, sir, and consequently a monster, sir, a greater monster than a husband, sir.

SIR JASPER. A husband! how, sir?

HORNER. So, sir; but I make no more cuckolds, sir. [*makes horns*]⁶

SIR JASPER. Ha! ha! ha! Mercury! Mercury!⁷

LADY FIDGET. Pray, Sir Jasper, let us be gone from this rude fellow.

MRS. DAINTY FIDGET. Who, by his breeding, would think he had ever been in France?

LADY FIDGET. Foh! he's but too much a French fellow, such as hate women of quality and virtue for their love to their husbands. Sir Jasper, a woman is hated by 'em as much for loving her husband as for loving their money. But pray let's be gone.

HORNER. You do well, madam; for I have nothing that you came for. I have brought over not so much as a bawdy picture, no new

6. This stage direction obviously describes the action to go along with "So, sir." Horner has lifted his hands to his forehead, forefingers extended, making a pair of horns, the sign of the cuckold, indicating the "greater monster" a husband is.
7. Mercury was used in the treatment of venereal disease.

postures, nor the second part of the *Ecole des Filles;* nor—

QUACK. Hold, for shame, sir! what d'ye mean? you'll ruin yourself for ever with the sex—[*apart to* HORNER]

SIR JASPER. Ha! ha! ha! he hates women perfectly, I find.

MRS. DAINTY FIDGET. What pity 'tis he should!

LADY FIDGET. Ay, he's a base fellow for't. But affectation makes not a woman more odious to them than virtue.

HORNER. Because your virtue is your greatest affectation, madam.

LADY FIDGET. How, you saucy fellow! would you wrong my honour?

HORNER. If I could.

LADY FIDGET. How d'ye mean, sir?

SIR JASPER. Ha! ha! ha! no, he can't wrong your ladyship's honour, upon my honour. He, poor man—hark you in your ear—a mere eunuch. [*whispers*]

LADY FIDGET. O filthy French beast! foh! foh! why do we stay? let's be gone: I can't endure the sight of him.

SIR JASPER. Stay but till the chairs come; they'll be here presently.

LADY FIDGET. No.

SIR JASPER. Nor can I stay longer. 'Tis, let me see, a quarter and half quarter of a minute past eleven. The council will be sat; I must away. Business must be preferred always before love and ceremony with the wise, Mr. Horner.

HORNER. And the impotent, Sir Jasper.

SIR JASPER. Ay, ay, the impotent, Master Horner; hah! hah! hah!

LADY FIDGET. What, leave us with a filthy man alone in his lodgings?

SIR JASPER. He's an innocent man now, you know. Pray stay, I'll hasten the chairs to you.—Mr. Horner, your servant; I should be glad to see you at my house. Pray come and dine with me, and play at cards with my wife after dinner; you are fit for women at that game yet, ha! ha!—[*aside*] 'Tis as much a husband's prudence to provide innocent diversion for a wife as to hinder her unlawful pleasures; and he had better employ her than let her employ herself.—[*aloud*] Farewell.

HORNER. Your servant, Sir Jasper.

[*Exit* SIR JASPER.]

LADY FIDGET. I will not stay with him, foh!—

HORNER. Nay, madam, I beseech you stay, if it be but to see I can be as civil to ladies yet as they would desire.

LADY FIDGET. No, no, foh! you cannot be civil to ladies.

MRS. DAINTY FIDGET. You as civil as ladies would desire?

LADY FIDGET. No, no, no, foh! foh! foh!

[*Exeunt* LADY FIDGET *and* MRS. DAINTY FIDGET.]

QUACK. Now, I think, I, or you yourself, rather, have done your business with the women.

HORNER. Thou art an ass. Don't you see already, upon the report, and my carriage, this grave man of business leaves his wife in my lodgings, invites me to his house and wife, who before would not be acquainted with me out of jealousy?

QUACK. Nay, by this means you may be the more acquainted with the husbands, but the less with the wives.

HORNER. Let me alone; if I can but abuse the husbands, I'll soon disabuse the wives. Stay—I'll reckon you up the advantages I am like to have by my stratagem. First, I shall be rid of all my old acquaintances, the most insatiable sort of duns, that invade our lodgings in a morning; and next to the pleasure of making a new mistress is that of being rid of an old one, and of all old debts. Love, when it comes to be so, is paid the most unwillingly.

QUACK. Well, you may be so rid of your old acquaintances; but how will you get any new ones?

HORNER. Doctor, thou wilt never make a good chemist, thou art so incredulous and impatient. Ask but all the young fellows of the town if they do not lose more time, like huntsmen, in starting the game, than in running it down. One knows not where to find 'em; who will or will not. Women of quality are so civil, you can hardly distinguish love from good breeding, and a man is often mistaken: but now I can be sure she that shows an aversion to me loves the sport, as those women that are gone, whom I warrant to be right. And then the next thing is, your women of honour, as you call 'em, are only chary of their reputations, not their persons; and 'tis scandal they would avoid, not men. Now may I have, by the reputation of an eunuch, the privileges of one, and be seen in a lady's chamber in a morning as early as her husband; kiss virgins before their parents or lovers; and may be, in short, the *passe-partout* of the town. Now, doctor.

QUACK. Nay, now you shall be the doctor; and your process is so new that we do not know but it may succeed.

HORNER. Not so new neither; *probatum est,* doctor.

QUACK. Well, I wish you luck, and many patients, whilst I go to mine. [*Exit.*]

[*Enter* HARCOURT *and* DORILANT.]

HARCOURT. Come, your appearance at the play yesterday, has, I hope, hardened you for the future against the women's contempt, and the men's raillery; and now you'll abroad as you were wont.

HORNER. Did I not bear it bravely?

DORILANT. With a most theatrical impudence, nay, more than the orange-wenches show there, or a drunken vizard-mask,[8] or a great-bellied actress; nay, or the most impudent of creatures, an ill poet; or what is yet more impudent, a second-hand critic.

HORNER. But what say the ladies? have they no pity?

HARCOURT. What ladies? The vizard-masks, you know, never pity a man when all's gone, though in their service.

DORILANT. And for the women in the boxes, you'd never pity them when 'twas in your power.

HARCOURT. They say 'tis pity but all that deal with common women should be served so.

DORILANT. Nay, I dare swear they won't admit you to play at cards with them, go to plays with 'em, or do the little duties which other shadows of men are wont to do for 'em.

HORNER. What do you call shadows of men?

8. Prostitute.

DORILANT. Half-men.

HORNER. What, boys?

DORILANT. Ay, your old boys, old *beaux garçons*, who, like super-annuated stallions, are suffered to run, feed, and whinny with the mares as long as they live, though they can do nothing else.

HORNER. Well, a pox on love and wenching! Women serve but to keep a man from better company. Though I can't enjoy them, I shall you the more. Good fellowship and friendship are lasting, rational, and manly pleasures.

HARCOURT. For all that, give me some of those pleasures you call effeminate too; they help to relish one another.

HORNER. They disturb one another.

HARCOURT. No, mistresses are like books. If you pore upon them too much, they doze you, and make you unfit for company; but if used discreetly, you are the fitter for conversation by 'em.

DORILANT. A mistress should be like a little country retreat near the town; not to dwell in constantly, but only for a night and away, to taste the town the better when a man returns.

HORNER. I tell you, 'tis as hard to be a good fellow, a good friend, and a lover of women, as 'tis to be a good fellow, a good friend, and a lover of money. You cannot follow both, then choose your side. Wine gives you liberty, love takes it away.

DORILANT. Gad, he's in the right on't.

HORNER. Wine gives you joy; love, grief and tortures, besides surgeons. Wine makes us witty; love, only sots. Wine makes us sleep; love breaks it.

DORILANT. By the world he has reason, Harcourt.

HORNER. Wine makes—

DORILANT. Ay, wine makes us—makes us princes; love makes us beggars, poor rogues, egad—and wine—

HORNER. So, there's one converted.—No, no, love and wine, oil and vinegar.

HARCOURT. I grant it; love will still be uppermost.

HORNER. Come, for my part, I will have only those glorious manly pleasures of being very drunk and very slovenly.

[*Enter* BOY.]

BOY. Mr. Sparkish is below, sir. [*Exit.*]

HARCOURT. What, my dear friend! a rogue that is fond of me only, I think, for abusing him.

DORILANT. No, he can no more think the men laugh at him than that women jilt him; his opinion of himself is so good.

HORNER. Well, there's another pleasure by drinking I thought not of,—I shall lose his acquaintance, because he cannot drink: and you know 'tis a very hard thing to be rid of him; for he's one of those nauseous offerers at wit, who, like the worst fiddlers, run themselves into all companies.

HARCOURT. One that, by being in the company of men of sense, would pass for one.

HORNER. And may so to the short-sighted world; as a false jewel amongst true ones is not discerned at a distance. His company is as troublesome to us as a cuckold's when you have a mind to his wife's.

HARCOURT. No, the rogue will not let us enjoy one another, but ravishes our conversation; though he signifies no more to't than Sir Martin Mar-all's gaping, and awkward thrumming upon the lute, does to his man's voice and music.[9]

DORILANT. And to pass for a wit in town shows himself a fool every night to us, that are guilty of the plot.

HORNER. Such wits as he are, to a company of reasonable men, like rooks to the gamesters; who only fill a room at the table, but are so far from contributing to the play, that they only serve to spoil the fancy of those that do.

DORILANT. Nay, they are used like rooks too, snubbed, checked, and abused; yet the rogues will hang on.

HORNER. A pox on 'em, and all that force nature, and would be still what she forbids 'em! Affectation is her greatest monster.

HARCOURT. Most men are the contraries to that they would seem. Your bully, you see, is a coward with a long sword; the little humbly fawning physician, with his ebony cane, is he that destroys men.

DORILANT. The usurer, a poor rogue, possessed of mouldy bonds and mortgages; and we they call spendthrifts, are only wealthy, who lay out his money upon daily new purchases of pleasure.

HORNER. Ay, your arrantest cheat is your trustee or executor; your jealous man, the greatest cuckold; your churchman the greatest atheist; and your noisy pert rogue of a wit, the greatest fop, dullest ass, and worst company, as you shall see; for here he comes.

[*Enter* SPARKISH.]

SPARKISH. How is't, sparks? how is't? Well, faith, Harry, I must rally thee a little, ha! ha! ha! upon the report in town of thee, ha! ha! ha! I can't hold i'faith; shall I speak?

HORNER. Yes; but you'll be so bitter then.

SPARKISH. Honest Dick and Frank here shall answer for me; I will not be extreme bitter, by the universe.

HARCOURT. We will be bound in a ten thousand pound bond, he shall not be bitter at all.

DORILANT. Nor sharp, nor sweet.

HORNER. What, not downright insipid?

SPARKISH. Nay then, since you are so brisk, and provoke me, take what follows. You must know, I was discoursing and rallying with some ladies yesterday, and they happened to talk of the fine new signs in town—

HORNER. Very fine ladies, I believe.

SPARKISH. Said I, I know where the best new sign is.—Where? says one of the ladies.—In Covent-Garden, I replied.—Said another, In what street?—In Russel-street, answered I.—Lord,

9. In John Dryden's *Sir Martin Mar-All*, the title character pretends to sing and accompany himself on a lute— a serenade to his mistress—while the real music comes from Sir Martin's man, who is hidden.

says another, I'm sure there was never a fine new sign there yesterday.—Yes, but there was, said I again; and it came out of France, and has been there a fortnight.

DORILANT. A pox! I can hear no more, prithee.

HORNER. No, hear him out; let him tune his crowd a while.

HARCOURT. The worst music, the greatest preparation.

SPARKISH. Nay, faith, I'll make you laugh.—It cannot be, says a third lady.—Yes, yes, quoth I again.—Says a fourth lady—

HORNER. Look to't, we'll have no more ladies.

SPARKISH. No—then mark, mark, now. Said I to the fourth, Did you never see Mr. Horner? he lodges in Russel-street, and he's a sign of a man, you know, since he came out of France; ha! ha! ha!

HORNER. But the devil take me if thine be the sign of a jest.

SPARKISH. With that they all fell a-laughing, till they bepissed themselves. What, but it does not move you, methinks? Well, I see one had as good go to law without a witness, as break a jest without a laugher on one's side.—Come, come, sparks, but where do we dine? I have left at Whitehall an earl, to dine with you.

DORILANT. Why, I thought thou hadst loved a man with a title, better than a suit with a French trimming to't.

HARCOURT. Go to him again.

SPARKISH. No, sir, a wit to me is the greatest title in the world.

HORNER. But go dine with your earl, sir; he may be exceptious. We are your friends, and will not take it ill to be left, I do assure you.

HARCOURT. Nay, faith, he shall go to him.

SPARKISH. Nay, pray, gentlemen.

DORILANT. We'll thrust you out, if you won't; what, disappoint anybody for us?

SPARKISH. Nay, dear gentlemen, hear me.

HORNER. No, no, sir, by no means; pray go, sir.

SPARKISH. Why, dear rogues—

DORILANT. No, no.

[*They all thrust him out of the room.*]

ALL. Ha! ha! ha!

[*Re-enter* SPARKISH.]

SPARKISH. But, sparks, pray hear me. What, d'ye think I'll eat then with gay shallow fops and silent coxcombs? I think wit as necessary at dinner, as a glass of good wine; and that's the reason I never have any stomach when I eat alone.—Come, but where do we dine?

HORNER. Even where you will.

SPARKISH. At Chateline's?

DORILANT. Yes, if you will.

SPARKISH. Or at the Cock?

DORILANT. Yes, if you please.

SPARKISH. Or at the Dog and Partridge?

HORNER. Ay, if you have a mind to't; for we shall dine at neither.

SPARKISH. Pshaw! with your fooling we shall lose the new play; and

I would no more miss seeing a new play the first day, than I would miss sitting in the wit's row. Therefore I'll go fetch my mistress, and away. [*Exit.*]

[*Enter* PINCHWIFE.]

HORNER. Who have we here? Pinchwife?

PINCHWIFE. Gentlemen, your humble servant.

HORNER. Well, Jack, by thy long absence from the town, the grumness of thy countenance, and the slovenliness of thy habit, I should give thee joy, should I not, of marriage?

PINCHWIFE. [*aside*] Death! does he know I'm married too? I thought to have concealed it from him at least.—[*aloud*] My long stay in the country will excuse my dress; and I have a suit of law that brings me up to town, that puts me out of humour. Besides, I must give Sparkish to-morrow five thousand pounds to lie with my sister.

HORNER. Nay, you country gentlemen, rather than not purchase, will buy anything; and he is a cracked title, if we may quibble. Well, but am I to give thee joy? I heard thou wert married.

PINCHWIFE. What then?

HORNER. Why, the next thing that is to be heard, is, thou'rt a cuckold.

PINCHWIFE. Insuppportable name! [*aside*]

HORNER. But I did not expect marriage from such a whoremaster as you; one that knew the town so much, and women so well.

PINCHWIFE. Why, I have married no London wife.

HORNER. Pshaw! that's all one. That grave circumspection in marrying a country wife, is like refusing a deceitful pampered Smithfield jade, to go and be cheated by a friend in the country.

PINCHWIFE. [*aside*] A pox on him and his simile!—[*aloud*] At least we are a little surer of the breed there, know what her keeping has been, whether foiled or unsound.

HORNER. Come, come, I have known a clap gotten in Wales; and there are cousins, justices' clerks, and chaplains in the country, I won't say coachmen. But she's handsome and young?

PINCHWIFE. [*aside*] I'll answer as I should do.—[*aloud*] No, no; she has no beauty but her youth, no attraction but her modesty: wholesome, homely, and huswifely; that's all.

DORILANT. He talks as like a grazier as he looks.

PINCHWIFE. She's too awkward, ill-favoured, and silly to bring to town.

HARCOURT. Then methinks you should bring her to be taught breeding.

PINCHWIFE. To be taught! no, sir, I thank you. Good wives and private soldiers should be ignorant—I'll keep her from your instructions, I warrant you.

HARCOURT. The rogue is as jealous as if his wife were not ignorant. [*aside*]

HORNER. Why, if she be ill-favoured, there will be less danger here for you than by leaving her in the country. We have such variety of dainties that we are seldom hungry.

DORILANT. But they have always coarse, constant, swingeing stomachs in the country.

HARCOURT. Foul feeders indeed!

DORILANT. And your hospitality is great there.

HARCOURT. Open house; every man's welcome.

PINCHWIFE. So, so, gentlemen.

HORNER. But prithee, why shouldst thou marry her? If she be ugly, ill-bred, and silly, she must be rich then.

PINCHWIFE. As rich as if she brought me twenty thousand pound out of this town; for she'll be as sure not to spend her moderate portion, as a London baggage would be to spend hers, let it be what it would: so 'tis all one. Then, because she's ugly, she's the likelier to be my own; and being ill-bred, she'll hate conversation; and since silly and innocent, will not know the difference betwixt a man of one-and-twenty and one of forty.

HORNER. Nine—to my knowledge. But if she be silly, she'll expect as much from a man of forty-nine, as from him of one-and-twenty. But methinks wit is more necessary than beauty; and I think no young woman ugly that has it, and no handsome woman agreeable without it.

PINCHWIFE. 'Tis my maxim, he's a fool that marries; but he's a greater that does not marry a fool. What is wit in a wife good for, but to make a man a cuckold?

HORNER. Yes, to keep it from his knowledge.

PINCHWIFE. A fool cannot contrive to make her husband a cuckold.

HORNER. No; but she'll club with a man that can: and what is worse, if she cannot make her husband a cuckold, she'll make him jealous, and pass for one: and then 'tis all one.

PINCHWIFE. Well, well, I'll take care for one. My wife shall make me no cuckold, though she had your help, Mr. Horner. I understand the town, sir.

DORILANT. His help! [*aside*]

HARCOURT. He's come newly to town, it seems, and has not heard how things are with him. [*aside*]

HORNER. But tell me, has marriage cured thee of whoring, which it seldom does?

HARCOURT. 'Tis more than age can do.

HORNER. No, the word is, I'll marry and live honest: but a marriage vow is like a penitent gamester's oath, and entering into bonds and penalties to stint himself to such a particular small sum at play for the future, which makes him but the more eager; and not being able to hold out, loses his money again, and his forfeit to boot.

DORILANT. Ay, ay, a gamester will be a gamester whilst his money lasts, and a whoremaster whilst his vigour.

HARCOURT. Nay, I have known 'em, when they are broke, and can lose no more, keep a fumbling with the box in their hands to fool with only, and hinder other gamesters.

DORILANT. That had wherewithal to make lusty stakes.

PINCHWIFE. Well, gentlemen, you may laugh at me; but you shall never lie with my wife: I know the town.

HORNER. But prithee, was not the way you were in better? is not keeping better than marriage?

PINCHWIFE. A pox on't! the jades would jilt me, I could never keep a whore to myself.

HORNER. So, then you only married to keep a whore to yourself. Well, but let me tell you, women, as you say, are like soldiers, made constant and loyal by good pay, rather than by oaths and covenants. Therefore I'd advise my friends to keep rather than marry, since too I find, by your example, it does not serve one's turn; for I saw you yesterday in the eighteenpenny place[1] with a pretty country-wench.

PINCHWIFE. How the devil! did he see my wife then? I sat there that she might not be seen. But she shall never go to a play again. [*aside*]

HORNER. What! dost thou blush, at nine-and-forty, for having been seen with a wench?

DORILANT. No, faith, I warrant 'twas his wife, which he seated there out of sight; for he's a cunning rogue, and understands the town.

HARCOURT. He blushes. Then 'twas his wife; for men are now more ashamed to be seen with them in public than with a wench.

PINCHWIFE. Hell and damnation! I'm undone, since Horner has seen her, and they know 'twas she. [*aside*]

HORNER. But prithee, was it thy wife? She was exceeding pretty: I was in love with her at that distance.

PINCHWIFE. You are like never to be nearer to her. Your servant, gentlemen. [*offers to go*]

HORNER. Nay, prithee stay.

PINCHWIFE. I cannot; I will not.

HORNER. Come, you shall dine with us.

PINCHWIFE. I have dined already.

HORNER. Come, I know thou hast not: I'll treat thee, dear rogue; thou sha't spend none of thy Hampshire money to-day.

PINCHWIFE. Treat me! So, he uses me already like his cuckold. [*aside*]

HORNER. Nay, you shall not go.

PINCHWIFE. I must; I have business at home. [*Exit.*]

HARCOURT. To beat his wife. He's as jealous of her, as a Cheapside husband of a Covent-garden wife.

HORNER. Why, 'tis as hard to find an old whoremaster without jealousy and the gout, as a young one without fear, or the pox:—

> As gout in age from pox in youth proceeds,
> So wenching past, then jealousy succeeds;
> The worst disease that love and wenching breeds.
> [*Exeunt.*]

1. At the theater, the middle gallery. The fashionable crowd would have been below, in the pit and boxes.

Act II

A *room* in PINCHWIFE's *House.*

[MRS. MARGERY PINCHWIFE *and* ALITHEA. PINCHWIFE *peeping behind at the door.*]

MRS. PINCHWIFE. Pray, sister, where are the best fields and woods to walk in, in London?

ALITHEA. [*aside*] A pretty question!—[*aloud*] Why, sister, Mulberry-garden and St. James's-park; and, for close walks, the New Exchange.

MRS. PINCHWIFE. Pray, sister, tell me why my husband looks so grum here in town, and keeps me up so close, and will not let me go a-walking, nor let me wear my best gown yesterday.

ALITHEA. O, he's jealous, sister.

MRS. PINCHWIFE. Jealous! what's that?

ALITHEA. He's afraid you should love another man.

MRS. PINCHWIFE. How should he be afraid of my loving another man, when he will not let me see any but himself?

ALITHEA. Did he not carry you yesterday to a play?

MRS. PINCHWIFE. Ay; but we sat amongst ugly people. He would not let me come near the gentry, who sat under us, so that I could not see 'em. He told me, none but naughty women sat there, whom they toused and moused. But I would have ventured, for all that.

ALITHEA. But how did you like the play?

MRS. PINCHWIFE. Indeed I was weary of the play; but I liked hugeously the actors. They are the goodliest, properest men, sister!

ALITHEA. O, but you must not like the actors, sister.

MRS. PINCHWIFE. Ay, how should I help it, sister? Pray, sister, when my husband comes in, will you ask leave for me to go a-walking?

ALITHEA. A-walking! ha! ha! Lord, a country-gentle-woman's pleasure is the drudgery of a footpost; and she requires as much airing as her husband's horses.—[*aside*] But here comes your husband: I'll ask, though I'm sure he'll not grant it.

MRS. PINCHWIFE. He says he won't let me go abroad for fear of catching the pox.

ALITHEA. Fy! the small-pox you should say.

[*Enter* PINCHWIFE.]

MRS. PINCHWIFE. O my dear, dear bud, welcome home! Why dost thou look so fropish? who has nangered thee?

PINCHWIFE. You're a fool.

[MRS. PINCHWIFE *goes aside, and cries.*]

ALITHEA. Faith, so she is, for crying for no fault, poor tender creature!

PINCHWIFE. What, you would have her as impudent as yourself, as arrant a jilflirt, a gadder, a magpie; and to say all, a mere notorious town-woman?

ALITHEA. Brother, you are my only censurer; and the honour of your family will sooner suffer in your wife there than in me, though I take the innocent liberty of the town.

PINCHWIFE. Hark you, mistress, do not talk so before my wife.— The innocent liberty of the town!

ALITHEA. Why, pray, who boasts of any intrigue with me? what lampoon has made my name notorious? what ill women frequent my lodgings? I keep no company with any women of scandalous reputations.

PINCHWIFE. No, you keep the men of scandalous reputations company.

ALITHEA. Where? would you not have me civil? answer 'em in a box at the plays, in the drawing-room at Whitehall, in St. James'-park, Mulberry-garden, or—

PINCHWIFE. Hold, hold! Do not teach my wife where the men are to be found: I believe she's the worse for your town-documents already. I bid you keep her in ignorance, as I do.

MRS. PINCHWIFE. Indeed, be not angry with her, bud, she will tell me nothing of the town, though I ask her a thousand times a day.

PINCHWIFE. Then you are very inquisitive to know, I find?

MRS. PINCHWIFE. Not I indeed, dear; I hate London. Our place-house in the country is worth a thousand of't: would I were there again!

PINCHWIFE. So you shall, I warrant. But were you not talking of plays and players when I came in?—[*to* ALITHEA] You are her encourager in such discourses.

MRS. PINCHWIFE. No, indeed, dear; she chid me just now for liking the playermen.

PINCHWIFE. [*aside*] Nay, if she be so innocent as to own to me her liking them, there is no hurt in't.—[*aloud*] Come, my poor rogue, but thou likest none better than me?

MRS. PINCHWIFE. Yes, indeed, but I do. The playermen are finer folks.

PINCHWIFE. But you love none better than me?

MRS. PINCHWIFE. You are my own dear bud, and I know you. I hate a stranger.

PINCHWIFE. Ay, my dear, you must love me only; and not be like the naughty town-women, who only hate their husbands, and love every man else; love plays, visits, fine coaches, fine clothes, fiddles, balls, treats, and so lead a wicked town-life.

MRS. PINCHWIFE. Nay, if to enjoy all these things be a town-life, London is not so bad a place, dear.

PINCHWIFE. How! if you love me, you must hate London.

ALITHEA. The fool has forbid me discovering to her the pleasures of the town, and he is now setting her agog upon them himself. [*aside*]

MRS. PINCHWIFE. But, husband, do the town-women love the playermen too?

PINCHWIFE. Yes, I warrant you.

MRS. PINCHWIFE. Ay, I warrant you.

PINCHWIFE. Why, you do not, I hope?

MRS. PINCHWIFE. No, no, bud. But why have we no playermen in the country?

PINCHWIFE. Ha!—Mrs. Minx, ask me no more to go to a play.

MRS. PINCHWIFE. Nay, why, love? I did not care for going: but when you forbid me, you make me, as 'twere, desire it.

ALITHEA. So 'twill be in other things, I warrant. [*aside*]

MRS. PINCHWIFE. Pray let me go to a play, dear.

PINCHWIFE. Hold your peace, I wo' not.

MRS. PINCHWIFE. Why, love?

PINCHWIFE. Why, I'll tell you.

ALITHEA. Nay, if he tell her, she'll give him more cause to forbid her that place. [*aside*]

MRS. PINCHWIFE. Pray why, dear?

PINCHWIFE. First, you like the actors; and the gallants may like you.

MRS. PINCHWIFE. What, a homely country girl! No, bud, nobody will like me.

PINCHWIFE. I tell you yes, they may.

MRS. PINCHWIFE. No, no, you jest—I won't believe you: I will go.

PINCHWIFE. I tell you then, that one of the lewdest fellows in town, who saw you there, told me he was in love with you.

MRS. PINCHWIFE. Indeed! who, who, pray who was't?

PINCHWIFE. I've gone too far, and slipped before I was aware; how overjoyed she is! [*aside*]

MRS. PINCHWIFE. Was it any Hampshire gallant, any of our neighbours? I promise you, I am beholden to him.

PINCHWIFE. I promise you, you lie; for he would but ruin you, as he has done hundreds. He has no other love for women but that; such as he look upon women, like basilisks, but to destroy 'em.

MRS. PINCHWIFE. Ay, but if he loves me, why should he ruin me? answer me to that. Methinks he should not, I would do him no harm.

ALITHEA. Ha! ha! ha!

PINCHWIFE. 'Tis very well; but I'll keep him from doing you any harm, or me either. But here comes company; get you in, get you in.

MRS. PINCHWIFE. But, pray, husband, is he a pretty gentleman that loves me?

PINCHWIFE. In, baggage, in. [*thrusts her in, and shuts the door*] [*Enter* SPARKISH *and* HARCOURT.] What, all the lewd libertines of the town brought to my lodging by this easy coxcomb! 'sdeath, I'll not suffer it.

SPARKISH. Here, Harcourt, do you approve my choice?— [*to* ALITHEA] Dear little rogue, I told you I'd bring you acquainted with all my friends, the wits and— [HARCOURT *salutes her.*]

PINCHWIFE. Ay, they shall know her, as well as you yourself will, I warrant you.

SPARKISH. This is one of those, my pretty rogue, that are to dance at your wedding to-morrow; and him you must bid welcome ever, to what you and I have.

PINCHWIFE. Monstrous! [*aside*]

SPARKISH. Harcourt, how dost thou like her, faith? Nay, dear, do not look down; I should hate to have a wife of mine out of countenance at anything.

PINCHWIFE. Wonderful! [*aside*]

SPARKISH. Tell me, I say, Harcourt, how dost thou like her? Thou hast stared upon her enough, to resolve me.

HARCOURT. So infinitely well, that I could wish I had a mistress too, that might differ from her in nothing but her love and engagement to you.

ALITHEA. Sir, Master Sparkish has often told me that his acquaintance were all wits and railleurs, and now I find it.

SPARKISH. No, by the universe, madam, he does not rally now; you may believe him. I do assure you, he is the honestest, worthiest, true-hearted gentleman—a man of such perfect honour, he would say nothing to a lady he does not mean.

PINCHWIFE. Praising another man to his mistress! [*aside*]

HARCOURT. Sir, you are so beyond expectation obliging, that—

SPARKISH. Nay, egad, I am sure you do admire her extremely; I see't in your eyes.—He does admire you, madam.—By the world, don't you?

HARCOURT. Yes, above the world, or the most glorious part of it, her whole sex: and till now I never thought I should have envied you, or any man about to marry, but you have the best excuse for marriage I ever knew.

ALITHEA. Nay, now, sir, I'm satisfied you are of the society of the wits and railleurs, since you cannot spare your friend, even when he is but too civil to you; but the surest sign is, since you are an enemy to marriage,—for that I hear you hate as much as business or bad wine.

HARCOURT. Truly, madam, I was never an enemy to marriage till now, because marriage was never an enemy to me before.

ALITHEA. But why, sir, is marriage an enemy to you now? because it robs you of your friend here? for you look upon a friend married, as one gone into a monastery, that is, dead to the world.

HARCOURT. 'Tis indeed, because you marry him; I see, madam, you can guess my meaning. I do confess heartily and openly, I wish it were in my power to break the match; by Heavens I would.

SPARKISH. Poor Frank!

ALITHEA. Would you be so unkind to me?

HARCOURT. No, no, 'tis not because I would be unkind to you.

SPARKISH. Poor Frank! no gad, 'tis only his kindness to me.

PINCHWIFE. Great kindness to you indeed! Insensible fop, let a man make love to his wife to his face! [*aside*]

SPARKISH. Come, dear Frank, for all my wife there, that shall be, thou shalt enjoy me sometimes, dear rogue. By my honour, we men of wit condole for our deceased brother in marriage, as much as for one dead in earnest: I think that was prettily said of me, ha, Harcourt?—But come, Frank, be not melancholy for me.

HARCOURT. No, I assure you, I am not melancholy for you.

SPARKISH. Prithee, Frank, dost think my wife that shall be there, a fine person?

HARCOURT. I could gaze upon her till I became as blind as you are.

SPARKISH. How as I am? how?

HARCOURT. Because you are a lover, and true lovers are blind, stock blind.

SPARKISH. True, true; but by the world she has wit too, as well as beauty: go, go with her into a corner, and try if she has wit; talk to her anything, she's bashful before me.

HARCOURT. Indeed if a woman wants wit in a corner, she has it nowhere.

ALITHEA. Sir, you dispose of me a little before your time—[aside to SPARKISH]

SPARKISH. Nay, nay, madam, let me have an earnest of your obedience, or—go, go, madam—

[HARCOURT courts ALITHEA aside.]

PINCHWIFE. How, sir! if you are not concerned for the honour of a wife, I am for that of a sister; he shall not debauch her. Be a pander to your own wife! bring men to her! let 'em make love before your face! thrust 'em into a corner together, then leave 'em in private! is this your town wit and conduct?

SPARKISH. Ha! ha! ha! a silly wise rogue would make one laugh more than a stark fool, ha! ha! I shall burst. Nay, you shall not disturb 'em; I'll vex thee, by the world. [struggles with PINCHWIFE to keep him from HARCOURT and ALITHEA]

ALITHEA. The writings are drawn, sir, settlements made; 'tis too late, sir, and past all revocation.

HARCOURT. Then so is my death.

ALITHEA. I would not be unjust to him.

HARCOURT. Then why to me so?

ALITHEA. I have no obligation to you.

HARCOURT. My love.

ALITHEA. I had his before.

HARCOURT. You never had it; he wants, you see, jealousy, the only infallible sign of it.

ALITHEA. Love proceeds from esteem; he cannot distrust my virtue: besides, he loves me, or he would not marry me.

HARCOURT. Marrying you is no more sign of his love than bribing your woman, that he may marry you, is a sign of his generosity. Marriage is rather a sign of interest than love; and he that marries a fortune covets a mistress, not loves her. But if you take marriage for a sign of love, take it from me immediately.

ALITHEA. No, now you have put a scruple in my head; but in short, sir, to end our dispute, I must marry him, my reputation would suffer in the world else.

HARCOURT. No; if you do marry him, with your pardon, madam, your reputation suffers in the world, and you would be thought in necessity for a cloak.

ALITHEA. Nay, now you are rude, sir.—Mr. Sparkish, pray come hither, your friend here is very troublesome, and very loving.

HARCOURT. Hold! hold!—[*aside to* ALITHEA]

PINCHWIFE. D'ye hear that?

SPARKISH. Why, d'ye think I'll seem to be jealous, like a country bumpkin?

PINCHWIFE. No, rather be a cuckold, like a credulous cit.

HARCOURT. Madam, you would not have been so little generous as to have told him.

ALITHEA. Yes, since you could be so little generous as to wrong him.

HARCOURT. Wrong him! no man can do't, he's beneath an injury: a bubble, a coward, a senseless idiot, a wretch so contemptible to all the world but you, that—

ALITHEA. Hold, do not rail at him, for since he is like to be my husband, I am resolved to like him: nay, I think I am obliged to tell him you are not his friend.—Master Sparkish, Master Sparkish!

SPARKISH. What, what?—[*to* HARCOURT] Now, dear rogue, has not she wit?

HARCOURT. Not so much as I thought, and hoped she had. [*speaks surlily*]

ALITHEA. Mr. Sparkish, do you bring people to rail at you?

HARCOURT. Madam—

SPARKISH. How! no; but if he does rail at me, 'tis but in jest, I warrant: what we wits do for one another, and never take any notice of it.

ALITHEA. He spoke so scurrilously of you, I had no patience to hear him; besides, he has been making love to me.

HARCOURT. True, damned tell-tale woman! [*aside*]

SPARKISH. Pshaw! to show his parts—we wits rail and make love often, but to show our parts: as we have no affections, so we have no malice, we—

ALITHEA. He said you were a wretch below an injury—

SPARKISH. Pshaw!

HARCOURT. Damned, senseless, impudent, virtuous jade! Well, since she won't let me have her, she'll do as good, she'll make me hate her. [*aside*]

ALITHEA. A common bubble—

SPARKISH. Pshaw!

ALITHEA. A coward—

SPARKISH. Pshaw, pshaw!

ALITHEA. A senseless, drivelling idiot—

SPARKISH. How! did he disparage my parts? Nay, then, my honour's concerned, I can't put up that, sir, by the world—brother, help me to kill him—[*aside*] I may draw now, since we have the odds of him:—'tis a good occasion, too, before my mistress—[*offers to draw*]

ALITHEA. Hold, hold!

SPARKISH. What, what?

ALITHEA. [*aside*] I must not let 'em kill the gentleman neither, for his kindness to me: I am so far from hating him, that I wish my gallant had his person and understanding. Nay, if my honour—

SPARKISH. I'll be thy death.

ALITHEA. Hold, hold! Indeed, to tell the truth, the gentleman said after all, that what he spoke was but out of friendship to you.

SPARKISH. How! say, I am, I am a fool, that is, no wit, out of friendship to me?

ALITHEA. Yes, to try whether I was concerned enough for you; and made love to me only to be satisfied of my virtue, for your sake.

HARCOURT. Kind, however. [aside]

SPARKISH. Nay, if it were so, my dear rogue, I ask thee pardon; but why would not you tell me so, faith?

HARCOURT. Because I did not think on't, faith.

SPARKISH. Come, Horner does not come; Harcourt, let's be gone to the new play.—Come, madam.

ALITHEA. I will not go, if you intend to leave me alone in the box, and run into the pit, as you use to do.

SPARKISH. Pshaw! I'll leave Harcourt with you in the box to entertain you, and that's as good; if I sat in the box, I should be thought no judge but of trimmings.—Come away, Harcourt, lead her down.

[Exeunt SPARKISH, HARCOURT, and ALITHEA.]

PINCHWIFE. Well, go thy ways, for the flower of the true town fops, such as spend their estates before they come to 'em, and are cuckolds before they're married. But let me go look to my own freehold.—How!

[Enter LADY FIDGET, MRS. DAINTY FIDGET, and MRS. SQUEAMISH.]

LADY FIDGET. Your servant, sir: where is your lady? We are come to wait upon her to the new play.

PINCHWIFE. New play!

LADY FIDGET. And my husband will wait upon you presently.

PINCHWIFE. [aside] Damn your civility.—[aloud] Madam, by no means; I will not see Sir Jasper here, till I have waited upon him at home; nor shall my wife see you till she has waited upon your ladyship at your lodgings.

LADY FIDGET. Now we are here, sir?

PINCHWIFE. No, Madam.

MRS. DAINTY FIDGET. Pray, let us see her.

MRS. SQUEAMISH. We will not stir till we see her.

PINCHWIFE. [aside] A pox on you all!—[goes to the door, and returns] She has locked the door, and is gone abroad.

LADY FIDGET. No, you have locked the door, and she's within.

MRS. DAINTY FIDGET. They told us below she was here.

PINCHWIFE. [aside] Will nothing do?—[aloud] Well, it must out then. To tell you the truth, ladies, which I was afraid to let you know before, lest it might endanger your lives, my wife has just now the small-pox come out upon her; do not be frightened; but pray be gone, ladies; you shall not stay here in danger of your lives; pray get you gone, ladies.

LADY FIDGET. No, no, we have all had 'em.

MRS. SQUEAMISH. Alack, alack!

MRS. DAINTY FIDGET. Come, come, we must see how it goes with her; I understand the disease.

LADY FIDGET. Come!

PINCHWIFE. [*aside*] Well, there is no being too hard for women at their own weapon, lying, therefore I'll quit the field. [*Exit.*]

MRS. SQUEAMISH. Here's an example of jealousy!

LADY FIDGET. Indeed, as the world goes, I wonder there are no more jealous, since wives are so neglected.

MRS. DAINTY FIDGET. Pshaw! as the world goes, to what end should they be jealous?

LADY FIDGET. Foh! 'tis a nasty world.

MRS. SQUEAMISH. That men of parts, great acquaintance, and quality, should take up with and spend themselves and fortunes in keeping little playhouse creatures, foh!

LADY FIDGET. Nay, that women of understanding, great acquaintance, and good quality, should fall a-keeping too of little creatures, foh!

MRS. SQUEAMISH. Why, 'tis the men of quality's fault; they never visit women of honour and reputation as they used to do; and have not so much as common civility for ladies of our rank, but use us with the same indifferency and ill-breeding as if we were all married to 'em.

LADY FIDGET. She says true; 'tis an arrant shame women of quality should be so slighted; methinks birth—birth should go for something; I have known men admired, courted, and followed for their titles only.

MRS. SQUEAMISH. Ay, one would think men of honour should not love, no more than marry, out of their own rank.

MRS. DAINTY FIDGET. Fy, fy, upon 'em! they are come to think cross breeding for themselves best, as well as for their dogs and horses.

LADY FIDGET. They are dogs and horses for't.

MRS. SQUEAMISH. One would think, if not for love, for vanity a little.

MRS. DAINTY FIDGET. Nay, they do satisfy their vanity upon us sometimes; and are kind to us in their report, tell all the world they lie with us.

LADY FIDGET. Damned rascals, that we should be only wronged by 'em! To report a man has had a person, when he has not had a person, is the greatest wrong in the whole world that can be done to a person.

MRS. SQUEAMISH. Well, 'tis an arrant shame noble persons should be so wronged and neglected.

LADY FIDGET. But still 'tis an arranter shame for a noble person to neglect her own honour, and defame her own noble person with little inconsiderable fellows, foh!

MRS. DAINTY FIDGET. I suppose the crime against our honour is the same with a man of quality as with another.

LADY FIDGET. How! no sure, the man of quality is likest one's husband, and therefore the fault should be the less.

MRS. DAINTY FIDGET. But then the pleasure should be the less.

LADY FIDGET. Fy, fy, fy, for shame, sister! whither shall we ramble? Be continent in your discourse, or I shall hate you.

MRS. DAINTY FIDGET. Besides, an intrigue is so much the more notorious for the man's quality.

MRS. SQUEAMISH. 'Tis true that nobody takes notice of a private man, and therefore with him 'tis more secret; and the crime's the less when 'tis not known.

LADY FIDGET. You say true; i'faith, I think you are in the right on't: 'tis not an injury to a husband, till it be an injury to our honours; so that a woman of honour loses no honour with a private person; and to say truth—

MRS. DAINTY FIDGET. So, the little fellow is grown a private person —with her—[*apart to* MRS. SQUEAMISH]

LADY FIDGET. But still my dear, dear honour—

[*Enter* SIR JASPER FIDGET, HORNER, *and* DORILANT.]

SIR JASPER. Ay, my dear, dear of honour, thou hast still so much honour in thy mouth—

HORNER. That she has none elsewhere. [*aside*]

LADY FIDGET. Oh, what d'ye mean to bring in these upon us?

MRS. DAINTY FIDGET. Foh! these are as bad as wits.

MRS. SQUEAMISH. Foh!

LADY FIDGET. Let us leave the room.

SIR JASPER. Stay, stay; faith, to tell you the naked truth—

LADY FIDGET. Fy, Sir Jasper! do not use that word naked.

SIR JASPER. Well, well, in short I have business at Whitehall, and cannot go to the play with you, therefore would have you go—

LADY FIDGET. With those two to a play?

SIR JASPER. No, not with t'other, but with Mr. Horner; there can be no more scandal to go with him than with Mr. Tattle, or Master Limberham.

LADY FIDGET. With that nasty fellow! no—no.

SIR JASPER. Nay, prithee, dear, hear me. [*whispers to* LADY FIDGET]

HORNER. Ladies—

[HORNER *and* DORILANT *draw near* MRS. SQUEAMISH *and* MRS. DAINTY FIDGET.]

MRS. DAINTY FIDGET. Stand off.

MRS. SQUEAMISH. Do not approach us.

MRS. DAINTY FIDGET. You herd with the wits, you are obscenity all over.

MRS. SQUEAMISH. And I would as soon look upon a picture of Adam and Eve, without fig-leaves, as any of you, if I could help it; therefore keep off, and do not make us sick.

DORILANT. What a devil are these?

HORNER. Why, these are pretenders to honour, as critics to wit, only by censuring others; and as every raw, peevish, out-of-humoured, affected, dull, tea-drinking, arithmetical fop, sets up for a wit by railing at men of sense, so these for honour, by railing at the court, and ladies of as great honour as quality.

SIR JASPER. Come, Mr. Horner, I must desire you to go with these ladies to the play, sir.

HORNER. I, sir?

SIR JASPER. Ay, ay, come, sir.

HORNER. I must beg your pardon, sir, and theirs; I will not be seen in women's company in public again for the world.

SIR JASPER. Ha, ha, strange aversion!

MRS. SQUEAMISH. No, he's for women's company in private.

SIR JASPER. He—poor man—he—ha! ha! ha!

MRS. DAINTY FIDGET. 'Tis a greater shame amongst lewd fellows to be seen in virtuous women's company, than for the women to be seen with them.

HORNER. Indeed, madam, the time was I only hated virtuous women, but now I hate the other too; I beg your pardon, ladies.

LADY FIDGET. You are very obliging, sir, because we would not be troubled with you.

SIR JASPER. In sober sadness, he shall go.

DORILANT. Nay, if he wo' not, I am ready to wait upon the ladies, and I think I am the fitter man.

SIR JASPER. You sir! no, I thank you for that. Master Horner is a privileged man amongst the virtuous ladies, 'twill be a great while before you are so; he! he! he! he's my wife's gallant; he! he! he! No, pray withdraw, sir, for as I take it, the virtuous ladies have no business with you.

DORILANT. And I am sure he can have none with them. 'Tis strange a man can't come amongst virtuous women now, but upon the same terms as men are admitted into the Great Turk's seraglio. But heavens keep me from being an ombre player with 'em!—But where is Pinchwife? [*Exit.*]

SIR JASPER. Come, come, man; what, avoid the sweet society of womankind? that sweet, soft, gentle, tame, noble creature, woman, made for man's companion—

HORNER. So is that soft, gentle, tame, and more noble creature a spaniel, and has all their tricks; can fawn, lie down, suffer beating, and fawn the more; barks at your friends when they come to see you, makes your bed hard, gives you fleas, and the mange sometimes. And all the difference is, the spaniel's the more faithful animal, and fawns but upon one master.

SIR JASPER. He! he! he!

MRS. SQUEAMISH. O the rude beast!

MRS. DAINTY FIDGET. Insolent brute!

LADY FIDGET. Brute! stinking, mortified, rotten French wether, to dare—

SIR JASPER. Hold, an't please your ladyship.—For shame, Master Horner! your mother was a woman—[*aside*] Now shall I never reconcile 'em.—[*aside to* LADY FIDGET] Hark you, madam, take my advice in your anger. You know you often want one to make up your drolling pack of ombre players, and you may cheat him easily; for he's an ill gamester, and consequently loves play. Besides, you know you have but two old civil gentlemen (with stinking breaths too) to wait upon you abroad; take in the third into your service. The other are but crazy; and a lady should have a supernumerary gentleman-usher as a supernumerary coach-horse, lest sometimes you should be forced to stay at home.

LADY FIDGET. But are you sure he loves play, and has money?

SIR JASPER. He loves play as much as you, and has money as much as I.

LADY FIDGET. Then I am contented to make him pay for his scurrility. Money makes up in a measure all other wants in men.— Those whom we cannot make hold for gallants, we make fine. [*aside*]

SIR JASPER. [*aside*] So, so; now to mollify, wheedle him.—[*aside to* HORNER] Master Horner, will you never keep civil company? methinks 'tis time now, since you are only fit for them. Come, come, man, you must e'en fall to visiting our wives, eating at our tables, drinking tea with our virtuous relations after dinner, dealing cards to 'em, reading plays and gazettes to 'em, picking fleas out of their smocks for 'em, collecting receipts, new songs, women, pages, and footmen for 'em.

HORNER. I hope they'll afford me better employment, sir.

SIR JASPER. He! he! he! 'tis fit you know your work before you come into your place. And since you are unprovided of a lady to flatter, and a good house to eat at, pray frequent mine, and call my wife mistress, and she shall call you gallant, according to the custom.

HORNER. Who, I?

SIR JASPER. Faith, thou sha't for my sake; come, for my sake only.

HORNER. For your sake—

SIR JASPER. Come, come, here's a gamester for you; let him be a little familiar sometimes; nay, what if a little rude? Gamesters may be rude with ladies, you know.

LADY FIDGET. Yes; losing gamesters have a privilege with women.

HORNER. I always thought the contrary, that the winning gamester had most privilege with women; for when you have lost your money to a man, you'll lose anything you have, all you have, they say, and he may use you as he pleases.

SIR JASPER. He! he! he! well, win or lose, you shall have your liberty with her.

LADY FIDGET. As he behaves himself; and for your sake I'll give him admittance and freedom.

HORNER. All sorts of freedom, madam?

SIR JASPER. Ay, ay, ay, all sorts of freedom thou canst take. And so go to her, begin thy new employment; wheedle her, jest with her, and be better acquainted one with another.

HORNER [*aside*] I think I know her already; therefore may venture with her my secret for hers.

[HORNER *and* LADY FIDGET *whisper.*]

SIR JASPER. Sister cuz, I have provided an innocent playfellow for you there.

MRS. DAINTY FIDGET. Who, he?

MRS. SQUEAMISH. There's a playfellow, indeed!

SIR JASPER. Yes sure.—What, he is good enough to play at cards, blindman's-buff, or the fool with, sometimes!

MRS. SQUEAMISH. Foh! we'll have no such playfellows.

MRS. DAINTY FIDGET. No, sir; you shan't choose playfellows for us, we thank you.

SIR JASPER. Nay, pray hear me. [*whispering to them*]

LADY FIDGET. But, poor gentleman, could you be so generous, so truly a man of honour, as for the sakes of us women of honour, to cause yourself to be reported no man? No man! and to suffer yourself the greatest shame that could fall upon a man, that none might fall upon us women by your conversation? but, indeed, sir, as perfectly, perfectly the same man as before your going into France, sir? as perfectly, perfectly, sir?

HORNER. As perfectly, perfectly, madam. Nay, I scorn you should take my word; I desire to be tried only, madam.

LADY FIDGET. Well, that's spoken again like a man of honour: all men of honour desire to come to the test. But, indeed, generally you men report such things of yourselves, one does not know how or whom to believe; and it is come to that pass, we dare not take your words no more than your tailor's, without some staid servant of yours be bound with you. But I have so strong a faith in your honour, dear, dear, noble sir, that I'd forfeit mine for yours, at any time, dear sir.

HORNER. No, madam, you should not need to forfeit it for me; I have given you security already to save you harmless, my late reputation being so well known in the world, madam.

LADY FIDGET. But if upon any future falling-out, or upon a suspicion of my taking the trust out of your hands, to employ some other, you yourself should betray your trust, dear sir? I mean, if you'll give me leave to speak obscenely, you might tell, dear sir.

HORNER. If I did, nobody would believe me. The reputation of impotency is as hardly recovered again in the world as that of cowardice, dear madam.

LADY FIDGET. Nay, then, as one may say, you may do your worst, dear, dear sir.

SIR JASPER. Come, is your ladyship reconciled to him yet? have you agreed on matters? for I must be gone to Whitehall.

LADY FIDGET. Why, indeed, Sir Jasper, Master Horner is a thousand, thousand times a better man than I thought him. Cousin Squeamish, sister Dainty, I can name him now. Truly, not long ago, you know, I thought his very name obscenity; and I would as soon have lain with him as have named him.

SIR JASPER. Very likely, poor madam.

MRS. DAINTY. I believe it.

MRS. SQUEAMISH. No doubt on't.

SIR JASPER. Well, well—that your ladyship is as virtuous as any she, I know, and him all the town knows—he! he! he! therefore now you like him, get you gone to your business together, go, go to your business, I say, pleasure, whilst I go to my pleasure, business.

LADY FIDGET. Come, then, dear gallant.

HORNER. Come away, my dearest mistress.

SIR JASPER. So, so; why, 'tis as I'd have it. [*Exit.*]

HORNER. And as I'd have it.

LADY FIDGET. Who for his business from his wife will run,

    Takes the best care to have her business done.

    [*Exeunt.*]

Act III

SCENE I.—A *Room in* PINCHWIFE'S *House.*

[*Enter* ALITHEA *and* MRS. PINCHWIFE.]

ALITHEA. Sister, what ails you? you are grown melancholy.

MRS. PINCHWIFE. Would it not make any one melancholy to see you go every day fluttering about abroad, whilst I must stay at home like a poor lonely sullen bird in a cage?

ALITHEA. Ay, sister; but you came young, and just from the nest to your cage: so that I thought you liked it, and could be as cheerful in't as others that took their flight themselves early, and are hopping abroad in the open air.

MRS. PINCHWIFE. Nay, I confess I was quiet enough till my husband told me what pure lives the London ladies live abroad, with their dancing, meetings, and junketings, and dressed every day in their best gowns; and I warrant you, play at nine-pins every day of the week, so they do.

[*Enter* PINCHWIFE.]

PINCHWIFE. Come, what's here to do? you are putting the town-pleasures in her head, and setting her a-longing.

ALITHEA. Yes, after nine-pins. You suffer none to give her those longings you mean but yourself.

PINCHWIFE. I tell her of the vanities of the town like a confessor.

ALITHEA. A confessor! just such a confessor as he that, by forbidding a silly ostler to grease the horse's teeth, taught him to do't.

PINCHWIFE. Come, Mrs. Flippant, good precepts are lost when bad examples are still before us: the liberty you take abroad makes her hanker after it, and out of humour at home. Poor wretch! she desired not to come to London; I would bring her.

ALITHEA. Very well.

PINCHWIFE. She has been this week in town, and never desired till this afternoon to go abroad.

ALITHEA. Was she not at a play yesterday?

PINCHWIFE. Yes; but she ne'er asked me; I was myself the cause of her going.

ALITHEA. Then if she ask you again, you are the cause of her asking, and not my example.

PINCHWIFE. Well, to-morrow night I shall be rid of you; and the next day, before 'tis light, she and I'll be rid of the town, and my dreadful apprehensions.—Come, be not melancholy; for thou sha't go into the country after to-morrow, dearest.

ALITHEA. Great comfort!

MRS. PINCHWIFE. Pish! what d'ye tell me of the country for?

PINCHWIFE. How's this! what, pish at the country?

MRS. PINCHWIFE. Let me alone; I am not well.

PINCHWIFE. Oh, if that be all—what ails my dearest?

MRS. PINCHWIFE. Truly, I don't know: but I have not been well since you told me there was a gallant at the play in love with me.

PINCHWIFE. Ha!—

ALITHEA. That's by my example too!

PINCHWIFE. Nay, if you are not well, but are so concerned, because a lewd fellow chanced to lie, and say he liked you, you'll make me sick too.

MRS. PINCHWIFE. Of what sickness?

PINCHWIFE. O, of that which is worse than the plague, jealousy.

MRS. PINCHWIFE. Pish, you jeer! I'm sure there's no such disease in our receipt-book at home.

PINCHWIFE. No, thou never met'st with it, poor innocent.—Well, if thou cuckold me, 'twill be my own fault—for cuckolds and bastards are generally makers of their own fortune. [*aside*]

MRS. PINCHWIFE. Well, but pray, bud, let's go to a play tonight.

PINCHWIFE. 'Tis just done, she comes from it. But why are you so eager to see a play?

MRS. PINCHWIFE. Faith, dear, not that I care one pin for their talk there; but I like to look upon the player-men, and would see, if I could, the gallant you say loves me: that's all, dear bud.

PINCHWIFE. Is that all, dear bud?

ALITHEA. This proceeds from my example!

MRS. PINCHWIFE. But if the play be done, let's go abroad, however, dear bud.

PINCHWIFE. Come have a little patience and thou shalt go into the country on Friday.

MRS. PINCHWIFE. Therefore I would see first some sights to tell my neighbours of. Nay, I will go abroad, that's once.

ALITHEA. I'm the cause of this desire too!

PINCHWIFE. But now I think on't, who, who was the cause of Horner's coming to my lodgings to-day? That was you.

ALITHEA. No, you, because you would not let him see your handsome wife out of your lodging.

MRS. PINCHWIFE. Why, O Lord! did the gentleman come hither to see me indeed?

PINCHWIFE. No, no.—You are not the cause of that damned question too, Mistress Alithea?—[*aside*] Well, she's in the right of it. He is in love with my wife—and comes after her—'tis so—but I'll nip his love in the bud; lest he should follow us into the country, and break his chariot-wheel near our house, on purpose for an excuse to come to't. But I think I know the town.

MRS. PINCHWIFE. Come, pray, bud, let's go abroad before 'tis late; for I will go, that's flat and plain.

PINCHWIFE. [*aside*] So! the obstinacy already of the town-wife; and I must, whilst she's here, humour her like one.—[*aloud*]

Sister, how shall we do, that she may not be seen, or known?

ALITHEA. Let her put on her mask.

PINCHWIFE. Pshaw! a mask makes people but the more inquisitive, and is as ridiculous a disguise as a stage-beard: her shape, stature, habit will be known. And if we should meet with Horner, he would be sure to take acquaintance with us, must wish her joy, kiss her, talk to her, leer upon her, and the devil and all. No, I'll not use her to a mask, 'tis dangerous; for masks have made more cuckolds than the best faces that ever were known.

ALITHEA. How will you do then?

MRS. PINCHWIFE. Nay, shall we go? The Exchange will be shut, and I have a mind to see that.

PINCHWIFE. So—I have it—I'll dress her up in the suit we are to carry down to her brother, little Sir James; nay, I understand the town-tricks. Come, let's go dress her. A mask! no—a woman masked, like a covered dish, gives a man curiosity and appetite; when, it may be, uncovered, 'twould turn his stomach: no, no.

ALITHEA. Indeed your comparison is something a greasy one: but I had a gentle gallant used to say, A beauty masked, like the sun in eclipse, gathers together more gazers than if it shined out.

[*Exeunt.*]

SCENE II.—*The New Exchange.*

[*Enter* HORNER, HARCOURT, *and* DORILANT.]

DORILANT. Engaged to women, and not sup with us!

HORNER. Ay, a pox on 'em all!

HARCOURT. You were much a more reasonable man in the morning, and had as noble resolutions against 'em, as a widower of a week's liberty.

DORILANT. Did I ever think to see you keep company with women in vain?

HORNER. In vain: no—'tis since I can't love 'em, to be revenged on 'em.

HARCOURT. Now your sting is gone, you looked in the box amongst all those women like a drone in the hive; all upon you, shoved and ill-used by 'em all, and thrust from one side to t'other.

DORILANT. Yet he must be buzzing amongst 'em still, like other beetle-headed liquorish drones. Avoid 'em, and hate 'em, as they hate you.

HORNER. Because I do hate 'em, and would hate 'em yet more, I'll frequent 'em. You may see by marriage, nothing makes a man hate a woman more than her constant conversation. In short, I converse with 'em, as you do with rich fools, to laugh at 'em and use 'em ill.

DORILANT. But I would no more sup with women, unless I could lie with 'em, than sup with a rich coxcomb, unless I could cheat him.

HORNER. Yes, I have known thee sup with a fool for his drinking; if he could set out your hand that way only, you were satisfied, and if he were a wine-swallowing mouth, 'twas enough.

HARCOURT. Yes, a man drinks often with a fool, as he tosses with a
marker, only to keep his hand in use. But do the ladies drink?

HORNER. Yes, sir; and I shall have the pleasure at least of laying
'em flat with a bottle, and bring as much scandal that way upon
'em as formerly t'other.

HARCOURT. Perhaps you may prove as weak a brother among 'em
that way as t'other.

DORILANT. Foh! drinking with women is as unnatural as scolding
with 'em. But 'tis a pleasure of decayed fornicators, and the basest
way of quenching love.

HARCOURT. Nay, 'tis drowning love, instead of quenching it. But
leave us for civil women too!

DORILANT. Ay, when he can't be the better for 'em. We hardly
pardon a man that leaves his friend for a wench, and that's a
pretty lawful call.

HORNER. Faith, I would not leave you for 'em, if they would not
drink.

DORILANT. Who would disappoint his company at Lewis's for a
gossiping?

HARCOURT. Foh! Wine and women, good apart, together are as
nauseous as sack and sugar. But hark you, sir, before you go, a
little of your advice; an old maimed general, when unfit for action, is fittest for counsel. I have other designs upon women than
eating and drinking with them; I am in love with Sparkish's
mistress, whom he is to marry to-morrow: now how shall I get
her?

[*Enter* SPARKISH, *looking about.*]

HORNER. Why, here comes one will help you to her.

HARCOURT. He! he, I tell you, is my rival, and will hinder my love.

HORNER. No; a foolish rival and a jealous husband assist their rival's
designs; for they are sure to make their women hate them, which
is the first step to their love for another man.

HARCOURT. But I cannot come near his mistress but in his company.

HORNER. Still the better for you; for fools are most easily cheated
when they themselves are accessaries: and he is to be bubbled
of his mistress as of his money, the common mistress, by keeping
him company.

SPARKISH. Who is that that is to be bubbled? Faith, let me snack; I
han't met with a bubble since Christmas. 'Gad, I think bubbles
are like their brother woodcocks, go out with the cold weather.

HARCOURT. A pox! he did not hear all, I hope. [*apart to* HORNER]

SPARKISH. Come, you bubbling rogues you, where do we sup?—Oh,
Harcourt, my mistress tells me you have been making fierce love
to her all the play long: ha! ha!—But I—

HARCOURT. I make love to her!

SPARKISH. Nay, I forgive thee, for I think I know thee, and I know
her; but I am sure I know myself.

HARCOURT. Did she tell you so? I see all women are like these of
the Exchange; who, to enhance the prize of their commodities,

report to their fond customers offers which were never made 'em.

HORNER. Ay, women are apt to tell before the intrigue, as men after it, and so show themselves the vainer sex. But hast thou a mistress, Sparkish? 'Tis as hard for me to believe it, as that thou ever hadst a bubble, as you bragged just now.

SPARKISH. O, your servant, sir: are you at your raillery, sir? But we are some of us beforehand with you to-day at the play. The wits were something bold with you, sir; did you not hear us laugh?

HORNER. Yes; but I thought you had gone to plays, to laugh at the poet's wit, not at your own.

SPARKISH. Your servant, sir: no, I thank you. 'Gad I go to a play as to a country treat; I carry my own wine to one, and my own wit to t'other, or else I'm sure I should not be merry at either. And the reason why we are so often louder than the players, is, because we think we speak more wit, and so become the poet's rivals in his audience: for to tell you the truth, we hate the silly rogues; nay, so much, that we find fault even with their bawdy upon the stage, whilst we talk nothing else in the pit as loud.

HORNER. But why shouldst thou hate the silly poets? Thou hast too much wit to be one; and they, like whores, are only hated by each other: and thou dost scorn writing, I'm sure.

SPARKISH. Yes; I'd have you to know I scorn writing: but women, women, that make men do all foolish things, make 'em write songs too. Everybody does it. 'Tis even as common with lovers, as playing with fans; and you can no more help rhyming to your Phillis, than drinking to your Phillis.

HARCOURT. Nay, poetry in love is no more to be avoided than jealousy.

DORILANT. But the poets damned your songs, did they?

SPARKISH. Damn the poets! they have turned 'em into burlesque, as they call it. That burlesque is a hocus-pocus trick they have got, which, by the virtue of *Hictius doctius topsy turvy*, they make a wise and witty man in the world, a fool upon the stage you know not how: and 'tis therefore I hate 'em too, for I know not but it may be my own case; for they'll put a man into a play for looking asquint. Their predecessors were contented to make serving-men only their stage-fools: but these rogues must have gentlemen, with a pox to 'em, nay, knights; and, indeed, you shall hardly see a fool upon the stage but he's a knight. And to tell you the truth, they have kept me these six years from being a knight in earnest, for fear of being knighted in a play, and dubbed a fool.

DORILANT. Blame 'em not, they must follow their copy, the age.

HARCOURT. But why shouldst thou be afraid of being in a play, who expose yourself every day in the play-houses, and at public places?

HORNER. 'Tis but being on the stage, instead of standing on a bench in the pit.

DORILANT. Don't you give money to painters to draw you like? and are you afraid of your pictures at length in a playhouse, where all your mistresses may see you?

SPARKISH. A pox! painters don't draw the small-pox or pimples in one's face. Come, damn all your silly authors whatever, all books and booksellers, by the world; and all readers, courteous or uncourteous!

HARCOURT. But who comes here, Sparkish?

[*Enter* PINCHWIFE *and* MRS. PINCHWIFE *in man's clothes,* ALITHEA, *and* LUCY.]

SPARKISH. Oh, hide me! There's my mistress too.

[SPARKISH *hides himself behind* HARCOURT.]

HARCOURT. She sees you.

SPARKISH. But I will not see her. 'Tis time to go to Whitehall, and I must not fail the drawing-room.

HARCOURT. Pray, first carry me, and reconcile me to her.

SPARKISH. Another time. Faith, the king will have supped.

HARCOURT. Not with the worse stomach for thy absence. Thou art one of those fools that think their attendance at the king's meals as necessary as his physicians, when you are more troublesome to him than his doctors or his dogs.

SPARKISH. Pshaw! I know my interest, sir. Prithee hide me.

HORNER. Your servant, Pinchwife.—What, he knows us not!

PINCHWIFE. Come along. [*to his wife aside*]

MRS. PINCHWIFE. Pray, have you any ballads? give me sixpenny worth.

BOOKSELLER. We have no ballads.

MRS. PINCHWIFE. Then give me "Covent Garden Drollery," and a play or two—Oh, here's "Tarugo's Wiles," and "The Slighted Maiden"; I'll have them.

PINCHWIFE. No; plays are not for your reading. Come along; will you discover yourself? [*apart to her*]

HORNER. Who is that pretty youth with him, Sparkish?

SPARKISH. I believe his wife's brother, because he's something like her: but I never saw her but once.

HORNER. Extremely handsome; I have seen a face like it too. Let us follow 'em.

[*Exeunt* PINCHWIFE, MRS. PINCHWIFE, ALITHEA, *and* LUCY; HORNER *and* DORILANT *following them.*]

HARCOURT. Come, Sparkish, your mistress saw you, and will be angry you go not to her. Besides, I would fain be reconciled to her, which none but you can do, dear friend.

SPARKISH. Well, that's a better reason, dear friend. I would not go near her now for her's or my own sake; but I can deny you nothing: for though I have known thee a great while, never go, if I do not love thee as well as a new acquaintance.

HARCOURT. I am obliged to you indeed, dear friend. I would be well with her, only to be well with thee still; for these ties to wives usually dissolve all ties to friends. I would be contented she should enjoy you a-nights, but I would have you to myself a-days as I have had, dear friend.

SPARKISH. And thou shalt enjoy me a-days, dear, dear friend, never stir: and I'll be divorced from her, sooner than from thee. Come along.

HARCOURT. [*aside*] So, we are hard put to't, when we make our rival our procurer; but neither she nor her brother would let me come near her now. When all's done, a rival is the best cloak to steal to a mistress under, without suspicion; and when we have once got to her as we desire, we throw him off like other cloaks.

[*Exit* SPARKISH, HARCOURT *following him. Re-enter* PINCH-WIFE *and* MRS. PINCHWIFE.]

PINCHWIFE. [*to* ALITHEA] Sister, if you will not go, we must leave you.[2]—[*aside*] The fool her gallant and she will muster up all the young saunterers of this place, and they will leave their dear sempstresses to follow us. What a swarm of cuckolds and cuckold-makers are here!—Come, let's be gone, Mistress Margery.

MRS. PINCHWIFE. Don't you believe that; I han't half my bellyfull of sights yet.

PINCHWIFE. Then walk this way.

MRS. PINCHWIFE. Lord, what a power of brave signs are here! stay —the Bull's-Head, the Ram's-Head, and the Stag's-Head, dear—

PINCHWIFE. Nay, if every husband's proper sign here were visible, they would be all alike.

MRS. PINCHWIFE. What d'ye mean by that, bud?

PINCHWIFE. 'Tis no matter—no matter, bud.

MRS. PINCHWIFE. Pray tell me: nay, I will know.

PINCHWIFE. They would be all Bulls, Stags, and Ramsheads.

[*Exeunt* PINCHWIFE *and* MRS. PINCHWIFE. *Re-enter* SPARK-ISH, HARCOURT, ALITHEA, *and* LUCY, *at the other side.*]

SPARKISH. Come, dear madam, for my sake you shall be reconciled to him.

ALITHEA. For your sake I hate him.

HARCOURT. That's something too cruel, madam, to hate me for his sake.

SPARKISH. Ay indeed, madam, too, too cruel to me, to hate my friend for my sake.

ALITHEA. I hate him because he is your enemy; and you ought to hate him too, for making love to me, if you love me.

SPARKISH. That's a good one! I hate a man for loving you! If he did love you, 'tis but what he can't help; and 'tis your fault, not his, if he admires you. I hate a man for being of my opinion! I'll n'er do't, by the world.

ALITHEA. Is it for your honour, or mine, to suffer a man to make love to me, who am to marry you to-morrow?

SPARKISH. Is it for your honour, or mine, to have me jealous? That he makes love to you, is a sign you are handsome; and that I am not jealous, is a sign you are virtuous. That I think is for your honour.

ALITHEA. But 'tis your honour too I am concerned for.

HARCOURT. But why, dearest madam, will you be more concerned

2. This line is spoken as he enters, directed off-stage where Alithea is pre-sumably talking to Sparkish and the others.

for his honour than he is himself? Let his honour alone, for my
sake and his. He! he has no honour—

SPARKISH. How's that?

HARCOURT. But what my dear friend can guard himself.

SPARKISH. O ho—that's right again.

HARCOURT. Your care of his honour argues his neglect of it, which
is no honour to my dear friend here. Therefore once more, let his
honour go which way it will, dear madam.

SPARKISH. Ay, ay; were it for my honour to marry a woman whose
virtue I suspected, and could not trust her in a friend's hands?

ALITHEA. Are you not afraid to lose me?

HARCOURT. He afraid to lose you, madam! No, no—you may see
how the most estimable and most glorious creature in the world
is valued by him. Will you not see it?

SPARKISH. Right, honest Frank, I have that noble value for her that
I cannot be jealous of her.

ALITHEA. You mistake him. He means, you care not for me, nor
who has me.

SPARKISH. Lord, madam, I see you are jealous! Will you wrest a
poor man's meaning from his words?

ALITHEA. You astonish me, sir, with your want of jealousy.

SPARKISH. And you make me giddy, madam, with your jealousy and
fears, and virtue and honour. 'Gad, I see virtue makes a woman
as troublesome as a little reading or learning.

ALITHEA. Monstrous!

LUCY. Well, to see what easy husbands these women of quality
can meet with! a poor chambermaid can never have such ladylike
luck. Besides, he's thrown away upon her. She'll make no use of
her fortune, her blessing, none to a gentleman, for a pure cuckold;
for it requires good breeding to be a cuckold. [*aside*]

ALITHEA. I tell you then plainly, he pursues me to marry me.

SPARKISH. Pshaw!

HARCOURT. Come, madam, you see you strive in vain to make him
jealous of me. My dear friend is the kindest creature in the world
to me.

SPARKISH. Poor fellow!

HARCOURT. But his kindness only is not enough for me, without
your favour, your good opinion, dear madam: 'tis that must
perfect my happiness. Good gentleman, he believes all I say:
would you would do so! Jealous of me! I would not wrong him
nor you for the world.

SPARKISH. Look you there. Hear him, hear him, and do not walk
away so.

[ALITHEA *walks carelessly to and fro.*]

HARCOURT. I love you, madam, so—

SPARKISH. How's that? Nay, now you begin to go too far indeed.

HARCOURT. So much, I confess, I say, I love you, that I would not
have you miserable, and cast yourself away upon so unworthy
and inconsiderable a thing as what you see here. [*clapping his
hand on his breast, points at* SPARKISH]

SPARKISH. No, faith, I believe thou wouldst not: now his meaning is plain; but I knew before thou wouldst not wrong me, nor her.

HARCOURT. No, no, Heavens forbid the glory of her sex should fall so low, as into the embraces of such a contemptible wretch, the least of mankind—my friend here—I injure him! [*embracing* SPARKISH]

ALITHEA. Very well.

SPARKISH. No, no, dear friend, I knew it.—Madam, you see he will rather wrong himself than me, in giving himself such names.

ALITHEA. Do not you understand him yet?

SPARKISH. Yes: how modestly he speaks of himself, poor fellow!

ALITHEA. Methinks he speaks impudently of yourself, since—before yourself too; insomuch that I can no longer suffer his scurrilous abusiveness to you, no more than his love to me. [*offers to go*]

SPARKISH. Nay, nay, madam, pray stay—his love to you! Lord madam, has he not spoke yet plain enough?

ALITHEA. Yes, indeed, I should think so.

SPARKISH. Well then, by the world, a man can't speak civilly to a woman now, but presently she says, he makes love to her. Nay, madam, you shall stay, with your pardon, since you have not yet understood him, till he has made an eclaircissement of his love to you, that is, what kind of love it is. Answer to thy catechism, friend; do you love my mistress here?

HARCOURT. Yes, I wish she would not doubt it.

SPARKISH. But how do you love her?

HARCOURT. With all my soul.

ALITHEA. I thank him, methinks he speaks plain enough now.

SPARKISH. [*to* ALITHEA] You are out still.—But with what kind of love, Harcourt?

HARCOURT. With the best and the truest love in the world.

SPARKISH. Look you there then, that is with no matrimonial love, I'm sure.

ALITHEA. How's that? do you say matrimonial love is not best?

SPARKISH. 'Gad, I went too far ere I was aware. But speak for thyself, Harcourt, you said you would not wrong me nor her.

HARCOURT. No, no, madam, e'en take him for Heaven's sake.

SPARKISH. Look you there, madam.

HARCOURT. Who should in all justice be yours, he that loves you most. [*claps his hand on his breast*]

ALITHEA. Look you there, Mr. Sparkish, who's that?

SPARKISH. Who should it be?—Go on, Harcourt.

HARCOURT. Who loves you more than women, titles, or fortune fools. [*points at* SPARKISH]

SPARKISH. Look you there, he means me still, for he points at me.

ALITHEA. Ridiculous!

HARCOURT. Who can only match your faith and constancy in love.

SPARKISH. Ay.

HARCOURT. Who knows, if it be possible, how to value so much beauty and virtue.

SPARKISH. Ay.

HARCOURT. Whose love can no more be equalled in the world, than that heavenly form of yours.

SPARKISH. No.

HARCOURT. Who could no more suffer a rival, than your absence, and yet could no more suspect your virtue, than his own constancy in his love to you.

SPARKISH. No.

HARCOURT. Who, in fine, loves you better than his eyes, that first made him love you.

SPARKISH. Ay—Nay, madam, faith, you shan't go till—

ALITHEA. Have a care, lest you make me stay too long.

SPARKISH. But till he has saluted you; that I may be assured you are friends, after his honest advice and declaration. Come, pray, madam, be friends with him.

[*Re-enter* PINCHWIFE *and* MRS. PINCHWIFE.]

ALITHEA. You must pardon me, sir, that I am not yet so obedient to you.

PINCHWIFE. What, invite your wife to kiss men? Monstrous! are you not ashamed? I will never forgive you.

SPARKISH. Are you not ashamed, that I should have more confidence in the chastity of your family than you have? You must not teach me, I am a man of honour, sir, though I am frank and free; I am frank, sir—

PINCHWIFE. Very frank, sir, to share your wife with your friends.

SPARKISH. He is an humble, menial friend, such as reconciles the differences of the marriage bed; you know man and wife do not always agree; I design him for that use, therefore would have him well with my wife.

PINCHWIFE. A menial friend!—you will get a great many menial friends, by showing your wife as you do.

SPARKISH. What then? It may be I have a pleasure in't, as I have to show fine cloths at a play-house, the first day, and count money before poor rogues.

PINCHWIFE. He that shows his wife or money, will be in danger of having them borrowed sometimes.

SPARKISH. I love to be envied, and would not marry a wife that I alone could love; loving alone is as dull as eating alone. Is it not a frank age? and I am a frank person; and to tell you the truth, it may be, I love to have rivals in a wife, they make her seem to a man still but as a kept mistress; and so good night, for I must to Whitehall.—Madam, I hope you are now reconciled to my friend; and so I wish you a good night, madam, and sleep if you can: for to-morrow you know I must visit you early with a canonical gentleman. Good night, dear Harcourt. [*Exit.*]

HARCOURT. Madam, I hope you will not refuse my visit tomorrow, if it should be earlier with a canonical gentleman than Mr. Sparkish's.

PINCHWIFE. This gentlewoman is yet under my care, therefore you must yet forbear your freedom with her, sir. [*coming between* ALITHEA *and* HARCOURT]

HARCOURT. Must, sir?

PINCHWIFE. Yes, sir, she is my sister.

HARCOURT. 'Tis well she is, sir—for I must be her servant, sir.— Madam—

PINCHWIFE. Come away, sister, we had been gone, if it had not been for you, and so avoided these lewd rake-hells, who seem to haunt us.

[*Re-enter* HORNER *and* DORILANT.]

HORNER. How now, Pinchwife!

PINCHWIFE. Your servant.

HORNER. What! I see a little time in the country makes a man turn wild and unsociable, and only fit to converse with his horses, dogs, and his herds.

PINCHWIFE. I have business, sir, and must mind it; your business is pleasure, therefore you and I must go different ways.

HORNER. Well, you may go on, but this pretty young gentleman— [*takes hold of* MRS. PINCHWIFE]

HARCOURT. The lady—

DORILANT. And the maid—

HORNER. Shall stay with us; for I suppose their business is the same with ours, pleasure.

PINCHWIFE. 'Sdeath, he knows her, she carries it so sillily! yet if he does not, I should be more silly to discover it first. [*aside*]

ALITHEA. Pray, let us go, sir.

PINCHWIFE. Come, come—

HORNER. [*to* MRS. PINCHWIFE] Had you not rather stay with us?— Prithee, Pinchwife, who is this pretty young gentleman?

PINCHWIFE. One to whom I'm a guardian.—[*aside*] I wish I could keep her out of your hands.

HORNER. Who is he? I never saw anything so pretty in all my life.

PINCHWIFE. Pshaw! do not look upon him so much, he's a poor bashful youth, you'll put him out of countenance.—Come away, brother. [*offers to take her away*]

HORNER. O, your brother!

PINCHWIFE. Yes, my wife's brother.—Come, come, she'll stay supper for us.

HORNER. I thought so, for he is very like her I saw you at the play with, whom I told you I was in love with.

MRS. PINCHWIFE. [*aside*] O jeminy! is that he that was in love with me? I am glad on't, I vow, for he's a curious fine gentleman, and I love him already, too.—[*to* PINCHWIFE] Is this he, bud?

PINCHWIFE. Come away, come away. [*to his wife*]

HORNER. Why, what haste are you in? why wont you let me talk with him?

PINCHWIFE. Because you'll debauch him; he's yet young and innocent, and I would not have him debauched for anything in the world.—[*aside*] How she gazes on him! the devil!

HORNER. Harcourt, Dorilant, look you here, this is the likeness of that dowdy he told us of, his wife; did you ever see a lovelier creature? The rogue has reason to be jealous of his wife, since she is like him, for she would make all that see her in love with her.

HARCOURT. And, as I remember now, she is as like him here as can be.

DORILANT. She is indeed very pretty, if she be like him.

HORNER. Very pretty? a very pretty commendation!—she is a glorious creature, beautiful beyond all things I ever beheld.

PINCHWIFE. So, so.

HARCOURT. More beautiful than a poet's first mistress of imagination.

HORNER. Or another man's last mistress of flesh and blood.

MRS. PINCHWIFE. Nay, now you jeer, sir; pray don't jeer me.

PINCHWIFE. Come, come.—[*aside*] By Heavens, she'll discover herself!

HORNER. I speak of your sister, sir.

PINCHWIFE. Ay, but saying she was handsome, if like him, made him blush.—[*aside*] I am upon a rack!

HORNER. Methinks he is so handsome he should not be a man.

PINCHWIFE. [*aside*] O, there 'tis out! he has discovered her! I am not able to suffer any longer.—[*to his wife*] Come, come away, I say.

HORNER. Nay, by your leave, sir, he shall not go yet.—[*aside to them*] Harcourt, Dorilant, let us torment this jealous rogue a little.

HARCOURT, DORILANT. How?

HORNER. I'll show you.

PINCHWIFE. Come, pray let him go, I cannot stay fooling any longer; I tell you his sister stays supper for us.

HORNER. Does she? Come then, we'll all go to sup with her and thee.

PINCHWIFE. No, now I think on't, having stayed so long for us, I warrant she's gone to bed.—[*aside*] I wish she and I were well out of their hands.—[*to his wife*] Come, I must rise early to-morrow, come.

HORNER. Well then, if she be gone to bed, I wish her and you a good night. But pray, young gentleman, present my humble service to her.

MRS. PINCHWIFE. Thank you heartily, sir.

PINCHWIFE. [*aside*] 'Sdeath, she will discover herself yet in spite of me.—[*aloud*] He is something more civil to you, for your kindness to his sister, than I am, it seems.

HORNER. Tell her, dear sweet little gentleman, for all your brother there, that you have revived the love I had for her at first sight in the playhouse.

MRS. PINCHWIFE. But did you love her indeed, and indeed?

PINCHWIFE. [*aside*] So, so.—[*aloud*] Away, I say.

HORNER. Nay, stay.—Yes, indeed, and indeed, pray do you tell her so, and give her this kiss from me. [*kisses her*]

PINCHWIFE. [*aside*] O Heavens! what do I suffer? Now 'tis too plain he knows her, and yet—

HORNER. And this, and this—[*kisses her again*]

MRS. PINCHWIFE. What do you kiss me for? I am no woman.

PINCHWIFE. [*aside*] So, there, 'tis out.—[*aloud*] Come, I cannot, nor will stay any longer.

HORNER. Nay, they shall send your lady a kiss too. Here, Harcourt, Dorilant, will you not? [*They kiss her.*]

PINCHWIFE. [*aside*] How! do I suffer this? Was I not accusing another just now for this rascally patience, in permitting his wife to be kissed before his face? Ten thousand ulcers gnaw away their lips.—[*aloud*] Come, come.

HORNER. Good night, dear little gentleman; madam, good night; farewell, Pinchwife.—[*apart to* HARCOURT *and* DORILANT] Did not I tell you I would raise his jealous gall?

[*Exeunt* HORNER, HARCOURT, *and* DORILANT.]

PINCHWIFE. So, they are gone at last; stay, let me see first if the coach be at this door. [*Exit.*]

[*Re-enter* HORNER, HARCOURT, *and* DORILANT.]

HORNER. What, not gone yet? Will you be sure to do as I desired you, sweet sir?

MRS. PINCHWIFE. Sweet sir, but what will you give me then?

HORNER. Anything. Come away into the next walk. [*exit, haling away* MRS. PINCHWIFE]

ALITHEA. Hold! hold! what d'ye do?

LUCY. Stay, stay, hold—

HARCOURT. Hold, madam, hold, let him present him—he'll come presently; nay, I will never let you go till you answer my question.

LUCY. For God's sake, sir, I must follow 'em.

[ALITHEA *and* LUCY, *struggling with* HARCOURT *and* DORILANT.]

DORILANT. No, I have something to present you with too, you shan't follow them.

[*Re-enter* PINCHWIFE.]

PINCHWIFE. Where?—how—what's become of?—gone!—whither?

LUCY. He's only gone with the gentleman, who will give him something, an't please your worship.

PINCHWIFE. Something!—give him something, with a pox!—where are they?

ALITHEA. In the next walk only, brother.

PINCHWIFE. Only, only! where, where? [*Exit and returns presently, then goes out again.*]

HARCOURT. What's the matter with him? why so much concerned? But, dearest madam—

ALITHEA. Pray let me go, sir; I have said and suffered enough already.

HARCOURT. Then you will not look upon, nor pity, my sufferings?

ALITHEA. To look upon 'em, when I cannot help 'em, were cruelty, not pity; therefore, I will never see you more.

HARCOURT. Let me then, madam, have my privilege of a banished lover, complaining or railing, and giving you but a farewell reason why, if you cannot condescend to marry me, you should not take that wretch, my rival.

ALITHEA. He only, not you, since my honour is engaged so far to him, can give me a reason why I should not marry him; but if he be true, and what I think him to me, I must be so to him. Your servant, sir.

HARCOURT. Have women only constancy when 'tis a vice, and are, like Fortune, only true to fools?

DORILANT. Thou sha't not stir, thou robust creature; you see I can deal with you, therefore you should stay the rather, and be kind. [*to* LUCY, *who struggles to get from him*]

[*Re-enter* PINCHWIFE.]

PINCHWIFE. Gone, gone, not to be found! quite gone! ten thousand plagues go with 'em! Which way went they?

ALITHEA. But into t'other walk, brother.

LUCY. Their business will be done presently sure, an't please your worship; it can't be long in doing, I'm sure on't.

ALITHEA. Are they not there?

PINCHWIFE. No, you know where they are, you infamous wretch, eternal shame of your family, which you do not dishonour enough yourself you think, but you must help her to do it too, thou legion of bawds—

ALITHEA. Good brother—

PINCHWIFE. Damned, damned sister!

ALITHEA. Look you here, she's coming.

[*Re-enter* MRS. PINCHWIFE *running, with her hat full of oranges and dried fruit under her arm,* HORNER *following.*]

MRS. PINCHWIFE. O dear bud, look you here what I have got, see!

PINCHWIFE. And what I have got here too, which you can't see. [*aside, rubbing his forehead*]

MRS. PINCHWIFE. The fine gentleman has given me better things yet.

PINCHWIFE. Has he so?—[*aside*] Out of breath and coloured!— I must hold yet.

HORNER. I have only given your little brother an orange, sir.

PINCHWIFE. [*to* HORNER] Thank you, sir.—[*aside*] You have only squeezed my orange, I suppose, and given it me again; yet I must have a city patience.—[*to his wife*] Come, come away.

MRS. PINCHWIFE. Stay, till I have put up my fine things, bud.

[*Enter* SIR JASPER FIDGET.]

SIR JASPER. O, Master Horner, come, come, the ladies stay for you; your mistress, my wife, wonders you make not more haste to her.

HORNER. I have stayed this half hour for you here, and 'tis your fault I am not now with your wife.

SIR JASPER. But, pray, don't let her know so much; the truth on't is, I was advancing a certain project to his majesty about—I'll tell you.

HORNER. No, let's go, and hear it at your house. Good night, sweet little gentleman; one kiss more, you'll remember me now, I hope. [*kisses her*]

DORILANT. What, Sir Jasper, will you separate friends? He promised to sup with us, and if you take him to your house, you'll be in danger of our company too.

SIR JASPER. Alas! gentlemen, my house is not fit for you; there are none but civil women there, which are not for your turn. He, you know, can bear with the society of civil women now, ha! ha! ha! besides, he's one of my family—he's—he! he! he!

DORILANT. What is he?

SIR JASPER. Faith, my eunuch, since you'll have it; he! he! he!

[*Exeunt* SIR JASPER FIDGET *and* HORNER.]

DORILANT. I rather wish thou wert his or my cuckold. Harcourt, what a good cuckold is lost there for want of a man to make him one? Thee and I cannot have Horner's privilege, who can make use of it.

HARCOURT. Ay, to poor Horner 'tis like coming to an estate at threescore, when a man can't be the better for't.

PINCHWIFE. Come.

MRS. PINCHWIFE. Presently, bud.

DORILANT. Come, let us go too.—[*to* ALITHEA] Madam, your servant.—[*to* LUCY] Good night, strapper.

HARCOURT. Madam, though you will not let me have a good day or night, I wish you one; but dare not name the other half of my wish.

ALITHEA. Good night, sir, for ever.

MRS. PINCHWIFE. I don't know where to put this here, dear bud, you shall eat it; nay, you shall have part of the fine gentleman's good things, or treat, as you call it, when we come home.

PINCHWIFE. Indeed, I deserve it, since I furnished the best part of it. [*strikes away the orange*]

> The gallant treats presents, and gives the ball;
> But 'tis the absent cuckold pays for all.

[*Exeunt.*]

Act IV

SCENE I.—PINCHWIFE'S *House in the morning.*

[*Enter* ALITHEA *dressed in new clothes, and* LUCY.]

LUCY. Well—madam, now have I dressed you, and set you out with so many ornaments, and spent upon you ounces of essence and pulvillio; and all this for no other purpose but as people adorn and perfume a corpse for a stinking second-hand grave: such, or as bad, I think Master Sparkish's bed.

ALITHEA. Hold your peace.

LUCY. Nay, madam, I will ask you the reason why you would banish poor Master Harcourt for ever from your sight; how could you be so hard-hearted?

ALITHEA. 'Twas because I was not hard-hearted.

LUCY. No, no; 'twas stark love and kindness, I warrant.

ALITHEA. It was so; I would see him no more because I love him.

LUCY. Hey day, a very pretty reason!

ALITHEA. You do not understand me.

LUCY. I wish you may yourself.

ALITHEA. I was engaged to marry, you see, another man, whom my justice will not suffer me to deceive or injure.

LUCY. Can there be a greater cheat or wrong done to a man than to give him your person without your heart? I should make a conscience of it.

ALITHEA. I'll retrieve it for him after I am married a while.

LUCY. The woman that marries to love better, will be as much mistaken as the wencher that marries to live better. No, madam, marrying to increase love is like gaming to become rich; alas! you only lose what little stock you had before.

ALITHEA. I find by your rhetoric you have been bribed to betray me.

LUCY. Only by his merit, that has bribed your heart, you see, against your word and rigid honour. But what a devil is this honour! 'tis sure a disease in the head, like the megrim or falling-sickness, that always hurries people away to do themselves mischief. Men lose their lives by it; women, what's dearer to 'em, their love, the life of life.

ALITHEA. Come, pray talk you no more of honour, nor Master Harcourt; I wish the other would come to secure my fidelity to him and his right in me.

LUCY. You will marry him then?

ALITHEA. Certainly, I have given him already my word, and will my hand too, to make it good, when he comes.

LUCY. Well, I wish I may never stick pin more, if he be not an arrant natural, to t'other fine gentleman.

ALITHEA. I own he wants the wit of Harcourt, which I will dispense withal for another want he has, which is want of jealousy, which men of wit seldom want.

LUCY. Lord, madam, what should you do with a fool to your husband? You intend to be honest, don't you? then that husbandly virtue, credulity, is thrown away upon you.

ALITHEA. He only that could suspect my virtue should have cause to do it; 'tis Sparkish's confidence in my truth that obliges me to be so faithful to him.

LUCY. You are not sure his opinion may last.

ALITHEA. I am satisfied, 'tis impossible for him to be jealous after the proofs I have had of him. Jealousy in a husband—Heaven defend me from it! it begets a thousand plagues to a poor woman, the loss of her honour, her quiet, and her—

LUCY. And her pleasure.

ALITHEA. What d'ye mean, impertinent?

LUCY. Liberty is a great pleasure, madam.

ALITHEA. I say, loss of her honour, her quiet, nay, her life sometimes; and what's as bad almost, the loss of this town; that is, she is sent into the country, which is the last ill-usage of a husband to a wife, I think.

LUCY. [*aside*] O, does the wind lie there?—[*aloud*] Then of necessity, madam, you think a man must carry his wife into the country, if he be wise. The country is as terrible, I find, to our young English ladies, as a monastery to those abroad; and on my virginity, I think they would rather marry a London jailer, than a high sheriff of a county, since neither can stir from his employment. Formerly women of wit married fools for a great estate, a fine seat, or the like; but now 'tis for a pretty seat only in Lincoln's-Inn-Fields, St. James's-Fields, or the Pall-Mall.[3]

[*Enter* SPARKISH, *and* HARCOURT, *dressed like a parson.*]

SPARKISH. Madam, your humble servant, a happy day to you, and to us all.

HARCOURT. Amen.

ALITHEA. Who have we here?

SPARKISH. My chaplain, faith—O madam, poor Harcourt remembers his humble service to you; and, in obedience to your last commands, refrains coming into your sight.

ALITHEA. Is not that he?

SPARKISH. No, fy, no; but to show that he ne'er intended to hinder our match, has sent his brother here to join our hands. When I get me a wife, I must get her a chaplain, according to the custom; that is his brother, and my chaplain.

ALITHEA. His brother!

LUCY. And your chaplain, to preach in your pulpit then—[*aside*]

ALITHEA. His brother!

SPARKISH. Nay, I knew you would not believe it.—I told you, sir, she would take you for your brother Frank.

ALITHEA. Believe it!

LUCY. His brother! ha! ha! he! he has a trick left still, it seems. [*aside*]

SPARKISH. Come, my dearest, pray let us go to church before the canonical hour is past.

ALITHEA. For shame, you are abused still.

SPARKISH. By the world, 'tis strange now you are so incredulous.

ALITHEA. 'Tis strange you are so credulous.

SPARKISH. Dearest of my life, hear me. I tell you this is Ned Harcourt of Cambridge, by the world; you see he has a sneaking college look. 'Tis true he's something like his brother Frank; and they differ from each other no more than in their age, for they were twins.

LUCY. Ha! ha! ha!

ALITHEA. Your servant, sir; I cannot be so deceived, though you are. But come, let's hear, how do you know what you affirm so confidently?

SPARKISH. Why, I'll tell you all. Frank Harcourt coming to me this morning to wish me joy, and present his service to you, I asked him if he could help me to a parson. Whereupon he told me, he had a brother in town who was in orders; and he went straight away, and sent him, you see there, to me.

ALITHEA. Yes, Frank goes and puts on a black coat, then tells you he is Ned; that's all you have for't.

3. Fashionable residential areas in London.

SPARKISH. Pshaw! pshaw! I tell you, by the same token, the mid-wife put her garter about Frank's neck, to know 'em asunder, they were so like.

ALITHEA. Frank tells you this too?

SPARKISH. Ay, and Ned there too: nay, they are both in a story.

ALITHEA. So, so; very foolish.

SPARKISH. Lord, if you won't believe one, you had best try him by your chambermaid there; for chambermaids must needs know chaplains from other men, they are so used to 'em.

LUCY. Let's see: nay, I'll be sworn he has the canonical smirk, and the filthy clammy palm of a chaplain.

ALITHEA. Well, most reverend doctor, pray let us make an end of this fooling.

HARCOURT. With all my soul, divine heavenly creature, when you please.

ALITHEA. He speaks like a chaplain indeed.

SPARKISH. Why, was there not soul, divine, heavenly, in what he said?

ALITHEA. Once more, most impertinent black coat, cease your persecution, and let us have a conclusion of this ridiculous love.

HARCOURT. I had forgot, I must suit my style to my coat, or I wear it in vain. [*aside*]

ALITHEA. I have no more patience left; let us make once an end of this troublesome love, I say.

HARCOURT. So be it, seraphic lady, when your honour shall think it meet and convenient so to do.

SPARKISH. 'Gad I'm sure none but a chaplain could speak so, I think.

ALITHEA. Let me tell you, sir, this dull trick will not serve your turn; though you delay our marriage, you shall not hinder it.

HARCOURT. Far be it from me, munificent patroness, to delay your marriage; I desire nothing more than to marry you presently, which I might do, if you yourself would; for my noble, good-natured, and thrice generous patron here would not hinder it.

SPARKISH. No, poor man, not I, faith.

HARCOURT. And now, madam, let me tell you plainly nobody else shall marry you; by Heavens! I'll die first, for I'm sure I should die after it.

LUCY. How his love has made him forget his function, as I have seen it in real parsons!

ALITHEA. That was spoken like a chaplain too? now you understand him, I hope.

SPARKISH. Poor man, he takes it heinously to be refused; I can't blame him, 'tis putting an indignity upon him, not to be suffered; but you'll pardon me, madam, it shan't be; he shall marry us; come away, pray madam.

LUCY. Ha! ha! he! more ado! 'tis late.

ALITHEA. Invincible stupidity! I tell you, he would marry me as your rival, not as your chaplain.

SPARKISH. Come, come, madam. [*pulling her away*]

LUCY. I pray, madam, do not refuse this reverend divine the honour and satisfaction of marrying you; for I dare say, he has set his heart upon't, good doctor.

ALITHEA. What can you hope or design by this?

HARCOURT. I could answer her, a reprieve for a day only, often revokes a hasty doom. At worst, if she will not take mercy on me, and let me marry her, I have at least the lover's second pleasure, hindering my rival's enjoyment, though but for a time. [*aside*]

SPARKISH. Come, madam, 'tis e'en twelve o'clock, and my mother charged me never to be married out of the canonical hours. Come, come; Lord, here's such a deal of modesty, I warrant, the first day.

LUCY. Yes, an't please your worship, married women show all their modesty the first day, because married men show all their love the first day.

[*Exeunt.*]

SCENE II.—A *Bedchamber in* PINCHWIFE's *House.*

[PINCHWIFE *and* MRS. PINCHWIFE *discovered.*]

PINCHWIFE. Come, tell me, I say.

MRS. PINCHWIFE. Lord! han't I told it a hundred times over?

PINCHWIFE. [*aside*] I would try, if in the repetition of the ungrateful tale, I could find her altering it in the least circumstance; for if her story be false, she is so too.—[*aloud*] Come, how was't, baggage?

MRS. PINCHWIFE. Lord, what pleasure you take to hear it sure!

PINCHWIFE. No, you take more in telling it I find; but speak, how was't?

MRS. PINCHWIFE. He carried me up into the house next to the Exchange.

PINCHWIFE. So, and you two were only in the room!

MRS. PINCHWIFE. Yes, for he sent away a youth that was there, for some dried fruit, and China oranges.

PINCHWIFE. Did he so? Damn him for it—and for—

MRS. PINCHWIFE. But presently came up the gentlewoman of the house.

PINCHWIFE. O, 'twas well she did; but what did he do whilst the fruit came?

MRS. PINCHWIFE. He kissed me a hundred times, and told me he fancied he kissed my fine sister, meaning me, you know, whom he said he loved with all his soul, and bid me be sure to tell her so, and to desire her to be at her window, by eleven of the clock this morning, and he would walk under it at that time.

PINCHWIFE. And he was as good as his word, very punctual; a pox reward him for't. [*aside*]

MRS. PINCHWIFE. Well, and he said if you were not within, he would come up to her, meaning me, you know, bud, still.

PINCHWIFE. [*aside*] So—he knew her certainly; but for this confession, I am obliged to her simplicity.—[*aloud*] But what, you stood very still when he kissed you?

MRS. PINCHWIFE. Yes, I warrant you; would you have had me discover myself?

PINCHWIFE. But you told me he did some beastliness to you, as you call it; what was't?

MRS. PINCHWIFE. Why, he put—

PINCHWIFE. What?

MRS. PINCHWIFE. Why, he put the tip of his tongue between my lips, and so mousled me—and I said, I'd bite it.

PINCHWIFE. An eternal canker seize it, for a dog!

MRS. PINCHWIFE. Nay, you need not be so angry with him neither, for to say truth, he has the sweetest breath I ever knew.

PINCHWIFE. The devil! you were satisfied with it then, and would do it again?

MRS. PINCHWIFE. Not unless he should force me.

PINCHWIFE. Force you, changeling! I tell you, no woman can be forced.

MRS. PINCHWIFE. Yes, but she may sure, by such a one as he, for he's a proper, goodly, strong man; 'tis hard, let me tell you, to resist him.

PINCHWIFE. [aside] So, 'tis plain she loves him, yet she has not love enough to make her conceal it from me; but the sight of him will increase her aversion for me and love for him; and that love instruct her how to deceive me and satisfy him, all idiot as she is. Love! 'twas he gave women first their craft, their art of deluding. Out of Nature's hands they came plain, open, silly, and fit for slaves, as she and Heaven intended 'em; but damned Love—well—I must strangle that little monster whilst I can deal with him.—[aloud] Go fetch pen, ink, and paper out of the next room.

MRS. PINCHWIFE. Yes, bud. [Exit.]

PINCHWIFE. Why should women have more invention in love than men? It can only be, because they have more desires, more soliciting passions, more lust, and more of the devil. [re-enter MRS. PINCHWIFE] Come, minx, sit down and write.

MRS. PINCHWIFE. Ay, dear bud, but I can't do't very well.

PINCHWIFE. I wish you could not at all.

MRS. PINCHWIFE. But what should I write for?

PINCHWIFE. I'll have you write a letter to your lover.

MRS. PINCHWIFE. O Lord, to the fine gentleman a letter!

PINCHWIFE. Yes, to the fine gentleman.

MRS. PINCHWIFE. Lord, you do but jeer: sure you jest.

PINCHWIFE. I am not so merry: come, write as I bid you.

MRS. PINCHWIFE. What, do you think I am a fool?

PINCHWIFE. [aside] She's afraid I would not dictate any love to him, therefore she's unwilling.—[aloud] But you had best begin.

MRS. PINCHWIFE. Indeed, and indeed, but I won't, so I won't.

PINCHWIFE. Why?

MRS. PINCHWIFE. Because he's in town; you may send for him if you will.

PINCHWIFE. Very well, you would have him brought to you; is it come to this? I say, take the pen and write, or you'll provoke me.

MRS. PINCHWIFE. Lord, what d'ye make a fool of me for? Don't I know that letters are never writ but from the country to London, and from London into the country? Now he's in town, and I am in town too; therefore I can't write to him, you know.

PINCHWIFE. [*aside*] So, I am glad it is no worse; she is innocent enough yet.—[*aloud*] Yes, you may, when your husband bids you, write letters to people that are in town.

MRS. PINCHWIFE. O, may I so? then I'm satisfied.

PINCHWIFE. Come, begin:—"Sir"—[*dictates*]

MRS. PINCHWIFE. Shan't I say, "Dear Sir?"—You know one says always something more than bare "sir."

PINCHWIFE. Write as I bid you, or I will write whore with this penknife in your face.

MRS. PINCHWIFE. Nay, good bud—"Sir"—[*writes*]

PINCHWIFE. "Though I suffered last night your nauseous, loathed kisses and embraces"—Write!

MRS. PINCHWIFE. Nay, why should I say so? You know I told you he had a sweet breath.

PINCHWIFE. Write!

MRS. PINCHWIFE. Let me but put out "loathed."

PINCHWIFE. Write, I say!

MRS. PINCHWIFE. Well then. [*writes*]

PINCHWIFE. Let's see, what have you writ?—[*takes the paper and reads*] "Though I suffered last night your kisses and embraces" —Thou impudent creature! where is "nauseous" and "loathed?"

MRS. PINCHWIFE. I can't abide to write such filthy words.

PINCHWIFE. Once more write as I'd have you, and question it not, or I will spoil thy writing with this. I will stab out those eyes that cause my mischief. [*holds up the penknife*]

MRS. PINCHWIFE. O Lord! I will.

PINCHWIFE. So—so—let's see now.—[*reads*] "Though I suffered last night your nauseous, loathed kisses and embraces"—go on— "yet I would not have you presume that you shall ever repeat them"—so—[*She writes.*]

MRS. PINCHWIFE. I have writ it.

PINCHWIFE. On, then—"I then concealed myself from your knowledge, to avoid your insolencies."—[*She writes.*]

MRS. PINCHWIFE. So—

PINCHWIFE. "The same reason, now I am out of your hands—" [*She writes.*]

MRS. PINCHWIFE. So—

PINCHWIFE. "Makes me own to you my unfortunate, though innocent frolic, of being in man's clothes"—[*She writes.*]

MRS. PINCHWIFE. So—

PINCHWIFE. "That you may for evermore cease to pursue her, who hates and detests you"—[*She writes on.*]

MRS. PINCHWIFE. So—heigh! [*sighs*]

PINCHWIFE. What, do you sigh?—"detests you—as much as she loves her husband and her honour—"

MRS. PINCHWIFE. I vow, husband, he'll ne'er believe I should write such a letter.

PINCHWIFE. What, he'd expect a kinder from you? Come, now your name only.

MRS. PINCHWIFE. What, shan't I say "Your most faithful humble servant till death?"

PINCHWIFE. No, tormenting fiend!—[*aside*] Her style, I find, would be very soft.—[*aloud*] Come, wrap it up now, whilst I go fetch wax and a candle; and write on the backside, "For Mr. Horner." [*Exit.*]

MRS. PINCHWIFE. "For Mr. Horner."—So, I am glad he has told me his name. Dear Mr. Horner! but why should I send thee such a letter that will vex thee, and make thee angry with me?— Well, I will not send it.—Ay, but then my husband will kill me— for I see plainly he won't let me love Mr. Horner—but what care I for my husband?—I won't, so I won't, send poor Mr. Horner such a letter—But then my husband—but oh, what if I writ at bottom my husband made me write it?—Ay, but then my husband would see't—Can one have no shift? ah, a London woman would have had a hundred presently. Stay—what if I should write a letter, and wrap it up like this, and write upon't too? Ay, but then my husband would see't—I don't know what to do.—But yet evads I'll try, so I will—for I will not send this letter to poor Mr. Horner, come what will on't.

"Dear, sweet Mr. Horner"—[*writes and repeats what she writes*]—so—"my husband would have me send you a base, rude, unmannerly letter; but I won't"—so—"and would have me forbid you loving me; but I won't"—so—"and would have me say to you, I hate you, poor Mr. Horner; but I won't tell a lie for him"—there—"for I'm sure if you and I were in the country at cards together"—so—"I could not help treading on your toe under the table"—so—"or rubbing knees with you, and staring in your face, till you saw me"—very well—"and then looking down, and blushing for an hour together"—so—"but I must make haste before my husband comes: and now he has taught me to write letters, you shall have longer ones from me, who am, dear, dear, poor, dear Mr. Horner, your most humble friend, and servant to command till death,—Margery Pinchwife."

Stay, I must give him a hint at bottom—so—now wrap it up just like t'other—so—now write "For Mr. Horner"—But oh now, what shall I do with it? for here comes my husband.

[*Re-enter* PINCHWIFE.]

PINCHWIFE. [*aside*] I have been detained by a sparkish coxcomb, who pretended a visit to me; but I fear 'twas to my wife—[*aloud*] What, have you done?

MRS. PINCHWIFE. Ay, ay, bud, just now.

PINCHWIFE. Let's see't: what d'ye tremble for? what, you would not have it go?

MRS. PINCHWIFE. Here—[*aside*] No, I must not give him that: so
I had been served if I had given him this.

[*He opens and reads the first letter.*]

PINCHWIFE. Come, where's the wax and seal?

MRS. PINCHWIFE. [*aside*] Lord, what shall I do now? Nay, then I
have it—[*aloud*] Pray let me see't. Lord, you think me so arrant
a fool, I cannot seal a letter; I will do't, so I will. [*snatches the
letter from him, changes it for the other, seals it, and delivers
it to him*]

PINCHWIFE. Nay, I believe you will learn that, and other things too,
which I would not have you.

MRS. PINCHWIFE. So, han't I done it curiously?—[*aside*] I think
I have; there's my letter going to Mr. Horner, since he'll needs
have me send letters to folks.

PINCHWIFE. 'Tis very well; but I warrant, you would not have it go
now?

MRS. PINCHWIFE. Yes, indeed, but I would, bud, now.

PINCHWIFE. Well, you are a good girl then. Come, let me lock you
up in your chamber, till I come back; and be sure you come not
within three strides of the window when I am gone, for I have
a spy in the street.—[*Exit* MRS. PINCHWIFE, PINCHWIFE *locks the
door.*] At least, 'tis fit she think so. If we do not cheat women,
they'll cheat us, and fraud may be justly used with secret enemies,
of which a wife is the most dangerous; and he that has a handsome one to keep, and a frontier town, must provide against
treachery, rather than open force. Now I have secured all within,
I'll deal with the foe without, with false intelligence. [*Holds up
the letter. Exit.*]

SCENE III.—HORNER'S *Lodging*

[*Enter* HORNER *and* QUACK.]

QUACK. Well, sir, how fadges the new design? have you not the
luck of all your brother projectors, to deceive only yourself at
last?

HORNER. No, good domine doctor, I deceive you, it seems, and
others too; for the grave matrons, and old, rigid husbands think
me as unfit for love, as they are; but their wives, sisters, and
daughters know, some of 'em, better things already.

QUACK. Already!

HORNER. Already, I say. Last night I was drunk with half-a-dozen
of your civil persons, as you call 'em, and people of honour, and
so was made free of their society and dressing-rooms for ever
hereafter; and am already come to the privileges of sleeping upon
their pallets, warming smocks, tying shoes and garters, and the
like, doctor, already, already, doctor.

QUACK. You have made good use of your time, sir.

HORNER. I tell thee, I am now no more interruption to 'em, when
they sing, or talk bawdy, than a little squab French page who
speaks no English.

QUACK. But do civil persons and women of honour drink, and sing bawdy songs?

HORNER. O, amongst friends, amongst friends. For your bigots in honour are just like those in religion; they fear the eye of the world more than the eye of Heaven; and think there is no virtue, but railing at vice, and no sin, but giving scandal. They rail at a poor, little, kept player, and keep themselves some young, modest pulpit comedian to be privy to their sins in their closets, not to tell 'em of them in their chapels.

QUACK. Nay, the truth on't is, priests, amongst the women now, have quite got the better of us lay-confessors, physicians.

HORNER. And they are rather their patients; but—

[*Enter* LADY FIDGET, *looking about her.*]

Now we talk of women of honour, here comes one. Step behind the screen there, and but observe, if I have not particular privileges with the women of reputation already, doctor, already.

[QUACK *retires.*]

LADY FIDGET. Well, Horner, am not I a woman of honour? you see, I'm as good as my word.

HORNER. And you shall see, madam, I'll not be behindhand with you in honour; and I'll be as good as my word too, if you please but to withdraw into the next room.

LADY FIDGET. But first, my dear sir, you must promise to have a care of my dear honour.

HORNER. If you talk a word more of your honour, you'll make me incapable to wrong it. To talk of honour in the mysteries of love, is like talking of Heaven or the Deity, in an operation of witchcraft, just when you are employing the devil: it makes the charm impotent.

LADY FIDGET. Nay, fy! let us not be smutty. But you talk of mysteries and bewitching to me; I don't understand you.

HORNER. I tell you, madam, the word money in a mistress's mouth, at such a nick of time, is not a more disheartening sound to a younger brother, than that of honour to an eager lover like myself.

LADY FIDGET. But you can't blame a lady of my reputation to be chary.

HORNER. Chary! I have been chary of it already, by the report I have caused of myself.

LADY FIDGET. Ay, but if you should ever let other women know that dear secret, it would come out. Nay, you must have a great care of your conduct; for my acquaintance are so censorious, (oh, 'tis a wicked, censorious world, Mr. Horner!) I say, are so censorious, and detracting, that perhaps they'll talk to the prejudice of my honour, though you should not let them know the dear secret.

HORNER. Nay, madam, rather than they shall prejudice your honour, I'll prejudice theirs; and, to serve you, I'll lie with 'em all, make the secret their own, and then they'll keep it. I am a Machiavel[4]

4. Machiavelli's name had become a common synonym for a cunning conniver. That is what comes of an author's name being better known than his book.

in love, madam.

LADY FIDGET. O, no sir, not that way.

HORNER. Nay, the devil take me, if censorious women are to be silenced any other way.

LADY FIDGET. A secret is better kept, I hope, by a single person than a multitude; therefore pray do not trust anybody else with it, dear, dear Mr. Horner. [*embracing him*]

[*Enter* SIR JASPER FIDGET.]

SIR JASPER. How now!

LADY FIDGET. [*aside*] O my husband!—prevented—and what's almost as bad, found with my arms about another man—that will appear too much—what shall I say?—[*aloud*] Sir Jasper, come hither: I am trying if Mr. Horner were ticklish, and he's as ticklish as can be. I love to torment the confounded toad; let you and I tickle him.

SIR JASPER. No, your ladyship will tickle him better without me, I suppose. But is this your buying china? I thought you had been at the china-house.

HORNER. [*aside*] China-house! that's my cue, I must take it.— [*aloud*] A pox! can't you keep your impertinent wives at home? Some men are troubled with the husbands, but I with the wives; but I'd have you to know, since I cannot be your journeyman by night, I will not be your drudge by day, to squire your wife about, and be your man of straw, or scarecrow only to pies and jays, that would be nibbling at your forbidden fruit; I shall be shortly the hackney gentleman-usher of the town.

SIR JASPER. [*aside*] He! he! he! poor fellow, he's in the right on't, faith. To squire women about for other folks is as ungrateful an employment, as to tell money for other folks.—[*aloud*] He! he! he! be'n't angry, Horner.

LADY FIDGET. No, 'tis I have more reason to be angry, who am left by you, to go abroad indecently alone; or, what is more indecent, to pin myself upon such ill-bred people of your acquaintance as this is.

SIR JASPER. Nay, prithee, what has he done?

LADY FIDGET. Nay, he has done nothing.

SIR JASPER. But what d'ye take ill, if he has done nothing?

LADY FIDGET. Ha! ha! ha! faith, I can't but laugh however; why, d'ye think the unmannerly toad would come down to me to the coach? I was fain to come up to fetch him, or go without him, which I was resolved not to do; for he knows china very well, and has himself very good, but will not let me see it, lest I should beg some; but I will find it out, and have what I came for yet.

HORNER. [*apart to* LADY FIDGET, *as he follows her to the door*] Lock the door, madam.—[*Exit* LADY FIDGET, *and locks the door.*]— [*aloud*] So, she has got into my chamber and locked me out. Oh the impertinency of woman-kind! Well, Sir Jasper, plain-dealing is a jewel; if ever you suffer your wife to trouble me again here, she shall carry you home a pair of horns; by my lord mayor she shall; though I cannot furnish you myself, you are sure, yet I'll find a way.

SIR JASPER. Ha! ha! he!—[*aside*] At my first coming in, and finding her arms about him, tickling him it seems, I was half jealous, but now I see my folly.—[*aloud*] He! he! he! poor Horner.

HORNER. Nay, though you laugh now, 'twill be my turn ere long. Oh women, more impertinent, more cunning, and more mischievous than their monkeys, and to me almost as ugly!—Now is she throwing my things about and rifling all I have; but I'll get into her the back way, and so rifle her for it.

SIR JASPER. Ha! ha! ha! poor angry Horner.

HORNER. Stay here a little, I'll ferret her out to you presently, I warrant. [*Exit at the other door.*]

[SIR JASPER *talks through the door to his wife, she answers from within.*]

SIR JASPER. Wife! my Lady Fidget! wife! he is coming in to you the back way.

LADY FIDGET. Let him come, and welcome, which way he will.

SIR JASPER. He'll catch you, and use you roughly, and be too strong for you.

LADY FIDGET. Don't you trouble yourself, let him if he can.

QUACK. [*aside*] This indeed I could not have believed from him, nor any but my own eyes.

[*Enter* MRS. SQUEAMISH.]

MRS. SQUEAMISH. Where's this woman-hater, this toad, this ugly, greasy, dirty sloven?

SIR JASPER. [*aside*] So, the women all will have him ugly: methinks he is a comely person, but his wants make his form contemptible to 'em; and 'tis e'en as my wife said yesterday, talking of him, that a proper handsome eunuch was as ridiculous a thing as a gigantic coward.

MRS. SQUEAMISH. Sir Jasper, your servant: where is the odious beast?

SIR JASPER. He's within in his chamber, with my wife; she's playing the wag with him.

MRS. SQUEAMISH. Is she so? and he's a clownish beast, he'll give her no quarter, he'll play the wag with her again, let me tell you: come, let's go help her—What, the door's locked?

SIR JASPER. Ay, my wife locked it.

MRS. SQUEAMISH. Did she so? let's break it open then.

SIR JASPER. No, no, he'll do her no hurt.

MRS. SQUEAMISH. [*aside*] But is there no other way to get in to 'em? whither goes this? I will disturb 'em. [*Exit at another door.*]

[*Enter* OLD LADY SQUEAMISH.]

LADY SQUEAMISH. Where is this harlotry, this impudent baggage, this rambling tomrigg?[5] O Sir Jasper, I'm glad to see you here; did you not see my vile grandchild come in hither just now?

SIR JASPER. Yes.

LADY SQUEAMISH. Ay, but where is she then? where is she? Lord, Sir Jasper, I have e'en rattled myself to pieces in pursuit of her: but can you tell what she makes here? they say below, no woman

5. Tomboy.

lodges here.

SIR JASPER. No.

LADY SQUEAMISH. No! what does she here then? say, if it be not a
woman's lodging, what makes she here? But are you sure no
woman lodges here?

SIR JASPER. No, nor no man neither, this is Mr. Horner's lodging.

LADY SQUEAMISH. Is it so, are you sure?

SIR JASPER. Yes, yes.

LADY SQUEAMISH. So; then there's no hurt in't, I hope. But where
is he?

SIR JASPER. He's in the next room with my wife.

LADY SQUEAMISH. Nay, if you trust him with your wife, I may with
my Biddy. They say, he's a merry harmless man now, e'en as
harmless a man as ever came out of Italy with a good voice, and
as pretty, harmless company for a lady, as a snake without his
teeth.

SIR JASPER. Ay, ay, poor man.

[*Re-enter* MRS. SQUEAMISH.]

MRS. SQUEAMISH. I can't find 'em.—Oh, are you here, grandmother?
I followed, you must know, my Lady Fidget hither; 'tis the prettiest lodging, and I have been staring on the prettiest pictures—

[*Re-enter* LADY FIDGET *with a piece of china in her hand,
and* HORNER *following.*]

LADY FIDGET. And I have been toiling and moiling for the prettiest
piece of china, my dear.

HORNER. Nay, she has been too hard for me, do what I could.

MRS. SQUEAMISH. Oh, lord, I'll have some china too. Good Mr.
Horner, don't think to give other people china and me none;
come in with me too.

HORNER. Upon my honour, I have none left now.

MRS. SQUEAMISH. Nay, nay, I have known you deny your china before now, but you shan't put me off so. Come.

HORNER. This lady had the last there.

LADY FIDGET. Yes indeed, madam, to my certain knowledge, he has
no more left.

MRS. SQUEAMISH. O, but it may be he may have some you could not
find.

LADY FIDGET. What, d'ye think if he had had any left, I would not
have had it too? for we women of quality never think we have
china enough.

HORNER. Do not take it ill, I cannot make china for you all, but I
will have a roll-waggon for you too, another time.

MRS. SQUEAMISH. Thank you, dear toad.

LADY FIDGET. What do you mean by that promise? [*aside to*
HORNER]

HORNER. Alas, she has an innocent, literal understanding. [*aside to*
LADY FIDGET]

LADY SQUEAMISH. Poor Mr. Horner! he has enough to do to please
you all, I see.

HORNER. Ay, madam, you see how they use me.

LADY SQUEAMISH. Poor gentleman, I pity you.

HORNER. I thank you, madam: I could never find pity, but from such reverend ladies as you are; the young ones will never spare a man.

MRS. SQUEAMISH. Come, come, beast, and go dine with us; for we shall want a man at ombre after dinner.

HORNER. That's all their use of me, madam, you see.

MRS. SQUEAMISH. Come, sloven, I'll lead you, to be sure of you. [*pulls him by the cravat*]

LADY SQUEAMISH. Alas, poor man, how she tugs him! Kiss, kiss her; that's the way to make such nice women quiet.

HORNER. No, madam, that remedy is worse than the torment; they know I dare suffer anything rather than do it.

LADY SQUEAMISH. Prithee kiss her, and I'll give you her picture in little, that you admired so last night; prithee do.

HORNER. Well, nothing but that could bribe me: I love a woman only in effigy, and good painting as much as I hate them.—I'll do't, for I could adore the devil well painted. [*kisses* MRS. SQUEAMISH]

MRS. SQUEAMISH. Foh, you filthy toad! nay, now I've done jesting.

LADY SQUEAMISH. Ha! ha! ha! I told you so.

MRS. SQUEAMISH. Foh! a kiss of his—

SIR JASPER. Has no more hurt in't than one of my spaniel's.

MRS. SQUEAMISH. Nor no more good neither.

QUACK. I will now believe anything he tells me. [*aside*]

[*Enter* PINCHWIFE.]

LADY FIDGET. O lord, here's a man! Sir Jasper, my mask, my mask! I would not be seen here for the world.

SIR JASPER. What, not when I am with you?

LADY FIDGET. No, no, my honour—let's be gone.

MRS. SQUEAMISH. Oh grandmother, let's be gone; make haste, make haste, I know not how he may censure us.

LADY FIDGET. Be found in the lodging of anything like a man!— Away.

[*Exeunt* SIR JASPER FIDGET, LADY FIDGET, OLD LADY SQUEAMISH, *and* MRS. SQUEAMISH.]

QUACK. What's here? another cuckold? he looks like one, and none else sure have any business with him. [*aside*]

HORNER. Well, what brings my dear friend hither?

PINCHWIFE. Your impertinency.

HORNER. My impertinency!—why, you gentlemen that have got handsome wives, think you have a privilege of saying anything to your friends, and are as brutish as if you were our creditors.

PINCHWIFE. No, sir, I'll ne'er trust you any way.

HORNER. But why not, dear Jack? why diffide⁶ in me thou know'st so well?

PINCHWIFE. Because I do know you so well.

HORNER. Han't I been always thy friend, honest Jack, always ready to serve thee, in love or battle, before thou wert married, and am

6. Distrust.

so still?

PINCHWIFE. I believe so, you would be my second now, indeed.

HORNER. Well then, dear Jack, why so unkind, so grum, so strange to me? Come, prithee kiss me, dear rogue: gad I was always, I say, and am still as much thy servant as—

PINCHWIFE. As I am yours, sir. What, you would send a kiss to my wife, is that it?

HORNER. So, there 'tis—a man can't show his friendship to a married man, but presently he talks of his wife to you. Prithee, let thy wife alone, and let thee and I be all one, as we were wont. What, thou art as shy of my kindness, as a Lombard-street alderman of a courtier's civility at Locket's!

PINCHWIFE. But you are over-kind to me, as kind as if I were your cuckold already; yet I must confess you ought to be kind and civil to me, since I am so kind, so civil to you, as to bring you this: look you there, sir. [*delivers him a letter*]

HORNER. What is't?

PINCHWIFE. Only a love-letter, sir.

HORNER. From whom?—how! this is from your wife—hum—and hum—[*reads*]

PINCHWIFE. Even from my wife, sir: am I not wondrous kind and civil to you now too?—[*aside*] But you'll not think her so.

HORNER. Ha! is this a trick of his or hers? [*aside*]

PINCHWIFE. The gentleman's surprised I find.—What, you expected a kinder letter?

HORNER. No faith, not I, how could I?

PINCHWIFE. Yes, yes, I'm sure you did. A man so well made as you are, must needs be disappointed, if the women declare not their passion at first sight or opportunity.

HORNER. [*aside*] But what should this mean? Stay, the postscript— [*reads aside*] "Be sure you love me, whatsoever my husband says to the contrary, and let him not see this, lest he should come home and pinch me, or kill my squirrel."—It seems he knows not what the letter contains.

PINCHWIFE. Come, ne'er wonder at it so much.

HORNER. Faith, I can't help it.

PINCHWIFE. Now, I think I have deserved your infinite friendship and kindness, and have showed myself sufficiently an obliging kind friend and husband; am I not so, to bring a letter from my wife to her gallant?

HORNER. Ay, the devil take me, art thou, the most obliging, kind friend and husband in the world, ha! ha!

PINCHWIFE. Well, you may be merry, sir; but in short I must tell you, sir, my honour will suffer no jesting.

HORNER. What dost thou mean?

PINCHWIFE. Does the letter want a comment? Then, know, sir, though I have been so civil a husband, as to bring you a letter from my wife, to let you kiss and court her to my face, I will not be a cuckold, sir, I will not.

HORNER. Thou art mad with jealousy. I never saw thy wife in my life but at the play yesterday, and I know not if it were she or no. I court her, kiss her!

PINCHWIFE. I will not be a cuckold, I say; there will be danger in making me a cuckold.

HORNER. Why, wert thou not well cured of thy last clap?

PINCHWIFE. I wear a sword.

HORNER. It should be taken from thee, lest thou shouldst do thyself a mischief with it; thou art mad, man.

PINCHWIFE. As mad as I am, and as merry as you are, I must have more reason from you ere we part. I say again, though you kissed and courted last night my wife in man's clothes, as she confesses in her letter—

HORNER. Ha! [*aside*]

PINCHWIFE. Both she and I say, you must not design it again, for you have mistaken your woman, as you have done your man.

HORNER. [*aside*] O—I understand something now—[*aloud*] Was that thy wife! Why wouldst thou not tell me 'twas she? Faith, my freedom with her was your fault, not mine.

PINCHWIFE. Faith, so 'twas. [*aside*]

HORNER. Fy! I'd never do't to a woman before her husband's face, sure.

PINCHWIFE. But I had rather you should do't to my wife before my face, than behind my back; and that you shall never do.

HORNER. No—you will hinder me.

PINCHWIFE. If I would not hinder you, you see by her letter she would.

HORNER. Well, I must e'en acquiesce then, and be contented with what she writes.

PINCHWIFE. I'll assure you 'twas voluntarily writ; I had no hand in't you may believe me.

HORNER. I do believe thee, faith.

PINCHWIFE. And believe her too, for she's an innocent creature, has no dissembling in her: and so fare you well, sir.

HORNER. Pray, however, present my humble service to her, and tell her, I will obey her letter to a tittle, and fulfil her desires, be what they will, or with what difficulty soever I do't; and you shall be no more jealous of me, I warrant her, and you.

PINCHWIFE. Well then, fare you well; and play with any man's honour but mine, kiss any man's wife but mine, and welcome. [*Exit.*]

HORNER. Ha! ha! ha! doctor.

QUACK. It seems, he has not heard the report of you, or does not believe it.

HORNER. Ha! ha!—now, doctor, what think you?

QUACK. Pray let's see the letter—hum—"for—dear—love you—" [*reads the letter*]

HORNER. I wonder how she could contrive it! What say'st thou to't? 'tis an original.

QUACK. So are your cuckolds too originals: for they are like no other common cuckolds, and I will henceforth believe it not impossible for you to cuckold the Grand Signior amidst his guards of eunuchs, that I say.

HORNER. And I say for the letter, 'tis the first love-letter that ever was without flames, darts, fates, destinies, lying and dissembling in't.

[*Enter* SPARKISH *pulling in* PINCHWIFE.]

SPARKISH. Come back, you are a pretty brother-in-law, neither go to church nor to dinner with your sister bride!

PINCHWIFE. My sister denies her marriage, and you see is gone away from you dissatisfied.

SPARKISH. Pshaw! upon a foolish scruple, that our parson was not in lawful orders, and did not say all the common-prayer; but 'tis her modesty only I believe. But let all women be never so modest the first day, they'll be sure to come to themselves by night, and I shall have enough of her then. In the mean time, Harry Horner, you must dine with me: I keep my wedding at my aunt's in the Piazza.

HORNER. Thy wedding! what stale maid has lived to despair of a husband, or what young one of a gallant?

SPARKISH. O, your servant, sir—this gentleman's sister then,—no stale maid.

HORNER. I'm sorry for't.

PINCHWIFE. How comes he so concerned for her? [*aside*]

SPARKISH. You sorry for't? why, do you know any ill by her?

HORNER. No, I know none but by thee; 'tis for her sake, not yours, and another man's sake that might have hoped, I thought.

SPARKISH. Another man! another man! what is his name?

HORNER. Nay, since 'tis past, he shall be nameless.—[*aside*] Poor Harcourt! I am sorry thou hast missed her.

PINCHWIFE. He seems to be much troubled at the match. [*aside*]

SPARKISH. Prithee, tell me—Nay, you shan't go, brother.

PINCHWIFE. I must of necessity, but I'll come to you to dinner. [*Exit.*]

SPARKISH. But, Harry, what, have I a rival in my wife already? But with all my heart, for he may be of use to me hereafter; for though my hunger is now my sauce, and I can fall on heartily without, the time will come, when a rival will be as good sauce for a married man to a wife, as an orange to veal.

HORNER. O thou damned rogue! thou hast set my teeth on edge with thy orange.

SPARKISH. Then let's to dinner—there I was with you again. Come.

HORNER. But who dines with thee?

SPARKISH. My friends and relations, my brother Pinchwife, you see, of your acquaintance.

HORNER. And his wife?

SPARKISH. No, 'gad, he'll ne'er let her come amongst us good fellows; your stingy country coxcomb keeps his wife from his friends, as he does his little firkin of ale, for his own drinking, and a gentleman can't get a smack on't; but his servants, when his back is turned, broach it at their pleasures, and dust it away, ha! ha!

ha!—'Gad, I am witty, I think, considering I was married today, by the world; but come—

HORNER. No, I will not dine with you, unless you can fetch her too.

SPARKISH. Pshaw! what pleasure canst thou have with women now,
Harry?

HORNER. My eyes are not gone; I love a good prospect yet, and will
not dine with you unless she does too; go fetch her, therefore,
but do not tell her husband 'tis for my sake.

SPARKISH. Well, I'll go try what I can do; in the meantime, come
away to my aunt's lodging, 'tis in the way to Pinchwife's.

HORNER. The poor woman has called for aid, and stretched forth
her hand, doctor; I cannot but help her over the pale out of the
briars.

[*Exeunt.*]

SCENE IV.—*A Room in* PINCHWIFE'S *House.*

[MRS. PINCHWIFE *alone, leaning on her elbow.—A table,
pen, ink and paper.*]

MRS. PINCHWIFE. Well, 'tis e'en so, I have got the London disease
they call love; I am sick of my husband, and for my gallant. I
have heard this distemper called a fever, but methinks 'tis like
an ague; for when I think of my husband, I tremble, and am in
a cold sweat, and have inclinations to vomit; but when I think
of my gallant, dear Mr. Horner, my hot fit comes, and I am all
in a fever indeed; and, as in other fevers, my own chamber is
tedious to me, and I would fain be removed to his, and then
methinks I should be well. Ah, poor Mr. Horner! Well, I cannot, will not stay here; therefore I'll make an end of my letter
to him, which shall be a finer letter than my last, because I have
studied it like anything. Oh sick, sick! [*takes the pen and writes*]

[*Enter* PINCHWIFE, *who seeing her writing, steals softly behind her and looking over her shoulder, snatches the paper
from her.*]

PINCHWIFE. What, writing more letters?

MRS. PINCHWIFE. O Lord, bud, why d'ye fright me so?

[*She offers to run out; he stops her, and reads.*]

PINCHWIFE. How's this? nay, you shall not stir, madam:—"Dear,
dear, dear Mr. Horner"—very well—I have taught you to write
letters to good purpose—but let us see't. "First, I am to beg
your pardon for my boldness in writing to you, which I'd have
you to know I would not have done, had not you said first you
loved me so extremely, which if you do, you will never suffer me
to lie in the arms of another man whom I loathe, nauseate,
and detest."—Now you can write these filthy words. But what
follows?—"Therefore, I hope you will speedily find some way to
free me from this unfortunate match, which was never, I assure
you, of my choice, but I'm afraid 'tis already too far gone; however, if you love me, as I do you, you will try what you can do;
but you must help me away before to-morrow, or else, alas! I shall
be for ever out of your reach, for I can defer no longer our—

our—" what is to follow "our"?—speak, what—our journey into the country I suppose—Oh woman, damned woman! and Love, damned Love, their old tempter! for this is one of his miracles; in a moment he can make those blind that could see, and those see that were blind, those dumb that could speak, and those prattle who were dumb before; nay, what is more than all, make these dough-baked, senseless, indocile animals, women, too hard for us their politic lords and rulers, in a moment. But make an end of your letter, and then I'll make an end of you thus, and all my plagues together. [*draws his sword*]

MRS. PINCHWIFE. O Lord, O Lord, you are such a passionate man, bud!

    [*Enter* SPARKISH.]

SPARKISH. How now, what's here to do?

PINCHWIFE. This fool here now!

SPARKISH. What! drawn upon your wife? You should never do that, but at night in the dark, when you can't hurt her. This is my sister-in-law, is it not? ay, faith, e'en our country Margery; [*pulls aside her handkerchief*] one may know her. Come, she and you must go dine with me; dinner's ready, come. But where's my wife? is she not come home yet? where is she?

PINCHWIFE. Making you a cuckold; 'tis that they all do, as soon as they can.

SPARKISH. What, the wedding-day? no, a wife that designs to make a cully of her husband will be sure to let him win the first stake of love, by the world. But come, they stay dinner for us: come, I'll lead down our Margery.

PINCHWIFE. No—sir, go, we'll follow you.

SPARKISH. I will not wag without you.

PINCHWIFE. This coxcomb is a sensible torment to me amidst the greatest in the world. [*aside*]

SPARKISH. Come, come, Madam Margery.

PINCHWIFE. No; I'll lead her my way: what, would you treat your friends with mine, for want of your own wife?—[*leads her to the other door, and locks her in and returns*] I am contented my rage should take breath—[*aside*]

SPARKISH. I told Horner this.

PINCHWIFE. Come now.

SPARKISH. Lord, how shy you are of your wife! but let me tell you, brother, we men of wit have amongst us a saying, that cuckolding, like the small-pox, comes with a fear; and you may keep your wife as much as you will out of danger of infection, but if her constitution incline her to't, she'll have it sooner or later, by the world, say they.

PINCHWIFE. [*aside*] What a thing is a cuckold, that every fool can make him ridiculous!—[*aloud*] Well, sir—but let me advise you, now you are come to be concerned, because you suspect the danger, not to neglect the means to prevent it, especially when the greatest share of the malady will light upon your own head, for

Hows'e'er the kind wife's belly comes to swell,
The husband breeds for her, and first is ill.
[*Exeunt.*]

Act V

SCENE I.—PINCHWIFE'S *House.*

[*Enter* PINCHWIFE *and* MRS. PINCHWIFE. A *table and candle.*]

PINCHWIFE. Come, take the pen and make an end of the letter, just as you intended; if you are false in a tittle, I shall soon perceive it, and punish you as you deserve.—[*lays his hand on his sword*] Write what was to follow—let's see—"You must make haste, and help me away before to-morrow, or else I shall be for ever out of your reach, for I can defer no longer our"—What follows "our"?

MRS. PINCHWIFE. Must all out, then, bud?—Look you there, then.
  [MRS. PINCHWIFE *takes the pen and writes.*]

PINCHWIFE. Let's see—"For I can defer no longer our—wedding —Your slighted Alithea."—What's the meaning of this? my sister's name to't? speak, unriddle.

MRS. PINCHWIFE. Yes, indeed, bud.

PINCHWIFE. But why her name to't? speak—speak, I say.

MRS. PINCHWIFE. Ay, but you'll tell her then again. If you would not tell her again—

PINCHWIFE. I will not:—I am stunned, my head turns round.— Speak.

MRS. PINCHWIFE. Won't you tell her, indeed, and indeed?

PINCHWIFE. No; speak, I say.

MRS. PINCHWIFE. She'll be angry with me; but I had rather she should be angry with me than you, bud; And, to tell you the truth, 'twas she made me write the letter, and taught me what I should write.

PINCHWIFE. [*aside*] Ha!—I thought the style was somewhat better than her own.—[*aloud*] Could she come to you to teach you, since I had locked you up alone?

MRS. PINCHWIFE. O, through the key-hole, bud.

PINCHWIFE. But why should she make you write a letter for her to him, since she can write herself?

MRS. PINCHWIFE. Why, she said because—for I was unwilling to do it—

PINCHWIFE. Because what—because?

MRS. PINCHWIFE. Because, lest Mr. Horner should be cruel, and refuse her; or be vain afterwards, and show the letter, she might disown it, the hand not being hers.

PINCHWIFE. [*aside*] How's this? Ha!—then I think I shall come to myself again.—This changeling could not invent this lie: but if she could, why should she? she might think I should soon discover it.—Stay—now I think on't too, Horner said he was sorry she had married Sparkish; and her disowning her marriage to me makes me think she has evaded it for Horner's sake: yet why should she take this course? But men in love are fools; women may well be so—[*aloud*] But hark you, madam, your sister went out in the morning, and I have not seen her within since.

MRS. PINCHWIFE. Alack-a-day, she has been crying all day above, it seems, in a corner.

PINCHWIFE. Where is she? let me speak with her.

MRS. PINCHWIFE. [*aside*] O Lord, then she'll discover all!—[*aloud*] Pray hold, bud; what, d'ye mean to discover me? she'll know I have told you then. Pray, bud, let me talk with her first.

PINCHWIFE. I must speak with her, to know whether Horner ever made her any promise, and whether she be married to Sparkish or no.

MRS. PINCHWIFE. Pray, dear bud, don't, till I have spoken with her, and told her that I have told you all; for she'll kill me else.

PINCHWIFE. Go then, and bid her come out to me.

MRS. PINCHWIFE. Yes, yes, bud.

PINCHWIFE. Let me see—[*pausing*]

MRS. PINCHWIFE. [*aside*] I'll go, but she is not within to come to him: I have just got time to know of Lucy her maid, who first set me on work, what lie I shall tell next; for I am e'en at my wit's end. [*Exit.*]

PINCHWIFE. Well, I resolve it, Horner shall have her: I'd rather give him my sister than lend him my wife; and such an alliance will prevent his pretensions to my wife, sure. I'll make him of kin to her, and then he won't care for her.

[*Re-enter* MRS. PINCHWIFE.]

MRS. PINCHWIFE. O Lord, bud! I told you what anger you would make me with my sister.

PINCHWIFE. Won't she come hither?

MRS. PINCHWIFE. No, no. Lack-a-day, she's ashamed to look you in the face: and she says, if you go in to her, she'll run away down stairs, and shamefully go herself to Mr. Horner, who has promised her marriage, she says; and she will have no other, so she won't.

PINCHWIFE. Did he so?—promise her marriage!—then she shall have no other. Go tell her so; and if she will come and discourse with me a little concerning the means, I will about it immediately. Go.—[*Exit* MRS. PINCHWIFE.] His estate is equal to Sparkish's, and his extraction as much better than his, as his parts are; but my chief reason is, I'd rather be akin to him by the name of brother-in-law than that of cuckold. [*Re-enter* MRS. PINCHWIFE.] Well, what says she now?

MRS. PINCHWIFE. Why, she says, she would only have you lead her to Horner's lodging; with whom she first will discourse the matter before she talks with you, which yet she cannot do; for alack, poor creature, she says she can't so much as look you in the face, therefore she'll come to you in a mask. And you must excuse her, if she make you no answer to any question of yours, till you have brought her to Mr. Horner; and if you will not chide her, nor question her, she'll come out to you immediately.

PINCHWIFE. Let her come: I will not speak a word to her, nor require a word from her.

MRS. PINCHWIFE. Oh, I forgot: besides she says, she cannot look you in the face, though through a mask; therefore would desire you to put out the candle.

PINCHWIFE. I agree to all. Let her make haste.—There, 'tis out—[*Puts out the candle. Exit* MRS. PINCHWIFE.] My case is something better: I'd rather fight with Horner for not lying with my sister, than for lying with my wife; and of the two, I had rather find my sister too forward than my wife. I expected no other from her free education, as she calls it, and her passion for the town. Well, wife and sister are names which make us expect love and duty, pleasure and comfort; but we find 'em plagues and torments, and are equally, though differently, troublesome to their keeper; for we have as much ado to get people to lie with our sisters as to keep 'em from lying with our wives.

[*Re-enter* MRS. PINCHWIFE *masked, and in hoods and scarfs, and a night-gown and petticoat of* ALITHEA'S.]

What, are you come, sister? let us go then.—But first, let me lock up my wife. Mrs. Margery, where are you?

MRS. PINCHWIFE. Here, bud.

PINCHWIFE. Come hither, that I may lock you up: get you in.—[*locks the door*] Come, sister, where are you now?

[MRS. PINCHWIFE *gives him her hand; but when he lets her go, she steals softly on to the other side of him, and is led away by him for his sister,* ALITHEA.]

SCENE II.—HORNER'S *Lodging.*

[HORNER *and* QUACK.]

QUACK. What, all alone? not so much as one of your cuckolds here, nor one of their wives! They use to take their turns with you, as if they were to watch you.

HORNER. Yes, it often happens that a cuckold is but his wife's spy, and is more upon family duty when he is with her gallant abroad, hindering his pleasure, than when he is at home with her playing the gallant. But the hardest duty a married woman imposes upon a lover is keeping her husband company always.

QUACK. And his fondness wearies you almost as soon as hers.

HORNER. A pox! keeping a cuckold company, after you have had his wife, is as tiresome as the company of a country squire to a witty fellow of the town, when he has got all his money.

QUACK. And as at first a man makes a friend of the husband to get the wife, so at last you are fain to fall out with the wife to be rid of the husband.

HORNER. Ay, most cuckold-makers are true courtiers; when once a poor man has cracked his credit for 'em, they can't abide to come near him.

QUACK. But at first, to draw him in, are so sweet, so kind, so dear! just as you are to Pinchwife. But what becomes of that intrigue

372 · *William Wycherley*

with his wife?

HORNER. A pox! he's as surly as an alderman that has been bit; and since he's so coy, his wife's kindness is in vain, for she's a silly innocent.

QUACK. Did she not send you a letter by him?

HORNER. Yes; but that's a riddle I have not yet solved. Allow the poor creature to be willing, she is silly too, and he keeps her up so close—

QUACK. Yes, so close, that he makes her but the more willing, and adds but revenge to her love; which two, when met, seldom fail of satisfying each other one way or other.

HORNER. What! here's the man we are talking of, I think.

[*Enter* PINCHWIFE, *leading in his wife masked, muffled, and in her sister's gown.*]

Pshaw!

QUACK. Bringing his wife to you is the next thing to bringing a love-letter from her.

HORNER. What means this?

PINCHWIFE. The last time, you know, sir, I brought you a love-letter; now, you see, a mistress; I think you'll say I am a civil man to you.

HORNER. Ay, the devil take me, will I say thou art the civilest man I ever met with; and I have known some. I fancy I understand thee now better than I did the letter. But, hark thee, in thy ear—

PINCHWIFE. What?

HORNER. Nothing but the usual question, man: is she sound, on thy word?

PINCHWIFE. What, you take her for a wench, and me for a pimp?

HORNER. Pshaw! wench and pimp, paw[7] words; I know thou art an honest fellow, and hast a great acquaintance among the ladies, and perhaps hast made love for me, rather than let me make love to thy wife.

PINCHWIFE. Come, sir, in short, I am for no fooling.

HORNER. Nor I neither: therefore prithee, let's see her face presently. Make her show, man: art thou sure I don't know her?

PINCHWIFE. I am sure you do know her.

HORNER. A pox! why dost thou bring her to me then?

PINCHWIFE. Because she's a relation of mine—

HORNER. Is she, faith, man? then thou art still more civil and obliging, dear rogue.

PINCHWIFE. Who desired me to bring her to you.

HORNER. Then she is obliging, dear rogue.

PINCHWIFE. You'll make her welcome for my sake, I hope.

HORNER. I hope she is handsome enough to make herself welcome. Prithee let her unmask.

PINCHWIFE. Do you speak to her; she would never be ruled by me.

HORNER. Madam—[MRS. PINCHWIFE *whispers to* HORNER.] She says she must speak with me in private. Withdraw, prithee.

7. Naughty.

PINCHWIFE. [*aside*] She's unwilling, it seems, I should know all her indecent conduct in this business—[*aloud*] Well then, I'll leave you together, and hope when I am gone, you'll agree; if not, you and I shan't agree, sir.

HORNER. What means the fool? if she and I agree 'tis no matter what you and I do. [*whispers to* MRS. PINCHWIFE, *who makes signs with her hand for him to be gone*]

PINCHWIFE. In the mean time I'll fetch a parson, and find out Sparkish, and disabuse him. You would have me fetch a parson, would you not? Well then—now I think I am rid of her, and shall have no more trouble with her—our sisters and daughters, like usurers' money, are safest when put out; but our wives, like their writings, never safe, but in our closets under lock and key. [*Exit.*]

[*Enter* BOY.]

BOY. Sir Jasper Fidget, sir, is coming up. [*Exit.*]

HORNER. Here's the trouble of a cuckold now we are talking of. A pox on him! has he not enough to do to hinder his wife's sport, but he must other women's too?—Step in here, madam.

[*Exit* MRS. PINCHWIFE. *Enter* SIR JASPER FIDGET.]

SIR JASPER. My best and dearest friend.

HORNER. [*aside to* QUACK] The old style, doctor.—[*aloud*] Well, be short, for I am busy. What would your impertinent wife have now?

SIR JASPER. Well guessed, i'faith; for I do come from her.

HORNER. To invite me to supper! Tell her, I can't come: go.

SIR JASPER. Nay, now you are out, faith; for my lady, and the whole knot of the virtuous gang, as they call themselves, are resolved upon a frolic of coming to you to-night in masquerade, and are all dressed already.

HORNER. I shan't be at home.

SIR JASPER. [*aside*] Lord, how churlish he is to women!—[*aloud*] Nay, prithee don't disappoint 'em; they'll think 'tis my fault: prithee don't. I'll send in the banquet and the fiddles. But make no noise on't; for the poor virtuous rogues would not have it known, for the world, that they go a-masquerading; and they would come to no man's ball but yours.

HORNER. Well, well—get you gone; and tell 'em, if they come, t'will be at the peril of their honour and yours.

SIR JASPER. He! he! he!—we'll trust you for that: farewell. [*Exit.*]

HORNER. Doctor, anon you too shall be my guest,
But now I'm going to a private feast.
[*Exeunt.*]

SCENE III.—*The Piazza of Covent Garden.*

[*Enter* SPARKISH *with a letter in his hand,* PINCHWIFE *following.*]

SPARKISH. But who would have thought a woman could have been false to me? By the world, I could not have thought it.

PINCHWIFE. You were for giving and taking liberty: she has taken

374 · *William Wycherley*

it only, sir, now you find in that letter. You are a frank person, and so is she, you see there.

SPARKISH. Nay, if this be her hand—for I never saw it.

PINCHWIFE. 'Tis no matter whether that be her hand or no; I am sure this hand, at her desire, led her to Mr. Horner, with whom I left her just now, to go fetch a parson to 'em at their desire too, to deprive you of her for ever; for it seems yours was but a mock marriage.

SPARKISH. Indeed, she would needs have it that 'twas Harcourt himself, in a parson's habit, that married us; but I'm sure he told me 'twas his brother Ned.

PINCHWIFE. O, there 'tis out; and you were deceived, not she: for you are such a frank person. But I must be gone.—You'll find her at Mr. Horner's. Go, and believe your eyes. [*Exit.*]

SPARKISH. Nay, I'll to her, and call her as many crocodiles, sirens, harpies, and other heathenish names, as a poet would do a mistress who had refused to hear his suit, nay more, his verses on her.—But stay, is not that she following a torch at t'other end of the Piazza? and from Horner's certainly—'tis so.

[*Enter* ALITHEA *following a torch, and* LUCY *behind.*]

You are well met, madam, though you don't think so. What, you have made a short visit to Mr. Horner? but I suppose you'll return to him presently, by that time the parson can be with him.

ALITHEA. Mr. Horner and the parson, sir!

SPARKISH. Come, madam, no more dissembling, no more jilting; for I am no more a frank person.

ALITHEA. How's this?

LUCY. So, 'twill work, I see. [*aside*]

SPARKISH. Could you find out no easy country fool to abuse? none but me, a gentleman of wit and pleasure about the town? But it was your pride to be too hard for a man of parts, unworthy false woman! false as a friend that lends a man money to lose; false as dice, who undo those that trust all they have to 'em.

LUCY. He has been a great bubble, by his similes, as they say. [*aside*]

ALITHEA. You have been too merry, sir, at your wedding-dinner, sure.

SPARKISH. What, d'ye mock me too?

ALITHEA. Or you have been deluded.

SPARKISH. By you.

ALITHEA. Let me understand you.

SPARKISH. Have you the confidence, (I should call it something else, since you know your guilt,) to stand my just reproaches? you did not write an impudent letter to Mr. Horner? who I find now has clubbed with you in deluding me with his aversion for women, that I might not, forsooth, suspect him for my rival.

LUCY. D'ye think the gentleman can be jealous now, madam? [*aside*]

ALITHEA. I write a letter to Mr. Horner!

SPARKISH. Nay, madam, do not deny it. Your brother showed it me just now; and told me likewise, he left you at Horner's lodging to fetch a parson to marry you to him: and I wish you joy, madam, joy, joy; and to him too, much joy; and to myself more joy, for not marrying you.

ALITHEA. [*aside*] So, I find my brother would break off the match; and I can consent to't, since I see this gentleman can be made jealous.—[*aloud*] O Lucy, by his rude usage and jealousy, he makes me almost afraid I am married to him. Art thou sure 'twas Harcourt himself, and no parson, that married us?

SPARKISH. No, madam, I thank you. I suppose, that was a contrivance too of Mr. Horner's and yours, to make Harcourt play the parson; but I would as little as you have him one now, no, not for the world. For, shall I tell you another truth? I never had any passion for you till now, for now I hate you. 'Tis true, I might have married your portion, as other men of parts of the town do sometimes; and so, your servant. And to show my unconcernedness, I'll come to your wedding, and resign you with as much joy, as I would a stale wench to a new cully; nay, with as much joy as I would after the first night, if I had been married to you. There's for you; and so your servant, servant. [*Exit.*]

ALITHEA. How was I deceived in a man!

LUCY. You'll believe then a fool may be made jealous now? for that easiness in him that suffers him to be led by a wife, will likewise permit him to be persuaded against her by others.

ALITHEA. But marry Mr. Horner! my brother does not intend it, sure: if I thought he did, I would take thy advice, and Mr. Harcourt for my husband. And now I wish, that if there be any overwise woman of the town, who, like me, would marry a fool for fortune, liberty, or title, first, that her husband may love play, and be a cully to all the town but her, and suffer none but Fortune to be mistress of his purse; then, if for liberty, that he may send her into the country, under the conduct of some huswifely mother-in-law; and if for title, may the world give 'em none but that of cuckold.

LUCY. And for her greater curse, madam, may he not deserve it.

ALITHEA. Away, impertinent! Is not this my old Lady Lanterlu's?

LUCY. Yes, madam.—[*aside*] And here I hope we shall find Mr. Harcourt.

[*Exeunt.*]

SCENE IV.—HORNER's *Lodging. A table, banquet, and bottles.*

[*Enter* HORNER, LADY FIDGET, MRS. DAINTY FIDGET, *and* MRS. SQUEAMISH.]

HORNER. A pox! they are come too soon—before I have sent back my new mistress. All that I have now to do is to lock her in, that they may not see her. [*aside*]

LADY FIDGET. That we may be sure of our welcome, we have brought our entertainment with us, and are resolved to treat thee, dear toad.

MRS. DAINTY FIDGET. And that we may be merry to purpose, have left Sir Jasper and my old Lady Squeamish, quarrelling at home at backgammon.

MRS. SQUEAMISH. Therefore let us make use of our time, lest they should chance to interrupt us.

LADY FIDGET. Let us sit then.

HORNER. First, that you may be private, let me lock this door and that, and I'll wait upon you presently.

LADY FIDGET. No, sir, shut 'em only, and your lips for ever; for we must trust you as much as our women.

HORNER. You know all vanity's killed in me; I have no occasion for talking.

LADY FIDGET. Now, ladies, supposing we had drank each of us our two bottles, let us speak the truth of our hearts.

MRS. DAINTY FIDGET *and* MRS. SQUEAMISH. Agreed.

LADY FIDGET. By this brimmer, for truth is nowhere else to be found —[*aside to* HORNER] not in thy heart, false man!

HORNER. You have found me a true man, I'm sure. [*aside to* LADY FIDGET]

LADY FIDGET. [*aside to* HORNER] Not every way.—But let us sit and be merry. [*sings*]

> Why should our damned tyrants oblige us to live
> On the pittance of pleasure which they only give?
> We must not rejoice
> With wine and with noise:
> In vain we must wake in a dull bed alone,
> Whilst to our warm rival the bottle they're gone.
> Then lay aside charms,
> And take up these arms.
>
> 'Tis wine only gives 'em their courage and wit:
> Because we live sober, to men we submit.
> If for beauties you'd pass,
> Take a lick of the glass,
> 'Twill mend your complexions, and when they are gone,
> The best red we have is the red of the grape:
> Then, sisters, lay't on,
> And damn a good shape.

MRS. DAINTY FIDGET. Dear brimmer! Well, in token of our open-ness and plain-dealing, let us throw our masks over our heads.

HORNER. So, 'twill come to the glasses anon. [*aside*]

MRS. SQUEAMISH. Lovely brimmer! let me enjoy him first.

LADY FIDGET. No, I never part with a gallant till I've tried him. Dear brimmer! that makest our husbands short-sighted.

MRS. DAINTY FIDGET. And our bashful gallants bold.

MRS. SQUEAMISH. And, for want of a gallant, the butler lovely in our eyes.—Drink, eunuch.

LADY FIDGET. Drink, thou representative of a husband.—Damn a husband!

MRS. DAINTY FIDGET. And, as it were a husband, an old keeper.

MRS. SQUEAMISH. And an old grandmother.

HORNER. And an English bawd, and a French surgeon.

LADY FIDGET. Ay, we have all reason to curse 'em.

HORNER. For my sake, ladies?

LADY FIDGET. No, for our own; for the first spoils all young gallants' industry.

MRS. DAINTY FIDGET. And the other's art makes 'em bold only with common women.

MRS. SQUEAMISH. And rather run the hazard of the vile distemper amongst them, than of a denial amongst us.

MRS. DAINTY FIDGET. The filthy toads choose mistresses now as they do stuffs, for having been fancied and worn by others.

MRS. SQUEAMISH. For being common and cheap.

LADY FIDGET. Whilst women of quality, like the richest stuffs, lie untumbled, and unasked for.

HORNER. Ay, neat, and cheap, and new, often they think best.

MRS. DAINTY FIDGET. No, sir, the beasts will be known by a mistress longer than by a suit.

MRS. SQUEAMISH. And 'tis not for cheapness neither.

LADY FIDGET. No; for the vain fops will take up druggets, and embroider 'em. But I wonder at the depraved appetites of witty men; they use to be out of the common road, and hate imitation. Pray tell me, beast, when you were a man, why you rather chose to club with a multitude in a common house for an entertainment, than to be the only guest at a good table.

HORNER. Why, faith, ceremony and expectation are unsufferable to those that are sharp bent. People always eat with the best stomach at an ordinary, where every man is snatching for the best bit.

LADY FIDGET. Though he get a cut over the fingers.—But I have heard, that people eat most heartily of another man's meat, that is, what they do not pay for.

HORNER. When they are sure of their welcome and freedom; for ceremony in love and eating is as ridiculous as in fighting: falling on briskly is all should be done on those occasions.

LADY FIDGET. Well then, let me tell you, sir, there is no where more freedom than in our houses; and we take freedom from a young person as a sign of good breeding; and a person may be as free as he pleases with us, as frolic, as gamesome, as wild as he will.

HORNER. Han't I heard you all declaim against wild men?

LADY FIDGET. Yes; but for all that, we think wildness in a man as desirable a quality as in a duck or rabbit: a tame man! foh!

HORNER. I know not, but your reputations frightened me as much as your faces invited me.

LADY FIDGET. Our reputation! Lord, why should you not think that we women make use of our reputation, as you men of yours, only to deceive the world with less suspicion? Our virtue is like the statesman's religion, the quaker's word, the gamester's oath, and the great man's honour; but to cheat those that trust us.

MRS. SQUEAMISH. And that demureness, coyness, and modesty, that you see in our faces in the boxes at plays, is as much a sign of a kind woman, as a vizard-mask in the pit.

MRS. DAINTY FIDGET. For, I assure you, women are least masked when they have the velvet vizard on.

LADY FIDGET. You would have found us modest women in our denials only.

MRS. SQUEAMISH. Our bashfulness is only the reflection of the men's.

MRS. DAINTY FIDGET. We blush when they are shamefaced.

HORNER. I beg your pardon, ladies, I was deceived in you devilishly. But why that mighty pretence to honour?

LADY FIDGET. We have told you; but sometimes 'twas for the same reason you men pretend business often, to avoid ill company, to enjoy the better and more privately those you love.

HORNER. But why would you ne'er give a friend a wink then?

LADY FIDGET. Faith, your reputation frightened us, as much as ours did you, you were so notoriously lewd.

HORNER. And you so seemingly honest.

LADY FIDGET. Was that all that deterred you?

HORNER. And so expensive—you allow freedom, you say.

LADY FIDGET. Ay, ay.

HORNER. That I was afraid of losing my little money, as well as my little time, both which my other pleasures required.

LADY FIDGET. Money! foh! you talk like a little fellow now: do such as we expect money?

HORNER. I beg your pardon, madam, I must confess, I have heard that great ladies, like great merchants, set but the higher prices upon what they have, because they are not in necessity of taking the first offer.

MRS. DAINTY FIDGET. Such as we make sale of our hearts?

MRS. SQUEAMISH. We bribed for our love? foh!

HORNER. With your pardon ladies, I know, like great men in offices, you seem to exact flattery and attendance only from your followers; but you have receivers about you, and such fees to pay, a man is afraid to pass your grants. Besides, we must let you win at cards, or we lose your hearts; and if you make an assignation, 'tis at a goldsmith's, jeweller's, or china-house; where for your honour you deposit to him, he must pawn his to the punctual cit, and so paying for what you take up, pays for what he takes up.

MRS. DAINTY FIDGET. Would you not have us assured of our gallants' love?

MRS. SQUEAMISH. For love is better known by liberality than by jealousy.

LADY FIDGET. For one may be dissembled, the other not.—[*aside*] But my jealousy can be no longer dissembled, and they are telling ripe.—[*aloud*]—Come, here's to our gallants in waiting, whom we must name, and I'll begin. This is my false rogue. [*claps him on the back*]

MRS. SQUEAMISH. How!

HORNER. So, all will out now. [*aside*]

MRS. SQUEAMISH. Did you not tell me, 'twas for my sake only you reported yourself no man? [*aside to* HORNER]

MRS. DAINTY FIDGET. Oh, wretch! did you not swear to me, 'twas for my love and honour you passed for that thing you do? [*aside to* HORNER]

HORNER. So, so.

LADY FIDGET. Come, speak, ladies: this is my false villain.

MRS. SQUEAMISH. And mine too.

MRS. DAINTY FIDGET. And mine.

HORNER. Well then, you are all three my false rogues too, and there's an end on't.

LADY FIDGET. Well then, there's no remedy; sister sharers, let us not fall out, but have a care of our honour. Though we get no presents, no jewels of him, we are savers of our honour, the jewel of most value and use, which shines yet to the world unsuspected, though it be counterfeit.

HORNER. Nay, and is e'en as good as if it were true, provided the world think so; for honour, like beauty now, only depends on the opinion of others.

LADY FIDGET. Well, Harry Common, I hope you can be true to three. Swear; but 'tis to no purpose to require your oath, for you are as often forsworn as you swear to new women.

HORNER. Come, faith, madam, let us e'en pardon one another; for all the difference I find betwixt we men and you women, we forswear ourselves at the beginning of an amour, you as long as it lasts.

[*Enter* SIR JASPER FIDGET, *and* OLD LADY SQUEAMISH.]

SIR JASPER. Oh, my Lady Fidget, was this your cunning, to come to Mr. Horner without me? but you have been nowhere else, I hope.

LADY FIDGET. No, Sir Jasper.

LADY SQUEAMISH. And you came straight hither, Biddy?

MRS. SQUEAMISH. Yes, indeed, lady grandmother.

SIR JASPER. 'Tis well, 'tis well; I knew when once they were thoroughly acquainted with poor Horner, they'd ne'er be from him: you may let her masquerade it with my wife and Horner, and I warrant her reputation safe.

[*Enter* BOY.]

BOY. O, sir, here's the gentleman come, whom you bid me not suffer to come up, without giving you notice, with a lady too, and other gentlemen.

HORNER. Do you all go in there, whilst I send 'em away; and, boy, do you desire 'em to stay below till I come, which shall be immediately.

[*Exeunt* SIR JASPER FIDGET, LADY FIDGET, OLD LADY SQUEAMISH, MRS. SQUEAMISH, *and* MRS. DAINTY FIDGET.]

BOY. Yes, sir. [*Exit.*]

[*Exit* HORNER *at the other door, and returns with* MRS. PINCHWIFE.]

HORNER. You would not take my advice, to be gone home before your husband came back, he'll now discover all; yet pray, my dearest, be persuaded to go home, and leave the rest to my management; I'll let you down the back way.

MRS. PINCHWIFE. I don't know the way home, so I don't.

HORNER. My man shall wait upon you.

MRS. PINCHWIFE. No, don't you believe that I'll go at all; what, are you weary of me already?

HORNER. No, my life, 'tis that I may love you long, 'tis to secure my love, and your reputation with your husband; he'll never receive you again else.

MRS. PINCHWIFE. What care I? d'ye think to frighten me with that? I don't intend to go to him again; you shall be my husband now.

HORNER. I cannot be your husband, dearest, since you are married to him.

MRS. PINCHWIFE. O, would you make me believe that? Don't I see every day at London here, women leave their first husbands, and go and live with other men as their wives? pish, pshaw! you'd make me angry, but that I love you so mainly.

HORNER. So, they are coming up—In again, in, I hear 'em.—[*exit* MRS. PINCHWIFE] Well, a silly mistress is like a weak place, soon got, soon lost, a man has scarce time for plunder; she betrays her husband first to her gallant, and then her gallant to her husband.

[*Enter* PINCHWIFE, ALITHEA, HARCOURT, SPARKISH, LUCY, *and a* PARSON.]

PINCHWIFE. Come, madam, 'tis not the sudden change of your dress, the confidence of your asseverations, and your false witness there, shall persuade me I did not bring you hither just now; here's my witness, who cannot deny it, since you must be confronted.—Mr. Horner, did not I bring this lady to you just now?

HORNER. Now must I wrong one woman for another's sake,—but that's no new thing with me, for in these cases I am still on the criminal's side against the innocent. [*aside*]

ALITHEA. Pray speak, sir.

HORNER. It must be so. I must be impudent, and try my luck; impudence uses to be too hard for truth. [*aside*]

PINCHWIFE. What, you are studying an evasion or excuse for her! Speak, sir.

HORNER. No, faith, I am something backward only to speak in women's affairs or disputes.

PINCHWIFE. She bids you speak.

ALITHEA. Ay, pray, sir, do, pray satisfy him.

HORNER. Then truly, you did bring that lady to me just now.

PINCHWIFE. O ho!

ALITHEA. How, sir?

HARCOURT. How, Horner?

ALITHEA. What mean you, sir? I always took you for a man of

honour.

HORNER. Ay, so much a man of honour, that I must save my mistress, I thank you, come what will on't. [*aside*]

SPARKISH. So, if I had had her, she'd have made me believe the moon had been made of a Christmas pie.

LUCY. Now could I speak, if I durst, and solve the riddle, who am the author of it. [*aside*]

ALITHEA. O unfortunate woman! A combination against my honour! which most concerns me now, because you share in my disgrace, sir, and it is your censure, which I must now suffer, that troubles me, not theirs.

HARCOURT. Madam, then have no trouble, you shall now see 'tis possible for me to love too, without being jealous; I will not only believe your innocence myself, but make all the world believe it.—[*aside to* HORNER] Horner, I must now be concerned for this lady's honour.

HORNER. And I must be concerned for a lady's honour too.

HARCOURT. This lady has her honour, and I will protect it.

HORNER. My lady has not her honour, but has given it me to keep, and I will preserve it.

HARCOURT. I understand you not.

HORNER. I would not have you.

MRS. PINCHWIFE. What's the matter with 'em all? [*peeping in behind*]

PINCHWIFE. Come, come, Mr. Horner, no more disputing; here's the parson, I brought him not in vain.

HARCOURT. No, sir, I'll employ him, if this lady please.

PINCHWIFE. How! what d'ye mean?

SPARKISH. Ay, what does he mean?

HORNER. Why, I have resigned your sister to him, he has my consent.

PINCHWIFE. But he has not mine, sir; a woman's injured honour, no more than a man's, can be repaired or satisfied by any but him that first wronged it; and you shall marry her presently, or— [*lays his hand on his sword*]

[*Re-enter* MRS. PINCHWIFE.]

MRS. PINCHWIFE. O Lord, they'll kill poor Mr. Horner! besides, he shan't marry her whilst I stand by, and look on; I'll not lose my second husband so.

PINCHWIFE. What do I see?

ALITHEA. My sister in my clothes!

SPARKISH. Ha!

MRS. PINCHWIFE. Nay, pray now don't quarrel about finding work for the parson, he shall marry me to Mr. Horner; or now, I believe, you have enough of me. [*to* PINCHWIFE]

HORNER. Damned, damned loving changeling! [*aside*]

MRS. PINCHWIFE. Pray, sister, pardon me for telling so many lies of you.

HORNER. I suppose the riddle is plain now.

LUCY. No, that must be my work.—Good sir, hear me. [*kneels to*

PINCHWIFE, *who stands doggedly with his hat over his eyes*]

PINCHWIFE. I will never hear woman again, but make 'em all silent thus—[*offers to draw upon his wife*]

HORNER. No, that must not be.

PINCHWIFE. You then shall go first, 'tis all one to me. [*offers to draw on* HORNER, *but is stopped by* HARCOURT]

HARCOURT. Hold!

[*Re-enter* SIR JASPER FIDGET, LADY FIDGET, OLD LADY SQUEAMISH, MRS. DAINTY FIDGET, *and* MRS. SQUEAMISH.]

SIR JASPER. What's the matter? what's the matter? pray, what's the matter, sir? I beseech you communicate, sir.

PINCHWIFE. Why, my wife has communicated, sir, as your wife may have done too, sir, if she knows him, sir.

SIR JASPER. Pshaw, with him! ha! ha! he!

PINCHWIFE. D'ye mock me, sir? a cuckold is a kind of a wild beast; have a care, sir.

SIR JASPER. No, sure, you mock me, sir. He cuckold you! it can't be, ha! ha! he! why, I'll tell you, sir—[*offers to whisper*]

PINCHWIFE. I tell you again, he has whored my wife, and yours too, if he knows her, and all the women he comes near; 'tis not his dissembling, his hypocrisy, can wheedle me.

SIR JASPER. How! does he dissemble? is he a hypocrite? Nay, then—how—wife—sister, is he a hypocrite?

LADY SQUEAMISH. A hypocrite! a dissembler! Speak, young harlotry, speak, how?

SIR JASPER. Nay, then—O my head too!—O thou libidinous lady!

LADY SQUEAMISH. O thou harloting harlotry! hast thou done't then?

SIR JASPER. Speak, good Horner, art thou a dissembler, a rogue? hast thou—

HORNER. So!

LUCY. I'll fetch you off, and her too, if she will but hold her tongue. [*apart to* HORNER]

HORNER. Canst thou? I'll give thee—[*apart to* LUCY]

LUCY. [*to* PINCHWIFE] Pray have but patience to hear me, sir, who am the unfortunate cause of all this confusion. Your wife is innocent, I only culpable; for I put her upon telling you all these lies concerning my mistress, in order to the breaking off the match between Mr. Sparkish and her, to make way for Mr. Harcourt.

SPARKISH. Did you so, eternal rotten tooth? Then, it seems, my mistress was not false to me, I was only deceived by you. Brother, that should have been, now man of conduct, who is a frank person now, to bring your wife to her lover, ha?

LUCY. I assure you, sir, she came not to Mr. Horner out of love, for she loves him no more—

MRS. PINCHWIFE. Hold, I told lies for you, but you shall tell none for me, for I do love Mr. Horner with all my soul, and nobody shall say me nay; pray, don't you go to make poor Mr. Horner believe to the contrary; 'tis spitefully done of you, I'm sure.

HORNER. Peace, dear idiot. [*aside to* MRS. PINCHWIFE]

MRS. PINCHWIFE. Nay, I will not peace.

PINCHWIFE. Not till I make you.

[*Enter* DORILANT *and* QUACK.]

DORILANT. Horner, your servant; I am the doctor's guest, he must excuse our intrusion.

QUACK. But what's the matter, gentlemen? for Heaven's sake, what's the matter?

HORNER. Oh, 'tis well you are come. 'Tis a censorious world we live in; you may have brought me a reprieve, or else I had died for a crime I never committed, and these innocent ladies had suffered with me; therefore, pray satisfy these worthy, honourable, jealous gentlemen—that—[*whispers*]

QUACK. O, I understand you, is that all?—Sir Jasper, by Heavens, and upon the word of a physician, sir—[*whispers to* SIR JASPER]

SIR JASPER. Nay, I do believe you truly.—Pardon me, my virtuous lady, and dear of honour.

LADY SQUEAMISH. What, then all's right again?

SIR JASPER. Ay, ay, and now let us satisfy him too.

[*They whisper with* PINCHWIFE.]

PINCHWIFE. An eunuch! Pray, no fooling with me.

QUACK. I'll bring half the chirurgeons in town to swear it.

PINCHWIFE. They!—they'll swear a man that bled to death through his wounds, died of an apoplexy.

QUACK. Pray, hear me, sir—why, all the town has heard the report of him.

PINCHWIFE. But does all the town believe it?

QUACK. Pray, inquire a little, and first of all these.

PINCHWIFE. I'm sure when I left the town, he was the lewdest fellow in't.

QUACK. I tell you, sir, he has been in France since; pray, ask but these ladies and gentlemen, your friend Mr. Dorilant. Gentlemen and ladies, han't you all heard the late sad report of poor Mr. Horner?

ALL THE LADIES. Ay, ay, ay.

DORILANT. Why, thou jealous fool, dost thou doubt it? he's an arrant French capon.

MRS. PINCHWIFE. 'Tis false, sir, you shall not disparage poor Mr. Horner, for to my certain knowledge—

LUCY. O, hold!

MRS. SQUEAMISH. Stop her mouth! [*aside to* LUCY]

LADY FIDGET. Upon my honour, sir, 'tis as true—[*to* PINCHWIFE]

MRS. DAINTY FIDGET. D'ye think we would have been seen in his company?

MRS. SQUEAMISH. Trust our unspotted reputations with him?

LADY FIDGET. This you get, and we too, by trusting your secret to a fool. [*aside to* HORNER]

HORNER. Peace, madam.—[*aside to* QUACK] Well, doctor, is not this a good design, that carries a man on unsuspected, and brings him off safe?

PINCHWIFE. Well, if this were true—but my wife—[*aside*]

384 · *William Wycherley*

[DORILANT *whispers with* MRS. PINCHWIFE.]

ALITHEA. Come, brother, your wife is yet innocent, you see; but have a care of too strong an imagination, lest, like an over-concerned timorous gamester, by fancying an unlucky cast, it should come. Women and fortune are truest still to those that trust 'em.

LUCY. And any wild thing grows but the more fierce and hungry for being kept up, and more dangerous to the keeper.

ALITHEA. There's doctrine for all husbands, Mr. Harcourt.

HARCOURT. I edify, madam, so much, that I am impatient till I am one.

DORILANT. And I edify so much by example, I will never be one.

SPARKISH. And because I will not disparage my parts, I'll ne'er be one.

HORNER. And I, alas! can't be one.

PINCHWIFE. But I must be one—against my will to a country wife, with a country murrain to me!

MRS. PINCHWIFE. And I must be a country wife still too, I find; for I can't, like a city one, be rid of my musty husband, and do what I list. [*aside*]

HORNER. Now, sir, I must pronounce your wife innocent, though I blush whilst I do it; and I am the only man by her now exposed to shame, which I will straight drown in wine, as you shall your suspicion; and the ladies' troubles we'll divert with a ballad.—Doctor, where are your maskers?

LUCY. Indeed, she's innocent, sir, I am her witness; and her end of coming out was but to see her sister's wedding; and what she has said to your face of her love to Mr. Horner, was but the usual innocent revenge on a husband's jealousy;—was it not, madam, speak?

MRS. PINCHWIFE. [*aside to* LUCY *and* HORNER] Since you'll have me tell more lies—[*aloud*] Yes, indeed, bud.

PINCHWIFE. For my own sake fain I would all believe;
Cuckolds, like lovers, should themselves deceive.
But—[*sighs*]
His honour is least safe (too late I find)
Who trusts it with a foolish wife or friend.
[*A Dance of Cuckolds.*]

HORNER. Vain fops but court and dress, and keep a pother,
To pass for women's men with one another;
But he who aims by women to be prized,
First by the men, you see, must be despised.
[*Exeunt.*]

Epilogue

SPOKEN BY MRS. KNEP[7]

Now you the vigorous, who daily here
O'er vizard-mask in public domineer,

7. The actress who played Lady Fidget.

And what you'd do to her, if in place where;
Nay, have the confidence to cry, "Come out!"
Yet when she says, "Lead on!" you are not stout;
But to your well-dressed brother straight turn round,
And cry "Pox on her, Ned, she can't be sound!"
Then slink away, a fresh one to engage,
With so much seeming heat and loving rage,
You'd frighten listening actress on the stage;
Till she at last has seen you huffing come,
And talk of keeping in the tiring-room,
Yet cannot be provoked to lead her home.
Next, you Falstaffs of fifty, who beset
Your buckram maidenheads, which your friends get;
And whilst to them you of achievements boast,
They share the booty, and laugh at your cost.
In fine, you essenced boys, both old and young,
Who would be thought so eager, brisk, and strong,
Yet do the ladies, not their husbands wrong;
Whose purses for your manhood make excuse,
And keep your Flanders mares for show not use;
Encouraged by our woman's man to-day,
A Horner's part may vainly think to play;
And may intrigues so bashfully disown,
That they may doubted be by few or none;
May kiss the cards at picquet, ombre, loo,
And so be taught to kiss the lady too;
But, gallants, have a care, faith, what you do.
The world, which to no man his due will give,
You by experience know you can deceive,
And men may still believe you vigorous,
But then we women—there's no cozening us.

Troilus and Cressida

WILLIAM SHAKESPEARE

It is not possible with *Troilus and Cressida*, as it is with most plays, to insist on a particular date of composition or to point with certainty at the day on which it was first performed. With Shakespeare, too much is conjectural. It is now generally assumed that the play was written around 1602 and performed sometime before February 7, 1603, when it was entered in the Stationers' Register for copyright. This was the period in which two strange and tough Shakespearean comedies, *All's Well That Ends Well* and *Measure for Measure*, were written, although neither of them has as strong a bite as *Troilus*.

Shortly after the quarto appeared in 1609, it was reissued with the identifying title page ("As it was acted by the Kings Majesties servants at the Globe") removed and two new leaves inserted. One contained a sort of preface, "A Never Writer to an Ever Reader," which pushed the play as caviar to the general and attempted snob appeal by suggesting that the play had never been performed and was the better "for not being sullied with the smoky breath of the multitude." Although such an appeal is often used in advertising today, most of us really know that the quality of a play depends on something inherent in it and not on the selectness, any more than on the largeness, of its audience. A more useful quotation from that slightly priggish preface is the statement that the author's comedies "are so framed to the life that they serve for the most common commentaries of all the actions of our lives . . ." This is certainly true of *Troilus and Cressida*—if not of "all the actions" at least of some of the most important. As Thersites says, "Still wars and lechery! Nothing else holds fashion."

The text is pretty much that of the quarto with a few words or sentences doctored according to the folio, or the learned guesses or wild conjectures of later editors. Stage directions in angle brackets—⟨ ⟩—are additions to the quarto text, usually from the folio. Neither the quarto nor the folio has act-scene divisions; the conventional ones, those of the Globe edition, which are often used in critical and scholarly discussions of Shakespeare, are indicated in angle brackets.

Troilus and Cressida

⟨Dramatis Personae⟩

PRIAM, *King of Troy*

HECTOR
TROILUS
PARIS ⟩ *his sons*
DEIPHOBUS
HELENUS

MARGARELON, *a bastard son of* PRIAM

AENEAS ⟩ *Trojan commanders*
ANTENOR

CALCHAS, *a Trojan priest, taking part with the Greeks*

PANDARUS, *uncle to* CRESSIDA

AGAMEMNON, *the Greek general*
MENELAUS, *his brother*
ACHILLES ⟩ *Greek commanders*
AJAX

ULYSSES
NESTOR
DIOMEDES ⟩ *Greek commanders*
PATROCLUS

THERSITES, *a deformed and scurrilous Greek*

ALEXANDER, *servant to* CRESSIDA
SERVANT *to* TROILUS
SERVANT *to* PARIS
SERVANT *to* DIOMEDES

HELEN, *wife to* MENELAUS
ANDROMACHE, *wife to* HECTOR
CASSANDRA, *daughter to* PRIAM, *a prophetess*
CRESSIDA, *daughter to* CALCHAS

TROJAN *and* GREEK SOLDIERS, *and* ATTENDANTS

THE SCENE: *Troy and the Greek camp before it.*⟩

PROLOGUE

In Troy, there lies the scene. From isles of Greece
The princes orgillous,¹ their high blood chafed,
Have to the port of Athens sent their ships
Fraught with the ministers and instruments
Of cruel war. Sixty and nine that wore　　　　　　5
Their crownets regal from th' Athenian bay
Put forth toward Phrygia; and their vow is made
To ransack Troy, within whose strong immures²
The ravished Helen, Menelaus' queen,
With wanton Paris sleeps—and that's the quarrel.　10
To Tenedos they come,
And the deep-drawing barks do there disgorge
Their war-like fraughtage.³ Now on Dardan plains
The fresh and yet unbruiséd Greeks do pitch
Their brave pavilions: Priam's six-gated city,　　15
Dardan, and Tymbria, Helias, Chetas, Troien,
And Antenorides, with massy staples
And corresponsive and fulfilling bolts,
Sperr up⁴ the sons of Troy.

1. Proud.
2. Walls.
3. Cargo, i.e., soldiers.
4. Shut up.

Now expectation, tickling skittish spirits   20
On one and other side, Troyan and Greek,
Sets all on hazard—and hither am I come
A Prologue armed, but not in confidence
Of author's pen or actor's voice, but suited
In like conditions as our argument,[5]   25
To tell you, fair beholders, that our play
Leaps o'er the vaunt and firstlings[6] of those broils,
Beginning in the middle; starting thence away
To what may be digested in a play.
Like or find fault; do as your pleasures are;   30
Now good or bad, 'tis but the chance of war.

⟨I. i⟩

[*Enter* TROILUS *armed, and* PANDARUS.]

TROILUS. Call here my varlet; I'll unarm again.
Why should I war without the walls of Troy
That find such cruel battle here within?
Each Troyan that is master of his heart,
Let him to field; Troilus, alas, hath none!   5
PANDARUS. Will this gear[7] ne'er be mended?
TROILUS. The Greeks are strong, and skilful to their strength,
Fierce to their skill, and to their fierceness valiant;
But I am weaker than a woman's tear,
Tamer than sleep, fonder than ignorance,   10
Less valiant than the virgin in the night,
And skilless as unpractised infancy.
PANDARUS. Well, I have told you enough of this; for my part, I'll
not meddle nor make no farther. He that will have a cake out
of the wheat must needs tarry the grinding.   15
TROILUS. Have I not tarried?
PANDARUS. Ay, the grinding; but you must tarry the bolting.[8]
TROILUS. Have I not tarried?
PANDARUS. Ay, the bolting; but you must tarry the leavening.
TROILUS. Still have I tarried.   20
PANDARUS. Ay, to the leavening; but here's yet in the word
'hereafter' the kneading, the making of the cake, the heating
of the oven, and the baking; nay, you must stay the cooling
too, or you may chance to burn your lips.
TROILUS. Patience herself, what goddess e'er she be,   25
Doth lesser blench at suff'rance than I do.
At Priam's royal table do I sit;
And when fair Cressid comes into my thoughts—
So, traitor, then she comes when she is thence.
PANDARUS. Well, she looked yesternight fairer than ever I saw   30

5. Subject. The speaker of the Prologue (21–25) is apparently dressed
for battle.
6. First part.
7. Business. Since *gear* is also
"armor," Pandarus is using a wartime

metaphor, but the business he is speaking of is probably Troilus' infatuation with Cressida and not the war
against the Greeks.
8. Sifting.

her look, or any woman else.

TROILUS. I was about to tell thee: when my heart,
As wedgéd with a sigh, would rive in twain,
Lest Hector or my father should perceive me,
I have, as when the sun doth light a storm,
Buried this sigh in wrinkle of a smile. 35
But sorrow that is couched in seeming gladness
Is like that mirth fate turns to sudden sadness.

PANDARUS. An her hair were not somewhat darker than Helen's
—well, go to—there were no more comparison between the 40
women. But, for my part, she is my kinswoman; I would not,
as they term it, praise her, but I would somebody had heard
her talk yesterday, as I did. I will not dispraise your sister Cassandra's wit; but—

TROILUS. O Pandarus! I tell thee, Pandarus— 45
When I do tell thee there my hopes lie drowned,
Reply not in how many fathoms deep
They lie indrenched. I tell thee I am mad
In Cressid's love. Thou answer'st 'She is fair'—
Pourest in the open ulcer of my heart 50
Her eyes, her hair, her cheek, her gait, her voice;
Handlest in thy discourse, O, that her hand,[9]
In whose comparison all whites are ink
Writing their own reproach; to whose soft seizure
The cygnet's down is harsh, and spirit of sense[1] 55
Hard as the palm of ploughman! This thou tell'st me,
As true thou tell'st me, when I say I love her;
But, saying thus, instead of oil and balm,
Thou lay'st in every gash that love hath given me
The knife that made it. 60

PANDARUS. I speak no more than truth.

TROILUS. Thou dost not speak so much.

PANDARUS. Faith, I'll not meddle in it. Let her be as she is: if
she be fair, 'tis the better for her; an she be not, she has the
mends[2] in her own hands. 65

TROILUS. Good Pandarus! How now, Pandarus!

PANDARUS. I have had my labour for my travail, ill thought on of
her and ill thought on of you; gone between and between, but
small thanks for my labour.

TROILUS. What, art thou angry, Pandarus? What, with me? 70

PANDARUS. Because she's kin to me, therefore she's not so fair as
Helen. An she were not kin to me, she would be as fair a Friday as Helen is on Sunday. But what care I? I care not an she
were a blackamoor; 'tis all one to me.

TROILUS. Say I she is not fair? 75

PANDARUS. I do not care whether you do or no. She's a fool to
stay behind her father. Let her to the Greeks; and so I'll tell

9. That hand of hers.
1. An extremely thin bodily substance
supposed to transmit sense impressions
through the nerves.
2. Remedies. She can put on make-up.

her the next time I see her. For my part, I'll meddle nor make
no more i' th' matter.

TROILUS. Pandarus!   80

PANDARUS. Not I.

TROILUS. Sweet Pandarus!

PANDARUS. Pray you, speak no more to me: I will leave all as I
found it, and there an end.   [*Exit. Sound alarum.*[3]]

TROILUS. Peace, you ungracious clamours! Peace, rude sounds!   85
Fools on both sides! Helen must needs be fair,
When with your blood you daily paint her thus.
I cannot fight upon this argument;
It is too starved a subject for my sword.
But Pandarus—O gods, how do you plague me!   90
I cannot come to Cressid but by Pandar;
And he's as tetchy to be wooed to woo
As she is stubborn-chaste against all suit.
Tell me, Apollo, for thy Daphne's[4] love,
What Cressid is, what Pandar, and what we?   95
Her bed is India; there she lies, a pearl;
Between our Ilium[5] and where she resides
Let it be called the wild and wand'ring flood;
Ourself the merchant, and this sailing Pandar
Our doubtful hope, and our convoy, and our bark.   100
          [*Alarum. Enter* AENEAS.]

AENEAS. How now, Prince Troilus! Wherefore not afield?

TROILUS. Because not there. This woman's answer sorts,
For womanish it is to be from thence.
What news, Aeneas, from the field to-day?

AENEAS. That Paris is returned home, and hurt.   105

TROILUS. By whom, Aeneas?

AENEAS.   Troilus, by Menelaus.

TROILUS. Let Paris bleed: 'tis but a scar to scorn;
Paris is gored with Menelaus' horn.[6]   [*Alarum.*]

AENEAS. Hark what good sport is out of town to-day!

TROILUS. Better at home, if 'would I might' were 'may'.   110
But to the sport abroad. Are you bound thither?

AENEAS. In all swift haste.

TROILUS.   Come, go we then together. [*Exeunt.*]

⟨I. ii⟩

          [*Enter* CRESSIDA *and her man* ⟨ALEXANDER⟩.]

CRESSIDA. Who were those went by?

MAN.   Queen Hecuba and Helen.

CRESSIDA. And whither go they?

---

3. Battle signal.
4. Daphne, to escape Apollo, asked
the gods for help and they turned her
into a laurel tree. Troilus is probably
right in calling on Apollo, since the
two of them were after the same thing,
but the juxtaposition of Cressida and
Daphne is a little ironic.

5. Latin name for Troy, used here
and elsewhere in the play for Priam's
palace. In this speech, it means simply
"here" or "home," in contrast to "where
she resides."
6. Sign of a cuckold. Paris, after all,
carried off Menelaus' wife.

MAN.   Up to the eastern tower,
  Whose height commands as subject all the vale,
  To see the battle. Hector, whose patience
  Is as a virtue fixed, to-day was moved.
  He chid Andromache, and struck his armourer;   5
  And, like as there were husbandry in war,
  Before the sun rose he was harnessed light,
  And to the field goes he, where every flower
  Did as a prophet weep what it foresaw   10
  In Hector's wrath.

CRESSIDA.   What was his cause of anger?

MAN. The noise goes, this: there is among the Greeks
  A lord of Troyan blood, nephew to Hector;
  They call him Ajax.

CRESSIDA.   Good; and what of him?

MAN. They say he is a very man per se.   15
  And stands alone.

CRESSIDA. So do all men, unless they are drunk, sick, or have no
  legs.

MAN. This man, lady, hath robbed many beasts of their particular
  additions: he is as valiant as the lion, churlish as the bear, slow   20
  as the elephant—a man into whom nature hath so crowded
  humours that his valour is crushed into folly, his folly sauced
  with discretion. There is no man hath a virtue that he hath
  not a glimpse of, nor any man an attaint but he carries some
  stain of it; he is melancholy without cause and merry against   25
  the hair;[7] he hath the joints of everything; but everything so
  out of joint that he is a gouty Briareus, many hands and no
  use, or purblind Argus, all eyes and no sight.

CRESSIDA. But how should this man, that makes me smile, make
  Hector angry?   30

MAN. They say he yesterday coped Hector in the battle and struck
  him down, the disdain and shame whereof hath ever since kept
  Hector fasting and waking.

      [*Enter* PANDARUS.]

CRESSIDA. Who comes here?

MAN. Madam, your uncle Pandarus.   35

CRESSIDA. Hector's a gallant man.

MAN. As may be in the world, lady.

PANDARUS. What's that? What's that?

CRESSIDA. Good morrow, uncle Pandarus.

PANDARUS. Good morrow, cousin Cressid. What do you talk of?   40
  —Good morrow, Alexander.—How do you, cousin? When
  were you at Ilium?

CRESSIDA. This morning, uncle.

PANDARUS. What were you talking of when I came? Was Hector
  armed and gone ere you came to Ilium? Helen was not up, was   45
  she?

CRESSIDA. Hector was gone, but Helen was not up.

7. Unnaturally.

PANDARUS. E'en so. Hector was stirring early.

CRESSIDA. That were we talking of, and of his anger.

PANDARUS. Was he angry? 50

CRESSIDA. So he says here.

PANDARUS. True, he was so; I know the cause too; he'll lay about him today, I can tell them that. And there's Troilus will not come far behind him; let them take heed of Troilus, I can tell them that too. 55

CRESSIDA. What, is he angry too?

PANDARUS. Who, Troilus? Troilus is the better man of the two.

CRESSIDA. O Jupiter! there's no comparison.

PANDARUS. What, not between Troilus and Hector? Do you know a man if you see him? 60

CRESSIDA. Ay, if I ever saw him before and knew him.

PANDARUS. Well, I say Troilus is Troilus.

CRESSIDA. Then you say as I say, for I am sure he is not Hector.

PANDARUS. No, nor Hector is not Troilus in some degrees.[8]

CRESSIDA. 'Tis just to each of them: he is himself. 65

PANDARUS. Himself? Alas, poor Troilus! I would he were!

CRESSIDA. So he is.

PANDARUS. Condition[9] I had gone barefoot to India.

CRESSIDA. He is not Hector.

PANDARUS. Himself? no, he's not himself. Would 'a were himself! 70 Well, the gods are above; time must friend or end. Well, Troilus, well! I would my heart were in her body! No, Hector is not a better man than Troilus.

CRESSIDA. Excuse me.

PANDARUS. He is elder. 75

CRESSIDA. Pardon me, pardon me.

PANDARUS. Th' other's not come to't[1]; you shall tell me another tale when th' other's come to't. Hector shall not have his wit this year.

CRESSIDA. He shall not need it if he have his own. 80

PANDARUS. Nor his qualities.

CRESSIDA. No matter.

PANDARUS. Nor his beauty.

CRESSIDA. 'Twould not become him: his own's better.

PANDARUS. You have no judgment, niece. Helen herself swore th' 85 other day that Troilus, for a brown favour,[2] for so 'tis, I must confess—not brown neither—

CRESSIDA. No, but brown.

PANDARUS. Faith, to say truth, brown and not brown.

CRESSIDA. To say the truth, true and not true. 90

PANDARUS. She praised his complexion above Paris.

CRESSIDA. Why, Paris hath colour enough.

PANDARUS. So he has.

CRESSIDA. Then Troilus should have too much. If she praised him above, his complexion is higher than his; he having colour 95

8. By some distance.
9. Even if.

1. Reached manhood.
2. Complexion.

enough, and the other higher, is too flaming a praise for a good complexion. I had as lief Helen's golden tongue had commended Troilus for a copper nose.

PANDARUS. I swear to you I think Helen loves him better than Paris. 100

CRESSIDA. Then she's a merry Greek indeed.

PANDARUS. Nay, I am sure she does. She came to him th' other day into the compassed window—and you know he has not past three or four hairs on his chin—

CRESSIDA. Indeed a tapster's arithmetic[3] may soon bring his particulars therein to a total. 105

PANDARUS. Why, he is very young, and yet will he within three pound lift as much as his brother Hector.

CRESSIDA. Is he so young a man and so old a lifter?[4]

PANDARUS. But to prove to you that Helen loves him: she came and puts me her white hand to his cloven chin— 110

CRESSIDA. Juno have mercy! How came it cloven?

PANDARUS. Why, you know, 'tis dimpled. I think his smiling becomes him better than any man in all Phrygia.

CRESSIDA. O, he smiles valiantly! 115

PANDARUS. Does he not?

CRESSIDA. O yes, an 'twere a cloud in autumn!

PANDARUS. Why, go to, then! But to prove to you that Helen loves Troilus—

CRESSIDA. Troilus will stand to the proof, if you'll prove it so. 120

PANDARUS. Troilus? Why, he esteems her no more than I esteem an addle egg.

CRESSIDA. If you love an addle egg as well as you love an idle head, you would eat chickens i' th' shell.

PANDARUS. I cannot choose but laugh to think how she tickled 125 his chin. Indeed, she has a marvell's white hand, I must needs confess.

CRESSIDA. Without the rack.

PANDARUS. And she takes upon her to spy a white hair on his chin.

CRESSIDA. Alas, poor chin! Many a wart is richer. 130

PANDARUS. But there was such laughing! Queen Hecuba laughed that her eyes ran o'er.

CRESSIDA. With millstones.

PANDARUS. And Cassandra laughed.

CRESSIDA. But there was a more temperate fire under the pot of 135 her eyes. Did her eyes run o'er too?

PANDARUS. And Hector laughed.

CRESSIDA. And what was all this laughing?

PANDARUS. Marry, at the white hair that Helen spied on Troilus' chin. 140

CRESSIDA. An't had been a green hair I should have laughed too.

PANDARUS. They laughed not so much at the hair as at his pretty answer.

---

3. The idea is that a bartender, a tapster, would not be able to count very far.
4. Thief.

CRESSIDA. What was his answer?

PANDARUS. Quoth she 'Here's but two and fifty hairs on your 145 chin, and one of them is white'.

CRESSIDA. This is her question.

PANDARUS. That's true; make no question of that. 'Two and fifty hairs,' quoth he 'and one white. That white hair is my father, and all the rest are his sons.' 'Jupiter!' quoth she 'which of 150 these hairs is Paris my husband?' 'The forked⁵ one;' quoth he 'pluck't out and give it him.' But there was such laughing! and Helen so blushed, and Paris so chafed; and all the rest so laughed that it passed.

CRESSIDA. So let it now; for it has been a great while going by. 155

PANDARUS. Well, cousin, I told you a thing yesterday; think on't.

CRESSIDA. So I do.

PANDARUS. I'll be sworn 'tis true; he will weep you, an 'twere a man born in April.

CRESSIDA. And I'll spring up in his tears, an 'twere a nettle against 160 May.   [*Sound a retreat.*]

PANDARUS. Hark! they are coming from the field. Shall we stand up here and see them as they pass toward Ilium? Good niece, do, sweet niece Cressida.

CRESSIDA. At your pleasure. 165

PANDARUS. Here, here, here's an excellent place; here we may see most bravely. I'll tell you them all by their names as they pass by; but mark Troilus above the rest.

                       [AENEAS *passes.*]

CRESSIDA. Speak not so loud.

PANDARUS. That's Aeneas. Is not that a brave man? He's one of 170 the flowers of Troy, I can tell you. But mark Troilus; you shall see anon.

                       [ANTENOR *passes.*]

CRESSIDA. Who's that?

PANDARUS. That's Antenor. He has a shrewd wit, I can tell you; and he's a man good enough; he's one o' th' soundest judg- 175 ments in Troy, whosoever, and a proper⁶ man of person. When comes Troilus? I'll show you Troilus anon. If he see me, you shall see him nod at me.

CRESSIDA. Will he give you the nod?⁷

PANDARUS. You shall see. 180

CRESSIDA. If he do, the rich shall have more.

                       [HECTOR *passes.*]

PANDARUS. That's Hector, that, that, look you, that; there's a fellow! Go thy way, Hector! There's a brave man, niece. O brave Hector! Look how he looks. There's a countenance! Is't not a brave man? 185

CRESSIDA. O, a brave man!

PANDARUS. Is 'a not? It does a man's heart good. Look you what hacks are on his helmet! Look you yonder, do you see? Look

5. A suggestion of the cuckold's horn.   7. Cressida is calling Pandarus a fool,
6. Handsome.   playing on the word *noddy*.

you there. There's no jesting; there's laying on, take't off who
will,[8] as they say. There be hacks.   190
CRESSIDA. Be those with swords?
PANDARUS. Swords! anything, he cares not; and the devil come to
  him, it's all one. By God's lid, it does one's heart good. Yonder
  comes Paris, yonder comes Paris.
    [PARIS *passes.*]
  Look ye yonder, niece; is't not a gallant man too, is't not?   195
  Why, this is brave now. Who said he came hurt home to-day?
  He's not hurt. Why, this will do Helen's heart good now, ha!
  Would I could see Troilus now! You shall see Troilus anon.
    [HELENUS *passes.*]
CRESSIDA. Who's that?
PANDARUS. That's Helenus. I marvel where Troilus is. That's   200
  Helenus. I think he went not forth to-day. That's Helenus.
CRESSIDA. Can Helenus fight, uncle?
PANDARUS. Helenus! no. Yes, he'll fight indifferent well. I marvel
  where Troilus is. Hark! do you not hear the people cry 'Troi-
  lus'? Helenus is a priest.   205
CRESSIDA. What sneaking fellow comes yonder?
    [TROILUS *passes.*]
PANDARUS. Where? yonder? That's Deiphobus. 'Tis Troilus.
  There's a man, niece. Hem! Brave Troilus, the prince of chivalry!
CRESSIDA. Peace, for shame, peace!   210
PANDARUS. Mark him; note him. O brave Troilus! Look well upon
  him, niece; look you how his sword is bloodied, and his helm
  more hacked than Hector's; and how he looks, and how he
  goes! O admirable youth! he never saw three and twenty. Go
  thy way, Troilus, go thy way. Had I a sister were a grace or a   215
  daughter a goddess, he should take his choice. O admirable
  man! Paris? Paris is dirt to him; and, I warrant, Helen, to
  change, would give an eye to boot.
CRESSIDA. Here comes more.
    [COMMON SOLDIERS *pass.*]
PANDARUS. Asses, fools, dolts! chaff and bran, chaff and bran! por-   220
  ridge after meat! I could live and die in the eyes of Troilus.
  Ne'er look, ne'er look; the eagles are gone. Crows and daws,
  crows and daws! I had rather be such a man as Troilus than
  Agamemnon and all Greece.
CRESSIDA. There is amongst the Greeks Achilles, a better man   225
  than Troilus.
PANDARUS. Achilles? A drayman, a porter, a very camel!
CRESSIDA. Well, well.
PANDARUS. Well, well! Why, have you any discretion? Have you
  any eyes? Do you know what a man is? Is not birth, beauty,   230
  good shape, discourse, manhood, learning, gentleness, virtue,

---

8. Pandarus, who free associated long
before the term was invented, naturally
follows *lay on* with *take off.* He means

something like "whatever the circumstances," a reinforcement of *laying on*
(fighting).

youth, liberality, and such like, the spice and salt that season a
man?

CRESSIDA. Ay, a minced[9] man; and then to be baked with no date
in the pie, for then the man's date is out.   235

PANDARUS. You are such a woman! A man knows not at what
ward[1] you lie.

CRESSIDA. Upon my back, to defend my belly; upon my wit, to
defend my wiles; upon my secrecy, to defend mine honesty;
my mask, to defend my beauty; and you, to defend all these;   240
and at all these wards I lie, at a thousand watches.[2]

PANDARUS. Say one of your watches.

CRESSIDA. Nay, I'll watch you for that; and that's one of the chief-
est of them too. If I cannot ward what I would not have hit, I
can watch you for telling how I took the blow; unless it swell   245
past hiding, and then it's past watching.

PANDARUS. You are such another!

    [*Enter* ⟨TROILUS'⟩ BOY.]

BOY. Sir, my lord would instantly speak with you.

PANDARUS. Where?

BOY. At your own house; there he unarms him.   250

PANDARUS. Good boy, tell him I come.   [*Exit* BOY.]
    I doubt he be hurt. Fare ye well, good niece.

CRESSIDA. Adieu, uncle.

PANDARUS. I will be with you, niece, by and by.

CRESSIDA. To bring,[3] uncle.   255

PANDARUS. Ay, a token from Troilus.

CRESSIDA. By the same token, you are a bawd.   [*Exit* PANDARUS.]
    Words, vows, gifts, tears, and love's full sacrifice,
    He offers in another's enterprise;
    But more in Troilus thousand-fold I see   260
    Than in the glass of Pandar's praise may be,
    Yet hold I off. Women are angels, wooing:
    Things won are done; joy's soul lies in the doing.
    That she beloved knows nought that knows not this:
    Men prize the thing ungained more than it is.   265
    That she was never yet that ever knew
    Love got so sweet as when desire did sue;
    Therefore this maxim out of love I teach:
    Achievement is command; ungained, beseech.
    Then though my heart's content firm love doth bear,   270
    Nothing of that shall from mine eyes appear.   [*Exit.*]

⟨I. iii⟩

    [⟨*Sennet.*⟩[4] *Enter* AGAMEMNON, NESTOR, ULYSSES, DIOME-
    DES, MENELAUS, *and* OTHERS.]

---

9. Cressida picks up Pandarus' *salt*
and *spice* to make a pun suggesting
mincing, effeminacy. Although the exact slang meaning of *date* and *pie* is
uncertain, it is clear that the rest of
her statement is a recipe for sexual

insufficiency.
1. Defensive position, in fencing.
2. Times for being on guard; she
means at night.
3. Get even.
4. A trumpet signal.

AGAMEMNON. Princes,
　What grief hath set the jaundice o'er your cheeks?
　The ample proposition that hope makes
　In all designs begun on earth below
　Fails in the promised largeness; checks and disasters　　5
　Grow in the veins of actions highest reared,
　As knots, by the conflux[5] of meeting sap,
　Infects the sound pine, and diverts his grain
　Tortive[6] and errant from his course of growth.
　Nor, princes, is it matter new to us　　　　　　　10
　That we come short of our suppose[7] so far
　That after seven years' siege yet Troy walls stand;
　Sith every action that hath gone before,
　Whereof we have recórd, trial did draw
　Bias and thwart, not answering the aim,　　　　　15
　And that unbodied figure of the thought
　That gave't surmiséd shape. Why then, you princes,
　Do you with cheeks abashed behold our works
　And call them shames, which are, indeed, nought else
　But the protractive trials of great Jove　　　　　20
　To find persistive constancy in men;
　The fineness of which metal is not found
　In fortune's love? For then the bold and coward,
　The wise and fool, the artist and unread,
　The hard and soft, seem all affined and kin.　　　25
　But in the wind and tempest of her frown
　Distinction, with a broad and powerful fan,
　Puffing at all, winnows the light away;
　And what hath mass or matter by itself
　Lies rich in virtue and unmingled.　　　　　　　30
NESTOR. With due observance of thy godlike seat,
　Great Agamemnon, Nestor shall apply
　Thy latest words. In the reproof of chance
　Lies the true proof of men. The sea being smooth,
　How many shallow bauble boats dare sail　　　　35
　Upon her patient breast, making their way
　With those of nobler bulk!
　But let the ruffian Boreas once enrage
　The gentle Thetis,[8] and anon behold
　The strong-ribbed bark through liquid mountains cut,　40
　Bounding between the two moist elements
　Like Perseus' horse. Where's then the saucy boat,
　Whose weak untimbered sides but even now
　Co-rivalled greatness? Either to harbour fled
　Or made a toast for Neptune. Even so　　　　　45
　Doth valour's show and valour's worth divide

5. Confluence.
6. Distorted.
7. Expectation.
8. In describing the water, stirred up by the north wind (*Boreas*), Nestor uses *Thetis*, a sea nymph, to stand for the whole sea. Since she is Achilles' mother, he touches on the Greeks' problem without actually mentioning it.

In storms of fortune; for in her ray and brightness
The herd hath more annoyance by the breese[9]
Than by the tiger; but when the splitting wind
Makes flexible the knees of knotted oaks,   50
And flies fled under shade—why, then the thing of courage,
As roused with rage, with rage doth sympathise,
And with an accent tuned in self-same key
Retorts to chiding fortune.

ULYSSES.   Agamemnon,
Thou great commander, nerve and bone of Greece,   55
Heart of our numbers, soul and only spirit
In whom the tempers and the minds of all
Should be shut up—hear what Ulysses speaks.
Besides the applause and approbation
The which, [*to* AGAMEMNON] most mighty, for thy place and
    sway,   60
[*to* NESTOR] And, thou most reverend, for thy stretched-out life,
I give to both your speeches—which were such
As Agamemnon and the hand of Greece
Should hold up high in brass; and such again
As venerable Nestor, hatched in silver,   65
Should with a bond of air, strong as the axle-tree
On which heaven rides, knit all the Greekish ears
To his experienced tongue—yet let it please both,
Thou great, and wise, to hear Ulysses speak.

AGAMEMNON. Speak, Prince of Ithaca; and be't of less expect   70
That matter needless, of importless burden,
Divide thy lips than we are confident,
When rank Thersites opes his mastic[1] jaws,
We shall hear music, wit, and oracle.

ULYSSES. Troy, yet upon his basis, had been down,   75
And the great Hector's sword had lacked a master,
But for these instances:
The specialty of rule[2] hath been neglected;
And look how many Grecian tents do stand
Hollow upon this plain, so many hollow factions.   80
When that the general is not like the hive,
To whom the foragers shall all repair,
What honey is expected? Degree being vizarded,
Th' unworthiest shows as fairly in the mask.
The heavens themselves, the planets, and this centre,   85
Observe degree, priority, and place,
Insisture,[3] course, proportion, season, form,
Office, and custom, in all line of order;
And therefore is the glorious planet Sol
In noble eminence enthroned and sphered   90
Amidst the other, whose med'cinable eye
Corrects the ill aspects of planets evil,

9. Gadfly.   2. Rights of authority.
1. Abusive.   3. Regularity of position.

And posts, like the commandment of a king,
Sans check, to good and bad. But when the planets
In evil mixture to disorder wander,   95
What plagues and what portents, what mutiny,
What raging of the sea, shaking of earth,
Commotion in the winds! Frights, changes, horrors,
Divert and crack, rend and deracinate,
The unity and married calm of states   100
Quite from their fixture! O, when degree is shaked,
Which is the ladder of all high designs,
The enterprise is sick! How could communities,
Degrees in schools, and brotherhoods in cities,
Peaceful commerce from dividable shores,   105
The primogenity and due of birth,
Prerogative of age, crowns, sceptres, laurels,
But by degree, stand in authentic place?
Take but degree away, untune that string,
And hark what discord follows! Each thing meets   110
In mere oppugnancy: the bounded waters
Should lift their bosoms higher than the shores,
And make a sop of all this solid globe;
Strength should be lord of imbecility,[4]
And the rude son should strike his father dead;   115
Force should be right; or, rather, right and wrong—
Between whose endless jar justice resides—
Should lose their names, and so should justice too.
Then everything includes itself in power,
Power into will, will into appetite;   120
And appetite, an universal wolf,
So doubly seconded with will and power,
Must make perforce an universal prey,
And last eat up himself. Great Agamemnon,
This chaos, when degree is suffocate,   125
Follows the choking.
And this neglection of degree it is
That by a pace goes backward, with a purpose
It hath to climb. The general's disdained
By him one step below, he by the next,   130
That next by him beneath; so every step,
Exampled by the first pace that is sick
Of his superior, grows to an envious fever
Of pale and bloodless emulation.
And 'tis this fever that keeps Troy on foot,   135
Not her own sinews. To end a tale of length,
Troy in our weakness stands, not in her strength.
NESTOR. Most wisely hath Ulysses here discovered
   The fever whereof all our power is sick.
AGAMEMNON. The nature of the sickness found, Ulysses,   140
   What is the remedy?

4. Weakness.

ULYSSES. The great Achilles, whom opinion crowns
  The sinew and the forehand of our host,
  Having his ear full of his airy fame,
  Grows dainty[5] of his worth, and in his tent   145
  Lies mocking our designs; with him Patroclus
  Upon a lazy bed the livelong day
  Breaks scurril jests;
  And with ridiculous and awkward action—
  Which, slanderer, he imitation calls—   150
  He pageants us. Sometime, great Agamemnon,
  Thy topless deputation he puts on;
  And like a strutting player—whose conceit
  Lies in his hamstring, and doth think it rich
  To hear the wooden dialogue and sound   155
  'Twixt his stretched footing and the scaffoldage—[6]
  Such to-be-pitied and o'er-wrested seeming
  He acts thy greatness in; and when he speaks
  'Tis like a chime a-mending, with terms unsquared,[7]
  Which, from the tongue of roaring Typhon[8] dropped,   160
  Would seem hyperboles. At this fusty stuff
  The large Achilles, on his pressed bed lolling,
  From his deep chest laughs out a loud applause;
  Cries 'Excellent! 'tis Agamemnon just.
  Now play me Nestor; hem, and stroke thy beard,   165
  As he being drest to some oration'.
  That's done, as near as the extremest ends
  Of parallels, as like[9] as Vulcan and his wife;
  Yet god Achilles still cries 'Excellent!
  'Tis Nestor right. Now play him me, Patroclus,   170
  Arming to answer in a night alarm'.
  And then, forsooth, the faint defects of age
  Must be the scene of mirth: to cough and spit
  And, with a palsy-fumbling on his gorget,
  Shake in and out the rivet. And at this sport   175
  Sir Valour dies; cries 'O, enough, Patroclus;
  Or give me ribs of steel! I shall split all
  In pleasure of my spleen'. And in this fashion
  All our abilities, gifts, natures, shapes,
  Severals and generals of grace exact,   180
  Achievements, plots, orders, preventions,
  Excitements to the field or speech for truce,
  Success or loss, what is or is not, serves
  As stuff for these two to make paradoxes.
NESTOR. And in the imitation of these twain—   185
  Who, as Ulysses says, opinion crowns
  With an imperial voice—many are infect.
  Ajax is grown self-willed and bears his head

5. Particular about.
6. Stage.
7. Unsuited.
8. A hundred-headed, big-voiced monster that Zeus destroyed.
9. Vulcan was crippled; his wife, Venus, beautiful.

In such a rein,[1] in full as proud a place
As broad Achilles; keeps his tent like him;   190
Makes factious feasts; rails on our state of war
Bold as an oracle, and sets Thersites,
A slave whose gall[2] coins slanders like a mint,
To match us in comparisons with dirt,
To weaken and discredit our exposure,   195
How rank[3] soever rounded in with danger.
ULYSSES. They tax our policy and call it cowardice,
    Count wisdom as no member of the war,
    Forestall prescience, and esteem no act
    But that of hand. The still and mental parts   200
    That do contrive how many hands shall strike
    When fitness calls them on, and know, by measure
    Of their observant toil, the enemies' weight—
    Why, this hath not a finger's dignity:
    They call this bed-work, mapp'ry, closet-war;   205
    So that the ram that batters down the wall,
    For the great swinge and rudeness of his poise,
    They place before his hand that made the engine,
    Or those that with the fineness of their souls
    By reason guide his execution.   210
NESTOR. Let this be granted, and Achilles' horse
    Makes many Thetis' sons.   [*Tucket*][4]
AGAMEMNON. What trumpet? Look, Menelaus.
MENELAUS. From Troy.
            [*Enter* AENEAS.]
AGAMEMNON. What would you fore our tent?   215
AENEAS. Is this great Agamemnon's tent, I pray you?
AGAMEMNON. Even this.
AENEAS. May one that is a herald and a prince
    Do a fair message to his kingly eyes?
AGAMEMNON. With surety stronger than Achilles' arm   220
    Fore all the Greekish heads, which with one voice
    Call Agamemnon head and general.
AENEAS. Fair leave and large security. How may
    A stranger to those most imperial looks
    Know them from eyes of other mortals?   225
AGAMEMNON.   How?
AENEAS. Ay;
    I ask, that I might waken reverence,
    And bid the cheek be ready with a blush
    Modest as Morning when she coldly eyes
    The youthful Phoebus.   230
    Which is that god in office, guiding men?
    Which is the high and mighty Agamemnon?
AGAMEMNON. This Troyan scorns us, or the men of Troy

1. As high.   3. Thickly.
2. Source of bile, the humor that was   4. A trumpet flourish.
supposed to cause resentment, malice.

Are ceremonious courtiers.

AENEAS. Courtiers as free, as debonair, unarmed,   235
   As bending angels; that's their fame in peace.
   But when they would seem soldiers, they have galls,
   Good arms, strong joints, true swords; and, Jove's accord,[5]
   Nothing so full of heart. But peace, Aeneas,
   Peace, Troyan; lay thy finger on thy lips.   240
   The worthiness of praise distains his worth,
   If that the praised himself bring the praise forth;
   But what the repining enemy commends,
   That breath fame blows; that praise, sole pure, transcends.

AGAMEMNON. Sir, you of Troy, call you yourself Aeneas?   245

AENEAS. Ay, Greek, that is my name.

AGAMEMNON. What's your affair, I pray you?

AENEAS. Sir, pardon; 'tis for Agamemnon's ears.

AGAMEMNON. He hears nought privately that comes from Troy.

AENEAS. Nor I from Troy come not to whisper him;   250
   I bring a trumpet to awake his ear,
   To set his sense on the attentive bent,
   And then to speak.

AGAMEMNON.   Speak frankly as the wind;
   It is not Agamemnon's sleeping hour.
   That thou shalt know, Troyan, he is awake,   255
   He tells thee so himself.

AENEAS.   Trumpet, blow loud,
   Send thy brass voice through all these lazy tents;
   And every Greek of mettle, let him know
   What Troy means fairly shall be spoke aloud. [*Sound trumpet.*]
   We have, great Agamemnon, here in Troy   260
   A prince called Hector—Priam is his father—
   Who in this dull and long-continued truce
   Is resty grown; he bade me take a trumpet
   And to this purpose speak: Kings, princes, lords!
   If there be one among the fair'st of Greece   265
   That holds his honour higher than his ease,
   That seeks his praise more than he fears his peril,
   That knows his valour and knows not his fear,
   That loves his mistress more than in confession
   With truant vows to her own lips he loves,[6]   270
   And dare avow her beauty and her worth
   In other arms than hers—to him this challenge.
   Hector, in view of Troyans and of Greeks,
   Shall make it good or do his best to do it:
   He hath a lady wiser, fairer, truer,   275
   Than ever Greek did compass in his arms;
   And will to-morrow with his trumpet call
   Mid-way between your tents and walls of Troy
   To rouse a Grecian that is true in love.
   If any come, Hector shall honour him;   280

5. God willing.   6. More than he says he does.

If none, he'll say in Troy, when he retires,
The Grecian dames are sunburnt[7] and not worth
The splinter of a lance. Even so much.

AGAMEMNON. This shall be told our lovers, Lord Aeneas.
If none of them have soul in such a kind,   285
We left them all at home. But we are soldiers;
And may that soldier a mere recreant prove
That means not, hath not, or is not in love.
If then one is, or hath, or means to be,
That one meets Hector; if none else, I am he.   290

NESTOR. Tell him of Nestor, one that was a man
When Hector's grandsire sucked. He is old now;
But if there be not in our Grecian mould
One noble man that hath one spark of fire
To answer for his love, tell him from me   295
I'll hide my silver beard in a gold beaver,
And in my vantbrace[8] put this withered brawn,
And, meeting him, will tell him that my lady
Was fairer than his grandame, and as chaste
As may be in the world. His youth in flood,   300
I'll prove this truth with my three drops of blood.

AENEAS. Now heavens forfend such scarcity of youth!

ULYSSES. Amen.

AGAMEMNON. Fair Lord Aeneas, let me touch your hand;
To our pavilion shall I lead you first.   305
Achilles shall have word of this intent;
So shall each lord of Greece, from tent to tent.
Yourself shall feast with us before you go,
And find the welcome of a noble foe.

[⟨*Exeunt all but* ULYSSES *and* NESTOR⟩]

ULYSSES. Nestor!   310

NESTOR. What says Ulysses?

ULYSSES. I have a young conception in my brain;
Be you my time to bring it to some shape.

NESTOR. What is't?

ULYSSES. This 'tis: 315
Blunt wedges rive hard knots. The seeded pride
That hath to this maturity blown up
In rank Achilles must or now be cropped
Or, shedding, breed a nursery of like evil
To overbulk us all.

NESTOR.   Well, and how?   320

ULYSSES. This challenge that the gallant Hector sends,
However it is spread in general name,
Relates in purpose only to Achilles.

NESTOR. True. The purpose is perspicuous as substance
Whose grossness little characters sum up;   325

---

7. Dark. A common insult since, according to Elizabethan fashion, light-complexioned ladies were more beautiful than others. Cf. I.ii, where Pandarus and Cressida quibble about whether or not Troilus is brown.
8. Armor for the forearm.

And, in the publication, make no strain
But that Achilles, were his brain as barren
As banks of Libya—though, Apollo knows,
'Tis dry enough—will with great speed of judgment,
Ay, with celerity, find Hector's purpose   330
Pointing on him.

ULYSSES. And wake him to the answer, think you?

NESTOR. Why, 'tis most meet. Who may you else oppose
That can from Hector bring his honor off,
If not Achilles? Though't be a sportful combat,   335
Yet in this trial much opinion dwells;
For here the Troyans taste our dear'st repute
With their fin'st palate; and trust to me, Ulysses,
Our imputation shall be oddly poised
In this vild action[9]; for the success,   340
Although particular, shall give a scantling
Of good or bad unto the general;
And in such indexes, although small pricks
To their subséquent volumes, there is seen
The baby figure of the giant mass   345
Of things to come at large. It is supposed
He that meets Hector issues from our choice;
And choice, being mutual act of all our souls,
Makes merit her election,[1] and doth boil,
As 'twere from forth us all, a man distilled   350
Out of our virtues; who miscarrying,
What heart receives from hence a conquering part,
To steel a strong opinion to themselves?
Which entertained, limbs are his[2] instruments,
In no less working than are swords and bows   355
Directive by the limbs.

ULYSSES.   Give pardon to my speech.
Therefore 'tis meet Achilles meet not Hector.
Let us, like merchants, show our foulest wares,
And think perchance they'll sell; if not,
The lustre of the better yet to show,   360
Shall show the better. Do not consent
That ever Hector and Achilles meet;
For both our honour and our shame in this
Are dogged with two strange followers.

NESTOR. I see them not with my old eyes. What are they?   365

ULYSSES. What glory our Achilles shares from Hector,
Were he not proud, we all should wear with him;
But he already is too insolent;
And it were better parch in Afric sun
Than in the pride and salt scorn of his eyes,   370
Should he scape Hector fair. If he were foiled,
Why, then we do our main opinion crush

9. Our reputation shall be unequally
balanced in this trivial action.

1. Reason for choosing.
2. That is, of the strong opinion.

In taint of our best man. No, make a lott'ry;
And, by device, let blockish Ajax draw
The sort to fight with Hector. Among ourselves   375
Give him allowance for the better man;
For that will physic the great Myrmidon,[3]
Who broils[4] in loud applause, and make him fall
His crest, that prouder than blue Iris bends.
If the dull brainless Ajax come safe off,   380
We'll dress him up in voices; if he fail,
Yet go we under our opinion still
That we have better men. But, hit or miss,
Our project's life this shape of sense assumes—
Ajax employed plucks down Achilles' plumes.   385
NESTOR. Now, Ulysses, I begin to relish thy advice;
And I will give a taste thereof forthwith
To Agamemnon. Go we to him straight.
Two curs shall tame each other: pride alone
Must tarre[5] the mastiffs on, as 'twere their bone.   [*Exeunt.*] 390

⟨II. i⟩

[*Enter* AJAX *and* THERSITES.]

AJAX. Thersites!

THERSITES. Agamemnon—how if he had boils full, all over, generally?

AJAX. Thersites!

THERSITES. And those boils did run—say so. Did not the general   5
run then? Were not that a botchy core?

AJAX. Dog!

THERSITES. Then would come some matter from him; I see none
now.

AJAX. Thou bitch-wolf's son, canst thou not hear? Feel, then.   10
[⟨*Strikes him.*⟩]

THERSITES. The plague of Greece upon thee, thou mongrel beef-
witted lord!

AJAX. Speak, then, thou vinewed'st[1] leaven, speak. I will beat
thee into handsomeness.

THERSITES. I shall sooner rail thee into wit and holiness; but I   15
think thy horse will sooner con an oration than thou learn a
prayer without book. Thou canst strike, canst thou? A red
murrain o' thy jade's tricks!

AJAX. Toadstool, learn me the proclamation.

THERSITES. Dost thou think I have no sense, thou strikest me   20
thus?

AJAX. The proclamation!

THERSITES. Thou art proclaimed fool, I think.

AJAX. Do not, porpentine,[2] do not; my fingers itch.

---

3. Achilles. His followers were called
Myrmidons.
4. A pun probably. He is sunning himself in loud applause, but he is also

quarreling as a result of too much
praise.
5. Incite.
1. Very mouldy.
2. Porcupine.

THERSITES. I would thou didst itch from head to foot and I had 25
the scratching of thee; I would make thee the loathsomest
scab in Greece. When thou art forth in the incursions, thou
strikest as slow as another.

AJAX. I say, the proclamation.

THERSITES. Thou grumblest and railest every hour on Achilles; 30
and thou art as full of envy at his greatness as Cerberus is at
Proserpina's beauty—ay, that thou bark'st at him.

AJAX. Mistress Thersites!

THERSITES. Thou shouldst strike him.

AJAX. Cobloaf! 35

THERSITES. He would pun thee into shivers with his fist, as a
sailor breaks a biscuit.

AJAX. You whoreson cur! [⟨*Strikes him.*⟩]

THERSITES. Do, do.

AJAX. Thou stool for a witch! 40

THERSITES. Ay, do, do; thou sodden-witted lord! Thou hast no
more brain than I have in mine elbows; an assinico may tutor
thee. Thou scurvy valiant ass! Thou art here but to thrash
Troyans, and thou art bought and sold among those of any
wit like a barbarian slave. If thou use to beat me, I will begin at 45
thy heel and tell what thou art by inches, thou thing of no
bowels, thou!

AJAX. You dog!

THERSITES. You scurvy lord!

AJAX. You cur! [⟨*Strikes him.*⟩] 50

THERSITES. Mars his idiot![3] Do, rudeness; do, camel; do, do.

[*Enter* ACHILLES *and* PATROCLUS.]

ACHILLES. Why, how now, Ajax! Wherefore do you thus?
How now, Thersites! What's the matter, man?

THERSITES. You see him there, do you?

ACHILLES. Ay, what's the matter? 55

THERSITES. Nay, look upon him.

ACHILLES. So I do. What's the matter?

THERSITES. Nay, but regard him well.

ACHILLES. Well! why, so I do.

THERSITES. But yet you look not well upon him; for whosomever 60
you take him to be, he is Ajax.

ACHILLES. I know that, fool.

THERSITES. Ay, but that fool knows not himself.

AJAX. Therefore I beat thee.

THERSITES. Lo, lo, lo, lo, what modicums of wit he utters! His 65
evasions have ears thus long.[4] I have bobbed his brain more
than he has beat my bones. I will buy nine sparrows for a
penny, and his pia mater[5] is not worth the ninth part of a
sparrow. This lord, Achilles, Ajax—who wears his wit in his
belly and his guts in his head—I'll tell you what I say of him. 70

---

3. Mars's idiot, i.e., war's fool, a man
fit only to fight.
4. I.e., he's an ass.

5. The membrane that covers the
brain. Here, the brain itself. It is
probably a pun on "pie," magpie.

ACHILLES. What?

THERSITES. I say this Ajax—   [⟨AJAX *offers to strike him.*⟩]

ACHILLES. Nay, good Ajax.

THERSITES. Has not so much wit—

                    [⟨AJAX *again offers to strike him.*⟩]

ACHILLES. Nay, I must hold you.   75

THERSITES. As will stop the eye of Helen's needle, for whom he comes to fight.

ACHILLES. Peace, fool.

THERSITES. I would have peace and quietness, but the fool will not—he there; that he; look you there.   80

AJAX. O thou damned cur! I shall—

ACHILLES. Will you set your wit to a fool's?

THERSITES. No, I warrant you, the fool's will shame it.

PATROCLUS. Good words, Thersites.

ACHILLES. What's the quarrel?   85

AJAX. I bade the vile owl go learn me the tenour of the proclamation, and he rails upon me.

THERSITES. I serve thee not.

AJAX. Well, go to, go to.

THERSITES. I serve here voluntary.   90

ACHILLES. Your last service was suff'rance; 'twas not voluntary. No man is beaten voluntary. Ajax was here the voluntary, and you as under an impress.

THERSITES. E'en so; a great deal of your wit too lies in your sinews, or else there be liars. Hector shall have a great catch an 95 he knock out either of your brains: 'a were as good crack a fusty nut with no kernel.

ACHILLES. What, with me too, Thersites?

THERSITES. There's Ulysses and old Nestor—whose wit was mouldy ere your grandsires had nails on their toes—yoke you 100 like draught oxen, and make you plough up the wars.

ACHILLES. What, what?

THERSITES. Yes, good sooth. To Achilles, to Ajax, to—

AJAX. I shall cut out your tongue.

THERSITES. 'Tis no matter; I shall speak as much as thou after- 105 wards.

PATROCLUS. No more words, Thersites; peace!

THERSITES. I will hold my peace when Achilles' brach bids me, shall I?

ACHILLES. There's for you, Patroclus.   110

THERSITES. I will see you hanged like clotpoles[6] ere I come any more to your tents. I will keep where there is wit stirring, and leave the faction of fools.   [*Exit.*]

PATROCLUS. A good riddance.

ACHILLES. Marry, this, sir, is proclaimed through all our host, 115
   That Hector, by the fifth hour of the sun,
   Will with a trumpet 'twixt our tents and Troy,
   To-morrow morning, call some knight to arms

6. Clotpoles, blockheads.

That hath a stomach; and such a one that dare
Maintain I know not what; 'tis trash. Farewell.   120
AJAX. Farewell. Who shall answer him?
ACHILLES. I know not; 'tis put to lott'ry. Otherwise
He knew his man.
AJAX. O, meaning you! I will go learn more of it.   [⟨*Exeunt.*⟩]

⟨II. ii⟩

[*Enter* PRIAM, HECTOR, TROILUS, PARIS, *and* HELENUS.]
PRIAM. After so many hours, lives, speeches spent,
Thus once again says Nestor from the Greeks:
'Deliver Helen, and all damage else—
As honour, loss of time, travail, expense,
Wounds, friends, and what else dear that is consumed   5
In hot digestion of this cormorant war—
Shall be struck off'. Hector, what say you to't?
HECTOR. Though no man lesser fears the Greeks than I,
As far as toucheth my particular,[7]
Yet, dread Priam,   10
There is no lady of more softer bowels,
More spongy to suck in the sense of fear,
More ready to cry out 'Who knows what follows?'
Than Hector is. The wound of peace is surety,
Surety secure[8]; but modest doubt is called   15
The beacon of the wise, the tent[9] that searches
To th' bottom of the worst. Let Helen go.
Since the first sword was drawn about this question,
Every tithe soul 'mongst many thousand dismes[1]
Hath been as dear as Helen—I mean, of ours.   20
If we have lost so many tenths of ours
To guard a thing not ours, nor worth to us,
Had it our name, the value of one ten,
What merit's in that reason which denies
The yielding of her up?
TROILUS.   Fie, fie, my brother!   25
Weigh you the worth and honour of a king
So great as our dread father in a scale
Of common ounces? Will you with counters sum
The past proportion of his infinite,
And buckle in a waist most fathomless   30
With spans and inches so diminutive
As fears and reasons? Fie, for godly shame!
HELENUS. No marvel, though you bite so sharp at reasons,
You are so empty of them. Should not our father

7. Concerns me personally.
8. The sense is that their own feeling of security, of invulnerability makes a healthy peace impossible.
9. A role of lint used as a surgical probe. A follow-up for the wound-of-peace metaphor.

1. Whatever Shakespeare means by "every tenth soul of many thousand tenths," it is clear that Hector is saying that Helen is no more valuable than any man lost in the war for her.

Bear the great sway of his affairs with reason, 35
Because your speech hath none that tells him so?
TROILUS. You are for dreams and slumbers, brother priest;
You fur your gloves with reason. Here are your reasons:
You know an enemy intends you harm;
You know a sword employed is perilous, 40
And reason flies the object of all harm.
Who marvels, then, when Helenus beholds
A Grecian and his sword, if he do set
The very wings of reason to his heels
And fly like chidden Mercury from Jove, 45
Or like a star disorbed? Nay, if we talk of reason,
Let's shut our gates and sleep. Manhood and honour
Should have hare hearts, would they but fat their thoughts
With this crammed reason. Reason and respect
Make livers pale and lustihood deject. 50
HECTOR. Brother, she is not worth what she doth cost
The keeping.
TROILUS. What's aught but as 'tis valued?
HECTOR. But value dwells not in particular will:[2]
It holds his estimate and dignity
As well wherein 'tis precious of itself 55
As in the prizer.[3] 'Tis mad idolatry
To make the service greater than the god;
And the will dotes that is attributive[4]
To what infectiously itself affects,
Without some image of th' affected merit.[5] 60
TROILUS. I take to-day a wife, and my election
Is led on in the conduct of my will;
My will enkindled by mine eyes and ears,
Two traded[6] pilots 'twixt the dangerous shores
Of will and judgment. How may I avoid, 65
Although my will distaste what it elected,
The wife I chose? There can be no evasion
To blench from this and to stand firm by honour.
We turn not back the silks upon the merchant
When we have soiled them, nor the remainder viands 70
We do not throw in unrespective sieve,[7]
Because we now are full. It was thought meet
Paris should do some vengeance on the Greeks;
Your breath with full consent bellied his sails;
The seas and winds, old wranglers, took a truce, 75

2. A thing is not valuable because a particular person wants to give it value.
3. Appraiser.
4. Suggests paying tribute, in both senses, and thus means subservient.
5. To what it is strongly drawn without some conception of the merit it seeks. *Infectiously*, of course, suggests that there is something sick about such doting.
6. Experienced.

7. Container that does not care what is put in it. It is a strange metaphor for Troilus to be using because surely a garbage can is where one puts *remainder viands*, particularly if one is a prince of Troy; Shakespeare, having grown up in Stratford, may be thinking that the sieve ought to be more "respective," that the leftovers can be sorted for use later.

And did him service. He touched the ports desired;
And for an old aunt[8] whom the Greeks held captive
He brought a Grecian queen, whose youth and freshness
Wrinkles Apollo's, and makes stale the morning.
Why keep we her? The Grecians keep our aunt.   80
Is she worth keeping? Why, she is a pearl
Whose price hath launched above a thousand ships,
And turned crowned kings to merchants.
If you'll avouch 'twas wisdom Paris went—
As you must needs, for you all cried 'Go, go'—   85
If you'll confess he brought home worthy prize—
As you must needs, for you all clapped your hands,
And cried 'Inestimable!'—why do you now
The issue of your proper wisdoms rate,
And do a deed that never fortune did—   90
Beggar the estimation which you prized
Richer than sea and land? O theft most base,
That we have stol'n what we do fear to keep!
But thieves unworthy of a thing so stol'n,
That in their country did them that disgrace[9]   95
We fear to warrant[1] in our native place!

CASSANDRA. [*within*] Cry, Troyans, cry.
PRIAM. What noise, what shriek is this?
TROILUS. 'Tis our mad sister; I do know her voice.
CASSANDRA. [*within*] Cry, Troyans.   100
HECTOR. It is Cassandra.

[*Enter* CASSANDRA, *raving.*]

CASSANDRA. Cry, Troyans, cry. Lend me ten thousand eyes,
    And I will fill them with prophetic tears.
HECTOR. Peace, sister, peace.
CASSANDRA. Virgins and boys, mid-age and wrinkled eld,   105
    Soft infancy, that nothing canst but cry,
    Add to my clamours. Let us pay betimes
    A moiety of that mass of moan to come.
    Cry, Troyans, cry. Practise your eyes with tears.
    Troy must not be, nor goodly Ilion stand;   110
    Our firebrand brother, Paris, burns us all.
    Cry, Troyans, cry! A Helen and a woe!
    Cry, cry. Troy burns, or else let Helen go.   [*Exit.*]
HECTOR. Now, youthful Troilus, do not these high strains
    Of divination in our sister work   115
    Some touches of remorse, or is your blood
    So madly hot that no discourse of reason,
    Nor fear of bad success in a bad cause,
    Can qualify the same?
TROILUS.   Why, brother Hector,
    We may not think the justness of each act   120

---

8. Hesione, Priam's sister, mother of
Ajax. See IV. v, where Aeneas makes
much of Hector's being Ajax's cousin.

9. The carrying off of Helen.
1. Defend.

Such and no other than event doth form it,
Nor once deject the courage of our minds
Because Cassandra's mad. Her brain-sick raptures
Cannot distaste the goodness of a quarrel
Which hath our several honours all engaged   125
To make it gracious. For my private part,
I am no more touched than all Priam's sons;
And Jove forbid there should be done amongst us
Such things as might offend the weakest spleen
To fight for and maintain.   130

PARIS. Else might the world convince of levity
As well my undertakings as your counsels;
But I attest the gods, your full consent
Gave wings to my propension, and cut off
All fears attending on so dire a project.   135
For what, alas, can these my single arms?
What propugnation[2] is in one man's valour
To stand the push and enmity of those
This quarrel would excite? Yet, I protest,
Were I alone to pass[3] the difficulties,   140
And had as ample power as I have will,
Paris should ne'er retract what he hath done
Nor faint in the pursuit.

PRIAM.   Paris, you speak
Like one besotted on your sweet delights.
You have the honey still, but these the gall;   145
So to be valiant is no praise at all.

PARIS. Sir, I propose not merely to myself
The pleasures such a beauty brings with it;
But I would have the soil of her fair rape
Wiped off in honourable keeping her.   150
What treason were it to the ransacked[4] queen,
Disgrace to your great worths, and shame to me,
Now to deliver her possession up
On terms of base compulsion! Can it be
That so degenerate a strain as this   155
Should once set footing in your generous bosoms?
There's not the meanest spirit on our party
Without a heart to dare or sword to draw
When Helen is defended; nor none so noble
Whose life were ill bestowed or death unfamed   160
Where Helen is the subject. Then, I say,
Well may we fight for her whom we know well
The world's large spaces cannot parallel.

HECTOR. Paris and Troilus, you have both said well;
And on the cause and question now in hand   165
Have glozed, but superficially; not much
Unlike young men, whom Aristotle thought

2. Defense.   4. Carried off.
3. Undergo.

412 · *William Shakespeare*

Unfit to hear moral philosophy.
The reasons you allege do more conduce
To the hot passion of distempered blood 170
Than to make up a free determination
'Twixt right and wrong; for pleasure and revenge
Have ears more deaf than adders to the voice
Of any true decision. Nature craves
All dues be rendered to their owners. Now, 175
What nearer debt in all humanity
Than wife is to the husband? If this law
Of nature be corrupted through affection[5];
And that great minds, of partial indulgence
To their benumbéd wills, resist the same; 180
There is a law in each well-ordered nation
To curb those raging appetites that are
Most disobedient and refractory.
If Helen, then, be wife to Sparta's king—
As it is known she is—these moral laws 185
Of nature and of nations speak aloud
To have her back returned. Thus to persist
In doing wrong extenuates not wrong,
But makes it much more heavy. Hector's opinion
Is this, in way of truth. Yet, ne'er the less, 190
My spritely brethren, I propend to you
In resolution to keep Helen still;
For 'tis a cause that hath no mean dependence
Upon our joint and several dignities.

TROILUS. Why, there you touched the life of our design. 195
Were it not glory that we more affected
Than the performance of our heaving spleens,
I would not wish a drop of Troyan blood
Spent more in her defence. But, worthy Hector,
She is a theme of honour and renown, 200
A spur to valiant and magnanimous deeds,
Whose present courage may beat down our foes,
And fame in time to come canonize us;
For I presume brave Hector would not lose
So rich advantage of a promised glory 205
As smiles upon the forehead of this action
For the wide world's revenue.

HECTOR.   I am yours,
You valiant offspring of great Priamus.
I have a roisting[6] challenge sent amongst
The dull and factious nobles of the Greeks 210
Will strike amazement to their drowsy spirits.

---

5. Either "inclination" or "appetite,"   6. Swaggering.
probably the latter since it is used in
line 181.

I was advertised their great general slept,
Whilst emulation in the army crept.
This, I presume, will wake him.   [*Exeunt.*]

⟨II. iii⟩

          [*Enter* THERSITES, *solus.*]

THERSITES. How now, Thersites! What, lost in the labyrinth of
thy fury? Shall the elephant Ajax carry it thus? He beats me,
and I rail at him. O worthy satisfaction! Would it were otherwise: that I could beat him, whilst he railed at me! 'Sfoot, I'll
learn to conjure and raise devils, but I'll see some issue of my   5
spiteful execrations. Then there's Achilles, a rare engineer! If
Troy be not taken till these two undermine it, the walls will
stand till they fall of themselves. O thou great thunder-darter
of Olympus, forget that thou art Jove, the king of gods, and,
Mercury, lose all the serpentine craft of thy caduceus, if ye   10
take not that little, little, less than little wit from them that
they have; which short-armed ignorance itself knows is so
abundant scarce, it will not in circumvention deliver a fly from
a spider without drawing their massy irons and cutting the
web. After this, the vengeance on the whole camp! or, rather,   15
the Neapolitan bone-ache![7] for that, methinks, is the curse depending on those that war for a placket.[8] I have said my prayers; and devil Envy say 'Amen'. What ho! my Lord Achilles!

          [*Enter* PATROCLUS.]

PATROCLUS. Who's there? Thersites! Good Thersites, come in
and rail.   20

THERSITES. If I could 'a' rememb'red a gilt counterfeit, thou
wouldst not have slipped out of my contemplation; but it is no
matter; thyself upon thyself! The common curse of mankind,
folly and ignorance, be thine in great revenue! Heaven bless
thee from a tutor, and discipline come not near thee! Let thy   25
blood[9] be thy direction till thy death. Then if she that lays
thee out says thou art a fair corse, I'll be sworn and sworn
upon't she never shrouded any but lazars. Amen. Where's
Achilles?

PATROCLUS. What, art thou devout? Wast thou in prayer?   30

THERSITES. Ay, the heavens hear me!

PATROCLUS. Amen.

          [*Enter* ACHILLES.]

ACHILLES. Who's there?

PATROCLUS. Thersites, my lord.

ACHILLES. Where, where? O, where? Art thou come? Why, my   35
cheese, my digestion, why hast thou not served thyself in to
my table so many meals? Come, what's Agamemnon?

THERSITES. Thy commander, Achilles. Then tell me, Patroclus,

7. Syphilis.   9. Violent passions.
8. Petticoat, i.e., Helen.

what's Achilles?

PATROCLUS. Thy lord, Thersites. Then tell me, I pray thee, what's 40
thyself?

THERSITES. Thy knower, Patroclus. Then tell me, Patroclus, what
art thou?

PATROCLUS. Thou must tell that knowest.

ACHILLES. O, tell, tell! 45

THERSITES. I'll decline[1] the whole question. Agamemnon commands Achilles; Achilles is my lord; I am Patroclus' knower;
and Patroclus is a fool.

PATROCLUS. You rascal!

THERSITES. Peace, fool! I have not done. 50

ACHILLES. He is a privileged man. Proceed, Thersites.

THERSITES. Agamemnon is a fool; Achilles is a fool; Thersites is a
fool; and, as aforesaid, Patroclus is a fool.

ACHILLES. Derive this; come.

THERSITES. Agamemnon is a fool to offer to command Achilles; 55
Achilles is a fool to be commanded of Agamemnon; Thersites
is a fool to serve such a fool; and this Patroclus is a fool positive.

PATROCLUS. Why am I a fool?

THERSITES. Make that demand of the Creator. It suffices me thou 60
art. Look you, who comes here?

[*Enter* AGAMEMNON, ULYSSES, NESTOR, DIOMEDES, AJAX,
and CALCHAS.]

ACHILLES. Patroclus, I'll speak with nobody. Come in with me,
Thersites. [*Exit.*]

THERSITES. Here is such patchery, such juggling, and such knav-
ery. All the argument is a whore and a cuckold—a good quarrel 65
to draw emulous factions and bleed to death upon. Now the
dry serpigo on the subject, and war and lechery confound all!
[⟨*Exit.*⟩]

AGAMEMNON. Where is Achilles?

PATROCLUS. Within his tent; but ill-disposed, my lord.

AGAMEMNON. Let it be known to him that we are here. 70
He shent[2] our messengers; and we lay by
Our appertainments, visiting of him.
Let him be told so, lest, perchance, he think
We dare not move the question of our place
Or know not what we are.

PATROCLUS.   I shall say so to him. [⟨*Exit.*⟩] 75

ULYSSES. We saw him at the opening of his tent.
He is not sick.

AJAX. Yes, lion-sick, sick of proud heart. You may call it melan-
choly, if you will favour the man; but, by my head, 'tis pride.
But why, why? Let him show us a cause. A word, my lord. 80
[⟨*Takes* AGAMEMNON *aside.*⟩]

NESTOR. What moves Ajax thus to bay at him?

ULYSSES. Achilles hath inveigled his fool from him.

1. Go through, as the declensions of a 2. Reviled.
noun.

NESTOR. Who, Thersites?
ULYSSES. He.
NESTOR. Then will Ajax lack matter, if he have lost his argument. 85
ULYSSES. No; you see he is his argument that has his argument—
    Achilles.
NESTOR. All the better; their fraction is more our wish than their
    faction. But it was a strong composure³ a fool could disunite!
ULYSSES. The amity that wisdom knits not, folly may easily untie. 90
    [⟨*Enter* PATROCLUS.⟩]
    Here comes Patroclus.
NESTOR. No Achilles with him.
ULYSSES. The elephant hath joints, but none for courtesy; his legs
    are legs for necessity, not for flexure.⁴
PATROCLUS. Achilles bids me say he is much sorry 95
    If any thing more than your sport and pleasure
    Did move your greatness and this noble state⁵
    To call upon him; he hopes it is no other
    But for your health and your digestion sake,
    An after-dinner's breath.
AGAMEMNON.   Hear you, Patroclus. 100
    We are too well acquainted with these answers;
    But his evasion, winged thus swift with scorn,
    Cannot outfly our apprehensions.
    Much attribute he hath, and much the reason
    Why we ascribe it to him. Yet all his virtues, 105
    Not virtuously on his own part beheld,
    Do in our eyes begin to lose their gloss;
    Yea, like fair fruit in an unwholesome dish,
    Are like to rot untasted. Go and tell him
    We come to speak with him; and you shall not sin 110
    If you do say we think him over-proud
    And under-honest, in self-assumption greater
    Than in the note of judgment⁶; and worthier than himself
    Here tend the savage strangeness he puts on,
    Disguise the holy strength of their command, 115
    And underwrite in an observing kind
    His humorous predominance; yea, watch
    His pettish lunes,⁷ his ebbs, his flows, as if
    The passage and whole carriage of this action
    Rode on his tide. Go tell him this, and add 120
    That if he overhold his price so much
    We'll none of him; but let him, like an engine
    Not portable, lie under this report:
    Bring action hither; this cannot go to war.
    A stirring dwarf we do allowance⁸ give 125
    Before a sleeping giant. Tell him so.
PATROCLUS. I shall, and bring his answer presently.   [⟨*Exit.*⟩]

3. Union.
4. Bending. This refers to an old myth that the elephant's legs were not jointed.
5. The accompanying nobles.
6. Regard of men of judgment.
7. Mad fits. Here, a suggestion of moons, since the whole sentence has to do with tides.
8. Approbation.

AGAMEMNON. In second voice we'll not be satisfied;
We come to speak with him. Ulysses, enter you.

[⟨*Exit* ULYSSES.⟩]

AJAX. What is he more than another? 130

AGAMEMNON. No more than what he thinks he is.

AJAX. Is he so much? Do you not think he thinks himself a better
man than I am?

AGAMEMNON. No question.

AJAX. Will you subscribe his thought and say he is? 135

AGAMEMNON. No, noble Ajax; you are as strong, as valiant, as
wise, no less noble, much more gentle, and altogether more
tractable.

AJAX. Why should a man be proud? How doth pride grow? I
know not what pride is. 140

AGAMEMNON. Your mind is the clearer, Ajax, and your virtues the
fairer. He that is proud eats up himself. Pride is his own glass,
his own trumpet, his own chronicle; and whatever praises itself
but in the deed devours the deed in the praise.

AJAX. I do hate a proud man as I do hate the engend'ring of 145
toads.

NESTOR. [*aside*] And yet he loves himself: is't not strange?

[⟨*Enter* ULYSSES.⟩]

ULYSSES. Achilles will not to the field to-morrow.

AGAMEMNON. What's his excuse?

ULYSSES.   He doth rely on none;
But carries on the stream of his dispose, 150
Without observance or respect of any,
In will peculiar and in self-admission.

AGAMEMNON. Why will he not, upon our fair request,
Untent his person and share the air with us?

ULYSSES. Things small as nothing, for request's sake only,[9] 155
He makes important; possessed he is with greatness,
And speaks not to himself but with a pride
That quarrels at self-breath. Imagined worth
Holds in his blood such swol'n and hot discourse
That 'twixt his mental and his active parts 160
Kingdomed[1] Achilles in commotion rages,
And batters down himself. What should I say?
He is so plaguy proud that the death tokens of it
Cry 'No recovery'.

AGAMEMNON.   Let Ajax go to him.
Dear lord, go you and greet him in his tent. 165
'Tis said he holds you well, and will be led
At your request a little from himself.

ULYSSES. O Agamemnon, let it not be so!
We'll consecrate the steps that Ajax makes
When they go from Achilles. Shall the proud lord 170
That bastes his arrogance with his own seam[2]

9. Because they are requested.   in a civil war.
1. Achilles is like a kingdom involved   2. Fat.

And never suffers matter of the world
Enter his thoughts, save such as doth revolve
And ruminate himself—shall he be worshipped
Of that we hold an idol more than he?   175
No, this thrice-worthy and right valiant lord
Shall not so stale his palm,[3] nobly acquired,
Nor, by my will, assubjugate[4] his merit,
As amply titled as Achilles is,
By going to Achilles.   180
That were to enlard his fat-already pride,
And add more coals to Cancer when he burns
With entertaining great Hyperion.[5]
This lord go to him! Jupiter forbid,
And say in thunder 'Achilles go to him'.   185
NESTOR. [aside] O, this is well! He rubs the vein of him.
DIOMEDES. [aside] And how his silence drinks up this applause!
AJAX. If I go to him, with my arméd fist I'll pash him o'er the
    face.
AGAMEMNON. O, no, you shall not go.   190
AJAX. An 'a be proud with me I'll pheeze his pride.
    Let me go to him.
ULYSSES. Not for the worth that hangs upon our quarrel.
AJAX. A paltry, insolent fellow!
NESTOR. [aside] How he describes himself!   195
AJAX. Can he not be sociable?
ULYSSES. [aside] The raven chides blackness.
AJAX. I'll let his humours blood.[6]
AGAMEMNON. [aside] He will be the physician that should be the
    patient.   200
AJAX. An all men were a my mind—
ULYSSES. [aside] Wit would be out of fashion.
AJAX. 'A should not bear it so, 'a should eat swords first. Shall
    pride carry it?
NESTOR. [aside] An 'twould, you'd carry half.   205
ULYSSES. [aside] 'A would have ten shares.
AJAX. I will knead him, I'll make him supple.
NESTOR. [aside] He's not yet through[7] warm. Force him with
    praises; pour in, pour in; his ambition is dry.
ULYSSES. [to AGAMEMNON] My lord, you feed too much on this 210
    dislike.
NESTOR. Our noble general, do not do so.
DIOMEDES. You must prepare to fight without Achilles.
ULYSSES. Why 'tis this naming of him does him harm.
    Here is a man—but 'tis before his face;   215
    I will be silent.
NESTOR.   Wherefore should you so?
    He is not emulous, as Achilles is.

---

3. Cheapen his glory.   6. Cure his humors by bleeding.
4. Degrade.   7. Thoroughly.
5. Add heat to summer.

ULYSSES. Know the whole world, he is as valiant.

AJAX. A whoreson dog, that shall palter with us thus! Would he were a Troyan! 220

NESTOR. What a vice were it in Ajax now—

ULYSSES. If he were proud.

DIOMEDES. Or covetous of praise.

ULYSSES. Ay, or surly borne.

DIOMEDES. Or strange, or self-affected. 225

ULYSSES. Thank the heavens, lord, thou art of sweet composure;
Praise him that got thee, she that gave thee suck;
Famed be thy tutor, and thy parts of nature
Thrice-famed beyond, beyond all erudition;
But he that disciplined thine arms to fight— 230
Let Mars divide eternity in twain
And give him half; and for thy vigour,
Bull-bearing Milo[8] his addition yield
To sinewy Ajax. I will not praise thy wisdom,
Which, like a bourn, a pale, a shore, confines 235
Thy spacious and dilated parts. Here's Nestor,
Instructed by the antiquary times—[9]
He must, he is, he cannot but be wise;
But pardon, father Nestor, were your days
As green as Ajax' and your brain so tempered, 240
You should not have the eminence of him,
But be as Ajax.

AJAX.   Shall I call you father?

NESTOR. Ay, my good son.

DIOMEDES.   Be ruled by him, Lord Ajax.

ULYSSES. There is no tarrying here; the hart Achilles
Keeps thicket. Please it our great general 245
To call together all his state of war;
Fresh kings are come to Troy. To-morrow
We must with all our main of power stand fast;
And here's a lord—come knights from east to west
And cull their flower, Ajax shall cope the best. 250

AGAMEMNON. Go we to council. Let Achilles sleep.
Light boats sail swift, though greater hulks draw deep.

[Exeunt.]

⟨III. i⟩

[⟨*Music sounds within.*⟩ *Enter* PANDARUS ⟨*and a* SERVANT⟩.]

PANDARUS. Friend, you—pray you, a word. Do you not follow the young Lord Paris?

SERVANT. Ay, sir, when he goes before me.

PANDARUS. You depend[1] upon him, I mean?

SERVANT. Sir, I do depend upon the lord. 5

PANDARUS. You depend upon a noble gentleman; I must needs praise him.

8. Title. Milo, the famous athlete, should give his fame to Ajax.   9. Times studied by an antiquary.
1. Are a dependent of.

SERVANT. The lord be praised!

PANDARUS. You know me, do you not?

SERVANT. Faith, sir, superficially.   10

PANDARUS. Friend, know me better: I am the Lord Pandarus.

SERVANT. I hope I shall know your honour better.

PANDARUS. I do desire it.

SERVANT. You are in the state of grace.[2]

PANDARUS. Grace! Not so, friend; honour and lordship are my   15
titles. What music is this?

SERVANT. I do but partly know sir; it is music in parts.

PANDARUS. Know you the musicians?

SERVANT. Wholly, sir.

PANDARUS. Who play they to?   20

SERVANT. To the hearers, sir.

PANDARUS. At whose pleasure, friend?

SERVANT. At mine, sir, and theirs that love music.

PANDARUS. Command, I mean, friend.

SERVANT. Who shall I command, sir?   25

PANDARUS. Friend, we understand not one another: I am too
courtly, and thou too cunning. At whose request do these men
play?

SERVANT. That's to't, indeed, sir. Marry, sir, at the request of
Paris my lord, who is there in person; with him the mortal   30
Venus, the heart-blood of beauty, love's invisible soul—

PANDARUS. Who, my cousin, Cressida?

SERVANT. No, sir, Helen. Could you not find out that by her at-
tributes?

PANDARUS. It should seem, fellow, that thou hast not seen the   35
Lady Cressida. I come to speak with Paris from the Prince
Troilus; I will make a complimental assault upon him, for my
business seethes.

SERVANT. Sodden business! There's a stewed[3] phrase indeed!

[*Enter* PARIS *and* HELEN.]

PANDARUS. Fair be to you, my lord, and to all this fair company!   40
Fair desires, in all fair measure, fairly guide them—especially
to you, fair queen! Fair thoughts be your fair pillow.

HELEN. Dear lord, you are full of fair words.

PANDARUS. You speak your fair pleasure, sweet queen. Fair prince,
here is good broken[4] music.   45

PARIS. You have broke it, cousin; and by my life, you shall make
it whole again; you shall piece it out with a piece of your performance. Nell, he is full of harmony.

PANDARUS. Truly, lady, no.

HELEN. O, sir—   50

PANDARUS. Rude, in sooth; in good sooth, very rude.

PARIS. Well said, my lord. Well, you say so in fits.[5]

PANDARUS. I have business to my lord, dear queen. My lord, will

2. Duke's title.
3. The servant picks up Pandarus'
cooking metaphor, but *stew* also
means brothel; so his pun brings him

closer to Pandarus' seething business
than the metaphor does.
4. Arranged for various instruments.
5. Parts of a song.
2. Duke's title.
3. The servant picks up Pandarus'
cooking metaphor, but *stew* also
means brothel; so his pun brings him

closer to Pandarus' seething business
than the metaphor does.
4. Arranged for various instruments.
5. Parts of a song.

420 · *William Shakespeare*

you vouchsafe me a word?

HELEN. Nay, this shall not hedge us out. We'll hear you sing, 55
certainly.

PANDARUS. Well, sweet queen, you are pleasant with me. But,
marry, thus, my lord: my dear lord and most esteemed friend,
your brother Troilus—

HELEN. My Lord Pandarus, honey-sweet lord— 60

PANDARUS. Go to, sweet queen, go to—commends himself most
affectionately to you—

HELEN. You shall not bob us out of our melody. If you do, our
melancholy upon your head!

PANDARUS. Sweet queen, sweet queen; that's a sweet queen, i' 65
faith.

HELEN. And to make a sweet lady sad is a sour offence.

PANDARUS. Nay, that shall not serve your turn; that shall it not,
in truth, la. Nay, I care not for such words; no, no.—And, my
lord, he desires you that, if the King call for him at supper, you 70
will make his excuse.

HELEN. My Lord Pandarus!

PANDARUS. What says my sweet queen, my very very sweet queen?

PARIS. What exploit's in hand? Where sups he to-night?

HELEN. Nay, but, my lord— 75

PANDARUS. What says my sweet queen?—My cousin will fall out
with you.

HELEN. You must not know where he sups.

PARIS. I'll lay my life, with my disposer[6] Cressida.

PANDARUS. No, no, no such matter; you are wide. Come, your dis- 80
poser is sick.

PARIS. Well, I'll make's excuse.

PANDARUS. Ay, good my lord. Why should you say Cressida? No,
your poor disposer's sick.

PARIS. I spy. 85

PANDARUS. You spy! What do you spy?—Come, give me an instrument. Now, sweet queen.

HELEN. Why, this is kindly done.

PANDARUS. My niece is horribly in love with a thing you have,
sweet queen. 90

HELEN. She shall have it, my lord, if it be not my Lord Paris.

PANDARUS. He! No, she'll none of him; they two are twain.

HELEN. Falling in, after falling out, may make them three.

PANDARUS. Come, come. I'll hear no more of this; I'll sing you a
song now. 95

HELEN. Ay, ay, prithee now. By my troth, sweet lord, thou hast
a fine forehead.

PANDARUS. Ay, you may, you may.[7]

HELEN. Let thy song be love. This love will undo us all. O

6. One who rules me. It is difficult to
see how Cressida rules Paris, except as
any pretty woman rules any man; the
phrase may be simply a compliment,
but if Pandarus is right in line 92 where

he says *they two are twain*, meaning
"at odds," then there's a barb in the
phrase.
7. I.e., make a joke.

Cupid, Cupid, Cupid!   100
PANDARUS. Love! Ay, that it shall, i' faith.
PARIS. Ay, good now, love, love, nothing but love.
PANDARUS. In good troth, it begins so.   [⟨*Sings.*⟩]

> Love, love, nothing but love, still love, still more!
>   For, oh, love's bow   105
>   Shoots buck and doe;
>   The shaft confounds
>   Not that it wounds,
> But tickles still the sore.[8]
> These lovers cry, O ho, they die!   110
>   Yet that which seems the wound to kill
> Doth turn O ho! to ha! ha! he!
>   So dying love lives still.
> O ho! a while, but ha! ha! ha!
> O ho! groans out for ha! ha! ha!—hey ho!   115

HELEN. In love, i' faith, to the very tip of the nose.
PARIS. He eats nothing but doves, love; and that breeds hot blood, and hot blood begets hot thoughts, and hot thoughts beget hot deeds, and hot deeds is love.
PANDARUS. Is this the generation of love: hot blood, hot thoughts, 120 and hot deeds? Why, they are vipers. Is love a generation of vipers? Sweet lord, who's a-field today?
PARIS. Hector, Deiphobus, Helenus, Antenor, and all the gallantry of Troy. I would fain have armed to-day, but my Nell would not have it so. How chance my brother Troilus went not? 125
HELEN. He hangs the lip at something. You know all, Lord Pandarus.
PANDARUS. Not I, honey-sweet queen. I long to hear how they sped to-day. You'll remember your brother's excuse?
PARIS. To a hair.   130
PANDARUS. Farewell, sweet queen.
HELEN. Commend me to your niece.
PANDARUS. I will, sweet queen.   [⟨*Exit.*⟩ *Sound a retreat.*]
PARIS. They're come from the field. Let us to Priam's hall
  To greet the warriors. Sweet Helen, I must woo you   135
  To help unarm our Hector. His stubborn buckles,
  With these your white enchanting fingers touched,
  Shall more obey than to the edge of steel
  Or force of Greekish sinews; you shall do more
  Than all the island kings—disarm great Hector.   140
HELEN. 'Twill make us proud to be his servant, Paris;
  Yea, what he shall receive of us in duty
  Gives us more palm in beauty than we have,
  Yea, overshines ourself.
PARIS. Sweet, above thought I love thee.   [*Exeunt.*]   145

8. A pun, probably, since *sore* is not only "wound," but a fourth-year buck.

⟨III. ii⟩

[*Enter* PANDARUS ⟨*and*⟩ TROILUS' MAN.]

PANDARUS. How now! Where's thy master? At my cousin Cressida's?

MAN. No, sir; he stays for you to conduct him thither.

[⟨*Enter* TROILUS.⟩]

PANDARUS. O, here he comes. How now, how now!

[⟨*Exit* MAN.⟩] 150

PANDARUS. Have you seen my cousin?

TROILUS. No, Pandarus. I stalk about her door
Like a strange soul upon the Stygian banks
Staying for waftage. O, be thou my Charon,
And give me swift transportance to these fields   155
Where I may wallow in the lily beds
Proposed for the deserver! O gentle Pandar,
From Cupid's shoulder pluck his painted wings,
And fly with me to Cressid!

PANDARUS. Walk here i' th' orchard, I'll bring her straight.   160

[⟨*Exit.*⟩]

TROILUS. I am giddy; expectation whirls me round.
Th' imaginary relish is so sweet
That it enchants my sense; what will it be
When that the wat'ry palate tastes indeed
Love's thrice-repuréd nectar? Death, I fear me,   165
Sounding⁹ destruction or some joy too fine,
Too subtle-potent, tuned too sharp in sweetness,
For the capacity of my ruder powers.
I fear it much; and I do fear besides
That I shall lose distinction¹ in my joys;   170
As doth a battle, when they charge on heaps
The enemy flying.

[*Re-enter* PANDARUS.]

PANDARUS. She's making her ready, she'll come straight; you must
be witty² now. She does so blush, and fetches her wind so short,
as if she were frayed with a sprite.³ I'll fetch her. It is the pret- 175
tiest villain; she fetches her breath as short as a new-ta'en sparrow. [*Exit.*]

TROILUS. Even such a passion doth embrace my bosom.
My heart beats thicker than a feverous pulse,
And all my powers do their bestowing lose,   180
Like vassalage at unawares encount'ring
The eye of majesty.

[*Re-enter* PANDARUS *with* CRESSIDA.]

PANDARUS. Come, come, what need you blush? Shame's a baby.—
Here she is now; swear the oaths now to her that you have
sworn to me.—What, are you gone again? You must be 185

9. Swooning.
1. Ability to distinguish one from another.
2. Have your wits about you.
3. Frightened by a ghost.

oted.

watched[4] ere you be made tame, must you? Come your ways, come your ways; an you draw backward, we'll put you i' th' fills.[5]—Why do you not speak to her?—Come, draw this curtain[6] and let's see your picture. Alas the day, how loath you are to offend daylight! An 'twere dark, you'd close sooner. So, so; rub on, and kiss the mistress.[7] How now, a kiss in fee-farm![8] Built there, carpenter; the air is sweet. Nay, you shall fight your hearts out ere I part you. The falcon as the tercel, for all the ducks i' th' river.[9] Go to, go to.

TROILUS. You have bereft me of all words, lady.

PANDARUS. Words pay no debts, give her deeds; but she'll bereave you o' th' deeds too, if she call your activity in question. What, billing again? Here's 'In witness whereof the parties interchangeably'. Come in, come in; I'll go get a fire. [⟨*Exit.*⟩]

CRESSIDA. Will you walk in, my lord?

TROILUS. O Cressid, how often have I wished me thus!

CRESSIDA. Wished, my lord! The gods grant—O my lord!

TROILUS. What should they grant? What makes this pretty abruption? What too curious[1] dreg espies my sweet lady in the fountain of our love?

CRESSIDA. More dregs than water, if my fears have eyes.

TROILUS. Fears make devils of cherubims; they never see truly.

CRESSIDA. Blind fear, that seeing reason leads, finds safer footing than blind reason stumbling without fear. To fear the worst oft cures the worse.

TROILUS. O, let my lady apprehend no fear! In all Cupid's pageant there is presented no monster.

CRESSIDA. Nor nothing monstrous neither?

TROILUS. Nothing, but our undertakings when we vow to weep seas, live in fire, eat rocks, tame tigers, thinking it harder for our mistress to devise imposition enough than for us to undergo any difficulty imposed. This is the monstruosity in love, lady, that the will is infinite, and the execution confined; that the desire is boundless, and the act a slave to limit.

CRESSIDA. They say all lovers swear more performance than they are able, and yet reserve an ability that they never perform; vowing more than the perfection of ten, and discharging less than the tenth part of one. They that have the voice of lions and the act of hares, are they not monsters?

TROILUS. Are there such? Such are not we. Praise us as we are tasted,[2] allow us as we prove; our head shall go bare till merit crown it. No perfection in reversion[3] shall have a praise in present. We will not name desert before his birth; and, being

4. Kept awake. The term is from the training of hawks, as almost everything Pandarus says in this speech is from some sport other than the one he is selling.
5. Shafts. As a horse, to keep from bolting.
6. I.e., veil.
7. At bowls, to *rub on* was to meet

obstacles in the way of the object-ball, sometimes called a *mistress.*
8. In perpetuity.
9. Will back the female hawk (*falcon*) against the male (*tercel*) to bring down the most game.
1. Causing anxiety.
2. Tested.
3. In right of future possession.

born, his addition shall be humble. Few words to fair faith: Troilus shall be such to Cressid as what envy can say worst ₂₃₀ shall be a mock for his truth[4]; and what truth can speak truest not truer than Troilus.

CRESSIDA. Will you walk in, my lord?

[*Enter* PANDARUS.]

PANDARUS. What, blushing still? Have you not done talking yet?

CRESSIDA. Well, uncle, what folly I commit, I dedicate to you. ₂₃₅

PANDARUS. I thank you for that; if my lord get a boy of you, you'll give him me. Be true to my lord; if he flinch, chide me for it.

TROILUS. You know now your hostages: your uncle's word and my firm faith. ₂₄₀

PANDARUS. Nay, I'll give my word for her too: our kindred, though they be long ere they be wooed, they are constant being won; they are burrs, I can tell you; they'll stick where they are thrown.

CRESSIDA. Boldness comes to me now and brings me heart. ₂₄₅
Prince Troilus, I have loved you night and day
For many weary months.

TROILUS. Why was my Cressid then so hard to win?

CRESSIDA. Hard to seem won; but I was won, my lord,
With the first glance that ever—pardon me. ₂₅₀
If I confess much, you will play the tyrant.
I love you now; but not, till now, so much
But I might master it. In faith, I lie;
My thoughts were like unbridled children, grown
Too headstrong for their mother. See, we fools! ₂₅₅
Why have I blabbed? Who shall be true to us,
When we are so unsecret to ourselves?
But, though I loved you well, I wooed you not;
And yet, good faith, I wished myself a man,
Or that we women had men's privilege
Of speaking first. Sweet, bid me hold my tongue, ₂₆₀
For in this rapture I shall surely speak
The thing I shall repent. See, see, your silence,
Cunning in dumbness, from my weakness draws
My very soul of counsel.[5] Stop my mouth.

TROILUS. And shall, albeit sweet music issues thence. ₂₆₅

PANDARUS. Pretty, i' faith.

CRESSIDA. My lord, I do beseech you, pardon me;
'Twas not my purpose thus to beg a kiss.
I am ashamed. O heavens! what have I done?
For this time will I take my leave, my lord. ₂₇₀

TROILUS. Your leave, sweet Cressid!

PANDARUS. Leave! An you take leave till to-morrow morning—

CRESSIDA. Pray you, content you.

TROILUS. What offends you, lady?

4. The worst thing envy can do is scorn his constancy.   5. Inmost secrets.

CRESSIDA. Sir, mine own company. 275
TROILUS. You cannot shun yourself.
CRESSIDA. Let me go and try.
  I have a kind of self resides with you;
  But an unkind self, that itself will leave
  To be another's fool. I would be gone. 280
  Where is my wit? I know not what I speak.
TROILUS. Well know they what they speak that speak so wisely.
CRESSIDA. Perchance, my lord, I show more craft than love;
  And fell so roundly to a large confession
  To angle for your thoughts; but you are wise, 285
  Or else you love not; for to be wise and love
  Exceeds man's might; that dwells with gods above.
TROILUS. O that I thought it could be in a woman—
  As, if it can, I will presume in you—
  To feed for aye her lamp and flames of love; 290
  To keep her constancy in plight and youth,[6]
  Outliving beauty's outward, with a mind
  That doth renew swifter than blood decays!
  Or that persuasion could but thus convince me
  That my integrity and truth to you 295
  Might be affronted[7] with the match and weight
  Of such a winnowed purity in love.
  How were I then uplifted! but, alas,
  I am as true as truth's simplicity,
  And simpler than the infancy of truth. 300
CRESSIDA. In that I'll war with you.
TROILUS.   O virtuous fight,
  When right with right wars who shall be most right!
  True swains in love shall in the world to come
  Approve their truth by Troilus, when their rhymes,
  Full of protest, of oath, and big compare, 305
  Want similes, truth tired with iteration—
  'As true as steel, as plantage to the moon,
  As sun to day, as turtle to her mate,
  As iron to adamant,[8] as earth to th' centre'—
  Yet, after all comparisons of truth, 310
  As truth's authentic author to be cited,
  'As true as Troilus' shall crown up the verse
  And sanctify the numbers.
CRESSIDA.   Prophet may you be!
  If I be false, or swerve a hair from truth,
  When time is old and hath forgot itself,
  When waterdrops have worn the stones of Troy, 315
  And blind oblivion swallowed cities up,
  And mighty states characterless are grated
  To dusty nothing—yet let memory
  From false to false, among false maids in love, 320

6. As it was first plighted, and as fresh.
7. Faced.
8. Loadstone, which is magnetic.

Upbraid my falsehood when th' have said 'As false
As air, as water, wind, or sandy earth,
As fox to lamb, as wolf to heifer's calf,
Pard to the hind, or stepdame to her son'—
Yea, let them say, to stick the heart of falsehood,   325
'As false as Cressid'.

PANDARUS. Go to, a bargain made; seal it, seal it; I'll be the witness. Here I hold your hand; here my cousin's. If ever you
prove false one to another, since I have taken such pains to
bring you together, let all pitiful goers-between be called to the   330
world's end after my name—call them all Pandars; let all constant men be Troiluses, all false women Cressids, and all
brokers between Pandars. Say 'Amen'.

TROILUS. Amen.

CRESSIDA. Amen.   335

PANDARUS. Amen. Whereupon I will show you a chamber which
bed,[9] because[1] it shall not speak of your pretty encounters,
press it to death. Away!

> [*Exeunt* ⟨TROILUS *and* CRESSIDA⟩.]

And Cupid grant all tongue-tied maidens here,
Bed, chamber, pander, to provide this gear!   [*Exit*.]   340

⟨III. iii⟩

> [⟨*Flourish*.⟩ *Enter* ULYSSES, DIOMEDES, NESTOR, AGAMEM-
> NON, ⟨MENELAUS, AJAX,⟩ *and* CALCHAS.]

CALCHAS. Now, Princes, for the service I have done,
Th' advantage of the time prompts me aloud
To call for recompense. Appear it to your mind
That, through the sight I bear in things to come,
I have abandoned Troy, left my possession,   5
Incurred a traitor's name, exposed myself
From certain and possessed conveniences
To doubtful fortunes, sequest'ring from me all
That time, acquaintance, custom, and condition,
Made tame and most familiar to my nature;   10
And here, to do you service, am become
As new into the world, strange, unacquainted—
I do beseech you, as in way of taste,
To give me now a little benefit
Out of those many regist'red in promise,   15
Which you say live to come in my behalf.

AGAMEMNON. What wouldst thou of us, Troyan? Make demand.

CALCHAS. You have a Troyan prisoner called Antenor,
Yesterday took; Troy holds him very dear.
Oft have you—often have you thanks therefor—
Desired my Cressid in right great exchange,[2]   20
Whom Troy hath still denied; but this Antenor,

9. In which the bed.
1. In order that.

2. In exchange for someone important.

I know, is such a wrest³ in their affairs
That their negotiations all must slack
Wanting his manage; and they will almost   25
Give us a prince of blood, a son of Priam,
In change of him. Let him be sent, great Princes,
And he shall buy my daughter; and her presence
Shall quite strike off all service I have done
In most accepted pain.

AGAMEMNON.   Let Diomedes bear him,   30
And bring us Cressid hither. Calchas shall have
What he requests of us. Good Diomed,
Furnish you fairly for this interchange;
Withal, bring word if Hector will to-morrow
Be answered in his challenge. Ajax is ready.   35

DIOMEDES. This shall I undertake, and 'tis a burden
Which I am proud to bear.   [*Exit* ⟨*with* CALCHAS⟩.]
    [ACHILLES *and* PATROCLUS *stand in their tent.*]

ULYSSES. Achilles stands i' th' entrance of his tent.
Please it our general pass strangely by him,
As if he were forgot; and, Princes all,
Lay negligent and loose regard upon him.   40
I will come last. 'Tis like he'll question me
Why such unplausive⁴ eyes are bent, why turned on him?
If so, I have derision med'cinable
To use between your strangeness and his pride,   45
Which his own will shall have desire to drink.
It may do good. Pride hath no other glass
To show itself but pride; for supple knees
Feed arrogance and are the proud man's fees.

AGAMEMNON. We'll execute your purpose, and put on   50
A form of strangeness as we pass along.
So do each lord; and either greet him not,
Or else disdainfully, which shall shake him more
Than if not looked on. I will lead the way.

ACHILLES. What comes the general to speak with me?   55
You know my mind. I'll fight no more 'gainst Troy.

AGAMEMNON. What says Achilles? Would he aught with us?

NESTOR. Would you, my lord, aught with the general?

ACHILLES. No.

NESTOR. Nothing, my lord.

AGAMEMNON. The better.   60

ACHILLES. Good day, good day.

MENELAUS. How do you? How do you?

ACHILLES. What, does the cuckold scorn me?

AJAX. How now, Patroclus?

ACHILLES. Good morrow, Ajax.   65

AJAX. Ha?

ACHILLES. Good morrow.

---

3. Tuning key, for a harp.   4. Disapproving.

AJAX. Ay, and good next day too.   [*Exeunt.*]

ACHILLES. What mean these fellows? Know they not Achilles?   70

PATROCLUS. They pass by strangely. They were used to bend,
    To send their smiles before them to Achilles,
    To come as humbly as they used to creep
    To holy altars.

ACHILLES.   What, am I poor of late?
    'Tis certain, greatness, once fall'n out with fortune,   75
    Must fall out with men too. What the declined is,
    He shall as soon read in the eyes of others
    As feel in his own fall; for men, like butterflies,
    Show not their mealy wings but to the summer;
    And not a man for being simply man   80
    Hath any honour, but honour for those honours
    That are without him, as place, riches, and favour,
    Prizes of accident, as oft as merit;
    Which when they fall, as being slippery standers,
    The love that leaned on them as slippery too,   85
    Doth one pluck down another, and together
    Die in the fall. But 'tis not so with me:
    Fortune and I are friends; I do enjoy
    At ample point all that I did possess
    Save these men's looks; who do, methinks, find out   90
    Something not worth in me such rich beholding
    As they have often given. Here is Ulysses.
    I'll interrupt his reading.
    How now, Ulysses.

ULYSSES.   Now, great Thetis' son.

ACHILLES. What are you reading?

ULYSSES.   A strange fellow here   95
    Writes me that man—how dearly ever parted,[5]
    How much in having, or without or in[6]—
    Cannot make boast to have that which he hath,
    Nor feels not what he owes, but by reflection;
    As when his virtues shining upon others   100
    Heat them, and they retort that heat again
    To the first giver.

ACHILLES.   This is not strange, Ulysses.
    The beauty that is borne here in the face
    The bearer knows not, but commends itself
    To others' eyes; nor doth the eye itself—   105
    That most pure spirit of sense—behold itself,
    Not going from itself; but eye to eye opposed
    Salutes each other with each other's form;
    For speculation[7] turns not to itself
    Till it hath travelled, and is married there   110
    Where it may see itself. This is not strange at all.

ULYSSES. I do not strain at the position—

5. However well endowed.
6. However much one possesses, ex-   ternally or internally.
7. Power of vision.

It is familiar—but at the author's drift;
Who, in his circumstance, expressly proves
That no man is the lord of anything,   115
Though in and of him there be much consisting,
Till he communicate his parts to others;
Nor doth he of himself know them for aught
Till he behold them formed in th' applause
Where th' are extended[8]; who,[9] like an arch, reverb'rate   120
The voice again; or, like a gate of steel
Fronting the sun, receives and renders back
His figure and his heat. I was much rapt in this;
And apprehended here immediately
The unknown Ajax.   125
Heavens, what a man is there! A very horse,
That has he knows not what. Nature, what things there are
Most abject in regard and dear in use!
What things again most dear in the esteem
And poor in worth! Now shall we see to-morrow—   130
An act that very chance doth throw upon him—
Ajax renowned. O heavens, what some men do,
While some men leave to do!
How some men creep in skittish Fortune's hall,
Whiles others play the idiots in her eyes!   135
How one man eats into another's pride,
While pride is fasting in his wantonness![1]
To see these Grecian lords!—why, even already
They clap the lubber Ajax on the shoulder,
As if his foot were on brave Hector's breast,   140
And great Troy shrinking.
ACHILLES. I do believe it; for they passed by me
As misers do by beggars, neither gave to me
Good word nor look. What, are my deeds forgot?
ULYSSES. Time hath, my lord, a wallet at his back,   145
Wherein he puts alms for oblivion,
A great-sized monster of ingratitudes.
Those scraps are good deeds past, which are devoured
As fast as they are made, forgot as soon
As done. Perseverance, dear my lord,   150
Keeps honour bright. To have done is to hang
Quite out of fashion, like a rusty mail
In monumental mock'ry. Take the instant[2] way;
For honour travels in a strait so narrow
Where one but goes abreast. Keep then the path,   155
For emulation hath a thousand sons
That one by one pursue; if you give way,
Or hedge aside from the direct forthright,
Like to an ent'red tide they all rush by
And leave you hindmost;   160

8. By which they are publicized.   1. Self-satisfaction.
9. Which.   2. Immediate.

Or, like a gallant horse fall'n in first rank,
Lie there for pavement to the abject rear,[3]
O'er-run and trampled on. Then what they do in present,
Though less than yours in past, must o'ertop yours;
For Time is like a fashionable host,   165
That slightly shakes his parting guest by th' hand;
And with his arms out-stretched, as he would fly,
Grasps in the comer. The welcome ever smiles,
And farewell goes out sighing. Let not virtue seek
Remuneration for the thing it was;   170
For beauty, wit,
High birth, vigour of bone, desert in service,
Love, friendship, charity, are subjects all
To envious and calumniating Time.
One touch of nature makes the whole world kin,   175
That all with one consent praise new-born gawds,[4]
Though they are made and moulded of things past,
And give to dust that is a little gilt
More laud than gilt o'er-dusted.
The present eye praises the present object.   180
Then marvel not, thou great and complete man,
That all the Greeks begin to worship Ajax,
Since things in motion sooner catch the eye
Than what not stirs. The cry went once on thee,
And still it might, and yet it may again,   185
If thou wouldst not entomb thyself alive
And case thy reputation in thy tent,
Whose glorious deeds but in these fields of late
Made emulous missions 'mongst the gods themselves,
And drave great Mars to faction.[5]

ACHILLES.   Of this my privacy   190
I have strong reasons.

ULYSSES.   But 'gainst your privacy
The reasons are more potent and heroical.
'Tis known, Achilles, that you are in love
With one of Priam's daughters.

ACHILLES.   Ha! known!

ULYSSES. Is that a wonder?   195
The providence that's in a watchful state
Knows almost every grain of Plutus' gold;
Finds bottom in th' uncomprehensive[6] deeps;
Keeps place with thought, and almost, like the gods,
Does thoughts unveil in their dumb cradles   200
There is a mystery—with whom relation
Durst never meddle—in the soul of state,
Which hath an operation more divine
Than breath or pen can give expressure to.

3. The miserable creatures bringing up
the rear.
4. Toys, showy ornaments.
5. The gods took sides in the battle;
the suggestion is that they did so out
of jealousy at Achilles' reputation.
6. Unfathomab.e.

All the commerce that you have had with Troy   205
As perfectly is ours as yours, my lord;
And better would it fit Achilles much
To throw down Hector than Polyxena.[7]
But it must grieve young Pyrrhus[8] now at home,
When fame shall in our island, sound her trump,   210
And all the Greekish girls shall tripping sing
'Great Hector's sister did Achilles win;
But our great Ajax bravely beat down him'.
Farewell, my lord. I as your lover speak.
The fool slides o'er the ice that you should break.   [⟨*Exit.*⟩] 215
PATROCLUS. To this effect, Achilles, have I moved you.
  A woman impudent and mannish grown
  Is not more loathed than an effeminate man
  In time of action. I stand condemned for this;
  They think my little stomach to the war   220
  And your great love to me restrains you thus.
  Sweet, rouse yourself; and the weak wanton Cupid
  Shall from your neck unloose his amorous fold,
  And, like a dew-drop from the lion's mane,
  Be shook to air.
ACHILLES.   Shall Ajax fight with Hector?   225
PATROCLUS. Ay, and perhaps receive much honour by him.
ACHILLES. I see my reputation is at stake;
  My fame is shrewdly gored.[9]
PATROCLUS.   O, then, beware!
  Those wounds heal ill that men do give themselves.
  Omission to do what is necessary   230
  Seals a commission to a blank of danger[1];
  And danger, like an ague, subtly taints
  Even then when we sit idly in the sun.
ACHILLES. Go call Thersites hither, sweet Patroclus.
  I'll send the fool to Ajax, and desire him   235
  T' invite the Troyan lords, after the combat,
  To see us here unarmed. I have a woman's longing,
  An appetite that I am sick withal,
  To see great Hector in his weeds of peace;
  To talk with him, and to behold his visage,   240
  Even to my full of view.
      [*Enter* THERSITES.]
               A labour saved!
THERSITES. A wonder!
ACHILLES. What?
THERSITES. Ajax goes up and down the field asking for himself.
ACHILLES. How so?   245
THERSITES. He must fight singly to-morrow with Hector, and is

---

7. Priam's daughter with whom Achilles is in love, if we believe Ulysses (lines 192–3).
8. Achilles' son.
9. Seriously wounded.

1. Binds one to face unknown dangers. A blank commission was given to royal agents to use in collecting imposts and making arrests.

so prophetically proud of an heroical cudgelling that he raves
in saying nothing.

ACHILLES. How can that be?

THERSITES. Why, 'a stalks up and down like a peacock—a stride 250
and a stand; ruminates like an hostess that hath no arithmetic
but her brain to set down her reckoning, bites his lip with a
politic regard,[2] as who should say 'There were wit in this head,
an 'twould out'; and so there is; but it lies as coldly in him as
fire in a flint, which will not show without knocking. The 255
man's undone for ever; for if Hector break not his neck i' th'
combat, he'll break't himself in vainglory. He knows not me.
I said 'Good morrow, Ajax'; and he replies 'Thanks, Agamemnon'. What think you of this man that takes me for the general? He's grown a very land fish, languageless, a monster. A 260
plague of opinion! A man may wear it on both sides, like a
leather jerkin.

ACHILLES. Thou must be my ambassador to him, Thersites.

THERSITES. Who, I? Why, he'll answer nobody; he professes not
answering. Speaking is for beggars; he wears his tongue in's 265
arms. I will put on his presence.[3] Let Patroclus make demands
to me, you shall see the pageant of Ajax.

ACHILLES. To him, Patroclus. Tell him I humbly desire the valiant Ajax to invite the most valorous Hector to come unarmed
to my tent; and to procure safe conduct for his person of the 270
magnanimous and most illustrious six-or-seven-times-honoured
Captain General of the Grecian army, Agamemnon, et cetera.
Do this.

PATROCLUS. Jove bless great Ajax!

THERSITES. Hum! 275

PATROCLUS. I come from the worthy Achilles—

THERSITES. Ha!

PATROCLUS. Who most humbly desires you to invite Hector to his
tent—

THERSITES. Hum! 280

PATROCLUS. And to procure safe conduct from Agamemnon.

THERSITES. Agamemnon!

PATROCLUS. Ay, my lord.

THERSITES. Ha!

PATROCLUS. What say you to't? 285

THERSITES. God be wi' you, with all my heart.

PATROCLUS. Your answer, sir.

THERSITES. If to-morrow be a fair day, by eleven of the clock it
will go one way or other. Howsoever, he shall pay for me ere
he has me. 290

PATROCLUS. Your answer, sir.

THERSITES. Fare ye well, with all my heart.

ACHILLES. Why, but he is not in this tune, is he?

THERSITES. No, but out of tune thus. What music will be in him
when Hector has knocked out his brains I know not; but, I am 295

2. Intelligent look.   3. Pretend to be him.

sure, none, unless the fiddler Apollo get his sinews to make catlings on.

ACHILLES. Come, thou shalt bear a letter to him straight.

THERSITES. Let me bear another to his horse; for that's the more capable creature. 300

ACHILLES. My mind is troubled, like a fountain stirred;
And I myself see not the bottom of it.

> [⟨*Exeunt* ACHILLES *and* PATROCLUS.⟩]

THERSITES. Would the fountain of your mind were clear again, that I might water an ass at it. I had rather be a tick in a sheep than such a valiant ignorance.   [⟨*Exit*.⟩] 305

⟨IV. i⟩

> [*Enter, at one door,* AENEAS *with a torch; at another,* PARIS, DEIPHOBUS, ANTENOR, DIOMEDES *the Grecian,* ⟨*and* OTHERS,⟩ *with torches.*]

PARIS. See, ho! Who is that there?

DEIPHOBUS.   It is the Lord Aeneas.

AENEAS. Is the Prince there in person?
Had I so good occasion to lie long
As you, Prince Paris, nothing but heavenly business   5
Should rob my bed-mate of my company.

DIOMEDES. That's my mind too. Good morrow, Lord Aeneas.

PARIS. A valiant Greek, Aeneas—take his hand:
Witness the process of your speech, wherein
You told how Diomed, a whole week by days,[1]
Did haunt you in the field.

AENEAS.   Health to you, valiant sir,   10
During all question of the gentle truce;
But when I meet you armed, as black defiance
As heart can think or courage execute.

DIOMEDES. The one and other Diomed embraces.
Our bloods are now in calm; and so long health!   15
But when contention and occasion meet,
By Jove, I'll play the hunter for thy life
With all my force, pursuit, and policy.

AENEAS. And thou shalt hunt a lion, that will fly
With his face backward. In humane gentleness,   20
Welcome to Troy! now, by Anchises' life,
Welcome indeed! By Venus' hand I swear
No man alive can love in such a sort
The thing he means to kill, more excellently.

DIOMEDES. We sympathise. Jove let Aeneas live,   25
If to my sword his fate be not the glory,
A thousand complete courses of the sun!
But in mine emulous honour let him die
With every joint a wound, and that to-morrow!

AENEAS. We know each other well.

DIOMEDES. We do; and long to know each other worse.   30

1. Day by day.

PARIS. This is the most despiteful gentle greeting
   The noblest hateful love, that e'er I heard of.
   What business, lord, so early?

AENEAS. I was sent for to the King; but why, I know not. 35

PARIS. His purpose meets you; it was to bring this Greek
   To Calchas' house, and there to render him,
   For the enfreed Antenor, the fair Cressid.
   Let's have your company; or, if you please,
   Haste there before us. I constantly² do think— 40
   Or rather call my thought a certain knowledge—
   My brother Troilus lodges there to-night.
   Rouse him and give him note of our approach,
   With the whole quality³ wherefore; I fear
   We shall be much unwelcome.

AENEAS.   That I assure you: 45
   Troilus had rather Troy were borne to Greece
   Than Cressid borne from Troy.

PARIS.   There is no help;
   The bitter disposition of the time
   Will have it so. On, lord; we'll follow you.

AENEAS. Good morrow, all.   [⟨*Exit.*⟩] 50

PARIS. And tell me, noble Diomed—faith, tell me true,
   Even in the soul of sound good-fellowship—
   Who in your thoughts deserves fair Helen best,
   Myself or Menelaus?

DIOMEDES.   Both alike:
   He merits well to have her that doth seek her, 55
   Not making any scruple of her soilure,
   With such a hell of pain and world of charge;
   And you as well to keep her that defend her,
   Not palating the taste of her dishonour,
   With such a costly loss of wealth and friends. 60
   He like a puling cuckold would drink up
   The lees and dregs of a flat tamed piece;
   You, like a lecher, out of whorish loins
   Are pleased to breed out your inheritors.
   Both merits poised, each weighs nor less nor more; 65
   But he as he, the heavier for a whore.

PARIS. You are too bitter to your country-woman.

DIOMEDES. She's bitter to her country. Hear me, Paris:
   For every false drop in her bawdy veins
   A Grecian's life hath sunk; for every scruple 70
   Of her contaminated carrion weight
   A Troyan hath been slain; since she could speak,
   She hath not given so many good words breath
   As for her Greeks and Troyans suff'red death.

PARIS. Fair Diomed, you do as chapmen do, 75
   Dispraise the thing that you desire to buy;
   But we in silence hold this virtue well,

2. Firmly.   3. Explanation.

We'll not commend what we intend to sell.
Here lies our way.   [*Exeunt.*]

⟨IV. ii⟩

[*Enter* TROILUS *and* CRESSIDA.]

TROILUS. Dear, trouble not yourself; the morn is cold.
CRESSIDA. Then, sweet my lord, I'll call mine uncle down;
He shall unbolt the gates.
TROILUS.   Trouble him not;
To bed, to bed! Sleep kill those pretty eyes,
And give as soft attachment to thy senses
As infants' empty of all thought!
CRESSIDA.   Good morrow, then.
TROILUS. I prithee now, to bed.
CRESSIDA.   Are you aweary of me?
TROILUS. O Cressida! but that the busy day,
Waked by the lark, hath roused the ribald crows,
And dreaming night will hide our joys no longer,
I would not from thee.
CRESSIDA.   Night hath been too brief.
TROILUS. Beshrew the witch! with venomous wights[4] she stays
As tediously as hell, but flies the grasps of love
With wings more momentary-swift than thought.
You will catch cold, and curse me.
CRESSIDA.   Prithee tarry.
You men will never tarry.
O foolish Cressid! I might have still held off,
And then you would have tarried. Hark! there's one up.
PANDARUS. [*within*] What's all the doors open here?
TROILUS. It is your uncle.
CRESSIDA. A pestilence on him! Now will he be mocking.
I shall have such a life!
      [*Enter* PANDARUS.]
PANDARUS. How now, how now! How go maidenheads? Here, you
maid! Where's my cousin Cressid?
CRESSIDA. Go hang yourself, you naughty mocking uncle.
You bring me to do, and then you flout me too.
PANDARUS. To do what? to do what? Let her say what. What
have I brought you to do?
CRESSIDA. Come, come, beshrew your heart! You'll ne'er be good,
Nor suffer others.
PANDARUS. Ha, ha! Alas, poor wretch! a poor capocchia![5] hast not
slept to-night? Would he not, a naughty man, let it sleep? A
bugbear take him!
CRESSIDA. Did not I tell you? Would he were knocked i' th' head!
                                                    [*One knocks.*]

4. Men out doing evil deeds.
5. In Italian, a knob on a club, or the head of a pin, some small protuberance on a stick. If Pandarus means this, it is probably some kind of forgotten mild obscenity directed at Cressida. He may mean *capocchio* ("blockhead"), but that seems not particularly appropriate to the occasion.

Who's that at door? Good uncle, go and see.   35
My lord, come you again into my chamber.
You smile and mock me, as if I meant naughtily.
TROILUS. Ha! ha!
CRESSIDA. Come, you are deceived, I think of no such thing.
[*Knock.*]
How earnestly they knock! Pray you come in: 40
I would not for half Troy have you seen here.
[*Exeunt ⟨*TROILUS *and* CRESSIDA⟩.*]
PANDARUS. Who's there? What's the matter? Will you beat down
the door? How now? What's the matter?
[⟨*Enter* AENEAS.⟩]
AENEAS. Good morrow, lord, good morrow.
PANDARUS. Who's there? My lord Aeneas? By my troth,   45
I knew you not. What news with you so early?
AENEAS. Is not Prince Troilus here?
PANDARUS. Here! What should he do here?
AENEAS. Come, he is here, my lord; do not deny him.
It doth import him much to speak with me.   50
PANDARUS. Is he here, say you? It's more than I know, I'll be
sworn. For my own part, I came in late. What should he do
here?
AENEAS. Who!—nay, then. Come, come, you'll do him wrong
ere you are ware; you'll be so true to him to be false to him.   55
Do not you know of him, but yet go fetch him hither; go.
[⟨*Enter* TROILUS.⟩]
TROILUS. How now? What's the matter?
AENEAS. My lord, I scarce have leisure to salute you,
My matter is so rash.[6] There is at hand
Paris your brother, and Deiphobus,   60
The Grecian Diomed, and our Antenor
Delivered to us; and for him forthwith,
Ere the first sacrifice, within this hour,
We must give up to Diomedes' hand
The Lady Cressida.
TROILUS.   Is it concluded so?   65
AENEAS. By Priam, and the general state of Troy.
They are at hand and ready to effect it.
TROILUS. How my achievements mock me!
I will go meet them; and, my lord Aeneas,
We met by chance; you did not find me here.   70
AENEAS. Good, good, my lord, the secrets of nature
Have not more gift in taciturnity.
[*Exeunt ⟨*TROILUS *and* AENEAS⟩.*]
PANDARUS. Is't possible? No sooner got but lost? The devil take
Antenor! The young prince will go mad. A plague upon An-
tenor! I would they had broke's neck.   75
[*Enter* CRESSIDA.]
CRESSIDA. How now? What's the matter? Who was here?
6. Urgent.

PANDARUS. Ah, ah!

CRESSIDA. Why sigh you so profoundly? Where's my lord? Gone?
Tell me, sweet uncle, what's the matter?

PANDARUS. Would I were as deep under the earth as I am above! 80

CRESSIDA. O the gods! What's the matter?

PANDARUS. Pray thee, get thee in. Would thou hadst ne'er been
born! I knew thou wouldst be his death! O, poor gentleman!
A plague upon Antenor!

CRESSIDA. Good uncle, I beseech you, on my knees I beseech you, 85
what's the matter?

PANDARUS. Thou must be gone, wench, thou must be gone; thou
art changed for Antenor; thou must to thy father, and be gone
from Troilus. 'Twill be his death; 'twill be his bane; he cannot
bear it. 90

CRESSIDA. O you immortal gods! I will not go.

PANDARUS. Thou must.

CRESSIDA. I will not, uncle. I have forgot my father;
I know no touch of consanguinity,
No kin, no love, no blood, no soul so near me
As the sweet Troilus. O you gods divine, 95
Make Cressid's name the very crown of falsehood,
If ever she leave Troilus! Time, force, and death,
Do to this body what extremes you can,
But the strong base and building of my love
Is as the very centre of the earth, 100
Drawing all things to it. I'll go in and weep—

PANDARUS. Do, do.

CRESSIDA. Tear my bright hair, and scratch my praiséd cheeks,
Crack my clear voice with sobs and break my heart, 105
With sounding 'Troilus'. I will not go from Troy.   [⟨Exeunt.⟩]

⟨IV. iii⟩

[Enter PARIS, TROILUS, AENEAS, DEIPHOBUS, ANTENOR,
DIOMEDES.]

PARIS. It is great morning,[7] and the hour prefixed
For her delivery to this valiant Greek
Comes fast upon. Good my brother Troilus,
Tell you the lady what she is to do
And haste her to the purpose.

TROILUS.   Walk into her house. 5
I'll bring her to the Grecian presently[8];
And to his hand when I deliver her,
Think it an altar, and thy brother Troilus
A priest, there off'ring to it his own heart.   [⟨Exit.⟩]

PARIS. I know what 'tis to love,
And would, as I shall pity, I could help! 10
Please you walk in, my lords.   [Exeunt.]

7. Broad daylight.   8. Immediately.

438 · *William Shakespeare*

⟨IV. iv⟩

[Enter PANDARUS *and* CRESSIDA.]

PANDARUS. Be moderate, be moderate.

CRESSIDA. Why tell you me of moderation?
　The grief is fine, full, perfect, that I taste,
　And violenteth in a sense as strong
　As that which causeth it. How can I moderate it?　5
　If I could temporize with my affections
　Or brew it to a weak and colder palate,
　The like allayment could I give my grief.
　My love admits no qualifying dross;
　No more my grief, in such a precious loss.　10
　　[Enter TROILUS.]

PANDARUS. Here, here, here he comes. Ah, sweet ducks!

CRESSIDA. O Troilus! Troilus!　　　　[⟨*Embracing him.*⟩]

PANDARUS. What a pair of spectacles is here!
　Let me embrace too. 'O heart', as the goodly saying is,
　　　　　O heart, heavy heart,
　　　　　Why sigh'st thou without breaking?　15
　where he answers again
　　　　　Because thou canst not ease thy smart
　　　　　By friendship nor by speaking.
　There was never a truer rhyme. Let us cast away nothing, for　20
　we may live to have need of such a verse. We see it, we see it.
　How now, lambs!

TROILUS. Cressid, I love thee in so strained⁹ a purity
　That the blessed gods, as angry with my fancy,¹
　More bright in zeal than the devotion which　25
　Cold lips blow to their deities, take thee from me.

CRESSIDA. Have the gods envy?

PANDARUS. Ay, ay, ay; 'tis too plain a case.

CRESSIDA. And is it true that I must go from Troy?

TROILUS. A hateful truth.

CRESSIDA.　　　　　What, and from Troilus too?　30

TROILUS. From Troy and Troilus.

CRESSIDA.　　　　　Is't possible?

TROILUS. And suddenly, where injury of chance
　Puts back leave-taking, justles roughly by
　All time of pause, rudely beguiles our lips
　Of all rejoindure,² forcibly prevents　35
　Our locked embrasures, strangles our dear vows
　Even in the birth of our own labouring breath.
　We two, that with so many thousand sighs
　Did buy each other, must poorly sell ourselves
　With the rude brevity and discharge of one.　40
　Injurious time now with a robber's haste
　Crams his rich thievery up, he knows not how.

9. Filtered, i.e., a purity so pure.　　2. Reunion.
1. Love.

Troilus and Cressida: ⟨IV. iv⟩ · 439

As many farewells as be stars in heaven,
With distinct breath and consigned kisses to them,
He fumbles up into a loose adieu,
And scants us with a single famished kiss,
Distasted with the salt of broken tears.

AENEAS. [*within*] My lord, is the lady ready?

TROILUS. Hark! you are called. Some say the Genius[3]
Cries so to him that instantly must die.
Bid them have patience; she shall come anon.

PANDARUS. Where are my tears? Rain, to lay this wind, or my
heart will be blown up by the root? [⟨*Exit.*⟩]

CRESSIDA. I must then to the Grecians?

TROILUS.   No remedy.

CRESSIDA. A woeful Cressid 'mongst the merry Greeks!
When shall we see again?

TROILUS. Hear me, my love. Be thou but true of heart—

CRESSIDA. I true! how now! What wicked deem[4] is this?

TROILUS. Nay, we must use expostulation kindly,
For it is parting from us.
I speak not 'Be thou true' as fearing thee,
For I will throw my glove[5] to Death himself
That there's no maculation in thy heart;
But 'Be thou true' say I to fashion in
My sequent protestation[6]: be thou true,
And I will see thee.

CRESSIDA. O, you shall be exposed, my lord, to dangers
As infinite as imminent! But I'll be true.

TROILUS. And I'll grow friend with danger. Wear this sleeve.

CRESSIDA. And you this glove. When shall I see you?

TROILUS. I will corrupt the Grecian sentinels
To give thee nightly visitation.
But yet be true.

CRESSIDA.   O heavens! 'Be true' again!

TROILUS. Hear why I speak it, love.
The Grecian youths are full of quality;
They're loving, well composed with gifts of nature,
And swelling o'er with arts and exercise.[7]
How novelty may move, and parts with person,[8]
Alas, a kind of godly jealousy,
Which I beseech you call a virtuous sin,
Makes me afeard.

CRESSIDA.   O heavens! you love me not.

TROILUS. Die I a villain, then!
In this I do not call your faith in question
So mainly as my merit. I cannot sing,
Nor heel the high lavolt,[9] nor sweeten talk,

3. The spirit that attends man through life.
4. Thought.
5. Challenge.
6. Set a pattern for my own oath
which follows.
7. In theory and practice.
8. A mixture of accomplishment and charm.
9. A spirited dance.

Nor play at subtle games—fair virtues all,
To which the Grecians are most prompt and pregnant;
But I can tell that in each grace of these
There lurks a still and dumb-discoursive[1] devil
That tempts most cunningly. But be not tempted.   90

CRESSIDA. Do you think I will?

TROILUS. No.
But something may be done that we will not;
And sometimes we are devils to ourselves,
When we will tempt the frailty of our powers,   95
Presuming on their changeful potency.[2]

AENEAS. [*within*] Nay, good my lord!

TROILUS.   Come, kiss; and let us part.

PARIS. [*within*] Brother Troilus!

TROILUS.   Good brother, come you hither;
And bring Aeneas and the Grecian with you.

CRESSIDA. My lord, will you be true?   100

TROILUS. Who, I? Alas, it is my vice, my fault!
Whiles others fish with craft for great opinion,
I with great truth catch mere simplicity;
Whilst some with cunning gild their copper crowns,
With truth and plainness I do wear mine bare.   105
Fear not my truth: the moral of my wit
Is 'plain and true'; there's all the reach of it.

[⟨*Enter* AENEAS, PARIS, ANTENOR, DEIPHOBUS, *and* DIO-
MEDES.⟩]

Welcome, Sir Diomed! Here is the lady
Which for Antenor we deliver you;
At the port,[3] lord, I'll give her to thy hand,   110
And by the way possess thee what she is.
Entreat[4] her fair, and, by my soul, fair Greek,
If e'er thou stand at mercy of my sword,
Name Cressid, and thy life shall be as safe
As Priam is in Ilion.

DIOMEDES.   Fair Lady Cressid,   115
So please you, save the thanks this prince expects.
The lustre in your eye, heaven in your cheek,
Pleads your fair usage; and to Diomed
You shall be mistress, and command him wholly.

TROILUS. Grecian, thou dost not use me courteously   120
To shame the zeal of my petition to thee
In praising her. I tell thee, lord of Greece,
She is as far high-soaring o'er thy praises
As thou unworthy to be called her servant.
I charge thee use her well, even for my charge;   125
For, by the dreadful Pluto, if thou dost not,
Though the great bulk Achilles be thy guard,
I'll cut thy throat.

1. Silently articulate.   3. Gate.
2. Inconstant power.   4. Treat.

DIOMEDES. O, be not moved, Prince Troilus.
    Let me be privileged by my place and message   130
    To be a speaker free. When I am hence
    I'll answer to my lust[5]; and know you, lord,
    I'll nothing do on charge. To her own worth
    She shall be prized; but that you say 'Be't so',
    I'll speak it in my spirit and honour, 'No'.   135
TROILUS. Come, to the port. I'll tell thee, Diomed,
    This brave shall oft make thee to hide thy head.
    Lady, give me your hand; and, as we walk,
    To our own selves bend we our needful talk.

        [⟨*Exeunt* TROILUS, CRESSIDA, *and* DIOMEDES.⟩]
                       [*Sound trumpet.*]

PARIS. Hark! Hector's trumpet.   140
AENEAS. How have we spent this morning!
    The Prince must think me tardy and remiss,
    That swore to ride before him to the field.
PARIS. 'Tis Troilus' fault. Come, come to field with him.
DEIPHOBUS. Let us make ready straight.   145
AENEAS. Yea, with a bridegroom's fresh alacrity
    Let us address to tend on Hector's heels.
    The glory of our Troy doth this day lie
    On his fair worth and single chivalry.   [*Exeunt.*]

⟨IV. v⟩

    [*Enter* AJAX, *armed;* ACHILLES, PATROCLUS, AGAMEMNON,
      MENELAUS, ULYSSES, NESTOR, *&c.*]

AGAMEMNON. Here art thou in appointment[6] fresh and fair,
    Anticipating time. With starting courage
    Give with thy trumpet a loud note to Troy,
    Thou dreadful Ajax, that the appallèd air
    May pierce the head of the great combatant,   5
    And hale him hither.
AJAX. Thou, trumpet, there's my purse.
    Now crack thy lungs and split thy brazen pipe;
    Blow, villain, till thy spheréd bias[7] cheek
    Out-swell the colic of puffed Aquilon.[8]
    Come, stretch thy chest, and let thy eyes spout blood: 10
    Thou blowest for Hector.   [⟨*Trumpet sounds.*⟩]
ULYSSES. No trumpet answers.
ACHILLES.   'Tis but early days.[9]
AGAMEMNON. Is not yond Diomed, with Calchas' daughter?
ULYSSES. 'Tis he, I ken the manner of his gait;
    He rises on the toe. That spirit of his   15
    In aspiration lifts him from the earth.

        [⟨ENTER DIOMEDES, *with* CRESSIDA.⟩]

AGAMEMNON. Is this the lady Cressid?

---

5. Do as I please.   8. North wind.
6. Equipment.   9. In the day.
7. Swollen.

DIOMEDES.   Even she.

AGAMEMNON. Most dearly welcome to the Greeks, sweet lady.

NESTOR. Our general doth salute you with a kiss.

ULYSSES. Yet is the kindness put particular;   20
   'Twere better she were kissed in general.

NESTOR. And very courtly counsel. I'll begin.
   So much for Nestor.

ACHILLES. I'll take that winter from your lips, fair lady.
   Achilles bids you welcome.   25

MENELAUS. I had good argument for kissing once.

PATROCLUS. But that's no argument for kissing now;
   For thus popped Paris in his hardiment,[1]
   And parted thus you and your argument.

ULYSSES. O deadly gall, and theme of all our scorns!   30
   For which we lose our heads to gild his horns.

PATROCLUS. The first was Menelaus' kiss; this, mine—
   Patroclus kisses you.

MENELAUS.   O, this is trim!

PATROCLUS. Paris and I kiss evermore for him.

MENELAUS. I'll have my kiss, sir. Lady, by your leave.   35

CRESSIDA. In kissing, do you render or receive?

PATROCLUS. Both take and give.

CRESSIDA.   I'll make my match to live,[2]
   The kiss you take is better than you give;
   Therefore no kiss.

MENELAUS. I'll give you boot; I'll give you three for one.   40

CRESSIDA. You are an odd man; give even or give none.

MENELAUS. An odd man, lady? Every man is odd.

CRESSIDA. No, Paris is not; for you know 'tis true
   That you are odd, and he is even with you.

MENELAUS. You fillip me o' th' head.

CRESSIDA.   No, I'll be sworn.   45

ULYSSES. It were no match, your nail against his horn.
   May I, sweet lady, beg a kiss of you?

CRESSIDA. You may.

ULYSSES.   I do desire it.

CRESSIDA.   Why, beg then.

ULYSSES. Why then, for Venus' sake give me a kiss
   When Helen is a maid again, and his.   50

CRESSIDA. I am your debtor; claim it when 'tis due.

ULYSSES. Never's my day, and then a kiss of you.

DIOMEDES. Lady, a word. I'll bring you to your father.

                  [⟨*Exit with* CRESSIDA.⟩]

NESTOR. A woman of quick sense.

ULYSSES.   Fie, fie upon her!
   There's a language in her eye, her cheek, her lip;   55
   Nay, her foot speaks; her wanton spirits look out
   At every joint and motive[3] of her body.

1. Boldness.   3. Moving part.
2. Bet my life.

O these encounterers so glib of tongue
That give accosting welcome ere it comes,
And wide unclasp the tables of their thoughts 60
To every ticklish reader! Set them down
For sluttish spoils of opportunity,
And daughters of the game.

[*Flourish. Enter all of Troy* ⟨HECTOR, PARIS, AENEAS,
HELENUS, TROILUS, *and* ATTENDANTS⟩.]

ALL ⟨THE GREEKS⟩. The Troyans' trumpet.

AGAMEMNON.   Yonder comes the troop.

AENEAS. Hail, all the state of Greece! What shall be done 65
To him that victory commands? Or do you purpose
A victor shall be known? Will you the knights
Shall to the edge of all extremity
Pursue each other, or shall they be divided
By any voice or order of the field? 70
Hector bade ask.

AGAMEMNON.   Which way would Hector have it?

AENEAS. He cares not; he'll obey conditions.

ACHILLES. 'Tis done like Hector; but securely[4] done,
A little proudly, and great deal misprizing
The knight opposed.

AENEAS.   If not Achilles, sir,
What is your name? 75

ACHILLES.   If not Achilles, nothing.

AENEAS. Therefore Achilles. But whate'er, know this:
In the extremity of great and little
Valour and pride excel themselves in Hector;
The one almost as infinite as all, 80
The other blank as nothing. Weigh him well,
And that which looks like pride is courtesy.
This Ajax is half made of Hector's blood,
In love whereof half Hector stays at home;
Half heart, half hand, half Hector comes to seek 85
This blended knight, half Troyan and half Greek.

ACHILLES. A maiden battle[5] then? O, I perceive you!

[⟨*Enter* DIOMEDES.⟩]

AGAMEMNON. Here is Sir Diomed. Go, gentle knight,
Stand by our Ajax. As you and Lord Aeneas
Consent upon the order of their fight,
So be it; either to the uttermost, 90
Or else a breath.[6] The combatants being kin
Half stints their strife before their strokes begin.

[AJAX *and* HECTOR *enter the lists.*⟩]

ULYSSES. They are opposed already.

AGAMEMNON. What Troyan is that same that looks so heavy? 95

ULYSSES. The youngest son of Priam, a true knight;

4. Overconfidently.
5. A bloodless one, like that of men
in training. He obviously wants to
suggest that there is something girlish
about such a battle.
6. Mild exercise.

Not yet mature, yet matchless; firm of word;
Speaking in deeds and deedless in his tongue;
Not soon provoked, nor being provoked soon calmed;
His heart and hand both open and both free;   100
For what he has he gives, what thinks he shows,
Yet gives he not till judgment guide his bounty,
Nor dignifies an impare thought[7] with breath;
Manly as Hector, but more dangerous;
For Hector in his blaze of wrath subscribes   105
To tender objects,[8] but he in heat of action
Is more vindicative than jealous love.
They call him Troilus, and on him erect
A second hope as fairly built as Hector.
Thus says Aeneas, one that knows the youth   110
Even to his inches,[9] and, with private soul,[1]
Did in great Ilion thus translate him to me.
                    [*Alarum.* ⟨HECTOR *and* AJAX *fight.*⟩]
AGAMEMNON. They are in action.
NESTOR. Now, Ajax, hold thine own!
TROILUS.   Hector, thou sleep'st;
Awake thee.   115
AGAMEMNON. His blows are well disposed. There, Ajax!
                                         [*Trumpets cease.*]
DIOMEDES. You must no more.
AENEAS.   Princes, enough, so please you.
AJAX. I am not warm yet; let us fight again.
DIOMEDES. As Hector pleases.
HECTOR.   Why, then will I no more.
Thou art, great lord, my father's sister's son,   120
A cousin-german to great Priam's seed;
The obligation of our blood forbids
A gory emulation 'twixt us twain.
Were thy commixtion Greek and Troyan so
That thou could'st say 'This hand is Grecian all,   125
And this is Troyan; the sinews of this leg
All Greek, and this all Troy; my mother's blood
Runs on the dexter cheek, and this sinister
Bounds in my father's', by Jove multipotent,
Thou shouldst not bear from me a Greekish member   130
Wherein my sword had not impressure made
Of our rank feud. But the just gods gainsay
That any drop thou borrowedst from thy mother,
My sacred aunt, should by my mortal sword
Be drained! Let me embrace thee, Ajax.   135
By him that thunders, thou hast lusty arms;
Hector would have them fall upon him thus.

---

7. One that is unequal to his judg-   9. From top to toe.
ment.   1. In confidence.
8. Gives terms to the weak.

Cousin, all honour to thee!

AJAX.   I thank thee, Hector.
Thou art too gentle and too free a man.
I came to kill thee, cousin, and bear hence   140
A great addition earnéd in thy death.

HECTOR. Not Neoptolemus[2] so mirable,[3]
On whose bright crest Fame with her loud'st Oyes
Cries 'This is he' could promise to himself
A thought of added honour torn from Hector.   145

AENEAS. There is expectance here from both the sides
What further you will do.

HECTOR.   We'll answer it.
The issue is embracement. Ajax, farewell.

AJAX. If I might in entreaties find success,
As seld[4] I have the chance, I would desire   150
My famous cousin to our Grecian tents.

DIOMEDES. 'Tis Agamemnon's wish; and great Achilles
Doth long to see unarmed the valiant Hector.

HECTOR. Aeneas, call my brother Troilus to me,
And signify this loving interview   155
To the expecters of our Troyan part.[5]
Desire them home. Give me thy hand, my cousin;
I will go eat with thee, and see your knights.

[AGAMEMNON *and the rest approach them.*]

AJAX. Great Agamemnon comes to meet us here.

HECTOR. The worthiest of them tell me name by name;   160
But for Achilles, mine own searching eyes
Shall find him by his large and portly size.

AGAMEMNON. Worthy all arms! as welcome as to one
That would be rid of such an enemy.
But that's no welcome. Understand more clear,   165
What's past and what's to come is strewed with husks
And formless ruin of oblivion;
But in this extant moment, faith and troth,
Strained purely from all hollow bias-drawing,[6]
Bids thee with most divine integrity,   170
From heart of very heart, great Hector, welcome.

HECTOR. I thank thee, most imperious Agamemnon.

AGAMEMNON. [*to* TROILUS] My well-famed lord of Troy, no less
to you.

MENELAUS. Let me confirm my princely brother's greeting.
You brace of warlike brothers, welcome hither.   175

HECTOR. Who must we answer?

AENEAS.   The noble Menelaus.

HECTOR. O you, my lord? By Mars his gauntlet, thanks!

2. Achilles' son, but here Shake-   5. The Trojans waiting for news.
speare must mean Achilles himself.   6. Oblique turnings, as the bias pulls
3. Wonderful.   the bowl in bowling.
4. Seldom.

Mock not that I affect the untraded[7] oath;
Your quondam wife swears still by Venus' glove.
She's well, but bade me not commend her to you.   180
MENELAUS. Name her not now, sir; she's a deadly theme.
HECTOR. O, pardon; I offend.
NESTOR. I have, thou gallant Troyan, seen thee oft,
    Labouring for destiny,[8] make cruel way
    Through ranks of Greekish youth; and I have seen thee,   185
    As hot as Perseus, spur thy Phrygian steed,
    Despising many forfeits and subduements,[9]
    When thou hast hung thy advancéd sword i' th' air,
    Not letting it decline on the declinéd;
    That I have said to some my standers-by   190
    'Lo, Jupiter is yonder, dealing life!'
    And I have seen thee pause and take thy breath,
    When that a ring of Greeks have hemmed thee in,
    Like an Olympian wrestling. This have I seen;
    But this thy countenance, still locked in steel,   195
    I never saw till now. I knew thy grandsire,
    And once fought with him. He was a soldier good,
    But, by great Mars, the captain of us all,
    Never like thee. Let an old man embrace thee;
    And, worthy warrior, welcome to our tents.   200
AENEAS. 'Tis the old Nestor.
HECTOR. Let me embrace thee, good old chronicle,
    That hast so long walked hand in hand with time.
    Most reverend Nestor, I am glad to clasp thee.
NESTOR. I would my arms could match thee in contention   205
    As they contend with thee in courtesy.
HECTOR. I would they could.
NESTOR. Ha!
    By this white beard, I'd fight with thee to-morrow.
    Well, welcome, welcome! I have seen the time.   210
ULYSSES. I wonder now how yonder city stands,
    When we have here her base and pillar by us.
HECTOR. I know your favour,[1] Lord Ulysses, well.
    Ah, sir, there's many a Greek and Troyan dead,
    Since first I saw yourself and Diomed   215
    In Ilion on your Greekish embassy.
ULYSSES. Sir, I foretold you then what would ensue.
    My prophecy is but half his journey yet;
    For yonder walls, that pertly front your town,
    Yond towers, whose wanton tops do buss the clouds,   220
    Must kiss their own feet.
HECTOR.   I must not believe you.

7. Unhackneyed. It is appropriate that
he swear by Mars's gauntlet, as Helen
by Venus' glove, since Mars and
Venus represent war and love. Mars
and Venus are also the classic adul-
terous couple, having cuckolded Vulcan, but this allusion would be stronger
if the line were Paris'.
8. Doing destiny's work, i.e., killing.
9. Ignoring the defeated whose lives
were forfeit.
1. Face.

There they stand yet; and modestly I think
The fall of every Phrygian stone will cost
A drop of Grecian blood. The end crowns all;
And that old common arbitrator, Time,   225
Will one day end it.

ULYSSES.   So to him we leave it.
Most gentle and most valiant Hector, welcome.
After the General, I beseech you next
To feast with me and see me at my tent.

ACHILLES. I shall forestall thee, Lord Ulysses, thou!   230
Now, Hector, I have fed mine eyes on thee;
I have with exact view perused thee, Hector,
And quoted joint by joint.

HECTOR.   Is this Achilles?

ACHILLES. I am Achilles.

HECTOR. Stand fair, I prithee; let me look on thee.   235

ACHILLES. Behold thy fill.

HECTOR.   Nay, I have done already.

ACHILLES. Thou art too brief. I will the second time,
As I would buy thee, view thee limb by limb.

HECTOR. O, like a book of sport thou'lt read me o'er;
But there's more in me than thou understand'st.   240
Why dost thou so oppress me with thine eye?

ACHILLES. Tell me, you heavens, in which part of his body
Shall I destroy him? Whether there, or there, or there?
That I may give the local wound a name,
And make distinct the very breach whereout   245
Hector's great spirit flew. Answer me, heavens.

HECTOR. It would discredit the blest gods, proud man,
To answer such a question. Stand again.
Think'st thou to catch my life so pleasantly
As to prenominate in nice² conjecture   250
Where thou wilt hit me dead?

ACHILLES.   I tell thee yea.

HECTOR. Wert thou an oracle to tell me so,
I'd not believe thee. Henceforth guard thee well;
For I'll not kill thee there, nor there, nor there;
But, by the force that stithied Mars his helm,   255
I'll kill thee everywhere, yea, o'er and o'er.
You wisest Grecians, pardon me this brag.
His insolence draws folly from my lips;
But I'll endeavour deeds to match these words,
Or may I never—

AJAX.   Do not chafe thee, cousin;   260
And you, Achilles, let these threats alone
Till accident or purpose bring you to't.
You may have every day enough of Hector,
If you have stomach. The general state, I fear,
Can scarce entreat you to be odd with him.   265

2. Precise.

HECTOR. I pray you let us see you in the field;
    We have had pelting wars since you refused
    The Grecians' cause.
ACHILLES.   Dost thou entreat me, Hector?
    To-morrow do I meet thee, fell as death;
    To-night all friends.
HECTOR.   Thy hand upon that match.   270
AGAMEMNON. First, all you peers of Greece, go to my tent;
    There in the full convive we[3]; afterwards,
    As Hector's leisure and your bounties shall
    Concur together, severally entreat him
    To taste your bounties. Let the trumpets blow,   275
    That this great soldier may his welcome know.
                 [⟨Exeunt all but TROILUS and ULYSSES.⟩]
TROILUS. My Lord Ulysses, tell me, I beseech you,
    In what place of the field doth Calchas keep?
ULYSSES. At Menelaus' tent, most princely Troilus.
    There Diomed doth feast with him tonight,   280
    Who neither looks upon the heaven nor earth,
    But gives all gaze and bent of amorous view
    On the fair Cressid.
TROILUS. Shall I, sweet lord, be bound to you so much,
    After we part from Agamemnon's tent,   285
    To bring me thither?
ULYSSES.   You shall command me, sir.
    As gentle tell me of, what honour was
    This Cressida in Troy? Had she no lover there
    That wails her absence?
TROILUS. O, sir, to such as boasting show their scars   290
    A mock is due. Will you walk on, my lord?
    She was beloved, she loved; she is, and doth;
    But still sweet love is food for fortune's tooth.   [Exeunt.]

⟨V. i⟩

        [Enter ACHILLES and PATROCLUS.]
ACHILLES. I'll heat his blood with Greekish wine to-night,
    Which with my scimitar I'll cool to-morrow.
    Patroclus, let us feast him to the height.
PATROCLUS. Here comes Thersites.
        [Enter THERSITES.]
ACHILLES.   How now, thou core of envy!
    Thou crusty batch of nature, what's the news?   5
THERSITES. Why, thou picture of what thou seemest, and idol of
    idiot worshippers, here's a letter for thee.
ACHILLES. From whence, fragment?
THERSITES. Why, thou full dish of fool, from Troy.
PATROCLUS. Who keeps the tent now?   10
THERSITES. The surgeon's box or the patient's wound.[1]

3. We all feast together.

1. Thersites' unnecessary answer is a play on *tent* as a surgical probe.

PATROCLUS. Well said Adversity! and what needs these tricks?

THERSITES. Prithee, be silent, boy; I profit not by thy talk; thou art said to be Achilles' male varlet.

PATROCLUS. Male varlet, you rogue! What's that? 15

THERSITES. Why, his masculine whore. Now, the rotten diseases of the south, the guts-griping ruptures, catarrhs, loads o' gravel in the back, lethargies, cold palsies, raw eyes, dirt-rotten livers, wheezing lungs, bladders full of imposthume, sciaticas, lime-kilns i' th' palm, incurable bone-ache, and the rivelled fee- 20 simple of the tetter, take and take again such preposterous discoveries!

PATROCLUS. Why, thou damnable box of envy, thou, what means thou to curse thus?

THERSITES. Do I curse thee? 25

PATROCLUS. Why, no, you ruinous butt; you whoreson indistin-guishable cur, no.

THERSITES. No! Why art thou, then, exasperate, thou idle im-material skein of sleave silk,[2] thou green sarcenet[3] flap for a sore eye, thou tassel of a prodigal's purse, thou? Ah, how the 30 poor world is pest'red with such water-flies—diminutives of nature!

PATROCLUS. Out, gall!

THERSITES. Finch egg!

ACHILLES. My sweet Patroclus, I am thwarted quite 35
From my great purpose in to-morrow's battle.
Here is a letter from Queen Hecuba,
A token from her daughter, my fair love,
Both taxing me and gaging me to keep
An oath that I have sworn. I will not break it. 40
Fall Greeks; fail fame; honour or go or stay;
My major vow lies here, this I'll obey.
Come, come, Thersites, help to trim my tent;
This night in banqueting must all be spent.
Away, Patroclus!   [*Exit* ⟨*with* PATROCLUS⟩.] 45

THERSITES. With too much blood and too little brain these two may run mad; but, if with too much brain and too little blood they do, I'll be a curer of madmen. Here's Agamemnon, an honest fellow enough, and one that loves quails,[4] but he has not so much brain as ear-wax; and the goodly transformation 50 of Jupiter[5] there, his brother, the bull, the primitive statue and oblique memorial of cuckolds, a thrifty shoeing-horn in a chain, hanging at his brother's leg—to what form but that he is, should wit larded with malice, and malice forced with wit, turn him to? To an ass, were nothing: he is both ass and ox. 55 To an ox, were nothing: he is both ox and ass. To be a dog, a mule, a cat, a fitchew,[6] a toad, a lizard, an owl, a puttock,[7] or a

2. Silk floss.
3. Silk.
4. Loose women.
5. Jupiter once turned himself into a bull (to seduce Europa), but Thersites is using the image for its horns, to describe the cuckold Menelaus.
6. Polecat.
7. A kite, a carrion-feeding hawk.

herring without a roe, I would not care; but to be Menelaus, I would conspire against destiny. Ask me not what I would be, if I were not Thersites; for I care not to be the louse of a lazar, so I were not Menelaus. Hey-day! spirits and fires! 60

[*Enter* ⟨HECTOR, TROILUS, AJAX,⟩ AGAMEMNON, ULYSSES, NESTOR, ⟨MENELAUS,⟩ *and* DIOMEDES, *with lights.*]

AGAMEMNON. We go wrong, we go wrong.

AJAX.   No, yonder 'tis;
There, where we see the lights.

HECTOR.   I trouble you.

AJAX. No, not a whit.

ULYSSES. Here comes himself to guide you.   65

[⟨*Enter* ACHILLES.⟩]

ACHILLES. Welcome, brave Hector; welcome Princes all.

AGAMEMNON. So now, fair Prince of Troy, I bid good night;
Ajax commands the guard to tend on you.

HECTOR. Thanks, and good night to the Greeks' general.

MENELAUS. Good night, my lord.   70

HECTOR. Good night, sweet Lord Menelaus.

THERSITES. Sweet draught![8] 'Sweet' quoth 'a?
Sweet sink, sweet sewer!

ACHILLES. Good night and welcome, both at once, to those
That go or tarry.   75

AGAMEMNON. Good night.

[*Exeunt* AGAM⟨EMNON *and*⟩ MENELAUS.]

ACHILLES. Old Nestor tarries; and you too, Diomed,
Keep Hector company an hour or two.

DIOMEDES. I cannot, lord; I have important business,
The tide[9] whereof is now. Good night, great Hector.   80

HECTOR. Give me your hand.

ULYSSES. [*aside to* TROILUS] Follow his torch; he goes to Calchas'
tent;
I'll keep you company.

TROILUS.   Sweet sir, you honour me.

HECTOR. And so, good night.

[⟨*Exit* DIOMEDES; ULYSSES *and* TROILUS *following.*⟩]

ACHILLES. Come, come, enter my tent.   85

[*Exeunt* ⟨*all but* THERSITES⟩.]

THERSITES. That same Diomed's a false-hearted rogue, a most unjust knave; I will no more trust him when he leers than I will a serpent when he hisses. He will spend his mouth and promise, like Brabbler the hound; but when he performs, astronomers foretell it, it is prodigious, there will come some 90 change; the sun borrows of the moon when Diomed keeps his word. I will rather leave to see[1] Hector than not to dog him. They say he keeps a Troyan drab, and uses the traitor Calchas' tent. I'll after. Nothing but lechery! All incontinent varlets!

[*Exit.*]

8. Privy.
9. Time.

1. Miss seeing.

⟨V. ii⟩

[*Enter* DIOMEDES.]

DIOMEDES. What, are you up here, ho? Speak.

CALCHAS. [*within*] Who calls?

DIOMEDES. Diomed. Calchas, I think. Where's your daughter?

CALCHAS. [*within*] She comes to you.

[*Enter* TROILUS *and* ULYSSES ⟨*after them* THERSITES⟩.]

ULYSSES. Stand where the torch may not discover us.   5

[*Enter* CRESSIDA.]

TROILUS. Cressid comes forth to him.

DIOMEDES. How now, my charge!

CRESSIDA. Now, my sweet guardian! Hark, a word with you.

[⟨*Whispers.*⟩]

TROILUS. Yea, so familiar!

ULYSSES. She will sing any man at first sight.   10

THERSITES. And any man may sing her, if he can take her cliff²;
she's noted.

DIOMEDES. Will you remember?

CRESSIDA. Remember? Yes.

DIOMEDES. Nay, but do, then;   15
And let your mind be coupled with your words.

TROILUS. What shall she remember?

ULYSSES. List!

CRESSIDA. Sweet honey Greek, tempt me no more to folly.

THERSITES. Roguery!   20

DIOMEDES. Nay, then—

CRESSIDA. I'll tell you what—

DIOMEDES. Fo, fo! come, tell a pin; you are a forsworn—

CRESSIDA. In faith, I cannot. What would you have me do?

THERSITES. A juggling trick, to be secretly open.   25

DIOMEDES. What did you swear you would bestow on me?

CRESSIDA. I prithee, do not hold me to mine oath;
Bid me do anything but that, sweet Greek.

DIOMEDES. Good night.

TROILUS. Hold, patience!   30

ULYSSES. How now, Troyan!

CRESSIDA. Diomed!

DIOMEDES. No, no, good night; I'll be your fool no more.

TROILUS. Thy better must.

CRESSIDA. Hark, one word in your ear.   35

TROILUS. O plague and madness!

ULYSSES. You are moved, Prince; let us depart, I pray you,
Lest your displeasure should enlarge itself
To wrathful terms. This place is dangerous;
The time right deadly; I beseech you, go.   40

TROILUS. Behold, I pray you.

ULYSSES.   Nay, good my lord, go off;
You flow to great distraction; come, my lord.

2. Clef.

TROILUS. I prithee stay.

ULYSSES.   You have not patience; come.

TROILUS. I pray you, stay; by hell and all hell's torments,
   I will not speak a word.

DIOMEDES. And so, good night.   45

CRESSIDA.   Nay, but you part in anger.

TROILUS. Doth that grieve thee? O withered truth!

ULYSSES. How now, my lord?

TROILUS.   By Jove, I will be patient.

CRESSIDA. Guardian! Why, Greek!

DIOMEDES.   Fo, fo! adieu! you palter.

CRESSIDA. In faith, I do not. Come hither once again.   50

ULYSSES. You shake, my lord, at something; will you go?
   You will break out.

TROILUS.   She strokes his cheek.

ULYSSES.   Come, come.

TROILUS. Nay, stay; by Jove, I will not speak a word.
   There is between my will and all offences
   A guard of patience. Stay a little while.   55

THERSITES. How the devil luxury,[3] with his fat rump and potato
finger, tickles these together! Fry, lechery, fry!

DIOMEDES. But will you, then?

CRESSIDA. In faith, I will, lo; never trust me else.

DIOMEDES. Give me some token for the surety of it.   60

CRESSIDA. I'll fetch you one.   [*Exit.*]

ULYSSES. You have sworn patience.

TROILUS.   Fear me not, my lord;
   I will not be myself, nor have cognition
   Of what I feel. I am all patience.
      [*Enter* CRESSIDA.]

THERSITES. Now the pledge; now, now, now!   65

CRESSIDA. Here, Diomed, keep this sleeve.

TROILUS. O beauty! where is thy faith?

ULYSSES.   My lord!

TROILUS. I will be patient; outwardly I will.

CRESSIDA. You look upon that sleeve; behold it well.
   He loved me—O false wench!—Give't me again.   70

DIOMEDES. Whose was't?

CRESSIDA. It is no matter, now I ha't again.
   I will not meet with you to-morrow night.
   I prithee, Diomed, visit me no more.

THERSITES. Now she sharpens.[4] Well said, whetstone.   75

DIOMEDES. I shall have it.

CRESSIDA.   What, this?

DIOMEDES.   Ay, that.

CRESSIDA. O all you gods! O pretty, pretty pledge!
   Thy master now lies thinking in his bed
   Of thee and me, and sighs, and takes my glove,
   And gives memorial dainty kisses to it,   80

3. Lechery.   4. Whets his desire.

As I kiss thee. Nay, do not snatch it from me;
He that takes that doth take my heart withal.
DIOMEDES. I had your heart before; this follows it.
TROILUS. I did swear patience.
CRESSIDA. You shall not have it, Diomed; faith, you shall not; 85
I'll give you something else.
DIOMEDES. I will have this. Whose was it?
CRESSIDA. It is no matter.
DIOMEDES. Come, tell me whose it was.
CRESSIDA. 'Twas one's that loved me better than you will.
But, now you have it, take it.
DIOMEDES. Whose was it? 90
CRESSIDA. By all Diana's waiting women yond,
And by herself,[5] I will not tell you whose.
DIOMEDES. To-morrow will I wear it on my helm,
And grieve his spirit that dares not challenge it.
TROILUS. Wert thou the devil and wor'st it on thy horn, 95
It should be challenged.
CRESSIDA. Well, well, 'tis done, 'tis past; and yet it is not;
I will not keep my word.
DIOMEDES. Why, then farewell;
Thou never shalt mock Diomed again.
CRESSIDA. You shall not go. One cannot speak a word 100
But it straight starts you.
DIOMEDES. I do not like this fooling.
THERSITES. Nor I, by Pluto; but that that likes not you
Pleases me best.
DIOMEDES. What, shall I come? The hour—
CRESSIDA. Ay, come—O Jove! Do come. I shall be plagued.[6] 105
DIOMEDES. Farewell till then.
CRESSIDA. Good night. I prithee come.
[⟨*Exit* DIOMEDES.⟩]
Troilus, farewell! One eye yet looks on thee;
But with my heart the other eye doth see.
Ah, poor our sex! this fault in us I find,
The error of our eye directs our mind. 110
What error leads must err; O, then conclude,
Minds swayed by eyes are full of turpitude. [*Exit.*]
THERSITES. A proof of strength[7] she could not publish more,
Unless she said 'My mind is now turned whore'.
ULYSSES. All's done, my lord.
TROILUS. It is.
ULYSSES. Why stay we, then? 115
TROILUS. To make a recordation to my soul
Of every syllable that here was spoke.
But if I tell how these two did coact,
Shall I not lie in publishing a truth?
Sith yet there is a credence in my heart, 120

5. By the moon (Diana) and the stars.
6. Punished.
7. Strong proof (of her inconstancy).

An esperance so obstinately strong,
That doth invert th' attest of eyes and ears;
As if those organs had deceptious functions
Created only to calumniate.
Was Cressid here?

ULYSSES.   I cannot conjure, Troyan.   125

TROILUS. She was not, sure.

ULYSSES.   Most sure she was.

TROILUS. Why, my negation hath no taste of madness.

ULYSSES. Nor mine, my lord. Cressid was here but now.

TROILUS. Let it not be believed for womanhood.
Think, we had mothers; do not give advantage   130
To stubborn critics, apt, without a theme,
For depravation, to square the general sex
By Cressid's rule. Rather think this not Cressid.

ULYSSES. What hath she done, Prince, that can soil our mothers?

TROILUS. Nothing at all, unless that this were she.   135

THERSITES. Will he swagger himself out on 's own eyes?

TROILUS. This she? No; this is Diomed's Cressida.
If beauty have a soul, this is not she;
If souls guide vows, if vows be sanctimonies,
If sanctimony be the god's delight,   140
If there be rule in unity itself,
This was not she. O madness of discourse,
That cause sets up with and against itself!
Bifold authority! where reason can revolt
Without perdition, and loss assume all reason   145
Without revolt. This is, and is not, Cressid.
Within my soul there doth conduce[8] a fight
Of this strange nature, that a thing inseparate[9]
Divides more wider than the sky and earth;
And yet the spacious breadth of this division   150
Admits no orifice for a point as subtle
As Ariachne's broken woof[1] to enter.
Instance, O instance! strong as Pluto's gates:
Cressid is mine, tied with the bonds of heaven.
Instance, O instance! strong as heaven itself: 155
The bonds of heaven are slipped, dissolved, and loosed;
And with another knot, five-finger-tied,
The fractions of her faith, orts of her love,
The fragments, scraps, the bits, and greasy relics
Of her o'er-eaten faith,[2] are bound to Diomed.   160

---

8. Is brought about.
9. He is talking about Cressida. Throughout this speech he is trying to make sense of the contrast between his Cressida (the image of beauty and true love) and the flirt he has watched with Diomedes. Not wanting to believe what he sees, he tries to reason it away.
1. Shakespeare most probably means

Arachne, who spun so fine that Minerva turned her into a spider. The line suggests that despite the breadth of the division, there is no room for a needle to enter to sew the split together, i.e., that the two Cressidas are unreconcilable.
2. Cressida ate the words of love she pledged Troilus.

ULYSSES. May worthy Troilus be half attached
  With that which here his passion doth express?[3]
TROILUS. Ay, Greek; and that shall be divulged well
  In characters as red as Mars his heart
  Inflamed with Venus. Never did young man fancy   165
  With so eternal and so fixed a soul.
  Hark, Greek: as much as I do Cressid love,
  So much by weight hate I her Diomed.
  That sleeve is mine that he'll bear on his helm;
  Were it a casque composed by Vulcan's skill   170
  My sword should bite it. Not the dreadful spout
  Which shipmen do the hurricano call,
  Constringed in mass by the almighty sun,
  Shall dizzy with more clamour Neptune's ear
  In his descent than shall my prompted sword   175
  Falling on Diomed.
THERSITES. He'll tickle it for his concupy.[4]
TROILUS. O Cressid! O false Cressid! false, false, false!
  Let all untruths stand by thy stainéd name,
  And they'll seem glorious.
ULYSSES.   O, contain yourself;   180
  Your passion draws ears hither.
     [Enter AENEAS.*]*
AENEAS. I have been seeking you this hour, my lord.
  Hector, by this, is arming him in Troy;
  Ajax, your guard, stays to conduct you home.
TROILUS. Have with you, Prince. My courteous lord, adieu.   185
  Farewell, revolted fair!—and, Diomed,
  Standfast and wear a castle on thy head.
ULYSSES. I'll bring you to the gates.
TROILUS. Accept distracted thanks.
     [Exeunt TROILUS, AENEAS, *and* ULYSSES.*]*
THERSITES. Would I could meet that rogue Diomed! I would   190
  croak like a raven; I would bode, I would bode. Patroclus will
  give me anything for the intelligence of this whore; the parrot
  will not do more for an almond than he for a commodious
  drab. Lechery, lechery! Still wars and lechery! Nothing else
  holds fashion. A burning devil take them!   *[Exit.]* 195

⟨V. iii⟩

    [Enter HECTOR *and* ANDROMACHE.*]*
ANDROMACHE. When was my lord so much ungently tempered
  To stop his ears against admonishment?
  Unarm, unarm, and do not fight to-day.
HECTOR. You train[5] me to offend[6] you; get you in.
  By all the everlasting gods, I'll go.
ANDROMACHE. My dreams will, sure, prove ominous to the day.[7]   5

3. Can you be even half as moved as you sound?
4. Diomedes will pay for his lust.
5. Tempt.
6. Do harm to.
7. Prophetic of the day's events.

HECTOR. No more, I say.
    [*Enter* CASSANDRA.]
CASSANDRA.   Where is my brother Hector?
ANDROMACHE. Here, sister, armed, and bloody in intent.
  Consort with me in loud and dear petition,
  Pursue we him on knees; for I have dreamt   10
  Of bloody turbulence, and this whole night
  Hath nothing been but shapes and forms of slaughter.
CASSANDRA. O, 'tis true!
HECTOR.   Ho! bid my trumpet sound.
CASSANDRA. No notes of sally, for the heavens, sweet brother!
HECTOR. Be gone, I say. The gods have heard me swear.   15
CASSANDRA. The gods are deaf to hot and peevish vows;
  They are polluted off'rings, more abhorred
  Than spotted livers in the sacrifice.
ANDROMACHE. O, be persuaded! Do not count it holy
  To hurt by being just. It is as lawful,
  For we would give much, to use violent thefts   20
  And rob in the behalf of charity.
CASSANDRA. It is the purpose that makes strong the vow;
  But vows to every purpose must not hold.
  Unarm, sweet Hector.
HECTOR.   Hold you still, I say.   25
  Mine honour keeps the weather[8] of my fate.
  Life every man holds dear; but the dear man[9]
  Holds honour far more precious dear than life.
    [*Enter* TROILUS.]
  How now, young man! Mean'st thou to fight to-day?
ANDROMACHE. Cassandra, call my father to persuade.   30
                     [*Exit* CASSANDRA.]
HECTOR. No, faith, young Troilus; doff thy harness, youth;
  I am to-day i' th' vein of chivalry.
  Let grow thy sinews till their knots be strong,
  And tempt not yet the brushes of the war.
  Unarm thee, go; and doubt thou not, brave boy,   35
  I'll stand to-day for thee and me and Troy.
TROILUS. Brother, you have a vice of mercy in you
  Which better fits a lion than a man.
HECTOR. What vice is that, good Troilus?
  Chide me for it.   40
TROILUS. When many times the captive Grecian falls,
  Even in the fan and wind of your fair sword,
  You bid them rise and live.
HECTOR. O, 'tis fair play!
TROILUS.   Fool's play, by heaven, Hector.
HECTOR. How now! how now!
TROILUS.   For th' love of all the gods,   45
  Let's leave the hermit Pity with our mother;

8. Keeps to windward (the advan-   9. Man of worth.
tageous position).

And when we have our armours buckled on,
The venomed vengeance ride upon our swords,
Spur them to ruthful[1] work, rein them from ruth!
HECTOR. Fie, savage, fie!
TROILUS.   Hector, then 'tis wars.[2]   50
HECTOR. Troilus, I would not have you fight to-day.
TROILUS. Who should withhold me?
    Not fate, obedience, nor the hand of Mars
    Beck'ning with fiery truncheon[3] my retire;
    Not Priamus and Hecuba on knees,   55
    Their eyes o'ergallèd with recourse of tears;
    Nor you, my brother, with your true sword drawn,
    Opposed to hinder me, should stop my way,
    But by my ruin.
            [*Enter* PRIAM *and* CASSANDRA.]
CASSANDRA. Lay hold upon him, Priam, hold him fast;   60
    He is thy crutch; now if thou lose thy stay,
    Thou on him leaning, and all Troy on thee,
    Fall all together.
PRIAM.   Come, Hector, come, go back.
    Thy wife hath dreamed; thy mother hath had visions;
    Cassandra doth foresee; and I myself   65
    Am like a prophet suddenly enrapt
    To tell thee that this day is ominous.
    Therefore, come back.
HECTOR.   Aeneas is a-field;
    And I do stand engaged to many Greeks,
    Even in the faith of valour, to appear   70
    This morning to them.
PRIAM.   Ay, but thou shalt not go.
HECTOR. I must not break my faith.
    You know me dutiful; therefore, dear sir,
    Let me not shame respect; but give me leave
    To take that course by your consent and voice   75
    Which you do here forbid me, royal Priam.
CASSANDRA. O Priam, yield not to him!
ANDROMACHE.   Do not, dear father.
HECTOR. Andromache, I am offended with you.
    Upon the love you bear me, get you in.   [*Exit* ANDROMACHE.]
TROILUS. This foolish, dreaming, superstitious girl   80
    Makes all these bodements.
CASSANDRA.   O, farewell, dear Hector!
    Look how thou diest. Look how thy eye turns pale.
    Look how thy wounds do bleed at many vents.
    Hark how Troy roars; how Hecuba cries out;
    How poor Andromache shrills her dolours forth;   85
    Behold distraction, frenzy, and amazement,
    Like witless antics, one another meet,

1. Pitiful.
2. *C'est la guerre.*
3. A truncheon was used to signal the end of combat between two champions.

And all cry, Hector! Hector's dead! O Hector!

TROILUS. Away, away!

CASSANDRA. Farewell!—yet, soft! Hector I take my leave. 90
Thou dost thyself and all our Troy deceive.   [⟨*Exit.*⟩]

HECTOR. You are amazed, my liege, at her exclaim.
Go in, and cheer the town; we'll forth, and fight,
Do deeds worth praise and tell you them at night.

PRIAM. Farewell. The gods with safety stand about thee. 95

[⟨*Exeunt* PRIAM *and* HECTOR.⟩ *Alarum.*]

TROILUS. They are at it, hark! Proud Diomed, believe
I come to lose my arm or win my sleeve.

[*Enter* PANDARUS.]

PANDARUS. Do you hear, my lord? Do you hear?

TROILUS. What now?

PANDARUS. Here's a letter come from yond poor girl. 100

TROILUS. Let me read.

PANDARUS. A whoreson tisick,[4] a whoreson rascally tisick so troubles me, and the foolish fortune of this girl, and what one
thing, what another, that I shall leave you one o' these days;
and I have a rheum in mine eyes too, and such an ache in my 105
bones that unless a man were cursed I cannot tell what to
think on't. What says she there?

TROILUS. Words, words, mere words, no matter from the heart;
Th' effect doth operate another way.   [⟨*Tearing the letter.*⟩]
Go, wind, to wind, there turn and change together. 110
My love with words and errors still she feeds,
But edifies another with her deeds.

[*Exeunt.*]

⟨V. iv⟩

[*Excursions. Enter* THERSITES.]

THERSITES. Now they are clapper-clawing one another; I'll go look
on. That dissembling abominable varlet, Diomed, has got that
same scurvy doting foolish young knave's sleeve of Troy there
in his helm. I would fain see them meet, that that same young
Troyan ass that loves the whore there might send that Greek- 5
ish whoremasterly villain with the sleeve back to the dissembling luxurious drab of a sleeveless errand. O' th' t'other side,
the policy of those crafty swearing[5] rascals—that stale old
mouse-eaten dry cheese, Nestor, and that same dog-fox, Ulysses—is not proved worth a blackberry. They set me up, in 10
policy, that mongrel cur, Ajax, against that dog of as bad a
kind, Achilles; and now is the cur Ajax prouder than the cur
Achilles, and will not arm today; whereupon the Grecians begin to proclaim barbarism, and policy grows into an ill opinion.[6] 15

[⟨*Enter* DIOMEDES *and* TROILUS.⟩]

4. Cough.
5. So cunning that they would swear
falsely.

6. Declare that they will not be gov-
erned by policy.

Soft! here comes sleeve, and t'other.

TROILUS. Fly not; for shouldst thou take the river Styx
I would swim after.

DIOMEDES.   Thou dost miscall retire.
I do not fly; but advantageous care
Withdrew me from the odds of multitude.[7]   20
Have at thee.

THERSITES. Hold thy whore, Grecian; now for thy whore, Troyan
—now the sleeve, now the sleeve!
                    [⟨*Exeunt* TROILUS *and* DIOMEDES *fighting.*⟩]
        [*Enter* HECTOR.]

HECTOR. What art thou, Greek? Art thou for Hector's match?
Art thou of blood and honour?   25

THERSITES. No, no—I am a rascal, a scurvy railing knave, a very
filthy rogue.

HECTOR. I do believe thee. Live.   [⟨*Exit.*⟩]

THERSITES. God-a-mercy, that thou wilt believe me; but a plague
break thy neck for fighting me! What's become of the wench-   30
ing rogues? I think they have swallowed one another. I would
laugh at that miracle. Yet, in a sort, lechery eats itself. I'll seek
them.   [*Exit.*]

⟨V. v⟩

        [*Enter* DIOMEDES *and* SERVANT.]

DIOMEDES. Go, go, my servant, take thou Troilus' horse;
Present the fair steed to my lady Cressid.
Fellow, commend my service to her beauty;
Tell her I have chastised the amorous Troyan,
And am her knight by proof.

SERVANT.   I go, my lord.   [⟨*Exit.*⟩]   5
        [*Enter* AGAMEMNON.]

AGAMEMNON. Renew, renew! The fierce Polydamus
Hath beat down Menon; bastard Margarelon
Hath Doreus prisoner,
And stands colossus-wise, waving his beam,[8]
Upon the pashed corses of the kings   10
Epistrophus and Cedius. Polixenes is slain;
Amphimacus and Thoas deadly hurt;
Patroclus ta'en, or slain; and Palamedes
Sore hurt and bruised. The dreadful Sagittary
Appals our numbers. Haste we, Diomed,   15
To reinforcement, or we perish all.
        [*Enter* NESTOR.]

NESTOR. Go, bear Patroclus' body to Achilles,
And bid the snail-paced Ajax arm for shame.
There is a thousand Hectors in the field;
Now here he fights on Galathe his horse,
And there lacks work; anon he's there afoot,   20

7. Caution made me withdraw from   8. Lance.
facing heavy odds.

And there they fly or die, like scaléd sculls[9]
Before the belching whale; then is he yonder,
And there the strawy Greeks, ripe for his edge,
Fall down before him like the mower's swath.   25
Here, there, and everywhere, he leaves and takes;
Dexterity so obeying appetite
That what he will he does, and does so much
That proof is called impossibility.
          [*Enter* ULYSSES.]
ULYSSES. O, courage, courage, Princes! Great Achilles   30
   Is arming, weeping, cursing, vowing vengeance.
   Patroclus' wounds have roused his drowsy blood,
   Together with his mangled Myrmidons,
   That noseless, handless, hacked and chipped, come to him,
   Crying on Hector. Ajax hath lost a friend   35
   And foams at mouth, and he is armed and at it,
   Roaring for Troilus; who hath done to-day
   Mad and fantastic execution,
   Engaging and redeeming of himself
   With such a careless force and forceless care   40
   As if that luck, in very spite of cunning,
   Bade him win all.
          [*Enter* AJAX.]
AJAX. Troilus! thou coward Troilus!   [*Exit.*]
DIOMEDES. Ay, there, there.
NESTOR. So, so, we draw together.   [*Exit.*] 45
          [*Enter* ACHILLES.]
ACHILLES. Where is this Hector?
   Come, come, thou boy-queller, show thy face;
   Know what it is to meet Achilles angry.
   Hector! where's Hector? I will none but Hector. [*Exeunt.*]

⟨V. vi⟩

          [*Enter* AJAX.]
AJAX. Troilus, thou coward Troilus, show thy head.
          [*Enter* DIOMEDES.]
DIOMEDES. Troilus, I say! Where's Troilus?
AJAX.   What wouldst thou?
DIOMEDES. I would correct him.
AJAX. Were I the general, thou shouldst have my office
   Ere that correction. Troilus, I say! What, Troilus!   5
          [*Enter* TROILUS.]
TROILUS. O traitor Diomed! Turn thy false face, thou traitor,
   And pay thy life thou owest me for my horse.
DIOMEDES. Ha! art thou there?
AJAX. I'll fight with him alone. Stand, Diomed.
DIOMEDES. He is my prize. I will not look upon.   10
TROILUS. Come, both, you cogging Greeks; have at you both.
          [⟨*Exeunt fighting.*⟩]

9. Schools of fish.

[⟨*Enter* HECTOR.⟩]

HECTOR. Yea, Troilus? O, well fought, my youngest brother!

[*Enter* ACHILLES.]

ACHILLES. Now do I see thee. Have at thee, Hector! [⟨*They fight.*⟩]

HECTOR. Pause, if thou wilt.

ACHILLES. I do disdain thy courtesy, proud Troyan.   15
  Be happy that my arms are out of use.
  My rest and negligence befriends thee now,
  But thou anon shalt hear of me again;
  Till when, go seek thy fortune.   [*Exit.*]

HECTOR.   Fare thee well.
  I would have been much more a fresher man,   20
  Had I expected thee. How now, my brother!

[*Enter* TROILUS.]

TROILUS. Ajax hath ta'en Aeneas. Shall it be?
  No, by the flame of yonder glorious heaven,
  He shall not carry him; I'll be ta'en too,
  Or bring him off. Fate, hear me what I say: 25
  I reck not though thou end my life to-day.   [*Exit.*]

[*Enter* ONE *in armour.*]

HECTOR. Stand, stand, thou Greek; thou art a goodly mark.
  No? wilt thou not? I like thy armour well;
  I'll frush[1] it and unlock the rivets all,
  But I'll be master of it. Wilt thou not, beast, abide?   30
  Why then, fly on; I'll hunt thee for thy hide.

[*Exit* ⟨*in pursuit*⟩.]

⟨V. vii⟩

[*Enter* ACHILLES, *with* MYRMIDONS.]

ACHILLES. Come here about me, you my Myrmidons;
  Mark what I say. Attend me where I wheel;
  Strike not a stroke, but keep yourselves in breath;
  And when I have the bloody Hector found,
  Empale[2] him with your weapons round about;   5
  In fellest manner execute your arms.
  Follow me, sirs, and my proceedings eye.
  It is decreed Hector the great must die.

[*Exit* ⟨*with* MYRMIDONS⟩.]

[*Enter* THERSITES, MENELAUS, PARIS ⟨*the last two fighting*⟩.]

THERSITES. The cuckold and the cuckold-maker are at it. Now,
  bull! now, dog! 'Loo, Paris, 'loo! now my double-horned Spar-   10
  tan! 'loo, Paris, 'loo! The bull has the game.[3] Ware horns, ho!

[*Exeunt* PARIS *and* MENELAUS.]

[*Enter* BASTARD ⟨MARGARELON⟩.]

BASTARD. Turn, slave, and fight.

THERSITES. What art thou?

BASTARD. A bastard son of Priam's.

THERSITES. I am a bastard too; I love bastards. I am a bastard be-   15

1. Batter.   3. Wins.
2. Fence him in.

got, bastard instructed, bastard in mind, bastard in valour, in everything illegitimate. One bear will not bite another, and wherefore should one bastard? Take heed, the quarrel's most ominous to us: if the son of a whore fight for a whore, he tempts judgment. Farewell, bastard.   [⟨*Exit.*⟩]   20
BASTARD. The devil take thee, coward!   [*Exit.*]

⟨V. viii⟩

[⟨*Enter* HECTOR.⟩]
HECTOR. Most putrified core so fair without,
    Thy goodly armour thus hath cost thy life.
    Now is my day's work done; I'll take good breath.
    Rest, sword; thou hast thy fill of blood and death!
                                          [⟨*Disarms.*⟩]

[*Enter* ACHILLES *and his* MYRMIDONS.]
ACHILLES. Look, Hector, how the sun begins to set;   5
    How ugly night comes breathing at his heels.
    Even with the vail and dark'ning of the sun,
    To close the day up, Hector's life is done.
HECTOR. I am unarmed; forego this vantage, Greek.
ACHILLES. Strike, fellows, strike; this is the man I seek.   10
                                          [⟨HECTOR *falls.*⟩]
    So, Ilion, fall thou next! Come, Troy, sink down;
    Here lies thy heart, thy sinews, and thy bone.
    On, Myrmidons, and cry you all amain,
    'Achilles hath the mighty Hector slain'.
                                          [*Retreat.*]
    Hark, a retire upon our Grecian part.   15
MYRMIDONS. The Troyan trumpets sound the like, my lord.
ACHILLES. The dragon wing of night o'erspreads the earth
    And, stickler-like,[4] the armies separates.
    My half-supped sword, that frankly would have fed,
    Pleased with this dainty bait, thus goes to bed.   20
                                          [⟨*Sheathes his sword.*⟩]
    Come, tie his body to my horse's tail;
    Along the field I will the Troyan trail.   [*Exeunt.*]

⟨V. ix⟩

[*Enter* AGAMEMNON, AJAX, MENELAUS, NESTOR, DIOMEDES,
    and the rest, marching. ⟨*Sound retreat. Shout.*⟩]
AGAMEMNON. Hark! hark! what shout is that?
NESTOR. Peace, drums!
SOLDIERS. [*within*] Achilles! Achilles! Hector's slain. Achilles!
DIOMEDES. The bruit is Hector's slain, and by Achilles.
AJAX. If it be so, yet bragless let it be;   5
    Great Hector was as good a man as he.
AGAMEMNON. March patiently along. Let one be sent
    To pray Achilles see us at our tent.

---

4. The stickler was the man who   for the stick he carried to part the
parted combatants in contests, named   duelists.

If in his death the gods have us befriended;
Great Troy is ours, and our sharp wars are ended.   *[Exeunt.]* 10

⟨V. x⟩

    [Enter AENEAS, PARIS, ANTENOR, *and* DEIPHOBUS.]
AENEAS. Stand, ho! yet are we masters of the field.
  Never go home; here starve we out the night.
    [Enter TROILUS.]
TROILUS. Hector is slain.
ALL.   Hector! The gods forbid!
TROILUS. He's dead, and at the murderer's horse's tail,
  In beastly sort, dragged through the shameful field.   5
  Frown on, you heavens, effect your rage with speed.
  Sit, gods, upon your thrones, and smite all Troy.
  I say at once let your brief plagues be mercy,[5]
  And linger not our sure destructions on.
AENEAS. My lord, you do discomfort all the host.   10
TROILUS. You understand me not that tell me so.
  I do not speak of flight, of fear of death,
  But dare all imminence that gods and men
  Address their dangers in. Hector is gone.
  Who shall tell Priam so, or Hecuba?   15
  Let him that will a screech-owl aye be called
  Go in to Troy, and say there 'Hector's dead'.
  There is a word will Priam turn to stone;
  Make wells and Niobes of the maids and wives,
  Cold statues of the youth; and, in a word,   20
  Scare Troy out of itself. But, march away;
  Hector is dead; there is no more to say.
  Stay yet. You vile abominable tents,
  Thus proudly pight[6] upon our Phrygian plains,
  Let Titan[7] rise as early as he dare,   25
  I'll through and through you. And, thou great-sized coward,[8]
  No space of earth shall sunder our two hates;
  I'll haunt thee like a wicked conscience still,
  That mouldeth goblins swift as frenzy's thoughts.
  Strike a free march to Troy. With comfort go;   30
  Hope of revenge shall hide our inward woe.
    [Enter PANDARUS.]
PANDARUS. But hear you, hear you!
TROILUS. Hence, broker-lackey. Ignomy and shame
  Pursue thy life and live aye with thy name!
              [Exeunt all but PANDARUS.]
PANDARUS. A goodly medicine for my aching bones! O world!   35
  world! world! thus is the poor agent despised! O traitors and
  bawds, how earnestly are you set a work, and how ill requited!
  Why should our endeavour be so loved, and the performance

5. Make the destruction mercifully short.   7. The sun.
6. Pitched.   8. He means Achilles.

so loathed? What verse for it? What instance for it? Let me
see: 40

> Full merrily the humble-bee doth sing
> Till he hath lost his honey and his sting;
> And being once subduéd in armed tail,
> Sweet honey and sweet notes together fail.

Good traders in the flesh, set this in your painted cloths.[9]   45
As many as be here of pander's hall,
Your eyes, half out, weep out at Pandar's fall;
Or, if you cannot weep, yet give some groans,
Though not for me, yet for your aching bones.
Brethren and sisters of the hold-door trade,   50
Some two months hence my will shall here be made.
It should be now, but that my fear is this,
Some galléd goose of Winchester[1] would hiss.
Till then I'll sweat[2] and seek about for eases,
And at that time bequeath you my diseases.   [*Exit.*]   55

9. Cloth hangings, sometimes used as advertisement.
1. Prostitute. The term *Winchester goose* came from the fact that the brothels in Southwark had once been under the jurisdiction of the Bishop of Winchester.
2. One of the treatments for venereal disease.

Tonight We Improvise

LUIGI PIRANDELLO

Tonight We Improvise was first performed in Italy in 1930. Although written rather late in Luigi Pirandello's career, it belongs with the philosophical comedies of the early twenties, in which the playwright worries the problem of reality and illusion, particularly with *Six Characters in Search of an Author* and *Each in His Own Way*, which make use of a theatrical setting. In his Preface to *Six Characters*, Pirandello wrote: "To me it was never enough to present a man or a woman and what is special and characteristic about them simply for the pleasure of presenting them; to narrate a particular affair, lively or sad, simply for the pleasure of narrating it; to describe a landscape simply for the pleasure of describing it." So, the melodramatic story of the jealous Sicilian husband, which might have been another playwright's complete play, becomes only one element in *Tonight We Improvise*. Separating the playwrights who tell stories from those who use them, what he calls the "historical writers" from the "philosophical writers," Pirandello added, "I have the misfortune to belong to these last."

The version of *Tonight* here printed was translated by Marta Abba, the Italian actress who played the lead in many of Pirandello's plays. In 1959, *Tonight We Improvise*, in a version by Claude Fredericks, became an off-Broadway success in New York; the production came just at the right moment, when the wide variety of offerings in the off-Broadway theater had stimulated a strong interest in plays that take liberties with the realistic form.

Tonight We Improvise†

Characters

DR. HINKFUSS

THE LEADING ACTOR—RICO VERRI

THE LEADING ACTRESS—MOMMINA
THE CHARACTER ACTOR—SAMPOGNETTA
THE CHARACTER ACTRESS—SIGNORA IGNAZIA
TOTINA
DORINA
NENE
POMARICI ⎤
SARALLI ⎟
MANGINI ⎬ *Five Air Force Officers*
POMETTI ⎟
NARDI ⎦
THE SECRETARY
TWO LITTLE GIRLS*
THREE GIRLS
THREE BLOND DANCERS
6 OR 8 CUSTOMERS
THE JOKING CUSTOMER
NIGHTCLUB SINGER
A GENTLEMAN FROM THE ORCHESTRA ⎤
A GENTLEMAN FROM THE BALCONY ⎟
A GENTLEMAN FROM A BOX ⎟
A VERY OLD GENTLEMAN FROM A BOX ⎟
AN OLD LADY ⎬ *In the audience*
HER HUSBAND ⎟
A YOUNG SPECTATOR NEARBY ⎟
A YOUNG SPECTATOR IN THE ORCHESTRA ⎟
POET FROM THE BALCONY ⎦
4 CHOIRBOYS* ⎤
4 YOUNG GIRLS* ⎟
JOSEPH—AN OLD MAN* ⎟
MARY* ⎟
SHEPHERD* ⎬ *Procession*
YOUNG SHEPHERD* ⎟
A GROUP OF PEASANTS* ⎟
MUSICIANS AND CHOIR ⎟
8 OR 9 MEN AND WOMEN* ⎦

Act One

The theatre is filled tonight with that particular audience that always appears at the premiere of any new play.

The announcements, in the papers and on posters, of the unusual event of an improvised performance has given rise to a great deal of curiosity in everyone. Only the critics from the papers seem to show none. They already feel quite sure they can chalk it all up tomorrow as a fiasco. ("Good Lord, for sure a bit like commedia dell'arte turned upside down. But where now can you get actors

45th St., New York 36, N.Y., or 7623 Sunset Blvd., Hollywood 46, Calif., or, if in Canada, to Samuel French (Can-

ada) Ltd., 27 Grenville St., Toronto. Ont.
* Non-speaking.

who can improvise the way those possessed performers of the commedia dell'arte used to? It was a good deal easier then, anyhow, with the ancient plots, traditional masks, and a repertory which facilitated the work.") One sees in their faces, instead, a certain irritation, since they have neither read in the announcements nor otherwise been able to learn the name of the author who tonight has given the actors and their director whatever scenario they are using. Lacking any clue to remind them of judgments they have already made, they are uneasy, afraid to jump at certain conclusions which could show a contradiction on their part. Punctually at the hour designated for the performance, the lights in the theatre go down and the footlights on stage softly come up.

The audience, unexpectedly plunged into darkness, is at first attentive. Then, not hearing the buzzer that usually announces the parting of the curtains, they begin to rustle about in their seats. And all the more because from the stage, through the closed curtains, confused and excited voices are heard—as though the actors were protesting about something, and someone else, reprimanding them, was trying to restore order and silence the uproar.

A GENTLEMAN FROM THE ORCHESTRA. [*looks around and loudly asks*] What's happening up there?

ANOTHER FROM THE BALCONY. Sounds like a fight.

A THIRD FROM A BOX. Maybe it's all part of the show.

[*Someone laughs.*]

A VERY OLD GENTLEMAN FROM A BOX. [*as though the uproar were a personal insult to his seriousness as playgoer*] What kind of scandalous behaviour is this? When has one ever had to put up with anything like it?

AN OLD LADY. [*leaping up from her seat in the last rows of the orchestra like a frightened hen*] God help us, it isn't a fire, is it?

HER HUSBAND. [*immediately grabbing hold of her*] Are you crazy? Fire indeed! Sit down and be quiet.

A YOUNG SPECTATOR NEARBY. [*with a melancholy smile of supportation*] Don't you say it even as a joke. Anyhow, lady, they'd have let the safety curtain down.

[*Finally the buzzer is heard on stage.*]

SOME OF THE AUDIENCE. Ah!—at last!

OTHERS. Sssshhhh! Be quiet.

[*But the curtains do not part. The buzzer instead is heard still again. To this, from the back of the theatre, the irritated voice of the director, DR. HINKFUSS, is heard replying. He violently pulls open the door at the back and angrily hurries down the aisle that divides in two the rows of the orchestra.*]

DR. HINKFUSS. Why the buzzer? Why the buzzer? Who ordered it rung? I'll order it, I alone, when it's time to. [*These words are shouted by DR. HINKFUSS as he comes down the aisle and climbs the three steps that join stage to orchestra. Then, controlling his nervous trembling with admirable speed, he turns to the audience. In a frock coat, a little scroll of paper under one arm, DR. HINKFUSS is one of those unfortunate creatures whose fate it is to be a tiny man hardly five feet tall. He compensates for this, in his way, with a great bushy head of hair. First he glances at his little hands, so small they perhaps inspire disgust even in him, scrawny and with the fingers as white and hairy as maggots, and then without giving much weight to his words says]* I am deeply grieved by the momentary confusion the audience must have noticed going on behind the curtains just now, and I must ask their indulgence—though perhaps after all I might be said to wish it all to be taken as a sort of involuntary prologue—

THE GENTLEMAN FROM THE ORCHESTRA. *[delightedly interrupting]* Ah, there! Didn't I say so myself?

DR. HINKFUSS. *[with cold severity]* What is it that the gentleman wishes to observe?

THE GENTLEMAN FROM THE ORCHESTRA. Nothing at all. I'm just pleased with myself for having guessed the whole thing.

DR. HINKFUSS. For having guessed exactly what?

THE GENTLEMAN FROM THE ORCHESTRA. That those noises on stage were all part of the show.

DR. HINKFUSS. Ah, yes? Is that so? It seemed to you that it was all being done as a trick? The very evening when I propose to myself to play with all my cards on the table. You're fooling only yourself, my dear sir. I said *involuntary* prologue, and, I will add, perhaps not at all inappropriate to a spectacle as unusual as the one you are about to witness this evening. But I must ask the audience not to interrupt me. Here it is, ladies and gentlemen. *[He takes from under his arm the little paper scroll.]* I have in this scroll of a few pages all I need. Almost nothing. A tale, hardly more, here and there interspersed with a little dialogue by a writer unknown to you.

SEVERAL IN THE AUDIENCE. What's the name? Who is it?

SOMEONE IN THE BALCONY. Who is it?

DR. HINKFUSS. Please, please, ladies and gentlemen. It is not at all my habit to call my audiences to attention. I do indeed wish to answer for all I have done, but I shall not allow you to call me to account during the performance itself.

THE GENTLEMAN FROM THE ORCHESTRA. But you said it hadn't started yet.

DR. HINKFUSS. Ah, yes, it has. And the very person who has the least right of any to deny it is exactly you, my dear sir, who took the noises on stage a few minutes ago as the start of the show. If I am here before you, the performance has begun.

THE VERY OLD GENTLEMAN IN THE BOX. *[clearing his throat]* I thought you were out here to apologize for those scandalous noises. I'll have you know—I've not come here to listen to a lecture by you or anyone else.

DR. HINKFUSS. A lecture indeed! How dare you think I'm out here to make you listen to a lecture? And how dare you proclaim such lies here in front of everyone? *[THE VERY OLD GENTLEMAN IN THE BOX, highly indignant at this apostrophe, leaps to his feet and muttering to himself leaves his box.]* Oh, so you can get up and leave, can you? No one's stopping you, my dear sir! I am here before you, ladies and gentlemen, solely to prepare you for the —unusual in what you are this evening about to see. I think I deserve your attention. You wish to know the author of this little tale? I could easily tell you.

SEVERAL IN THE AUDIENCE. Tell us. Go ahead and tell us. Do.

DR. HINKFUSS. All right, I will. Pirandello!

[*Exclamations from the audience: "Uhhh—"*]

THE GENTLEMAN IN THE BALCONY. [*loudly, over the exclamations*] And who is he?

[*Many of those in the boxes and the orchestra break out laughing.*]

DR. HINKFUSS. [*laughing a little himself*] Yes, it's always him, the incorrigible man. But though he did get away with it with two of my esteemed colleagues, giving the first of them six characters lost and looking for an author—what a really wretched innovation of the stage *that* was, unsettling everyone!—and the next time cunningly writing a *commedia a chiave* at which my other colleague saw his production broken off by the audience up in arms, this time there's no danger of his doing any such thing.[1] Rest assured. I have—*eliminated* him. His name doesn't figure even on the posters. But then it would hardly have been fair of me to have made him responsible ever so slightly for this evening's performance. The only individual responsible for this evening is myself. I have taken one of his stories, as I would have taken one by anyone else. I preferred to take one of his because, of all writers writing for the theatre, it is perhaps he alone who has shown himself fully aware of the fact that the work of a writer is *finished* the moment he has finished putting the last word down on paper. He is responsible for the work to readers, of course, and to book reviewers, but neither can, nor should be, to theatregoers and to drama critics, who pass judgment sitting in a theatre.

VOICES IN THE THEATRE. Ah, no? Oh, lovely!

DR. HINKFUSS. No, ladies and gentlemen. For in the theatre the work of the writer no longer exists!

THE GENTLEMAN IN THE BALCONY. What's left, then?

DR. HINKFUSS. The scenic creation. The scenic creation I myself make of it and which is entirely my own. I must again ask the audience not to interrupt me. And let me caution you now (though I can already see some of the critics laughing) that I am firmly convinced of this theory of mine. The critics are masters at not taking such ideas seriously, of continuing to upbraid —unjustly, I maintain—the *writer* for what goes on in a theatre,

---

1. He is referring to two earlier Pirandello plays—*Six Characters in Search of an Author* and *Each in His Own Way*—in which the playwright used theatrical production, as he does here, as the main device around which to organize his action and his ideas. A *commedia a chiave*, by the way, is what, if it were a novel, we would call a *roman à clef*, a literary work in which the characters are thinly disguised fictions of recognizable people; of course, in *Each in His Own Way*, Pirandello invented both the real and the fictional people.

even when they are quite willing to concede that the writer can laugh at their reviews just as they now are laughing at me and my theory of the theatre. Laugh, that is—it must be understood —if the reviews are unfavorable. If they're not, it would hardly be fair—would it?—for the writer to take for himself praise that belongs to *me?* My theory is based on solid reasons. Here in my hands is the work of the writer. [*He again shows the audience the same little scroll.*] What do I *do* with it? I take it for the subject of my scenic creation and *use* it—in the very way I use the skill of the actors I have cast, to play their roles according to the interpretations I have made, and of the designer whom I commission to design the sets, and of the stagehands who put them up, and of the electricians who light them—all according to instructions, advice, and indications, that I myself have given them. In a different theatre, with different actors and different sets, with different directions and different lighting, you will surely grant me the scenic creation would certainly be—different. Is it not then obvious from this that what one judges sitting in the theatre is never the work the writer had in his head but this or that scenic creation that had been made of it, each one different from the other—many, where the writer is unique? To judge a text it is necessary to know it. And in the theatre, where performed by certain actors it is one thing and by others necessarily another, one cannot. The work could be unique only if it could give *itself,* no longer employing actors but rather its own characters that, by some miracle, had assumed flesh and voice. In that case, yes, it could be judged in the theatre. But is such a miracle ever possible? To this day no one has ever seen it happen. And so, ladies and gentlemen, it is that which the director, with more or less dedication, tries for each night with his actors. The only thing he *can* do. To remove from what I am saying every appearance of paradox, I ask you to consider the fact that a finished work of art is fixed forever in an immutable form. This immutable form represents the poet's release from the toil of creation, the perfect quiet attained after all the agitation such toil entails. Good. Does it seem to you, ladies and gentlemen, that there can still be life where nothing any longer moves? Where all reposes in perfect stillness? Life must obey two imperatives, which, one equipoised against the other, permit it neither perpetually to be still nor always to be in movement. If life were always in movement, it would never be still. If it everlastingly were still, it would never move again. And life must both move and be still.

But the poet deludes himself when he thinks he has found release and tranquility in his work of art fixing life forever in immutable form. He has only ceased to live his own labor. Complete peace, complete tranquility is had only at the price of life itself. And how many people there are who suffer from this miserable delusion—who believe themselves still alive, when in fact they are so far gone they can't even smell the stench of their own corpses. If a work of art survives, it is only because we can still lift it out of the rigidity of its own form and let it loose inside ourselves, with our own life endow it with life—differently at different times for each of us. A work of art has many lives, not one. As one can infer even from the continual discussions born from not wanting to believe that it is so, it is *we* who give this life. Thus it is impossible for the life I give to a work of art to be like the life someone else is giving it. I ask your indulgence, ladies and gentlemen, for the round about way I have had to take in order to come to this, the point I wished to come to.

Someone could ask me: "But who told you art must be life? Life, yes, must obey the two opposing imperatives you speak of, and just for that very reason is not art. Just as art is not life, exactly because it succeeds in freeing itself from these same imperatives and reposes forever in the immutability of its own form. Exactly because of this, art is the kingdom of perfected creation, where life is as it ought to be, in an infinitely various and continually changing state of becoming. Each of us is seeking to create himself and his own life with those very faculties of the spirit that the poet employs in creating his work of art, and in fact he who is best instructed in these things and best knows how to use them succeeds both in reaching a higher state of being and in making it endure more constantly. But it will never be a true creation, first of all because it is doomed to wither and perish with us, in time; secondly, because, moving towards an end to be arrived at, it will never be free; and lastly, because, exposed to all the unforeseen and unforeseeable circumstances, to all the obstacles that others throw up against it, it perpetually risks being opposed, deviated, deformed. Art vindicates life, in a certain sense, because its creation, insofar as it is true creation, is freedom from time and from circumstances and has no end but itself."

Ah, yes, ladies and gentlemen, I reply, that's exactly how it is. Many times, however, I have happened to consider with anguished dismay the eternity of a work of art as an unreachable divine solitude from which even the artist himself, as soon as he has created it, is excluded. Terrible in its changelessness is the attitude assumed by a statue; terrible, this eternal solitude of immutable forms cast outside time. Every sculptor, I do not know but I imagine, after having created a statue, if he truly thinks he has given it a life which stands forever outside of time, should believe that his statue, like a living thing, could change its position and walk and speak. But then it would stop being a statue. It would become a living person. But only on *this* condition, ladies and gentlemen, can that which art has fixed in the immutability of form be brought to life, and turn, and move—on the condition that this form receive its movement from us who are alive; a life various and diverse and momentary, whatever each of us is capable of embuing it with. Today let us willingly leave works of art in that divine solitude they have, outside time. The audience, after a day full of worries and difficulties, anxieties and ordeals of every sort, in the evening, in the theatre, wish to be amused.

THE GENTLEMAN FROM THE ORCHESTRA. Good God! With Pirandello?

[*Laughter.*]

DR. HINKFUSS. You don't have anything to worry about. Rest assured. [*He once more shows the audience the little scroll.*] This is Pirandello. A mere trifle. The rest I do myself. I myself, all alone. And let me confide to you that I have created for you a delightful spectacle indeed, if the sets and scenes turn out with the same attention in each detail, and if my actors respond in every way to the faith I have placed in them. But in any case I shall be here with you, ready to intervene whenever necessary to lead the play back if it goes astray ever so slightly, to supplement any faulty workmanship with clarifications and explanations. And that, I like to think, will make you find the novelty of this effort at improvisation even more amusing. I have divided the performance tonight into a great many short scenes with brief pauses between, often only a moment of darkness from which a new scene will unexpectedly arise on the stage or, yes, even among you. Yes, in the theatre I've purposely left empty a box that will later be used by the actors, and then all of you will participate in the action. You will also be allowed an intermission so that you can get up and go out—but not to catch your breath, let me warn you now. I have prepared a new surprise for you even in the lobby. One last and very brief word—so that you can orient yourselves at once. The action takes place in a city in the interior of Sicily. Passions there, as you must know, are very strong, smoulder a long time and then flare forth with great violence. Above all, the fiercest passion is jealousy. Our tale in fact tells of one of these cases of the worst sort of jealousy. Worst because irremediable. Irremediable because it is that of time past. And it takes place exactly in the family where it least should have. For among the almost monastic seclusion of the other families in the city, it is the only one that has opened its doors to foreigners. It is a family with an excess of hospitality, given almost as if on purpose to challenge the inevitable gossip and scandal the whole town will make of it. The LaCroce family is composed, as you will see, of the father, Signor Palmiro, a mining engineer, who because of his continual absent-minded whistling is called Sampognetta, the toy whistle, by everyone; of the mother, Signora Ignazia, who comes from Naples and is known in her present surroundings as "The General"; and of four pretty daughters, shapely and flirtatious, vivacious and passionate: Mommina, Totina, Dorina, and Nene. And now, with your permission. [*He claps his hands as a signal for the actors and, pulling back one of the curtains a little, yells backstage.*] The buzzer. [*The buzzer is heard.*] I'm calling the actors out to introduce the characters.

[*The curtains part. Towards the front of the stage a green scrim or a thin green traveller is seen that can be parted in the middle.* DR. HINKFUSS *pulls back the scrim or traveller a little and calls.*] Please, Mr. ———. [*He pronounces the name of* THE LEADING ACTOR, *who will play the part of* RICO VERRI. *But* THE LEADING ACTOR, *though there behind the scrim or traveller, is unwilling to come out.*] Please come out here, Mr. ———. Surely you'll not keep up our little argument here in front of the audience.

THE LEADING ACTOR. [*Dressed as* RICO VERRI *in the uniform of an air force officer, he emerges from behind the scrim or traveller greatly excited.*] I shall, sir. And all the more if you now go so far, here in front of the audience, as to call me by my real name.

DR. HINKFUSS. Have I offended you?

THE LEADING ACTOR. Yes, and continue to, not realizing what you're doing—keeping me here to discuss the matter with you after you've already forced me against my will to come out on the stage.

DR. HINKFUSS. Who asked you to discuss it? *You're* the only one discussing it. I called you out here merely to do what you are supposed to.

THE LEADING ACTOR. And I'm ready to. As soon as the play starts. [*He withdraws, using the green curtain scornfully.*]

DR. HINKFUSS. [*with difficulty staying where he is*] I wanted to introduce you—

THE LEADING ACTOR. [*coming back out*] Never, sir. You shall not introduce me to a public that already knows me. Don't think for a minute I'm some little puppet in your hands. I am not to be shown off to the audience like that box you left empty up there, or a chair put here rather than there, all for some special scenic effect.

DR. HINKFUSS. [*muttering between his teeth*] You are at this moment profiting from the forbearance I must of necessity—

THE LEADING ACTOR. [*quickly interrupting*] No, my dear sir. No forbearance at all. You must remember that here, beneath these clothes, Mr. ——— [*He says his own name.*] no longer exists. He has given you his word to improvise this evening, and to do so, to have on his lips those lines that must rise from the depths of the character he represents, with the action that goes with them, with all the gestures completely natural, Mr. ——— must live the character of Rico Verri. And *is* already. So much so that, as I was just saying to you, I do not know how much longer I shall be able to endure all these accidents and surprises, these little games of light and shade you've prepared in order to amuse the audience. Do you understand?

[*There is heard at this point the reverberating whack of a slap, delivered behind the curtain, and immediately afterwards, the protests of* THE CHARACTER ACTOR, *who will play the part of* SAMPOGNETTA.]

THE CHARACTER ACTOR. Ohi! How do you like that? By God I

didn't expect you to really hit me.

[*The protest is received with laughter behind the green curtain.*]

DR. HINKFUSS. [*peering through the green curtain*] What the devil's happening now? Can something else be wrong?

THE CHARACTER ACTOR. [*coming out from behind the green curtain, his hand still nursing his cheek. Dressed up as* SAMPO-GNETTA] Just this—that I will not stand for Miss ——— [*the name of* THE CHARACTER ACTRESS] with the mere excuse she's *improvising* to haul off and slap me so hard. You must have heard it. It has among other things—[*He unveils his cheek.*] ruined my makeup.

THE CHARACTER ACTRESS. [*coming out dressed and made up as* SIGNORA IGNAZIA] Good heavens. Why not withdraw and try not to get hit by me? My slap was just a perfectly instinctive gesture.

THE CHARACTER ACTOR. And how do I shelter myself from you if you hit me suddenly and without notice?

THE CHARACTER ACTRESS. Whenever you deserve it, dear.

THE CHARACTER ACTOR. All right, but I have no way of knowing when I'm going to deserve it.

THE CHARACTER ACTRESS. Then you'll always have to be on guard because you're going to always be in need of a good whack or two. And, if one is really improvising, I cannot after all slap you at some moment decided on in advance.

THE CHARACTER ACTOR. But there's no need to really hit me!

THE CHARACTER ACTRESS. And just what should I do then? *Pretend* to hit you? I haven't a written part to play. My lines come from here [*She makes a gesture from the stomach up.*] and I do not stand on ceremony, understand? You'll grab at me, and I'll let you have it.

DR. HINKFUSS. Ladies and gentlemen, ladies and gentlemen, not here in front of the audience, please.

THE CHARACTER ACTRESS. We're already in our parts, Dr. Hinkfuss.

THE CHARACTER ACTOR. [*putting his hand again to his cheek*] You said it!

DR. HINKFUSS. So that's how it is, is it?

THE CHARACTER ACTRESS. Excuse me, but I thought *you* wanted to introduce us. Here we are introducing ourselves. One slap and this imbecile of a husband is good and introduced. [THE CHARACTER ACTOR, *as* SAMPOGNETTA, *starts whistling.*] There, see? He's whistling. Perfectly in character.

DR. HINKFUSS. But does it seem possible to you to have it done this way? In a chaos before the curtain and outside of the scenery?

THE CHARACTER ACTRESS. It does not matter. It does not matter.

DR. HINKFUSS. What do you mean it does not matter? Just what do you expect the audience to think?

THE LEADING ACTOR. They'll get it. They'll get it all the better this way. Leave it all up to us. We're all in character already.

THE CHARACTER ACTRESS. Everything will seem—you must believe it—much easier and more natural this way. None of the problems and restraints of a set place and action. We'll not forget to do everything you've planned for this evening. But just now, with your permission, I'm going to introduce my daughters. [*She pulls back the green curtain and calls.*] Come here, girls! Girls, come here! [*She takes the first by the arm and pulls her out on the stage.*] Mommina. [*And then the second.*] Totina. [*And then the third.*] Dorina. [*And then the fourth.*] Nene. [*All except the first make a graceful curtsey.*] Tocchi di ragazze! Thank God—all *four* of them deserve to be queens! Who'll ever guess they had *him* for a father? [THE CHARACTER ACTOR, *seeing that he is being pointed out, immediately averts his face and starts whistling.*] Whistle! Yes, go ahead and whistle. All you need in that sulphur mine of yours is for a little gas to get in your nose—just the way I might take a little pinch of snuff—and there you are, stretched out cold. And in one fine moment right before my eyes you're taken from me forever.

TOTINA. [*running with* DORINA *to stop her*] Please, Mama, please, don't start that.

DORINA. [*at the same time*] Let it pass, Mama, please.

THE CHARACTER ACTRESS. Just look at him whistle, look at him! [*Then, coming out of character, to* DR. HINKFUSS] Everything's going like clockwork, isn't it?

DR. HINKFUSS. [*with a wicked little gleam in his eye, finding here a way to get out of his predicament and save his battered prestige*] As the audience must already have guessed, this rebellion against my orders among the actors was faked, agreed on in advance between them and me, in order to make the performance seem more authentic. [*At this underhanded getaway, the actors stop and stare at him suddenly, like so many mannequins, in various poses of astonishment.* DR. HINKFUSS *notices it at once. He turns and looks at them and then points them out to the audience.*] Faked, too, this astonishment.

THE LEADING ACTOR. [*trembling with indignation*] A dirty trick! The audience must not believe a word of it. My protest was not in any way faked. [*He pushes back the green curtain as at first and strides off angrily.*]

DR. HINKFUSS. [*at once, confidently to the audience*] Acting, acting, all acting, even this outburst. I should perhaps, after all, have conceded something to the ego of an actor like Mr. ———, indeed one of the very best on the stage today. But you surely understand that whatever happens here on this stage cannot be other than faked. [*turning to* THE CHARACTER ACTRESS] Yes, go on, go on, Miss ———, it is indeed going splendidly. But I could hardly have expected less from you.

THE CHARACTER ACTRESS. [*disconcerted, dumbfounded by such impudence, not knowing any longer what to do*] So, you want—you want me to go on? And—and—excuse me, please—go on with exactly what?

DR. HINKFUSS. Good God, with the performance, Miss ———,—it's off to such a splendid start, just as we planned it.

THE CHARACTER ACTRESS. No, listen, please. Don't say "just as we

planned it" if you don't want me to stand here not able to say
one single word.

DR. HINKFUSS. [again to the audience, as though in confidence]
Marvelous. She's marvelous!

THE CHARACTER ACTRESS. You really want to make people believe
that this emergence of our roles was agreed on between us
ahead of time?

DR. HINKFUSS. Just ask the audience if they think we are not at this
moment really improvising?

> [THE GENTLEMAN IN THE ORCHESTRA, FOUR OTHERS IN THE
> ORCHESTRA, and THE GENTLEMAN IN THE BALCONY start ap-
> plauding. They stop at once if the real audience does not
> contagiously follow their example.]

THE CHARACTER ACTRESS. But yes, of course, we are really improvising now. We're out of our roles and we're improvising, I as
much as you.

DR. HINKFUSS. All right, then—keep it up, keep it up. Call the
other actors out and introduce them.

THE CHARACTER ACTRESS. Right away. [calling behind the green cur-
tain] All right boys, all of you come out here! Don't worry, Dr.
Hinkfuss, I'm in character! Out here, my friends!

> [Five young AIR FORCE OFFICERS enter noisily, in uniform.
> First they vigorously salute SIGNORA IGNAZIA.]

THE FIVE OFFICERS. Cara Signora! Long live the General! Santa
Pretettrice! [And other similar exclamations. Then they greet
THE FOUR GIRLS, who gaily reply. ONE OF THE OFFICERS goes
over and also greets SAMPOGNETTA. SIGNORA IGNAZIA tries to interrupt all the uproar, indeed this time actually improvised.]

SIGNORA IGNAZIA. Quiet, quiet, my dears. Let's not make too much
noise. Wait, wait. Here, Pomerici, you're just what I've always
dreamed of for my little Totina. Here, take her by the arm—
like this! And you, Sarelli, you over here with Dorina.

THE THIRD OFFICER. Look here, Dorina's mine. [holding her by the
arm] Let's not joke about it.

SARELLI. [pulling DORINA by her other arm] Come on, lay off. Let
me have her. If her mother says she's mine, she's mine.

THE THIRD OFFICER. Not at all. We have an understanding, the
signorina and I.

SARELLI. [to DORINA] So, you have an understanding, do you? Congratulations! [denouncing them] Signora Ignazia, do you hear
that?

THE CHARACTER ACTRESS. Understanding?

DORINA. [irritated] But of course, Miss ——— [the name of THE
CHARACTER ACTRESS] An understanding—about the roles we're
playing.

THE THIRD OFFICER. I have to ask you, Miss ——— [the name of
THE CHARACTER ACTRESS], not to interfere with what's already
been decided on.

THE CHARACTER ACTRESS. Oh dear. I'm sorry. Excuse me. Now I
do remember. You, Sarelli, are with Nene.

NENE. [*to* SARELLI, *taking his arm*] With *me!* Don't you remember that that's how we planned it?

SARELLI. Anyhow, we are here only to make noise.

DR. HINKFUSS. [*to* THE CHARACTER ACTRESS] Attention, attention, Miss ————. I beg of you.

THE CHARACTER ACTRESS. Yes, yes. I'm terribly sorry. With so many of them I get all mixed up. [*turning around to look*] But Verri? Where is Verri? He ought to be here with his friends.

THE LEADING ACTOR. [*at once sticking his head out between the green curtain*] Fine friends they are, giving your daughters here lessons in—modesty.

SIGNORA IGNAZIA. What do you want them to do? Treat them like nuns and teach them to embroider? Don't be old-fashioned, my dear. [*She goes and drags him out by the hand.*] Come now, be a sport. Come out here. Look at them. They're not a bit conceited and they have virtues, too. That can be said of very few girls now-a-days. All the virtues of good little wives—you who talks about modesty. Mommina is wonderful in the kitchen.

MOMMINA. [*reproachfully, as though her* MOTHER *had betrayed a shameful secret*] Mama!

SIGNORA IGNAZIA. Totina can patch and mend—

TOTINA. [*as* MOMMINA] But what are you saying, Mama?

SIGNORA IGNAZIA. And Nene—

NENE. [*quickly, aggressively threatening to clamp her hand on her mother's mouth*] Mama, are you going to be still?

SIGNORA IGNAZIA. Find me anyone to equal the way she can take any old dress and make it over as good as new—

NENE. [*as before*] Really, Mama, that's quite enough!

SIGNORA IGNAZIA. Get the spots out—

NENE. [*clamping her hand on her mother's mouth*] I said that was enough, Mama.

SIGNORA IGNAZIA. [*pulling* NENE'S *hand away*] Turning collars—and Dorina takes care of the accounts!

DORINA. *Now* have you scraped bottom?

SIGNORA IGNAZIA. What have things come to? They're *ashamed* of it.

SAMPOGNETTA. Just as if they were secret vices!

SIGNORIA IGNAZIA. And they aren't vain, either. They're happy with so very little. Just so long as they get to the theatre now and then, they're willing to go hungry. Our old opera, that is. Even I like it a great deal.

NENE. [*who comes in with a rose in her hand*] But, Mama, don't forget *Carmen,* too. [*She puts the rose between her teeth and sings, wiggling her hips impudently*]

> "E l'amore uno strano augello
> che non si puo domesticar—"

SIGNORA IGNAZIA. *Carmen's* all right, too, but it doesn't start your heart pounding the way our old opera does. Innocence cries out and no one believes her. And then, the lover in despair, "Ah!

quell' infame l'onore ha venduto." Get Mommina to speak about
all this. Basta! [*turning around to* VERRI] The first time you came
to our house, remember?—you were introduced by these boys
here—

THE THIRD OFFICER. If only we'd never done it—

THE SECOND OFFICER. He was an officer at our airfield—

THE LEADING ACTOR. Please, merely a reserve officer, for only six
months and then, done with, God willing, and done with *their*
good times, too, enjoying life at my expense.

POMERICI. Us? At your expense?

SARELLI. Now listen here—

SIGNORA IGNAZIA. This is not the question. What I wanted to say
was that neither I, nor my daughters here, nor their father over
there— [*Again* SAMPOGNETTA, *the moment he is mentioned
turns his face and starts whistling.*] Stop it, or I'll smack you in
the face with this purse. [*It is a large purse.* SAMPOGNETTA *stops
at once.*] Not one of us had the least idea at the start that you
had that damned Sicilian blood in your veins—

VERRI. I'm proud of it!

SIGNORA IGNAZIA. Ah! How I know it. God, how I know it!

DR. HINKFUSS. Please, please, Miss ——— [*He pronounces* THE
CHARACTER ACTRESS' *name.*] Let's not give the plot away.

THE CHARACTER ACTRESS. No, don't worry, I won't.

DR. HINKFUSS. Only the introduction, clear and simple. That's all
we want just now.

THE CHARACTER ACTRESS. Clear and simple, yes, don't you worry.
But as I was saying, at first he didn't boast about it. Like the
rest of us, he looked down cn all those savages in town who
thought it was shameful, our living *alla continentale*, our having
in a few of the officers from the field and letting them have fun
the way, my God, the way young people should, without anything shameful about it. And he had fun too, with my Mommina— [*She looks around her.*] Where is she? There she is.
Come here, come over here, my poor girl. It's not time for you to
stand there like that. [THE LEADING ACTRESS, *who will play*
MOMMINA's *part, is pulled by the hand, but pulls back.*] Come.
Come along.

THE LEADING ACTRESS. Let me alone, Miss ———. *Please* let me
alone. [*She pronounces the name of* THE CHARACTER ACTRESS.
Then resolutely she turns and faces DR. HINKFUSS.] Dr. Hinkfuss,
I simply cannot do it this way. I told you so right from the start.
It simply is not possible for me. You sketched out the action for
us and gave us the sequence of all scenes. All right. Then it
should be that way. I'm supposed to sing. I must feel secure, in
my place, in the action I've been assigned. I simply can't change
every five minutes.

THE LEADING ACTOR. And why not? Possibly because Miss ———
[*He pronounces* THE LEADING ACTRESS' *name.*] has already written down the lines she wants to say and memorized them.

THE LEADING ACTRESS. I am prepared. Of course I am. And you perhaps are not?

THE LEADING ACTOR. Yes, but not with the very lines I'm going to say. Let's get this straight now. You are trying, aren't you, to get me to say certain things so you can use lines you've already prepared? I shall say what I feel like saying myself. [*An outburst of simultaneous comments from the actors follows this argument.*] "That would be fine, wouldn't it?" "To have one get the other to say what suits *him!*" "There goes our improvisation!" "She might as well sit down and write out everybody's part!"

DR. HINKFUSS. [*cutting short the uproar*] Ladies and gentlemen, please. I have already told you to say as little as possible, as little as possible. Enough for now. Introductions are over. What we need is more action and fewer words. You must pay attention to me. I assure you that your lines will come all by themselves, spontaneously, if you go through the action I've worked out for you. Do this and you can't go wrong. Let yourself be guided by me, just the way we agreed on. Come now. Off stage. Let's have the curtain dropped. [*The stage curtain is closed.* DR. HINKFUSS, *remaining before the footlights and turning to the audience, adds*] I must apologize, ladies and gentlemen. The performance is really ready to begin. Five minutes, just five minutes, with your kind permission, while I go and see that everything is ready. [*He withdraws, pushing aside the stage curtain. A five-minute pause.*]

Act Two

The stage curtain again opens. But DR. HINKFUSS *continues to put the audience off. It has occurred to him that it would be a good idea to start off with a religious procession, thereby giving the audience some Sicilian atmosphere. "It will add a little color," he says to himself. And he has seen to everything. For now just such a procession moves from the entrance of the theatre towards the stage, down the aisle that divides in two the rows of the orchestra. They enter in this order:*

1. FOUR CHOIRBOYS, *in black tunics and white shirts trimmed in lace, two before and two after, each bearing a lit taper in his hand;*

2. FOUR YOUNG GIRLS, *the "little virgins," dressed all in white and swathed in white veils, with white crocheted gloves so large their little hands seem clumsy in them—two before and two after. And each bearing one of the four supports of a little baldachin of sky-blue silk;*

3. *Under the baldachin, the Holy Family, consisting of* AN OLD MAN *dressed like the St. Joseph one sees in holy pictures of the nativity, a purple halo on his head and on one hand a long staff, flowered at the crook; and beside him a beautiful blond young woman, with her eyes lowered, a modest smile on her lips, dressed like the* VIRGIN MARY. *She too has a halo on her head, and in her arms she carries a big beautiful wax doll, representing the Christ*

*child, like the ones still seen today in crude Christmas pageants
in Sicily; they are accompanied by* MUSICIANS *and* CHOIR;

4. *A* SHEPHERD *in a wool beret and coat, his trousers of goat-
skin, and* ANOTHER SHEPHERD, *somewhat younger; one is playing
the bagpipes and the other the flute;*

5. *Bringing up the rear a* GROUP OF PEASANTS *of every age, the
women in long skirts thickly pleated at the hips, veils on their
heads, the men in short jackets and bell trousers, with wide belts
of colored silk. In their hands are black cotton stocking caps with
tassels on the ends. They come into the theatre singing, to the accompaniment of bagpipes:*

> *Oggi e sempre sia lodato*
> *nostro Dio sagramentato;*
> *e lodata sempre sia*
> *nostra vergine Maria.*

6. DR. HINKFUSS, *on the tail of the procession, watches the performance seated in the first row of the orchestra in a place reserved
for him.*

*Meanwhile on stage one sees a street in the city. The rough
white wall of a house runs from left to right across more than three
quarters of the stage and then abruptly turns and runs upstage at an
obtuse angle. At the corner, on a bracket attached to the wall, is a
street light. Beyond the street light, in the wall, one sees the entrance to a night club, lit with colored lights, and, almost opposite
but a little beyond and in relief, the portal of an old church with
three steps leading up to it.*

*A little before the curtains are opened and the procession has
entered the theatre, one hears on stage the sound of church bells
and, hardly audible, the boom of an organ playing inside the
church. When the curtains part and while the procession is mounting the stage, there is seen along the wall and to the right, MEN
and WOMEN (not more than eight or nine) kneeling. These have
just happened to be passing by. The WOMEN are crossing themselves; the MEN baring their heads. When, having crossed the stage,
the PROCESSION has entered the church, these MEN and WOMEN
join onto the end and enter, too. When the last has gone in, the
sound of the church bell stops. Now more clearly audible, the
sound of the organ persists a moment longer in the silence, but it
grows softer and softer and the lights dim out. Suddenly, the very
moment the organ stops, there breaks out in shattering contrast
the sound of a jazz band in the night club across the street; and at
the same moment the white wall that runs across the stage becomes transparent. One sees the inside of the night club, glittering with colored lights. At the right, near the entrance, is the bar,
and, behind it,* THREE GIRLS *in low-cut dresses with too much
make-up crudely smeared on their faces. Against the wall in back,
next to the bar, a long drapery of flaming red velvet is hung, and,
against it, composed like a bas relief, is a night club singer, dressed
all in black gauze, her face pale, her head dropped to one side, her*

eyes closed. She is mournfully singing blues songs. THREE BLOND
DANCERS *move their arms and legs in rhythm and in unison turn
their shoulders towards the bar. Only a small amount of space is
left for them between the bar and the first row of small round
tables. At the tables a* FEW CUSTOMERS *are seated with their drinks
before them. Among the customers is* SAMPOGNETTA, *an old
crumpled hat in his hand and a long cigar in his mouth. A* JOKING
CUSTOMER *sitting behind him in the second row of tables, seeing
him intently watching the movements of the* THREE BLOND DANCERS,
*begins preparing a hideous joke: two long horns cut out of the
light cardboard on which the wine list and program are printed.
The* OTHER CUSTOMERS *are quite aware of what he is doing and,
delighted by the whole thing, urge him with winks and gestures to
hurry. After the two horns are cut out, long and straight, from the
circle of cardboard that forms their base, the* JOKING CUSTOMER *gets
up and with great caution places them on* SAMPOGNETTA'S *crumpled
hat.* EVERYONE *starts laughing and applauding.* SAMPOGNETTA,
thinking the laughter and applause are for the THREE BLOND
DANCERS, *who have just finished their number, begins himself to
laugh and applaud and, doing so, causes the others to laugh all
the harder and applaud more noisily. He seems unable to understand why everyone is looking at him, including the* THREE GIRLS
at the bar. Even the THREE BLOND DANCERS, *who have to exit, are
laughing.* SAMPOGNETTA *is bewildered. He stops applauding. Then
the strange* NIGHT CLUB SINGER, *overwhelmed with indignation,
leaves her velvet backdrop and goes over and grabs the mocking
trophy from* SAMPOGNETTA'S *head, crying.*

NIGHT CLUB SINGER. No, poor old man—[*to the others*] Away, all
   of you. You ought to be ashamed! [*The* CUSTOMERS *push her
   back, all crying out at once in great confusion.*]

THE CUSTOMERS. Stay out there, stupid! Shut up and get back where
   you belong. Where's the poor old man? Leave it alone! You
   keep out of this! He's got what he deserves! He deserves it!

NIGHT CLUB SINGER. [*continues to protest and, restrained by the
   others, struggles to get free*] You cowards, let go of me! Why
   does he deserve it? What has he done to you?

SAMPOGNETTA. [*more bewildered than ever, now stands up*] I deserve what? What do I *deserve?*

THE JOKING CUSTOMER. Come on, why don't you get out of here?
   This is no place for you, sir! [*He, with the help of the others,
   pushes* SAMPOGNETTA *towards the door.*]

THIRD CUSTOMER. We know perfectly well what *you* deserve, Signor
   Palmiro!

   [SAMPOGNETTA *is led out with the horns still on his head.
   The lights are extinguished behind the transparent wall,
   and it becomes a wall again. The cries of those trying to restrain the night club singer continue to be heard. Then a big
   burst of laughter and the jazz starts up again.*]

SAMPOGNETTA. [*to the two or three* CUSTOMERS *who have pushed
   him out into the street and who now stand relishing the sight of*

him with his crown underneath the street light.] What I'd like to know is what happened?

SECOND CUSTOMER. Nothing, really. It's all because of the little incident the other night.

THIRD CUSTOMER. Everyone knows you care about that night club singer—

SECOND CUSTOMER. Just for laughs they were hoping she would slap you as she did the other night—

THIRD CUSTOMER. Exactly—saying it was what you *deserved!*

SAMPOGNETTA. Ah, I understand now! I understand!

FIRST CUSTOMER. Look—hey, look up there in the sky, all of you. Stars!

SECOND CUSTOMER. Stars?

THIRD CUSTOMER. What are you talking about? *Stars?*

FIRST CUSTOMER. They're moving. They're moving.

SECOND CUSTOMER. Come on. Come on.

SAMPOGNETTA. Is it possible?

FIRST CUSTOMER. Yes, yes, just look. It's as though, with a couple of poles, you could reach right up and touch them. [*He raises his arms, making the shape of two horns.*]

THIRD CUSTOMER. You think those bulbs there are stars?

SECOND CUSTOMER. You were saying, Signor Palmiro—?

SAMPOGNETTA. Ah, yes, yes. I was trying to say that this evening, I don't know if you noticed it, I expressly kept my eyes fixed all the time on the little dancers, without once turning my head towards her. She makes such an impression on me, ah, such an impression, that poor soul, when she sings: her eyes closed and those tears streaming down her face!

SECOND CUSTOMER. That's an act, Signor Palmiro! Do not pay any attention to those tears. It's all part of the show.

SAMPOGNETTA. [*seriously shaking his head and waving "no" with his finger*] No, no, ah, no, no, not at all. An act indeed! That woman suffers. She really and truly suffers. And then her voice is the very voice of my eldest girl. Exactly. Exactly. And she's told me herself, in confidence of course, she too comes from a very good family—

THIRD CUSTOMER. Ah yea? Just listen. A daughter of some engineer perhaps—?

SAMPOGNETTA. That I wouldn't know. But I do know that misfortunes can befall anyone. And every time I hear her sing, I become grieved and dismayed—

[*At this point enter from the left, marching, TOTINA on POMARICI'S arm, NENE on SARELLI'S, DORINA on that of THE THIRD OFFICER, MOMMINA at RICO VERRI'S side, and SIGNORA IGNAZIA on the arm of THE OTHER TWO OFFICERS. POMARICI is beating out the time for all of them, even before they come on stage. The THREE CUSTOMERS, who have now become a group of four or more, hearing a voice, withdraw towards the entrance to the night club, leaving SAMPOGNETTA alone under the street light. The horns are still on his head.*]

POMARICI. One—two, one—two, one—two—

[*They march in, facing the audience. The* FOUR DAUGHTERS *and* SIGNORA IGNAZIA *are dressed up in gaudy evening dresses.*]

TOTINA. [*seeing her father with horns on his head*] Oh God, Papa —what have they done to you?

POMARICI. Those filthy cowards!

SAMPOGNETTA. To me? What are you talking about?

NENE. But take that thing off your head!

SIGNORA IGNAZIA. [*while her husband feels around his hat with his hands*] Horns?

DORINA. Rascals—who did it?

TOTINA. Just look over there!

SAMPOGNETTA. [*taking off the horns*] On me—horns? Ah then, it was *this* all along. Scoundrels.

SIGNORA IGNAZIA. And he's still holding them in his hand. Throw them away, you idiot. All you're good for is to be the butt of every rogue in town.

MOMMINA. [*to her mother*] That's all we need now, for you to scold *him* for it—

TOTINA. —while those filthy cowards are to blame.

VERRI. [*Going towards the entrance to the night club. To* THE CUSTOMERS *who have been standing by watching and laughing*] Which of you did it? Which of you did it? [*He grabs one of them by the chest.*] You? Was it you?

NENE. They're *laughing!*

THE CUSTOMER. [*trying to get free*] Let go of me. I had nothing to do with it. You better keep your hands off me!

VERRI. Then tell me who did it.

POMARICI. Come on, Verri. Let's get out of here.

SARELLI. What's the point of remaining for a row?

SIGNORA IGNAZIA. No, no, no. I must have an apology, a personal apology, from the proprietor of this—den of iniquity.

TOTINA. Let's go, Mama, please.

SECOND CUSTOMER. Careful how you speak there, Signora. There are also gentlemen around here.

MOMMINA. Do gentlemen behave this way?

DORINA. You filthy fools!

THIRD OFFICER. Let's go, Signorina, let's go.

FOURTH CUSTOMER. Just the boys, playing a little joke—

POMARICI. So you call it a joke, do you?

SECOND CUSTOMER. We all have the highest regard for Signor Palmiro here—

THIRD CUSTOMER. [*to* SIGNORA IGNAZIA] But as for you, Signora, not one damned bit!

SECOND CUSTOMER. Everyone in town's talking about your behavior.

VERRI. [*going towards him with raised arms*] Watch out what you say there, or I'll knock you down.

FOURTH CUSTOMER. We'll report you to the Colonel.

THIRD CUSTOMER. Such conduct in an officer.

VERRI. Who'll report it?

THE CUSTOMERS. [*also those inside the night club*] All of us—we all will!

POMARICI. You started this. You insult the ladies walking down the street in our company, and it's our duty to defend them.

FOURTH CUSTOMER. No one insulted them!

THIRD CUSTOMER. No—it was the Signora who started insulting us!

SIGNORA IGNAZIA. I—never! I insulted no one. All I did was tell you to your dirty faces what you are—fools, imbeciles, rogues— that's what you are, and you ought to be under lock and key in cages, the way wild animals are. There. That's what I think of you. [*All* THE CUSTOMERS *laugh a little awkwardly.*] Go ahead. Laugh. Laugh, you scoundrels, savages.

POMARICI. [*with* THE OTHER OFFICERS *and* THE DAUGHTERS, *trying to calm her down*] Come, come, Signora, let's go—

SARELLI. We've had enough of this.

THIRD OFFICER. Let's get on to the show.

NENE. Mama, don't you debase yourself by having anything more to do with them.

FOURTH OFFICER. Let's go. We're already late.

TOTINA. The first act'll be over, I'm sure.

MOMMINA. Yes, yes, let's go, Mama. Leave them to their dirty tricks.

POMARICI. Signor Palmiro, you come on to the theatre with us.

SIGNORA IGNAZIA. Him at the theatre? Oh, no! Get home! Get home this minute! You have to get up early tomorrow for the mine. Go on! Go home! [THE CUSTOMERS *turn and laugh at this peremptory order from the wife to her husband.*]

SARELLI. And we must get to the theatre. Let's not lose any more time.

SIGNORA IGNAZIA. Imbeciles. Cretins. Go ahead and laugh. Laugh at your ignorance.

POMARICI. Enough of this now. Enough of this!

THE OTHER OFFICERS. Yes, let's get to the theatre, to the theatre.

DR. HINKFUSS. [*at this point he gets up and cries*] Yes, quite enough, quite enough. Now off to the theatre! Everyone off stage. The customers get back in the night club and the rest of you exit right. And pull the curtains too, just a little, on both sides.

[*The actors exit. The stage curtain is pulled a little from either side so that there is left exposed in the center the section of the white wall that will serve as the screen for the film about to be shown of the opera. Only* THE CHARACTER ACTOR (SAMPOGNETTA) *has stayed on the stage after the others have exited. If the theatre does not have boxes, at this point and during the next few speeches of* DR. HINKFUSS *and* THE CHARACTER ACTOR, *stage hands can bring onstage a very simple box arrangement and set it up downstage right. They also bring on straight chairs and a bench and place them within the framework of the box, so that when the actors and actresses enter they will sit on an angle facing the screen—three quarters of each face towards the audience.*]

THE CHARACTER ACTOR. [*to* DR. HINKFUSS] But if I'm not going to the theatre with them, I should go off left, shouldn't I?

DR. HINKFUSS. What a question! Of course you should go off left.

THE CHARACTER ACTOR. No, I wanted only you to consider, my dear director, that they didn't let me say a single word. Too much confusion!

DR. HINKFUSS. Not at all. It went—beautifully!! Go on, get off stage.

THE CHARACTER ACTOR. I have to clarify that it is *I* who always have to pay for everything.

DR. HINKFUSS. Very well. Now you have, and now you can get off the stage. We're going to have the theatre scene now. [THE CHARACTER ACTOR *exits left.*] Is the turntable ready? And the projector? Start them up.

[DR. HINKFUSS *turns to sit down in his seat. Meanwhile, at the right of the stage behind the stage curtain drawn to hide the corner edge where the wall bracket with the street light is, the stage hands have set up a phonograph on which they have put the end of the first act of an Italian opera, "La Forza del Destino" or "Un Ballo in Maschera" or some other. It is synchronized with the film being shown on the white wall that serves as a screen. The sound and the projection have barely begun, however, before the box that has been left empty, or the box set up onstage, is lit up, with a strong light whose source one cannot see, and* SIGNORA IGNAZIA *is seen entering with her* FOUR DAUGHTERS, RICO VERRI, *and* THE OTHER OFFICERS. *Their entrance is noisy and immediately arouses protests from the audience.*]

SIGNORA IGNAZIA. Now see if I wasn't right! It's already the first act finale.

TOTINA. Ohhhh, how we've rushed! Auf. [*She sinks down in the first seat in the box, opposite her mother.*] God, it's hot here!

POMARICI. [*making a fan of his cap*] Here I am, Signorina, at your service!

DORINA. Of course! On close ranks! One—two, one—two—

VOICES IN THE THEATRE. But *really!* Silence! Is this any way to enter a theatre?

MOMMINA. [*to* TOTINA] You've got my seat. Get up.

TOTINA. Well, if Dorina and Nene are sitting down in the middle—

DORINA. We thought Mommina would want to sit in back with Verri, like the other time—

VOICES IN THE THEATRE. Sssshhhhhh—quiet. Quiet. The same people again. It's simply indecent. And the really shocking thing is they're *officers!* Isn't there anyone here to make them be still?

[*Meanwhile there is great confusion in the box while everyone changes places.* TOTINA *gives up her place to* MOMMINA

and takes DORINA'S. DORINA *has moved over into the place
left empty by* NENE, *who has gone over and sat on the
divan next to her mother.* RICO VERRI *sits next to* MOMMINA
on the divan opposite. Behind TOTINA, POMARICI. *Behind*
DORINA, THE THIRD OFFICER. *And in back,* SARELLI *and* THE
OTHER TWO OFFICERS.]

MOMMINA. Gently, gently, for God's sake!

NENE. Yes, gently! First you cause all this mixup—

MOMMINA. I?

NENE. Yes, making everyone get up and change seats—

DORINA. *Let* them talk!

TOTINA. As if they'd never heard ———[*She names the opera.*]
before.

POMARICI. Still one ought to have a little respect for the ladies.

VOICES IN THE THEATRE. Shut up, you. It's simply shocking. Throw
them out! Can it really be the box the officers are in that's making all the noise? Out! Out!

SIGNORA IGNAZIA. Cannibals! Is it our fault if we happen to get
here a little late? Do you call *this* civilization? First we're as-
saulted on the street, and now here in the theatre we're shouted
at and insulted. Cannibals!

TOTINA. This is the way it's done on the continent!

DORINA. One comes to the theatre when one feels like it.

NENE. And with us are people who know how one lives and does
things on the continent.

VOICES IN THE THEATRE. Enough. Enough.

DR. HINKFUSS. [*getting up and turning to the box where the actors
are*] Yes, enough, enough. Let's not carry it too far, I beg of you.

SIGNORA IGNAZIA. But it pleases me to carry it this far. We're
being egged on from down there. It is an absolutely insup-
portable persecution, don't you see? to have all these insults
thrown at us just because we happen to make a bit of noise
getting into our seats—

DR. HINKFUSS. All right. All right. This is enough for now. Anyhow
the act's over.

VERRI. Over? Thank God. Let's get out then.

DR. HINKFUSS. Excellent. Yes, out, out!

TOTINA. I'm so thirsty. [*She leaves box.*]

NENE. Let us hope to find some ice cream.

SIGNORA IGNAZIA. Come, let's get out of here, or I'm going to blow
up!

[*The film is done. The phonograph is silent. The curtain
closes completely now.* DR. HINKFUSS *gets up on the stage
and turns to the audience as the lights come on in the
theatre.*]

DR. HINKFUSS. Those of the audience who usually go out between
acts are free to do so now if they like. They can have a good
look at the scandal that those dear people have aroused, even
out in the lobby—not willfully but because by now everything
they do is scrutinized and examined and becomes still some-

thing else for people to gossip about. Go on, then. But not
everyone, please. I don't want it too crowded outside with everyone trying to see what more or less has already been seen in
the box. I can assure you that whoever stays here in his seat
will miss absolutely nothing of consequence. You will see, out
there mixing with the audience during the usual intermission
between acts, the same people you saw leave their box a moment ago. I myself, here in the theatre, shall profit from this
interruption to change scenes, doing so right here in front
of you, ladies and gentlemen, clearly in view, to offer you
who are staying in your seats something a little out of the ordinary, too. [*He claps his hands as a signal and commands*]
Open the curtains!

[*The curtains open.*]

Interlude

Simultaneous performances in the lobby and on stage: In the
lobby the actors and actresses, each of course still in his role, behave
with complete freedom and naturalness, as though he was merely
a part of the audience during intermission. They group themselves
at four different places in the lobby and there, each group, in-
dependent from the other, performs a simultaneous scene: NENE
and TOTINA, *who go with* POMARICI *and* SARELLI *to the far end of*
the lobby where there is a counter at which coffee, beer, soft drinks,
caramels, and other such things are sold; DORINA *walks up and down*
as she talks with THE THIRD OFFICER (NARDI); RICO VERRI *with*
SIGNORA IGNAZIA, *sitting on a bench, with the* OTHER TWO OFFICERS
(POMETTI *and* MANGINI) *and* MOMMINA. *These little scenes,*
though taking place simultaneously and in different parts of the
lobby, are written here, because of space, one after the other.

I

[NENE, TOTINA, POMARICI, *and* SARELLI *at the counter at*
the far end of the lobby.]

NENE. What, you don't have any ice cream? Oh, what a shame.
Give me a soft drink, then, but it *must* be cold. I insist. Yes,
cherry's all right.

TOTINA. And lemonade for me.

POMARICI. And a little bag of chocolates, and some caramels, too.

NENE. No, don't get any caramels, Pomarici. Thank you.

TOTINA. They won't be any good. They are? Well, get them, then,
go ahead and get them. It's one of the nicest things in the
world—

POMARICI. Caramels?

TOTINA. No—for us women—to make men pay for things.

POMARICI. It is such a little thing. I'm sorry we did not go to the
drugstore before coming to the theatre—

SARELLI. With what has happened—?

TOTINA. Didn't you say he'd be on leave, the *beast*, and very soon?

NENE. I simply don't see why not. All I want to do really is fly over town just for the pleasure of leaning out and spitting on it. Can't I really, can't I?

SARELLI. Go up? It's absolutely out.

NENE. No, I mean spit—puh! like that, just once. Well, you'll have to do it for me, then.

II

[DORINA *and* NARDI, *the* THIRD OFFICER, *walking up and down.*]

NARDI. But didn't you know? Your father's simply crazy about that night club singer!

DORINA. Papa? What are you telling me?

NARDI. Papa. Papa. I'm telling you myself. And everyone in town knows all about it.

DORINA. You aren't serious. Papa in love? [*She bursts out laughing and all the audience turns to look at her.*]

NARDI. Didn't you *see* her over there in the night club?

DORINA. For God's sake, don't let Mama know about it. She'd skin him alive. But who is she? Do you know her?

NARDI. I've seen her once. Some crazy girl all broken up over something or other.

DORINA. Broken up? How?

NARDI. They say she always cries when she sings, with her eyes closed. Real tears. And sometimes she even faints and falls down on the floor, from whatever it is that makes her cry so. Drunk.

TOTINA. Good lord. Even if he is my father I must say he does go out of his way looking for trouble, going to places like that.

POMARICI. [*putting a chocolate in her mouth*] Don't you worry about it. Don't worry about it.

NENE. [*opening her mouth like a little bird*] Don't I get one, too?

POMARICI. [*putting one in her mouth too*] There you are, baby, but you get a caramel instead.

NENE. Are you sure this is the way people on the continent behave?

POMARICI. What do you mean? Feed the pretty girls candy? Absolutely.

SARELLI. That, and a good deal more, too.

NENE. What else? What else?

POMARICI. Oh, if you only wanted to do *everything* just the way we do it on the continent.

TOTINA. [*provocative*] What, for example?

SARELLI. Can't show you here.

NENE. And then tomorrow the four of us are storming the airfield—

TOTINA. And if you don't take us up for a ride, we'll never have anything more to do with you.

POMARICI. We'll love seeing you, but as for going up to fly with us, well—

SARELLI. Against regulations!

POMARICI. With that commander we have in charge out there—

DORINA. Oh? Then it's being drunk that does it.

NARDI. Maybe. Or maybe she drinks because she's so miserable.

DORINA. Oh God, and Papa—? Poor dear. But does he know everyone's talking about him? No, no, I don't believe it.

NARDI. You don't believe it? Even if I told you that one night— maybe he was a little high, too—he made a fool of himself in front of everyone in the night club, getting up and going over —with tears in his eyes, too, and a handkerchief in his hand— to dry her tears, while she stood there singing with her eyes closed?

DORINA. But, no—you aren't serious!

NARDI. And you know what she did? She let go with a terrific slap!

DORINA. She slapped Papa? She, too? Poor Papa. Mama gives him enough as it is.

NARDI. That's what he said himself, right there before everyone, with all of them laughing. "You do it, too, you ungrateful girl. My wife gives me plenty of them as it is."

[*By now they are near the counter.* DORINA *sees her sisters,* TOTINA *and* NENE, *and with* NARDI *she rushes towards them.*]

III

[*In front of the counter:* NENE, TOTINA, DORINA, POMARICI, SARELLI, *and* NARDI.]

DORINA. Can you imagine what Nardi's been telling me? Papa's in love. With that night club singer.

TOTINA. No!

NENE. Do you believe it? It's just a joke.

DORINA. No, no, it's *true*. It's true.

NARDI. I can prove it's true.

SARELLI. Sure. I knew it all along.

DORINA. And if you only knew what he did—

NENE. What?

DORINA. He got slapped by her, too, right in front of everyone, in the night club.

NENE. Slapped?

TOTINA. But why?

DORINA. He wanted to dry her tears.

TOTINA. Her tears?

DORINA. Yes, you see, they say she's a girl who always crying—

TOTINA. There. Wasn't I right when I said it just now? It's he who causes it all. What can you expect? Why shouldn't people laugh at him?

SARELLI. If you want proof, just reach in the inside pocket of his coat. He ought to have the picture of the singer tucked away there. He showed it to me the other day, with tears and comments. Poor Signor Palmiro.

IV

[RICO VERRI *and* MOMMINA, *apart from the others.*]

MOMMINA. [*a little frightened by the gloomy look with which* VERRI *came out of theatre box*] What's the matter?

VERRI. [*hiding awkwardly his annoyance*] Me? Nothing. What do
you mean, "What's the matter?"

MOMMINA. But then why are you acting like this?

VERRI. I don't know. All I know is that if I'd been cooped up in
that box one more minute, I'd have committed a crime for sure.

MOMMINA. I can't bear such a life any longer!

VERRI. [*loudly and angrily*] Have you noticed it just now?

MOMMINA. Please, please, don't speak so loudly. Everyone's looking
at us.

VERRI. That's what I say. That's exactly what I say.

MOMMINA. I've gotten to the point I hardly dare raise my hand
or say a single word.

VERRI. What I'd like to know is what business they have looking
at us like that, standing here listening to every word you and
I say to each other.

MOMMINA. Please, be good and do me this one favor—don't
provoke them.

VERRI. Aren't we here like everyone else? What's so funny about
us at this moment that they just stand and stare at us? I ask
you, is it possible—

MOMMINA. Yes—to really live—I've already told you—to even
make a single gesture any more, raise one's eyes even, when
everyone's always staring. Look over there, around my sisters,
and over there around Mama.

VERRI. Just as if we were here giving a performance in a play.

MOMMINA. Exactly.

VERRI. Unfortunately, your sisters over there—I am sorry to say—

MOMMINA. What?

VERRI. Nothing. I'd rather not pay any attention to it. But it seems
to me they rather enjoy—

MOMMINA. Enjoy what?

VERRI. Being stared at.

MOMMINA. But they aren't doing anything wrong. They're laughing and talking—that's all.

VERRI. It's a challenge. That bold behaviour!

MOMMINA. But *your* friends are to blame—

VERRI. I know. To lead them on. Believe me, they're beginning to
get in my hair—Sarelli there, and Pomarici, and Nardi.

MOMMINA. They're simply having a little fun.

VERRI. Fun? At the expense of the reputations of three young
women. They could at least keep from doing certain things,
certain little familiarities here in public—

MOMMINA. Yes, you're right, about that.

VERRI. I, for example, would no longer tolerate one of them permitting himself with you—

MOMMINA. First of all, I would not allow it. You know that.

VERRI. Let me go on, please. Even you, even you at first let them.

MOMMINA. But not any more, not for a long time. You know that.

VERRI. It isn't that I know it. They must know it, too.

MOMMINA. They do. They do.

VERRI. They do not. More than once they've tried to show me they don't—just to prove to me they can.

MOMMINA. Not at all. When? Please, please. Don't get such ideas—

VERRI. They ought to know they can't joke with me about these things.

MOMMINA. They do—you can be sure of that. But the more you let on how it upsets you, even as a joke, the more they'll try and do it, just to show you they weren't malicious about it in the first place.

VERRI. So then, you forgive them?

MOMMINA. No, it isn't that at all. I'm saying all this just for you, so you won't be so upset. And for myself, too. Knowing how you feel, I live in a continual state of trepidation. Let's go now. Let's go. Mama just motioned to me. I think she's ready to go back in.

V

[SIGNORA IGNAZIA, *sitting on a bench, with* POMETTI *and* MANGINI, *flanking her.*]

SIGNORA IGNAZIA. Ah, boys, you could acquire many merits in the eyes of—civilization.

MANGINI. Us? How, Signora?

SIGNORA IGNAZIA. How? Why in giving a few lessons at your club.

POMETTI. Lessons, Signora? To whom?

SIGNORA IGNAZIA. To these rude, uncouth, boorish villagers. If only an hour a day.

MANGINI. Lessons in what?

POMETTI. In manners?

SIGNORA IGNAZIA. No, no, no, in behavior. In how it's done. In comme il faut. One little lesson a day, one hour a day, just to show them how one really lives outside this island in great cities. You—where do you come from, my dear Mangini?

MANGINI. I? From Venice, Signora.

SIGNORA IGNAZIA. Venice. God, Venice—the city of my dreams. And you, you, Pometti?

POMETTI. From Milan.

SIGNORA IGNAZIA. Ah, Milan. Milano. Think of it. El nost Milan —I myself come from Naples, from Naples, which is—I don't want to insult Milan, but I must say it—and fully granting the charms of Venice—is, is, in its very essence a paradise. Chiaia. Posillipo. I can't help it. I simply can't help crying every time I think of Napoli. The things there are there, the things. Oh, that Vesuvius. And Capri. You, you of course have the Duomo, and the Galleria, and La Scala. And you, ah, the Piazza San Marco, the Grand Canal. Such things they are! While here, all these "*fetenzierie!*" They stink! And would this be seen only outside in the streets!

MANGINI. Don't say it to their faces so loudly, please, Signora.

SIGNORA IGNAZIA. No, no, I want to speak loudly. Fetenzierie! They have it in their blood, in their very bones. Always growling about something. Isn't that the impression you get? That they're ready to slit your throat at the drop of a pin?

MANGINI. Really, as far as I personally am concerned—

SIGNORA IGNAZIA. Come, come, doesn't it seem so to you? Of course it does. They're all burning up with a—what shall we call it? Yes, with a rage they must have been born with, that makes them turn on each other like wild animals. All you have to do—I don't know—is look here instead of there, or blow your nose a little hard, or smile from something you are thinking. God save us! "He's laughing at me! He blew his nose like that just as an affront! He looked around like that just to insult me!" You can't do anything without their thinking there's an insult intended. Just because, all of them, have the very devil down inside them. Just look in their eyes. It scares the breath straight out of you. The eyes of wolves—! *Su. Su. Su.* Let's get up. It's time to go back in. Let's go and rescue those poor girls.

[*The time each of the four groups need for saying its lines, each in its designated place in the lobby, has been measured. Lines have been cut or added where necessary so that all four groups finish at the same time and simultaneously start towards each other in leaving the lobby. This interlude must also be synchronized with the time needed for* DR. HINKFUSS *onstage to perform the scenic miracles he has planned. Such miracles could simply be left up to* DR. HINKFUSS' *bizarre powers of invention, but since it was he himself, and not the author of the short story, who chose to make* RICO VERRI *and the other* OFFICERS *aviators, it seems likely he did so in order to have the pleasure at this point of preparing for the public left in the theatre the beautiful scenic effects of an airfield at night, under a magnificent starry sky. Everything on the ground is small, to give the impression of infinite space bounded only by star-strewn sky; in back, the white buildings that house the* OFFICERS, *with their small lit windows, here and there scattered about the field two or three airplanes, all very small. One hears the roar of an airplane out of sight, flying in the tranquil night.*

[*We shall let* DR. HINKFUSS *take the pleasure of producing all this even if not a single member of the audience remains in the theatre. In this case, which of course one must be prepared for, the simultaneous performances both in the lobby and onstage do not of course take place.* DR. HINKFUSS *orders the curtains opened, but, seeing that he is unable to keep even a small part of the audience in the theatre, he retires into the wings, somewhat annoyed, to give proof of his scenic bravura only when the performances in the lobby are over and the audience, recalled by the buzzer, have come back into the theatre and taken their seats again.*

[*What is important is that the audience be made to see things that, if not exactly superfluous, are certainly quite peripheral. But granted that one can see, by many different signs, that the audience takes great delight in all this and goes after it more greedily than simpler fare, still* DR. HINK-FUSS *should put it to good use.* DR. HINKFUSS *says clearly and with the disdain of a great lord who permits himself certain extravagances,* "The airfield scene could be omitted since it is not, strictly speaking, necessary. But, although a little time will be lost in creating a certain beautiful effect, you will understand that one does not want to lose time so another scene will be skipped that can easily be omitted without damage to our play." *We, for our part, shall omit the directions* DR. HINKFUSS *can readily think up for himself, to the scene changers and electricians and stagehands, for the setting up of the airfield. Barely done, he gets down off the stage and into the orchestra, plants himself firmly in the middle of the aisle to direct with still other appropriate commands the lighting effects. And when he has them just right, he goes back onstage.*]

DR. HINKFUSS. No! no! no! Clear everything! Clear everything! Stop the motor of the airplane. Turn the lights off. I'm thinking that we can do better without this scene. Yes, the effect we have is very pretty, but, with the means we have at our disposal, we can get other effects no less pretty that further the action even more effectively. Luckily this evening I am quite frank with you, ladies and gentlemen, completely honest with you, and I trust it will not displease you to see just how one puts a show on, not only under your very eyes but even (and indeed why not?) with your collaboration. You see, ladies and gentlemen, the theatre is the yawning mouth of a gigantic machine that is—hungry: a hunger, I should add, that these gentlemen the poets—

A POET FROM THE BALCONY. If you please—don't call poets gentlemen. Poets are not gentlemen.

DR. HINKFUSS. [*straight off*] Nor that matter are critics. In this sense at least. But still I call them gentlemen—out of a certain polemical affectation that, without really offending anyone, in this case at least I can be allowed. A hunger, I was saying, that these gentlemen, the poets, profoundly err in not trying to satisfy. It is indeed deplorable that the invention of our poets, far behind everyone else, no longer succeeds in discovering adequate nourishment for this vast machine we call the theatre that, like other machines, has in recent years enormously and wondrously grown and developed. I would not have you think that I consider the theatre mere spectacle. Art it is indeed— but *life* as well. Creation it is indeed—but not enduring creation. A thing of the moment. A miracle. A statue that moves. A miracle, ladies and gentlemen, that can by its very nature only be of the moment, transitory, caught up in time. To create, in a single moment, before your eyes, a scene—and within this one, another, and within this, still another, and within this, still another yet. A moment of darkness—a sudden change—a suggestive play of light. Here, I'll do it right before you. [*He claps his hands and commands.*] Lights out!

[*The stage is dark. The curtains are slightly drawn behind* DR. HINKFUSS'S *shoulders. The lights in the theatre go up while the buzzers in the lobby ring to recall the audience to their seats. In the event that everyone in the audience left the theatre, and* DR. HINKFUSS, *simultaneous performances both in the lobby and onstage not taking place, was compelled to wait for the return of the audience into the theatre to commence the staging of the airfield scene and its consequent chatter, it is of course understood that the curtains are not at this point drawn and that he, before the whole audience already seated in the theatre, will order the light out and give the other directions necessary for going on with the performance. Here, one assumes that both performances, in the lobby and onstage, have, as one would wish, been given at the same time. One should indeed try and find a way to make this possible. The curtains are closed, and the lights come up again in the theatre.* DR. HINKFUSS *continues.*]

Let us wait till all the audience are in their seats again. We must also allow time for Signora Ignazia and her daughters, accompanied by their young officer friends, to get back home after the theatre. [*turning to* THE GENTLEMAN IN THE BALCONY, *who by now is again in his seat*] Meanwhile, if you, my dear sir, my intrepid and dauntless interruptor, might wish to inform those who remained here in their seats whether anything new was disclosed in the lobby—

THE GENTLEMAN IN THE BALCONY. Are you speaking to me, sir?

DR. HINKFUSS. Yes, to you. If you could be so kind as to—

THE GENTLEMAN IN THE BALCONY. No, nothing new to speak of. Simply a rather charming diversion. They all gossiped about each other. The only thing was that one learned that this clown Palmiro, Sampognetta, is crazy about that night club singer.

DR. HINKFUSS. Ah, yes. But then this one could already have deduced. Anyhow, it has little importance.

THE YOUNG SPECTATOR IN THE ORCHESTRA. No, I'm sorry, one also came to realize that that Officer Rico Verri—

THE LEADING ACTOR. [*pushing his head between the curtains and over the shoulder of* DR. HINKFUSS.] That's quite enough of this officer business. I'll soon be out of this uniform.

DR. HINKFUSS. [*turning around to* THE LEADING ACTOR, *who has already pulled his head back in*] May I please ask why you are interrupting us in this fashion?

THE LEADING ACTOR. [*sticking his head out again*] Because this tag gripes me and I want to get things straight right now. I am not an officer. Not by profession, that is. I am a reserve officer. [*He draws his head back in again.*]

DR. HINKFUSS. You made this quite clear some time ago. That's quite enough. [*turning again to* THE YOUNG SPECTATOR IN THE

ORCHESTRA] I'm very sorry. Excuse me. You were saying—?

THE YOUNG SPECTATOR IN THE ORCHESTRA. [*intimidated and embarrassed*] Nothing really—I was just saying that—that even out there, in the lobby, this Signor Verri made it quite clear that he has a very bad temper and that—and that he's beginning to get fed up with the scandals these young ladies and their mother are always creating—

DR. HINKFUSS. Yes, yes, that's very good. But this, too, one could have guessed right from the start. In any case, thank you very much, very much indeed. [*behind the curtain is heard the sound of a piano playing Siebel's aria from Faust: "Le parlate d'amor— o cari fior—"*] There—that's the piano. Everything's ready now. [*He pushes back the curtain a little and yells behind stage.*] Buzzer. Buzzer. [*At the sound of the buzzer he goes back down into his seat in the orchestra, and the curtain opens again.*]

Act Three

At the right, in the rear, is the frame of a wall made of panes of glass, with a door in the middle through which one catches a glimpse—a bit of color, a lit lamp—of the hall beyond. The set is divided in half by another wall; this too with an open door in the middle that leads from the living room at the right into the dining room. The dining room is roughly sketched in, with a pretentious sideboard, a table spread with a red cloth over which hangs, from the ceiling, a lamp, now extinguished, with an enormous bellshaped shade of orange and green. On the sideboard, among other things, are a candlestick with a candle in it, a box of matches, and a cork bottle-stopper. In the living room, besides the piano, are a sofa, a few small tables, and some chairs.

When the curtains part, POMARICI is seen seated at the piano playing. NENE is waltzing to the music with SARELLI, and DORINA with NARDI. They have just returned from the theatre. Because of a toothache, SIGNORA IGNAZIA has a black silk handkerchief tied around her face like a bandage. RICO VERRI has run to an all-night pharmacy looking for medicine that might made the toothache go away. MOMMINA is seated beside her mother on the sofa. Near them is POMETTI. TOTINA is offstage with MANCINI.

MOMMINA.[*to her mother, while* POMARICI *continues to play and the couples to dance*] Does it hurt terribly? [*She starts to put her hand to her mother's cheek.*]

SIGNORA IGNAZIA. I am going mad! Don't touch me!

POMETTI. Verri's gone to the drugstore. He'll be back any minute with something.

SIGNORA IGNAZIA. Oh, they won't open up for him! They won't open up for him!

MOMMINA. But they have to. It's an all-night drug store, isn't it?

SIGNORA IGNAZIA. Indeed! Indeed! As though you didn't know perfectly well what people are like in this town! Ayi! Ayi! Don't make me talk. I am going mad! They're quite capable of not opening up at all, if they find out it's for me.

POMETTI. Oh, you just wait and see. Verri will make them open up.
He's quite capable of knocking the door down if they don't.

NENE. [calmly, continuing to dance] Of course, Mama. You can be
sure of that.

DORINA. [in the same tone] Think of them not opening up! If he
puts himself to it he is more beastly than they are!

SIGNORA IGNAZIA. No, no, poor boy. Don't talk like that. He's so
good. He went right away.

MOMMINA. He did. Only he did it. All by himself. The rest of you
kept right on dancing.

SIGNORA IGNAZIA. Let them, let them dance. At any rate the pain
will not go away if they stand around asking me how I am. [to
POMETTI] It's the rage, it's the rage that these people in town
arise in me; just fire in my blood. They are the cause of all my
grief.

NENE. [stops dancing and turns to her mother, excited by the idea
she has to propose] Mama, and if you said the Ave Maria like
the other time?

POMETTI. There you have it! That's an idea!

NENE. [persisting] Don't you remember how the pain went away as
soon as you said it?

POMETTI. Come on, give it a try, Signora. Give it a try.

DORINA. [as she continues to dance] Yes, yes, do, Mama. You'll
see, the pain'll go away.

NENE. Yes, but you must stop dancing.

POMETTI. Sure, and Pomarici stop playing.

NENE. Mama's going to say the Ave Maria like the other time!

POMARICI. [getting up from the piano and rushing over] Fine. Fine.
Let's see if we can get that miracle repeated.

SARELLI. And do it in Latin. In Latin, Signora Ignazia.

NARDI. Sure. It'll have more effect in Latin.

SIGNORA IGNAZIA. No, no, let me alone. What is it you're asking
me to do?

NENE. But, Mama, you know it worked the other time. It went
away then.

DORINA. We have to do it in the dark, too! In the dark.

NENE. And we must all get in a group! Pomarici, turn off the lights.

POMARICI. But where's Totina?

DORINA. She's in the other room with Mangini. Stop thinking about
Totina and turn off the lights.

SIGNORA IGNAZIA. Not at all. We have to have a candle at least. And
hands where they should be. And Totina must come back in
here.

MOMMINA. [calling] Totina! Totina!

DORINA. There's a candle out there.

NENE. You go get it. I'm going for the little statue of the Madonna.
[She runs off to the rear. DORINA goes into the dining room
with NARDI to get the candle off the sideboard. Before lighting it, in the dark, NARDI embraces DORINA and kisses her

passionately.]

SIGNORA IGNAZIA. [*yelling back to* NENE *who is already offstage*] No, no, don't bother. Forget it. Why the Madonna? We don't need all that.

POMARICI. [*also yelling back at* NENE] Make Totina come back in, instead.

SIGNORA IGNAZIA. Yes, that's right. Totina, here! Right away!

POMETTI. We need a little table for the altar. [*He goes and gets it.*]

DORINA. [*coming back with the candle lit, as* POMARICI *turns off the light*] Here's the candle.

POMETTI. Put it here on the table.

NENE. [*from the rear, with the little statue of the Madonna*] And here's the Madonna.

POMARICI. And Totina?

NENE. She's coming now. Don't be silly calling Totina all the time.

SIGNORA IGNAZIA. Could we know just what they're doing in there?

NENE. Nothing, really. Getting ready with a surprise. You'll see. [*then bidding everyone with her gesture*] Here, back in here. Everyone, get close to her. Concentrate, Mama.

[*Tableau: In the darkness, scarcely lessened by the quavering light of the candle,* DR. HINKFUSS *has prepared a most exquisite effect: the suffusion of a gentle green "miracle light"—psychological effect, of course—almost as though it was emanating from the hope that the miracle take place. All this almost at the very moment* SIGNORA IGNAZIA, *seated before the Madonna that has been placed with the candle on the little table, begins, with clasped hands, to recite, in a slow, deep voice, the words of the prayer, half expecting, after each word, that the pain will pass.*]

SIGNORA IGNAZIA. Ave Maria, Gratia plena, Dominus tecum—

[*Suddenly thunder and the devilish glare of a bright red light breaks up everything.* TOTINA, *dressed as a man, in* MANGINI'S *uniform, enters singing, followed by* MANGINI, *who has put on a very long bathrobe, belonging to* SIGNOR PALMIRO. *One realizes almost at once that the thunder is the voice of* TOTINA *singing and the red light is the light that* MANGINI *turns on in the living room coming in.*]

TOTINA. "Le parlate d'amor—O cari fior—"

[*A loud and unanimous cry of protest.*]

NENE. You fool. Shut up.

MOMMINA. She has spoiled everything!

TOTINA. [*stunned*] What's the matter?

DORINA. Mama was saying the Ave Maria.

TOTINA. [*to* NENE] You *could* have told me!

NENE. Is that so? Was I to guess you'd come crashing in at just this very moment?

TOTINA. I was already dressed up when you came and got the Madonna.

NENE. Well then, you should have guessed what we were doing.

DORINA. Enough, enough! What do we do now?

POMARICI. Start all over again; start all over again.

SIGNORA IGNAZIA. I don't know. I'm not sure—

MOMMINA. [*happily*] Has it gone?

SIGNORA IGNAZIA. I don't know. Maybe it was the devil—or the Madonna— [*Her whole face is contorted in a new fit of pain.*] No. No. Ayi! Ayi! Again. I thought it was gone. Ayyyyiiiii! Good God, what torture! [*all of a sudden getting hold of herself, grinding her heel into the floor and commanding*] No! I'll not give in! Sing, sing, girls! Sing, boys! Do me this favor. Sing! Woe if I'll lose my nerve because of an infernal toothache! Go ahead, Mommina. "Stride la vampa!"

MOMMINA. [*while everyone, applauding, yells, "Yes, yes, that's it, the chorus from 'Trovatore'"*] No, no, Mama. I don't feel like it. No.

SIGNORA IGNAZIA. [*angrily insisting*] Do me this one favor, Mommina. It's for the tooth's ache.

NENE. Come on. Please her just this once.

TOTINA. She's telling you she's trying to keep her courage up under the pain.

SARELLI *and* NARDI. Yes, yes. Come on. Humor her, Mommina.

DORINA. God, how you like to be coaxed!

NENE. You think we don't know why you don't want to sing any more?

POMARICI. No, no. Mommina *will* sing.

SARELLI. If it's on account of Verri, don't you worry. We'll see to it that he keeps in his place.

POMARICI. Singing will charm away the pain! I swear it!

SIGNORA IGNAZIA. Yes, yes. Do it. Do it for your poor mama's sake.

POMETTI. What terrific courage the general's got.

SIGNORA IGNAZIA. You, Totina, will be Manrico?

TOTINA. Of course. I'm already dressed for it!

SIGNORA IGNAZIA. Paint the moustache on her. Paint the moustache on this girl.

MANGINI. Here, I'll do it myself.

POMARICI. No, if you please, *I'll* do it.

NENE. Here's the cork, Pomarici. I'll go get the big hat with the feather. And a yellow handkerchief and a red shawl for Azucena. [*She leaves by the rear and returns a moment later with the objects she spoke of.*]

POMARICI. [*to* TOTINA, *as he paints on the moustache*] Stay still, please.

SIGNORA IGNAZIA. Wonderful, Mommina as Azucena—

MOMMINA. [*by this time speaking almost to herself but without strength left to refuse*] No, no, no—I can't—

SIGNORA IGNAZIA. [*continuing*] Totina as Manrico—

SARELLI. And the rest of us the gypsy chorus!

SIGNORA IGNAZIA. [*commencing the music*] "All'opra, all'opra! Dagli. Martella. Chi del gitana la vita abbella?" [*Singing, she asks some of them the question. They keep looking at her, uncertain whether she is asking them seriously or jokingly. And then turning to others she repeats*] "Chi del gitano la vita abbella?" [*But these too look at her as the others did. She can endure her pain no longer and furiously she once again asks all of them, insisting on a reply.*] "Chi del gitano la vita abbella?"[2]

ALL. [*understanding at last, intone the reply*] "La zingareeee— eeeella!"

SIGNORA IGNAZIA. [*taking a deep breath at finally being understood*] Ahhhhhhhhhhhh! [*then while the others hold the note, to herself, writhing in pain*] Let me get hold of myself! I can't stand it any more. Go ahead, go ahead! Children, quick, sing, sing!

POMARICI. No, wait, for God's sake, till I finish.

DORINA. More than this? That's enough!

SARELLI. She looks marvelous.

NENE. Adorable! Now for the hat! The hat! [*She gives it to her and turns to* MOMMINA.] And you, no more excuses! Put the handkerchief on your head! [*to* SARELLI] Tie it in back for her. [SARELLI *does so.*] And the shawl. Like this.

DORINA. [*giving* MOMMINA, *who has remained immobile, a shake*] Wake up. Come to!

POMARICI. Oh, but we have to have something to beat time on!

NENE. I know just the thing. Those brass finger-bowls in there. [*She goes and gets them from the sideboard in the dining room. She returns and hands them out.*]

POMARICI. [*going to the piano*] Now attention. We're starting from the beginning. "Vedi le fosche notturne spoglie." [*He begins to play the gypsy chorus that opens the second act of "Il Trovatore."*]

CHORUS. [*on the beat*]
   "Vedi le fosche notturne spoglie
   de' cieli sveste l'immensa volta:
   sembra una vedova che alfin si toglie
   i bruni panni ond' era involta."
    [*then beating the fingerbowls*]
   "All'opra, all'opra! Dagli. Martella.
   Chi del gitano la vita abbella?"
    [*and three times*]
   "La zingarella!"

POMARICI. [*to* MOMMINA] Attention, Miss. Mommina, it's your turn. And all of you get around her.

MOMMINA. [*coming forward*]
   "Stride la vampa! la folla indomita
   corre a quel foco, lieta in sembianza!
   Urli di gioja intorno echeggiano:
   cinta di sgherri donna s'avanza."[3]

2. The use of Verdi's *Il Trovatore* at this point seems mainly a preparation for its extended use at the end of the act. Still, it is worth considering that Signora Ignazia's question, "Who brightens the gypsy's life?" and the answer she finally elicits, "The gypsy girl," are an ironic comment on the Ignazia girls and their soldier visitors as well as the Signora's attempt to get the music started.

3. At the beginning of Act II of the opera, after the gypsy chorus sings its welcome to the morning (part of which we have here), Azucena sings, "*Stride la vampa,*" the famous aria in

[*While the others are singing, first the chorus and then* MOMMINA *alone,* SIGNORA IGNAZIA, *seated in a chair, squirming constantly, beating her feet, first one and then the other, mutters in cadenza, as if in her pain she was reciting a litany.*]

SIGNORA IGNAZIA. God, I'm dying, dying. Have pity on my sins. God, God, what agony! Hit me, God! Make me suffer, yes, me alone! Make me alone pay, God, for all the amusements the girls have. Sing, sing, yes, yes, enjoy yourselves, girls! I'll sit here and suffer all alone. It's penance for my sins. I want you happy, gay, gay, just like this. Yes, "dagli, martella," hit me, me alone, dear God, and let the girls enjoy themselves. Oh, God, the joy I never had—never, never, God, never, never—I want *them* to have it. They *should*. *Should* have it. *I'll* pay for it. Yes, I'll pay for everything, God, even if they break your commandments, dear God. [*She joins in with the others while the tears trickle down her cheeks.*] "La zingareeee—eeeéllaaaaa!" Silence. Now Mommina's singing, the voice of a true *artiste*. "La vampa"—yes. Ah, that's what I've got in my jaw, fire, fire! "Lieta, yes, lieta in sembianza"—

[RICO VERRI *unexpectedly appears in the door at the rear. For a moment he stands there suspended, as if his bewilderment were a precipice opened up before his anger. Then he leaps into the room and rushes up to* POMARICI. *He yanks him off the piano stool and hurls him to the floor, yelling.*]

RICO VERRI. God damn you all! So this is the way you make fun of me behind my back, is it?

[*There follows at first a bewilderment in them all that is expressed by certain silly and incongruous exclamations.*]

NENE. But just look at his manners!

DORINA. Are you crazy?

[*Then a general uproar, as* POMARICI *gets up and throws himself on* VERRI *and the others get between them, trying to separate them and keep them apart. Everyone talks at once, in great confusion.*]

POMARICI. You'll pay for this, Verri!

VERRI. [*violently pushing him back*] I'm not through with you yet!

SARELLI *and* NARDI. We're here, too. You'll answer us for this, too.

VERRI. Every damned one of you. I'll break all your noses.

TOTINA. Who made you master in our house?

VERRI. I was sent out to get medicine for her tooth—

SIGNORA IGNAZIA. The medicine, yes, and—?

VERRI. [*pointing to* MOMMINA] And I come back and find her dressed up like this.

SIGNORA IGNAZIA. Get out of my house this minute!

MOMMINA. I didn't want to. I didn't want to. I told everyone I

which she describes how her mother was burned as a witch. In the part that Mommina sings here, she describes how the crowds pushed in eagerly to see the burning, a description that may have some relation to Mommina's reaction to the audience during the Interlude.

didn't want to.

DORINA. Look what we have here. The little fool's apologizing to him.

NENE. He's just taking advantage of the fact we have no man in our house to kick him out. That's what he deserves.

SIGNORA IGNAZIA. [*to* NENE] Go get your father immediately. Make him get up and come in here at once.

SARELLI. If that's what you want, Signora, we can throw him out.

NENE. [*running to call her father*] Papa, Papa. [*She runs off.*]

VERRI. [*to* SARELLI] You? I'd like to see you. Go ahead and throw me out! [*to* NENE *as she runs off*] Yes, call Papa, call him. I'll answer the head of this house for what I'm doing—demanding from *them* a little respect for you ladies.

SIGNORA IGNAZIA. And who has asked you to? How dare you demand it?

VERRI. How? The Signorina knows. [*He points to* MOMMINA.]

MOMMINA. Oh, but not like this, with such violence.

VERRI. Am I the one who's being violent? Isn't it the *others* towards *you?*

SIGNORA IGNAZIA. I repeat. I want to know nothing about all this! There's the door. Get out!

VERRI. You can't say this to me.

SIGNORA IGNAZIA. My daughter will also tell you this. Anyhow, I am the lady of the house and I command.

DORINA. We'll all say the same thing to you.

VERRI. That's not enough. Not if the Signorina's with me. I'm the only man in this room with—honorable intentions!

SARELLI. Listen to him! *Honorable!*

NARDI. No one's doing a thing here he shouldn't!

VERRI. The Signorina knows the truth.

POMARICI. Buffoon!

VERRI. Buffoons, the god-damned lot of you! [*brandishing a chair*] Watch out—don't any of you butt in or it'll end right now.

POMETTI. [*to the others*] Come on. Let's get out of here.

DORINA. No. Why?

TOTINA. Don't leave us alone. He's not the master in our house.

VERRI. You, Nardi, don't you feign any sickness tomorrow. We've got a date.

NENE. [*returning in great distress*] Papa's not in the house!

SIGNORA IGNAZIA. Not in the house?

NENE. I've looked all over. I can't find him anywhere.

DORINA. What's this? Didn't he come home?

NENE. He didn't come home.

MOMMINA. Where is he?

SIGNORA IGNAZIA. Still out, at this hour?

SARELLI. He must have gone back to the night club.

POMARICI. Signora, we're leaving.

SIGNORA IGNAZIA. No, wait—

MANGINI. Of course, wait. I certainly can't leave like this!

TOTINA. Oh, I'm sorry. I'd completely forgotten I had your uniform on. I'll go and change right away. [*She slips away.*]

POMARICI. [*to* MANGINI] You wait and get your uniform. We're going on.

SIGNORA IGNAZIA. But excuse me—I don't understand—

VERRI. They understand. They understand all right, even if you, Signora, don't choose to.

SIGNORA IGNAZIA. I'll tell you once more. You're the one who's getting out of here.

VERRI. No, Signora, they must leave. They know there's no place here any more for their dirty jokes—face to face with a man who has serious intentions.

POMARICI. Yeah, yeah, you'll see tomorrow whether we're joking or not!

MOMMINA. Please, Verri. Please!

VERRI. [*trembling*] You should not plead, *anyone!*

MOMMINA. I'm not pleading. I only want to say that the fault's all mine, who gave in. I shouldn't have, knowing that you—

NARDI. As an earnest, upright Sicilian, couldn't take a joke.

SARELLI. We aren't taking any more jokes now, either.

VERRI. [*to* MOMMINA, *as he would speak to* THE LEADING ACTRESS, *by now spontaneously coming out of his part, with the irritation of* THE LEADING ACTOR *who has been forced to say what he does not wish to say*] Excellent. Are you pleased?

MOMMINA. [*as* THE LEADING ACTRESS, *disconcerted*] With what?

VERRI. [*as before*] With having said what you shouldn't have. Why does all this guilt come in right here at the end?

MOMMINA. It just came to me spontaneously.

VERRI. And doing so you made them start in on me again! It's I who must be the last one to shout that they have to deal with me, every one of them.

MANGINI. Even I, like this, in a bathrobe? [*He arches his legs clumsily as though on guard.*] Pronto. Opla!

NENE *and* DORINA. [*laughing and applauding*] Oh, that's lovely! Bravo!

VERRI. [*as before, indignantly*] What do you mean, "bravo"? Idiocy! That's how the whole scene gets spoiled. And it will never come to an end!

DR. HINKFUSS. [*getting up from his seat in the orchestra*] Why not? It was all going very, very well. Keep on. Keep on.

[*There is heard, getting increasingly louder, a knock in the hall at the back, as though on the street door.*]

MANGINI. [*excusing himself*] I am standing here in a bathrobe. What's more natural than to make a joke?

NENE. But of course.

VERRI. [*scornfully to* MANGINI] Go play cards or something, then. Don't come here to act!

MOMMINA. If Mr. ——— [*She says the name of* THE LEADING ACTOR.] would like to play his role all by himself, while we sit here and twiddle our thumbs, let him say so, and we can all leave.

VERRI. No, it's I who must leave, if everyone else wants to do things *his* way, the way that suits *him*; even to timing everything all wrong!

SIGNORA IGNAZIA. But good heavens, it was beautiful, our timing was perfect. You know it was. That cry of Mommina's: "The fault's mine, who gave in—"

POMARICI. [*to* VERRI] Look here, after all, we're in this show too, you know.

SARELLI. We must live *our* parts, too.

NARDI. He wants to be the whole show all by himself. But everyone's got to say what he has to say.

DR. HINKFUSS. [*yelling*] Enough. This is quite enough. Get on with the scene. It seems to me that it is exactly you, Mr. ——— [*the name of* THE LEADING ACTOR], who has spoiled everything.

VERRI. No, no, please, I do indeed want everyone to speak who ought to, and to answer me just as he should. For three hours I keep hammering at the same thing: "The Signorina knows, the Signorina knows—" And the Signorina does not find one single word to back me up. Always this same old pose of martyred victim.

MOMMINA. [*exasperated, almost in tears*] But I am, I *am* the victim! The victim of my sisters, of the house, of you; the victim of everyone.

[*At this point, pushing between the actors all turned towards the footlights to speak with* DR. HINKFUSS, THE CHARACTER ACTOR, *or rather* SAMPOGNETTA, *makes his way; his face like a dead man's; his bloody hands on his stomach, where he has been wounded by a knife; his coat and trousers smeared with blood.*]

SAMPOGNETTA. Look here, Dr. Hinkfuss. I'm standing out there knocking, knocking, knocking. Smeared with blood, like this. I've got my guts in my fists, and I'm supposed to come in here and die. Onstage. Which isn't very easy anyhow for a character actor. And no one lets me in. When I finally do get in, what do I find? Complete and utter confusion. The whole effect I've been promising myself I'd create with my entrance is completely ruined. I'm dripping with blood, and dying, and I'm drunk, too. I ask you, *now* what do I do?

DR. HINKFUSS. It's all very simple. You're leaning on the shoulder of the night club singer. Where is she?

NIGHT CLUB SINGER. Here I am.

ONE OF THE CUSTOMERS FROM THE NIGHT CLUB. I'm here, too, to help hold him up.

DR. HINKFUSS. Very well. Hold him up.

SAMPOGNETTA. I had the stairs to climb, carried on the shoulders of these two—

DR. HINKFUSS. Good God. Pretend all that's been done. And each of you get back in your places. And all of you begin to cry in despair. Can you drown in a tea cup? [*He returns to his seat muttering to himself.*] And all this ruined for a silly punctilious

504 · *Luigi Pirandello*

point of view.

[*The action is resumed.* SAMPOGNETTA *appears now at the rear, supported by the* NIGHT CLUB SINGER *on one side and the* CUSTOMER FROM THE NIGHT CLUB *on the other. Almost the first moment* SIGNORA IGNAZIA *and the daughters see him, they suddenly start screaming. But* SAMPOGNETTA *remains motionless while the women vent their feelings, a tolerant smile playing on his lips that seems to say, "When you're done, I shall speak." He lets the* NIGHT CLUB SINGER *and the* CUSTOMER FROM THE NIGHT CLUB *make a few replies to the anguished questions with which he is overwhelmed, even though he would clearly prefer for them to be quiet and wait for the truth he himself is visibly preparing to disclose when everyone else has finished speaking. The others, seeing him before them in such a subdued manner, do not have the least idea what he intends to do and play their parts as best they can.*]

SIGNORA IGNAZIA. Oh God, what's happened?

MOMMINA. Papa, my Papa!

NENE. You've been wounded!

VERRI. Who did it?

DORINA. Where is he wounded? Where?

THE CUSTOMER. In the belly.

SARELLI. With a knife?

NIGHT CLUB SINGER. Ripped right open. He's lost all his blood getting here.

NARDI. But who did it? Who did it?

POMETTI. Was it at the night club?

MANGINI. Get him to lie down, for Christ's sake.

POMARICI. Here. Over here on the sofa.

SIGNORA IGNAZIA. [*as the* NIGHT CLUB SINGER *and the* CUSTOMER *take* SAMPOGNETTA *over to the sofa*] So he did go back to the night club. Didn't he?

NENE. But, Mama, don't talk about it now. Can't you see he's wounded?

SIGNORA IGNAZIA. I see how he's come home, all right—and look, look, at the clutch she's got on him. Who are you?

NIGHT CLUB SINGER. A woman, Signora, with more of a heart than you.

THE CUSTOMER. Think, Signora, it's your own husband who stands here dying.

MOMMINA. But how did it happen? How did it happen?

THE CUSTOMER. He was trying to defend her— [*He indicates the* NIGHT CLUB SINGER.]

SIGNORA IGNAZIA. [*with a sardonic smile*] There, see! He thinks he's Sir Galahad!

THE CUSTOMER. [*continuing*] A fight started—

NIGHT CLUB SINGER. And that cutthroat—

THE CUSTOMER. Turned from her and threw himself on *him!*

VERRI. Did they get him?

THE CUSTOMER. No, he got away, waving his knife wildly at every-one.

NARDI. At least you know who he is?

THE CUSTOMER. [*gesturing to the* NIGHT CLUB SINGER] She knows him very well—

SARELLI. Your lover?

NIGHT CLUB SINGER. My murderer! My murderer!

THE CUSTOMER. He was ready for a massacre.

NENE. But someone has to go and get a doctor right away!

[TOTINA *appears, still only half dressed.*]

TOTINA. What's happened? What's happened? Oh God, Papa! Who wounded him?

MOMMINA. Speak, speak, Papa, say *something*—

DORINA. Why are you staring at us like that?

NENE. He just stares at us and smiles.

TOTINA. But where did it happen? How did it happen?

SIGNORA IGNAZIA. [*to* TOTINA] At the night club. Now don't you understand? [*She points to the* NIGHT CLUB SINGER.] Of course!

NENE. A doctor, a doctor! We can't let him die like this.

MOMMINA. Who'll go and get one?

MANGINI. I'd go, except that like this— [*He motions to the bath-robe.*]

TOTINA. Oh, I'd forgotten. Go get your uniform. It's in there on the bed.

NENE. You go, Sarelli, please.

SARELLI. Yes, yes, of course. I'm off. I'm off. [*He goes off rear with* MANGINI.]

VERRI. But why doesn't he say a word? [*He is alluding to* SAMPOG-NETTA.] He ought to say *something*—

TOTINA. Papa! Papa!

NENE. He keeps on looking at us and smiling.

MOMMINA. Papa, here we all are, at your side!

VERRI. Could it be that's what he wants—to die without saying a word?

POMARICI. This is fine. He stands there neither dead nor alive. What in God's name is he waiting for?

NARDI. I can't think of another thing to do. Sarelli's gone to get the doctor and Mangini to get his uniform.

SIGNORA IGNAZIA. [*to her husband*] Speak up! Speak up! Don't you even have brains enough to say a solitary word? If you'd only listened to me, if you'd only stopped to think you had four little girls at home who now very well may go without a bite of bread to eat—

NENE. [*having waited a moment, with the others*] Not a word, nothing. Look at him there! He just smiles.

MOMMINA. It isn't natural. [*meaning his acting*]

DORINA. You can't just smile like that, Papa, and stare at us.

THE CUSTOMER. Maybe he drunk a little too much—

MOMMINA. It isn't natural. If someone has a drink and it makes him sad, then he's quiet and peaceful. But if it makes him smile, then he talks. He shouldn't be smiling, then!

SIGNORA IGNAZIA. Can you at least tell us why you are smiling like this?

[*Once more they all wait in suspense.*]

SAMPOGNETTA. Because I'm simply delighted by the fact that all of you are much, much better actors than I.

VERRI. [*as the others look at each other, all suddenly frozen in their make-believe*] But what is he saying?

SAMPOGNETTA. I'm saying that I, like this, having no idea how I got in this house if no one came to let me in, and after I'd stood there at the door knocking so long and so hard—

DR. HINKFUSS. [*furiously getting up from his seat*] Again? The same thing all over again?

SAMPOGNETTA. I simply cannot die like this, Dr. Hinkfuss. I can't help smiling, seeing how good they all are, and I just don't die. The maid—[*He looks around.*] where is *she?* I don't see her—should have run in and cried, "Oh God, the Master. Oh God, the Master! They're bringing him home wounded!"

DR. HINKFUSS. But why are you harping on this now? Didn't we say we'd take your entrance for granted?

SAMPOGNETTA. Now all I have to do then is die, die without a word.

DR. HINKFUSS. Not at all. You must speak. You must have a big scene—and *then* die.

SAMPOGNETTA. All right. We've had the scene. We'll take that for granted, too. [*He drops back on the sofa.*] I'm dead!

DR. HINKFUSS. Not like that!

SAMPOGNETTA. [*getting up on his feet and coming toward the footlights*] My dear sir, then *you* come up here and finish me off. What do you want me to say? I repeat, I can't die just like that, without help from anyone. I am not, please remember, some old accordion that you push and pull, that comes up with a tune everytime you press on the keys.

DR. HINKFUSS. But your colleagues—

SAMPOGNETTA. [*quickly*] Are more gifted than I. I admit the fact quite freely, and it delights me. I cannot do it. The scene-entrance was everything for me. You dropped it. And without the maid's cry, I cannot get into the right feeling. And then— Death himself should have entered into the room with me, introducing himself here into the shameless uproar of my own house; Death the drunkard, as we'd already established it, drunk with a wine that turns to blood. And I should have spoken, yes, *that* I know—tried to speak in the midst of all this horror—taking courage from the wine, and the blood, supported only by this woman here [*going over to the* NIGHT CLUB SINGER *and leaning on her, his arm around her neck*] like this!—saying wild, senseless, terrible things to my wife, and to my daughters, and to these young men. I should have proved to them all that if I've behaved like a fool, it's because they've been vile—vile wife, vile daughters, vile friends. I'm not a fool. It is I who am good. It is they who are bad; only I who am intelligent, and they who are stupid;

I, in all my cleverness, and they, in their corrupt bestiality, yes, yes—[*growing angry as though someone were contradicting him*] intelligent, intelligent, as babes are intelligent—(well, not all of them—those who grew up, heartbroken in the midst of the adult brutality). But I should have said all these things like a drunkard, in a delirium, and smeared my bloody hands on my face—like this—and befouled myself with blood—[*asking the other actors*] am I smeared with blood? [*and as they nod yes*] Good—[*and resuming*] terrify you all and make you cry—but *really* cry—hardly able to get my breath and puckering up my lips like this [*He tries to form a whistle that does not come: fhhhhh, fhhhhh.*] to make my very last little whistle and then—[*calling the* CUSTOMER *over to him*] you come here, too—[*He hangs onto his neck with his other arm.*] like this—between the two of you—but nearer you, sweetheart—drop my head, the quick little way birds do, and die. [*He drops his head on the breast of the* NIGHT CLUB SINGER. *His arms go limp after a moment, and he falls on the floor dead.*]

NIGHT CLUB SINGER. Oh God! [*She tries to hold him up and then lets go of him.*] He's dead! He's dead!

MOMMINA. [*throwing herself on him*] Papa, my Papa, my Papa—[*and she begins to cry. This outburst of actual emotion in* THE LEADING ACTRESS *provokes emotion in the other actors, who give themselves up to tears, too. And then* DR. HINKFUSS *leaps up from his seat shouting.*]

DR. HINKFUSS. Excellent. Lights out, please. Lights out. [*The stage is darkened.*] Everyone offstage. The four sisters and their mother around the dining table, six days later. The living room is dark. The only light is from the lamp in the dining room.

MOMMINA. [*in the dark*] But, Dr. Hinkfuss, we have to change costumes first. We're supposed to be in mourning.

DR. HINKFUSS. Ah, yes. In mourning. The curtains should have been dropped after the death scene. It does not matter. Go and get in your mourning clothes. And drop the curtains. Lights up in the theatre, please. [*The curtains are closed. The lights in the theatre come up.* DR. HINKFUSS *smiles sadly.*] We've lost part of the effect to be sure. But I promise you we'll get it all tomorrow evening. And it will be truly overwhelming. You must know, ladies and gentlemen, that in life as well, an effect one has worked at and counted on can, even at best, just not come off—and then our reproaches go to the wife, to the daughters. "You ought to have done this!" and "You ought to have done that!" It's true that here it was a question of death. It's a shame my fine Mr. ———— [*He names* THE CHARACTER ACTOR.] was so stubborn about his entrance. But he's a good actor. Tomorrow evening he'll acquit himself of the scene marvelously. And a great scene it is, ladies and gentlemen, for all the consequences it brings. I made it up myself. It isn't in the story at all and, moreover, I'm sure the author would never have put it in, for scruples I myself had no reason to respect: those of spreading the idea, already quite widespread, that in Sicily the knife is very much used. If he'd had the idea at all that the character should die, he would have had him die of a stroke, or a heart attack, or some such thing as that. But you yourself can see what a different sort of theatrical effect you get from the death as *I* have conceived it, with the wine, and the blood, and his arm around the neck of that singer. The father has to die. Through his death the family falls into wretched poverty. Without that it seems highly unlikely that Mommina would ever consent to marry that Rico Verri, resisting every objection her mother and sisters can possibly raise. They have learned, from a few questions sent to the town he comes from, that he is, yes, from a very well-to-do family, but that his father is infamous in the whole area not only as an outrageous miser but also as a man so possessed by jealousy that he had, in a few short years, made his poor wife— Rico Verri's mother—die of a broken heart. And can you imagine the fate awaiting this sweet young girl? Think of all the things Rico Verri, marrying the girl out of spite to get even with his fellow officers, must have agreed on with that jealous, stingy, old father of his? And the other promises he must have made to himself, not only to recompense himself for the sacrifice his honor was costing him but also to be able to face his fellow townsmen, to whom the notoriety of his wife's family was all too well known. Who knows how he will make her pay for the pleasure she's gotten out of life the years she was living at home with her mother and her sisters? His feelings are quite reasonable, as you shall see. But my gifted heroine, Miss ——— [*He names* THE LEADING ACTRESS.] is not really of my opinion. Mommina is for her the most aware of the four sisters, the one who has been sacrificed, who has always arranged amusements for the others but who herself has never enjoyed any except at the price of effort, vigilance, and many unhappy thoughts. The responsibility for the whole family falls on her shoulders. And she comes to an understanding of many things: first of all, that time passes, and that the father, with all the disorder at home, was unable to set aside anything for all of them, and that no young man in town will marry any of them, while Verri—ah, Verri will fight for her, not one, but three duels with those officers, who of course immediately, at the first whiff of misfortune, slip away, disappear, evaporate. At the bottom of it, the passion that makes up all melodrama—which Mommina has in common with her sisters—Raul, Ernani, Don Alvaro—"Ne toglier mi potro, l'imagin suo dal cuor—,"[4] keeps a firm attitude

<hr/>

4. Ernani (from *Ernani*) and Don Alvaro (from *La Forza del Destino*) are heroes of Verdi operas. By analogy, I assume that Raul is Raoul de Nangis of Meyerbeer's *Les Huguenots*. Each of these characters (like Manrico in *Il Trovatore*, who figures so prominently later in the play) is the male half of a pair of true lovers who can never get together, but who cannot be parted except by the last-act death of one or both. The quotation, which I do not recognize, must surely be from such an opera; it says, "I am unable to tear his (her) image from my heart," an appropriate sentiment in this context. Just why Dr. Hinkfuss, describing Mommina's melodramatic passion, should name the tenors instead of the sopranos is unclear. Per-

and marries him. [DR. HINKFUSS *has continued talking in order to give his actresses time to change, but now he has nothing more to say. He takes a little leap and, pulling back one of the curtains, yells inside*] Is it really possible that the ladies still are not ready? Where's the buzzer? [*and pretending to speak with someone behind the curtain he adds*] No? What else must be done? What? They no longer wish to act? And what could that mean? With the audience out here waiting? Come here at once.

[DR. HINKFUSS' SECRETARY *appears, embarrassed and confused.*]

THE SECRETARY. But they say—

DR. HINKFUSS. What *is* it they say?

THE LEADING ACTOR. [*behind the curtain, to* THE SECRETARY] Speak up. Speak up clearly and tell him why.

DR. HINKFUSS. Ah, Mr. ——— once again.

[*He names* THE LEADING ACTOR. *But now the other actors and actresses come out in front of the curtain, beginning with* THE CHARACTER ACTRESS, *who takes off her wig in front of the audience, and* THE CHARACTER ACTOR; THE LEADING ACTOR, *next, has by this time taken off his uniform.*]

THE CHARACTER ACTRESS. No, no, Dr. Hinkfuss, it's all of us.

THE LEADING ACTRESS. We simply can't go on.

THE OTHERS. Impossible! Out of the question!

THE CHARACTER ACTOR. I've finished my part, to be sure, but I'm right here—

DR. HINKFUSS. In God's name, what's happened now?

THE CHARACTER ACTOR. [*The last phrase of* THE CHARACTER ACTOR'S *comes out tranquilly over* DR. HINKFUSS' *speech like a cold shower.*] —square behind my colleagues.

DR. HINKFUSS. Square behind your colleagues. Just what do you mean by that?

THE CHARACTER ACTOR. That we're all walking out.

DR. HINKFUSS. Walking out? Where?

SEVERAL. Out! Out!

THE LEADING ACTOR. Unless *you* do.

THE OTHERS. It's either you or us!

DR. HINKFUSS. I? *You* dare intimidate *me* like this?

THE ACTORS. All right then, we'll go! We're leaving. We're through with being puppets. Let's get out of here. [*They are wildly agitated.*]

DR. HINKFUSS. [*parrying*] Where? Are you mad? We've got the audience out here. They've already paid for their seats. How can you explain this to *them*?

THE CHARACTER ACTOR. You figure that one out for yourself. We're giving you a choice. You or us—

DR. HINKFUSS. I'll ask you again. *What has happened now?*

THE LEADING ACTOR. What now? Does what's already happened

haps because Hinkfuss is a man. Perhaps because he is familiar with the play he is putting on and so knows

that her big scene will end with her trying to sing an aria of Manrico's.

seem unimportant to you?

DR. HINKFUSS. But wasn't that all taken care of?

THE CHARACTER ACTOR. Taken care of how?

THE CHARACTER ACTRESS. You pretend we're improvising—

DR. HINKFUSS. It's in your contracts—

THE CHARACTER ACTOR. But look here—not like this, with you jumping up here onstage every five minutes, ordering me to die just like that—

THE CHARACTER ACTRESS. Starting us cold in the middle of a scene—

THE LEADING ACTRESS. We no longer find words—

THE LEADING ACTOR. There, just as I said at the beginning, the words ought to spring up spontaneously!

THE LEADING ACTRESS. Just a minute, my dear, you were the first one to pay no attention to the words spontaneously springing up in *me*—

THE LEADING ACTOR. You're right. But it isn't my fault.

POMARICI. Yes, he's the one who started it all.

THE LEADING ACTOR. But let me finish. I'm telling you it isn't my fault—it's *his*. [*He points to* DR. HINKFUSS.]

DR. HINKFUSS. Mine? Why mine?

THE LEADING ACTOR. Because you're here with your damned *theatre*. The devil take it.

DR. HINKFUSS. My theatre? But have you all gone crazy? Where are we? Are we not in a theatre?

THE LEADING ACTOR. We're in a theatre? Excellent. Then give us parts—

THE LEADING ACTRESS. Act by act, scene by scene—

NENE. —with speeches written, word for word—

THE CHARACTER ACTOR. Cut them as much as you like. Make us jump around just as you like. But at points designated beforehand.

THE LEADING ACTOR. First you let life loose inside us—

THE LEADING ACTRESS. Real feelings—

THE CHARACTER ACTRESS. The more we say the more excited we get—

NENE. All of us in one big uproar—

THE LEADING ACTRESS. All of us trembling—

TOTINA. [*pointing to* THE LEADING ACTOR] I could kill him!

DORINA. This blusterer coming in and laying down the law in our own house.

DR. HINKFUSS. But all the better, all the better that way!

THE LEADING ACTOR. What do you mean "all the better" if at the same time you insist on our being so damned careful throughout the scene—

THE CHARACTER ACTOR. —not to miss the least effect you've planned—

THE LEADING ACTOR. —because of "theatre"! How can you expect us to think any more of "theatre"—yours or anyone else's—if we must *live* our parts? Don't you see what happens? How even

I got to thinking for a moment that the scene should end the way you'd told us it should, with the last line mine. And then I get in with Miss ——— [*pointing to* THE LEADING ACTRESS *and saying her name*] who was right, yes, absolutely right, at that point to beg—

THE LEADING ACTRESS. I was begging for you—

THE LEADING ACTOR. Yes, exactly—[*to the actor playing* MANGINI] just as you were joking about that bathrobe—and I apologize. It's I who was stupid to have paid any attention to him. [*He points to* DR. HINKFUSS.]

DR. HINKFUSS. Watch what you say, Mr. ——— [*He names* THE LEADING ACTOR.]

THE LEADING ACTOR. [*ignoring* DR. HINKFUSS *and again turning impetuously to* THE LEADING ACTRESS] Don't interrupt me now—! You are truly the victim. I see it. I feel it. You are filled with your part, as I am with mine. I suffer all the agonies of hell just seeing you there before me [*He takes her face between his hands.*] with these eyes and this mouth. You're quivering all over. You're dying of fright right here in my hands. The audience is still here—we can't get rid of *them*, but we can't keep on, neither you nor I, trying to play the usual kind of theatre. As you cry out your despair, your martyrdom, I must cry out my feelings, too, the feelings that make me commit my crime. Good. Let *them* stay. They'll be like a jury hearing a case and judging it. [*With a leap he turns back to* DR. HINKFUSS.] But not you. You're getting out of here!

DR. HINKFUSS. [*stunned*] I?

THE LEADING ACTOR. Yes. And leave us alone. Leave the two of us alone!

NENE. Excellent.

THE CHARACTER ACTRESS. To act what they feel.

THE CHARACTER ACTOR. To act what they feel inside them. Splendid.

ALL THE OTHERS. [*pushing* DR. HINKFUSS *off the stage*] Yes, yes, get out, get out!

DR. HINKFUSS. You're driving me out of my own theatre?

THE CHARACTER ACTOR. We don't need you any more.

ALL THE OTHERS. [*now pushing him down the aisle*] Get out. Get out.

DR. HINKFUSS. This is unheard of insolence. You want to turn this into a courtroom.

THE LEADING ACTOR. Real theatre.

THE CHARACTER ACTOR. The one you scatter away every evening so all the scenes of the play could be made for the eyes alone, sensational!

THE CHARACTER ACTRESS. Theatre is real when you let your passion be alive and then a mere suggestion would be enough.

THE LEADING ACTRESS. A passionate feeling is no joking matter.

THE LEADING ACTOR. To sacrifice everything for a stage effect! You ought to do farce, not drama.

ALL THE ACTORS. Get out! Get out!

DR. HINKFUSS. I am your director.

THE LEADING ACTOR. When life comes to life it cannot be pushed around by anyone.

THE CHARACTER ACTRESS. Even the playwright has to obey it.

THE LEADING ACTRESS. Obey, yes, obey.

THE CHARACTER ACTOR. And whoever wants to give orders get out of here.

ALL THE OTHERS. Out! Out!

DR. HINKFUSS. [*with his shoulders against the exit door of the theatre*] I'll sue! I'll sue!! I'll file charges. It's a scandal! I'm your direct—

> [*He is driven out of the theatre. Meanwhile, the curtains have again opened. The stage is now dark and bare.* THE SECRETARY, THE STAGE HANDS, THE ELECTRICIANS, ALL THE BACKSTAGE PERSONNEL *have come out to see the extraordinary sight of a director driven out by his own actors.*]

THE LEADING ACTOR. [*to* THE LEADING ACTRESS, *inviting her to get back onstage*] Come. Let's get back on. Quickly.

THE CHARACTER ACTRESS. We'll do the whole thing ourselves.

THE LEADING ACTOR. We don't need anything!

POMARICI. We'll stage the scene ourselves—

THE CHARACTER ACTOR. Good! I'll work the lights!

THE CHARACTER ACTRESS. No, it's better like this. Dark and bare.

THE LEADING ACTOR. Just enough light to outline the figures!

THE LEADING ACTRESS. And no scenery?

THE CHARACTER ACTRESS. We don't need scenery.

THE LEADING ACTRESS. Not even the walls of my jail?

THE LEADING ACTOR. Yes, but only as one can perceive them—there —for a moment—at the touch of your fingers—and then—darkness again—to illustrate after all that it is no longer the scenery that counts in the theatre.

THE CHARACTER ACTRESS. It's enough that you *feel* yourself there, child, inside your jail. It will seem to be there. Everyone will see it, just as if it really were.

THE LEADING ACTRESS. But at least I have to do something to my make-up.

THE CHARACTER ACTRESS. Wait! I have an idea! [*to a* STAGE HAND] Go get a chair. Quickly. [STAGE HAND *exits.*]

THE LEADING ACTRESS. What are you going to do?

THE CHARACTER ACTRESS. You'll see. [*to the other actors*] Meanwhile, all of you get the stage ready, but just what is barely needed. Two chairs, the small ones for the little girls, see if they are ready for us.

> [*The* STAGE HAND *brings in a chair.*]

THE LEADING ACTRESS. I was saying that I must change my make-up—

THE CHARACTER ACTRESS. [*giving her the chair*] Yes, yes. Sit here, my child.

THE LEADING ACTRESS. [*puzzled as though she did not know where she was*] Here?

THE CHARACTER ACTRESS. Yes, here. And you will begin to see all the sorrow— Nene, run get the make-up box and a towel. And don't forget—the nightgowns for the children.

THE LEADING ACTRESS. But what are you doing? What is all this?

THE CHARACTER ACTRESS. Leave it to us; to me, your mother, and to your sisters. We'll do your make-up ourselves. Go, Nene.

TOTINA. Get a mirror, too.

THE LEADING ACTRESS. And my dress.

DORINA. [*to* NENE, *who has already run off toward the dressing rooms*] Get her dress, too.

THE LEADING ACTRESS. It's a skirt and coat—they're in my dressing room. [NENE *nods assent and goes off right.*]

THE CHARACTER ACTRESS. You see, it must be our suffering—mine, your mother's who knows what age is—to make you grow old before your time—

TOTINA. And ours, who once helped make you beautiful and now shall make you ugly—

DORINA. And lay waste your loveliness—

THE LEADING ACTRESS. And condemn me for wanting that man?

THE CHARACTER ACTRESS. Yes, condemn you, but torn inside ourselves in doing so—

TOTINA. You detached yourself from us—

THE LEADING ACTRESS. But you mustn't think I did it out of fear, fear of the poverty in store for us all with Papa dead—

DORINA. And what else could it have been? Love? Could you ever have been in love with a monster like that?

THE LEADING ACTRESS. No!—out of gratitude—

TOTINA. For what?

THE LEADING ACTRESS. For having *believed*—when no one else did —with all the scandal that was going about—

TOTINA. So people could see that at least one of us still could get married?

DORINA. A big deal, to marry *him*!

THE CHARACTER ACTRESS. What did you gain after you married him? Now—now—you'll see.

NENE. [*returning with a make-up box, a mirror, a towel, the skirt and coat*] Here's everything. I couldn't find—

THE CHARACTER ACTRESS. Give the box to me. [*She opens the box and begins to do* MOMMINA'S (THE LEADING ACTRESS') *make-up.*] Hold up your face. Oh, my child, my child. If you only knew how they talk in town; how they still say, just the way they do of a girl who's dead: "What a pretty girl she was! and what a big heart she had!"—Gone, now—just like this—there,—like this—like this—the face of one who no longer breathes air nor any longer sees the sun—

TOTINA. And the bags under the eyes, the bags under the eyes now.

THE CHARACTER ACTRESS. Yes, there—like this!

DORINA. Not too much!

NENE. What are you saying? On the contrary, a lot, a lot—

TOTINA. The eyes of one who'll die of a broken heart—

NENE. And at the temples, the hair—

THE CHARACTER ACTRESS. Yes, yes—

DORINA. Not white! Not white!

NENE. No, not white—

THE LEADING ACTRESS. My dearest Dorina—

TOTINA. There—fine—like this—at barely thirty years old—

THE CHARACTER ACTRESS. —dusty with age—

THE LEADING ACTRESS. He will no longer even want me to comb my hair—

THE CHARACTER ACTRESS. [*ruffling her daughter's hair*] Then wait a minute, like this—like this—

NENE. [*bringing her the mirror*] Now take a look at yourself.

THE LEADING ACTRESS. [*immediately pushing the mirror away with both hands*] No! He's had all the mirrors in the house taken away. But I still can see myself, though. You know where? In the window panes, like a ghost, or all deformed in the quivering water of a washtub. I stand there stunned, looking.

THE CHARACTER ACTRESS. Wait, her mouth! Her mouth!

THE LEADING ACTRESS. Yes—paint all the red out. I no longer have blood in my veins.

TOTINA. And the wrinkles, the wrinkles at the corners of her mouth—

THE LEADING ACTRESS. Even at thirty, I have lost some of my teeth.

DORINA. [*in an outburst of emotion, embracing her*] No, no, my sweet Mommina, no, no.

NENE. [*almost angrily, she too caught up by emotion and pushing* DORINA *away*] Now her dress—her dress. Let us change her dress—

THE CHARACTER ACTRESS. No. Put the skirt and jacket on over the dress.

TOTINA. Wonderful—she'll look awkward that way.

THE CHARACTER ACTRESS. And her shoulders must be stooped just the way mine are, an old woman's—

DORINA. Trying to get your breath, you go around the house—

THE LEADING ACTRESS. Stunned with grief—

THE CHARACTER ACTRESS. Dragging your feet—

NENE. A walking corpse—

[*Each one, as she says her last line, withdraws into the darkness at the right.* THE LEADING ACTRESS, *left alone between the three bare walls of her prison—put up in the dark during the make-up scene—presses her forehead first against the wall at the right, and then against the one in back, then against the one at the left. At the touch of her forehead a blinding light from overhead makes the walls visible for a moment, and then they disappear again into darkness.*]

MOMMINA [THE LEADING ACTRESS]. [*in a dismal tone that deepens in intensity as she speaks, knocking her head against the three walls like a crazed animal in a cage*] This is wall—this is wall— this is wall— [*She goes and sits on the chair with the look of one who is insane. After she has sat there a moment there rises out of the darkness at the right, where the mother and sisters have withdrawn, a voice, the voice of the mother,* SIGNORA IGNAZIA, *who speaks as if she were reading a story from a book.*]

SIGNORA IGNAZIA. —She was imprisoned in the highest house in town. The doors were locked and all the windows locked, both casements and shutters—only one window, and that very small, was open on the faraway countryside and the faraway sea. Of the town, high on the hill, she saw only rooftops and steeples—roofs, roofs, dripping roofs, dripping here a little more, here a little less, the gutters of many filled up—roof tiles, nothing but roof tiles. Only in the evening could she appear at that window and take some air.

[*In the wall at the rear a little window is lit up, as veiled and faraway, through which shines the soft glimmer of moonlight.*]

NENE. [*from the darkness, softly, happily, with a childlike wonder, while far, far away is heard a feeble sound of a gentle serenade*] Oh, the window. Look, it's really a window—

DORINA. Sssshhhh.

[*The prisoner has remained immobile. The mother again begins to speak, and always it is as though she were reading.*]

SIGNORA IGNAZIA. —All those rooftops, like so many black dice, used to swim before her feverish eyes in the dusky light the street lamps used to cast in the narrow winding streets of the town. In the heavy silence of nearer alleys she used to hear sounds of echoing footsteps, the voice of some woman who perhaps was waiting as she herself was waiting, or the howling of a dog, or—more painful yet to hear—the sound of the bell in the nearby church, tolling the hour. But why does the clock keep counting the minutes? For whom does it toll the hour? Everything is dead.

[*After a moment five strokes of a bell are heard, muffled and faraway. It is the clock in the church.* RICO VERRI *appears, sombre and serious. He has just returned home. He still has his hat on his head. The collar of his overcoat is turned up. There is a scarf around his neck. He looks at his wife still sitting motionless in the chair. Then suspiciously he glances at the window.*]

VERRI. What have you been doing?

MOMMINA. Nothing! I was waiting for you.

VERRI. Were you at the window?

MOMMINA. No.

VERRI. You know you're there every evening.

MOMMINA. Not this evening.

VERRI. [*after throwing his coat, his hat, and his scarf on the other big chair*] Don't you ever get tired of thinking?

MOMMINA. I never think.

VERRI. Are the children in bed?

MOMMINA. Where else would they be at this hour?

VERRI. I ask the question only to remind you of the single thought you ought to have—of them.

MOMMINA. I've thought of them all day long.

VERRI. And what are you thinking of now?

MOMMINA. [*understanding now why he keeps returning with such insistence to this question, first stares at him scornfully and then, taking up again her pose of motionless apathy, replies*] Of throwing myself in bed—dead tired—

VERRI. You're lying. I want to know what you're thinking about. What have you been thinking about all the time you've been waiting for me to come? [*an expectant pause, during which she does not answer*] You won't answer me? You don't dare tell me! [*another pause*] So you admit it?

MOMMINA. Admit what?

VERRI. That you're thinking things you don't dare tell me.

MOMMINA. I've told you what I've been thinking of. Going to sleep.

VERRI. Of going to sleep? With those eyes and that voice—? You mean—to *dream!*

MOMMINA. I never dream.

VERRI. That's not true. Everyone dreams. It's not possible to sleep and not to dream.

MOMMINA. I never dream.

VERRI. You're lying, I tell you. It's not possible.

MOMMINA. All right, then, I dream. Have it your way.

VERRI. So you dream, then, do you? You dream. You dream, and you get back at me. You think, and you get back at me. What is it you dream about? Tell me what it is you dream about.

MOMMINA. I don't know.

VERRI. What do you mean you don't know?

MOMMINA. I don't know. It's you who said I dream. I'm so tired at night, my body's so heavy, I'm hardly in bed before I fall asleep, like lead. I no longer know what dreaming means. If I dream and, awakening, no longer recall what it was I dreamt, it's the same as if I'd never dreamt at all. It's perhaps a way God has of helping me.

VERRI. God? *God* helps you?

MOMMINA. Helps me endure a life that would be all the more hideous if for a while dreams had made me think I was leading some other life and then I had to open my eyes on this life again. You know that perfectly well. You know it. What do you want from me? You wish I were dead. Dead. That I no longer thought; that I no longer dreamed. And yet—and yet—to think implies an act of will, but dreaming—if one could dream—would not be an act of will but merely sleeping, and *how* could you forbid me that?

VERRI. [*agitated, flying into a rage like a beast in a cage*] That's it! that's it! that's it! I lock the doors, I lock the windows; I put bars up, and grills; but what good does it do me if right here in this prison I'm still betrayed? Here inside you, *inside* you, in this dead body—alive—still alive—betrayal—if you think, if you dream, if you remember. You're standing here before me. You're looking at me. Can I knock open your skull and look inside and find out what it is you're thinking? I ask you what you're thinking, and you say "nothing," and all the while you're thinking, dreaming, remembering, right before my very eyes, *looking at me* while deep down inside you may be remembering *someone else.* How can I find out who it is? How can I see who it is?

MOMMINA. But what do you think there is left inside me, if now I'm no longer anything? Don't you see me standing here? Not even yet another being. No longer anything. I'm burned up. An ash, a mere ash. What can you expect me to remember?

VERRI. Don't talk that way! Don't talk that way! You know you only make it all the worse when you talk that way!

MOMMINA. All right. I won't. Be calm.

VERRI. Even if you went blind, all the things your eyes had already seen, memories, memories you have fixed in your eyes, would be in your mind. And if I tore your lips off, those lips that have kissed other men's lips, inside you'd still keep experiencing the pleasure, the pleasure, the very taste of those other kisses, re-membering them till you died from the pleasure of it. You can't deny it. If you deny it, you're lying. You can't do anything but cry, scared of all I suffer on account of you, living with you, of all the evil you've done me, all your mother and your sisters taught you. You can't deny it. You've done them. You've done them, all those horrible things, and you know how I suffer be-cause of them, suffer to the point I think I'm going stark mad. It isn't my fault. The only sign of madness I've ever shown was my madness in marrying you.

MOMMINA. Madness, yes, madness—you knew yourself and what you were like. You should never have done it—

VERRI. What *I* was like? Is that what you're saying? What *I* was like, you say? Knowing what *you* were like, you *should* say—the kind of life you were leading there, with your mother and your sisters!

MOMMINA. Yes, yes. That, too. That, too. But don't forget that you were perfectly aware that I did not approve of the way they lived—

VERRI. But you lived that way, too—

MOMMINA. Because I had to. I was there—

VERRI. And only when you met me, did you stop approving of it—

MOMMINA. No. Even before that, even before that. Anyhow, it's true that in those days you yourself believed I was superior to the others—I don't say this for my own sake, to accuse the others and excuse myself, no, I say it for your sake. So you'll have pity not for me, not for me, if you're happier in *not* doing so, or rather in showing others you have none—*be* hard on me, *be* hard on me, but at least take pity on yourself and remember you *did* believe in me once, that even there in the midst of the life you despise, you believed you could love me—

VERRI. Enough to marry you! Of course I believed you were better than the others, but what does that do? How does that excuse what I did? If I remember I loved you, that I could love you even there, leading the kind of life you were leading—what good does that do me?

MOMMINA. But don't you see? Recognizing that there was at least something in me that partly excuses the madness you committed in marrying me. There. I'll say it for you.

VERRI. Doesn't that make it all the worse? Do I, with that, cancel out the life you led before I fell in love with you? To have married you because you were better than the others doesn't excuse anything. It only makes it all the worse—since the better you were, all the more hideous, all the more hideous becomes the sinfulness of the life you had led. I've not lifted you up out of it— you've sucked me down into it with you, dragging me down and locking me up here in this prison of yours, to expiate with you all this, as though I'd committed it all myself. Feeling myself eaten alive by it but kept alive by everything I know about your mother and your sisters.

MOMMINA. I no longer know anything about them.

NENE. [*rising up out of the dark*] How meanly he is talking about us now.

VERRI. [*hideously yelling*] Shut up, you! You're not here!

SIGNORA IGNAZIA. [*coming to the wall out of the darkness*] Beast, beast! You've got her there between your teeth, in that cage, and you're ripping her to pieces!

VERRI. [*touching the walls two times with his hands and, two times at his touch, making the walls visible*] This is wall! This is wall! *You are not here!*

TOTINA. [*also coming forward toward the wall with the others, aggressively*] And you take advantage of it, monster, by telling her filthy lies about us.

DORINA. We were starving, Mommina.

NENE. We'd touched bottom.

VERRI. And how did you get up again?

SIGNORA IGNAZIA. Scoundrel. You dare throw that in our faces while all the time you're slowly *murdering* our Mommina with your cruelty?

NENE. We have an enjoyable life.

VERRI. You sold yourselves. You're dishonored.

TOTINA. And the honor you've kept for her, how do you make up to her for that?

DORINA. Mama's getting along fine now, Mommina. Just see how well she looks. How she dresses! What a gorgeous fur coat she has now!

SIGNORA IGNAZIA. Thanks to Totina. She's become a great singer.

DORINA. Totina La Croce.

NENE. All the theatres are clamoring for her.

SIGNORA IGNAZIA. Parties! One triumph after another!

VERRI. Dishonor!

NENE. I'm all for it, if honor is what you're giving to your wife.

MOMMINA. [*suddenly, with an impulse of affection and pity for her husband, who has his face in his hands, and seems depressed*] No, no, I'm not saying that. I'm not saying that. I'm complaining of nothing—

VERRI. They want to condemn me—

MOMMINA. No, no, I understand why you have to shout, to release the torment pent up inside you. You cannot help it.

VERRI. But it's they who keep me in torment. If you only knew the scandals they keep causing. Everyone talks about them. Think how I feel. The success they've had has made them let go completely. They're more shameless than ever.

MOMMINA. Dorina, too?

VERRI. All of them. Even Dorina. But most of all, Nene. The little whore—[MOMMINA *covers her face.*]—yes, yes, even in public.

MOMMINA. And Totina has begun to sing?

VERRI. Yes, in theatres—in country towns, of course, where scandals are all the worse, with that mother and those sisters—

MOMMINA. She takes them all with her?

VERRI. All of them. One continuous party—What's the matter? Does it get you excited thinking about it?

MOMMINA. No—it's just that I am learning of all this for the first time. I knew nothing about it before—

VERRI. And you feel yourself all stirred up inside? The theatre, eh? *You* used to sing, didn't you? With that beautiful voice of yours. The most beautiful voice of all was yours. Just think what a different sort of life it would have been for you. To be singing in a big theatre. That was your passion, to sing. Lights, glitter, publicity—

MOMMINA. But, no—

VERRI. Don't say no. You're standing there thinking about it right now.

MOMMINA. I tell you no.

VERRI. What do you mean *no?* If you'd just stuck with them and kept away from me—what a different life you'd have had—instead of this—

MOMMINA. But it's you who are making me think about it. How do you expect me to think any more about anything, when I'm what I am now?

VERRI. You've got that pain again?

MOMMINA. My heart's in my throat—

VERRI. That's it! The pain is showing up again—

MOMMINA. You want to kill me!

VERRI. I? Your sisters, what you were once, your past—that's what's churning up your insides and making your heart jump up in your throat!

MOMMINA. [*panting, her hands on her chest*] Please—please—I beg you. I can't get my breath any more—

VERRI. But you see it's true, you see, it's true what I'm telling you.

MOMMINA. Have pity on me—

VERRI. The girl you were—those same thoughts, those same feel-ings—you thought they were all gone, done with, put out? It isn't true. The merest reminder—and there they all are again, come to life again inside you—

MOMMINA. It's you who remind me of them—

VERRI. No, anything reminds you of them. They're always there, alive, inside you. You don't know it but they're there, beyond anything you know about. You always have inside you the whole life you've lived. All you need is a word, a sound, nothing at all —the smallest sensation. Take me. All I have to do is smell sage and I'm in the country. It's August and I'm a little boy of eight again, behind the gardener's house, in the shade of an old olive tree, afraid of a big blue hornet; miserable because it's buzzing so greedily inside a white flower. I still see that flower trembling on its stalk at being raped by the terrible greed of that hornet that scares me so. And I have it here still, here in my loins, that same fear, I have it right here! Let's just imagine you, and all that fine life you used to lead, and all the things that used to happen between you girls and all those young men who came to the house, shut up alone in this or that room. Don't deny it! I've seen—things. That Nene. One time with Sarelli. They thought they were alone and they'd left the door ajar. I could see them. Nene pretended to go off toward the other room, in the back—there were green curtains there— She went out but came right back, between the green curtains. She'd uncovered her little breasts, pulling down her pink silk slip—and with one hand she was pretending to offer her breast and then right away with the same hand was hiding it. I saw it myself. Beautiful little breasts, you know. Each one just the size you could cup whole in your hand—license to do what one pleases. Before I came to your house—you with Pomarici. Yes, I knew all about it. But before Pomarici—yes, who knows how many others you were with? For years that same life; the house wide open to anyone who came along— [*He stands over her trembling.*] You, certain things—certain things—that you did *first* with me—if up till then you really, as you said, didn't know about them—you couldn't have known how to do them with me—

MOMMINA. No, no, I swear it. Never, never, before I met you—

VERRI. But hugs—embraces—with that Pomarici, yes,—his arms, his arms, didn't they hug you like this? Like this?

MOMMINA. Ahi—you're hurting me.

VERRI. You liked that didn't you? Didn't you? Around your waist, around your waist, like this? Like this?

MOMMINA. Please, please, let go, I'm dying.

VERRI. [*furiously grabbing her with one hand by the nape of the neck*] And your mouth, your mouth? How did he kiss your mouth? Like this? Like this? [*And he kisses her, and bites her, and breaks out into loud laughter, and pulls her hair as though crazed.* MOMMINA, *trying to get free, screams desperately.*]

MOMMINA. Help! Help!
> [*In their long nightgowns,* THE TWO LITTLE CHILDREN, *girls, terrified by the noises, run in and cling to their mother.* VERRI *runs out of the room, grabbing from the chair only his hat.*]

VERRI. [*yelling*] I'm going crazy! I'm going crazy! I'm going crazy!
MOMMINA. [*protecting herself and making a shield of her body for* THE TWO CHILDREN] Get out of here, get out, get out, monster! Leave me alone with my babies— [*She sinks down exhausted on the chair.* THE TWO CHILDREN *are beside her, and she holds them tightly, embracing them, one on one side and one on the other.*] My little ones, my little ones, the things you've had to see! Locked up here with me—with your waxen faces and your great big eyes wide open with fear. He's gone now. He's gone now. Don't tremble any more like this. You can stay here with me a little while. Here with me. Are you sure you aren't cold? The window's closed. It's so late already. You're always glued to the window there, like two little beggars begging for—a glimpse of the world. Always counting the white sails of the sloops at sea, aren't you? And the little cottages scattered across the fields where you've never been. And you're always asking me what it's like, the sea—and the fields. Oh, children, children, what a life you've had. Worse than mine. But at least you don't know it. And your mother's so sick—so sick here, in her heart. It beats so hard, here in her breast, it's like a gallop, like the gallop of a runaway horse. Here, here, give me your little hands—feel it, feel it! May God not make him pay for it—for your sakes, children. But he'll make martyrs out of you, because he can't help it. It's his nature. He made himself a martyr, too—but you're innocent. You are innocent—
> [*She presses the little hands of* THE TWO CHILDREN *to her cheeks and remains like this. From the right, at the wall, emerging from the darkness like conspirators, the mother,* SIGNORA IGNAZIA, *and the daughters approach her, gorgeously dressed and making a colorful scene. They are, it should be noted, effectively lit from overhead.*]

SIGNORA IGNAZIA. [*softly calling*] Mommina—Mommina—
MOMMINA. Who is it?
DORINA. It's us, Mommina.
NENE. We're here. All of us.
MOMMINA. Here? Where?
TOTINA. Here. In the town. I've come to sing.
MOMMINA. Totina—you? to sing here?
NENE. Yes, in the theatre here.
MOMMINA. Oh God, here? And when? When?
NENE. This evening. This very evening.
SIGNORA IGNAZIA. My dears, leave something for me to say. Listen, Mommina, look—what was it I wanted to say? Oh, yes. Look, you want proof of it? Your husband left his coat over there, there on that chair—

MOMMINA. [*turning to look*] Yes, he did.

SIGNORA IGNAZIA. Look in one of the pockets of the coat and see what you find there. [*softly to the girls*] We must help her get into her big scene now. We're near the end of the performance.

MOMMINA. [*getting up and going to search feverishly in the pockets of the coat*] What is it I'm looking for? What is it I'm looking for?

NENE. [*softly to* SIGNORA IGNAZIA] Will you answer her?

SIGNORA IGNAZIA. No, no, you— What a fuss!

NENE. [*loudly to* MOMMINA] It's a handbill—you know, a little yellow sheet, the kind they pass out in cafes, in country towns—

SIGNORA IGNAZIA. There you'll find Totina's name, printed in large letters—the name of the prima donna.

[*They vanish.*]

MOMMINA. [*finding it*] Here it is! Here it is! [*She opens it and reads.*] *Il Trovatore. Il Trovatore.* Lenora—soprano—Totina La Croce—this evening. Your aunt, children, your aunt. It's your aunt who's singing Lenora. And your grandmother and your other aunts are all here, are *here!* You don't know them. You've never seen them—nor have I, for many years. They're here. [*thinking of her husband's anger*] Ah, it was all because of this —they here in town, Totina singing in the theatre here. There is a theatre here, then? I didn't even know there was one. Aunt Totina. Then it's true. Perhaps, with study, her voice— Surely, if she can sing in public— But, my children, my poor little children, you don't even know what a theatre is—a theatre, a theatre—now I shall tell you what a theatre is. Tonight your Aunt Totina is singing in one. And oh how beautiful she'll be as Lenora— [*She tries to sing.*]

> "Tacea la notte placida
> e bella in ciel sereno
> la luna il viso argenteo
> mostrava lieto e pieno—"

You see. I too can sing. Yes, yes. I too can sing. I used to sing all the time once. Yes, I did. I know all of *Trovatore* by heart. And I'm going to sing it for you now. I'll make the theatre for you first—you who've never seen one, my poor little chicks, shut up in your prison here with your mummy. Sit down, sit down here in front of me, right here on your little chairs. I'll make a theatre for you. First I'll tell you what it's like. [*She sits before the two stunned children. She herself is trembling all over, and from moment to moment she will become increasingly excited until finally her heart will fail her and she will suddenly fall dead on the floor.*] A hall, a big, big hall, with many rows of boxes all around; five, six rows, full of beautiful women, with feathers and jewels and fans and flowers. And the gentlemen all in tails, with little pearls for buttons on their shirts. And with white ties. And so many, many people everywhere, even below, in red plush chairs, in the orchestra. A sea of heads. And lights, lights

everywhere. A great chandelier in the center that hangs down
as though it were hanging down from heaven itself, and all
covered with glittering crystals. Oh, how dazzling it is. It makes
you dizzy. You can't imagine how dazzling the light is and how
dizzy it makes you— Noise and movement—the ladies are all
talking with elegant gentlemen, greeting each other from one
box to the next; some who take their places below in the orchestra; others who are looking with their glasses—like the ones
of mother-of-pearl that I've made you look at the fields with—
yes, those—I used to carry them—yes, your own mother used
to carry them—when she went to the theatre and used them to
look around, ah, yes, some time ago. All of a sudden the lights
go down. Only the little green lights on the desks of the orchestra—in front of the seats—there below the curtain—stay lit.
The players are already in their places—oh, so many of them—
and they're all tuning up. And the curtains are like window
curtains, but large, and heavy, all red velvet splattered with gold,
magnificent things really. When they open—for the conductor's
come out with his baton to lead the players—the opera begins.
And you see the stage now. There's a forest, or a square, or a
palace. And Aunt Totina's coming out and singing with the
others, and the orchestra is playing—that's the theatre— But I
once, I once had the more beautiful voice, not your Aunt Totina.
I, I had a very much more beautiful voice. I had a voice that
made everyone say I should sing opera. I. Your own mother. Instead it's your Aunt Totina who's done it. Ah, she had the
courage to do it. The curtain's opening now. Listen. They draw
it back from both sides. Once it's open you see on the stage a
hall in a great palace, and armed men that march up and down
in the rear. And many knights, including a certain Ferrando.
They're all waiting for their captain, the Conte di Luna. They're
dressed up in a funny old-fashioned way, with velvet coats and
plumed hats and swords and padded legs. It's night. They're tired
of waiting for the count who, in love with a great lady in the
Spanish court—her name is Lenora—is jealous of her and stays
hidden under her balcony to spy on her. In the gardens of the
palace. He knows that every night a trovatore, a troubadour, a
man who is both a singer and a knight, comes and sings her this
song. [*She sings.*]

"Deserto sulla terra—"

[*She interrupts herself for a moment to say, almost to herself.*]
Oh God, my heart—[*and immediately begins to sing again, but
with effort, struggling with the pain caused, of course, by the
excitement of hearing herself sing again*]

"Col rio destino in guerra
é sola speme un cor—"
    [*sung three times and then*]
"un cor—al Trovator—"

I can't sing any more—I—I—can't get my breath—the heart —my heart hurts so—I haven't sung for a great many years— but perhaps little by little, my breath, my voice, will come back to me— You must understand that this troubadour is a brother of the Conte di Luna—yes, but the count, of course, does not know this, and the troubadour himself does not know it, either —for he was kidnapped by a gypsy when he was a little baby. It's a terrible story you're about to hear. You'll see this gypsy in the second act. Her name is Azucena. Yes, that was my part, that was my part, the role of Azucena. She stole the baby, this Azucena, to revenge her mother's death, her mother, who was innocently burned alive by the father of the Conte di Luna. Gypsies are vagabonds that tell your fortune and read the future, and they still exist. They're still said to kidnap children, so much so that mama is very careful about them. But this Azucena steals the son of the count, as I've just told you, to revenge the death of her own mother, and she plans to give him the very death her own mother suffered. And she gets the fire going big. But in the fury of her revenge, half-crazed, she grabs up her own child, her own little boy, instead of the count's and throws *him* on the fire. You understand? "Il figlio mio—il figlio mio—" I can't— I can't sing it for you. You don't know, my children, what this evening means to me, and especially *Trovatore*—this song of the gypsy—it's the one I was singing one night, with everyone around me— [*She sings, crying at the same time.*]

"Chi del gitano la vita abbella?
La zingarella!"

My father that night, my father—your grandfather—was brought back home all covered with blood—and he had with him a kind of gypsy that night—and that night, that very night, children, my fate—my fate was sealed—my fate— [*She gets up desperately and sings with all her strength.*]

"Ah che la morte ognora
é tarda nel venir
a chi desia
a chi desia morir!
Addio,
addio, Lenora, addio—"[5]

[*She suddenly collapses on the floor, dead.* THE TWO CHIL-
DREN, *more bewildered than ever, have no inkling of what*

5. In the performance that she attempts to give for her children,
Mommina describes the second scene
of Act I of the opera, in which
Leonora confides to her attendant
that she loves an unknown knight
(Manrico) whom she calls *il trovatore*
(the troubadour). The two arias she
tries to sing are *"Tacea la notte
placida,"* in which she describes the
beauty of the evening on which she
was first serenaded, and *"Deserto sulla
terra,"* Manrico's bid for her love.
From this point on, Mommina so
confuses the events in the opera with
those in her own story that when she
finally sings *"Ah che la morte organa"*
(Ah, how death always comes late to
the one who wants to die), Manrico's
Act IV plaint has become her own.

has happened. *They think it is still the opera that their
mother is doing for them. And they sit there motionless in
their little chairs, waiting. The silence and the immobility
become unbearable. Finally, in the darkness, from the rear
at the left, come the anxious voices of* RICO VERRI, *of*
SIGNORA IGNAZIA, *of* TOTINA, DORINA, *and* NENE.]

VERRI. She was singing. Did you hear it? It was *her* voice—

SIGNORA IGNAZIA. Yes. A bird in a cage!

TOTINA. Mommina! Mommina!

DORINA. It's us—we're here with him. He's admitted he was
wrong—

NENE. It was Totina's triumph that did it—he understood—the
town went delirious— [*She starts to say "delirious" but she
breaks off in the middle, terrified like the others at the sight
of the lifeless body there on the floor before them and of* THE
TWO CHILDREN *that are still waiting, motionless.*]

VERRI. What's the matter?

SIGNORA IGNAZIA. Dead?

DORINA. She was playing theatre for the children!

TOTINA. Mommina—

NENE. Mommina—

> [*They stand in fixed poses. From the door into the hall of
> the theatre, running down the aisle straight onto the stage,*
> DR. HINKFUSS *enthusiastically rushes to them.*]

DR. HINKFUSS. Magnificent! A truly magnificent scene! You did it
just as I told you to. *This* is not in the story at all.

SIGNORA IGNAZIA. [*as* THE CHARACTER ACTRESS] He's here again!

THE CHARACTER ACTOR. [*appearing from the left*] But he was here
all the time, hidden over there with the electricians, seeing to
all the lighting effects.

NENE. So that explains it—they were beautiful—

TOTINA. I guessed it. When we appeared together— [*She points
to the other side of the stage, to the right, behind the wall.*] that
beautiful effect from overhead—

THE CHARACTER ACTRESS. [*pointing again to* MOMMINA (THE LEAD-
ING ACTRESS) *lying on the floor*] But why don't you get up, Miss
————? She's still lying there—

THE CHARACTER ACTOR. She couldn't really be dead, could she?

> [*All gently bend down over* THE LEADING ACTRESS.]

THE LEADING ACTOR. [*calling to her and lifting her up*] Miss ————

THE CHARACTER ACTRESS. Are you really sick?

NENE. Good God, she's fainted. Let's lift her up.

THE LEADING ACTRESS. [*getting up herself*] No—thank you. It really
is my heart, though. Let me get my breath. Let me get my
breath—

THE CHARACTER ACTOR. Of course, of course—if you really want
us to *live* our roles, this is what happens. But get this, we aren't
here to do this kind of thing. We're here to play written parts,
memorized before hand, learned by heart. Don't you think for
a minute that every evening each of us is going to get out of his

own skin like this—

THE LEADING ACTOR. We need the author.

DR. HINKFUSS. The author, no. Written parts, yes, if we must—just so they can for one moment be endowed with the life we alone can give them and—[*He turns to the audience.*] without a repetition of this evening's errors, for which I must beg—the audience's forgiveness. [*He bows.*]

CURTAIN

The Lark

JEAN ANOUILH

The Lark was first performed in Paris on October 14, 1953. In a note in the program, Jean Anouilh wrote, "The play that follows makes no attempt to explain the mystery of Joan." Instead, although Anouilh does not go on to say so, he uses Joan for his own purposes, as authors—particularly dramatists—have been doing for years. Joan's story is sprinkled with incidents—the convincing of Beaudricourt, the winning over of Charles, the coronation of Charles, the trial—which have a dramatic potential that seems to make a playwright itch to get his hands on them, to twist them so that the audience can see them from another, perhaps a new angle. Anouilh not only chose to use these incidents to say what he wanted about man in relation to abstract ideas, but he chose to order them in a way that violated the form of the traditional history play, so that his dramatic structure, too, could make its comment—on Joan as myth. Christopher Fry's version of the play, which is very close to the original, first played in London on May 11, 1955; later that year, another version, an adaptation by Lillian Hellman, opened in New York.

The Lark†

Characters

BEAUCHAMP, *Earl of Warwick*	BOUDOUSSE, *a guard*
CAUCHON, *Bishop of Beauvais*	AGNES SOREL
JOAN	THE YOUNG QUEEN
HER FATHER	CHARLES, *the Dauphin*
HER MOTHER	QUEEN YOLANDE
HER BROTHER	ARCHBISHOP OF RHEIMS
THE PROMOTER	M. DE LA TREMOUILLE
THE INQUISITOR	PAGE TO THE DAUPHIN
BROTHER LADVENU	CAPTAIN LA HIRE
ROBERT DE BEAUDRICOURT,	THE HANGMAN
Squire of Vaucouleurs	AN ENGLISH SOLDIER

527

528 · *Jean Anouilh*

Part One

A simple, neutral setting. The stage is empty at first; then the characters enter by twos and threes. The costumes are plain. JOAN *wears man's clothes throughout the play.* WARWICK *is the last to enter.*

WARWICK. Well, now; is everyone here? If so, let's have the trial and be done with it. The sooner she is found guilty and burned the better for all concerned.

CAUCHON. But, my lord, before we do that we have the whole story to play: Domremy, the Voices, Vaucouleurs, Chinon, the Coronation.

WARWICK. Theatrical poppycock! You can tell that story to the children: the beautiful white armour, the fluttering standard, the gentle and implacable warrior maid. The statues of her can tell that story, later on, when policies have changed. We might even put up a statue ourselves in London, though I know at the moment that sounds wildly improbable: but you never know, in a few hundred years it might suit His Majesty's Government for some reason or other. But, as for now, I am Beauchamp, Earl of Warwick; and I've got my grubby little witch lying on the straw in the dungeon at Rouen, and a fine packet of trouble she has been, and a pretty sum she has cost us; but the money's been paid, and the next thing is to put her on trial and burn her.

CAUCHON. Not immediately. Before we come to that, there's the whole of her life to go through. It won't take very long, my lord.

WARWICK. [*going to a corner resignedly*] Well, if you insist. An Englishman knows how to wait. [*anxiously*] I hope you're not expecting me to stand by while you go through that monstrous farce of a coronation again. And all the battles as well—Orleans, Patay, Beaugency?—I may as well tell you now, I should find that in very poor taste.

CAUCHON. [*smiling*] Put your mind at rest, my lord. There are too few of us here to stage the battles.

WARWICK. Good.

CAUCHON. Joan.
[*She looks up.*]
You may begin.

JOAN. May I begin wherever I like?

CAUCHON. Yes.

JOAN. I like remembering the beginning: at home, in the fields, when I was still a little girl looking after the sheep, the first time I heard the Voices, that is what I like to remember. . . . It is after the evening Angelus. I am very small and my hair is still in pigtails. I am sitting in the field, thinking of nothing at all. God is good and keeps me safe and happy, close to my mother and my father and my brother, in the quiet countryside of Domremy, while the English soldiers are looting and burning

villages up and down the land. My big sheep-dog is lying with
his head in my lap; and suddenly I feel his body ripple and
tremble, and a hand seems to have touched my shoulder, though
I know no one has touched me, and the voice says——

SOMEONE IN THE CROWD. Who is going to be the voice?

JOAN. I am, of course. I turned to look. A great light was filling
the shadows behind me. The voice was gentle and grave. I had
never heard it before, and all it said to me was: "Be a good and
sensible child, and go often to church." But I *was* good, and
I *did* go to church often, and I showed I was sensible by running
away to safety. That was all that happened the first time. And
I didn't say anything about it when I got home; but after supper
I went back. The moon was rising; it shone on the white sheep;
and that was all the light there was. And then came the second
time; the bells were ringing for the noonday Angelus. The light
came again, in bright sunlight, but brighter than the sun, and
that time I saw him.

CAUCHON. You saw whom?

JOAN. A man in a white robe, with two white wings reaching from
the sky to the ground. He didn't tell me his name that day, but
later on I found out that he was the blessed St. Michael.

WARWICK. Is it absolutely necessary to have her telling these ab-
surdities all over again?

CAUCHON. Absolutely necessary, my lord.

[WARWICK *goes back to his corner in silence, and smells the
rose he has in his hand.*]

JOAN. [*in the deep voice of the Archangel*]—Joan, go to the help
of the King of France, and give him back his kingdom. [*She
replies in her own voice.*] Oh sir, you haven't looked at me; I
am only a young peasant girl, not a great captain who can lead
an army.—You will go and search out Robert de Beaudricourt,
the Governor of Vaucouleurs. He will give you a suit of clothes
to dress you like a man, and he will take you to the Dauphin.
St. Catherine and St. Margaret will protect you. [*She suddenly
drops to the floor sobbing with fear.*]—Please, please pity me,
holy sir! I'm a little girl; I'm happy here alone in the fields. I've
never had to be responsible for anything, except my sheep. The
Kingdom of France is far beyond anything I can do. If you will
only look at me you will see I am small, and ignorant. The realm
of France is too heavy, sir. But the King of France has famous
Captains, as strong as you could need and they're used to doing
these things. If they lose a battle they sleep as soundly as ever.
They simply say the snow or the wind was against them; and
they just cross all the dead men off their roll. But I should always
remember I had killed them. Please have pity on me! . . . No
such thing. No pity. He had gone already, and there I was, with
France on my shoulders. Not to mention the work on the farm,
and my father, who wasn't easy.

[*Her* FATHER, *who has been wandering around her* MOTHER,
suddenly speaks.]

FATHER. Where has that girl got to?

MOTHER. [*going on with her knitting*] She is out in the fields.

FATHER. Well, I was out in the fields, and I'm back home again. It's six o'clock. She's no business to be out in the fields.

BROTHER. She's sitting under the Fairy Tree, staring at nothing. I saw her when I went to fetch in the bull.

PROMOTER. [*from among the crowd*] The Fairy Tree! Note that, gentlemen, if you will. Note the superstition. The beginning of witchcraft already. The Fairy Tree! I ask you to note that!

CAUCHON. There are Fairy Trees all over France, my Lord Promoter. It's in our own interest not to refuse the fairies to these little girls.

PROMOTER. [*primly*] We have our saints. That should be sufficient.

CAUCHON. [*conciliating him*] Later on, certainly. But I mean while they are still very young; as Joan was; not yet fifteen.

PROMOTER. By fifteen they know everything: they're as old as Eve.

CAUCHON. Not Joan: Joan at that time was very simple and innocent. It will be another matter when we come to the trial; I shan't spare her Voices then. But a little girl shall keep her fairies. [*firmly*] And these discussions are under my charge.

[*The* PROMOTER *bows, and retires, unmollified.*]

FATHER. [*bursting out afresh, to the* BROTHER] So that's where you say she is? And what does she think she's doing there, sitting under the tree?

BROTHER. Try and find out! She's just staring in front of her as if she was expecting something. And it isn't the first time either.

FATHER. Well, why didn't you tell me when you saw her before, then? Aren't you old enough to know what trouble there is with girls of her age, you little fool? What do you think she was expecting, eh? Somebody, not something, idiot! She's got a lover, and you know it! Give me my stick!

MOTHER. [*gently, still knitting*] You know quite well, Joan's as innocent as a baby.

FATHER. Maybe she is. And girls as innocent as babies can come to you one evening and hold up their faces to be kissed, and the next morning, though you've kept them locked in their room all night, what has happened? You can't see into their eyes at all: they're avoiding you, and lying to you. They're the devil, all at once.

PROMOTER. [*raising a finger*] The word has been said, my lords, and by her father!

MOTHER. How do you know that? The day I married you I was as innocent as Joan, and I daresay you could look into my eyes just as well next morning.

FATHER. [*muttering*] That's nothing to do with it.

MOTHER. Who are these other girls you've known, then, that you've never told me about?

FATHER. [*thundering to cover his embarrassment*] I tell you it's got nothing to do with it! We're not talking about other girls, we're talking about Joan! Hand me that stick. I'm going to look for

her, and if she's been meeting somebody on the quiet I'll skin
them alive!

JOAN. [*smiling gently*] I was meeting someone on the quiet, and
his solemn voice was saying: "Joan! Joan! What are you waiting
for? There's a great sorrow in the realm of France."—"Holy Sir
of Heaven, I'm so afraid; I'm only a young village girl; surely
you've made a mistake?"—"Does God make mistakes, Joan?"
[*She turns to her Judges.*] How could I have answered Yes?

PROMOTER. [*shrugging*] You should have made the sign of the cross.

JOAN. I did, and the Archangel made it, too, all the time keeping
his eyes carefully on mine, and the church clock sounded.

PROMOTER. You should have cried: Vade retro Satanus!

JOAN. I don't know Latin, my Lord.

PROMOTER. Don't be an idiot! The devil understands French. You
should have cried: Get thee behind me, foul Satan, and don't
tempt me again.

JOAN. But, my Lord, it was St. Michael.

PROMOTER. [*sneering*] So he told you. And you were fool enough
to believe him.

JOAN. Yes, I believed him. He couldn't have been the devil. He
shone with light; he was beautiful.

PROMOTER. [*losing his temper*] So is the devil, so is the devil, I
tell you!

JOAN. [*scandalised*] Oh, my Lord!

CAUCHON. [*calming the* PROMOTER *with a gesture*] These subtle
theological points, my lord Promoter, are proper for debating
between ourselves, but they're beyond the understanding of this
poor girl. No good is served by shocking her.

JOAN. [*to the* PROMOTER] You're telling a lie, Canon! I haven't
any of your learning, but I know the devil is ugly, and all that's
beautiful is the work of God.

PROMOTER. [*sneering*] Very charming, simple and stupid! Do you
think the devil is stupid? He's a thousand times more intelligent
than you and I put together. Do you think when he comes to
snare a soul he would come like a horror of the flesh, with black
ploughed skin and a snouting tusk like a rhinoceros? If he did,
souls would fly to virtue at the sight of him. I tell you he
chooses a moonlit summer night, and comes with coaxing hands,
with eyes that receive you into them like water that drowns you,
with naked women's flesh, transparent, white . . . beautiful——

CAUCHON. [*stopping him sternly*] Canon! You are losing your way!
This is very far from Joan's devil, if she has seen one. I beg you
not to confuse your devil with hers.

PROMOTER. [*flushed and confused in front of the smiling crowd*]
I beg your pardon, my lord; there is only one devil.

CAUCHON. Go on, Joan.

JOAN. [*still troubled*] If the devil is beautiful, how can we know
him?

PROMOTER. By asking your parish priest.

JOAN. Can we never know by ourselves?

PROMOTER. No. That is why there is no salvation outside the church.

JOAN. Only rich people have a parish priest always at hand. It's hard for the poor.

PROMOTER. It is hard for everyone to escape damnation.

CAUCHON. My lord Promoter, let her talk with her Voices in peace and quiet. It is the beginning of the story. We mustn't reproach her with them yet.

JOAN. [*continuing*] Another time it was St. Catherine and St. Margaret who came to me. [*She turns to the* PROMOTER *with a slightly mischievous defiance.*] They were beautiful, too.

PROMOTER. [*blushing, but unable to prevent himself*] Did they appear to you naked?

JOAN. [*smiling*] Oh, my lord! Do you imagine that God can't afford clothes for the saints in heaven?

[*The* CROWD *chuckles at this answer, and the* PROMOTER *sits down confused.*]

CAUCHON. You see, you make us all smile with your questions, my lord Promoter. Be wise enough to keep your interruptions until we come to the serious heart of this business. And when we do so, particularly when we come to judge her, remember that the soul in this little arrogant body is in our care. Aren't you risking very much confusion in her mind, to suggest to her that good and evil are no more than a question of clothes? It is true certainly, that our saints are traditionally represented as clothed; yet, on the other hand——

JOAN. [*to the* PROMOTER] Our Lord is naked on the cross.

CAUCHON. [*turning to her*] I was going to say so, Joan, if you had not prevented me. It isn't for you to correct the reverend Canon. You forget who you are; you forget that we are your priests, your masters and your judges. Beware of your pride, Joan. If the devil one day wins you for his own, that is the way he will come to you.

JOAN. I know I am proud. But if God didn't mean me to be proud, why did He send an Archangel to see me, and saints with the light of heaven on them to speak to me? Why did He promise I should persuade all the people I have persuaded—men as learned and as wise as you—and say I should ride in white armour, with a bright sword given me by the King, to lead France into battle: and it has been so. He had only to leave me looking after the sheep, and I don't think pride would ever have entered my head.

CAUCHON. Weigh your words, Joan; weigh your thoughts. It is your Saviour you are accusing now.

JOAN. [*crossing herself*] God guide me. His will be done, if His will is to make me proud and damned. That is His right, as well.

PROMOTER. [*unable to contain himself*] Terrible! What she says is terrible! God's will to damn a soul? And you all listen to this without a murmur, my lords? I see here the seed of a fearful heresy which will one day tear the Church apart.

[*The* INQUISITOR *has risen. He is an intelligent looking man, spare and hard, speaking with great quietness.*]

INQUISITOR. Listen carefully to what I am going to ask you, Joan. Do you think you are in a state of grace at this moment?

JOAN. [*firmly*] At what moment, my lord? Is it the beginning, when I hear my Voices, or the end, when my King and all my friends have deserted me, when I doubt and recant and the Church receives me again?

INQUISITOR. Don't evade my question. Do you think you are in a state of grace?

[*All the* PRIESTS *are watching her in silence; it seems a dangerous question.*]

LADVENU. [*rising*] My lord Inquisitor, it is a formidable question for a simple girl who believes in all sincerity that God has called her. I ask that her reply shall not be held against her: she is risking quite unwittingly——

INQUISITOR. Quiet, Brother Ladvenu! I ask what I consider good to ask. Let her answer my question. Do you think you are in a state of grace, Joan?

JOAN. If I am not, may God in His goodness set me there. If I am, may God in His goodness keep me so.

[*The* PRIESTS *murmur. The* INQUISITOR *sits again, inscrutable.*]

LADVENU. [*quietly*] Well answered, Joan.

PROMOTER. [*muttering, annoyed by* JOAN'S *success*] What of it? The devil has cunning, or he wouldn't be the devil. It isn't the first time he has been asked that question. We know what he is; he has his answers all ready.

WARWICK. [*bored, to* CAUCHON] No doubt this is all very interesting, my lord, but if you go on at this rate we shall never get to the trial, never have her burnt, never get anywhere. I said she could take us over the old ground again, if you thought it so necessary, but let her get on with it. And let us come to the essentials. His Majesty's Government have to discredit this wretched little Charles Valois, at once; it's imperative that we should let Christendom know that the Coronation was all a humbug, the performance of a witch, a heretic, an army's whore.

CAUCHON. My lord, we're trying her only for heresy.

WARWICK. I know that; but I have to make more of it for the sake of the troops. The findings of your trial, I'm afraid, will be too rarefied for my soldiers. Propaganda, my lord Archbishop, is black or white. The main thing is to say something pretty staggering, and repeat it often enough until you turn it into a truth. It's a new idea, but, believe me, it will make its way. The essential thing, so far as I am concerned, is that the girl should be a nonentity, whatever she is in fact. And what she is in fact is of no particular importance to His Majesty's Government. Personally, I must admit, I find the girl attractive. The way she takes the wind out of your sails gives me a lot of pleasure; and her seat on a horse is very good: that's rare in a woman. If the circumstances had been different, and she had belonged to my own set, I should have enjoyed a day's hunting with her. But unfortunately there's been this damned Coronation, and that was nobody's notion but hers in the first place. Really, my lords, what impudence! To have himself crowned King of France right under our noses: a Valois, King of France! and to do it at Rheims, our territory! To dare to pick France out of our pockets, and pilfer the English heritage! Luckily, God is on the side of England, as he satisfactorily proved at Agincourt. God and our right. Two ideas completely synonymous. And moreover, inscribed on our coat-of-arms. So rattle her through the rest of it, and have her burned, and not so much talk. Earlier on I was joking. I give it ten years, and this whole incident will have been forgotten.

CAUCHON. [*sighing*] God grant so, my lord.

WARWICK. Where had we got to?

FATHER. [*coming forward with his stick*] To where I was going out to find her, sitting under her tree, waiting to get herself into trouble, the little bitch. And I can tell you she'll be sorry she ever began it! [*He drags* JOAN *up by the wrists.*] What are you doing here, eh? Tell me what you're waiting about here for, when you know you ought to be indoors, eating your supper!

JOAN. [*stammering, shy at being surprised, raising her arm to protect her face*] I didn't know it was so late. I had lost count of the time.

FATHER. That's it, you lost count of the time! And what else have you lost that you daren't tell me? [*He shakes her abominably.*] Who made you forget it was so late? I heard you as I came along, calling out goodbye to somebody. Well, who was it?

JOAN. St. Michael, father.

FATHER. [*giving her a resounding slap on the face*] You make fun at your father, you'll be sorry! I won't have any girl of mine sitting out in the fields waiting for any man who wants to find her. You'll marry the decent fellow we choose for you, or I'll break every bone in your body!

JOAN. I've done nothing wrong, father: truthfully it was the blessed St. Michael who spoke to me.

FATHER. And when you can't hide your sinning any longer, and every day it grows bigger in you for all to see, and you've killed your mother with grief, and your brothers have to join the army to get away from the scandal in the village, it will be the Holy Ghost who brought it on us, I suppose? I'll tell the priest: not content with whoring, you have to blaspheme: and you'll be shut up in a convent on bread and water, my girl.

JOAN. [*kneeling before him*] Father, stop shouting, you can't hear what I say. I promise you, by our Saviour, I'm telling you the truth. They've been coming for a long time now to ask things of me. It is always at the mid-day Angelus or the evening Angelus; always when I'm praying, when I am least sinful and nearest to God. Above all doubt, surely it must be true. St.

Michael has appeared to me, and St. Margaret, and St. Catherine. They speak to me, and they answer when I question them, and each one says the same as the others.

FATHER. [*pulling her about*] Why should St. Michael speak to you, you little idiot? Does he speak to me? Natural enough, if he had something to say to us, he'd say it to me, the head of the family. Does he speak to our priest?

JOAN. Father, as well as shaking me and shouting at me, try to understand what I'm saying. I'm so alone, and they want me to do so much. For three years I've been trying not to believe them, but all that time they've been saying the same thing. These voices I hear: I can't go on fighting them all by myself. I've got to do what they say.

FATHER. The voices you hear? Do you want to drive me mad?

JOAN. They say it can't wait any longer; the time has come when I have to say yes.

FATHER. What can't wait any longer, idiot? What are they telling you to do, what you call these Voices? Voices! Well, it's better than being deaf!

JOAN. They tell me to go and save the realm of France which is in grave danger of being destroyed. Is it true?

FATHER. Heavens above! Of course the realm of France is in danger of being destroyed. It isn't the first time, and it won't be the last: and she always gets out of it. Leave it in God's hands; there's nothing you can do about it, you poor girl. Even a man can't do anything about it, unless he's a soldier.

JOAN. But I can. My voices have said so.

FATHER. [*laughing*] Oh, you can, can you? Dear me! You're sharper than all our great captains, of course, who can't do anything these days except be beaten every time they fight?

JOAN. Yes, father.

FATHER. Yes, father! Perhaps you're not a bad girl, but worse. You're a mad, idiot girl. What do you think you can do then, poor idiot?

JOAN. What my Voices tell me. I can ask the Squire of Beaudricourt for an armed escort. And when I've got my escort, I can go straight to the Dauphin at Chinon, to tell him that he's the rightful King; and I can lead him out at the head of the soldiers to save Orleans; and then I can persuade him to be consecrated with holy oil by the Archbishop, and then we can hurl the English into the sea.

FATHER. [*suddenly understanding*] Now you're explaining yourself, at last, you filthy little slut! You want to go off with the soldiers, like the lowest of the low?

JOAN. [*smiling mysteriously*] No, father, like the highest under God, riding first into the battle, and not looking back until I have saved France. [*suddenly sad*] And after that is done, what happens is God's will.

FATHER. I've heard enough shameless lying! I won't stand any more of it! I'll teach you what happens to girls who go chasing after soldiers, pretending to save France!

[*He savagely and unmercifully beats and kicks her.*]

JOAN. [*crying*] Stop, father, stop! stop!

[*The* FATHER *has taken off his belt, and starts to leather her, gasping with effort.*]

LADVENU. [*rising, very pale*] This must be stopped! He means to injure her.

CAUCHON. [*gently*] We can do nothing, Brother Ladvenu. At this part of the story we have never met Joan; we don't get to know her until the trial. We can only act our parts, each his own, good or bad, as they are written, and in his turn. And later on, you know, we shall do worse things than this to her. [*He turns to* WARWICK.] This domestic scene is not very pleasant to witness, my lord?

WARWICK. [*with a gesture*] Why not? We're firm believers in corporal punishment in England; it forms the character. I myself have been flogged many times as a boy; and I took it extremely well.

[*The* FATHER, *at last too exhausted to go on, wipes the sweat off his forehead, and shouts at* JOAN, *lying crumpled at his feet.*]

FATHER. There! you carrion! Do you still want to save France? [*He turns to the others, rather ashamed of himself.*] Well, sirs, what would you have done in my place if your daughter had said that to you?

MOTHER. [*coming forward*] Have you killed her?

FATHER. Not this time. But if she talks any more about going off with the soldiers, I'll drown that girl of yours in the river with my own hands, do you hear me? And if I'm nowhere about, I give her brother full permission to do it for me. [*He strides off.*]

[*The* MOTHER *bends over* JOAN *and dries her face.*]

MOTHER. Joan, my little Joan, my little Joan. Did he hurt you?

JOAN. [*giving a pathetic smile when she recognises her* MOTHER] Yes. He meant me to feel it.

MOTHER. He's your father, Joan; you must bear it patiently.

JOAN. [*in a small voice*] I do bear it, mother. I prayed while he beat me: prayed that our heavenly Father would forgive him.

MOTHER. [*shocked*] Our heavenly Father doesn't have to forgive fathers for beating their daughters. It's their right.

JOAN. And I prayed for him to understand.

MOTHER. [*fondling her*] Understand what, my silly one? Why did you have to tell him all this nonsense?

JOAN. [*in agony*] Someone has to understand; otherwise I'm by myself, and I have to face them alone!

MOTHER. [*rocking her in her arms*] Now, now, now, you don't have to upset yourself. You remember when you were little, we would rock away your nightmares together. But now you're nearly a woman: nearly too big to hold in my arms any more, and I can tell you it's no good breaking your heart to make men understand anything. All you can do is say "yes" to whatever they think, and wait till they've gone out to the fields. Then you can be mistress in your own house again. Your father's a good man; but if I didn't trick him sometimes for his own good I don't know where we should be. Who is it, Joan? You can tell your mother. Don't you even know his name, perhaps? And yet I don't know but it must be someone in the village. Why, your father might even agree to him; he's not against a good marriage for you. We might even be able to persuade him he chose the boy himself, the poor old stupid. You know what men are: roar a lot, and lay down the law, and bang you about: but, the same as with a bull, you can lead them by the nose.

JOAN. It isn't marriage that I have to think of, mother. The blessed St. Michael has told me I should leave the village, put on a man's clothes, and go and find his highness the Dauphin, to save the realm of France.

MOTHER. [*severely*] Joan, I speak nicely and gently to you, but I won't have you talking wickedness. And I won't have you put on a man's clothes, not if you beg at my grave. Have my daughter a man! You let me catch you, my goodness!

JOAN. But, mother, I should have to, if I'm to ride horseback with the soldiers. It's the blessed St. Michael who says so.

MOTHER. I don't care what the blessed St. Michael says, you shall never go off on a horse. Joan of Arc on a horse! It would be the talk of the village.

JOAN. But the lady of Vaucouleurs rides a horse to hawking.

MOTHER. You will not ride a horse, never! It isn't the station of life you were born to. Such grand ideas, indeed!

JOAN. But if I don't ride a horse, how can I lead the soldiers?

MOTHER. And you won't go with the soldiers, either, you wicked girl! I'd rather see you cold and dead. You see, how you make me talk the same as your father. There are some things we feel the same about. A daughter spins, and scrubs, and stays at home. Your grandmother never left this village, and neither have I, and neither will you, and when you have a daughter of your own, neither will she. [*She suddenly bursts into tears.*] Going off with the soldiers! Do you want to kill me?

JOAN. [*throwing herself into her mother's arms, crying too*] No, mother!

MOTHER. You do: I can see you do. And you'll destroy yourself in the end if you don't soon get these thoughts out of your head. [*exit*]

> [JOAN *straightens herself up, still in tears, while her* MOTHER *goes back to the* CROWD.]

JOAN. You see, holy St. Michael, it isn't possible; they won't ever understand. No one will. It is better that I should give up at once. Our Lord has said that we have to obey our father and mother. [*She speaks with the voice of the Archangel.*]

——But first, Joan, you have to obey God.

——But if God commands the impossible?

——Then you have to attempt the impossible, calmly and

quietly. It is a cause for pride, Joan, that God gives you something of His burden to carry.

[*After a pause.*]

——My Lord, do you think our Saviour can want a daughter to make her parents weep, and leave them alone to break their hearts, perhaps to die? That's hard to understand.

——He has said, I come to bring not peace, but a sword. I am come to set the brother against the sister and the son against the father. God came to bring struggle, Joan; not to make the way easy, but to make the way harder. He doesn't ask the impossible of everybody, but He does ask it of you. That is all. [JOAN *looks up, and says simply.*]——Well, I will go.

A VOICE. [*from somewhere out of the shadows behind*] Proud and arrogant!

JOAN. [*disturbed*] Who is calling me proud and arrogant?

[*After a pause, in the voice of the Archangel.*]

——It was you, Joan. And when you begin to do what God is asking, it will be what the world calls you. But if you give yourself humbly into the hands of God, you can bear this blame of pride.

——It is heavy to bear, my Lord!

——Yes, it is heavy. But God knows that you are strong.

[*A silence. She looks straight in front of her, and suddenly becomes a little girl again, happy and decided.*]

All right, then. It's all decided. I shall go and find my Uncle Durand. With him I always get my own way. He's as easy to manage as a tame sparrow. I shall kiss him on both cheeks, and on the top of his head, and sit on his lap, and he will say "Oh Lord, Oh Lord," and take me to Vaucouleurs!

BROTHER. You're a silly donkey! Why did you have to go and tell the old people all that stuff? Next time, if you give me a ha'penny, I won't say a word about where I saw you.

JOAN. [*leaping cheerfully at him*] Oh, so it was you who told them, you beastly little pig? Sneak, sneak, I'll give you a tweak! Tell tales out of school, duck him in a muddy pool! There's your halfpenny, lardy-head. Tell-tale-tit, your tongue shall be split, and all the children in the town shall have a little bit!

[*They fight like urchins. She chases straight across the stage towards* BEAUDRICOURT *who has come forward to take the centre of the stage.*]

BEAUDRICOURT. Well, what is it? What does she want? What is it you want, you infernal nuisance? What's this nonsensical story I hear——

[JOAN *collides head first with* BEAUDRICOURT's *great paunch. He is half winded, gives a yell of pain, grabs her by the arm and lifts her level with his nose, apoplectic with rage.*]

What the devil do you want, you horrible mosquito? What the devil do you mean, playing the fool outside my gates for three days on end? What the devil are these tales you've been telling the guards until their eyes pop out as far as their noses?

JOAN. [*breathless with her running and poised on tip-toe in the arms of the giant*] I want a horse, my lord, a man's clothes, and an escort, to go to Chinon to see his highness the Dauphin.

BEAUDRICOURT. And my boot, you want that, too, of course?

JOAN. If you like, my lord, and a good clout, as long as I get the horse as well.

BEAUDRICOURT. [*still holding her*] You know about me and you know what I want; the village girls have told you all about it, haven't they? They come along to see me, usually to beg for the life of a brother, or their old father who's been caught poaching on my lands. If the girl is pretty, I always hook him down off the gallows, being amiable at heart. If she's ugly, I hang the old chap, to make an example of him. But it's always the pretty ones who come; they manage to dig up one in the family somehow; with the admirable result that I have a fine reputation for benevolence in the neighbourhood. So now you know the rate of exchange, and we can come to terms.

JOAN. [*simply*] I don't know what you're trying to say, my lord. The blessed St. Michael sent me to you.

BEAUDRICOURT. [*crossing himself anxiously with his free hand*] You don't have to bring the saints into this. That was all right for the guards, to get you in to see me. But now you're here, and you can leave the saints in their proper places. And I wouldn't be surprised if you get your horse. An old jade for a young maid; it's a reasonable bargain. Are you a virgin?

JOAN. Yes, my lord.

BEAUDRICOURT. [*looking at her all the time*] I agree to the horse.

JOAN. That isn't all I want, my lord.

BEAUDRICOURT. A greedy child, I see! Well, go on; you're amusing me. If I pay well for my pleasures it helps me to believe I really want them. You understand where this conversation is leading?

JOAN. [*frankly*] No, my lord.

BEAUDRICOURT. Splendid. The bed's no place for brains. What else do you want beside the horse? The taxes are coming in very well this autumn; I don't mind being generous.

JOAN. An escort of men-at-arms, my lord, to accompany me to Chinon.

BEAUDRICOURT. [*freeing her, changing his tone*] Now listen to me, if we're to get on together: I may be easygoing, but I won't stand any impudence. I'm the master here and you're using up my patience fast. I can just as well have you whipped for forcing your way in here, and send you home with nothing except the marks on your backside. So behave yourself. Why do you want to go to Chinon?

JOAN. To find his highness the Dauphin.

BEAUDRICOURT. Well, well, you mean to get on! Why not the Duke of Burgundy while you're about it? In theory, you might have a sporting chance with him: the Duke's as hot as a buck rabbit. Whereas, as you probably know, the Dauphin when it comes to war and women . . . I don't know what you expect to get from him.

JOAN. An army, my lord, which I can lead to Orleans.

BEAUDRICOURT. Ah: if you're mad it's another thing altogether. I'm not getting involved in any scandal. [*He turns to the crowd upstage.*] Hey, there, Boudousse!

[A GUARD *comes forward.*]

Take her away and give her a ducking, and then lock her up. You can send her back to her father tomorrow evening. But no beating, I don't want any trouble; the girl's mad.

JOAN. [*calmly, held by the* GUARD] You can lock me up, my lord: I don't mind that; but when they let me out tomorrow evening I shall come back again. So it would be simpler if you let me talk to you now.

BEAUDRICOURT. Ten million thunders! Don't I frighten you?

JOAN. No, my lord. Not at all.

BEAUDRICOURT. [*to the* GUARD] Get back to your post! you don't need to stand about, listening to this.

[*The* GUARD *goes, and when he has gone* BEAUDRICOURT *asks uneasily*]

And why don't I frighten you? I frighten everybody.

JOAN. [*quietly*] You are very good, my lord.

BEAUDRICOURT. Good? Good? I've told you, that depends on the price.

JOAN. And what's more, very intelligent. There are many people I will have to convince before I can do everything my Voices want; so it's lucky the first person I have to deal with, the one everything really depends on, should turn out to be the most intelligent.

BEAUDRICOURT. [*slightly puzzled, asks in a casual voice while he pours himself some wine*] You're an odd girl, in your way. How did you come to notice that I'm intelligent?

JOAN. Because you're very handsome, my lord.

BEAUDRICOURT. [*with a furtive glance into the metal mirror beside him*] Oh, tush! I suppose, twenty years ago, I might say that I pleased the ladies; and I've taken care of myself, not let myself get too old too soon; that's all it is.—It's quite peculiar and unsettling to have a conversation like this with a farm girl I've never heard of, who happens to drop in like a stray kitten. [*He sighs.*] On the whole I vegetate here. My lieutenants are a poor bunch: hardly a brain between them. And while we're on the subject, what's this connection you find between intellect and beauty? I've usually heard quite the opposite: handsome people are always stupid; that's the general opinion.

JOAN. That's the opinion of the plain people, who like to believe God can't manage both things at once.

BEAUDRICOURT. [*flattered*] Ah, well, you've made a point there. But then, take myself for example. I know, as you so kindly say, I'm not one of the plain people; but I wonder sometimes, am I, after all, very intelligent? No, no, don't protest. It's a question

I have to ask now and again. I can tell you this, between ourselves, as you're not anyone in particular. Obviously I'm more
intelligent than my lieutenants, that's only natural, being officer in command. If that wasn't an established fact there
wouldn't be an army at all. But even so, I sometimes meet with
problems which I find very troublesome. They ask me to decide
something, some tactical or administrative point, and quite suddenly, I don't know why, my mind is a blank. There it is, nothing but a sort of fog. Mark you, nobody knows that. I get out of
it, without my face showing any change of expression; I make a
decision all right. And that's the essential thing when you're in
command, of course: make a decision, whatever it is. Until
you've had some experience you're apt to get flustered: but you
realise after a bit, it all amounts to the same thing, whatever you
decide. Still, I should like to see myself doing better. Vaucouleurs, as you see, is of no great size. I'm looking forward to
the day when I make a really important decision: one of those
momentous decisions, of great consequence to the nation: not a
question of somebody who hasn't paid his taxes, or half a dozen
prisoners to be hanged: but something a bit exceptional, which
would get me noticed and talked about higher up. [*He stops
dreaming, and looks at her.*] I don't know what in the world I'm
doing telling you all this. You can't do anything about it, and
God help you, you're half crazy into the bargain.

JOAN. [*smiling gently*] I know why. I knew it would happen, because they told me so. Listen, Robert—

BEAUDRICOURT. [*startled*] What are you doing calling me by my
Christian name?

JOAN. It's God's name for you, Robert. Now listen, Robert, and
don't bluster again, because it isn't any use. What is the important decision, which will get you noticed and talked about
higher up? I can tell you, Robert. It's me.

BEAUDRICOURT. What are you talking about?

JOAN. [*coming to him*] I'll tell you, if you'll listen. First of all, you
have to stop thinking of me as a girl, that's what is getting you
confused. And I don't mean much to you anyway, do I?

[*He hesitates, afraid of being cheated; she flares up.*]
Robert, if you want to help yourself, you have to help me, too!
When I tell you the truth, acknowledge it and say Yes: other-
wise we shall never get anywhere.

BEAUDRICOURT. [*muttering, rather shamefaced*] Well, no . . .

JOAN. [*severely*] What do you mean, no?

BEAUDRICOURT. I mean, yes, it's true. I'm not particular about you.
[*adding politely*] Though, mind you, you're a pretty enough
little thing . . .

JOAN. All right, you don't have to think you've upset me. I'm very
happy the point is cleared up. And now you can imagine you
have already given me the suit of clothes I asked for, and we can
discuss things together, sensibly and calmly, as man to man.

BEAUDRICOURT. [*still suspicious*] Discuss what?

JOAN. [*sitting on the edge of the table, finishing the dregs in the wine glass*] Your own important decision, my splendid Robert. Your great achievement which will make everyone take notice of you. Think of all of them, there at Bourges. They don't know whether they're praying or cursing, or which saint to turn to next. The English are everywhere. And you know the French army. Good boys, who have still got fight in them, but they're discouraged. They've got it into their heads that the English will always be the strongest, and there's nothing to be done. Dunois the Bastard; he's a good captain; intelligent, which is rare in the army, but no one listens to him any more, and he's getting tired of it. So he spends his days having a high old time with the women in the camp (and that's something else I shall have to deal with): and he's far too cock-a-hoop, like all bastards. "The affairs of France aren't his concern: let that milksop Charles get his country out of the tangle for himself." Then there's La Hire, and there's Xantrailles: prize angry bulls: they always want to charge in head first, slashing and thrusting like old heroes in the chronicles. They belong among the champions of single combat, who don't understand how to use their cannons, and always get killed to no purpose whatever, the way they did at Agincourt. They're wonderful at getting killed, but it isn't any help. That's true, isn't it, Robert. You can't treat war like a tournament. You have to win. You have to be cunning. [*She touches her forehead.*] You have to wage it here. With all your intelligence, Robert, you know that better than I do.

BEAUDRICOURT. I've always said so. Nowadays we don't think enough. Take my lieutenants: always spoiling for a fight, and that's all they can think of. And the men who know how to think get overlooked; nobody dreams of using them.

JOAN. Nobody. So they have to think for themselves. It's a lucky thing you have had such a tremendous idea. It's certain to alter everything.

BEAUDRICOURT. [*uneasily*] I have an idea?

JOAN. Don't question it, Robert; be very proud of it. Your brain is working at great speed, clearly and concisely. It's a sad thing to think that, in the whole of France at this moment, no one sees things clearly, except you.

BEAUDRICOURT. You believe so?

JOAN. I tell you so.

BEAUDRICOURT. And what is it I see?

JOAN. You see simply that the people of France have to be given a spirit and a faith. And it so happens that you have with you at this moment a young country girl. St. Michael has appeared to her, and St. Catherine and St. Margaret, or at least she says they have. You are not so sure about it, but for the time being it's not important. And this is where you show yourself to be so remarkable. You say to yourself: Here's a little peasant girl, of no consequence at all; all right. If by any chance she really has been sent by God, then nothing could stop her, and it can't be proved one way or the other whether God sent her or not. She certainly got in to see me, without my permission, and I've been listening to her for half an hour; nobody could deny that. And then, like a sword of lightning, the idea strikes home to you. You say to yourself: If she has the power to convince me, why shouldn't she convince the Dauphin and Dunois and the Archbishop? They're men, just as I'm a man; as a matter of fact, between ourselves, rather less intelligent. Moreover, why shouldn't she convince our soldiers that the English in the main are exactly like themselves, half courage and half a wish to save their skins; pummel them hard enough at the right moment, and you send them staggering out of Orleans. It's magnificent how you marshal the whole situation in your mind. What our fellows need, you are saying to yourself: what they need is someone to rouse their spirit and prove to them that God is still with them. This is where you show yourself a born leader, Robert.

BEAUDRICOURT. [*pitifully*] You think that?

JOAN. I know it. And very soon so will everyone else. Like all great politicians, you're a realist, Robert. You say to yourself: I, Beaudricourt, have my doubts about her coming from God, but I'll send her off to them, and if they think she is, it will have the same effect whether it's true or false. By a stroke of good luck my courier is leaving for Bourges tomorrow morning——

BEAUDRICOURT. Who told you that? It's a secret.

JOAN. I found it out. [*She continues.*] I pick half a dozen strong men for an escort, give her a horse and send her off with the courier. At Chinon, as far as I can see, she will work things out for herself. [*She looks at him admiringly.*] My word, my word, Robert!

BEAUDRICOURT. What?

JOAN. You have a marvellous intelligence to think of all that.

BEAUDRICOURT. [*wiping his forehead, worn out*] Yes.

JOAN. Only, please give me a quiet horse, because I don't know how to ride one yet.

BEAUDRICOURT. [*delighted*] You're going to break your neck, my girl!

JOAN. I don't think so. St. Michael will hold me on. I tell you what, Robert: I'll have a wager with you. I'll bet you a suit of clothes—the man's clothes which you still haven't said you'll give me—against a punch on the nose. Bring two horses into the courtyard and we'll gallop them together. If I fall off, you can lose faith in me. Is that fair? [*She offers him her hand.*] Agreed? And whoever doesn't pay up is a man of mud!

BEAUDRICOURT. [*getting up*] Agreed! I need to move about a bit. I wouldn't have believed how tiring it is to think so much. [*He calls.*] Boudousse!

[*Enter the* GUARD.]

GUARD. Do I take her away and give her a ducking, sir?

BEAUDRICOURT. No, you idiot! You fetch her some breeches, and bring us a couple of horses. We're taking a gallop together.

GUARD. What about the Council, sir? It's four o'clock.

BEAUDRICOURT. It can wait till tomorrow. Today I've used my brains quite enough.

> [*He goes.* JOAN *passes the astonished* GUARD *and sticks out her tongue. They lose themselves in the crowd up stage.*]

WARWICK. [*to* CAUCHON] I can see this girl had quality. Very entertaining, to watch her playing the old fish, didn't you think so?

CAUCHON. Rather too crude for my taste, my lord. Something subtler than that will be needed when she comes to deal with Charles.

WARWICK. My lord Bishop, the tricks that you and I use in our way of business aren't so remarkably different from hers. Whether we're ruling the world with a mace or a crozier, in the long run, we do it by persuading fools that what we make them think is their own opinion. No need for any intervention of God in that. Which is why I found it so entertaining. [*He bows politely towards the* BISHOP.] Entertaining, at least, if one isn't professionally concerned, of course, as you are. Have you faith yourself, my lord Bishop? Forgive my bluntness; but between ourselves. I'm interested to know.

CAUCHON. [*simply*] A child's faith, my lord. And that is why I shall make problems for you during the trial, and why we shall go as far as ever we can to save Joan, even though we have been sincere collaborators with the English rule, which seemed to us then the only reasonable solution to chaos. It was very easy for those who were at Bourges to call us traitors, when they had the protection of the French army. We were in occupied Rouen.

WARWICK. I don't like the word "occupied": You forget the Treaty of Troyes. You were quite simply on His Majesty's territory.

CAUCHON. In the midst of His Majesty's army, and the execution of His Majesty's hostages; submitting to the curfew, and the condescension of His Majesty's food-supplies. We were men, with the frailty of men, who wanted to go on living, and yet at the same time to save Joan if we could. It was not in any way a happy part that we were called upon to fill.

WARWICK. [*smiling*] There was nothing to stop you becoming martyrs, my dear fellow, if that would have made it more inspiring for you. My eight hundred soldiers were quite ready.

CAUCHON. We knew it. They took great pleasure in shouting their insults at us, hammering on the door with the butts of their halberds, to remind us they were there. We temporised for nine months before we would deliver Joan up to you; this little girl, forsaken by everyone; nine months to make her say Yes. Future times will be pleased to say we were barbarous. But I fancy, for all their fine principles, they will take to expediency faster than we did; in every camp.

WARWICK. Nine months, that's quite true. What a difficult confinement this trial has been. Our Holy Mother Church takes her time, when she's asked to give birth to a small matter of policy. But the nightmare is over. The mother and child are both doing well.

CAUCHON. I have pondered deeply over these things, my lord. The health of the mother, as you put it, is our one concern. And that is why, when we saw there could be no alternative, we sacrificed the child in good faith. Ever since that day of Joan's arrest, God has been dead to us. Neither she, whatever she may imagine, nor we, certainly, have heard Him any more. We have gone on, following our daily custom; our pre-eminent duty, to defend the old house, this great and wise human building which is all that remains to us in the absence of God. From the time we were fifteen years old, we were taught how to defend it. Joan had no such help, and yet, though her faith fell on dreadful days, when she was left alone by men and by God, she also has gone on, recovering at once after the single moment when she weakened, bearing herself with her curious mixture of humility and insolence, of grandeur and good sense, even up to execution and death. We weren't able to understand it then; we had our eyes buried in our mother's skirts, like children grown old. And yet, precisely in this loneliness, in the desert of a vanished God, in the privation and misery of the animal, the man is indeed great who continues to lift his head. Greatly alone.

WARWICK. Yes, well, no doubt. But if our business is politics we can't afford to brood about such men. We seem fated, as a rule, to meet them among the people we condemn to execution.

CAUCHON. [*quietly, after a pause*] It is a consolation to me sometimes to think of those old priests who, though they were deeply offended by her insolent answers, nevertheless, even with English swords at their back, tried for nine months not to commit the irreparable.

WARWICK. Enough of fine phrases, Bishop. Nothing is irreparable in politics. I tell you we shall raise a handsome statue to her in London one day, when the right time comes.

[*He turns towards the people of Chinon, who have been putting up a small palace set during this conversation.*]

But now let's come to Chinon, my lord. I've got a profound disrespect for that lounging little idler, Charles, but he's a character who never fails to amuse me.

[CHARLES *is with the two* QUEENS *and* AGNES SOREL.]

AGNES. But Charles, it's impossible! You can't let me appear at the ball looking such a frump. Your mistress in one of last year's steeple-hats.

QUEEN. And your Queen, Charles! The Queen of France! What would they say?

CHARLES. [*playing cup-and-ball, dropping into his throne*] They would say the King of France isn't worth a farthing. Which is quite right.

QUEEN. And think how the English court would laugh! The Duchess of Bedford, and Gloucester's wife, to say nothing of the Cardinal of Winchester's mistress! Now there's someone who

546 · *Jean Anouilh*

knows how to dress.

AGNES. Imagine, Charles, if they're wearing our newest fashions over there before we are!

CHARLES. At least they pay for them. Fashion is practically the only thing we can sell them: our fashions and our cooking. They are the only things which still give us some prestige with the foreigners.

YOLANDE. We have to defend this prestige. The girls aren't altogether wrong, Charles. It's most important there should be no question at this ball that ladies of the court of France are the best dressed women in the world. No one has ever been able to decide, remember, exactly where triviality begins. A steeple-hat the English have never seen before might be as good as a great victory.

CHARLES. [*with a dry laugh*] A victory which isn't going to stop them making off with Orleans, mother-in-law! According to the latest reports, Orleans is lost. And you think we should counterattack with a new fashion.

AGNES. Certainly. You've no idea what a dangerous blow it will be to their confidence. If you want a victory, Charles, here is one you can have for nothing.

CHARLES. For nothing? You make me laugh! How much did you say these steeple-hats would come to?

AGNES. Six thousand francs, my darling. That's next to nothing, when you remember they're completely embroidered with pearls. And the pearls are a good investment. When the steeple-hat isn't fashionable any more you can always sell the pearls at a profit and put it towards the army's back pay.

CHARLES. Six thousand francs! But where do you think I can find six thousand francs, you poor little fool?

QUEEN. [*softly*] Twelve thousand francs, Charles, because there are two of us, remember. You wouldn't want your mistress to be better dressed than your wife.

CHARLES. [*raising his hands to heaven*] Twelve thousand francs! They've gone out of their minds!

AGNES. Of course there's a simpler model, but I wouldn't advise it. You would forfeit the moral effect we should have on the stupid English. And that, after all, is the effect we're after.

CHARLES. Twelve thousand francs! Enough to pay three-quarters of Dunois's army. I don't understand how you can encourage them, mother-in-law, a woman of your good judgment.

YOLANDE. It's because I'm a woman of good judgment that I support them, Charles. Have you ever found me opposing anything that might be for your good or the dignity of the throne? I am the mother of your Queen, and yet it was I who introduced you to Agnes when I saw clearly how it might help you.

QUEEN. Please, mother, don't brag about it!

YOLANDE. Daughter, Agnes is a very charming girl who perfectly knows her place. It was quite as important to you as to me, that Charles should decide to become a man. And the kingdom had even more need of it than we had. A little more pride, dear girl; at the moment you have thoughts like a tradesman's wife! Before Charles could become a man he had to be given a woman.

QUEEN. [*acidly*] I was a woman, it seems to me, and his wife, what is more.

YOLANDE. I don't want to wound you, my dearest girl: but only slightly a woman. I can say this to you, because I was very much the same. Good sense, intelligence—more than you have—but that was all. Which is why I was always willing that the King, your father, should have his mistresses. Be his Queen, run his house, give him a son and heir, and leave the rest to other people. We can't do everything. And anyway, love is scarcely an honest woman's concern. We don't do well at it. Besides, you will thank me later on: one sleeps so much better alone. And Charles is far more manly since he knew Agnes. You are more manly, aren't you, Charles?

CHARLES. Yesterday I said "No" to the Archbishop. He tried to scare me, he sent La Tremouille in first to roar at me, and then he threatened to excommunicate me. All the old tricks. But I held firm.

AGNES. And thanks to whom?

CHARLES. Thanks to Agnes! We had rehearsed the whole scene in bed.

YOLANDE. What did the Archbishop want? You didn't tell me.

CHARLES. [*caressing* AGNES *absent-mindedly*] I can't remember. To give up Paris to the Duke of Burgundy, or something of the sort, in return for a year's truce. I might say it wouldn't really have meant anything at all. The Duke's in Paris already. But it was a matter of principle: Paris is France, and France is mine. At least I encourage myself to believe it so. So I said "No." The Archbishop made such a great fuss about it, the Duke must have promised him a pretty good sum.

AGNES. And what would have happened, Charles dear, if you had said "yes" in spite of me?

CHARLES. You would have had a headache for a week, and although, I suppose, if I had to, I could do without Paris, I couldn't do without you.

AGNES. Well, then, my darling, if I have helped you to save Paris, you can surely buy me the new steeple-hat, and one for your little Queen, too, because you have said some very hurtful things to her, without noticing it, as usual, you bad boy. You don't want me to be ill for a whole week, do you? You wouldn't know what to do with yourself.

CHARLES. All right, then, order your steeple-hats. I always have to say "yes" to somebody, if it isn't the Archbishop, it's you. But I may as well tell you, I haven't the least idea how I'm going to pay for them.

AGNES. You're going to sign a draft on the Treasury, Charles, and we will see what happens later. Come along, little Majesty, we will try them on together. Would you rather have this rose-coloured one, or the sky-blue? I think myself the rose is the one which will suit you best.

CHARLES. What do you mean? Have you got them already?

AGNES. You're very slow at understanding, my dearest! Surely you can see, if we were to have them in time for the ball we had to order them a month ago? But we were so sure you would say "yes," weren't we, Your Majesty? You shall see what a sensation this causes in London! It's a great victory for France, you know, Charles!

[*They take to their heels.*]

CHARLES. [*sitting back on his throne again*] There's nothing you can do but laugh, the way they harp on victories. La Tremouille, Dunois, they're all the same! There is always going to be a great victory. But everything has to be paid for, including great victories, these days. And suppose I can't afford a great victory? Suppose France is above my means? [*He takes his writing desk, muttering.*] Ah well, we shall see! I can always sign a draft on the Treasury. Let's hope it will please the tradesmen. The Treasury is empty, but there's nothing on this paper to say so. [*He turns towards the* QUEEN YOLANDE.] You wouldn't like a steeple-hat too, while I'm doing it? You needn't mind saying so. My signature isn't worth the ink it's written in.

YOLANDE. [*coming to him*] I'm past the age for steeple-hats, Charles. I want something else.

CHARLES. [*wearily*] To make me a great King, I know! It gets very boring in the end, everybody wants to make me a great King. Even Agnes. Even in bed. Imagine how jolly that is. I wish you would all try and get it into your heads, I'm an unimportant, insignificant Valois, and to make a King of me would need a miracle. I know my grandfather Charles was a great king; but he lived before the war when everything was much cheaper. Besides, he was rich. But my father and mother spent it all, so whether you like it or not, I can't afford to be a great king; I haven't got the money, and I haven't got the courage; you all know I haven't. Courage is far too dangerous in a world full of bullying brutes. That fat pig La Tremouille was in a raging temper the other day, and drew his sword on me. We were alone together: nobody there to defend me. He was quite prepared to give me a jab with it, the beastly hooligan! I only just had time to dodge behind the throne. So you see what we've come to. Drawing his sword on the King! I should have sent for the constable to arrest him, except that unfortunately he is the constable, and I'm not sure that I am the King. That's why they treat me like this; they know that I may be only a bastard.

YOLANDE. It's nobody but yourself, Charles, who is always saying so.

CHARLES. When I look at the legitimate faces all round me I hope I am a bastard. It's a charming day and age to live in, when a man isn't considered anybody unless he can brandish an eight-pound sword, and stroll about in a suit of armour which would

sink a galleon. When they put it on me, I'm welded into the
ground; a great help to my dignity. And I don't like fighting. I
don't like hitting, and I don't like being hit. And what's more,
if you want to know, I'm frightened of it. [*He turns towards her
crossly.*] What other impossibilities do you want me to do?

YOLANDE. I want you to receive this girl from Vaucouleurs. She
says God sent her; and furthermore she says she has come to
deliver Orleans. The people can think and talk of nothing else,
and they're only waiting now to hear that you agree to receive
her.

CHARLES. Then they're going to find I'm not as ridiculous as they
think I am. Give audience to an eccentric peasant girl? Really,
mother-in-law, for a woman of good sense you disappoint me.

YOLANDE. I've given you Agnes, because I thought it was for your
good, Charles, though against my interest as a mother. Now I
tell you to accept this girl from Domremy. She seems to possess
some exceptional power, or so everybody says, which is a point
to be considered.

CHARLES. [*bored*] I don't like virgins. I know, you're going to tell
me again that I'm not virile enough. But they frighten me. And,
anyway, I have Agnes, who still pleases me quite well enough.
Don't think I'm reproaching you, but for someone who is a
queen and my mother-in-law, you have a very remarkable vocation.

YOLANDE. [*smiles*] You don't understand me, Charles, or else you're
pretending not to. I'm asking you to take this peasant girl into
your counsel, not into your bed.

CHARLES. In that case, in spite of all the respect I owe you, I have
to tell you you're absolutely mad. Into my council, with the
Archbishop, and La Tremouille, who believes that he sprang
from Jupiter's thigh? Do you want them to knock my head off?

YOLANDE. [*gently*] I think a peasant in your counsels is exactly what
you all need. The nobility governs the kingdom, which is as it
should be; God has entrusted it into their hands. But, without
presuming to criticise the wisdom of providence, I wonder sometimes that he hasn't given them what he gives so generously to
humbler men, a better measure of simplicity and common sense.

CHARLES. [*ironically*] And courage!

YOLANDE. [*gently*] And courage, Charles.

CHARLES. As far as I can understand you, you recommend turning
the government over to the people? To the good people who
have all the virtues. You've read the history of tyrants, I suppose?

YOLANDE. No, Charles. In my day, knowledge was not encouraged
in young women.

CHARLES. But I've read it: the endless procession of horrors and
scandals; and I amuse myself sometimes by imagining how the
procession will go on in the future. They will certainly try what
you recommended. They'll try everything. Men of the people
will become masters of the kingdoms, maybe for centuries, the

time it takes for a meteor to cross the sky; and that will be the time for massacres and the most monstrous errors. And what will they find, at the great account, when all is done? They'll find that not even the most vile, capricious, and cruel of the princes have cost the world as much as one of these virtuous men. Give France a powerful man of action, born of the people, whose ambition is to make the people happy, whatever it may entail, and see how they'll come to wish to God they had their poor lazy Charles back again, with his everlasting game of cup-and-ball. At least I've no theories about organizing the happy life. A negative virtue, perhaps, but more valuable than they realise yet.

YOLANDE. You should give up this cup-and-ball game, Charles, and this habit of sitting upside down on your throne. It's no behaviour for a king.

CHARLES. You would be sensible to let me be as I am. When the ball misses the cup, it drops on to my nose and nobody else's. But sit me on the throne the right way up, with the orb in one hand and the sceptre in the other, then whenever I make a mistake the ball will drop on everybody's nose.

[*Enter the* ARCHBISHOP *and* LA TREMOUILLE. *He sits like a king on his throne.*]

CHARLES. Archbishop, Constable, you've come at the perfect moment. I am starting to govern. You see I have here the orb and the sceptre.

ARCHBISHOP. [*taking his eye-glass*] It's a cup-and-ball!

CHARLES. Unimportant, Archbishop; symbolism, after all. That isn't something I have to teach a prince of the Church. Your announced visit to me, my lord, must mean you wish for an audience.

ARCHBISHOP. I haven't come to be playful, Sire. I know very well the minority opinion, which cares to intrigue and agitate on every possible occasion, is trying to persuade you to see this notorious peasant girl you have heard of. The Constable and I are here, Sire, to say it is not our intention to admit her.

CHARLES. [*to* QUEEN YOLANDE] What did I tell you?——I have taken note of what you recommend, my lord, and I shall consider what course to follow. Now you may go; the audience is over.

ARCHBISHOP. I will remind you, Sire, we are not here for your amusement.

CHARLES. Whenever I talk like a king for a moment, they always think I'm amusing myself. [*He lies back on his throne with the cup and ball.*] Very well, then; leave me to amuse myself in peace.

ARCHBISHOP. This girl's miraculous reputation is spreading across the country ahead of her; it was here before she arrived; it's already causing excitement in besieged Orleans. God has taken her by the hand and leads her: this is the story. God has decided that she shall save France and drive the English back across the sea;

and other such nonsense. God will expect you to receive her into the royal presence, and nothing is going to prevent her. I don't know why they're so anxious that God should concern Himself in their affairs. And naturally she has performed miracles; it would have surprised me more if she hadn't. A soldier called her I don't know what when she arrived at Chinon. She told him that he was wrong to swear, because soon he would be standing before his Redeemer. And an hour later this boorish fellow missed his footing, and fell into the well in the servants' yard, and drowned himself. That blundering step of a drunkard has done more for the girl's reputation than a great victory ever did for Dunois. Apparently the opinion is unanimous, from the lowest kennel-boy to the highest lady in your court: only this wretched girl can save us. A preposterous infatuation!——I speak to you, sir, of the gravest matters of the realm, and you play at cup-and-ball.

CHARLES. My lord, let us be clear about this. Do you want me to play at cup-and-ball, or do you want me to govern? [*He sits up.*] Do you want me to govern?

ARCHBISHOP. [*disturbed*] Sir, we don't ask you to go as far as that. We wish you to notice and appreciate the efforts we are making . . .

CHARLES. I assure you, I notice them; I appreciate them; and I find them quite useless, my lord. Everyone expects me to see this girl, isn't it so?

ARCHBISHOP. I haven't said that!

CHARLES. Well, I'm not at all curious to see her. I'm not fond of new faces; we have to know too many people as it is. And messengers from God aren't usually very enlivening. But I want to be a good king, and content my people. I shall see this peasant girl, if only to take the wind out of her sails. Have you spoken to her yourself, Archbishop?

ARCHBISHOP. I have other things to do, sir, when you consider that I carry the whole burden of the kingdom's affairs.

CHARLES. Quite so. And I have nothing else to do except play at cup-and-ball. So I shall see her to save you the trouble: and I shall tell you frankly what I think of her. You can trust me to do that, my lord. I know you don't easily credit me with any qualities worth having, but at least you will agree that I'm a frivolous man: a quite useful condition for this interview. I'm very soon bored by anyone who takes himself seriously. I am going to receive this girl, and if she can make me want to listen to her talking about the welfare of the kingdom, which no one has ever done yet without making me yawn, then there's no doubt about her performing miracles.

ARCHBISHOP. [*muttering*] A peasant girl in the presence of the king!

CHARLES. [*simply*] You will remember, I think, that some of all kinds have been admitted to my presence. I don't mean M. de la Tremouille, who springs, of course, direct from Jupiter's thigh.

But, for instance, yourself, my lord:—I think I remember being told you were the grandson of a wine merchant. There is no reproach in that. What could be more natural? You have carried the wine from your cellars to the altar. And as for myself, as you frequently have told me, it's a moot point whether I'm the son of a king. So we'd better not play the ancestry game, my lord, or we shall be making ourselves altogether ridiculous. [*to* QUEEN YOLANDE] Come with me, and help me get ready for her. I've thought of a very amusing joke. We can disguise one of the pages in a royal doublet, if we can find one that isn't too shabby; sit him on the throne, which I am sure he will manage better than I can, and I shall hide myself in the crowd. Then we can listen to a solemn harangue from the messenger of God to a pageboy! It ought to be irresistible, don't you think so?

[*They go out.*]

ARCHBISHOP. [*to* LA TREMOUILLE] Do we let him do it? It's a game to him, like everything else. It shouldn't be dangerous. And once he has seen her, the people may very well calm down again. In a fortnight they will have found some other messenger of God to infatuate them, and the girl will be forgotten.

LA TREMOUILLE. I command the army, Archbishop, and I can only tell you, the official doctor of the nation has nothing more to say. We're now entirely in the hands of the bone-setters, the faith-healers, the quacks. In other words, what you call messengers from God. What do we risk?

ARCHBISHOP. [*anxiously*] Constable, wherever God concerns himself everything is a risk. If the unlikely should be true, and He really has sent this girl to us: if, in fact, He means to take our part, then our troubles are only beginning. We shall be shaken out of all custom and orthodoxy, contrive to win four or fve battles, and then will come the problems, the complications. Long experience as a man, both in the church and in government, teaches me that never, never must we draw God's attention to us. It is better to remain very small, Constable, very small and unnoticed.

[*The* COURTIERS *take their places with the* QUEENS; *a* PAGE *sits on the throne;* CHARLES *slips into the crowd. The* ARCHBISHOP *concludes in an undertone. Everybody is grouped round the throne where the little* PAGE *sits;* CHARLES *is in the crowd.* JOAN *enters alone, looking very small and simple among the armour and the court fashions. They make a way for her to pass to the throne. She is about to kneel, hesitates, blushes, looking at the* PAGE.]

YOLANDE. [*whispering in her ear*] You must kneel, child, before the king.

[JOAN *turns towards her, puzzled; then suddenly she looks at all the silent people who are watching her, and advances silently in the crowd, who make way for her. She goes towards* CHARLES, *who tries to hide from her. When he sees that she is about to reach him, he almost runs to hide be-*

*hind the others, but she follows him, almost running, too.
She finds him in a corner and falls on her knees.*]

CHARLES. [*embarrassed in the silence*] What do you want with me?

JOAN. Gentle Dauphin, I am called Joan the Maid. God has brought
me to you, to tell you that you will be anointed and crowned in
the city of Rheims. You will be viceroy of the King of Heaven,
who is King of France.

CHARLES. [*awkwardly*] Well, that is very nice. But Rheims belongs
to the English, I understand. How would I get there?

JOAN. [*still on her knees*] By your own strength, gentle Dauphin;
by beating them. We will start with Orleans, and then we can
go to Rheims.

LA TREMOUILLE. [*coming up*] Little lunatic! Isn't that what all the
army commanders have been trying to do for months? I am the
head of them; I know something about it. And they haven't got
there.

JOAN. [*getting up*] I will get there.

LA TREMOUILLE. Will you indeed? And how will you get there?

JOAN. With the help of God Who sends me.

LA TREMOUILLE. I see. So God has arranged for us to retake Orleans?

JOAN. Yes, my lord; and to hunt the English out of France.

LA TREMOUILLE. [*jeering*] A very beautiful thought! But God can't
convey His own messages Himself? He has to have you to do it
for Him?

JOAN. Yes, my lord.

ARCHBISHOP. [*approaching her*] Young woman . . .

[JOAN *sees him, kneels and kisses the hem of his robe. He
gives her his ring to kiss, and motions her to rise.*]

You say that God wishes to deliver the kingdom of France. If
such is indeed His will, He has no need of armies, or you to
lead them.

JOAN. Oh, my lord, does God care for those who have no care?
First the soldiers must fight, and then He will give the victory.

CHARLES. How did you recognise me without my crown?

JOAN. Gentle Dauphin, it was a good joke to put your crown on
this boy, it doesn't take much to see that he's really a little nobody.

CHARLES. You're mistaken. The boy is the son of a great lord.

JOAN. Great lords are not the king.

CHARLES. [*troubled*] Who told you I was the king? I don't look
like a king.

JOAN. God told me, gentle Dauphin: Who appointed you from the
beginning of time, through your father and your grandfather and
all the line of kings, to be viceroy of His kingdom.

[*The* ARCHBISHOP *and* LA TREMOUILLE *exchange a look of
annoyance.*]

ARCHBISHOP. Sire. The girl's answers are interesting: they show a
remarkable good sense. But in a matter as delicate as this you
cannot surround yourself with precautions too strict or thorough.

A commission of learned theologians must question and examine her very closely. We will then discuss their report in Council, and decide if it is timely for you to give this girl a longer hearing. There's no need for her to importune you any further today. First of all I shall interrogate her myself. Come here, my daughter.

CHARLES. Not at all. [*He stops* JOAN.] Stay where you are. [*He turns to the* ARCHBISHOP, *taking* JOAN's *hand to give himself courage.*] I was the one she recognised. I was the one she spoke to. I wish you to leave me alone with her: all of you.

ARCHBISHOP. This blunt dismissal, sir: it is quite extraordinary, it is improper! Apart from all else, you should at least think of your own security . . .

CHARLES. [*fearful for a moment, but he looks at* JOAN *and pulls himself together*] I am the only judge of that. [*He recites:*] Through my father, my grandfather, and all the line of kings . . . [*He winks at* JOAN.] Isn't that right? [*He turns to the others, imperturbable.*] Leave us, my lords, when the king commands it.

[*They* ALL *bow, and go.* CHARLES *keeps his regal pose for a moment, and then explodes with laughter.*]

They've gone, they've gone! Did I do that, or did you? It's the first time in my life I have ever made myself obeyed. [*He looks at her, suddenly anxious.*] I hope there is nothing in what the Archbishop was trying to suggest. You haven't come here to kill me? There isn't a knife hidden about you somewhere?

[*He looks at her, and she smiles gravely.*]

No. You reassure me. I had forgotten, among all these pirates in my court, how reassuring a smile could be. Are there many of you in my kingdom with such honest faces?

JOAN. [*still smiling gravely*] Yes, sir, very many.

CHARLES. But I never see you. Only ruffians, hypocrites, and whores: my entourage. Though of course there's my little queen, who has a certain amount of charm but not many brains. [*He goes back to his throne, his feet on the rail, and sighs.*] Well, there you are. I suppose now you have to start boring me. You're going to tell me to become a great king.

JOAN. [*gently*] Yes, Charles.

CHARLES. Don't let's bother. We shall have to stay shut up here together for an hour at least, to impress them. If you talk to me about God and the kingdom of France for an hour, I shall never last out. I propose instead we talk about something quite different. Do you play cards?

JOAN. [*opening her eyes wide*] I don't know what it is.

CHARLES. It's an amusing game they invented for Papa, to distract him during his illness. You'll see, I shall teach you. I've played so often now I've got tired of it, but I think you may like it if you've never played before. [*He goes to rummage about in a chest.*] I hope they haven't stolen them from me. They steal everything here. And a pack of cards, you know, costs a lot of money. Only the royal princes have them. Mine were left to me by my father. I shall never have enough money to buy myself another pack. If those devils have stolen them . . . No, here they are. [*He returns with the cards.*] You knew Papa was mad, did you? Sometimes I hope I'm really his son, so that I can be sure I'm the true king; and then, at other times I hope I'm a bastard, so that I don't have to dread going mad before I'm thirty.

JOAN. [*gently*] And which of the two would you prefer, Charles?

CHARLES. [*turning in surprise*] Good heavens, are you calling me Charles? This is turning out to be a most surprising day. I believe I'm not going to be bored, for once; it's marvellous.

JOAN. Not now, Charles, or ever again.

CHARLES. Extraordinary.—Which of the two would I prefer? Well, I suppose on the days when I have some courage I would rather take the risk of going mad, and be the true king; and on the days when I haven't I would rather let everything go, and retire on my twopence-ha'penny to somewhere abroad, and live in peace. Have you met Agnes?

JOAN. No.

CHARLES. [*shuffling the cards*] No, of course you haven't. Retiring wouldn't do for her. And I couldn't afford her then. She is always wanting me to buy her things.

JOAN. [*suddenly grave*] And today: are you feeling brave today, Charles?

CHARLES. Today? [*He ponders a moment.*] Yes, it seems to me I feel fairly brave. Not very, but fairly. Well, you saw how I packed off the Archbishop.

JOAN. How would you like to be brave all the time, from today onwards?

CHARLES. [*leaning forward, interested*] Do you mean you know the secret?

JOAN. Yes.

CHARLES. Are you some sort of a witch? You needn't be afraid to tell me; it isn't something I object to. I promise you I won't repeat it. Those executions horrify me. I was taken once to see them burn a heretic. I was sick all night.

JOAN. [*smiling*] No, I'm not a witch, Charles. But I know the secret.

CHARLES. Would you sell it to me, without letting the others know about it? I'm not very well off, but I could make you a draft on the Treasury.

JOAN. I will give it to you, Charles.

CHARLES. [*suspiciously*] For nothing?

JOAN. Yes.

CHARLES. Then I'm not interested. A secret is either no good, or far beyond my means. Disinterested people are too rare, at any price. [*He shuffles the cards.*] I've taken to behaving like a fool, so that I shall be left in peace, but I know more than you think I know. I'm not so easily gulled.

JOAN. You know too much.

CHARLES. Too much? You can never know too much.

JOAN. Sometimes; it is possible.

CHARLES. I have to defend myself. You would soon see, if you were here in my position! If you were alone, among a lot of brutes whose one idea is to stab you when you are least expecting it, and if you've been born a weak sort of fellow, as I was, you would soon realise the only way to steer safely through it is by being more clever than they are. And I am; much more clever. Which is why I more or less hang on to my throne.

JOAN. [puts her hand on his arm] I shall be with you now, defending you.

CHARLES. Do you think you will?

JOAN. And I'm strong. I'm not afraid of anything.

CHARLES. [sighing] You're very lucky! [He deals the cards.] Sit down on the cushion; I'm going to teach you to play cards.

JOAN. [smiling, sitting close to the throne] All right. And then I'll teach you something.

CHARLES. What?

JOAN. Not to be afraid. And not to know too much.

CHARLES. Now pay attention. You see the cards, and these pictures on them? There's something of everything here: knaves, queens, kings: the same as in the world: and here are the commoners: spades, hearts, clubs, diamonds. Those are the troops. There are plenty of them, you can lose as many as you like. You deal the cards without looking at them, and fate either gives you a good hand, or a bad hand, and then the battle begins. The higher cards can capture the lower cards. Which do you think is the strongest?

JOAN. The king is.

CHARLES. Well, he is almost the strongest, but there's one stronger still. This card here, for instance, the single heart. Do you know what it's called?

JOAN. God, of course: because He's the only one who commands kings.

CHARLES. [annoyed] No, it isn't at all. For goodness sake let God alone for five minutes. For the time being we're playing cards. It's called the ace.

JOAN. Then the game of cards is ridiculous. What can be stronger than a king, except God?

CHARLES. The ace, in fact. The ace, or God if you like; but there's one in each camp. You see: ace of hearts, ace of spades, ace of clubs, ace of diamonds. One for each of them. You're not so intelligent as I thought you were. Do you think the English don't say their prayers, as well as us? And, what's more, to a God who protects them, and gives them victories over us. And my cousin, the Duke of Burgundy, he has a God for Burgundy, in just the same way: a smallish one, maybe, but a bold one, a cunning one, who gets my cousin out of difficulties very well. God is with everybody, my girl. He marks the points, and keeps the score. But, in the long run, He plumps for the people who have the most money and the biggest armies. So why do you imagine He should be with France, now that France has got nothing at all?

JOAN. Perhaps for that reason: because she has nothing at all, Charles.

CHARLES. [*shrugging his shoulders*] You don't know Him!

JOAN. I do. God isn't with the strongest; He is with the bravest. There's the difference. God hasn't any love for cowards.

CHARLES. Then He doesn't love me. And if He doesn't love me, why do you expect me to love Him? All He had to do was to give me some courage. I don't ask for anything better.

JOAN. [*severely*] Do you think He's your nurse, with no one else to think about but you? Why can't you make the best of what you have got; I know He has made you weak in the legs . . .

CHARLES. You've noticed that? He ought to have managed better than that. Particularly with the present fashions. It's because of my legs that Agnes can't bring herself to love me. If He had only an eye for proportion, and hadn't given me my big knees as well . . .

JOAN. Well, I grant you that. He didn't go to much trouble over your knees. But there was something else that more concerned Him; His eye was on your head and your heart, Charles, where you most resemble Him. And there it is He makes you free, to be whatever you will. You can use them to play cards, or to outmanœuvre the Archbishop for a time, though in the end you have to pay for it; or else you can use them to make the house of Valois glorious again, and remake the kingdom. Your little queen gave you a son, Charles. What are you going to leave the boy when you die? This wretched scrap of France, nibbled by the English? If so, when he grows up, the boy will be able to say, as you did just now, that God hasn't any interest in him. You are God, Charles, to your little son; and you have to take care of him.

CHARLES. [*groans*] But I keep telling you, everything frightens me.

JOAN. [*coming nearer to him*] You shall have the secret now, Charles. But don't give me away when I tell you first that everything frightens me, too. Do you know why M. de la Tremouille isn't afraid of anything?

CHARLES. Because he is strong.

JOAN. No. Because he is stupid. He never imagines anything. Wild boars, and bulls, and barrel-headed oxen are never afraid of anything, either. And I tell you this: it has been even more complicated for me to get to you than it will be for you to get to Orleans and refashion your kingdom. I had to explain to my father, and that was a bad enough beginning. He wouldn't believe I wanted anything, except to go dragging off after the soldiers; and so he beat me, and, my goodness, the English don't hit any harder than he does. And then I had to make my mother cry; there was nothing worse than that; and then to convince

Beaudricourt, who didn't want to think of anything except adding one more to his list of sins. Don't think I haven't been afraid. I was afraid all the time, from the very beginning.

CHARLES. Then how have you done it?

JOAN. Just as I should have done without the fear. That's all the difficulty there is, Charles. Try it once, and see. You say: one thing is obvious, I'm frightened, which is nobody's business but mine, and now on I go. And on you go. And if you see something ahead which nothing can overcome . . .

CHARLES. Like Tremouille enjoying one of his rages—

JOAN. Yes, if you like. Or the unshakeable English facing Orleans in their fortress built like rocks. You say: Here it is—they outnumber us, their walls are as thick as the length of a giant's arm, their cannons out-thunder thunder, their arrows out-rain the rain. So be it. I'm frightened. Now I've realised how frightening it is, on we go.—And the English are so astonished, they begin to be frightened themselves, and you get through! You get through because you think deeper, imagine more, and get your fear over first. That's the secret of it.

CHARLES. But is it always so successful?

JOAN. Always. As long as you turn and face what frightens you. But the first step has to be yours; He waits for that.

CHARLES. [after a pause] You think we could try your secret?

JOAN. We have to try it.

CHARLES. [suddenly frightened by his temerity] Tomorrow, perhaps. By tomorrow I shall have had time to prepare for it.

JOAN. No, Charles; now; you're ready now.

CHARLES. Do you mean that I'm ready to call the Archbishop and La Tremouille? That I'm ready to tell them that I've given you command of the army, and then sit calmly back and watch their faces?

JOAN. Absolutely ready.

CHARLES. I'm scared out of my life.

JOAN. Then the worst is over. One thing is essential: you mustn't be still frightened after you've called them. Are you sure you are as frightened as you possibly can be?

CHARLES. [his hand on his belly] Oh yes, I agree with you.

JOAN. Wonderful! That's an enormous advantage. When they start to be frightened, you will have got over it already. The whole scheme is to be afraid first, before the battle begins. You'll soon see. I'll call them. [She calls offstage.] My Lord Archbishop, M. de la Tremouille! M. le Dauphin wishes to speak to you.

CHARLES. [taken by panic] Oh dear, I'm so frightened! Goodness, goodness, I'm so frightened.

JOAN. That's it, that's right Charles; more frightened still!

CHARLES. [his teeth chattering] I can't be more frightened: it's impossible!

JOAN. Then we have the victory! God has joined you; He says "Charles is afraid, but still he calls them." In eight hours we shall hold Orleans!

[*Enter the* ARCHBISHOP *and* LA TREMOUILLE, *surprised.*]

ARCHBISHOP. You called us, your Highness?

CHARLES. [*suddenly, after a last look at* JOAN] Yes: I've come to a decision, my lord, and it also concerns you, M. de la Tremouille. I am giving the command of my royal army to this Maid here. [*He suddenly shouts.*] If you don't agree, M. de la Tremouille, I must ask you to surrender your sword to me. You are under arrest!

[LA TREMOUILLE *and the* ARCHBISHOP *stand petrified.*]

JOAN. [*clapping her hands*] Well done! Now you know how simple it is! Do you see their faces, Charles? Look at them: do look at them! Who is frightened now, Charles?

[*She bursts out laughing;* CHARLES *begins to laugh as well: they rock with laughter, unable to stop; and the* ARCHBISHOP *and* LA TREMOUILLE *seem turned to stone.*

JOAN *drops suddenly on to her knees, crying* Thank you, God!]

CHARLES. [*also kneeling*] On your knees, M. de la Tremouille, on to your knees! And give us your blessing, Archbishop: no hesitating: give us your blessing! Now that we've all been thoroughly frightened, we must make straight for Orleans!

[LA TREMOUILLE *is on his knees, stupefied by the blow. The* ARCHBISHOP, *bewildered, mechanically gives his blessing.*]

Part Two

WARWICK. [*laughing and coming forward with* CAUCHON] In point of fact, that wasn't exactly how it happened. They called a meeting of the Council, and discussed the matter for hours. In the end they agreed to use Joan as a sort of flagpole to nail their colours to: an attractive little mascot, well qualified to charm the general public into letting themselves be killed. The best we could do to restore the balance was to treble the men's drink ration before they went into action, though it had nothing like as good an effect. We started being beaten from that time on, against all the laws of strategy. I know some people have said there was nothing miraculous about that. They maintain that our system of isolated forts around Orleans was ludicrous, and all the enemy had to do was attack: which is what Joan made them agree to try. But that's not true. Sir John Talbot was no fool. He knew his job thoroughly well; as he has proved again and again, both before this regrettable business, and since. His system of fortification was theoretically impregnable. No: we must have the grace to admit there was more in it than that: a strong element of the imponderable—or God, as you might say, my Lord Bishop—which the rules of strategy don't provide for. Without question, it was Joan: singing like a lark in the sky over the heads of your French armies on the march. I am very fond of France, my Lord: which is why I should be most unhappy if we lost her. This lark singing in the sky, while we all

560 · Jean Anouilh

take aim to shoot her down: that seems very like France to me.
Or at least like the best of her. In her time she has had plenty
of fools, rogues and blunderers; but every now and then a lark
sings in her sky, and the fools and the rogues can be forgotten.
I am very fond of France.

CAUCHON. [*gently*] But still you take aim and shoot her down.

WARWICK. A man is a mass of contradictions, my lord Bishop. It
isn't unusual in him to kill what he loves. I love animals, but
I hunt them, too. [*He suddenly gets up, looking stern. He raps
with his stick on his boot, and makes a sign to* TWO SOLDIERS
who come forward.] Come along now: the lark has been caught.
The cage of Compiègne has shut her in. The singing is over;
and Charles and his court are leaving her there, without a
second glance. They're going back to their old political methods,
now that their little mascot isn't bringing them luck any more.
[*Indeed,* CHARLES, LA TREMOUILLE, *and the* ARCHBISHOP
have slyly got up and edged away from JOAN, *who is on her
knees, praying. She starts up astonished to be alone, and
sees* CHARLES *deserting her. The* GUARDS *begin to drag her
away.*]

CAUCHON. Your king has left you, Joan! There's no reason now to
go on defending him. Yesterday we read you the letter he has
sent to every town, telling them to say he repudiates you.

JOAN. [*after a pause, quietly*] He is my king.

CHARLES. [*in a low voice to the* ARCHBISHOP] That letter is going
to be thrown in our teeth for a long time yet.

ARCHBISHOP. [*also aside*] It had to be, sir: it was absolutely necessary. At this juncture, the cause of France cannot be linked
in any way with Joan's.

CAUCHON. Joan: listen carefully, and try to understand what I'm
saying. Your king is not our king. A treaty in rightful and due
form has made Henry the Sixth of Lancaster King of France and
England. Your trial is not a political trial. We are simply trying
with all our power and with all our faith to lead a lost sheep
back into the fold of our Holy Mother Church. But as men,
Joan, we consider ourselves to be faithful subjects of His Majesty
King Henry. We have as great and sincere a love of France as
you: and because of that we recognise him as our sovereign: so
that France can rise up again out of her ruins, dress her wounds,
and be free of this appalling, interminable war which has
drained all her strength. The useless resistance of the man you
call your king, and his absurd pretensions to a throne which isn't
his, appear to us to be acts of rebellion and terrorism against
a peace which was almost assured. The puppet whom you served
is not our master, be certain of that.

JOAN. Say what you like, you can't alter the truth. This is the king
God gave you. Thin as he is, with his long legs and his big,
bony knees.

CHARLES. [*to the* ARCHBISHOP] This is really most disagreeable.

ARCHBISHOP. For a little while we have to have patience; but they mean to hurry through the trial and burn her, and after that we shall not be disturbed. You must surely admit, sir, the English have done us a good turn, making themselves responsible for her arrest and execution. If they hadn't done it, we ourselves should have had to, some day or other. She was becoming impossible!

[*They withdraw, unnoticed.*]

CAUCHON. We know by many of your answers, insolent though they were, that you're not slow of understanding, Joan. Put yourself for a moment in our place. How can you suppose that we, men with most earnest human convictions, can agree that God has sent you to oppose the cause we defend? How can you think, only because you say voices have spoken to you, that we should believe God to be against us?

JOAN. You will know when we have beaten you.

CAUCHON. [*shrugging*] You are answering like a self-willed, obstinate child. Considering the question now as priests and defenders of our Holy Mother Church, have we any better reason to put faith in what you tell us? Do you think you are the first who has heard Voices?

JOAN. No, of course not.

CAUCHON. Neither the first, nor the last, Joan. Now, do you believe that each time a little girl goes to her village priest and says: I have seen some saint, or the Blessed Virgin, I have heard Voices which have told me to do one thing or another—that her priest should believe and encourage her: and how long then would the Church still remain?

JOAN. I don't know.

CAUCHON. You don't know; but you are full of good sense, and that is why I am trying to lead you to reason with me. Have you not been in command in battle, Joan?

JOAN. Yes, I was in command of hundreds of good soldiers who followed me, and believed me.

CAUCHON. You were in command. And if on the morning of some attack one of your soldiers had heard voices persuading him to attack by another gate than the one you had chosen, or not to attack at all, what would you have done?

JOAN. [*speechless for a moment, before she suddenly bursts out laughing*] My lord Bishop, it's easy to see you're a priest! It's clear you don't know much about our men. They can drink and swear and fight, but they're not ones for hearing Voices!

CAUCHON. A joke is no answer, Joan. But you gave your answer before you spoke, in the second of hesitation when you were held and disarmed by what I said to you. And you see it is true: that the Church militant is an army in a world still overrun by infidels and the powers of evil. The Church owes obedience to our Holy Father the Pope and his bishops, as your soldiers owed obedience to you and your lieutenants. If a soldier says on the morning of attack that Voices have told him not to advance, in yours or any army in the world he would be silenced. And far more brutally than this effort of ours to reason with you.

JOAN. [*gathering herself together, on the defensive*] You have a right to hit at me with all your power. And my right is to say No, and go on believing.

CAUCHON. Don't make yourself a prisoner of your own pride, Joan. You can surely see that we have no possible reason, either as men or as priests, to believe that your mission is divinely inspired. You alone have a reason to believe so; encouraged by the fiend who means to damn you, and also, as long as you were useful to them, by those whom you served. You served them; and yet the way they behaved before your capture, and their explicit repudiation since, certainly proves that the most intelligent of them never believed you. No one believes you, Joan, any longer, except the common people, who believe everything, and tomorrow they will believe half a dozen others. You are quite alone.

[JOAN *makes no reply, sitting small and quiet among them all.*]

I beg you not to imagine that your strong will and your stubborn resistance to us is a sign that God is upholding you. The devil has also got intelligence and a tough hide. His mind had the flash of a star among the angels before he rebelled.

JOAN. [*after a pause*] I am not intelligent, my lord. I am a peasant girl, the same as any other in my village. But when something is black I cannot say it is white, that is all.

[*Another pause.*]

PROMOTER. [*suddenly rising up behind her*] What was the sign you gave to the man you are calling your king, to make him trust you with his army?

JOAN. I don't know what you mean: what sign I gave.

PROMOTER. Did you make him sip mandragora, to be a protection against harm?

JOAN. I don't know what you mean by mandragora.

PROMOTER. Your secret has a name, whether it's a potion or a formula, and we mean to know it. What did you give him at Chinon to make him so heroic all of a sudden? A Hebrew name? The devil speaks all languages, but he delights in Hebrew.

JOAN. [*smiling*] No, my lord: it has a French name. I gave him courage.

CAUCHON. And so you think that God, or at least the power you believe to be God, took no part in this.

JOAN. He always takes part, my lord Bishop. When a girl speaks two words of good sense and someone listens, there He is. But He is thrifty; when those two words of good sense will do, He isn't likely to throw away a miracle.

LADVENU. [*quietly*] The answer's a good one, in all humility, my lord: it can't be held against her.

PROMOTER. [*with venom, to* JOAN] I see, I see! So you don't believe in such miracles as we are shown in the gospels? You deny what was done by Our Lord Jesus at the marriage of Cana? You deny that He raised Lazarus from the dead?

JOAN. No, my lord. What is written in Holy Scripture was surely done. He changed the water into wine just as easily as He created them. And it was no more extraordinary for Him, the Master of life and death, to make Lazarus live again, than for me to thread a needle.

PROMOTER. [*yelping*] Listen to that! Listen to that! She says there is no such thing as a miracle!

JOAN. No, my lord. I say that a true miracle is not done with a magic wand or incantation. The gypsies on our village green can do miracles of that sort. The true miracle is done by men themselves, with the mind and the courage which God has given to them.

CAUCHON. Are you measuring the gravity of your words, Joan? You seem to be telling us quite calmly that God's true miracle on earth is man, who is nothing but sin and error, blindness and futility. . . .

JOAN. And strength, too, and courage, and light sometimes when he is deepest in sin. I have seen men during the battles. . . .

LADVENU. My lord, Joan is talking to us in her rough and ready language about things which come instinctively from her heart, which may be wrong but are surely simple and genuine. Her thoughts are not so schooled that she can shape them to our way of argument. Perhaps by pressing her with questions we run the risk of making her say more than she meant, or something different from her belief.

CAUCHON. Brother Ladvenu, we shall try and estimate as fairly as we can what part lack of skill plays in her answers. But our duty is to question her to the last point of doubt. We are not perfectly sure, remember, that our concern now is *only* the question of Joan. So then, Joan, you excuse man all his faults, and think him one of God's greatest miracles, even the only one?

JOAN. Yes, my lord.

PROMOTER. [*yelping, beside himself*] It's blasphemy! Man is filth, lust, a nightmare of obscenity!

JOAN. Yes, my lord. He sins; he is evil enough. And then something happens: it may be he is coming out of a brothel, roaring out his bawdy songs in praise of a good time, and suddenly he has thrown himself at the reins of a runaway horse to save some child he has never seen before; his bones broken, he dies at peace.

PROMOTER. But he dies like an animal, without a priest, in the full damnation of sin.

JOAN. No, my lord; he dies in the light which was lighted within him when the world began. He behaved as a man, both in doing evil and doing good, and God created him in that contradiction to make his difficult way.

[A *storm of indignation from the* PRIESTS *when they hear this said. The* INQUISITOR *quietens them, and suddenly rises.*]

INQUISITOR. [*calmly*] Joan. I have let you speak throughout this trial, with scarcely a question to you. I wanted you to find your way clearly to your position. It has taken some time. The Promoter could see only the Devil, the Bishop only the pride of a young girl intoxicated with success; I waited for something else to show itself. Now it has happened—I represent the Holy Inquisition. My Lord the Bishop told you just now, with great humanity, how his human feelings linked him with the English cause, which he considers just; and how they were confounded by his sentiments as priest and bishop, charged with the defence of our Mother Church. But I have come from the heart of Spain. This is the first time I have been sent to France. I know nothing of either the Armagnac faction, or of the English. It is indifferent to me who shall rule France, whether your prince or Henry of Lancaster. As for that strict discipline of our Mother Church which will not tolerate those who play a lone hand, however well-intentioned, but directs them back into the fold: I'll not say that is indifferent to me; but it is perhaps a secondary task, which the Inquisition leaves to the Bishops and the parish priests. The Holy Inquisition has something higher and more secret to defend than the temporal integrity of the Church. She wrestles on an invisible ground, inwardly, with an enemy only she knows how to detect, of whom only she can estimate the danger. It has been her care sometimes to take up arms against an Emperor; at other times the same solemnity, the same vigilance, the same fixity of purpose have been deployed against some old apparently inoffensive scholar, or a herdsman buried away in a mountain village, or a young girl. The princes of the earth laugh very heartily to see the Inquisition give itself such endless care, when for them a piece of rope or a sergeant's signature on a death warrant would be enough. The Inquisition lets them laugh. It knows how to recognise the enemy; it knows better than to under-estimate him wherever he may be found. And its enemy is not the devil, not the devil with the cloven hooves, the chastener of troublesome children, whom my lord Promoter sees on every side. His enemy, you yourself spoke his name, when at last you came into the open: his only enemy, is man. Stand up, Joan, and answer me. I am your interrogator now.[1]

> [JOAN *rises and turns towards him. He asks in an expressionless voice.*]

Are you a Christian?

JOAN. Yes, my lord.

INQUISITOR. You were baptized, and in your earliest years you lived in the shadow of the church whose walls touched the walls of your home. The church bells ruled over your day, your playtime, your work, and your prayers. The emissaries we sent to your village have all come back with the same story: you were a little

---

1. If it disconcerts you to find *La Sainte Inquisition* called variously "she," "it" and "him" in the Inquisitor's speech, blame the translator; *elle* is both "she" and "it" in French and *ennemi* takes a masculine pronoun.

girl full of piety. Sometimes, instead of playing and running
about with other children, though you were not a solemn child,
you delighted to play, yet you would slip away into the church,
and for a long time you would be there alone, kneeling, not
even praying, but gazing at the coloured glass of the window.

JOAN. Yes. I was happy.

INQUISITOR. You had a friend you loved very dearly, a little girl
called Haumette.

JOAN. Yes, my lord.

INQUISITOR. And when you made up your mind to leave for Vaucouleurs, already believing that you would never go back, you
said goodbye to all your other friends, but you passed her house
by.

JOAN. Yes. I was afraid to be too unhappy.

INQUISITOR. But you cared for more than only those you loved most.
You cared for old people in sickness, children in poverty. And
later on, when you fought in your first battle, you stood among
the wounded and cried very bitterly.

JOAN. French blood was being shed; it was hard to bear.

INQUISITOR. Not only because it was French blood. A bully who
had captured two English soldiers in a skirmish outside Orleans,
knocked one of them down because he didn't move fast enough
for him. You jumped off your horse, took the man's head on
your knee, wiped the blood from his mouth, and helped him in
his dying, calling him your little son, and promising him Heaven.

JOAN. How is it you can know that, my lord?

INQUISITOR. The Holy Inquisition knows everything, Joan. It
weighed your human tenderness in the scales before it sent me
to judge you.

LADVENU. [*rising*] My Lord Inquisitor, I am happy to hear you re-
calling all these details which until now have been passed over in
silence. Yes, indeed, everything we know of Joan since her earliest
years has been gentleness, humility, and Christian charity.

INQUISITOR. [*turning upon him, suddenly stern*] Silence, Brother
Ladvenu! I ask you to remember that I stand here for the Holy
Inquisition, alone qualified to make the distinction between
Charity, the theological virtue, and the uncommendable, grace-
less, cloudy drink of the milk of human kindness. [*He passes his
eye over them all.*] Ah, my Masters! How quickly your hearts
can be melted. The accused has only to be a little girl, looking
at you with a pair of wide-open eyes, and with a ha'porth of
simple kindness, and you're all ready to fall over yourselves to
absolve her. Very good guardians of the faith we have here! I
see that the Holy Inquisition has enough to occupy it still: and
still so much has to be cut away, cut, cut, always the dead wood
to be cut away: and after us, others will go on, still pruning,
hacking away without mercy, clearing the ranks of unruliness, so
that the forest will be sound from root to branch.

[*A pause, and then* LADVENU *replies.*]

LADVENU. Our Saviour also loved with this loving-kindness, my lord.

He said: Suffer the little children to come unto me. He put His hand on the shoulder of the woman taken in adultery, and said to her: Go in peace.

INQUISITOR. I tell you to be silent, Brother Ladvenu! Otherwise I shall have to investigate your case as well as Joan's. Lessons from the Gospels are read to the congregations, and we ask the parish priests to explain them. But we have not translated them into the vulgar tongue, or put them into every hand to make of them what they will. How mischievous that would be, to leave untutored souls to let their imaginations play with the texts which only we should interpret. [*He quietens down.*] You are young, Brother Ladvenu, and you have a young man's generosity. But you must not suppose that youth and generosity find grace in the eyes of the faith's defenders. Those are transitory ills which experience will cure. I see that we should have considered your age, and not your learning which I believe is remarkable, before we invited you to join us here. Experience will soon make plain to you that youth, generosity, human tenderness are names of the enemy. At least, I trust it may. Surely you can see, if we were so unwise as to put these words you have spoken into the hands of simple people, they would draw from them a love of Man. And love of Man excludes the love of God.

LADVENU. [*quietly*] And yet He chose to become a man . . .

INQUISITOR. [*turning suddenly to* CAUCHON, *curtly*] My lord Bishop, in virtue of your discretionary power as president of these debates, I ask you to dispense for today with the collaboration of your young assessor. I shall inform you, when the session is over, what conclusions will be entered against him, if needs be. [*He suddenly thunders.*] Against him or against whomsoever! For no one is of too great importance to be put out of our care: understand so! I would denounce myself, if God should allow me to be misled. [*He gravely crosses himself and ends*] May He mercifully watch over me!

   [*A breath of fear whispers through the tribunal.* CAUCHON *says simply, with a gesture of distress to* BROTHER LADVENU.]

CAUCHON. Leave us, Brother Ladvenu.

LADVENU. [*before he moves off*] My lord Inquisitor, I owe you obedience, as I do my Reverend Lord Bishop. I will go, saying no more: except that my prayers must be to our Lord Jesus that He shall lead you to remember the fragility of your small enemy who faces you now.

INQUISITOR. [*not answering until he has gone, and then speaking quietly*] Small, fragile, tender, pure: and therefore formidable. [*He turns to* JOAN *and says in his neutral tone.*] The first time you heard your Voices you were not yet fifteen. On that occasion they simply said to you: "Be a good and sensible child, and go often to church." In fact you were a happy and contented little girl. And the unhappiness of France was only old men's talk. And yet one day you felt you should leave the village.

JOAN. My Voices told me that I must.

INQUISITOR. One day you felt that you must take upon yourself the unhappiness of others around you. And you knew even then everything that would come of it: how glorious your ride would be, how soon it would come to an end, and once your King had been anointed, how you would find yourself where you are now, surrounded and alone, the faggots heaped up in the market place, waiting to be set alight. You know this is——

JOAN. My Voices told me that I should be captured, and then delivered.

INQUISITOR. Delivered! They very well might use that word: and you guessed in what way it might be taken, how ambiguously as a word from heaven. Death is a deliverance, certainly. And you set off all the same, in spite of your father and mother, and in spite of all the grave difficulties ahead of you.

JOAN. Yes, my lord; it had to be. If I had been the daughter of a hundred mothers and a hundred fathers: still it would have had to be.

INQUISITOR. So that you could help your fellow men to keep possession of the soil where they were born, which they fondly imagine belongs to them.

JOAN. Our Lord couldn't want the English to pillage, and kill and overrule us in our own country. When they have gone back across the sea, they can be God's children then in their own land. I shall pick no quarrel with them then.

PROMOTER. Presumption! Pride! Don't you think you would have done better to go on with your sewing and spinning beside your mother?

JOAN. I had something else to do, my lord. There have always been plenty of women to do women's work.

INQUISITOR. When you found yourself in such direct communication with heaven did it never occur to you to consecrate your life to prayer, supplicating that heaven itself should expel the English from France?

JOAN. God likes to see action first, my lord. Prayer is extra. It was simpler to explain to Charles that he ought to attack, and he believed me, and gentle Dunois believed me, too. And so did La Hire and Xantrailles, my fine couple of angry bulls! We had some joyful battles, all of us together. It was good to face every new day with friends, ready to turn on the English, ready to rescue France, ready to——

PROMOTER. Kill, Joan? Ready to kill? And does Our Lord tell us to kill for what we want, as though we had fangs and claws?

[JOAN *does not reply.*]

CAUCHON. [*gently*] You loved the war, Joan . . .

JOAN. [*simply*] Yes. It is one of the sins which I have most need of God's forgiveness for. Though in the evening I would look across the battlefield and cry to see that the joyous beginning to the morning had gone down in a heap of dead.

PROMOTER. And the next day, you began again?

JOAN. God wished it. While there remained one Englishman in

France. It isn't difficult to understand. There was work to be done first, that was all. You are learned, and you think too much. You can't understand the simple things, but the dullest of my soldiers understands them. Isn't that true, La Hire?

[LA HIRE *strides forward, in huge armour, gay and alarming.*]

LA HIRE. You bet it's true.

[*Everybody finds himself pushed into the shade: this one figure is clear. A vague music of the fife is heard.* JOAN *goes quietly up to him, incredulous, and touches him with her finger.*]

JOAN. La Hire . . .

LA HIRE. [*taking up again the comradeship of the battle mornings*] Well, Miss, we've had the bit of praying we agreed to have: what's the next thing? Do we take a bash at them this morning?

JOAN. [*throwing herself into his arms*] It is La Hire, my dear, fat La Hire! You smell so good!

LA HIRE. [*embarrassed*] A glass of wine and an onion. It's my usual morning meal. Excuse me, Miss: I know you don't like it, but I did my praying beforehand so that God shouldn't take against my breath. Don't come too near: I know I stink in a way.

JOAN. [*pressed against him*] No: it's good.

LA HIRE. You don't want to make me feel awkward. Usually you tell me I stink and it's a shame for a Christian. Usually you say that if the wind carries in that direction I shall give us away to the goddams, I stink so much; and we shall ruin our ambush because of me. One quite small onion and two tots of red wine, no more. Of course, let's be honest, no water with it.

JOAN. Well, I was a fool if I said so. If an onion has a right to stink why shouldn't you?

LA HIRE. It's what war does for you. Be a clerk, or a priest, or a linen draper: no smell. But be a captain, you're bound to sweat. As for washing, up in the line: a man doesn't see the interest in it. There was no need to add the onion, I suppose: I ought to do with a bit of garlic sausage like the other fellows: it's better behaved when you come to conversation. But, look here, you wouldn't call it a sin, would you, eating the onion?

JOAN. [*smiling*] No, La Hire: not a sin.

LA HIRE. You never know with you, you know.

JOAN. Have I pestered you with sins, La Hire? I was silly to tease you so much: it's odd, but there you are, a great bear smelling of sweat and onions and red wine, and you kill, and swear, and think of nothing except the girls . . .

LA HIRE. [*very astonished*] Who, me?

JOAN. You. Yes. Look astonished, you old rogue. And yet you shine in the hand of God as bright as a new penny.

LA HIRE. Is that a fact? I should have thought I'd bitched my chance of paradise years ago. But you think if I keep on praying as arranged, a bit every day, I might still get there?

JOAN. They're expecting you. I know that God's paradise must be full of ruffians like you.

LA HIRE. Is that a fact? It would make all the difference to feel that there were a few kindred spirits around. I wasn't much looking forward to being in a crowd of saints and bishops looking like Heaven's village idiot.

JOAN. [*gaily thumping him*] Great jackass! Of course Heaven's full of dunces. Hasn't our Lord said so? It may even be they're the only ones who get in: the others have had so many brains to sin with, they never get past the door.

LA HIRE. [*uneasily*] You don't think, between ourselves, we'll get bored to death, do you, always on our best behaviour? Any fighting at all, do you imagine?

JOAN. All the day long.

LA HIRE. [*respectfully*] Wait, now. Only when God isn't looking at us.

JOAN. But He's looking at you all the time, crackpot! He sees everything. And what's more, He is going to enjoy watching you at it. "Go it, La Hire," He'll say: "Bash the stuffing out of old Xantraille! Pitch into him, now! Show him what you're made of!"

LA HIRE. Is that a fact?

JOAN. Not in those words perhaps, but in His own way.

LA HIRE. By God Almighty. [*enthusiastically*]

JOAN. [*suddenly stern*] La Hire!

LA HIRE. [*hanging his head*] Sorry, miss.

JOAN. [*pitilessly*] If you swear He will throw you out.

LA HIRE. [*stammering*] I was feeling pleased, you see: had to thank Him somehow.

JOAN. So He thought. But don't do it again! We've talked quite enough for one morning. Let's get up on horseback and take a look at the day.

LA HIRE. It's dead country this morning. Not a soul to see.

[*They ride imaginary horses side by side.*]

JOAN. Look, we've got France all to ourselves—shall we ever see the world to better advantage? Here on horseback side by side: this is how it will be, La Hire, when the English have gone. Smell the wet grass, La Hire, isn't this why men go fighting? To ride out together smelling the world when the light of day is just beginning to discover it.

LA HIRE. So anyone can who likes to take a walk in his garden.

JOAN. No. I think death has to be somewhere near before God will show us the world like this.

LA HIRE. Suppose we should meet some English, who might also be liking the good smells of the morning?

JOAN. We attack them, we smite them, and send them flying. That's what we're here for! [*A little pause. She suddenly cries.*] Stop! [*They draw in their horses.*] There are three English over there. They've seen us. They're running away! No! Now they've turned back again: they've seen there are only two of us. They're attacking. You're not afraid, La Hire? No use counting on me; I'm only a girl, and I've got no sword. Will you fight them alone?

LA HIRE. [*brandishing his sword with a delighted roar*] Hell, yes, by

God I will! [*shouting to the sky as he charges*] I didn't say anything, God, I didn't say anything. Pay no attention . . .

[*He charges into the middle of the Tribunal: they scatter as he swings his sword to left and right. He disappears still fighting.*]

JOAN. He didn't say anything, God. He didn't say anything! He is as good as a French loaf. So all my soldiers are, though they kill, and loot, and swear: good as your wolves are, God, whom you created innocent. I will answer for all of them!

[JOAN *is deep in prayer. The Tribunal has re-formed round her: the light has come back.* JOAN *raises her head, sees them, seems to shake herself free of a dream.*]

La Hire and Xantrailles! Oh, we're not at the end of things yet. You can be sure they will come and deliver me with two or three or four hundred men . . .

CAUCHON. [*quietly*] They came, Joan: right up to the gates of Rouen to find out how many of the English were in the town, and then they went away again.

JOAN. [*dashed*] Oh, they went away? Without fighting? [*A silence; she looks up.*] Why, they have gone to find reinforcements, of course. I myself taught them, it is no good to attack willynilly, as they did at Agincourt.

CAUCHON. They withdrew to the South of the Loire; Charles is down there, disbanding his armies. He is tired of the war, and if he can he will make a treaty, to secure at least his own small portion of France. They will never come back again, Joan.

JOAN. That isn't true! La Hire will come back, even if he hasn't a chance.

CAUCHON. La Hire is only the captain of an army of mercenaries, who sold himself and his men to another Prince as soon as he found that yours was out to make peace. He is marching at this moment towards Germany, to find another country to plunder; simply that.

JOAN. It isn't true!

CAUCHON. [*rising*] Have I ever lied to you, Joan? It is true. Then why will you sacrifice yourself to defend those who have deserted you? The only men on earth who are trying to save you—paradoxical though it may seem—are ourselves, your old enemies, and now your judges. Recant, Joan: your resistance helps no-one now; your friends are betraying you. Return to the arms of your Mother Church. Humble yourself, she will lift you up again. I am convinced that deep in your heart you have never ceased to be one of her daughters.

JOAN. Yes, I am a daughter of the Church!

CAUCHON. Then give yourself into the care of your mother, Joan, without question. She will weigh your burden of error, and so release you from the anguish of judging it for yourself. You needn't think of anything any more: you will do your penance, whether it be heavy or light, and at last you will be at peace. Surely you have a great need of peace.

JOAN. [*after a pause*] In what concerns the Faith, I trust myself to the Church. But what I have done I shall never wish to undo.

[A *stir among the priests. The* INQUISITOR *breaks in.*]

INQUISITOR. Do you hear, my masters? Do you see Man raising up his head, like a serpent ready to strike us dead? Do you understand now what it is you have to judge? These heavenly voices have deafened you as well as the girl, on my word they have! You have been labouring to discover what devil has been behind her actions. Would it were only a question of the devil. His trial would soon be over. The devil speaks our language. In his time he was an angel, and we understand him. The sum of his blasphemies, his insults, even his hatred of God, is an act of faith. But man, calm and transparent as he seems, frightens me infinitely more. Look at him: in chains, disarmed, deserted, no longer sure even in himself (isn't that so, Joan?) that the voices which have been silent for so long have ever truly spoken. Does he throw himself down, supplicating God to hold him again in his hand? Does he at least implore his Voices to come back and give light to his path? No. He turns away, suffers the torture, suffers humiliation and beating, suffers like a dumb animal, while his eyes fasten on the invincible image of himself; [*he thunders*] himself, his only true God! That is what I fear! And he replies— repeat it, Joan; you are longing to say it again; "But what I have done . . ."

JOAN. [*quietly*] . . . I shall never wish to undo.

INQUISITOR. [*repeats*] "But what I have done I shall never wish to undo!" You hear those words? And you will hear them said on the scaffold, at the stake, in the torture chamber, wherever they come to suffer for the errors they commit. And centuries hence they will be saying it; the hunting down of Man will go on endlessly. However powerful we become one day in one shape or another, however inexorably the Idea shall dominate the world, however rigorous, precise and subtle its organisation and its police, there will always be a man who has escaped, a man to hunt, who will presently be caught, presently be killed: a man who, even so, will humiliate the Idea at the highest point of its Power, simply because he will say "No" without lowering his eyes. [*He hisses through his teeth, looking at* JOAN *with hatred.*] An insolent breed! [*He turns again towards the Tribunal.*] Do you need to question her any more? Do you need to ask her why she threw herself from the height of the tower where she was imprisoned, whether to escape, or to destroy herself against the commandments of God? Why she has left her father and mother, put on the clothes of a man, and wears them still, against the commandments of the Church? She will give you the same reply, the reply of Man: What I have done, I have done. It is mine, and my doing. No-one can take it from me; no-one can make me disown it. All that you can do is kill me, to make me cry out no matter what under the torture, but make me say "Yes," you cannot do. [*He cries to them.*] Ah well: by some means or other he

572 · *Jean Anouilh*

must be taught to say Yes, whatever it may cost the world. As long as one man remains who will not be broken, the Idea, even if it dominates and pervades all the rest of mankind, will be in danger of perishing. That is why I require Joan's excommunication, her rejection from the bosom of the Church and that she should be given over to the secular arm for punishment. [*He adds neutrally, reciting a formula.*] Beseeching it nevertheless to limit its sentence on this side of death and the mutilation of the limbs. [*He turns to* JOAN.] This will be a paltry victory against you, Joan, but at least it will silence you. And, up to now, we have not thought of a better. [*He sits down again in silence.*]

CAUCHON. [*gently*] My Lord Inquisitor is the first to ask for your excommunication, Joan. In a moment I am afraid my Lord Promoter will ask for the same thing. Each one of us will speak his mind and then I shall have to give my decision. Before lopping the dead branch, which you have become, and casting it far from her, your Holy Mother Church, to whom the one lost sheep is more dear than all the others, remember that, entreats you now for the last time.

[CAUCHON *makes a sign, and a man comes forward.*]
Do you know this man, Joan?

[*She turns to look and gives a little shudder of fear.*]
It is the master hangman of Rouen. In a short while from now you will belong to him, unless you give your soul into our keeping so that we can save it. Is the stake ready, Master Hangman?

HANGMAN. Quite ready, my lord. Higher than the regulation stake, such was the orders: so that the girl can be got a good view of from all sides. The nuisance of it for her is that I shan't be able to help her at all, she will be too high up.

CAUCHON. What do you call helping her, Master Hangman?

HANGMAN. A trick of the trade, my lord: it's the custom, when there aren't any special instructions. You wait till the first flames get up, and then I climb up behind, under cover of the smoke, and strangle the party. Then it's only the corpse that burns, and it isn't so bad. But with the instructions I've had, it's too high, and I won't be able to get up there. [*He adds simply.*] So, naturally, it will take longer.

CAUCHON. Do you hear that, Joan?

JOAN. [*softly*] Yes.

CAUCHON. I am going to offer you once more the hand of your Mother, the great hand which opens towards you to take you back and save you. But the delay can't be for long. You hear the noise outside, as though the sea had come up to the door? That is the sound of the crowd, who already have been waiting for you since daybreak. They came early to get good places: and there they are still, eating the food they brought with them, grumbling at their children, joking and singing, and asking the soldiers how long it will be before things begin to happen. They are not bad people. They are the same men and women who would have cheered you if you had captured Rouen. But things

have turned out differently, that's all, and so instead they come
to see you burned. As nothing very much ever happens to them,
they make their adventures out of the triumphs or the deaths
of the world's great ones. You will have to forgive them, Joan.
All their lives long they pay dearly for being the common people;
they deserve these little distractions.

JOAN. [*quietly*] I do forgive them. And I forgive you, as well, my
lord.

PROMOTER. Appalling, abominable pride! My lord the Bishop troubles to talk to you like a father, in the hope of saving your miserable soul, and you have the effrontery to say that you forgive him!

JOAN. My lord talks to me gently, but I don't know whether it is
to save me or to overthrow me. And since in a little while he
will have to burn me anyway, I forgive him.

CAUCHON. Joan: try to understand that there is something absurd
in your refusal. You are not an unbeliever. The God you claim as
your own is ours also. And we are, in fact, those whom God has
ordained to guide you, through the apostle Peter upon whom
His Church is built. God did not say to His creatures: You will
understand My will from Me. He said "Thou art Peter, and upon
this rock I will build My church . . . and its priests will be your
shepherds . . . ". Do you think us unworthy priests, Joan?

JOAN. [*quietly*] No.

CAUCHON. Then why will you not do as God has said? Why will
you not resign your fault to the Church, as you did when you
were a small girl, at home in your village? Has your faith so
changed?

JOAN. [*crying out in anguish*] I want to submit to the Church. I
want to receive the Holy Sacrament, but you won't let me!

CAUCHON. We will give it to you after your confession, and when
your penance has begun; we only wait for you to say "Yes". You
are brave, we know that indeed: but your flesh is still frail: you
are surely afraid of dying?

JOAN. [*quietly*] Yes. I'm afraid. But what else can I do?

CAUCHON. I think well enough of you, Joan, to know that fear in
itself is not enough to make you draw back. But you should have
another, greater fear: the fear of being deceived, and of laying
yourself open to eternal damnation. Now, what risk do you run,
even if your voices are from God, if you perform the act of sub-
mission to the priests of His church? If we do not believe in your
Voices, and if nevertheless God has really spoken to you, then
it is we who have committed the monstrous sin of ignorance,
presumption and pride, and we who will have to make expiation
through all eternity. We will take this risk for you, Joan, and
you risk nothing. Say to us: "I submit to you," say simply "Yes,"
and you will be at peace, blameless, and safe in your redemp-
tion.

JOAN. [*suddenly exhausted*] Why will you torture me so gently, my
lord? I would far rather you beat me.

CAUCHON. [*smiling*] If I beat you, Joan, I should only add to your pride: your pride which wishes to see you persecuted and killed. I reason with you because God gifted you with reason and good sense. I beseech you, because I know you have gentle feeling. I am an old man, Joan; I have no more ambitions in this world, and, like each of us here, I have put many to death in defence of the Church, as you have put many to death in defence of your Voices. It is enough. I am tired. I wish to die without adding to those deaths the death of a little girl. Help me.

JOAN. [*after a pause*] What do I have to say?

CAUCHON. First of all you must understand that by insisting that God sent you, you no longer help anything or anyone. It is only playing into the hands of the English and the Executioner. Your king himself has declared in his letters that he doesn't in any way wish to owe the possession of his crown to a divine intervention of which you were the instrument.

[JOAN *turns towards* CHARLES *in distress.*]

CHARLES. Put yourself in my place, Joan! If there had to be a miracle to crown me King of France, it means I wasn't naturally king at all. It means I wasn't the true son of my father, or else my coronation would have followed of its own accord. All the other kings in my family have been crowned without needing a miracle. Divine help is all very well in its way, but suspect. And it's even more suspect when it stops. Since that unhappy Paris business, we've been beaten at every step; and then you let yourself be captured at Compiègne. They've got a little verdict up their sleeve for you, to denounce you as a witch, a heretic, the devil's intermediary, all in one. I prefer people to think you were never sent by anyone, God or devil. In that way, God has neither helped me, nor thrown me over. I won because I was the strongest at the time; I am being beaten now because I am the weakest, for the moment. That is healthy politics, if you understand?

JOAN. [*softly*] Yes, I understand.

CAUCHON. I'm thankful to see you're wiser at last. We have put so many questions to you, you became confused. I am going to ask you three more, three essential ones. If you answer "Yes" three times, we shall all of us be saved, you who are going to die, and we who are putting you to death.

JOAN. [*quietly, after a pause*] Ask them. I will see whether I can answer them.

CAUCHON. The first question is the really important one. If you answer "yes," the other answers will take care of themselves. Listen carefully, weighing each word: "Do you humbly put yourself into the hands of the Holy Apostolic Church of Rome; of our Holy Father the Pope and his bishops, that they shall estimate your deeds and judge you? Do you surrender yourself entirely and undoubtedly, and do you ask to be received again into the bosom of the Church?" It is enough for you to answer "yes."

[JOAN *after a pause, looks around her without moving. At last she speaks.*]

JOAN. Yes, but . . .

INQUISITOR. [*in a level voice*] With no "but."

JOAN. I do not wish to be made to deny what my Voices have said to me. I do not wish to be made to bear witness against my king, or to say anything which will dim the glory of his coronation which is his, irrevocably, now and for ever.

[*The* INQUISITOR *shrugs his shoulders.*]

INQUISITOR. Such is the voice of man. There is only one way of bringing him to silence.

CAUCHON. [*becoming angry*] Joan, Joan, Joan, are you mad? Do you not see this man in red who is waiting for you? Realise, understand, this is my last effort to save you, after this there is nothing more I can do. The Church still wishes to believe that you are one of her daughters. She has weighed with care the form her question should take, to help you on the path, and you cavil and try to bargain. There is no bargaining with your Mother, you impudent girl! You should beg her on your knees to wrap you in her cloak of love and protect you. Our Lord suffered far more than you in the humiliation and injustice of His Passion. Did He bargain or cavil when He came to die for you? Your suffering bears no comparison with His: scourged, mocked, spat upon: crowned with thorns, and nailed in a long agony between two thieves; you can never hope to rival His suffering! And He asks, through us, only one thing of you, that you submit to the judgment of His Church, and you hesitate.

JOAN. [*after a pause, tears in her eyes*] Forgive me, my lord. I hadn't thought that Our Saviour might wish it. It is true that He has surely suffered more than I. [*a short pause, again, and she says*] I submit.

CAUCHON. Do you humbly and without any restriction supplicate the Holy Catholic Church to receive you again into her bosom, and do you defer to her judgment?

JOAN. I humbly supplicate my Mother Church to receive me again into her bosom, and I surrender myself to her judgment.

CAUCHON. [*with a sigh of relief*] Good, Joan; well done. The rest will be simple enough now. Do you promise never again to take up arms?

JOAN. There is still work to be done . . .

CAUCHON. The work, as you call it, will be done by others. Don't be foolish, Joan. You are in chains, a prisoner, and in great danger of being burned. So whether you say yes or no the work will not be done by you. Your part is played out. The English have you in their grasp, and they'll not let you fight again. You said to us just now that when a girl has two words of good sense God is there performing His miracle. If God is protecting you, this is the time for Him to bring you the two words of good sense. So you promise never again to take up arms?

JOAN. [*groaning*] But if my King still needs me?

CHARLES. [*hastily*] Oh, goodness me! If it's me you're thinking about you can say yes at once. I don't need you any more.

JOAN. [*heavily*] Then, yes; yes.

CAUCHON. Do you promise never to wear again these man's clothes, which is contrary to all the rules of decency and Christian modesty?

JOAN. [*tired of the question*] You have asked me that ten times. The clothes are nothing. My Voices told me to wear them.

PROMOTER. The devil told you! Who except the devil would incite a girl to overthrow decency?

JOAN. [*quietly*] Common sense, my lord.

PROMOTER. [*sneering*] Common sense? Common sense is your strong card! Are breeches on a girl common sense?

JOAN. Of course, my lord. I had to ride horseback with the soldiers; I had to wear what they wore so that they wouldn't think of me as a girl, but as a soldier like themselves.

PROMOTER. A worthless reply! A girl who isn't damned to begin with wouldn't wish to ride with the soldiers!

CAUCHON. Even though it may be that these clothes had their purpose during the war, why do you still refuse to dress as a woman? The fighting's over, you are in our hands; yet you still refuse.

JOAN. It is necessary.

CAUCHON. Why?

JOAN. [*hesitating for a moment, blushing*] If I were in a Church prison, I wouldn't refuse then.

PROMOTER. You hear this nonsense, my lord? What hair splitting: what deliberate prevarication! Why should she agree to modesty in a Church prison, and not where she is? I don't understand it, and I don't wish to!

JOAN. [*smiling sadly*] And yet it is very easy to understand, my lord. You don't have to be very wise to see it.

PROMOTER. It is very easy to understand, and I don't understand because I'm a fool, I suppose? Will you note that, my lord? She insults me, in the exercise of my public office. She treats her indecency as something to glory in, boasts of it, in fact, takes a gross delight in it, I've no doubt! If she submits to the Church, as she apparently wants to, I may have to give up my chief accusation of heresy; but as long as she refuses to put off this diabolical dress, I shall persist in my charge of witchcraft, even though pressure is put upon me by the conspiracy to shield her which I see presides over this debate. I shall appeal, if necessary, to the Council of Basle! The devil is in this, my lord, the devil is in it! I can feel his terrible presence! He it is who is making her refuse to give up these clothes of immodesty and vice, no doubt of that.

JOAN. Put me in a Church prison, and I shall give them up.

PROMOTER. You shall not make your bargains with the Church: my lord has already told you so. You will give up this dress altogether, or you will be condemned as a witch and burnt!

CAUCHON. If you accept the principle, Joan, why don't you wish to obey us now, in the prison where you are?

JOAN. I'm not alone there.

PROMOTER. Well? you're not alone there. Well? What of that?

JOAN. The English soldiers are on guard in the cell, all through the day, and through the night.

PROMOTER. Well? [*a pause*] Do you mean to go on? Your powers of invention have failed you already, is that it? I should have thought the devil was more ingenious! You feel that you've been caught out, my girl, and it makes you blush.

CAUCHON. [*quietly*] You must answer him, Joan. I think I understand but it must be you who tells us so.

JOAN. [*after a moment of hesitation*] The nights are long, my lord. I am in chains. I do my best to keep awake, but sleep sometimes is too strong for me. [*She stops.*]

PROMOTER. [*more and more obtuse*] Well, what then? The nights are long, you are in chains, you want to sleep. What then?

JOAN. [*quietly*] I can defend myself better if I wear these clothes.

CAUCHON. [*heavily*] Has this been so all the time of the trial?

JOAN. Ever since I was captured, my lord, each night; and when you send me back there in the evening, it begins again. I've got into the way of not sleeping now, which is why my answers are so sleepy and muddled when I'm brought before you in the mornings. But each night seems longer; and the soldiers are strong, and full of tricks. I should as soon wear a woman's dress on the battlefield.

CAUCHON. Why don't you call the officer, and he would defend you?

JOAN. [*after a pause*] They told me they would be hanged if I called for help.

WARWICK. [*to* CAUCHON] Incredible. I never heard of such a thing! Quite possible in the French army. But in the English army, no, quite ridiculous. I shall inquire into this.

CAUCHON. If you would return, Joan, back to your Mother the Church who is waiting for you: promise to change from these clothes to the dress of a girl: the Church from now on would see you had no such fears.

JOAN. Then I do promise.

CAUCHON. [*giving a deep sigh*] Good. Thank you, Joan, you have helped me. I was afraid for a time we should have no power to save you. We shall read your promise to abjure your sins: the document is all ready, you have only to sign it.

JOAN. I don't know how to write.

CAUCHON. You will make a cross. My lord Inquisitor, allow me to recall Brother Ladvenu so that he may read this to the prisoner. It is Brother Ladvenu who is responsible, at my request, for drawing up this paper. And, moreover, we have all to be here now, to pronounce sentence, now that Joan has returned to us. [*He leans towards him.*] You should be gratified, my lord: Man has said "yes."

INQUISITOR. [*a pallid smile on his thin lips*] I am waiting until the conclusion; until the conclusion.

[CAUCHON *calls to the* GUARD.]

CAUCHON. Recall Brother Ladvenu!

PROMOTER. [*whispering*] My lord Inquisitor, you won't allow them to do this?

INQUISITOR. [*with a vague gesture*] If she has said "yes" . . .

PROMOTER. My lord Bishop has conducted the enquiry with an indulgence towards the girl which I can't begin to understand! And yet I have reliable information that he feeds well from the English manger. Does he feed even more rapaciously from the French? That is what I ask myself.

INQUISITOR. [*smiling*] It is not what I ask myself, my lord Promoter. It is not of eating, well or better, that I am thinking, but of something graver. [*He falls on to his knees, oblivious of all around him.*] O Lord! It has pleased You to grant that Man should humble himself at the eleventh hour in the person of this young girl. It has been Your will that this time he shall say "Yes." But why has it also pleased You to let an evident and earthly tenderness be born in the heart of this old man who was judging her? Will you never grant, O Lord, that this world should be unburdened of every trace of humanity, so that at last we may in peace consecrate it to Thy glory alone?

[BROTHER LADVENU *has come forward.*]

CAUCHON. She is saved, Brother Ladvenu, Joan is saved. She has agreed to return to us, and to Holy Mother Church. Read her the act of Abjuration, and she will sign it.

LADVENU. Thank you, Joan. I was praying for you, I prayed that this might be possible. [*he reads*] "I, Joan, known as the Maid, confess to having sinned, by pride, obstinacy, and wrong-doing, in pretending to receive revelation from Our Lord God, Father of all Men, through the means of His angels and His blessed Saints. I confess to having blasphemed by wearing immodest clothing, contrary to the ruling of our Holy Mother Church; and to having, by persuasion, incited men to kill one another. I foreswear and abjure all these sins; I vow upon the Holy Gospels no more to wear these clothes or to bear arms. I promise to surrender myself in humility to our Holy Mother Church, and to our Holy Father the Pope of Rome, and to his Bishops, that they shall weigh and estimate my sins and wickedness. I beseech the Church to receive me again into her bosom; and I declare myself ready to suffer the sentence which it will please her to inflict upon me. In token of which I have signed my name to this Act of Abjuration which I profess I have understood."

JOAN. [*who seems now like a shy and awkward girl*] Do I make a circle or a cross? I can't write my name.

LADVENU. I will guide your hand. [*He helps her to sign.*]

CAUCHON. There; it is done, Joan; and the Church rejoices to see her daughter safely returned: and you know she rejoices more for the one lost sheep than for the ninety-and-nine safely enfolded. Your soul is saved, and your body will not be delivered up to the executioner. We condemn you only, through the mercy and the grace of God, to live the rest of your days a prisoner, in penitence of these errors, eating the bread of sorrow, drinking the water of anguish, so that in solitary contemplation you may repent; and by these means we shall admit you free of the danger of excommunication into which you were fallen. You may go in peace. [*He makes the sign of the cross over her.*] Take her away.

> [*The* SOLDIERS *lead* JOAN *away. The assembly breaks up into groups, conversing among themselves.*]

WARWICK. [*coming up to* CAUCHON] Good enough, my lord; good enough. I was wondering for a moment or so what irresponsible whim was urging you to save the girl, and whether you hadn't a slight inclination to betray your king.

CAUCHON. Which king, my lord?

WARWICK. [*with a touch of frigidity*] I said your king. I imagine you have only one? Yes; very uncertain for a time whether His Majesty was going to get his money's worth, owing to this fancy of yours. But then, when I thought about it, I could see this method would discredit young Charles equally well, without the disadvantages of martyrdom, which are unpredictable, when you think of the sort of sentimental reactions we get from the public. The resolute, unshakeable girl, tied to the stake and burning in the flames, would have seemed, even so, something of a triumph for the French cause. This admission of guilt, on the other hand, is properly disgraceful. Perfect.

> [*The* CHARACTERS *move away. The lighting changes.* JOAN *is brought on by a* GUARD. AGNES SOREL *and* QUEEN YOLANDE *slip in beside her.*]

AGNES. [*coming forward*] Joan, Joan, my dear; we're so very happy it has all turned out well for you. Congratulations!

YOLANDE. Dying is quite useless, my little Joan: and whatever we do in life should have a use of some kind. People may have different opinions about the way my life has been lived, but at least I've never done anything absolutely useless.

AGNES. It was all so very stupid. Usually I adore political trials, and I particularly begged Charles to get me a seat; to watch someone fighting for his life is desperately exciting, as a rule. But really I didn't feel in the least happy when I was there. All the time I kept saying to myself: This is so very stupid: this poor little tomboy: she is going to get herself killed, and all for nothing. [*She takes* CHARLES's *arm.*] Being alive is much better, you know, in every way.

CHARLES. Yes, of course it is; and when you practically ruined your chances, just because of me—well, I was very touched, naturally, but I didn't know how to make you understand that you were getting everything quite wrong. In the first place, as you might expect, I had taken the precaution to disown you, on the advice of that old fox of an Archbishop; but, more than that, I don't like people being devoted to me. I don't like being loved. It creates obligations, and obligations are destestable.

> [JOAN *does not look at them; she hears their prattle without seeming to hear it. Then suddenly she speaks quietly.*]

JOAN. Take care of Charles. I hope he keeps his courage.

AGNES. Of course he will; why shouldn't he? My way with him is not so different from yours. I don't want him to be a poor little king who is always being beaten, any more than you do; and you shall see, I shall make our Charles a great King yet, and without getting myself burnt, either. [*She adds in a low voice.*] I suppose it may be rather disillusioning to say so, Joan, (though, of course, the two sexes are presumably what God wanted): but I do seem to get as much out of Charles by my little campaigns in the bedroom as ever you did with swords and angels.

JOAN. [*murmuring*] Poor Charles . . .

AGNES. Why poor? He is perfectly happy, like all egoists: and one of these days he is going to be a great king into the bargain.

YOLANDE. We shall see that done, Joan: not your way, but ours, and effectively enough.

AGNES. [*with a gesture to the little* QUEEN] Even her little Majesty will help. She has just given him a second son. It is all she can do, but she does it very well. So if the first son dies there is no feverish worry. The succession is assured. You can be quite happy, Joan, that you're leaving everything in good order at the Court of France.

CHARLES. [*after a sneeze*] Are you coming, my dear? This prison atmosphere is deadly, so damp it would really be healthier to sit in the river. Goodbye, Joan, for the moment; we'll come and visit you from time to time.

JOAN. Goodbye, Charles.

CHARLES. Goodbye, goodbye . . . I might say, if ever you come back to Court, you will have to call me Sire, like anybody else. I've seen to that, since my coronation. Even La Tremouille does it. It's a great victory.

[*They go off, rustling their robes.*]

JOAN. [*murmuring*] Goodbye, Sire. I am glad I got you that privilege at least.

[*The light changes again, as the* GUARD *leads her to a three-legged stool; she is alone now in her cell.*]

Blessed St Michael, blessed ladies Catherine and Margaret, are you never going to come again and speak to me? Why have you left me alone since the English captured me? You were there to see me safely to victory: but it's now, in the suffering time, that I need you most. I know it would be too simple, too easy, if God always held me by the hand: where would the merit be? I know He took my hand at the beginning because I was still too small to be alone, and later He thought I could make my own way. But I am not very big yet, God. It was very difficult to follow clearly everything the Bishop said to me. With the Canon it was easy: I could see where he was wrong, and where he was wicked, and I was ready to give him any answer which would make him furious. But the Bishop spoke so gently, and it often seemed to me he was right. Are you sure that you meant that, God? Did you mean me to feel so afraid of suffering, when the man said he would have no chance to strangle me before the flames could reach me? Are you sure that you want me to live? [*A pause. She seems to be waiting for an answer, her eyes on the sky.*] No word for me? I shall have to answer that question for myself, as well. [*A pause. She nods.*] Perhaps I am only proud and self-willed after all? Perhaps after all, I did imagine everything?

> [*Another pause. She suddenly burts into tears, her head on the stool.* WARWICK *comes quickly on to the stage, preceded by a* GUARD *who leaves them at once.* WARWICK *stops, and looks at* JOAN, *surprised.*]

WARWICK. Are you crying?

JOAN. Yes, my lord.

WARWICK. And I came here to congratulate you! That was a very happy solution to it all, I thought, the outcome of the trial, very. I told Cauchon, I was delighted you managed to avoid an execution. Quite apart from my own personal sympathy for you, the suffering is really frightful, you know, and quite useless, and most unpleasant to watch. I'm perfectly convinced you've done right to steer clear of martyrdom; better for us all. I congratulate you most sincerely. It was astonishing, considering the peasant stock you come from, that you should behave with such distinction. A gentleman is always ready, when he must, to die for his honour or his king, but it's only the riff-raff who get themselves killed for nothing. And then I was very entertained to see you queen the Inquisitor's pawn. A sinister character, that Inquisitor fellow! I detest intellectuals more than anybody. These fleshless people, what unpleasant fossils they are!—Are you really a virgin?

JOAN. Yes.

WARWICK. Well, yes, of course you are. No woman would have spoken quite in the way you did. My fiancée in England, who's a very innocent girl, reasons exactly like a boy herself, and, like you, there's no gainsaying her. There's an Indian proverb—I don't know whether you may have heard it—which says it takes a virgin to walk on water. [*He gives a little laugh.*] We shall see how long she manages that, once she becomes Lady Warwick! Being a virgin is a state of grace. We adore them, and revere them, and yet, the sad thing is, as soon as we meet one we're in the greatest possible hurry to make a woman of her: and we expect the miracle to go on as if nothing had happened. Madmen! Just as soon as ever this campaign is over—it won't be long now, I hope: your little Charles is tottering to a fall—but as soon as it is, back I go to England, to do that very same idiotic thing. Warwick Castle is a very beautiful place, a bit big, a bit severe, but very beautiful. I breed superb horses—and my fiancée rides rather well, not as well as you do, but rather well. So she ought to be very happy there. We shall go fox-hunting, of course, and entertain fairly lavishly from time to time. I'm only sorry the circumstances make it so difficult to invite you over. [*an awkward pause*] Well, there it is, I thought I'd pay you this visit, rather like shaking hands after a match, if you know what I mean. I hope I haven't disturbed you. Are my men behaving themselves now?

JOAN. Yes.

WARWICK. I should think they will certainly transfer you to a Church prison. But in any case, until they do, if there's any sign of a lapse, don't hesitate to report it to me. I'll have the blackguard hung. It's not really possible to have a whole army of gentlemen, but we can try. [*He bows.*] Madam.

[*He starts to go.* JOAN *calls him back.*]

JOAN. My lord!

WARWICK. [*returning*] Yes?

JOAN. [*without looking at him*] It would have been better, wouldn't it, if I had been burned?

WARWICK. I told you, for His Majesty's Government, the admission of guilt was just as good.

JOAN. But for me?

WARWICK. Unprofitable suffering. An ugly business. No, really, it wouldn't have been better. It would have been, as I told you just now, slightly plebeian, and ill-bred, and more than slightly stupid, to insist on dying just to embarrass everybody and make a demonstration.

JOAN. [*as though to herself*] But I am ill-bred, I am stupid. And then, remember, my lord, my life isn't prepared and perfected like yours, running so orderly and smoothly between war, hunting, and your beautiful bride waiting for you in England. What is left of me when I am not Joan any longer?

WARWICK. Life isn't going to be very gay for you, I agree, not at first, anyway. But things will adjust themselves in time, I don't think you need have any doubt of that.

JOAN. But I don't want things to adjust themselves. I don't want to live through however long this "in time" of yours will be. [*She gets up like a sleepwalker, and stares blindly ahead.*] Do you see Joan after living through it, when things have adjusted themselves: Joan, set free, perhaps, and vegetating at the French Court on her small pension?

WARWICK. [*impatient*] My dear girl, I can tell you, in six months there won't be a French Court!

JOAN. [*almost laughing, though sadly*] Joan accepting everything, Joan fat and complacent, Joan doing nothing but eat. Can you see Joan painted and powdered, trying to look fashionable, getting entangled in her skirts, fussing over her little dog, or trailing a man at her heels: who knows, perhaps with a husband?

WARWICK. Why not? Everything has to come to an end sometime. I'm going to be married myself.

JOAN. [*suddenly cries out in another voice*] But I don't want everything to come to an end! Or at least not an end like that, an end which is no end at all. Blessed St. Michael: St. Margaret: St. Catherine! You may be silent now, but I wasn't born until you first spoke to me, that day in the fields: my life truly began when I did what you told me to do, riding horseback with a sword in my hand. And that is Joan, and no other one. Certainly not one sitting placid in her convent, pasty-faced and going to pieces in comfort: continuing to live as a tolerable habit: set free, they would call it! You kept yourself silent, God, while all the priests were trying to speak at once, and everything became a confusion of words. But You told St. Michael to make it clear to me in the very beginning, that when You're silent You have then the most certain trust in us. It is the time when You let us take on everything alone. [*She draws herself up.*] Well, I take it on, O God: I take it upon myself! I give Joan back to You: true to what she is, now and forever! Call your soldiers, Warwick; call them, call them, quickly now: for I tell you I withdraw my admission of guilt: I take back my promises: they can pile their faggots, and set up their stake: they can have their holiday after all!

WARWICK. [*bored*] Now for God's sake don't let's have any such nonsense, I do implore you. I told you, I'm very satisfied with things as they are. And besides, I loathe executions. I couldn't bear to watch you going through anything of the kind.

JOAN. You have to have courage, that's all; I shall have courage. [*She looks at his pale face and puts a hand on his shoulder.*] You're a good dear fellow, in spite of your gentlemanly poker-face; but there isn't anything you can do: we belong, as you say, to different ways of life. [*She unexpectedly gives him a little kiss on the cheeks, and runs off, calling.*] Soldiers, goddams! Hey there, goddams! Fetch me the clothes I wore to fight in, and when I'm back in my breeches tell all my judges Joan is herself again!

[WARWICK *remains alone, wiping his cheek.*]

WARWICK. How out of place this all is. What bad form. It's impossible to get on well with these French for long.

[*A great clamour.*]

CROWD. Death to the witch! Burn the heretic! Kill her, kill her, kill her!

[*All the actors return quickly, grasping faggots: the* EXECU-TIONER *dragging* JOAN *with the help of* TWO ENGLISH SOL-DIERS.* LADVENU *follows, very pale. The movement is rapid and brutal. The* EXECUTIONER, *with someone's help, per-haps the* PROMOTER'S, *makes a stake with the benches from the trial scene. They make* JOAN *climb up, they tie her to the stake, and nail a defamatory inscription over her head. The* CROWD *yells.*]

CROWD. To the stake with the witch! To the stake! Shave her head, the soldier's bitch! To the stake! To the stake! Burn her!

WARWICK. Stupidity! Absurd stupidity! This is something we could have done without, perfectly well.

JOAN. A cross! Let me have a cross, a cross to hold: pity me!

PROMOTER. No, no! No cross for a witch!

JOAN. Give me a cross, a cross to hold, a crucifix!

CAUCHON. Ladvenu! To the parish church! Run, Ladvenu!

[LADVENU *runs off.*]

PROMOTER. [*to the* INQUISITOR] This is most irregular! Aren't you going to protest, my lord?

INQUISITOR. [*staring at* JOAN] With or without a cross, she has to be silenced, and quickly! Look at her, defying us. Are we never going to be able to master this flaunting spirit of man?

JOAN. A cross!

> [*An* ENGLISH SOLDIER *has taken two sticks, ties them together and calls to* JOAN.]

SOLDIER. Hold on, wait a bit, my girl: here you are! What are they talking about, these two priests? They make me vomit. She's got a right to a cross, like anybody else.

PROMOTER. [*rushing forward*] She is a heretic! I forbid you to give it to her!

SOLDIER. [*jostling him off*] You choke yourself.

> [*He offers the improvised cross to* JOAN, *who clasps it against her, and kisses it.*]

PROMOTER. [*rushing to* WARWICK] My lord! This man ought to be arrested as a heretic. I insist that you arrest him immediately!

WARWICK. You make me tired, sir. I have eight hundred men like that, each one more heretical than the others. They are what I use to fight the wars with.

INQUISITOR. [*to the* EXECUTIONER] Will you hurry and light the fire? Let the smoke cover her quickly, and hide her away out of our sight! [*to* WARWICK] We must make haste! In five minutes everybody will have swung to her side, they will all be for her!

WARWICK. I'm very much afraid that has already happened.

> [LADVENU *runs in with a cross.*]

PROMOTER. [*yelling*] Don't dare to give her the cross, Brother Ladvenu!

CAUCHON. Let him alone, Canon: I order you to let him alone.

PROMOTER. I shall refer this matter to the court of Rome!

CAUCHON. You can refer it to the devil, if you like: for the present moment, the orders to be obeyed here are mine.

> [*All this is rapid, hurly-burly, improvised, like a police operation.*]

INQUISITOR. [*running from one to the other nervously*] We must be quick! We must be quick! We must be quick!

LADVENU. [*who has climbed up to the stake*] Courage, Joan. We are all praying for you.

JOAN. Thank you, little brother. But get down: the flames will catch you: you will be burnt as well.

INQUISITOR. [*who can't bear it any more, to the* EXECUTIONER] Well, man, have you done it yet, have you done it?

EXECUTIONER. [*climbing down*] Yes, it's done, my lord, it's alight. In two minutes, you'll see, the flames will have reached her.

INQUISITOR. [*with a sigh of relief*] At last!

CAUCHON. [*falling on his knees*] O God, forgive us! [*They all kneel, and start the prayers for the dead. The* PROMOTER, *in a fury of hatred, remains standing.*] Get down on your knees, Canon!

> [*The* PROMOTER *looks like a cornered animal: he kneels.*]

INQUISITOR. [*who dare not look, to* LADVENU *who is near him and holding the cross for* JOAN] Is she looking straight in front of her?

LADVENU. Yes, my lord.

INQUISITOR. Without flinching?

LADVENU. Yes, my lord.

INQUISITOR. [*almost sorrowfully*] And there is almost a smile on her lips, is there not?

LADVENU. Yes, my lord.

INQUISITOR. [*with bowed head, overwhelmed, heavily*] I shall never be able to master him.

LADVENU. [*radiant with confidence and joy*] No, my lord!

JOAN. [*murmuring, already twisted with pain*] Blessed Michael, Margaret, and Catherine, you were brighter than these flames: let your voices burn me. O Lord Jesus, let them speak to me. Speak to me. In the fields, in the heat of the sun. Noon.

AGNES. [*kneeling in a corner with* CHARLES *and the* QUEEN] Poor little Joan. It is monstrous and stupid. Do you think she is suffering already?

CHARLES. [*wiping his forehead and looking away*] There is still the agony to come.

[*The murmur of the prayers for the dead drowns the voices. Suddenly* BEAUDRICOURT *bursts on to the stage, breathless from running.*]

BEAUDRICOURT. Stop! Stop! Stop!

[*Everyone is startled; a moment of uncertainty. To* CAUCHON] This can't be the way it goes! Grant a stay of execution, and let me have time to think! For, as I said to her when she first came to me, I don't think clearly when suddenly put to it. But one thing I do see: we haven't done what we said we'd do. We haven't performed the coronation! We said that we were going to play everything! And we haven't at all. It isn't justice to her. And she has a right to see the coronation performed: it's a part of her story.

CAUCHON. [*struck by this*] We did say so, indeed; you are right to remind us. You remember, gentlemen: the whole of her life to go through, was what we said. We were in too great a hurry to bring her to an end. We were committing an injustice!

CHARLES. You see! I knew they would forget my coronation. No one ever remembers my coronation. And look what it cost me.

WARWICK. Well, really! The Coronation, now! And at this time of the day, as though their little victory came last. It would be most improper for me to attend any such ceremony; I shall go away. As far as I'm concerned it is all over, and Joan is burnt. His Majesty's Government has obtained its political objective. [*He goes.*]

CAUCHON. Unchain her! Drag away the faggots! Give her the sword and the standard again! [*He goes.*]

[*Everyone joyously drags down the stage and faggots.*]

CHARLES. This man is quite right. The real end of Joan's story, the end which will never come to an end, which they will always tell, long after they have forgotten our names or confused them all together: it isn't the painful and miserable end of the cornered animal caught at Rouen: but the lark singing in the open sky. Joan at Rheims in all her glory. The true end of the story is a kind of joy. Joan of Arc: a story which ends happily.

[*They have quickly set up an altar where the stake was standing. Bells suddenly ring out proudly. A procession forms with* CHARLES, JOAN *a little behind him, then the* QUEENS, LA TREMOUILLE, *etc. The procession moves towards the altar.* EVERYONE *kneels. Only* JOAN *remains standing, leaning on her standard, smiling upward, like a statue of her. The* ARCHBISHOP *puts the crown on* CHARLES'S *head. Bells, a salute of cannon, a flight of doves, a play of light perhaps, which throws the reflection of the cathedral stained glass across the scene, transforming it. The curtain falls slowly on this beautiful illustration from a school prize.*]

Alcestis

EURIPIDES

Alcestis was produced in 438 B.C. It was the fourth play in the tetralogy (the other three have disappeared) that Euripides entered in that year's tragedy competition; he won second prize to Sophocles' first. Since the fourth play in a set was ordinarily a satyr-play, a burlesque of a hero of myth, *Alcestis*, which Richmond Lattimore calls "a tragedy with a happy ending," was an unusual play to appear in that position. It is an unusual play in any case, one that is open to a wide variety of interpretations. Admetus is generally taken as the play's central figure, and the differing opinions about the play have to do with the way one looks at that unhappy king of Thessaly. Some critics assume that Euripides is treating the character sympathetically, drawing a sharp portrait of a man who learns something about himself and about death; to others, Admetus is the object of Euripides' satire. Although these are the two sides of the conventional conflict about *Alcestis*, there are a few unusual readings of the play. According to one, Alcestis does not die at all, but simply swoons, and her supposed rescue from Death becomes part of the playwright's subdued poke at conventional theology. According to another, the drunken Heracles (a standard figure in Greek comedy) brings back not a live Alcestis, but the woman's dead body, and the play becomes a macabre comedy. Since the stage directions in any Greek play, as well as the assignment of lines to particular characters, are the work of the translator, it might be possible to play *Alcestis* in line with any of these theories without doing violence to the text. After all, classics in the theater change regularly from era to era, from actor to actor. In the case of the Greek drama, each generation gets not only new interpretations, but new translations. Richmond Lattimore is one of the men whose work has been instrumental in rescuing us and the Greek plays from the turn-of-the-century translations which once oppressed us.

Alcestis†

Characters

APOLLO

DEATH

CHORUS OF CITIZENS OF PHERAE

MAID, *attendant of* ALCESTIS

† Translated by Richmond Lattimore. From Richmond Lattimore and David Grene, eds., *The Complete Greek Trag-* *edies.* Copyright © 1955 by the University of Chicago Press. Reprinted by permission of the publisher.

ALCESTIS, *wife of* ADMETUS
ADMETUS OF PHERAE, *king of Thessaly*
BOY (EUMELUS), *son of* ADMETUS *and* ALCESTIS
HERACLES
PHERES, *father of* ADMETUS
SERVANT OF ADMETUS
GIRL, *daughter of* ADMETUS *and* ALCESTIS (*silent character*)
SERVANTS (*silent*)

SCENE: *Pherae, in Thessaly, before the house of* ADMETUS. *The front door of the house, or palace, is the center of the backdrop.*

[*Enter* APOLLO *from the house, armed with a bow.*]
APOLLO. House of Admetus, in which I, god though I am,
  had patience to accept the table of the serfs!
  Zeus was the cause. Zeus killed my son, Asclepius,
  and drove the bolt of the hot lightning through his chest.
  I, in my anger for this, killed the Cyclopes,   5
  smiths of Zeus's fire, for which my father made me serve
  a mortal man, in penance for my misdoings.
  I came to this country, tended the oxen of this host
  and friend, Admetus, son of Pheres. I have kept
  his house from danger, cheated the Fates to save his life   10
  until this day, for he revered my sacred rights
  sacredly, and the fatal goddesses allowed
  Admetus to escape the moment of his death
  by giving the lower powers someone else to die
  instead of him. He tried his loved ones all in turn,   15
  father and aged mother who had given him birth,
  and found not one, except his wife, who would consent
  to die for him, and not see daylight any more.
  She is in the house now, gathered in his arms and held
  at the breaking point of life, because the destiny marks   20
  this for her day of death and taking leave of life.
  The stain of death in the house must not be on me. I
  step therefore from these chambers dearest to my love.
  And here is Death himself, I see him coming, Death
  who dedicates the dying, who will lead her down   25
  to the house of Hades. He has come on time. He has
  been watching for this day on which her death falls due.
        [*Enter* DEATH, *armed with a sword, from the wing. He sees*
        APOLLO *suddenly and shows surprise.*]
DEATH. Ah!
  You at this house, Phoebus? Why do you haunt
  the place. It is unfair to take for your own   30
  and spoil the death-spirits' privileges.
  Was it not enough, then, that you blocked the death
  of Admetus, and overthrew the Fates

by a shabby wrestler's trick? And now
your bow hand is armed to guard her too,   35
Alcestis, Pelias' daughter, though she
promised her life for her husband's.

APOLLO. Never fear. I have nothing but justice and fair words
for you.

DEATH. If you mean fairly, what are you doing with a bow?

APOLLO. It is my custom to carry it with me all the time.   40

DEATH. It is your custom to help this house more than you
ought.

APOLLO. But he is my friend, and his misfortunes trouble me.

DEATH. You mean to take her body, too, away from me?

APOLLO. I never took *his* body away from you by force.

DEATH. How is it, then, that he is above ground, not below?   45

APOLLO. He gave his wife instead, and you have come for her
now.

DEATH. I have. And I shall take her down where the dead are.

APOLLO. Take her and go. I am not sure you will listen to me.

DEATH. Tell me to kill whom I must kill. Such are my orders.

APOLLO. No, only to put their death off. They must die in the
end.   50

DEATH. I understand what you would say and what you want.

APOLLO. Is there any way, then, for Alcestis to grow old?

DEATH. There is not. I insist on enjoying my rights too.

APOLLO. You would not take more than one life, in any case.

DEATH. My privilege means more to me when they die young.   55

APOLLO. If she dies old, she will have a lavish burial.

DEATH. What you propose, Phoebus, is to favor the rich.

APOLLO. What is this? Have you unrecognized talent for debate?

DEATH. Those who could afford to buy a late death would buy
it then.

APOLLO. I see. Are you determined not to do this for me?   60

DEATH. I will not do it. And you know my character.

APOLLO. I know it: hateful to mankind, loathed by the gods.

DEATH. You cannot always have your way where you should not.

APOLLO. For all your brute ferocity you shall be stopped.
The man to do it is on the way to Pheres' house   65
now, on an errand from Eurystheus, sent to steal
a team of horses from the wintry lands of Thrace.
He shall be entertained here in Admetus' house
and he shall take the woman away from you by force,
nor will you have our gratitude, but you shall still   70
be forced to do it, and to have my hate beside.

DEATH. Much talk. Talking will win you nothing. All the same,
the woman goes with me to Hades' house. I go
to take her now, and dedicate her with my sword,
for all whose hair is cut in consecration   75
by this blade's edge are devoted to the gods below.

[DEATH *enters the house.* APOLLO *leaves by the wing. The*

CHORUS *enters and forms a group before the gates.*]

CHORUS. It is quiet by the palace. What does it mean?
Why is the house of Admetus so still?
Is there none here of his family, none
who can tell us whether the queen is dead   80
and therefore to be mourned? Or does Pelias'
daughter Alcestis live still, still look
on daylight, she who in my mind appears
noble beyond
all women beside in a wife's duty?   85

[*Here they speak individually, not as a group.*]¹

FIRST CITIZEN. Does someone hear anything?
The sound a hand's stroke would make,
or outcry, as if something were done
and over?

SECOND CITIZEN. No. And there is not servant stationed
at the outer gates. O Paean,   90
healer, might you show in light
to still the storm of disaster.

THIRD CITIZEN. They would not be silent if she were dead.

FOURTH CITIZEN. No, she is gone.

FIFTH CITIZEN. They have not taken her yet from the house.

SIXTH CITIZEN. So sure? I know nothing. Why are you certain?   95
And how could Admetus have buried his wife
with none by, and she so splendid?

SEVENTH CITIZEN. Here at the gates I do not see
the lustral spring water, approved
by custom for a house of death.   100

EIGHTH CITIZEN. Nor are there cut locks of hair at the forecourts
hanging, such as the stroke of sorrow
for the dead makes. I can hear no beating
of the hands of young women.

NINTH CITIZEN. Yet this is the day appointed.   105

TENTH CITIZEN. What do you mean? Speak.

NINTH CITIZEN. On which she must pass to the world below.

ELEVENTH CITIZEN. You touch me deep, my heart, where it hurts.

TWELFTH CITIZEN. Yes. He who from the first has claimed to be
called
a good man himself   110
must grieve when good men are afflicted.

[*Henceforward all the* CHORUS *together.*]

Sailing the long sea, there is
not any place on earth
you could win, not Lycia,

---

1. It is the translator who has par-
celed out pieces of the chorus speech
to individual choristers. In some translations, this speech is divided among
semi-choruses. Since most of what we
know about the performance of the
Greek chorus is conjectural—and since
the translator has to assign all the
speeches in any play to particular
characters—either method is accepta-
ble. Given the nature of the lines, their
sense of confusion and contradiction,
Lattimore's designation seems sensible.

not the unwatered sands called
of Ammon,
to approach and redeem the life
of this unhappy woman. Her fate shows
steep and near. There is no god's hearth
I know you could reach and by sacrifice
avail to save.

There was only one. If the eyes
of Phoebus' son were opened
still, if he could have come
and left the dark chambers,
the gates of Hades.
He upraised those who were stricken
down, until from the hand of God
the flown bolt of thunder hit him.
Where is there any hope for life
left for me any longer?

For all has been done that can be done by our kings now,
and there on all the gods' altars
are blood sacrifices dripping in full,
but no healing comes for the evil.

[*Enter a* MAID *from the house.*]

CHORUS. But here is a serving woman coming from the house.
The tears break from her. What will she say has taken place?
We must, of course, forgive your sorrow if something
has happened to your masters. We should like to know
whether the queen is dead or if she is still alive.

MAID. I could tell you that she is still alive or that she is dead.

CHORUS. How could a person both be dead and live and see?

MAID. It has felled her, and the life is breaking from her now.

CHORUS. Such a husband, to lose such a wife. I pity you.

MAID. The master does not see it and he will not see it
until it happens.

CHORUS. There is no hope left she will live?

MAID. None. This is the day of destiny. It is too strong.

CHORUS. Surely, he must be doing all he can for her.

MAID. All is prepared so he can bury her in style.

CHORUS. Let her be sure, at least, that as she dies, there dies
the noblest woman underneath the sun, by far.

MAID. Noblest? Of course the noblest, who will argue that?
What shall the wife be who surpasses her? And how
could any woman show that she loves her husband more
than herself better than by consent to die for him?
But all the city knows that well. You shall be told
now how she acted in the house, and be amazed
to hear. For when she understood the fatal day
was come, she bathed her white body with water drawn
from running streams, then opened the cedar chest and took

her clothes out, and dressed in all her finery
and stood before the Spirit in the Hearth, and prayed:
"Mistress, since I am going down beneath the ground,
I kneel before you in this last of all my prayers.
Take care of my children for me. Give the little girl   165
a husband; give the little boy a generous wife;
and do not let my children die like me, who gave
them birth, untimely. Let them live a happy life
through to the end and prosper here in their own land."
Afterward she approached the altars, all that stand   170
in the house of Admetus, made her prayers, and decked them
    all
with fresh sprays torn from living myrtle. And she wept
not at all, made no outcry. The advancing doom
made no change in the color and beauty of her face.
But then, in their room, she threw herself upon the bed,   175
and there she did cry, there she spoke: "O marriage bed,
it was here that I undressed my maidenhood and gave
myself up to this husband for whose sake I die.
Goodbye. I hold no grudge. But you have been my death
and mine alone. I could not bear to play him false.   180
I die. Some other woman will possess you now.
She will not be better, but she might be happier."
She fell on the bed and kissed it. All the coverings
were drenched in the unchecked outpouring of her tears;
but after much crying, when all her tears were shed,   185
she rolled from the couch and walked away with eyes cast
    down,
began to leave the room, but turned and turned again
to fling herself once more upon the bed. Meanwhile
the children clung upon their mother's dress, and cried,
until she gathered them into her arms, and kissed   190
first one and then the other, as in death's farewell.
And all the servants in the house were crying now
in sorrow for their mistress. Then she gave her hand
to each, and each one took it, there was none so mean
in station that she did not stop and talk with him.   195
This is what Admetus and the house are losing. Had
he died, he would have lost her, but in this escape
he will keep the pain. It will not ever go away.
CHORUS. Admetus surely must be grieving over this
when such a wife must be taken away from him.   200
MAID. Oh yes, he is crying. He holds his wife close in his arms,
imploring her not to forsake him. What he wants
is impossible. She is dying. The sickness fades her now.
She has gone slack, just an inert weight on the arm.
Still, though so little breath of life is left in her,   205
she wants to look once more upon the light of the sun,
since this will be the last time of all, and never again.
She must see the sun's shining circle yet one more time.

Now I must go announce your presence. It is not
everyone who bears so much good will toward our kings   210
as to stand by ready to help in their distress.
But you have been my master's friends since long ago.
    [*Exit.*]
CHORUS. O Zeus, Zeus, what way out of this evil
is there, what escape from this
which is happening to our princes?
A way, any way? Must I cut short my hair   215
for grief, put upon me the black
costume that means mourning?
We must, friends, clearly we must; yet still
let us pray to the gods. The gods
have power beyond all power elsewhere.

Paean, my lord,   220
Apollo, make some way of escape for Admetus.
Grant it, oh grant it. Once you found
rescue in him. Be now
in turn his redeemer from death.
Oppose bloodthirsty Hades.   225

Admetus,
O son of Pheres, what a loss
to suffer, when such a wife goes.
A man could cut his throat for this, for this
and less he could bind the noose upon his neck
and hang himself. For this is   230
not only dear, but dearest of all,
this wife you will see dead
on this day before you.
    [ALCESTIS *is carried from the house on a litter, supported*
    by ADMETUS *and followed by her children and servants of*
    the household.]
But see, see,
she is coming out of the house and her husband is with her.
Cry out aloud, mourn, you land
of Pherae for the bravest   235
of wives fading in sickness and doomed
to the Death God of the world below.

I will never again say that marriage brings
more pleasure than pain. I judge by what
I have known in the past, and by seeing now   240
what happens to our king, who is losing a wife
brave beyond all others, and must live a life
that will be no life for the rest of time.
ALCESTIS. Sun, and light of the day,
O turning wheel of the sky, clouds that fly.   245
ADMETUS. The sun sees you and me, two people suffering,

who never hurt the gods so they should make you die.
ALCESTIS. My land, and palace arching my land,
and marriage chambers of Iolcus, my own country.
ADMETUS. Raise yourself, my Alcestis, do not leave me now.   250
I implore the gods to pity you. They have the power.
ALCESTIS. I see him there at the oars of his little boat in the lake,
the ferryman of the dead,
Charon, with his hand upon the oar,
and he calls me now: "What keeps you?   255
Hurry, you hold us back." He is urging me on
in angry impatience.
ADMETUS. The crossing you speak of is a bitter one for me;
ill starred; it is unfair we should be treated so.
ALCESTIS. Somebody has me, somebody takes me away, do you
      see,
don't you see, to the courts   260
of dead men. He frowns from under dark
brows. He has wings. It is Death.
Let me go, what are you doing, let go.
                                        Such is the road
most wretched I have to walk.
ADMETUS. Sorrow for all who love you, most of all for me
and for the children. All of us share in this grief.   265
ALCESTIS. Let me go now, let me down,
flat. I have no strength to stand.
Death is close to me.
The darkness creeps over my eyes. O children,
my children, you have no mother now,   270
not any longer. Daylight is yours,
my children. Look on it and be happy.
ADMETUS. Ah, a bitter word for me to hear,
heavier than any death of my own.
Before the gods, do not be so harsh   275
as to leave me, leave your children forlorn.
No, up, and fight it.
There would be nothing left of me if you died.
All rests in you, our life, our not
having life. Your love is our worship.
ALCESTIS. Admetus, you can see how it is with me. Therefore,   280
I wish to have some words with you before I die.
I put you first, and at the price of my own life
made certain you would live and see the daylight. So
I die, who did not have to die, because of you.
I could have taken any man in Thessaly   285
I wished and lived in queenly state here in this house.
But since I did not wish to live bereft of you
and with our children fatherless, I did not spare
my youth, although I had so much to live for. Yet
your father, and the mother who bore you, gave you up,   290
though they had reached an age when it was good to die

and good to save their son and end it honorably.
You were their only one, and they had no more hope
of having other children if you died. That way
I would be living and you would live the rest of our time,   295
and you would not be alone and mourning for your wife
and tending motherless children. No, but it must be
that some god has so wrought that things shall be this way.
So be it. But swear now to do, in recompense,
what I shall ask you—not enough, oh, never enough,   300
since nothing is enough to make up for a life,
but fair, and you yourself will say so, since you love
these children as much as I do; or at least you should.
Keep them as masters in my house, and do not marry
again and give our children to a stepmother   305
who will not be so kind as I, who will be jealous
and raise her hand to your children and mine. Oh no,
do not do that, do not. That is my charge to you.
For the new-come stepmother hates the children born
to a first wife, no viper could be deadlier.   310
The little boy has his father for a tower of strength.
He can talk with him and be spoken to in turn.
But you, my darling, what will your girlhood be like,
how will your father's new wife like you? She must not
make shameful stories up about you, and contrive   315
to spoil your chance of marriage in the blush of youth,
because your mother will not be there to help you
when you are married, not be there to give you strength
when your babies are born, when only a mother's help will do.
For I must die. It will not be tomorrow, not   320
the next day, or this month, the horrible thing will come,
but now, at once, I shall be counted among the dead.
Goodbye, be happy, both of you. And you, my husband,
can boast the bride you took made you the bravest wife,
and you, children, can say, too, that your mother was brave.   325
CHORUS. Fear nothing; for I dare to speak for him. He will
do all you ask. If he does not, the fault is his.
ADMETUS. It shall be so, it shall be, do not fear, since you
were mine in life, you still shall be my bride in death
and you alone, no other girl in Thessaly   330
shall ever be called wife of Admetus in your place.
There is none such, none so marked out in pride of birth
nor beauty's brilliance, nor in anything else. I have
these children, they are enough; I only pray the gods
grant me the bliss to keep them as we could not keep you.   335
I shall go into mourning for you, not for just
a year, but all my life while it still lasts, my dear,
and hate the woman who gave me birth always, detest
my father. These were called my own people. They were not.
You gave what was your own and dear to buy my life   340
and saved me. Am I not to lead a mourning life

when I have lost a wife like you? I shall make an end
of revelry and entertainment in my house,
the flowers and the music that were found here once.
No, I shall never touch the lutestrings ever again   345
nor have the heart to play music upon the flute
of Libya, for you took my joy in life with you.
I shall have the skilled hand of an artificer
make me an image of you to set in my room,
pay my devotions to it, hold it in my arms   350
and speak your name, and clasp it close against my heart,
and think I hold my wife again, though I do not,
cold consolation, I know it, and yet even so
I might drain the weight of sorrow. You could come
to see me in my dreams and comfort me. For they   355
who love find a time's sweetness in the visions of night.
Had I the lips of Orpheus and his melody
to charm the maiden daughter of Demeter and
her lord, and by my singing win you back from death,
I would have gone beneath the earth, and not the hound   360
of Pluto could have stayed me, not the ferryman
of ghosts, Charon at his oar. I would have brought you back
to life. Wait for me, then, in that place, till I die,
and make ready the room where you will live with me,
for I shall have them bury me in the same chest   365
as you, and lay me at your side, so that my heart
shall be against your heart, and never, even in death
shall I go from you. You alone were true to me.
CHORUS. And I, because I am your friend and you
are mine, shall help you bear this sorrow, as I should.   370
ALCESTIS. Children, you now have heard your father promise me
that he will never marry again and not inflict
a new wife on you, but will keep my memory.
ADMETUS. I promise. I will keep my promise to the end.
ALCESTIS. On this condition, take the children. They are yours.   375
ADMETUS. I take them, a dear gift from a dear hand.
ALCESTIS.   And now
you must be our children's mother, too, instead of me.
ADMETUS. I must be such, since they will no longer have you.
ALCESTIS. O children, this was my time to live, and I must go.
ADMETUS. Ah me, what shall I do without you all alone.   380
ALCESTIS. Time will soften it. The dead count for nothing at all.
ADMETUS. Oh, take me with you, for God's love, take me there
              too.
ALCESTIS. No, I am dying in your place. That is enough.
ADMETUS. O God, what a wife you are taking away from me.
ALCESTIS. It is true. My eyes darken and the heaviness comes.   385
ADMETUS. But I am lost, dear, if you leave me.
ALCESTIS.   There is no use
in talking to me any more. I am not there.
ADMETUS. No, lift your head up, do not leave your children thus.

ALCESTIS. I do not want to, but it is goodbye, children.
ADMETUS. Look at them, oh look at them.
ALCESTIS.   No. There is nothing more. ₃₉₀
ADMETUS. Are you really leaving us?
ALCESTIS.   Goodbye.
ADMETUS.   Oh, I am lost.
CHORUS. It is over now. Admetus' wife is gone from us.
BOY.² O wicked fortune. Mother has gone down there,
    father, she is not here with us
    in the sunshine any more.   395
    She was cruel and went away
    and left me to live all alone.
    Look at her eyes, look at her hands, so still.
    Hear me, mother, listen to me, oh please,   400
    listen, it is I, mother,
    I your little one lean and kiss
    your lips, and cry out to you.
ADMETUS. She does not see, she does not hear you. You and I
    both have a hard and heavy load to carry now.   405
BOY. Father, I am too small to be left alone
    by the mother I loved so much. Oh,
    it is hard for me to bear
    all this that is happening,
    and you, little sister, suffer   410
    with me too. Oh, father,
    your marriage was empty, empty, she did not live
    to grow old with you.
    She died too soon. Mother, with you gone away,
    the whole house is ruined.   415
        [ALCESTIS *is carried into the house, followed by children*
        and servants.]
CHORUS. Admetus, you must stand up to misfortune now.
    You are not the first, and not the last of humankind
    to lose a good wife. Therefore, you must understand
    death is an obligation claimed from all of us.
ADMETUS. I understand it. And this evil which has struck   420
    was no surprise. I knew about it long ago,
    and knowledge was hard. But now, since we must bury our
        dead,
    stay with me and stand by me, chant responsively
    the hymn of the unsacrificed-to god below.
    To all Thessalians over whom my rule extends   425
    I ordain a public mourning for my wife, to be
    observed with shaving of the head and with black robes.
    The horses that you drive in chariots and those
    you ride single shall have their manes cut short with steel,
    and there shall be no sound of flutes within the city,   430

2. Since Greek drama ordinarily al-   Admetus in this scene—it is probable
lowed for no more than two speaking   that a chorister spoke or sang the
actors on stage at any one time—and   Boy's lines.
since they are obviously Alcestis and

no sound of lyres, until twelve moons have filled and gone;
for I shall never bury any dearer dead
than she, nor any who loved me better. She deserves
my thanks. She died for me, which no one else would do.
    [*Exit into the house.*]

CHORUS. O daughter of Pelias   435
my wish for you is a happy life
in the sunless chambers of Hades.
Now let the dark-haired lord of Death himself, and the old man,
who sits at the steering oar   440
and ferries the corpses,
know that you are the bravest of wives, by far,
ever conveyed across the tarn
of Acheron in the rowboat.

Much shall be sung of you   445
by the men of music to the seven-strung mountain
lyre-shell, and in poems that have no music,
in Sparta when the season turns and the month Carneian
comes back, and the moon
rides all the night;   450
in Athens also, the shining and rich.
Such is the theme of song you left
in death, for the poets.

Oh that it were in my power   455
and that I had strength to bring you
back to light from the dark of death
with oars on the sunken river.
For you, O dearest among women, you only   460
had the hard courage
to give your life for your husband's and save
him from death. May the dust lie light
upon you, my lady. And should he now take
a new wife to his bed, he will win my horror and hatred,
mine, and your children's hatred too.   465

His mother would not endure
to have her body hidden in the ground
for him, nor the aged father.
He was theirs, but they had not courage to save him.
Oh shame, for the gray was upon them.   470
But you, in the pride
of youth, died for him and left the daylight.
May it only be mine to win
such wedded love as hers from a wife; for this
is given seldom to mortals; but were my wife such, I would
    have her
with me unhurt through her lifetime.   475

[*Enter* HERACLES *from the road, travel-stained.*]

HERACLES. My friends, people of Pherae and the villages
  hereby, tell me, shall I find Admetus at home?

CHORUS. Yes, Heracles, the son of Pheres is in the house.
  But tell us, what is the errand that brings you here
  to Thessaly and the city of Pherae once again?   480

HERACLES. I have a piece of work to do for Eurystheus
  of Tiryns.

CHORUS.   Where does it take you? On what far journey?

HERACLES. To Thrace, to take home Diomedes' chariot.

CHORUS. How can you? Do you know the man you are to meet?

HERACLES. No. I have never been where the Bistones live.   485

CHORUS. You cannot master his horses. Not without a fight.

HERACLES. It is my work, and I cannot refuse.

CHORUS.   You must
  kill him before you come back; or be killed and stay.

HERACLES. If I must fight, it will not be for the first time.

CHORUS. What good will it do you if you overpower their master?   490

HERACLES. I will take the horses home to Tiryns and its king.

CHORUS. It is not easy to put a bridle on their jaws.

HERACLES. Easy enough, unless their nostrils are snorting fire.

CHORUS. Not that, but they have teeth that tear a man apart.

HERACLES. Oh no! Mountain beasts, not horses, feed like that.   495

CHORUS. But you can see their mangers. They are caked with
      blood.

HERACLES. And the man who raises them? Whose son does he
      claim he is?

CHORUS. Ares'. And he is lord of the golden shield of Thrace.

HERACLES. It sounds like my life and the kind of work I do.
  It is a hard and steep way always that I go,   500
  having to fight one after another all the sons
  the war god ever got him, with Lycaon first,
  again with Cycnus, and now here is a third fight
  that I must have with the master of these horses. So—
  I am Alcmene's son, and the man does not live   505
  who will see me break before my enemy's attack.

CHORUS. Here is the monarch of our country coming
  from the house himself, Admetus.

      [*Enter* ADMETUS.]

ADMETUS.   Welcome and happiness
  to you, O scion of Perseus' blood and child of Zeus.

HERACLES. Happiness to you likewise, lord of Thessaly,   510
  Admetus.

ADMETUS. I could wish it. I know you mean well.

HERACLES. What is the matter? Why is there mourning and cut
      hair?

ADMETUS. There is one dead here whom I must bury today.

HERACLES. Not one of your children! I pray God shield them from
      that.

ADMETUS. Not they. My children are well and living in their   515 house.

HERACLES. If it is your father who is gone, his time was ripe.

ADMETUS. No, he is still there, Heracles. My mother, too.

HERACLES. Surely you have not lost your wife, Alcestis.

ADMETUS.   Yes
and no. There are two ways that I could answer that.

HERACLES. Did you say that she is dead or that she is still alive?   520

ADMETUS. She is, but she is gone away. It troubles me.

HERACLES. I still do not know what you mean. You are being
    obscure.

ADMETUS. You know about her and what must happen, do you
    not?

HERACLES. I know that she has undertaken to die for you.

ADMETUS. How can she really live, then, when she has promised   525
    that?

HERACLES. Ah, do not mourn her before she dies. Wait for the
    time.

ADMETUS. The point of death is death, and the dead are lost and
    gone.

HERACLES. Being and nonbeing are considered different things.

ADMETUS. That is your opinion, Heracles. It is not mine.

HERACLES. Well, but whose is the mourning now? Is it in the
    family?   530

ADMETUS. A woman. We were speaking of a woman, were we not?

HERACLES. Was she a blood relative or someone from outside?

ADMETUS. No relation by blood, but she meant much to us.

HERACLES. How does it happen that she died here in your house?

ADMETUS. She lost her father and came here to live with us.   535

HERACLES. I am sorry,
    Admetus. I wish I had found you in a happier state.

ADMETUS. Why do you say that? What do you mean to do?

HERACLES.   I mean
to go on, and stay with another of my friends.

ADMETUS. No, my lord, no. The evil must not come to that.

HERACLES. The friend who stays with friends in mourning is in   540
    the way.

ADMETUS. The dead are dead. Go on in.

HERACLES.   No. It is always wrong
for guests to revel in a house where others mourn.

ADMETUS. There are separate guest chambers. We can take you
    there.

HERACLES. Let me go, and I will thank you a thousand times.

ADMETUS. You shall not go to stay with any other man.   545
    You there: open the guest rooms which are across the court
    from the house, and tell the people who are there to provide
    plenty to eat, and make sure that you close the doors
    facing the inside court. It is not right for guests
    to have their pleasures interrupted by sounds of grief.   550
        [HERACLES *is ushered inside.*]

CHORUS. Admetus, are you crazy? What are you thinking of

to entertain guests in a situation like this?
ADMETUS. And if I had driven from my city and my house
the guest and friend who came to me, would you have approved
of me more? Wrong. My misery would still have been   555
as great, and I should be inhospitable too,
and there would be one more misfortune added to those
I have, if my house is called unfriendly to its friends.
For this man is my best friend, and he is my host
whenever I go to Argos, which is a thirsty place.   560
CHORUS. Yes, but then why did you hide what is happening here
if this visitor is, as you say, your best friend?
ADMETUS. He would not have been willing to come inside my
          house
if he had known what trouble I was in. I know.
There are some will think I show no sense in doing this.   565
They will not like it. But my house does not know how
to push its friends away and not treat them as it should.
[*He goes inside.*]
CHORUS. O liberal and forever free-handed house of this man,
the Pythian himself, lyric Apollo,   570
was pleased to live with you
and had patience upon your lands
to work as a shepherd,
and on the hill-folds and the slopes   575
piped to the pasturing of your flocks
in their season of mating.
And even dappled lynxes for delight in his melody
joined him as shepherds. From the cleft of Othrys descended 580
a red troop of lions,
and there, Phoebus, to your lyre's strain
there danced the bright-coated
fawn, adventuring from the deep   585
bearded pines, lightfooted for joy
in your song, in its kindness.

Therefore, your house is beyond
all others for wealth of flocks by the sweet waters
of Lake Boebias. For spread of cornland   590
and pasturing range its boundary stands
only there where the sun
stalls his horses in dark air by the Molossians.
Eastward he sways all to the harborless   595
Pelian coast on the Aegaean main.

Now he has spread wide his doors
and taken the guest in, when his eyes were wet
and he wept still for a beloved wife who died
In the house so lately. The noble strain   600
comes out, in respect for others.
All that wisdom means is there in the noble. I stand

in awe, and good hope has come again to my heart
that for this godly man the end will be good.   605
    [*Enter* ADMETUS *from the house, followed by servants with
    a covered litter.*]
ADMETUS. Gentlemen of Pherae, I am grateful for your company.
  My men are bearing to the burning place and grave
  our dead, who now has all the state which is her due.
  Will you then, as the custom is among us, say
  farewell to the dead as she goes forth for the last time?   610
CHORUS. Yes, but I see your father coming now. He walks
  as old men do, and followers carry in their hands
  gifts for your wife, to adorn her in the underworld.
    [*Enter* PHERES, *attended, from outside.*]
PHERES. I have come to bear your sorrows with you, son. I know,
  nobody will dispute it, you have lost a wife   615
  both good and modest in her ways. Nevertheless,
  you have to bear it, even though it is hard to bear.
  Accept these gifts to deck her body, bury them
  with her. Oh yes, she well deserves honor in death.
  She died to save your life, my son. She would not let   620
  me be a childless old man, would not let me waste
  away in sorrowful age deprived of you. Thereby,
  daring this generous action, she has made the life
  of all women become a thing of better repute
  than it was.
           O you who saved him, you who raised us up   625
  when we were fallen, farewell, even in Hades' house
  may good befall you.
              I say people ought to marry women
  like this. Otherwise, better not to marry at all.
ADMETUS. I never invited you to come and see her buried,
  nor do I count your company as that of a friend.   630
  She shall not wear anything that you bring her.
  She needs nothing from you to be buried in. Your time
  to share my sorrow was when I was about to die.
  But you stood out of the way and let youth take my place
  in death, though you were old. Will you cry for her now?   635
  It cannot be that my body ever came from you,
  nor did the woman who claims she bore me and is called
  my mother give me birth. I was got from some slave
  and surreptitiously put to your wife to nurse.
  You show it. Your nature in the crisis has come out.   640
  I do not count myself as any child of yours.
  Oh, you outpass the cowardice of all the world,
  you at your age, come to the very last step of life
  and would not, dared not, die for your own child. Oh, no,
  you let this woman, married into our family,   645
  do it instead, and therefore it is right for me
  to call her all the father and mother that I have.
  And yet you two should honorably have striven for

the right of dying for your child. The time of life
you had left for your living was short, in any case,   650
and she and I would still be living out our time
and I should not be hurt and grieving over her.
And yet, all that a man could have to bless his life
you have had. You had your youth in kingship. There was I
your son, ready to take it over, keep your house   655
in order, so you had no childless death to fear,
with the house left to be torn apart by other claims.
You cannot justify your leaving me to death
on grounds that I disrespected your old age. Always I
showed all consideration. See what thanks I get   660
from you and from the woman who gave me birth. Go on,
get you other children, you cannot do it too soon,
who will look after your old age, and lay you out
when you are dead, and see you buried properly.
I will not do it. This hand will never bury you.   665
I am dead as far as you are concerned, and if, because
I found another savior, I still look on the sun,
I count myself that person's child and fond support.
It is meaningless, the way the old men pray for death
and complain of age and the long time they have to live.   670
Let death only come close, not one of them still wants
to die. Their age is not a burden any more.
CHORUS. Stop, stop. We have trouble enough already, child.
   You will exasperate your father with this talk.
PHERES. Big words, son. Who do you think you are cursing out   675
like this? Some Lydian slave, some Phrygian that you bought?
I am a free Thessalian noble, nobly born
from a Thessalian. Are you forgetting that? You go
too far with your high-handedness. You volley brash
words at me, and fail to hit me, and then run away.   680
I gave you life, and made you master of my house,
and raised you. I am not obliged to die for you.
I do not acknowledge any tradition among us
that fathers should die for their sons. That is not Greek.
Your natural right is to find your own happiness   685
or unhappiness. All you deserve from me, you have.
You are lord of many. I have wide estates of land
to leave you, just as my father left them to me.
What harm have I done you then? What am I taking away
from you? Do not die for me, I will not die for you.   690
You like the sunlight. Don't you think your father does?
I count the time I have to spend down there as long,
and the time to live is little, but that little is sweet.
You fought shamelessly for a way to escape death,
and passed your proper moment, and are still alive   695
because you killed her. Then, you wretch, you dare to call
me coward, when you let your woman outdare you,
and die for her magnificent young man? I see.

You have found a clever scheme by which you *never* will die.
You will always persuade the wife you have at the time   700
to die for you instead. And you, so low, then dare
blame your own people for not wanting to do this.
Silence. I tell you, as you cherish your own life,
all other people cherish theirs. And if you call
us names, you will be called names, and the names are true.   705
CHORUS. Too much evil has been said in this speech and in
that spoken before. Old sir, stop cursing your own son.
ADMETUS. No, speak, and I will speak too. If it hurts to hear
the truth, you should not have made a mistake with me.
PHERES. I should have made a mistake if I had died for you.   710
ADMETUS. Is it the same thing to die old and to die young?
PHERES. Yes. We have only one life and not two to live.
ADMETUS. I think you would like to live a longer time than Zeus.
PHERES. Cursing your parents, when they have done nothing to
you?
ADMETUS. Yes, for I found you much in love with a long life.   715
PHERES. Who is it you are burying? Did not someone die?
ADMETUS. And that she died, you foul wretch, proves your cow-
ardice.
PHERES. You cannot say that we were involved in her death.
ADMETUS. Ah.
I hope that some day you will stand in need of me.   720
PHERES. Go on, and court more women, so they all can die.
ADMETUS. Your fault. You were not willing to.
PHERES.   No, I was not.
It is a sweet thing, this God's sunshine, sweet to see.
ADMETUS. That is an abject spirit, not a man's.
PHERES.   You shall
not mock an old man while you carry out your dead.
ADMETUS. You will die in evil memory, when you do die.   725
PHERES. I do not care what they say of me when I am dead.
ADMETUS. How old age loses all the sense of shame.
PHERES.   She was
not shameless, you found; she was only innocent.
ADMETUS. Get out of here now and let me bury my dead.
PHERES. I'll go. You murdered her, and you can bury her.   730
But you will have her brothers still to face. You'll pay,
for Acastus is no longer counted as a man
unless he sees you punished for his sister's blood.
ADMETUS. Go and be damned, you and that woman who lives
with you.
Grow old as you deserve, childless, although your son   735
still lives. You shall not come again under the same roof
with me. And if I had to proclaim by heralds that I
disowned my father's house, I should have so proclaimed.
      [PHERES *goes off.*]
Now we, for we must bear the sorrow that is ours,
shall go, and lay her body on the burning place.   740

CHORUS. Ah, cruel the price of your daring,
    O generous one, O noble and brave,
    farewell. May Hermes of the world below
    and Hades welcome you. And if, even there,
    the good fare best, may you have high honor   745
    and sit by the bride of Hades.

      [*The body is borne off, followed by* ADMETUS, SERVANTS,
      and CHORUS. *Thus the stage is empty. Then enter, from
      the house, the* SERVANT *who was put in charge of* HERA-
      CLES.]

SERVANT. I have known all sorts of foreigners who have come in
    from all over the world here to Admetus' house,
    and I have served them dinner, but I never yet
    have had a guest as bad as this to entertain.   750
    In the first place, he could see the master was in mourning,
    but inconsiderately came in anyway.
    Then, he refused to understand the situation
    and be content with anything we could provide,
    but when we failed to bring him something, demanded it,   755
    and took a cup with ivy on it in both hands
    and drank the wine of our dark mother, straight, until
    the flame of the wine went all through him, and heated him,
    and then he wreathed branches of myrtle on his head
    and howled, off key. There were two kinds of music now   760
    to hear, for while he sang and never gave a thought
    to the sorrows of Admetus, we servants were mourning
    our mistress; but we could not show before our guest
    with our eyes wet. Admetus had forbidden that.
    So now I have to entertain this guest inside,   765
    this ruffian thief, this highwayman, whatever he is,
    while she is gone away from the house, and I could not
    say goodbye, stretch my hand out to her in my grief
    for a mistress who was like a mother to all the house
    and me. She gentled her husband's rages, saved us all   770
    from trouble after trouble. Am I not then right
    to hate this guest who has come here in our miseries?

      [*Enter* HERACLES *from the house, drunk, but not hope-
      lessly so.*]

HERACLES. You there, with the sad and melancholy face, what is
    the matter with you? The servant who looks after guests
    should be polite and cheerful and not scowl at them.   775
    But look at you. Here comes your master's dearest friend
    to visit you, and you receive him with black looks
    and frowns, all because of some trouble somewhere else.
    Come here, I'll tell you something that will make you wise.
    Do you really know what things are like, the way they are?   780
    I don't think so. How could you? Well then, listen to me.
    Death is an obligation which we all must pay.
    There is not one man living who can truly say
    if he will be alive or dead on the next day.

Fortune is dark; she moves, but we cannot see the way   785
nor can we pin her down by science and study her.
There, I have told you. Now you can understand. Go on,
enjoy yourself, drink, call the life you live today
your own, but only that, the rest belongs to chance.
Then, beyond all gods, pay your best attention to   790
the Cyprian, man's sweetest. There's a god who's kind.
Let all this business go and do as I prescribe
for you, that is, if I seem to talk sense. Do I?
I think so. Well, then, get rid of this too-much grief,
put flowers on your head and drink with us, fight down   795
these present troubles; later, I know very well
that the wine splashing in the bowl will shake you loose
from these scowl-faced looks and the tension in your mind.
We are only human. Our thoughts should be human too,
since, for these solemn people and these people who scowl,   800
the whole parcel of them, if I am any judge,
life is not really life but a catastrophe.
SERVANT. I know all that. But we have troubles on our hands
now, that make revelry and laughter out of place.
HERACLES. The dead woman is out of the family. Do not mourn   805
too hard. The master and the mistress are still alive.
SERVANT. What do you mean, alive? Do you not know what hap-
        pened?
HERACLES. Certainly, unless your master has lied to me.
SERVANT. He is too hospitable, too much.
HERACLES.   Should I not then
have enjoyed myself, because some outside woman was dead?   810
SERVANT. She was an outsider indeed. That is too true.
HERACLES. Has something happened that he did not tell me
        about?
SERVANT. Never mind. Go. Our masters' sorrows are our own.
HERACLES. These can be no outsiders' troubles.
SERVANT.   If they were,
I should not have minded seeing you enjoy yourself.   815
HERACLES. Have I been scandalously misled by my own friends?
SERVANT. You came here when we were not prepared to take in
        guests.
You see, we are in mourning. You can see our robes
of black, and how our hair is cut short.
HERACLES.   Who is dead?
The aged father? One of the children who is gone?   820
SERVANT. My lord, Admetus' wife is dead.
HERACLES.   What are you saying?
And all this time you were making me comfortable?
SERVANT. He could not bear to turn you from this house of his.
HERACLES. My poor Admetus, what a helpmeet you have lost!
SERVANT. We are all dead and done for now, not only she.   825
HERACLES. I really knew it when I saw the tears in his eyes,
his shorn hair and his face; but he persuaded me

with talk of burying someone who was not by blood
related. So, unwillingly, I came inside
and drank here in the house of this hospitable man   830
when he was in this trouble! Worse, I wreathed my head
with garlands, and drank freely. But you might have said
something about this great disaster in the house.
Now, where shall I find her? Where is the funeral being held?
SERVANT. Go straight along the Larisa road, and when you clear   835
the city you will see the monument and the mound.

    [*He goes into the house, leaving* HERACLES *alone on the
    stage.*]

HERACLES. O heart of mine and hand of mine, who have endured
so much already, prove what kind of son it was
Alcmene, daughter of Electryon, bore to Zeus
in Tiryns. I must save this woman who has died   840
so lately, bring Alcestis back to live in this house,
and pay Admetus all the kindness that I owe.
I must go there and watch for Death of the black robes,
master of dead men, and I think I shall find him
drinking the blood of slaughtered beasts beside the grave.   845
Then, if I can break suddenly from my hiding place,
catch him, and hold him in the circle of these arms,
there is no way he will be able to break my hold
on his bruised ribs, until he gives the woman up
to me. But if I miss my quarry, if he does not come   850
to the clotted offering, I must go down, I must ask
the Maiden and the Master in the sunless homes
of those below; and I have confidence I shall bring
Alcestis back, and give her to the arms of my friend
who did not drive me off but took me into his house   855
and, though he staggered under the stroke of circumstance,
hid it, for he was noble and respected me.
Who in all Thessaly is a truer friend than this?
Who in all Greece? Therefore, he must not ever say
that, being noble, he befriended a worthless man.   860

    [*He goes out. Presently* ADMETUS *comes on, followed by
    the* CHORUS.]

ADMETUS. Hateful is this
return, hateful the sight of this house
widowed, empty. Where shall I go?
Where shall I stay? What shall I say?
How can I die?
My mother bore me to a heavy fate.   865
I envy the dead. I long for those
who are gone, to live in their houses, with them.
There is no pleasure in the sunshine
nor the feel of the hard earth under my feet.
Such was the hostage Death has taken   870
from me, and given to Hades.

    [*As they chant this,* ADMETUS *moans inarticulately.*]

CHORUS. Go on, go on. Plunge in the deep of the house.
    What you have suffered is enough for tears.
    You have gone through pain, I know,
    but you do no good to the woman who lies   875
    below. Never again to look on the face
    of the wife you loved hurts you.
ADMETUS. You have opened the wound torn in my heart.
    What can be worse for a man than to lose
    a faithful wife. I envy those   880
    without wives, without children. I wish I had not
    ever married her, lived with her in this house.
    We have each one life. To grieve for this
    is burden enough.
    When we could live single all our days   885
    without children, it is not to be endured
    to see children sicken or married love
    despoiled by death.
    [As before.]
CHORUS. Chance comes. It is hard to wrestle against it.
    There is no limit to set on your pain.   890
    The weight is heavy. Yet still
    bear up. You are not the first man to lose
    his wife. Disaster appears, to crush
    one man now, but afterward another.
ADMETUS. How long my sorrows, the pain for my loves   895
    down under the earth.
    Why did you stop me from throwing myself
    in the hollow cut of the grave, there to lie
    dead beside her, who was best on earth?
    Then Hades would have held fast two lives,   900
    not one, and the truest of all, who crossed
    the lake of the dead together.
CHORUS. There was a man
    of my people, who lost a boy
    any house would mourn for,   905
    the only child. But still
    he carried it well enough, though childless,
    and he stricken with age
    and the hair gray on him,
    well on through his lifetime.   910
ADMETUS. O builded house, how shall I enter you?
    How live, with this turn
    of my fortune? How different now and then.
    Then it was with Pelian pine torches,   915
    with marriage songs, that I entered my house,
    with the hand of a sweet bride on my arm,
    with loud rout of revelers following
    to bless her who now is dead, and me,
    for our high birth, for nobilities   920
    from either side which were joined in us.

Now the bridal chorus has changed for a dirge,
and for white robes the costumed black
goes with me inside
to where her room stands deserted.   925
CHORUS. Your luck had been
good, so you were inexperienced when
grief came. Still you saved
your own life and substance.
Your wife is dead, your love forsaken.   930
What is new in this? Before
now death has parted
many from their wives.
ADMETUS. Friends, I believe my wife is happier than I   935
although I know she does not seem to be. For her,
there will be no more pain to touch her ever again.
She has her glory and is free from much distress.
But I, who should not be alive, who have passed by
my moment, shall lead a sorry life. I see it now.   940
How can I bear to go inside this house again?
Whom shall I speak to, who will speak to me, to give
me any pleasure in coming home? Where shall I turn?
The desolation in my house will drive me out
when I see my wife's bed empty, when I see the chairs   945
she used to sit in, and all about the house the floor
unwashed and dirty, while the children at my knees
huddle and cry for their mother and the servants mourn
their mistress and remember what the house has lost.
So it will be at home, but if I go outside   950
meeting my married friends in Thessaly, the sight
of their wives will drive me back, for I cannot endure
to look at my wife's agemates and the friends of her youth.
And anyone who hates me will say this of me:
"Look at the man, disgracefully alive, who dared   955
not die, but like a coward gave his wife instead
and so escaped death. Do you call him a man at all?
He turns on his own parents, but he would not die
himself." Besides my other troubles, they will speak
about me thus. What have I gained by living, friends,   960
when reputation, life, and action all are bad?
CHORUS. I myself, in the transports
of mystic verses, as in study
of history and science, have found
nothing so strong as Compulsion,   965
nor any means to combat her,
not in the Thracian books set down
in verse by the school of Orpheus,
not in all the remedies Phoebus has given the heirs   970
of Asclepius to fight the many afflictions of man.

She alone is a goddess

without altar or image to pray
before. She heeds no sacrifice.   975
Majesty, bear no harder
on me than you have in my life before!
All Zeus even ordains
only with you is accomplished.
By strength you fold and crumple the steel of the Chalybes.   930
There is no pity in the sheer barrier of your will.

[*They turn and speak directly to* ADMETUS, *who remains
in the background.*]

Now she has caught your wife in the breakless grip of her
    hands.
Take it. You will never bring back, by crying,   985
the dead into the light again.
Even the sons of the gods fade
and go in death's shadow.   990
She was loved when she was with us.
She shall be loved still, now she is dead.
It was the best of all women to whom you were joined in mar-
    riage.

The monument of your wife must not be counted among the
    graves   995
of the dead, but it must be given its honors
as gods are, worship of wayfarers.
And as they turn the bend of the road   1000
and see it, men shall say:
"She died for the sake of her husband.
Now she is a blessed spirit.
Hail, majesty, be gracious to us." Thus will men speak in
    her presence.   1005

But here is someone who looks like Alcmene's son,
Admetus. He seems on his way to visit you.

[HERACLES *enters, leading a veiled woman by the hand.*]

HERACLES. A man, Admetus, should be allowed to speak his mind
to a friend, instead of keeping his complaints suppressed
inside him. Now, I thought I had the right to stand   1010
beside you and endure what you endured, so prove
my friendship. But you never told me that she, who lay
dead, was your wife, but entertained me in your house
as if your mourning were for some outsider's death.
And so I wreathed my head and poured libations out   1015
to the gods, in your house, though your house had suffered so.
This was wrong, wrong I tell you, to have treated me
thus, though I have no wish to hurt you in your grief.
Now, as for the matter of why I have come back again,
I will tell you. Take this woman, keep her safe for me,   1020
until I have killed the master of the Bistones
and come back, bringing with me the horses of Thrace.

If I have bad luck—I hope not, I hope to come
back home—I give her to the service of your house.
It cost a struggle for her to come into my hands.   1025
You see, I came on people who were holding games
for all comers, with prizes which an athlete might
well spend an effort winning.

[*Points to the woman.*]

                                   Here is the prize I won
and bring you. For the winners in the minor events
were given horses to take away, while those who won   1030
the heavier stuff, boxing and wrestling, got oxen,
and a woman was thrown in with them. Since I happened
to be there, it seemed wrong to let this splendid prize
go by. As I said, the woman is for you to keep.
She is not stolen. It cost me hard work to bring   1035
here here. Some day, perhaps, you will say I have done well.

ADMETUS. I did not mean to dishonor nor belittle you
when I concealed the fate of my unhappy wife,
but it would have added pain to pain already there
if you had been driven to shelter with some other host.   1040
This sorrow is mine. It is enough for me to weep.
As for the woman, if it can be done, my lord,
I beg you, have some other Thessalian, who has not
suffered as I have, keep her. You have many friends
in Pherae. Do not bring my sorrows back to me.   1045
I would not have strength to see her in my house and keep
my eyes dry. I am weak now. Do not add weakness
to my weakness. I have sorrow enough to weigh me down.
And where could a young woman live in this house? For
she is young, I can see it in her dress, her style.   1050
Am I to put her in the same quarters with the men?
And how, circulating among young men, shall she be kept
from harm? Not easy, Heracles, to hold in check
a young strong man. I am thinking of your interests.
Or shall I put her in my lost wife's chamber, keep   1055
her there? How can I take her to Alcestis' bed?
I fear blame from two quarters, from my countrymen
who might accuse me of betraying her who helped
me most, by running to the bed of another girl,
and from the dead herself. Her honor has its claim   1060
on me. I must be very careful. You, lady,
whoever you are, I tell you that you have the form
of my Alcestis; all your body is like hers.
Too much. Oh, for God's pity, take this woman away
out of my sight. I am beaten already, do not beat   1065
me again. For as I look on her, I think I see
my wife. It churns my heart to tumult, and the tears
break streaming from my eyes. How much must I endure
the bitter taste of sorrow which is still so fresh?

CHORUS. I cannot put a good name to your fortune; yet   1070 whoever you are, you must endure what the god gives.

HERACLES. I only wish that my strength had been great enough
for me to bring your wife back from the chambered deep
into the light. I would have done that grace for you.

ADMETUS. I know you would have wanted to. Why speak of it?   1075
There is no way for the dead to come back to the light.

HERACLES. Then do not push your sorrow. Bear it as you must.

ADMETUS. Easier to comfort than to suffer and be strong.

HERACLES. But if you wish to mourn for always, what will you
gain?

ADMETUS. Nothing. I know it. But some impulse of my love   1080
makes me.

HERACLES. Why, surely. Love for the dead is cause for tears.

ADMETUS. Her death destroyed me, even more than I can say.

HERACLES. You have lost a fine wife. Who will say you have not?

ADMETUS.   So fine
that I, whom you see, never shall be happy again.

HERACLES. Time will soften it. The evil still is young and strong.   1085

ADMETUS. You can say time will soften it, if time means death.

HERACLES. A wife, love, your new marriage will put an end to this.

ADMETUS. Silence! I never thought you would say a thing like
that.

HERACLES. What? You will not remarry but keep an empty bed?

ADMETUS. No woman ever shall sleep in my arms again.   1090

HERACLES. Do you believe you help the dead by doing this?

ADMETUS. Wherever she may be, she deserves my honors still.

HERACLES. Praiseworthy, yes, praiseworthy. And yet foolish, too.

ADMETUS. Call me so, then, but never call me a bridegroom.

HERACLES. I admire you for your faith and love you bear your
wife.   1095

ADMETUS. Let me die if I betray her, though she is gone.

HERACLES.   Well then,
receive this woman into your most generous house.

ADMETUS. Please, in the name of Zeus your father, no!

HERACLES.   And yet
you will be making a mistake if you do not;

ADMETUS. and eaten at the heart with anguish if I do.   1100

HERACLES. Obey. The grace of this may come where you need
grace.

ADMETUS. Ah.
I wish you had never won her in those games of yours.

HERACLES. Where I am winner, you are winner along with me.

ADMETUS. Honorably said. But let the woman go away.

HERACLES. She will go, if she should. First look. See if she
should.   1105

ADMETUS. She should, unless it means you will be angry with me.

HERACLES. Something I know of makes me so insistent with you.

ADMETUS. So, have your way. But what you do does not please
me.

HERACLES. The time will come when you will thank me. Only

obey.

ADMETUS. [*to attendants*] Escort her in, if she must be taken
into this house. 1110

HERACLES. I will not hand this lady over to attendants.

ADMETUS. You yourself lead her into the house then, if you wish.

HERACLES. I will put her into your hands and into yours alone.

ADMETUS. I will not touch her. But she is free to come inside.

HERACLES. No, I have faith in your right hand, and only yours. 1115

ADMETUS. My lord, you are forcing me to act against my wish.

HERACLES. Be brave. Reach out your hand and take the strangers'.

ADMETUS. So.
Here is my hand; I feel like Perseus killing the gorgon.

HERACLES. You have her?

ADMETUS. Yes, I have her.

HERACLES. Keep her, then. Some day
you will say the son of Zeus came as your generous guest. 1120
But look at her. See if she does not seem most like
your wife. Your grief is over now. Your luck is back.

ADMETUS. Gods, what shall I think! Amazement beyond hope,
as I
look on this woman, this wife. Is she really mine,
or some sweet mockery for God to stun me with? 1125

HERACLES. Not so. This is your own wife you see. She is here.

ADMETUS. Be careful she is not some phantom from the depths.

HERACLES. The guest and friend you took was no necromancer.

ADMETUS. Do I see my wife, whom I was laying in the grave?

HERACLES. Surely. But I do not wonder at your unbelief. 1130

ADMETUS. May I touch her, and speak to her, as my living wife?

HERACLES. Speak to her. All that you desired is yours.

ADMETUS. Oh, eyes
and body of my dearest wife, I have you now
beyond all hope. I never thought to see you again.

HERACLES. You have her. May no god hate you for your happiness. 1135

ADMETUS. O nobly sprung child of all-highest Zeus, may good
fortune go with you. May the father who gave you birth
keep you. You alone raised me up when I was down.
How did you bring her back from down there to the light?

HERACLES. I fought a certain deity who had charge of her. 1140

ADMETUS. Where do you say you fought this match with Death?

HERACLES. Beside
the tomb itself. I sprang and caught him in my hands.

ADMETUS. But why is my wife standing here, and does not speak?

HERACLES. You are not allowed to hear her speak to you until
her obligations to the gods who live below 1145
are washed away. Until the third morning comes. So now
take her and lead her inside, and for the rest of time,
Admetus, be just. Treat your guests as they deserve.
and now goodbye. I have my work that I must do,
and go to face the lordly son of Sthenelus. 1150

ADMETUS. No, stay with us and be the guest of our hearth.

HERACLES.   There still
will be a time for that, but I must press on now.

ADMETUS. Success go with you. May you find your way back here.

[HERACLES *goes.*]

I proclaim to all the people of my tetrarchy
that, for these blessed happenings, they shall set up
dances, and the altars smoke with sacrifice offered.   1155
For now we shall make our life again, and it will be
a better one.

I was lucky. That I cannot deny.

[*He takes* ALCESTIS *by the hand and leads her inside the
house.*]

CHORUS. [*going*][3] Many are the forms of what is unknown.
Much that the gods achieve is surprise.   1160
What we look for does not come to pass;
God finds a way for what none foresaw.
Such was the end of this story.

---

3. If the chorus' last speech seems only
vaguely appropriate as an ending to
this play, it is because it is a general
sentiment, suitable for most occasions,
of which Euripides was apparently
fond. He used it to end *Helen*, *Andromache*, *The Bacchae*, and, with varia-
tions, *Medea*.

Selected Bibliography

I. Secondary Reading, Historical and Critical

Bentley, Eric. *The Playwright as Thinker*, revised edition. New York: Meridian, 1955. (pb)[1]

Clark, Barrett H. *European Theories of the Drama* (revised edition with a Supplement on American Drama). New York: Crown, 1947.

Cole, Toby, editor. *Playwrights on Playwriting*. New York: Hill & Wang, 1961. (pb)

Downer, Alan S. *Fifty Years of American Drama, 1900–1950*. Chicago: University of Chicago Press, 1951.

Esslin, Martin. *The Theatre of the Absurd*. Garden City, N.Y.: Doubleday Anchor, 1961. (pb)

Fergusson, Francis. *The Idea of the Theatre*. Princeton, N.J.: Princeton University Press, 1949. (pb: Doubleday Anchor)

Gassner, John. *Form and Idea in Modern Theatre*. New York: Holt, Rinehart & Winston, 1956.

Gassner, John. *Masters of the Drama*, 3rd Edition. New York: Dover, 1953.

Gorelik, Mordecai. *New Theatres for Old*. New York: S. French, 1941. (pb: Dutton)

Granville-Barker, Harley. *On Dramatic Method*. London: Sidgwick & Jackson, 1931. (pb: Hill & Wang)

Kerr, Walter. *How Not to Write a Play*. New York: Simon & Schuster, 1960. (pb)

Krutch, Joseph Wood. *American Drama Since 1918*, revised edition. New York: Braziller, 1957.

Macgowan, Kenneth, and William Melnitz. *The Living Stage*. New York: Prentice-Hall, 1955.

Nelson, Robert J. *Play Within a Play*. New Haven: Yale University Press, 1958.

Norwood, Gilbert. *Greek Tragedy*. New York: Hill & Wang, 1960. (pb)

Peacock, Ronald. *The Poet in the Theatre*, enlarged edition. New York: Hill & Wang, 1960. (pb)

Weales, Gerald. *American Drama Since World War II*. New York: Harcourt, Brace & World, 1962.

1. Indicates the work is published in a paperbound edition.

Williams, Raymond. *Drama from Ibsen to Eliot.* New York: Oxford, 1953.

II. *Further Works by the Playwrights in This Volume*

1. Anouilh.

   Selected Plays, 2 vols. New York: Hill & Wang, 1958–59. (pb)

   Individual plays—including *The Waltz of the Toreadors, Becket* and *The Fighting Cock*—published by Coward-McCann, New York. (pb)

2. Barker.

   Three Plays. London: Sidgwick & Jackson, 1909.

   The Madras House, in *Edwardian Plays,* edited by Gerald Weales. New York: Hill & Wang, 1962.

3. Euripides.

   The Complete Greek Tragedies, edited by David Grene & Richmond Lattimore, Vols. 3 & 4. Chicago: University of Chicago Press, 1959. (pb: in five separate volumes)

4. Ibsen.

   The Collected Work, edited by William Archer, 11 vols. New York: Scribner's, 1909.

   The Oxford Ibsen, edited by James Walter McFarlane, Vols. II, V, & VI. London: Oxford, 1960–1962. (VI in pb)

   There are a host of pb editions of Ibsen plays, the most useful being the translations by Michael Meyer (Doubleday Anchor), Una Ellis-Fermor (Penguin), and Arvid Paulson (Bantam).

5. Miller.

   Collected Plays. New York: Viking, 1957.

   After the Fall. New York: Viking, 1964.

   Pb editions of various plays (Bantam, Compass).

6. Musset.

   Seven Plays, tr. Peter Meyers. New York: Hill & Wang, 1962. (pb)

7. Pirandello.

   The Mountain Giants and Other Plays, edited by Marta Abba. New York: Crown, 1958.

   Naked Masks, edited by Eric Bentley. New York: Dutton, 1958. (pb)

   Plays, edited by E. Martin Browne. Baltimore: Penguin, 1959. (pb)

   To Clothe the Naked, and Two Other Plays, translated by William Murray. New York: Dutton, 1962. (pb)

8. Shakespeare.

   There are innumerable editions of the *Complete Works* (I use the one edited by George Lyman Kittredge; New York:

Ginn, 1936) and an almost endless selection of pb collections and single volumes (the Penguin Shakespeare is consistently well edited).

9. Shaw
Complete Plays with Prefaces, 6 vols. New York: Dodd, Mead, 1962.
The Theatre of Bernard Shaw, edited by Alan S. Downer, 2 vols. (10 plays). New York: Dodd, Mead, 1961. (pb)
Many pb editions of Shaw, but Penguin has the best selection.

10. Wilder.
Long Christmas Dinner and Other Plays. New York: Harper, 1963.
Three Plays. New York: Harper, 1957. (pb: Bantam)

11. Wycherley.
The Complete Works, edited by Montague Summers, 4 vols. London: Nonesuch Press, 1924.